THE JOHN CHAPPELL NATURAL PHILOSOPHY SOCIETY

Papers by the members of the John Chappell Natural Philosophy Society
presented at their annual conference

University of British Columbia, Vancouver, Canada, 2017

Edited by

DAVID DE HILSTER
ROBERT DE HILSTER
NICK PERCIVAL

Caldeon, Michigan

THE PUBLISHER

2017

Published by the John Chappell Natural Philosophy Society, Caledonia, Michigan.

Library of Congress Cataloging-in-Publication Data:

CNPS 2017 Annual Proceedings / David de Hilster, Nick Percival . . . [et al.].
p. cm.-(CNPS series in science annuals)

"CNPS-Publications."
Includes bibliographical references and index.
ISBN 978-1-387-06289-8 (pbk.)
Printed in the United States of America.

10 9 8 7 6 5 4 3 2 1

At the time of publishing, the directors for the John Chappell Natural Philosophy Society (CNPS) are as follows:

July 19, 2017

Table of Contents

A Proposed Experiment to Disprove Special Relativity

Musa D. Abdullahi

12 Bujumbura Street, Wuse 2, Abuja, Nigeria, e-mail: musadab@outlook.com

According to classical and relativistic electrodynamics, a charged particle moving with velocity v should go straight through a crossed electric field of intensity E and a magnetic flux of intensity B, at right angles, without deflection, if the magnitude E = Bv. For a constant B, the relationship between E and v is linear, with Bc as the maximum value of E required for the particle to pass right through the crossed fields at the speed of light c. This paper shows that the relationship being E and v is not linear. Due to aberration of electric field, it is the electric field experienced by a moving charged particle, not the mass, which depends on velocity. For a particle to pass through the crossed fields without deflection, E should increase to an infinitely large value as v approaches the speed of light. An experiment, demonstrating this non-linearity, invalidates special relativity.

Keywords: Aberration, electric field, Lorentz force, magnetic flux, mass, special relativity, velocity

1. Introduction

An experiment, being in accordance with a theory, does not necessarily make the theory correct. But an experiment, contra-dicting a theory, should invalidate the theory. In this paper an experiment to disprove the theory of special relativity, with respect to the mass-velocity formula, is proposed. The theory of special relativity [1][2] predicts increase in the mass m of a particle with its speed v, relative to an observer, as:

$$m = \frac{m_o}{\sqrt{(1-\frac{v^2}{c^2})}} = \gamma m_o \tag{1}$$

where m_o is the rest mass, γ the Lorentz factor, and c the speed of light in a vacuum. Once the mass-velocity formula is shown to be incorrect, the theory of special relativity stands disproved.

In an alternative electrodynamics [3][4] the author showed that equation (69) is mathematically correct only where a charged particle is moving perpendicular to an electric field. This is so in circular revolution of an electron round a positively charged nucleus [5]. As the effect of an electric field is propagated at the speed of light, a charged particle, moving in an electric field, is subjected to aberration of the electric field.

2. Aberration of Electric Field

The English astronomer, James Bradley, discovered aberration of light in 1725. This was one of the most significant discoveries in science. In aberration of light, a distant star (considered as stationary) under observation, by a moving astronomer, appears displaced in the forward direction (from the instantaneous line joining the star and the observer) through a small angle α, called the angle of aberration. Aberration of electric field is a phenomenon similar to aberration of light. The effect of an electric field of magnitude E and intensity $\mathbf{E}$, in the direction of unit vector $\hat{\mathbf{u}}$, is propagated with the velocity of light $\mathbf{c}$, of magnitude c, so that:

$$\mathbf{E} = E\hat{\mathbf{u}} = \frac{E}{c}\mathbf{c} \tag{2}$$

Figure 4 depicts a particle of charge q and mass m at a point P moving with velocity $\mathbf{v}$ at an angle θ to the electric field of intensity $\mathbf{E}$, in the direction of unit vector $\hat{\mathbf{u}}$, from a source charge Q at O. The electric field appears to be propagated along NP with velocity of light $\mathbf{c}$, at aberration angle α from the line OP. The sine rule, in triangle PNR, gives the Bradley's equation:

$$sin(\alpha) = \frac{v}{c}sin(\theta) \tag{3}$$

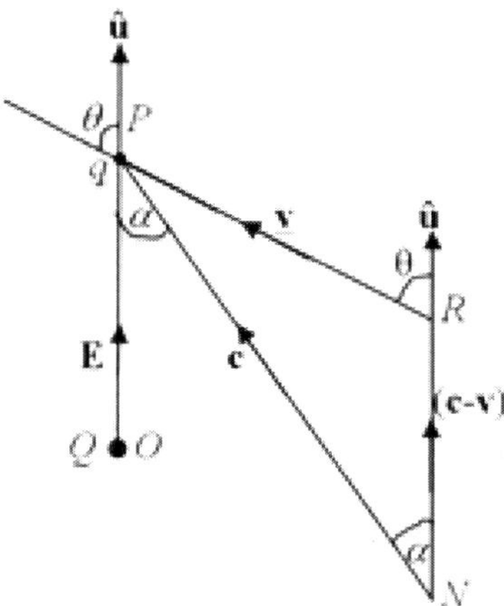

Figure 1. A particle of charge q at P moving with velocity **v** at angle to the electric field **E** due to source charge Q at O

Relative velocity between the particle moving with velocity v and the effect an electric field propagated with velocity of light **c**, is (**c-v**) in the $\hat{\mathbf{u}}$ field direction. In an alternative electrodynamics, field E_v, experienced by the moving particle, is put as vector:

$$\mathbf{E}_v = \frac{E}{c}(\mathbf{c}-\mathbf{v}) \tag{4}$$

The angle between the vectors **c** and **v** Figure (4) being $(\theta - \alpha)$ and the *modulus* of $(\mathbf{c} - \mathbf{v})$, gives equation (16) as vector:

$$\mathbf{E}_v = \frac{\mathbf{E}}{c}\sqrt{c^2 + v^2 - 2cvcos(\theta - \alpha)} \quad (5)$$

For a charged particle moving at speed v under acceleration in the direction of the electric field of intensity **E**, we have $\theta = 0$ with equations (15) and (17) giving E_v as vector:

$$\mathbf{E}_v = \mathbf{E}(1 - \frac{v}{c}) \quad (6)$$

For a charged particle moving at speed v under deceleration in the opposite direction of an electric field of intensity **E**, we have $\theta = \pi$ radians with equations (15) and (17) giving E_v as vector:

$$\mathbf{E}_v = \mathbf{E}(1 + \frac{v}{c}) \quad (7)$$

For a charged particle moving with speed v perpendicular to an electric field of intensity **E**, we have $\theta = \pi/2$ radians, with equations (15) and (17) giving $cos(\theta - \alpha) = sin(\alpha) = v/c$, and $\mathbf{E}_v$ becomes:

$$\mathbf{E}_v = \mathbf{E}\sqrt{1 - \frac{v^2}{c^2}} = \frac{\mathbf{E}}{\gamma} \quad (8)$$

An interesting case is where an electron of charge $q = -e$ and mass m revolves with speed v in a circle of radius r, perpendicular to a radial electric field of intensity $\mathbf{E} = E\,\hat{\mathbf{u}}$ from a positively charged nucleus. The accelerating force **F** and centripetal acceleration $(-v^2/r)\hat{\mathbf{u}}$, in accordance with equation (20) and Newton's second law of motion, with $m = m_o$, is vector:

$$\mathbf{F} = -e\mathbf{E}_v = -e\mathbf{E}\hat{\mathbf{u}}\sqrt{1 - \frac{v^2}{c^2}} = -m\frac{v^2}{r}\hat{\mathbf{u}} = -m_o\frac{v^2}{r}\hat{\mathbf{u}} \quad (9)$$

In relativistic electrodynamics, with $m \neq m_o$, accelerating force on an electron is regarded as $-eE\hat{\mathbf{u}}$, independent of speed of the electron in the field. In this case equation (21) gives:

$$eE = \frac{m_o}{\sqrt{1 - \frac{v^2}{c^2}}}\frac{v^2}{r} = m\frac{v^2}{r} \quad (10)$$

In equation (22), it is as if the force is constant at eE but the mass m varies with speed v in accordance with the relativistic equation (69). This is a mathematical misinterpretation of a physical phenomenon. The relativistic mass m in equations (69) and (22) is not a physical quantity but the ratio of electrostatic force eE to acceleration v^2/r in circular motion. This ratio can become infinitely large, for rectilinear motion, without any problem.

It is not the physical mass which increases with speed but the electric field which varies with speed in accordance with equations (18), (19) or (20). An experiment, proving equation (20) as correct, invalidates equation (69) of the theory of special relativity and the theory itself. This is what this paper sets out to prove with a proposed experiment in support.

3. Proposed Experiment

In the experiment, particles each of charge q, moving with velocity **v**, pass through a crossed electric field of intensity **v** and a magnetic flux of intensity **B**, at right angles, as shown in Figure 2. Here, the vectors **E** and **B** lie on the plane of the page and in the directions indicated by the arrows. The velocity v is directed perpendicularly into the plane of the page.

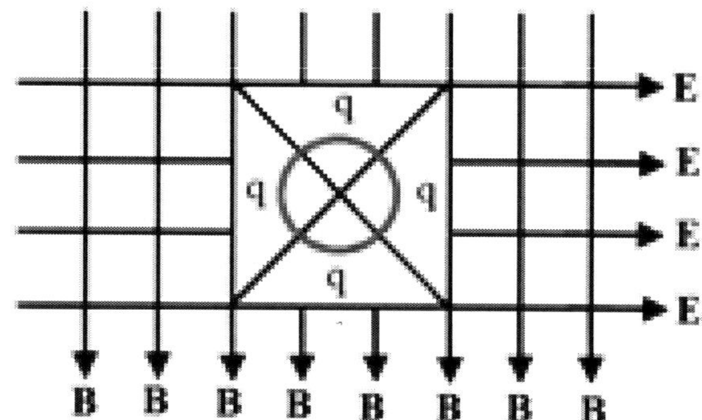

Figure 2. A particle of charge q passing with velocity **v** perpendicular to crossed electric field of intensity **E** and magnetic flux of intensity **B**.

A particle of charge q goes through the crossed fields at velocity **v**, without deflection, if it experiences zero electric field and zero force. This makes the sum of the Lorentz force, the vector product, $q\mathbf{v}X\mathbf{B}$, and the electrical force $q\mathbf{E}_v$ equal to zero, so that equation (20) gives the vector equation:

$$q\mathbf{E}\sqrt{1 - \frac{v^2}{c^2}} = -qv\mathbf{B} = \hat{\mathbf{u}}qvBsin(\theta) \quad (11)$$

where $\hat{\mathbf{u}}$ is a unit vector in the direction of the electric field **E** and θ is the angle between the vectors **v** and **B**. With **v** perpendicular to **B** ($\theta = \pi/2$ *radians*), the scalar equation is:

$$E\sqrt{1 - \frac{v^2}{c^2}} = vB; \quad \frac{E}{Bc} = \frac{v}{\sqrt{1 - \frac{v^2}{c^2}}} \quad (12)$$

Graphs of v/c against E/Bc are shown in Figure 3. Classical and relativistic electrodynamics give the solid line AL, indicating a linear relationship between E and v, with E reaching a maximum value Bc at the speed of light c. The alternative electrodynamics gives the dotted curve AK, for equation (24). It shows a non-linear relationship between E and v, where the magnitude E becomes infinitely large as the speed of light is approached.

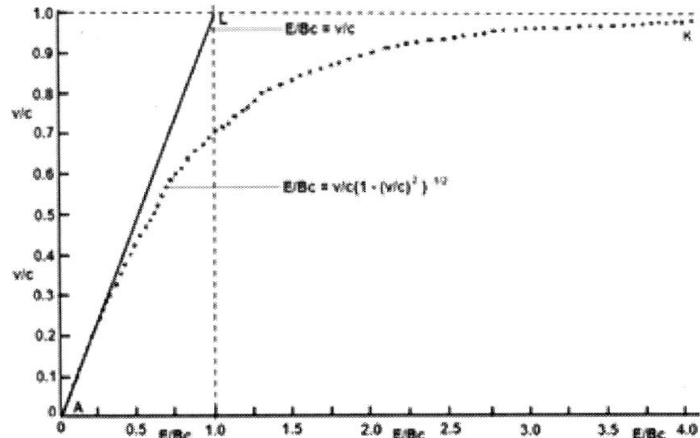

Figure 3. A particle of charge q passing with velocity v perpendicular to crossed electric field of intensity **E** and magnetic flux of intensity **B**.

4. Conclusions

The following conclusions may be drawn:

- As mass is not involved in obtaining equation (20) with the Lorentz factor γ, it is not the mass of a particle, but the electric field experienced, that depends on velocity of the particle in the field.
- It is wrong to assume that the force exerted by an electric field, on a moving charged particle, is independent of its speed.
- Equation (69) is a mathematical misinterpretation of a physical phenomenon. It is correct for circular revolution, not because mass increases with speed, but as a result of accelerating field decreasing with speed as in equations (18), (19), and (20).
- The relativistic mass $m = \gamma m_o$ equation (69) is not a physical quantity but the ratio of electrostatic force eE to acceleration v^2/r in circular motion. This ratio can be infinitely large. Equating m with physical mass is an (expensive ???) case of mistaken identity.
- Applying equation (69), in rectilinear motion, is wrong.
- An experiment giving a non-linear curve AK, in Figure 3, disproves equation (69), the relativistic the mass-velocity formula.

REFERENCES

1. A. Einstein, *On the Electrodynamics of Moving Bodies*, Ann. Phys., 17 (1905), 891.
2. Einstein and Lorentz, *The Principles of Relativity.*, Matheun, London, 1923
3. M. Abdullahi, *An Alternative Electrodynamics to the Theory of Special Relativity.*, `https:www.academia.edu/7973538/`, 2013
4. M. Abdullahi, *Aberration of Electric Field and Radiation Power due to a Moving Electron*, `www.academia.edu/16045596`
5. M. Abdullahi, *An Interpretation of Relativistic Mass in Circular Motion of an Electron*, `www.academia.edu/10962823`

An Explanation for the Cause of Force of Gravity

Musa D. Abdullahi

12 Bujumbura Street, Wuse 2, Abuja, Nigeria, e-mail: musadab@outlook.com

Space contains isolated regions of matter or bodies each composed of equal amounts of positive and negative electric charges as sources of electric fields. The fields, from neutral bodies, balance out exactly everywhere and vanish at infinitely long distances from the respective sources. While the strong electrical forces of repulsion and attraction, proportional to the charges, in accordance with Coulomb's law, balance out exactly everywhere in space, the weak gravitational forces of attraction, proportional to the squares of the charges and in accordance with Newton's law, remain and add up. The universal space, crisscrossed by electric fields emanating from charges in bodies, balancing out exactly everywhere and vanishing at infinity, constituting a medium supporting electromagnetic radiation and gravitation, is proposed to be the aether, as conceived by J. C. Maxwell and others.

Keywords: Aether, electric charge, electric field, force, gravity, light, mass, matter, space, speed.

1. Introduction

It is reasonable to suppose that there is an absolute medium, filling all space, which supports gravitation and in which light and other electromagnetic waves are propagated. This luminiferous medium is called aether [1], as conceived by Newton [2], Maxwell [3], Einstein [4] and others. The concept of the aether, as a medium uniformly filling the whole of infinite space, is untenable, since nature is not so infinitely extravagant. The only thing that could uniformly fill all of infinite space is nothingness or something, like an electric field, vanishing to zero at infinity.

The identification of what really constitutes the aether would go a long way to explaining the cause of gravity and resolving the difficulty with curvature or warping of four-dimensional space-time continuum of general relativity [5]. It may lead to the long awaited unification of electrostatic and gravitational forces.

In this paper, space is regarded as of one dimension –**displacement**– a vector with three orthogonal components. *Time* is taken as a separate dimension, not one of space. Speed of light, being a constant relative to its source, defines *time* in terms of displacement. The other fundamental dimensions should be *electric charge* and *electric potential*. The fundamental quantities are:

- Length or Displacement [L] $\hat{\mathbf{u}}$ in the direction of unit vector $\hat{\mathbf{u}}$
- Time [T]
- Electric charge or Electric flux [Q]
- Electric potential or Voltage [Φ]

Some of the derived quantities, vectors and scalars, expressed in terms of the four fundamental quantities, are:

- Velocity (v) - $[LT^{-1}]\hat{\mathbf{u}}$ in the plane of the page/paper
- Electric current (I) - $[QT^{-1}]$
- Electric field (E) - $[\Phi L^{-1}]\hat{\mathbf{u}}$
- Resistance (R) - $[\Phi TQ^{-1}]$
- Mass (M) - $[Q\Phi L^{-2}T^{2}]$
- Force (F) - $[Q\Phi L^{-1}]\hat{\mathbf{u}}$
- Energy or Work (W) - $[Q\Phi]$
- Power (P) - $[Q\Phi T^{-1}]$
- Capacitance (C) - $[Q\Phi^{-1}]$
- Inductance (K) - $[\Phi Q^{-1}T^{2}]$
- Magnetic field (H) - $[QL^{-1}T^{-1}]\hat{\mathbf{u}}$
- Magnetic flux (ψ) – $[\Phi T]$
- Magnetic vector potential (A) - $[\Phi TL^{-1}]\hat{\mathbf{u}}$
- Poynting vector (X) - $[Q\Phi T^{-1}]\hat{\mathbf{a}}$, normal to the page.
- Angular momentum (Λ) – $[Q\Phi T]\hat{\mathbf{a}}$ normal to the page.
- Vectors (in **boldface** type) are associated with displacement L.

An electric field is a quantity emanating from all bodies in space. Balanced electric fields, emanating from equal amounts of positive and negative charges of bodies in isolated regions of space, constitute a medium as the aether. Any imbalance in the electric fields in space gives rise to electromagnetic radiation.

2. Electromagnetic Radiation

An oscillating electric charge sets up a transverse magnetic field **H** and generates an electric field **E** in the opposite direction of acceleration. Maxwell's equations give the fields **H** and **E** as:

$$\nabla \times \mathbf{H} = \varepsilon_o \frac{\delta \mathbf{E}}{\delta t} \tag{13}$$

$$\nabla \times \mathbf{E} = -\mu_o \frac{\delta \mathbf{H}}{\delta t} \tag{14}$$

where ε_o is the permittivity and μ_o the permeability of space and $\nabla \times$ denotes the curl of a vector. Taking the curl of equations (69) and (14) in free space, where there is no electric current and no electric charge, gives:

$$\bigtriangledown\times\bigtriangledown\times\mathbf{H}=\bigtriangledown^2\mathbf{H}=\varepsilon_o\frac{\delta}{\delta t}\bigtriangledown\times\mathbf{E}=-\mu_o\varepsilon_o\frac{\delta^2\mathbf{H}}{\delta^2 t} \quad (15)$$

Equation (15) gives the wave velocity c as:

$$c=\sqrt{\frac{1}{\mu_o\varepsilon_o}} \quad (16)$$

Equation (16) is used in deriving the mass of an electric charge.

3. Mass of an Electric Charge

An electric charge Q oscillating with velocity v at time t is associated with magnetic vector potential A as:

$$\mathbf{A}=\mu_o\varepsilon_o\Phi\mathbf{v} \quad (17)$$

where Φ is the potential at a point due to the charge. If the charge is accelerated it generates an electric field E, as given by:

$$\mathbf{E}=-\frac{\delta\mathbf{A}}{\delta t}=-\mu_o\varepsilon_o\Phi\frac{d\mathbf{v}}{\delta t} \quad (18)$$

The electric field E is supposed to act on the same charge Q, producing it, to produce a reactive force equal and opposite to the accelerating force, such that:

$$q\mathbf{E}=-\mu_o\varepsilon_o Q\phi\frac{\delta\mathbf{v}}{\delta t}=-m\frac{\delta\mathbf{v}}{\delta t} \quad (19)$$

The product $Q\Phi$ of an electric charge Q in its own potential Φ is equal to twice the electrostatic energy W of the charge, thus:

$$m=\mu_o\varepsilon_o Q\phi=2\mu_o\varepsilon_o W \quad (20)$$

$$W=\frac{1}{2}mc^2 \quad (21)$$

If an electrically charged particle is to assume any configuration, it will most likely be a spherical shell of charge Q and radius a. Such a figure has intrinsic energy W, given by the well-known classical formula, and equation (20)and (21, as:

$$W=\frac{Q^2}{8\pi\varepsilon_o\alpha}=\frac{1}{2}mc^2 \quad (22)$$

$$m=\frac{Q^2}{4\pi\varepsilon_o c^2\alpha}=\frac{\mu_o Q^2}{4\pi\alpha} \quad (23)$$

Equation (23), where m is proportional to Q^2, will be used for a unification of electrostatic and gravitational forces.

4. Electrostatic and Gravitational Forces

Figure 4 shows two electric charges Q and K of radii a and b and masses $m1$ and $m2$ respectively, separated by a distance r in space. The force f between the charges is a combination of electrostatic forces given by Coulomb's law and gravitational force given by Newton's universal law, thus:

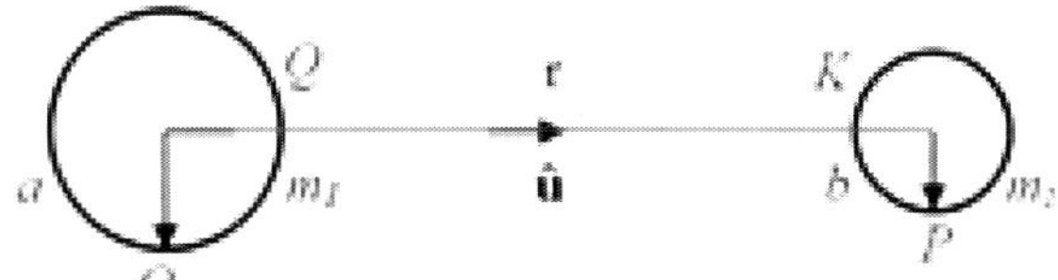

Figure 4. Electric charges Q and K at O separated by distance r

$$f=\frac{QK}{4\pi\varepsilon_o r^2}\hat{\mathbf{u}}-\gamma\frac{m_1m_2}{r^2}\hat{\mathbf{u}} \quad (24)$$

where $\hat{\mathbf{u}}$ is a unit vector in the direction of force of repulsion and γ is the gravitational constant. In equation (24) the force is repulsive (positive) between like charges or attractive (negative) between unlike charges. The force of gravity is always attractive.

Substituting for masses m_1 and m_2 from equation (23), where m is proportional to Q^2, into equation (24), gives:

$$f=\frac{QK}{4\pi\varepsilon_o r^2}\hat{\mathbf{u}}-\gamma\frac{m_1m_2}{r^2}\hat{\mathbf{u}}=\frac{QK}{4\pi\varepsilon_o r^2}\hat{\mathbf{u}}-\gamma\chi\frac{Q^2K^2}{r^2}\hat{\mathbf{u}} \quad (25)$$

where $\chi$is a constant. Equation (25) may be regarded as a unification of electrostatic and gravitational forces.

An interpretation of equation (25) is that the electric field of charge Q causes a kind of slight distortion of the charge K, such that force of repulsion is slightly decreased and force of attraction similarly increased. The result is a persistent force of attraction, irrespective of the sign of the charge Q or K. The force of attraction is in the longitudinal $(-\hat{\mathbf{u}})$ direction, pulling charge K. There is an equal and opposite force pulling charge Q towards K.

4.1. Force of Gravity between Neutral Bodies

A neutral body consists of equal numbers or equal amounts of positive and negative electric charges. It is obvious that a neutral body does not have a resultant electric field to exert any force of repulsion or attraction on other bodies or other charges, but the gravitational forces of attraction remain. The force of attraction F_G between one body of mass M_1 consisting of $N_1/2$ positive charges and $N_1/2$ negative charges, each of magnitude Q and another body of mass M_2 containing $N_2/2$ positive charges and $N_2/2$ negative charges, each of magnitude K, is obtained from equation (24) as:

$$F_G=-\gamma\frac{M_1M_2}{Z^2}\hat{\mathbf{u}}=-\frac{\gamma\chi}{Z^2}\sum_{n=1}^{N_1}Q_n^2\sum_{n=1}^{N_2}K_n^2\hat{\mathbf{u}}=\frac{\gamma\chi}{Z^2}N_1N_2QK\hat{\mathbf{u}} \quad (26)$$

where the product $\gamma\chi$ is a constant and Z is the distance between the centers of gravity of the masses. The numbers N_1 and/or N_2 may be very large. Equation (26) comes as a unification of electrostatic and gravitational forces.

5. Conclusions

The following conclusions may be drawn:

- The aether, as a medium uniformly filling the whole of infinite space, is untenable, as nothing can have an infinite expanse.
- Space contains isolated regions of matter or bodies, each with equal amounts or equal numbers of positive and negative electric charges, from which balanced electric fields emanate.
- Electric fields, emanating from matter or bodies, crisscrossing space, balancing out exactly everywhere and vanishing at infinitely long distances from their respective sources, constitute the aether as a physical medium filling the universal space and supporting propagation of light and universal gravitation.
- The aether exists in a vacuum providing the space, or balanced electric fields, for radiation and gravitation.
- Permittivity ε_o and permeability μ_o are properties of the universal space, the aether.
- Beyond the aether is a void, a vacuum, uniformly filling the rest of infinite space where nothing takes place.
- Electric fields, existing in the aether and balancing out exactly everywhere, exert no electrical force on neutral bodies or electric charges but the gravitational forces persist.
- Electromagnetic radiation is due to imbalance in the electrical fields of the aether as a result of oscillations of charges in matter.
- An electric charge moving in the aether carries along its electric field with the same velocity and the emitted radiation takes on the velocity of the source.
- Gravitation is electrical in nature with the strong electric forces of repulsion and attraction, between neutral bodies, cancelling out exactly everywhere, while the weak gravitational forces of attraction remain and add up.
- A body moves under the force of gravity without emitting any radiation but with change in potential energy equaling the change in kinetic energy.
- A unification of electrostatic and gravitational forces may have been achieved.

REFERENCES

1. http://www.spaceandmotion.com/Physics-Space-Aether-Ether.htm
2. Isaac Newton (1687) *Mathematical Principles of Natural Philosophy (Translated by F. Cajori), University of California Press* Berkeley (1964)
3. *J. Maxwell, A Treatise on Electricity and Magnetism, Oxford, 3rd ed, Part iv, Chap. 2* (1892)
4. A. Einstein *âĂIJOn the Electrodynamics of Moving BodiesâĂİ, Ann. Phys.,17* (1905)
5. *R. Geroch, General Relativity from A to B, Chicago: University of Chicago Press, ISBN 0-226-28864-1* (1981)
6. https://www.academia.edu/7692116/On_the_Energy_and_Mass_of_Electric_Charges_in_a_Body
7. http://www.musada.net/Papers/Paper6.pdf

Two Experimental Measurements to Define the Laws of Gravitational Force and Motion

James Carter

James Carter 29500 Green River Gorge Rd, Enumclaw, Wa 98022, circlon@gmail.com www.living-universe.com

The force of Earth's gravity is measured to come from within its own atoms and not from some infinite gravitational medium far beyond its surface.

Gravity is presented here as a principle of measurement and not a "theory". Conclusions of measurement are used to explain the dynamics of gravity and no metaphysical assumptions are made prior to measurement other than assuming the accuracy of measuring instruments. Two simple measurements can be made to easily illustrate the gravity principle in terms metaphysical gravitational theories. The first measurement quantifies the true natural dynamics of gravitational force and motion that is common to all gravitational theories. The second test measures the true direction and velocity of gravitational motion and the results can be used to either verify or falsify all four of the basic classes of gravity theories. The first test uses accelerometers to measure the upward force at Earth's surface and atomic clocks to measure the gravitational motion produced by both gravitational force and the inertial acceleration of rockets. The second gravity cannon experiment answers the age old paradox of what really happens when a gold ball is dropped into a bottomless pit. This second test is an opposite but complementary measurement of the first, in that it measures downward gravitational deceleration that balances measured upward gravitational acceleration. Whereas, the first test uses atomic clocks and accelerometers to measure gravitational motion and force at all points above Earth's center, the gravity cannon uses a video camera clock to measure gravitational motion and force at Earth's center.

Keywords: gravity, motion, gravity theory

1. The Gravity Cannon Experiment

The gravity cannon experiment is a very simple test that can provide decisive confirmation or falsification of all the different gravitational theories. Although it would have to be performed in the weightlessness of outer space, this experiment could otherwise be executed very easily and inexpensively. A Gold ball would be formed to loosely fit inside of a hollow shaft passing through the center of a large clear glass sphere. When a motionless ball is placed at the barrel's mouth, the gravitational force and motion, whatever might be its cause, is measured and recorded with a video camera. Each of the four different gravity theories has a different prediction for what will happen when a gold ball is placed in the barrel of a gravity cannon. Also, besides being able to differentiate between theories of gravitational force and motion, this experiment would also provide the means to verify and calibrate earthbound measurements and calculations of both the Newtonian force constant G and the gravitational velocity constant GV.

2. Four Possible Theories of Gravity

There are only four different basic theories of gravitational force and motion. These include the two pulling medium theories of the homogeneous field and infinite particle aether. The other two are the internal and pushing particle theories. Each idea uses different complementary equations to explain the two complementary measurements that can be made of gravitational force and motion. Depending on their various assumptions, all four of these theories can be made to predict the values of most measurements of gravity.

Both tests are based on the Newtonian momentum measurement principle of $F = maxd$. The gravity principle test shows that at its surface Earth produces an upward acceleration of about $10m/s^2$ and an upward escape/surface velocity of about $V_{es} = 11/s$. Newtonian force and motion is not a theory. It is the principle of measurement that theories of gravity attempt to explain. Both the aether and field theories base their ideas on the unmeasurable premise of a metaphysical gravitational force that extends to infinity but points downward toward the centers of all bodies. This force is calculated to be equivalent to and opposite of the upward force of gravity that is measured with Newtonian accelerometers. The external pushing particle theories are based on the metaphysical assumption that the universe is filled with rapidly moving unmeasured particles that push falling bodies toward Earth's center.

3. Aether, Spacetime, and Field Theories of Gravity

Aether, spacetime and continuum fields are defined as any description or condition of space that is not an infinite and eternal dimensionless void. Fields are local conditions of aether or spacetime that extend between and connect to bodies of mass. They can either be local pulling forces between atoms or they can be non-local infinite pulling forces between galaxies. There are two classes of gravitational pulling theories.

The first is the homogeneous field theories. They explain gravity as a single, universal, all pervasive field, spacetime continuum or some other universal medium that is either a continuous solid, liquid or gas. Curvatures, ripples, and waves within this universal substance cause bodies of mass to move toward Earth and other centers of mass. Newton's gravitational attraction theory is a homogeneous field theory.

The second class of gravity theory is the infinite particle theories. Gravity is explained by a potentially infinite number of gravitational fields that are usually, but not always, called gravitons. These calculated wave-particle dualities are generated at the center of each atom and then spread out in all directions to infinity at the speed of light. These particles are thought to move unheeded throughout the universe at the speed of light. Just how they are able to cause falling bodies to accelerate downward is unclear.

General Relativity that has been mathematically crafted into several interpretations. Its equations usually calculate a four-dimensional spacetime continuum that connects all matter and interacts with an apparent but otherwise undetectable force that causes equivalent gravitational motion. The presence of a body of mass causes the continuum to curve and produce an apparent but unmeasured pulling motion between all bodies of mass.

General Relativity is also sometimes classed as an infinite particle aether theory because in some versions, the force of gravity is spread from atom to atom across the universe by great numbers of tiny wave-particle dualities called gravitons. These wavelike particles move through the continuum at the speed of light and are calculated to cause portions of the spacetime to curve in such a way as to cause the appearance of gravitational pulling motion between bodies of matter.

4. Measuring Gravitational Force and Motion

This drawing shows the measured acceleration of Earth's gravity and the motion produced by that acceleration. The velocities shown for the clocks in different positions relative to Earth's center are the combined velocity vectors for orbital velocity and Earth's escape/surface velocity for that position. The measured clock intervals are:

$$t' = \frac{T}{\sqrt{v_1 - V_{es}^2 + \frac{V_o^2}{c^2}}} \tag{27}$$

Clock interval t' is equal to the Time interval T at Earth's center or at deep space rest divided by the square root of one minus escape surface velocity squared V_{es}^2 plus orbital velocity squared V_o^2 divided by the speed of light squared. Except for the rates at Earth's center and at deep space momentum rest, these clock rates have been experimentally verified many times.

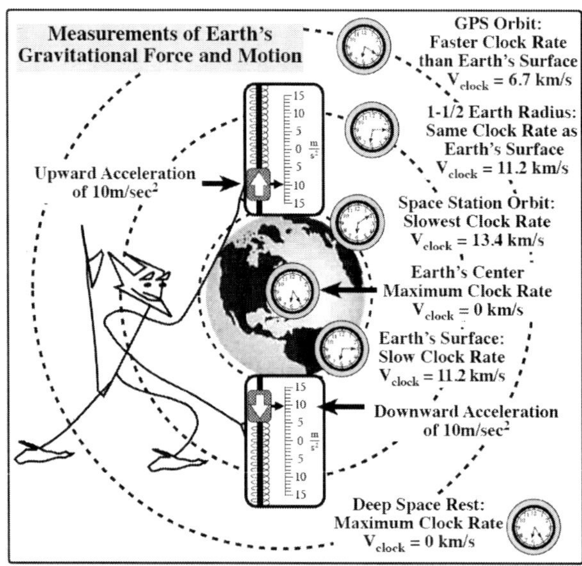

Figure 5. Measuring Gravitational Force and Motion

All accelerometer readings made at Earth's surface clearly show that the direction of the acceleration of gravity points away from Earth's center. Accelerometers placed on falling bodies, show that they are undergoing no change in inertial motion except for an upward acceleration caused by air resistance.

The above Lorentz transformation formula used to calculate atomic clocks rates was adopted by the Special and General Theories of Relativity for the purpose of calculation. It was a preexisting principle of measurement and not one of relativity's theoretical assumptions. In its GPS clock calculations, Special Relativity uses orbital velocity and General Relativity uses an unmeasurable metaphysical quantity called gravitational potential that is calculated from measurements of Earth's escape/surface velocity.

5. Pushing Particle Gravity Theories

Pushing theories of gravity are divided into external pushing particle theories and the internal pushing particle principle of the gravitational expansion of mass, space, and time.

The external theories explain gravity by assuming that bodies of matter like Earth are constantly being pushed inward toward their centers by great numbers of tiny undetectable particles impinging on them from all directions of space. These external theories claim that the downward motion of falling bodies is produced by the absorption of tiny undetectable extremely high speed particles that are assumed to exist uniformly distributed throughout all of space. Some of these theories predict slow moving particle speeds and others predict particles moving at many orders of magnitude greater than the speed of light. When these particles strike matter, they give it a slight push. These omnidirectional particles push the surface of Earth towards its center.

An external pushing gravity theory was first proposed by Nicolas Fatio in 1690. Later, similar theories were proposed by Le Sage and others. Rene Descartes had a pushing gravity theory in which numerous tiny whirlpools within the aether pushed matter towards Earth. Many NPA members have their own pushing gravity theories but no one has identified a particle.

While external pushing gravity theories have never gained much recent credibility among the physics establishment, they have a wide following among alternative and dissident gravitational theorists. Most of these theories have no explanation for Einstein's equivalence principle and generally ignore the concept altogether. All of these theories predict the Gold ball would be pushed back and forth from one side of the glass sphere to the other in a similar manner to the predictions of pulling gravity aether and field theories.

In the internal pushing particle principle of the gravitational expansion of mass, space, and time, the particles that do the pushing are the well established protons and electrons that make up the structure of atoms. This explanation of gravity is a purely mechanical principle of measurement and not a theory, because the outward physical force and motion of gravity is easily measured with accelerometers and atomic clocks. The motion of the gravity cannon ball can easily indicate the truth between the pulling and pushing theories of gravity.

In the internal pushing particle principle of gravity, the Gold ball would move from the surface of the sphere towards its center where it would gradually decelerate to a stop. All the other theories of gravity predict the Gold ball would oscillate back and forth through the shaft from one surface of the glass sphere to the other.

6. The Gravity Cannon Test

(See figure 6) The gravity cannon is a definitive experimental measurement of gravity that must be performed in the weightlessness of outer space. Once made, this test can easily differentiate between the four possible classes of gravitational theories.

A gold ball is placed at the opening of a shaft running through the center of a clear glass sphere. There are only two possible outcomes once the ball is released into the shaft. It will either accelerate down the shaft past center and then oscillate back and forth from one end of the shaft to the other, or it will appear to move toward the sphere's center and decelerate to a stop. A video camera is all that is needed to both confirm a theory of gravity and measure the speed of the gravitational constant.

This test is so simple and basic that once it has been performed, the results can be put up on You Tube to make it possible for the true nature of gravity to be seen and understood by everyone. Even small children will be able to clearly see and understand just how the gravity that they all feel with their bodies actually works.

7. Three Possible Gravities

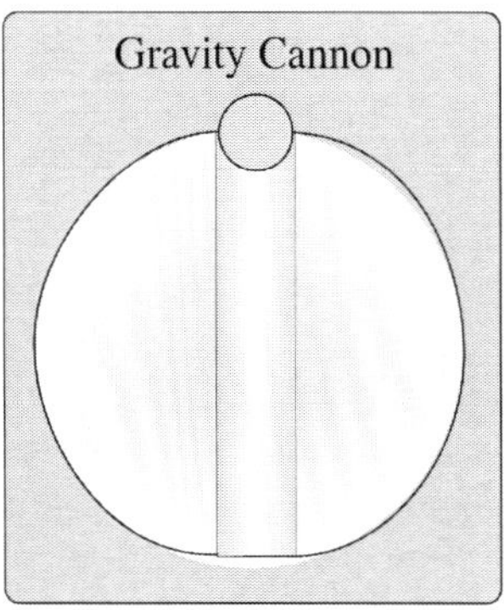

Figure 6. Gravity Cannon Test

Gravity can only be one of three possibilities. It can only be theorized as a downward pull, a downward push or an upward push. Even though everyone's subconscious is continually monitoring and adjusting the body's balance against the upward force and motion of gravity, almost everyone's conscious mind imagines it to be the downward pull of a curving spacetime field. A few others still believe the once common view that gravity is the downward push of impinging particles from outer space. All measurements clearly show gravity to be an upward push.

There can be only two possible outcomes to the gravity cannon experiment. This test easily decides the absolute physical truth between whether gravity points down with equivalent acceleration as has always been imagined and calculated or whether the force of gravity points up as has always been felt and measured. Either the Gold ball will just appear to move toward the center of the sphere and stop or it will be actually pulled or pushed back and forth from one end of the cannon barrel to the other. Does equivalent force add and then subtract equivalent momentum from the Gold ball as it moves through the glass sphere or does the momentum of both ball and glass sphere remain separate and conserved?

The internal proton/electron pushing principle of absolute gravitational force and motion predicts that the ball will appear to begin accelerating toward the center and then slow to a stop with decreasing deceleration at the sphere's center. The ball remains at rest while the outer surfaces of both ball and sphere move away from their inertial centers. There is no absolute motion between the inertial centers of ball and sphere.

8. Principle of the Gravitational Expansion of Mass, Space, and Time

Absolute gravitational motion and force is not a theory of gravity. It is just the measurement of gravity that reveals why we have always felt and measured the upward push of Earth's surface falling up!

in terms of its physical measurements with no metaphysical assumptions such as aethers, fields, actions at a distance, or unseen impinging particles from outer space. Expanding parameters of mass, space, and time show that our measurements of gravitational force are real and that the acceleration of gravity produces true upward motion. Gravity is merely the outward force produced by the gradual and constant dimensional expansion of mass, space, and time. A falling body does not accelerate downward because no such change in motion can be measured. Like the Gold ball in the gravity cannon, falling bodies do not change their state of motion while the surface of Earth moves upward with measured

Newtonian acceleration and velocity. Gravity and inertia are not just equivalent. They are exactly equal.

The gravity cannon test will provide a decisive experimental and mathematical difference between both aether theories and the many pushing gravity particle theories.

Most previous experimental measurements of gravity such as GPS clock rates and the Pound-Rebka measurements of gamma ray momentum shifts tended to yield the same predicted results for different gravity theories. However, this experiment will yield different results depending on which theory might be correct.

The ultimate financial benefits of putting a gravity cannon experiment in orbit could be enormous. Hundreds of millions of dollars have been spent to test one or another of General Relativity's many predictions. Just one example is the LIGO experiment that has probably been unsuccessful in detecting Einstein's continuum of gravitons and gravity waves. The gravity cannon would either verify General Relativity's curved relative space interpretation of gravity or prove the opposite curving matter interpretation of absolute Newtonian force and motion. What this experiment actually determines is the true intrinsic up or down direction of gravitational motion and force and whether gravity is a one-dimensional push or a two-dimensional pull.

9. The Gravity Cannon Ball

The gravity cannon (see figure 7) is a simple apparatus with two movable parts that react to the force and motion of gravity in the weightlessness of outer space. One of the two possible opposite motions of the cannonball will clearly determine which gravity theory is correct. General Relativity has long claimed that gravity was the relative motion between two bodies caused by the undetectable curving of the spacetime continuum. Perhaps the golden cannonball will show that gravity is the measurable curving of matter itself and not the unmeasured curvature spacetime. If gravity is not the infinite pulling and curving of spacetime throughout the universe then maybe the quantum nature of gravity is that it is just the purely local event of one atom pushing against another.

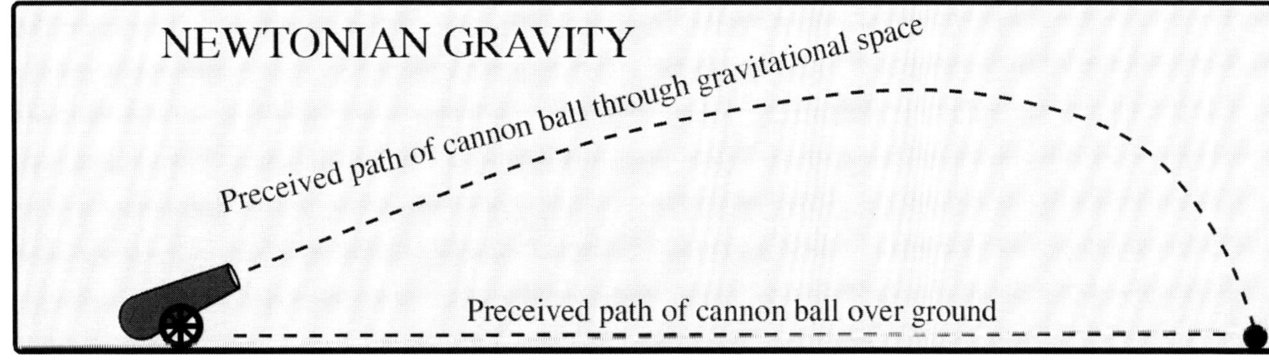

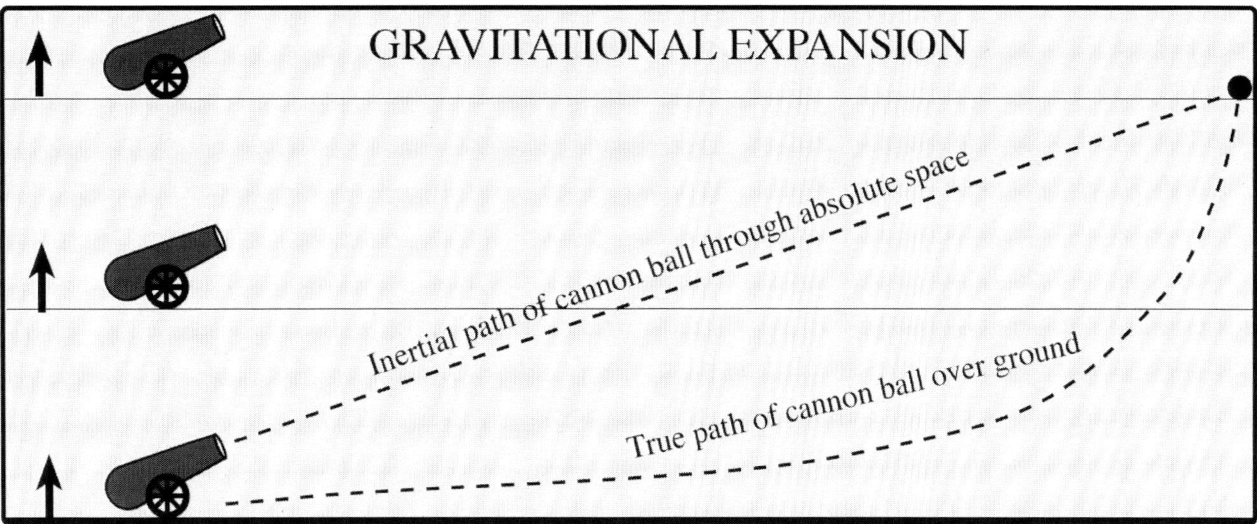

Figure 7. The Gravity Cannon Ball

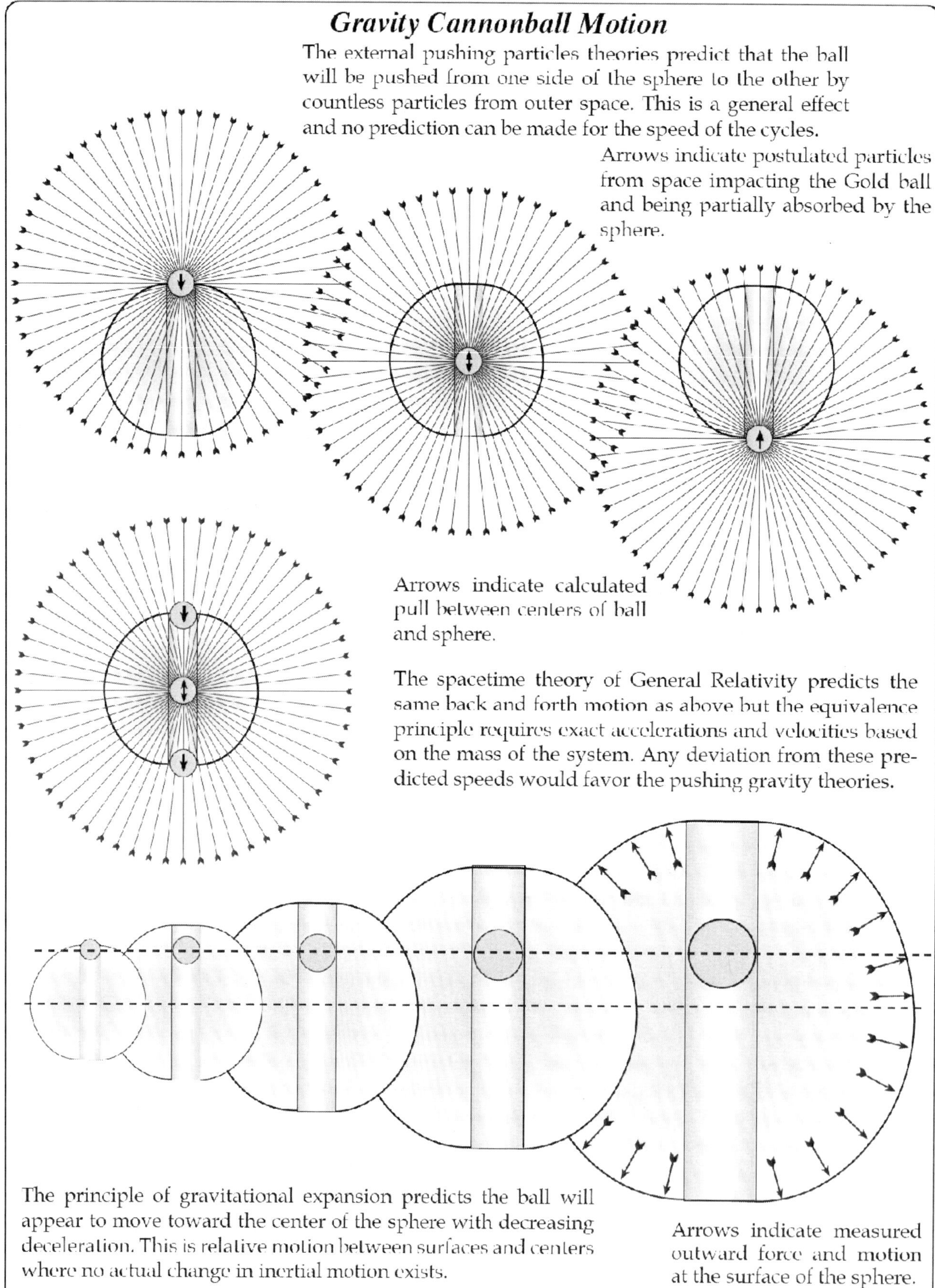

Gravity Cannonball Motion
The external pushing particles theories predict that the ball will be pushed from one side of the sphere to the other by countless particles from outer space. This is a general effect and no prediction can be made for the speed of the cycles.
Arrows indicate postulated particles from space impacting the Gold ball and being partially absorbed by the sphere.
Arrows indicate calculated pull between centers of ball and sphere.
The spacetime theory of General Relativity predicts the same back and forth motion as above but the equivalence principle requires exact accelerations and velocities based on the mass of the system. Any deviation from these predicted speeds would favor the pushing gravity theories.
The principle of gravitational expansion predicts the ball will appear to move toward the center of the sphere with decreasing deceleration. This is relative motion between surfaces and centers where no actual change in inertial motion exists.
Arrows indicate measured outward force and motion at the surface of the sphere.

Figure 8. Gravity Cannonball Motion

The Candle, The Light Bulb, and The Radio

Robert de Hilster

23344 Carolwood Ln #6409, Boca Raton, FL 33428, robert@dehilster.com

It's all about light waves and radio waves. There is a rainbow of light coming from a candle. There is white light coming from a light bulb. Radio waves come from a Radio station but the waves are not visible. But they all are based on the photon. The photon is considered both a particle and a wave since Einstein did his work on the photo-electric effect. This led to the wave particle duality of light. This paper investigates the candle and the light bulb to help understand light. It then replaces the photon with a stream of particles with a particle distribution that has a repetitive pattern. With this model there is no wave particle duality.

Keywords: Energy, Photon, Electron, Nucleon, G1 Particle

1. The Candle

Figure 9 is a drawing of a candle showing the various temperature zones and the corresponding color.

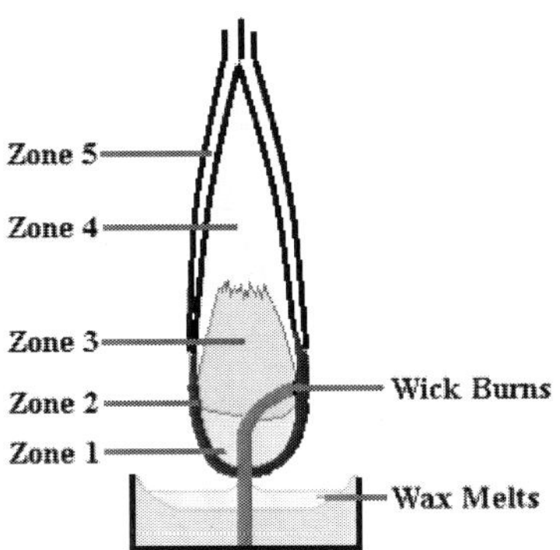

Figure 9. The Candle, Temperature, and Color

A candle is made of two parts, the fuel, which is some type of wax, and the wick, which is made of twine. The wick has to be absorbent or with a strong capillary action (the tendency of a liquid to move up in a thin tube). The absorbency of the wick allows it to carry the liquid wax to the flame. When the wick is lit, the wax that is on or near it melts. The wax is then vaporized by the flame and burns. A candle's flame can be divided into several zones: [1]

- Zone 1: Non-Luminous zone – There is not enough oxygen for the fuel to burn. The temperature is around 600 °*C* (The temperature in each zone changes among different candles and environments).
- Zone 2: Blue zone – There is plenty of oxygen and the flame burns with blue light. The temperature is around 800 °*C*.
- Zone 3: Dark zone – Pyrolysis (cracking) of the fuel begins due to a shortage of oxygen. This creates minute carbon particles. The temperature is around 1000 °*C*.
- Zone 4: Luminous zone – Pyrolysis continues due to a shortage of oxygen, carbon particles continue to heat as they rise until they ignite and emit the full spectrum of visible light (we see it as yellow). The temperature is around 1200 °*C*.
- Zone 5: Veil – There is plenty of oxygen so carbon particles burn more completely. The temperature is around 1400 °*C*.

It is quite remarkable that the color and the temperature are so closely related. Temperature is the measurement of the amount of heat that an object has. But, what is heat?

2. Heat

Matter is made up of atoms and molecules (groupings of atoms) and energy causes the atoms and molecules to always be in motion - either bumping into each other or vibrating back and forth. The motion of atoms and molecules creates a form of energy called heat or thermal energy which is present in all matter. [2]

An object has heat when its atoms are vibrating. An object whose atoms do not vibrate has no heat and the temperature is at absolute zero. When atoms of an object vibrate faster than the atoms of your finger, your finger will feel warmer. If the atoms of an object vibrate slower than the atoms of your finger, and you will feel cooler.

Atoms do not care how slow or fast they vibrate. As such heat is not real in nature. Heat is something humans care about because we must maintain a proper temperature for our bodies.

Vibration, Temperature, and Color

Atoms with a small amount of heat have a very small vibration. That means the distance it travels back and forth is small. Atoms with a large amount of heat will travel a longer distance as it vibrates. Chart 1 is a chart of temperature and color for short and long vibrations.

Item	Two Wavelengths	
Vibration	Short	Long
Temperature	800 °C	1400 °C
Color	Blue	Red

Chart 1 - Vibration, Temperature, and Color

There seems to be a correlation between vibrating atom and color. According to Figure 10, when the atom burns, it generates carbon dioxide gas, water vapor, soot, heat, and a photon. [3] But the atoms only contain protons, neutrons and electrons.

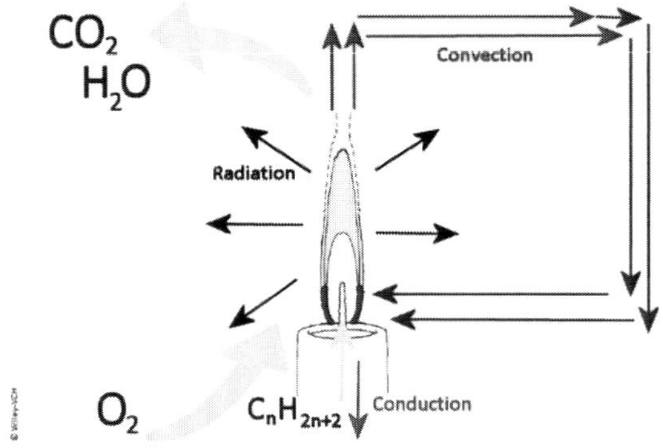

Figure 10. Burning Candle

Where do the photons come from?

3. The Light Bulb

The light bulb in Figure 11 has been burning for over 100 years.

Figure 11. The 100 Year Light Bulb

Livermore, California, is home to what residents say is the world's longest-burning light bulb. Made by the Shelby Electric Co. of Ohio, it's been shining bright, without a flicker, at the town's firehouse since 1901. [4]

And the filament is still working. The original atoms are still there.

In an electric light bulb, electrons pass through the filament causing it to heat up. The atoms in the filament vibrate at different rates. If there are atoms vibrating with different wavelengths, the light bulb can generate white light. However, when the electron passes through the filament, the atom vibrates and it releases photons.

Where do the photons come from?

4. The Atom

How Atoms Emit Photons

Figure 12 describes how an atom produces a photon. There are three steps: [5]

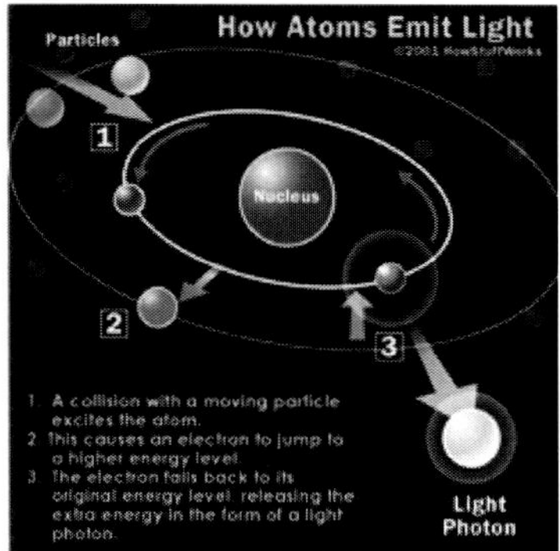

Figure 12. How Atoms Emit Light

- **Step 1**: A particle collides with and excites the atom. Colliding is understood. What is the state of an excited atom?
- **Step 2**: An electron jumps to a higher level. What force caused the electron to move? If there is motion, there must be a force. (Newton)
- **Step 3**: It falls back releasing energy in the form of a photon. How can energy create a particle?

Energy is Not Real

There are objects in nature that are clearly real. You can go outside get some dirt and hold it in your hand. These objects are real. Particles are considered real even though we cannot hold them in our hand. There are terms that are used to describe characteristics of an object or group of objects that are useful but not real.

Any term developed using mathematics is not real. Nature cannot do math. As such the following are not real: momentum, force, energy, frequency, and more. But they are useful.

Since energy is not real, there is light but no photon.

5. The Particle Model

This particle model was first described by Bob and Dave de Hilster at the CNPS 2015 Conference. [6] The particle model suggests that the atom is made of two particles; the Nucleon and the G1. The nucleon replaces the neutron and the proton. The G1 particle replaces the electron and the photon. Figure 13 is a diagram of the hydrogen atom using the particle model

All the atoms in the periodic table can be developed from these two particles. The G1 particle is held in orbit by an atomic binding force. And yes, there is no plus and minus charge. There is no negative electron and there is no positive proton.

5.1. Light

Light is a stream of G1 particles each moving at the speed of c and has a repetitive pattern. Figure 14 shows streams of particles whose patterns have the general form

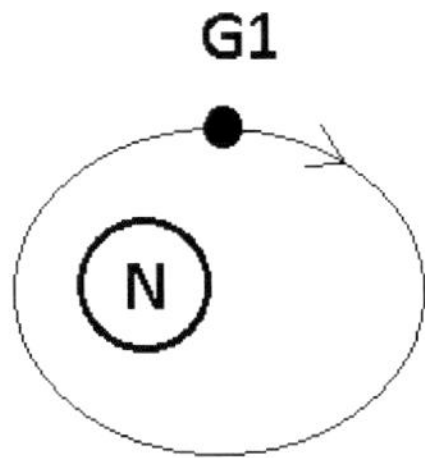

Figure 13. The Particle Model for Hydrogen

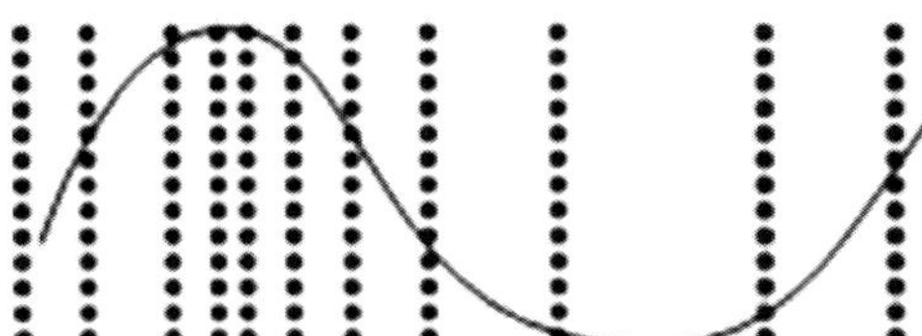

Figure 14. The Particle Model for Light

of a sine wave. A square wave, a triangular wave, a single pulse, and many other patterns can be generated.

Nature can generate any pattern that the atoms and molecules allow. Humans can generate any wave from radio waves to gamma waves using existing electronic technology.

Speed of Light

The particle model assumes that the speed of the G1 particle is c, but it is not constant.

Wavelength

Wave length is real. The wave length of Figure 14 is represented by the distance between peaks. The assigned value of the wavelength (the meter) is man made.

If the speed of the stream is c, then the frequency is speed divided by wavelength (c/λ). Since nature cannot do mathematics, frequency is not real. It is a man made construct.

Intensity

The intensity of light is the dependent on the number of particles per wave. Bright light has many particles and dim light has fewer particles. Although the number per wave is real, nature does not know or care how many are there.

6. Applying the Particle Model

The Candle

G1 particles come from the atoms in the wax and exit the candle while being modulated by the vibrating atoms. Not many G1s are needed since one candle has a very little light.

The Light Bulb

Since the G1 particles in the filament are not lost, the light from the bulb does not come from the atoms. The G1 particles flowing through the filament interact with atoms and cause them to heat up. They are also scattered by the atoms in patterns that match the the vibration rate of the atoms. The intensity of the light depends on the number of G1s (electrons) flowing through the filament. The greater the number of G1s, the more intense the light.

Radio Transmission

The G1 particle can easily enter and leave any object including an antenna. Figure 15 shows an electronic circuit guiding the G1 particle streams to the antenna.

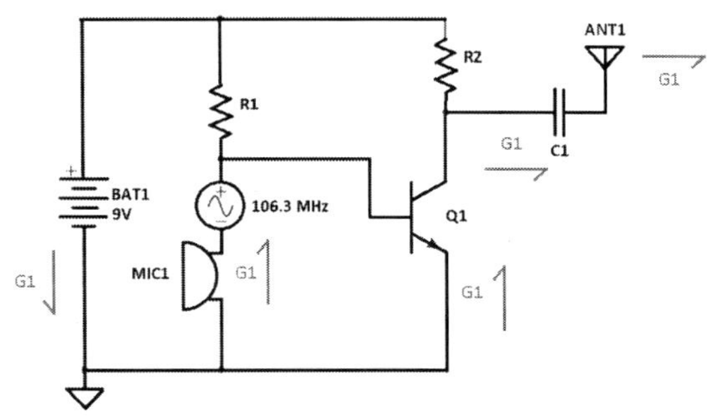

Figure 15. FM Transmitter

The FM circuit sends streams of G1s using constant amplitude and modulated wavelengths to the antenna. The modulated wavelengths contain the audio information. Figure 16 shows the streams entering the transmitting antenna with a format that matches the FM signal; that same stream leaves the antenna. The G1 streams enter the antenna of the FM receiver and they enter the FM receiver circuit.

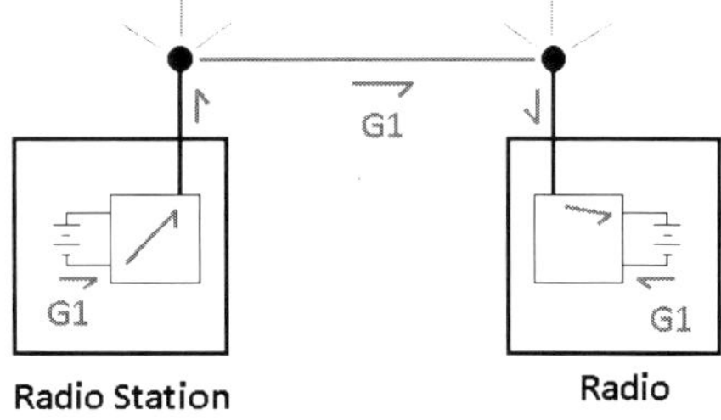

Figure 16. Radio Station and Radio

The G1 particle replaces the electron in the circuit and it replaces the photons between the radio station and the radio.

Wave Particle Duality

Light is made of one type of particle, the G1. The wave is not the motion of a medium. Light consists of a stream of these particles that has a repetitive pattern. The wavelength is the distance between the peaks (where most of the particles occur) of the wave. In this model there is no wave particle duality.

REFERENCES

1. Web Site: Pysanka
   URL: http://www.pysanky.info/Chemistry/Candle-Flame.html
2. Web Site: Cool Cosmos
   URL: http://coolcosmos.ipac.caltech.edu/cosmic-classroom/light-lessons/thermal/heat.html
3. Web Site: Cool Cosmos
   URL: http://www.chemistryviews.org/details/ezine/1393243/What-Makes-a-Candle-Flame.html
4. Web Site: abcnews.go.com
   URL: http://abcnews.go.com/blogs/business/2014/10/light-bulb-still-burning-after-100-plus-years-as-ge-brings-business-back-to-us/
5. Web Site: How Stuff Works, Home and garden
   URL: http://home.howstuffworks.com/light-bulb.htm
6. Title: Light, Gravity, and Mass
   Authors: Robert and David de Hilster,
   CNPS 2016 Proceedings

Comparing Aether with the Particle Model

David de Hilster

22936 Ironwedge Dr., Boca Raton, Florida 33433, david@dehilster.com

Until the emergence of a viable contender, aether theory for light has been one of the only alternatives to give physicality to light. With the emergence of the Particle Model for light, gravity, magnetic fields, electricity, and the atom as proposed by Robert and David de Hilster [7], it is now necessary to compare the two. Aether theory has had several hundred years to find a correct answer but to model light but has failed to do so for numerous reasons. This paper will compare and contrast the two models.

Keywords: aether theory, particle model

1. Introduction

Modern aether theory has been pursued for well over 100 years with the majority of aetherists working in the late 20th and early 21st centuries. The allure to aether to modern aetherists are the following:

1. Light is the result of something physical
2. Light acts like a wave through something
3. Therefore it is logical that light travels through a medium

Yet, there are problems with modern aether theory and include:

1. Aether cannot transmit transverse waves
2. The requirement of extremely high elasticity
3. High density
4. Highly stable and static
5. It cannot describe certain important phenomena like laser light

2. Enough Time to Crask

The other important point with aether models is that there have been many very intelligent people try to come up with a working aether theory and they all have failed. The number of scientists pursuing aether theory as documented in the Natural Philosophy Database has at least 85 people who have or are actively pursuing aether as an explanation for light.

3. Emotional Attachment to Aether

Given that light is all around us and can be seen in all directions, leads to the conclusion that in fact, light must be waves through a medium. Aetherists become so fixated with this model in their head, they cannot step back far enough to see the trees from the forest. Although this is not a scientific argument, it is important to understand the psychology of theory are well as the theory itself.

4. Wave-Particle Duality and the Particle Model

One of the great downfalls of modern physics is what is termed the "wave-particle duality" [3]. Light is said to sometimes behave as particles as in Albert Einstein's photo-electric effect [4], while most all of the other times we observe light, it behaves more like a wave. Where aether theory states that light is exclusively the result of collisions, the particle model says light is exclusively waves of particles.

The particle-wave duality is why quantum mechanics has gone astray. They claim to be shooting one photon or one electron toward a target and this causes all the silliness of spooky action at a distance. This is simply solved by the fact that light and electrons in the Particle Model are plural and not singular.

The particle model solves the wave-particle duality by allowing for "waves of particles" traveling at the same speed to be waves instead of "collisions in particles" being waves.

5. Comparing Aether with the Particle Model

Given that light is all around us and can be seen in all directions, leads to the conclusion that in fact, light must be waves through a medium.

5.1. Aether Light Transmission

The physical properties required by aether to transmit light at extreme distances involves extreme if not impossible properties.

The first, and most impossible, is elasticity. For waves to travel in a medium, the further they travel, the more elastic they must be. In the case of transmitting light waves over 12.6 billion light years which are the distance of the furthest galaxies, elasticity or "hardness" would have to be almost infinite.

Second, the density of such a material needs to be incredibly high in order to transmit the resolution needed for objects we see and can even magnify.

Third, aether must be fairly stable and unmoving in order for the waves to transmit long distances. In all intense and purposes, aether is would practically need to be close to an infinitely dense solid.

5.2. Particle Model Light Transmission

The particle model for light waves does not involve any

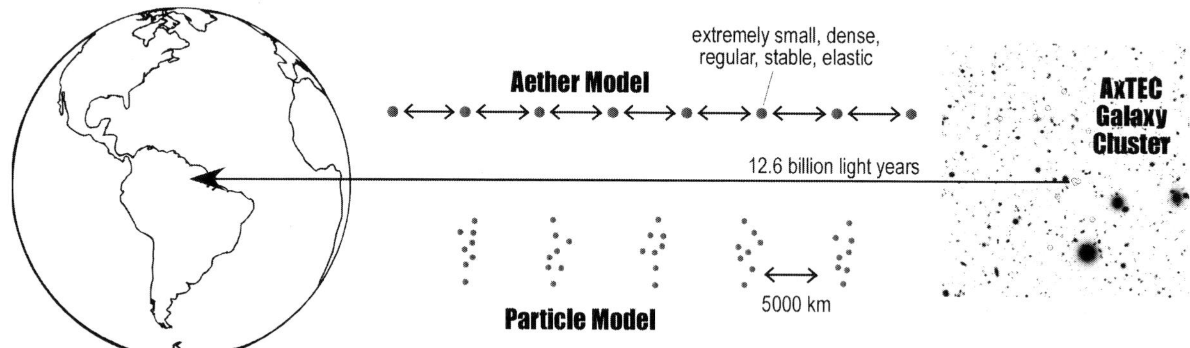

Figure 17. Comparing Aether Theory to the Particle Model of light from extreme distances

collisions. It involves the travel of waves of particles traveling through 99.9999% empty space. There is no problem with absurd elasticity or density of a matter.

A question from a fellow scientist wondered how the particle model could transmit light from a star at such a great distance when the particles sent out by a star spread throughout the universe. Starlight must in effect be very intermittent and not a solid image as we see them. Given that the eye must see 60 frames a second to not perceive flickering, at the speed of light, particle waves can be as far as 50,000 kilometers apart and we will still perceive the image as steady.

A comparison of the two models is see in figure 17.

5.3. Particle Model Versus Neo-Mechanics

Most aether models are not comprehensive models for the universe. They usually concentrate on modeling light and light waves. One exception to this is Pence and Bochardt's neo-mechanics [2] which is comprehensive in its use of infinity, but not conprensive when it comes to the wave-particle duality or magnetic fields.

The particle model as described by de Hilster and de Hilster shares many of the same assumptions including infinity. The particle model is also inspired by many of the concepts in neo-mechanics, like electricity being the same physical substance as light.

But the biggest difference between neo-mechanics is the failure of aether to solve the wave-particle duality. neo-mechanics suffers from all the same problems all aetherist theories suffer and with decades of work, no aetherist has yet to solve.

6. Conclusion

The particle model is a real alternative to aether theory. The major difference between aetherists and the particle model is that aetherists have concentrated on light and not a comprehensive model for the universe. Neo-mechanics, although much more comprehensive, still falls short in modeling the physicality of the entire universe. It is important to also note that emotional attachment to the idea that light must be a wave through some medium has kept aetherists from exploring different models such as the particle model.

REFERENCES

1. Robert de Hilster, David de Hilster, *A No-Math Physical Model of the Entire Universe*, John Chappell Natural Philosophy Society, 2017.
2. Steve Pence, Glenn Borchardt, *Universal Cycle Theory: Neomechanics of the Hierarchically Infinite Universe*, Outskirts Press, 2011.
3. Wikipedia, *Wave-Particle Duality*, https://en.wikipedia.org/wiki/Wave-particle_duality
4. Albert Einstein *The Photo Electric Effect*, https://en.wikipedia.org/wiki/Photoelectric_effect

Comparing "Models"

David de Hilster

22936 Ironwedge Dr., Boca Raton, Florida 33433, david@dehilster.com

One of the great downfalls of modern physics both in the mainstream and in dissident science is the overuse of the word "Model". The biggest offender is the "Standard Model" which for all intensive purposes is 100% non-physical in nature. Supposed "models" or "theories" of the universe employ lots of math, concepts, and words without giving any physicality to anything. When physicality is given, there is no justification for the shape or attributes to those structures. This is a grand failure in science.

Keywords: aether, particle model, standard model

1. Introduction

The use of language in physics is extremely important while at the same time extremely neglected. If you analyze the words and meaning of what words scientists use, you quickly discover a vast misuse of vocabulary, in modern physics and cosmology. The word "model" in Standard Model, the word "field", and there are many more. Not using our language properly leads to the usse of "magical" words being equated to magical theory and models.

2. Standard Model

The standard model of physics and their particles as Dr. Alexander Unzicker states[1], is made up of arbitrary packages with arbitrary attributes[1]. It is ironic that mainstream physics calls their theory a "model" when in fact, it completely theoretical. This is evident when one looks at the attributes that are imbued upon the particles in physics including isospin, color, upness, downess, strangeness, etc.

It is also evident is the lack of physicality of how particles are made from other particles and what keeps those particles together. The grand absence of any physicality makes it impossible for mainstream to even use the word "model" in their vocabulary when in reality, it is only theory.

Space-time is another concept that defy physical logic. Space-time is often referred to as the "fabric" of space-time yet no one knows or gives any physicality to that "fabric" but it's existence is completely dependent on the fact that it "bends". Only physical things bend yet space-time is a completely vacuous concept with no physicality.

The wave / particle duality describes a problem where light seems to be a wave in some material and at other times acts like a particle. This is a schizophrenic concept form at the outset and clearly shows the lack of a physical model which would clear up such a notion.

3. Fields

Everyone in physics both in the mainstream and dissident science talk about "fields" including electric fields, gravitation fields, and the like. Yet, they give no physicality to those fields. Their models depend 100% on some field yet they cannot name of give an explanation for the "stuff" those fields are made of.

Fields are one of the most common "ideas" in theories and models yet their physical description is nothing more than words.

4. Electric Universe

The Electric Universe main thesis is that the universe is much more electrical than thought. It relies on electric fields and electricity and it too suffers from no physical model to electrical phenomena in the universe. Without knowing what actually makes up electromagnetic fields, magnet fields and even electricity, it cannot be called a model. It is the application of "everything electrical" to any phenomena that happens or is said to have happened in the universe.

5. Toroid Models

Toroids are popular models in dissident physics. The claim is that toroids can persit for some time in liquids or gases [5] [6]. Yet, there is no explanation for the existence and makeup of the medium no as to why these toroids exist and what forces keep them in place and persistant.

6. Aether and Other Physical Light Theories

Aether in dissident science is a response to the fact that in modern physics, there is no physical explanation for light. Aether becomes the physical medium or physicality for light in the many hundreds of "aetherists" around the world. The major problem with this physicality is that it is fixated on putting physicality to light, and the rest of the universe is neglected.

The problems of aether theory are well documented among mainstream physics including the inability to transmit transverse waves and problems with extreme elasticity and density.

7. Neo-Mechanics

Neo-mechanics [2] solves many of the problems of other models by introducing infinity. Infinity allows for each level of the universe to have a supporting system below it to explain the existence of the structures in the level above.

Neo-mechanics however is an aether theory and suffers from the same problems as other aether theories and this problem exists at all levels.

8. The Particle Model

The Particle Model [7] is a model that looks to be the first complete physical model of the universe which is heavily based on neo-mechanics, yet resolves the problem with neo-mechanics and other aetherist's models. Where neo-mechanics suffers from all the problems of aether and does not address charge and atomic polarity. The particle model, using only Newtonian physics, describes the entire universe as moving mass in space providing a model for light, gravity, magnetic fields, electricity, charge, polarity, scattering, reflection, refraction, dispersion; and in general, atomic structure, and mass increase, to name a few.

The Particle Model solves the wave-particle duality and by describing light not as waves through a medium, but as waves of particles themselves traveling together in groups and therefore do not have any problems that are inherent in aether theory. The Particle Model in essence solves the wave-particle duality problem in physics.

9. Conclusion

All models, with the exception of the neo-mechanical and particle model, suffer from almost no physicality of any kind. Neo-mechanics tries to address this problem, but by definition, suffers from the problems inherent in aether, and therefore is incomplete. It is the opinion of this author that Particle Model is the first true physical model of the entire universe - right or wrong. It's model is very powerful in that it gives new insights and explanations to well-known phenomena as well as describes experiments that are inexplicable such as the double slit experiment with detector.

Science must create real physical models for everything in the universe so that we can make technological advances in science to control our world for the betterment of all people. This will never happen if we continue to follow theory and mathematics which masquerades as models, as is seen in the case with the Standard "Model" and many dissident theories. It is important for dissidents to try and create models that are comprehensive instead of dealing with abstract words that tell us nothing. Models that are physical and comprehensive are easier to understand and visualize.

REFERENCES

1. Dr. Alexander Unzickere, *The Higgs Fake*, Createspace Independent Pub, 2013.
2. Steve Pence, Glenn Borchardt, *Universal Cycle Theory: Neomechanics of the Hierarchically Infinite Universe*, Outskirts Press, 2011.
3. Wikipedia, *Wave-Particle Duality*, https://en.wikipedia.org/wiki/Wave-particle_duality
4. Albert Einstein *The Photo Electric Effect*, https://en.wikipedia.org/wiki/Photoelectric_effect
5. Carter, James The Next Great Impossible Discovery in Physics, Absolute Motion Institute; First B&W edition, 2013.
6. Dr. William Lucas A Classical Electromagnetic Theory of Everything, NPA Proceedings, 2010
7. Robert de Hilster, David de Hilster, *A No-Math Physical Model of the Entire Universe*, John Chappell Natural Philosophy Society, 2017.

A New Mechanism for Matter Increase within the Earth

John Eichler[1]

United States, jbeichler@ualr.edu

A plausible new argument suggests that, based on known physical phenomena, particles from the Sun may account for Earth expansion. It resolves questions on the source of new matter and how it penetrates the Earth, thereby lending support to Expansion Tectonics theory. According to Expansion Tectonics, geological data support the claim that the Earth has been gaining matter over geological time. The source of this new matter and the specific manner of how the Earth gains it remain a mystery which affects the viability of Expansion Tectonics. This article proposes a new mechanism for matter gain. In summary, based on the electric nature of our universe, it is suggested that this gain is primarily fed by solar particles that are transferred to the Earth's interior by electron and proton conduction. It is argued that such a process is plausible and has support based on theoretical and empirical studies appearing in existing scientific literature.

Keywords: expansion tectonics, mass increase

1. Expansion Tectonics

For over a century, many professional geologists have speculated on the possibility that the Earth has undergone a steadily increasing expansion. In the past 60 years, the two names most notable in this regard are Professor Samuel Warren Carey and his successor Dr James Maxlow, both geologists from Australia. These and other scientists have arrived at the conclusion that, based on sound empirical evidence, the observed geology of the Earth can only be explained if the Earth has been increasing its radius substantially over a time period of several billion years.

In the 1990s, Maxlow in his graduate research pursued the Earth expansion hypothesis in much greater detail. Maxlow initiated his studies soon after the Commission for the Geological Map of the World and UNESCO had completed worldwide geological mapping of the surface of the Earth—both on land and under the oceans—assembling extensive aging data of the entire crust. This mapping then formed the basis for Maxlow's research.

Maxlow determined that the Earth has undergone an exponential increase in radius since the beginning of Earth history some 4,000 plus million years ago. What this means is that, for over 90 per cent of its existence, the increase in Earth radius was much less than the thickness of a human hair per year, and then, about 200 million years ago, this rapidly increased to its present rate of 22 millimeters per year.

By systematically taking away the area represented by the oceans and constructing progressively smaller-radius Earth models, Maxlow demonstrated that it is possible to reduce the Earth's radius and fit all of the present continents together at about 55 per cent of the current Earth radius at the beginning of the Jurassic Period some 200 million years ago. Similarly, by investigation of ancient interior continental basins, Maxlow found that it was possible to extend this value downwards to approximately 27 per cent of the current value at the beginning of the Archaean Aeon some 4,000 million years ago. From the beginning of the Archaean to the present day, this represents about a 50-fold increase in volume. In all cases, Maxlow claims he was able to achieve a better than 99 per cent land-mass fit as he progressed stepwise back in time, providing compelling evidence for Expansion Tectonics.

A detailed technical discussion of the geological and other evidence supporting this expansion process—termed by Maxlow as Expansion Tectonics—is beyond the scope of this article but is covered extensively elsewhere [1, 2, 3].

Carey considered and subsequently rejected a number of possible causes of expansion such as

1. a pulsating Earth,
2. meteoric and asteroidal accretion,
3. a constant Earth matter with phase changes of an originally superdense core,
4. continual reduction of the universal gravitational constant, and
5. a cosmological cause involving a continual increase in matter.

The problem with each of these possible causes is that none seemed to account for the proposed magnitude of expansion. Furthermore, most of these possible causes involve esoteric theoretical speculation. Clearly, if the Earth has been gaining matter at the levels required (from what geological evidence suggests), there must be some other mechanism underlying this matter increase. Such a mechanism is suggested here, based on electron and proton conduction in solids, which is consistent with known empirically determined characteristics of matter.

[1] This is a slightly expanded version of an article originally published in Nexus Magazine, April-May 2011.

2. Ruling out the conversion of pure energy to matter

Some have put forth the speculation that energy impinging on the Earth has been converted into mass according to Einstein's famous (equation 28).

$$E = mc^2 \quad (28)$$

It has been experimentally observed that a quanta of light (i.e., a photon), may under certain conditions, create an electron and a positron (referred to as pair-formation). Actually, as pointed out by Feynman [4], positron creation is much more common than one might think. At much higher photon energies a proton and anti-proton may even be formed.[2] Could this account for the increase in the Earths matter?

Several technical issues would arise if this were so. In the case of an electron and positron, one must consider what minimum energy level a photon must possess for pair-formation to occur. To calculate this, the rest mass of each of these particles must be considered. If we take the rest mass (i.e., the smallest energy level equivalents) of each of these particles and add them together, using Einstein's equation the resultant energy level of the quanta needed to produce both particles is shown to be quite large (approximately 1.022 MeV) and photons at this energy level seldom reach the surface of the Earth having undergone particle collisions at high altitudes.

Moreover, there are so many electrons naturally occurring in the environment that any positrons produced would, on average, interact with existing electrons once again producing a new quanta of energy. For protons, whose mass is over 1,800 times that of an electron, the energy requirements are much higher for proton and anti-proton formation.

Furthermore, observation shows in most cases the energy being converted into mass (and vise-versa) does not occur through the above mechanism. Rather, a quanta of energy is converted into its mass equivalence by increasing the energy level of an already existing particle (usually an electron) with which it interacts. New matter, in the form of electrons and protons, is not produced. Instead, existing matter is changed via ionization, molecular bonding, or nuclear binding and their reverse processes. For example, our Sun does not produce energy by creating new, or destroying old, matter but rather alters existing matter to liberate nuclear binding energy through well-known nuclear processes. In summary, most common energy reactions we know of do not result in actual matter creation or destruction. Also, electrons and protons do not annihilate each other.[3] The best that can happen when these particles interact is that a neutron is formed which itself is unstable (except when present in an atomic nucleus) having a half-life of about 14 minutes.

3. A Proposed New Mechanism

Dr. Hannes Alfvén, Nobel laureate and recognized plasma physics expert who is considered the father of the field, has said that our universe is one where over 99 per cent of the matter present is in the form of plasma. Plasma currents consist of charged particles, both electrons and negatively or positively charged ions, which move in unison (although in opposite directions) under the influence of electric and magnetic fields. Subsequent exploration of space by artificial satellites and space probes has verified that such currents do exist. Even though these charged particles are widely separated—as is the case in the relative void of space—the sheer number of particles is so large that currents in the billions of amps or more are created by their motion [5]. This subject matter has been analyzed in detail in many technical books and papers (e.g., [6, 7, 8]). For our purposes, what is important here is that vast numbers of charged particles do indeed exist in space.

What is suggested here is that the constant bombardment of the Earth by charged particles, primarily from our Sun, provides a source for the matter necessary to account for the increase in matter within the Earth without the necessity of invoking esoteric theoretical processes. More importantly, all this occurs within the confines of known physics.

4. The Global Electric Circuit

Our Earth is very active, both from an electric and a magnetic standpoint. In a similar manner as to how a current flowing through a coil of wire produces a magnetic field, the Earth's magnetic field is inferred to be generated by currents of electricity within the Earth. Additionally, there is a large amount of electrical activity below, on and above the surface of our planet.

The ionosphere ranges from 50 to more than 400 kilometers above the Earth's surface. It is characterized by a mixture of free electrons and ions of various elements including hydrogen (whose ion is a single proton), thus creating a plasma current due to the Earth's magnetic field. From an electric point of view, there exists a voltage potential which ranges from 200,000 to 300,000 volts or more between the ionosphere and the surface of the Earth [9]. The atmosphere acts as an insulator, making it difficult for electric current to travel to and from the Earth's surface to the ionosphere except under special conditions. This also has been extensively studied by others. In effect, we live between the plates of a huge capacitor where one plate is the ionosphere and the other the surface of the Earth.

[2] Since the mass of a proton has been shown to be over 1,800 times that of an electron, the required energy of a photon to achieve this must be higher by a similar factor. For this reason, electron-positron pair formation is regarded as the best-case scenario as discussed herein.

[3] Both electrons and protons are required to produce stable mass and to merely imply that photons, i.e., energy, can somehow "condense" into new matter ignores some basic laws of physics.

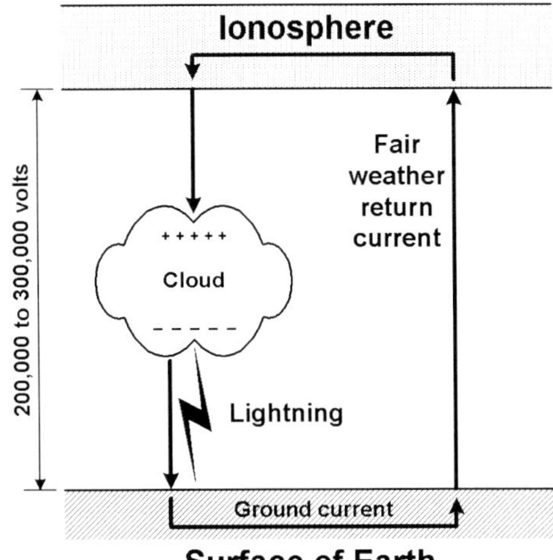

Figure 18. Shows global circuit

In thunderstorms, clouds build up large static charges in a similar way to how you might build up a charge on your body in cold weather by walking across a rug; when you reach for a door knob or other metallic device, a spark is generated between your hand and the device. Nature does the same thing, in essence, only it is called "lightning" and is vastly more intense. The potential between a cloud and the ground may extend upwards to several million volts, and the current that is discharged averages about a trillion watts [10]. It's not surprising that this amount of power is generated, considering that a lightning strike has such a high voltage together with estimated currents of up to 50,000 amperes. This means that there is a huge number of negatively charged electrons traveling between a cloud and the Earth's surface, conducted via an ionized path consisting of plasma.

With the advent of artificial satellites capable of recording lightning discharges with a high degree of accuracy, it has been estimated that about 45 to 50 lightning flashes occur every second worldwide from more than 1,500 to 2,000 thunderstorms in progress during that second. This means that every day approximately 4,000,000 lightning discharges take place, resulting in about 1.4 billion occurrences each year. About 80 per cent of the lightning flashes are between clouds, while the remaining 20 per cent are between clouds and the surface of the Earth.

Nature abhors with a vengeance an imbalance in electric charge distribution. After the lightning strike, the cloud has an unbalanced charge. It experiences an interaction with the ionosphere above it to try to become neutral again by the transfer of electrons to the cloud. But each lightning strike creates a more negative Earth by passing electrons to it. In an attempt to restore balance, some means must exist to transfer current back to the ionosphere to complete what is known as the "global electric circuit" [11] or the "global atmospheric electrical circuit" [12].

Figure 1 represents a simplified complete circuit. Lightning sends electrons to the ground where the charge spreads, since the surface layers of the Earth are good conductors of electricity. In what is referred to as the "fair-weather return current", the high potential between the ground and the ionosphere drives current flow through the air to the ionosphere to close the circuit.

It must be appreciated that in any electrical transfer, the large potential difference between the ground and the ionosphere also will drive positively charged ions down towards the ground because the Earth has a negative electrostatic charge. Any time there is a potential difference and there are charged particles present, these particles will move. And the ionosphere, under the influence of the magnetic field lines of the Earth, has all kinds of ionized particles as well as electrons moving primarily in a north-south direction. In addition, there are continual streams of electrons and ions from the Sun which serve as a potentially vast supply of available charged particles to account for the hypothesized matter gain within the Earth.

In summary, ours is a world where ionized particles abound whether from plasmas formed by the electric discharge in a bolt of lightning or plasmas present in the ionosphere due to particle bombardment from the Sun.

5. New Matter Requires Protons and Electrons

We are all familiar with electric conduction when it comes to the electric currents that we use every day to power devices around us. We know, for example, that copper and aluminum are excellent conductors of electricity. But current conduction is not limited to just metals. The Earth itself is an excellent conductor, which is why when you touch an electrical outlet while standing on the earth you feel a zap as electricity travels through your body between the outlet and the ground. We even know through this often accidental, simple experiment that the body itself is a good conductor of electricity.

Most discussions about the flow of electricity focus on the movement of electrons under conditions of voltage potential difference, since it is so common. Not so obvious in everyday life is the recognition that magnetic fields are also prime movers of electrons and other charged particles, and nowhere is this truer than within the magnetic field generated by the Earth itself.

The Earth is continually being bombarded by charged particles, both electrons and ions, from our Sun. These particles become entrapped in the Earth's magnetic flux lines in space, forming plasma sheaths which channel these particles away from most of the Earth with the exception of at its poles, where the magnetic lines of force converge. The beautiful aurora borealis and aurora australis (northern and southern lights) are ribbons of plasma where incoming charged particles enter our atmosphere, driven by the magnetic field of the Earth. But a magnet has two poles and each pole acts on particles of the same charge, be it negative or positive.

In a plasma, electrons and negative ions (atoms which have gained an extra electron, making them negative) flow in one direction, whereas protons (ionized hydrogen) and other positively charged ions flow in the opposite direction to that of the negatively charged particles. From a particle standpoint, there are differences to be noted. Electrons, being lightweight, as opposed to protons and other positive ions (made up of protons and neutrons in ionized atoms), travel with a higher velocity than do ions. But particles of each charge come under the same force provided in a magnetic field, only they have different movement characteristics.

When a thunder cloud moves over an area of land, the potential difference between the cloud and the ground creates a current flow of electrons to or from the ground directly below the cloud. This is a local effect. However, disregarding local effects, there is a component of magnetic force from the Earth which acts on charged particles. We know that currents flow within the Earth, so why shouldn't there be a similar flow of individual protons within the Earth?

It is good to reiterate at this point that new matter, in the form of atoms, requires both electrons and protons; either alone is not enough. When we are talking about matter increase within the Earth, we therefore must have both types of particles present. Is there such a phenomenon as proton flow within a liquid or solid?

6. Proton Conduction

There is a large amount of both theoretical and experimental evidence for proton conduction. Much of the recent research effort in this field has been motivated by the desire to find substances which can effectively separate charged particles in materials having practical applications, particularly in areas such as fuel cells, electrochemical sensors, electrochemical reactors and electrochromic devices [13].

What has been made clear from this research is that the mechanism of proton conduction is much different than that of electron conduction. Whereas electron current flow is generally based on freely mobile electrons as found in metals, protons don't move in a similar manner because free protons don't behave like free electrons. Protons tend to bind to the electrons in outer orbit around the atoms in a liquid or solid. Then the protons migrate in a molecule-to-molecule fashion when acted upon by a magnetic force field.

A couple of points to keep in mind are that protons are the same order of magnitude in size as electrons, and hence individual protons conduct in liquids and solids better than other heavier positively charged ions. The reason for this is that *the smallest atom is roughly 10,000 to 100,000 times larger than either an electron or a proton*. The theory behind proton conduction is complex, so only highlights will be discussed here. Individual protons are extremely active and tend to bind easily whenever atoms are present with outer-orbit electrons which may be shared.

There are two primary modes of proton conduction discussed in the literature (although others have been considered). The first mode is where the proton forms a bond with an existing atom. For example, the oxygen in a water molecule (H_2O) may temporarily gain an extra proton (H_3O). If the molecule is capable of rotation, the extra proton (whose bond is relatively weak) can create a bond with a nearby water molecule and then break loose from its existing bond with the first water molecule. In this manner, the proton is passed from molecule to molecule, which essentially provides a method for proton conduction [14]. Water (liquid or solid) is not the only type of molecule in which this effect has been studied [15].

The second mode of conduction is where a larger molecule exists which contains a number of tightly bound atoms. Of particular interest here is that materials exhibiting the structure of perovskite (a mineral with the same type of crystal structure as calcium titanium oxide, ($CaTiO_3$) have oxygen atoms which create an interactive electric-potential field where a proton finds a resting spot between such atoms [13]. Assuming that these molecules are in a matrix structure, as is frequently the case with solids, a virtual path is created that is analogous to a virtual proton-carrying wire, so that protons can travel almost unimpeded from molecule to molecule.

The point being made here is that proton conduction in both liquids and solids has been observed experimentally and has been intensively studied. Proton conduction is not just a theoretical phenomenon; it is empirically based.

Within the interior of the Earth, several well-defined layers have been found by using a variety of techniques, primarily by recording and analyzing seismic waves. Furthermore, studies have been conducted with regard to proton conduction in the materials of which these layers are composed [16]. The lower mantle, which constitutes the bulk of the material of the Earth, is believed to be composed primarily of perovskite, which, as mentioned above, has been found to be a conductor of protons. Consequently, it is argued here that there exists a probable pathway for likely conduction of protons deep within the Earth under the influence of the Earth's magnetic field, thus providing a viable method of proton transport. But what happens to this concentration of protons within the Earth?

7. Nucleosynthesis and Transmutation within the Earth from Protons and Electrons

Protons, being of like charge, normally repel each other with a vengeance. However, quantum and other effects come into play. The problem with nuclear fusion is trying to keep a group of charged particles together for sufficient enough time for fusion to occur, thus liberating energy. Protons in close proximity encounter what is known as the "Coulomb barrier". As the protons get closer together, the force of repulsion between them becomes exponentially greater. Theoretically this force should reach a near infinite level, making it impossible for nuclear fusion to occur.

Nucleosynthesis is the formation of atoms more complex than the hydrogen atom. It is generally believed that nucleosynthesis of the heavier elements only occurs in interiors of stars where extremely high temperatures and pressures are thought to occur, leading to the conclusion that most of the heavier elements found in the universe have been created in this manner.

To assume that the Earth is gaining matter and that this may be due to nucleosynthesis within the Earth seems to fly in the face of conventional wisdom and it does. However, if the geological evidence strongly suggests that the Earth's radius is getting larger with time (due to the Earth's gain of new matter), as Expansion Tectonics advocates maintain, then some mechanism must be at play to account for this additional matter. Clearly, the solid nature of the crust of the Earth is relatively impervious to the infusion of most matter, with the exception being electrons and the nuclei of the lightest elements, most likely hydrogen or an isotope of hydrogen.

Transmutation is the changing of one element into another by radioactive decay, nuclear bombardment or similar processes. New matter introduced into the Earth would require transmutation as well as nucleosynthesis. According to conventional physics, both processes normally occur when high energy levels of the interacting particles are present. The question here is whether or not these processes could happen should high-energy particles not be present. Over the last two decades, work has been going on in this area of research.

To understand this better, we turn our attention to the subject of what is generally referred to as "cold fusion". The research into this subject is complex, with many unanswered questions remaining.

In 1989, two researchers, Dr Martin Fleischmann and Dr Stanley Pons at the University of Utah, announced that they had achieved nuclear fusion in their laboratory. They claimed that this was done by electrolysis, using a palladium cathode with heavy water (deuterium oxide), with the result being that the energy output, based on measured heat, was greater than the energy input. They hypothesized that two atoms of deuterium (a stable isotope of hydrogen) fuse, creating a helium atom and liberating heat in the process. For them to have done this in a laboratory at low energies was thought to have been impossible. Since the 1950s, billions of dollars had been spent trying to accomplish fusion through expensive atom-smashing-type machines with very limited success. The hope had been to provide a cheap source of energy. Absent in Fleischmann and Pons's experiment were all the exotic by-products normally expected when high-energy fusion occurs under thermonuclear conditions with temperatures in the millions of degrees.

Below are the important points relevant to the discussion here. The best source of current information about cold fusion, i.e., low-energy nuclear reactions, is `http://www.lenr-canr.org`. I encourage interested readers to check out this website.

Cold fusion has been experimentally verified in a number of laboratories around the world, including in the USA. Because of the nature of the experimentation, the most difficult part of this effort is in carrying out the extensive instrumentation procedures required to obtain definitive results. However, scientists working with cold fusion generally agree that there is no question about its working. Excess energy is released through the fusion process, as predicted by nuclear physics, and has been measured.

Various theoretical analysis models have been proposed to explain the process, and headway is being made in this regard according to a number of investigators (e.g., [17, 18]). Although cold fusion of deuterium to create helium (and other atomic nuclei) ends with the same final result as hot fusion, the process by which this occurs is much different, primarily in the absence of high-energy by-products including radiation. Clearly, a new physical process seems to be at work that begs more theoretical attention.

It has been reported in many instances that once the electrolysis current was turned off, the heat generation process continued for extended durations, i.e., hours and/or days afterwards [17]. Presumably this is due to the palladium becoming saturated with deuterium, allowing continuation of the fusion effect independently of additional power input.

Some researchers have reported that atomic transmutation occurred in cathodes made of various materials. For example, one researcher using high-purity nickel-coated beads as the cathode found that after five weeks about 40 per cent of the nickel had been transmuted into a mixture of other elements including chromium, iron, copper, selenium, silver, cadmium, antimony and lead [17].

Over two decades ago, it was proposed that nucleosynthesis has perhaps been occurring in condensed matter within planets, moons, etc. Some research was done over that period in an attempt to prove or disprove this hypothesis [19]. This research involved looking for fusion by-products, primarily isotopes of hydrogen and helium. The principal radioactive isotope of hydrogen looked for is tritium, which has a half-life of 12.32 years.

Because of this short half-life, tritium in nature doesn't remain present for long and hence is quite rare. With helium, there are two stable isotopes (^{3}He, ^{4}He) which allow for a ratio of one to another to be calculated. The ratio of naturally occurring isotopes of helium is much different than the ratio produced in fusion reactions, allowing detection of these reactions. Gas analysis searches were conducted in two primary areas.

The first area included so-called "hot spot" volcanoes, like Kilauea in Hawai'i and Alcedo in the Galpagos, which produce magma from plumes which supposedly rise hundreds of kilometres from the core-mantle boundary, as opposed to crustal volcanoes which are regarded as rather shallow in comparison [20, 21]. The deeper volcanoes have yielded tritium presence and helium ratios (^{3}He/^{4}He) much higher, by factors of tens to hundreds, than do the shallower crustal volcanoes, indicating the possible by-products of fusion.

The second area is that of volcanic crater lakes [22]. Towards the bottom of many such lakes, the water does not mix with the upper-layer water so gases trapped in the bottom layers typically remain unaffected for thousands of years. Research has shown that the presence of tritium (with its short half-life) and high helium ratios strongly indicates that the source of these isotopes is from mantle degassing rather than from the Earth's surface. This unusually abnormal finding has led the researchers to the tentative conclusion that it fits with the hypothesis of what would be expected if fusion were occurring deep within the Earth.

8. Conclusions and Comments

For over a century, many professional scientists have maintained that expansion of the Earth has occurred. Numerous technical articles and books have expressed this hypothesis as a viable and indeed necessary one to explain the observed empirical geological facts known about our planet. Expansion Tectonics, as it is known today, alleviates the reliance on other theories that have been put forth, such as Continental Drift and Plate Tectonics.

However, Expansion Tectonics, in and of itself, has not inspired a paradigm shift away from the currently held paradigm of Plate Tectonics. When one asks why this is true, the response which most frequently comes back is the question, "If the Earth has undergone expansion, where did the increase in matter come from?" Carey, for one, spent the majority of his lifetime trying to provide an answer to this question. Time and again he considered possible mechanisms, mostly theoretical, to explain this question of increase in matter, only to reject such mechanisms for one reason or another. Any mechanism should have a foundation in the area of experimental physics rather than in purely theoretical physics abstractions.

This article proposes and examines what is considered a plausible answer to this question based upon physical processes that have been experimentally observed. It has never been observed, for example, that matter just pops into being where nothing was before. What is required is:

1. a source for new matter,
2. a means whereby this matter can penetrate into the Earth's interior, and
3. a mechanism by which heavier elements may be formed.

Empirical geological evidence strongly indicates that Expansion Tectonics is indeed valid, so the task confronted has always been to formulate a viable mechanism whereby this expansion occurs. In a plasma universe, the Earth is under constant bombardment with all the necessary components to reconstitute matter from its constituent parts deep within the Earth. Theoretical constructs that have never been experimentally observed are not required. The Earth, having a magnetic field strong enough to interact with impinging particles, gathers more than sufficient fundamental particles, namely electrons and protons, to account for a slow increase in matter internally over hundreds of millions of years. There is, therefore, no lack of component particles to create new matter deep within the body of the Earth. The exact process by which this occurs is complex in nature and, like the interior of the Earth itself, involves speculation as to its dynamics. It is argued that the avenue of approach proposed here is plausible and warrants further serious scientific investigation. If new matter has been added to the interior of the Earth, there must be an answer to the riddle of the dynamics of the process.

At the level of human perception it may seem that the Earth is an impenetrable solid, and this perception gives rise to the notion that it is impossible for new matter somehow, as if by magic, to make its way to the Earth's deep interior. But, as argued here, there are mechanisms which have an empirical basis whereby this may occur on a subatomic level. It is extremely doubtful that humans will ever penetrate much below the Earth's crust (the deepest hole depth obtained to date is approximately 0.1 per cent of the Earth's radius), so it is a near certainty that the best we will ever achieve are very-small-scale, time-limited experimental laboratory simulations based upon what we can only speculate is going on within the deep interior of the Earth.

Perhaps the time has come to stop ignoring the growing geological and other evidence against Plate Tectonics and in favor of Expansion Tectonics and begin to consider that we may, in fact, have an element-synthesizing factory right beneath the ground on which we walk.

9. Acknowledgements:

Special thanks go to Dr James Maxlow (Australia), Professor Andre K. T. Assis (Brazil) and Professor Charles M. Anderson (USA) for their helpful comments and suggestions in the preparation of this article.

10. About the Author:

John B. Eichler graduated from the Illinois Institute of Technology with majors in physics and mathematics. Under a contract from the US Atomic Energy Commission, he worked on computer analysis of blast shields for nuclear reactors and other government research activities at the IIT Research Institute. Later, his efforts were in the design and implementation of new computer systems. In 2015 he received a Masters degree in Interdisciplinary Studies from the University of Arkansas in Little Rock. His thesis titled *Rhetoric and Paradigm Change in Science: Three case studies* is available from several websites including `http://www.expansiontectonics.com/`. He is currently working on the manuscript for his forthcoming book *An Infinite Universe*. John's interest in Expansion Tectonics began in 1958 when he arrived at the conclusion that the Earth had undergone a significant expansion over time. His search for a viable mechanism to explain the matter gain utilizing empirical evidence has led to the writing of this article.

REFERENCES

1. S. Carey, *Earth, Universe, Cosmos.* University of Tasmania, Hobart, Australia, 2000.
2. J. Maxlow and A. Maxlow, *Terra non firma Earth: plate tectonics is a myth.* Terrella Press, 2005.

3. G. Scalera, "Samuel Warren Carey-commemorative memoir," in *Why expanding Earth? A book in honour of OC Hilgenberg*, G. Scalera and K.-H. Jacob, Eds. Rome, Italy: INGV, 2003, pp. 85–96.
4. R. P. Feynman and A. Zee, *QED: The strange theory of light and matter*. Princeton University Press, 2006.
5. E. Lerner, *The big bang never happened.* Vintage Books, New York, 1992.
6. H. Alfvén, "Model of the plasma universe," *IEEE transactions on plasma science*, vol. 14, no. 6, pp. 629–638, 1986.
7. A. L. Peratt, "The evidence for electrical currents in cosmic plasma," *IEEE Transactions on Plasma Science*, vol. 18, no. 1, pp. 26–32, 1990.
8. ——, "Introduction to plasma astrophysics and cosmology," in *Plasma Astrophysics and Cosmology*. Springer, 1995, pp. 3–11.
9. R. Markson and M. Muir, "Solar wind control of the earth's electric field," *Science*, vol. 208, no. 4447, pp. 979–990, 1980.
10. H. J. Christian and M. A. McCook, "A lightning primer," Lightning and Atmospheric Electricity Research at the GHCC, NASA, Tech. Rep., 2003. [Online]. Available: http://thunder.msfc.nasa.gov/primer/index.html
11. E. A. Bering III, A. A. Few, and J. R. Benbrook, "The global electric circuit," *Physics Today*, vol. 51, no. 10, pp. 24–30, 1998.
12. R. G. Harrison, "The global atmospheric electrical circuit and climate," *Surveys in Geophysics*, vol. 25, no. 5-6, pp. 441–484, 2004.
13. K.-D. Kreuer, "Proton conductivity: materials and applications," *Chemistry of Materials*, vol. 8, no. 3, pp. 610–641, 1996.
14. F. W. Poulsen, "An introduction to proton conduction in solids," Risø National Laboratory, DK 4000 Roskilde, Denmark, Tech. Rep., 1980.
15. L. Glasser, "Proton conduction and injection in solids," *Chemical Reviews*, vol. 75, no. 1, pp. 21–65, 1975.
16. T. Yoshino, "Laboratory electrical conductivity measurement of mantle minerals," *Surveys in Geophysics*, vol. 31, no. 2, pp. 163–206, 2010.
17. C. G. Beaudette, *Excess Heat: Why Cold Fusion Research Prevailed.* Oak Grove Press South Bristol, ME, 2002.
18. M. Fleischmann, S. Pons, and G. Preparata, "Possible theories of cold fusion," *Il Nuovo Cimento A (1965-1970)*, vol. 107, no. 1, p. 143, 1994.
19. J. O. Bockris and E. F. Mallove, "Is the occurrence of cold nuclear reactions widespread throughout nature?" *Infinite Energy*, vol. 27, pp. 29–38, 1999.
20. S. Jones and J. Ellsworth, "Geo-fusion and cold nucleosynthesis in tenth international conference on cold fusion," *Cambridge, MA: LENR-CANR. org*, 2003.
21. J. Tebbe, "Print and american culture," *American Quarterly*, vol. 32, no. 3, pp. 259–279, 1980.
22. S. Jiang, M. He, W. Yue, B. Qi, and J. Liu, "Observation of 3 he and 3 h in the volcanic crater lakes: possible evidence for natural nuclear fusion in deep earth," in *8th International Workshop on Anomalies in Hydrogen/Deuterium Loaded Metals, Sicily, Italy.* Citeseer, 2007.

The Ionic Growing Earth

Eugene Ellis

38178 Yacht Basin Road, Ocean View, DE, 19970, geneaellis@msn.com

The energy of the universe (as contained within the elements) is declining as it ages, some of which is being stored as potential energy by converting to mass within the existing elements and the rest to an entropy that heats the elemental mass:

E (energy) <===> m (mass) or E —-> e (entropy - heat and temperature).

Energy and mass can neither be created nor destroyed but are interconvertible. The flow of heat is from warmer to cooler and irreversible. In an open system, heat flows toward the empty space of the colder universe. Heat, unable to reverse flow, indicates it is not reverting to energy but causing the entropy of the universe to increase. The temperature of the universe (2.7 Kelvin) appears low because space is expanding much faster than the heat produced by the stars and elsewhere. Space is the container of entropy. Time is non-linear when space is expanding.

On Earth, the declining energy of eight elements (O, Fe, Si, Mg, S, Al, Ni and Ca) as exemplified by their ionization properties, is responsible for accumulating sufficient mass to double Earth's radius at least twice in the past billion years. Before that time, the energy converting to entropy from the same elements internally heated a near absolute zero planet for several billion years, cooling to a core, mantle, and crust. Afterwards, it provided sufficient heat to maintain a temperate environment to support life while exponentially growing to its present size. Ionization is responsible for oxygen becoming water and doubling in volume several times to incrementally fill the expanding ocean beds shown on the NOAA map, Age of the Ocean Floors.

Ionization is presented as a feasible mechanism for expanding and heating Earth and the other planets in the universe.

Keywords: expansion tectonics, mass increase

1. Introduction

In table 19, Mass Doubling Rates, in earlier Ionic Growing Earth (IGE) papers originally utilized five elements and a decay rate of 1 eV per 2 MY. This table was later designated as Table 2 using the same five elements and a rate of 1 eV per 1.75, MY which conforms to geological events better. Adding three elements (Al-1.4%, Ni-1.8%, and Ca-1.5%) to the five elements that make up 93.3% of Earth's matter brings the total to 98.8%. All the other elements combined make up the remaining 1.2%.

2. Growth Rates

The earlier work (IGE page 4) indicates exponential growth is of the order yx where x is the rate per 100 MY (CMY). The exponential growth equation for doubling the mass is yx = 2. Table 2 below is arranged to show what is presently known regarding the 8 elements and what is not known The third column is the element's atomic mass divided by the mass equivalent of 1 electron volt (1 eV ïĄÅ 1.073544 AMU). The "y" in column 7 is the percentage in column 5 (per 100 MY) divided by the mass in column 3. The total "y" in column 7 fixes the total "x" in column 6 by the doubling equation yx = 2.

Solving for x:

$$x \ln y = \ln 2 \tag{29}$$

or

$$x = \frac{\ln 2}{\ln y} \tag{30}$$

And for y:

$$y = x\sqrt{2} \tag{31}$$

From the known total in column 7, (y = 4.05379) one calculates a total for "x" in Column 6 (ln 2 / ln 4.05379 equals 0.495228 CMY or 49.5228 MY). Atomic Mass AMU/1.073544 Rate (MY) Percentages

Reverse engineering a decay rate of 1 eV per 1.595235 MY produces a total in column 6 matching the 49.5228 in column 8. The resulting rates in the fourth column is the third column times 1.595235 MY and provides the time it takes to double the mass of each element, i.e. oxygen doubles in mass around every 24 MY. This column 4 rate times the column 5 percentage is the "x" rate in column 6 (Figure 20).

The energy levels in Table 1 of NBS-34 are shown below for the 8 elements. Multiplying these levels by the energy decay rate (1 eV / 1.595235 MY) fixes the time at each level. The shaded areas in Table 3R (figure 21) are the times when no energy converts to mass.

Sequencing the shaded time of the 8 elements forms the first column of New Table 4 (figure 22) and one can use these times to calculate the duration of "t" in CMY (100

[1] This is a slightly expanded version of an article originally published in Nexus Magazine, April-May 2011.

TABLE 2 - MASS DOUBLING RATES - KNOWN VS UNKNOWN							
	Elemental			Total Earth			
	Atomic Mass	AMU/1.073544	Rate (MY)	Percentages	*x* (MY) % Rate	*y* (100 MY) Rate/≅ eV	*x* (MY) ln 2/ln *y*
O	15.9994	14.90335		30.10%		2.01968	
Fe	55.8470	52.02116		32.10%		0.61706	
Si	28.0855	26.16148		15.10%		0.57718	
Mg	24.3050	22.63997		13.90%		0.61396	
S	32.0600	29.86370		2.90%		0.09711	
Al	26.9815	25.13311		1.40%		0.05570	
Ni	58.7000	54.67871		1.80%		0.03292	
Ca	40.0800	37.33429		1.50%		0.04018	
Totals				98.80%		4.05379	49.5228

Figure 19. Mass Doubling Rates

TABLE 2R - MASS DOUBLING RATES (Energy = Mass) known factors							
	Elemental			Total Earth			
	Atomic Mass	AMU/1.073544	Rate (MY)	Percentages	*x* (MY) % Rate	*y* (100 MY) Rate/≅ eV	*x* (MY) ln 2/ln *y*
O	15.9994	14.90335	23.7743	30.10%	7.15608	2.01968	
Fe	55.8470	52.02116	82.9860	32.10%	26.63850	0.61706	
Si	28.0855	26.16148	41.7337	15.10%	6.30179	0.57718	
Mg	24.3050	22.63997	36.1161	13.90%	5.02013	0.61396	
S	32.0600	29.86370	47.6396	2.90%	1.38155	0.09711	
Al	26.9815	25.13311	40.0932	1.40%	0.56131	0.05570	
Ni	58.7000	54.67871	87.2254	1.80%	1.57006	0.03292	
Ca	40.0800	37.33429	59.5570	1.50%	0.89335	0.04018	
Totals				98.80%	49.5228	4.05379	49.5228

Figure 20. Mass Doubling Rates - Known Factors

TABLE 3R IONIZATION POTENTIALS of the 8 ELEMENTS

Energy in eV

	Ni	Fe	Ca	S	Si	Al	Mg	O
I	7.635	7.870	6.113	10.360	8.151	5.986	7.646	13.618
II	18.168	16.180	11.871	23.330	16.345	18.828	15.035	35.116
III	34.170	30.651	50.908	34.830	33.492	28.447	80.143	54.934
IV	54.900	54.800	67.100	47.300	45.141	119.990	109.240	77.412
V	75.500	75.000	84.410	72.680	166.770	153.710	141.260	113.896
VI	108.000	99.000	108.780	88.049	205.050	190.470	186.500	138.116
VII	133.000	125.000	127.700	280.930	246.520	241.430	224.940	739.315
VIII	162.000	151.060	147.240	328.230	303.170	284.590	265.900	871.387
IX	193.000	235.040	188.540	379.100	351.100	330.210	327.950	
X	224.500	262.100	211.270	447.090	401.430	398.570	367.530	
XI	321.200	290.400	591.250	504.780	476.060	442.070	1761.802	
XII	352.000	330.800	656.390	564.650	523.500	2085.983	1962.613	
XIII	384.000	361.000	726.030	651.630	2437.676	2304.080		
XIV	430.000	392.200	816.610	707.140	2673.108			
XV	464.000	457.000	895.120	3223.836				
XVI	499.000	489.500	947.000	3494.099				
XVII	571.000	1266.100	1087.000					

Time in MY

1.5952xeV	Ni	Fe	Ca	S	Si	Al	Mg	O
I	12.2	12.6	9.8	16.5	13.0	9.5	12.2	21.7
II	29.0	25.8	18.9	37.2	26.1	30.0	24.0	56.0
III	54.5	48.9	81.2	55.6	53.4	45.4	127.8	87.6
IV	87.6	87.4	107.0	75.5	72.0	191.4	174.3	123.5
V	120.4	119.6	134.7	115.9	266.0	245.2	225.3	181.7
VI	172.3	157.9	173.5	140.5	327.1	303.8	297.5	220.3
VII	212.2	199.4	203.7	448.1	393.3	385.1	358.8	1179.4
VIII	258.4	241.0	234.9	523.6	483.6	454.0	424.2	1390.1
IX	307.9	374.9	300.8	604.8	560.1	526.8	523.2	
X	358.1	418.1	337.0	713.2	640.4	635.8	586.3	
XI	512.4	463.3	943.2	805.2	759.4	705.2	2810.5	
XII	561.5	527.7	1047.1	900.7	835.1	3327.6	3130.8	
XIII	612.6	575.9	1158.2	1039.5	3888.7	3675.5		
XIV	686.0	625.7	1302.7	1128.1	4264.2			
XV	740.2	729.0	1427.9	5142.8				
XVI	796.0	780.9	1510.7	5573.9				
XVII	910.9	2019.7	1734.0					

Figure 21. Table 3R - Ionization Potentials of the 8 Elements

MY) in the second column. The present rate from Table 2R starts the "y" column at 4.05379.

A new column, ln 2/ln y, indicates Earth's mass doubling rate in MY and the last two columns indicates the active mass growing and heating percentages for the times specified in the first column. The highlighted years, beginning when the rate for oxygen (2.01968) is entered, are skewed and indicate all the corresponding "y" values are also skewed. The chart indicates that iron is growing between 241.0 MYA and 220.3 MYA while its graph below shows it declining and losing mass. A reason for this anomaly may involve an unknown ... how much of the 30.1% oxygen on Earth became water 1,400 MYA? Or possibly because water having a density of one, neither adds to nor subtracts from or contributes to the physical expansion of the planet. Upon growing, it merely fills holes and cracks and lies on or near the surface. An unusual build up of density before a severe split in the cracks is also a possibility.

The chart also indicates the Earth's radius would double 700 MYA (100% mass/64= 1.56%)... a physical impossibility. Some of the elements just started to grow prior to that time (from 20.6% to 52.7%) and it takes an 8-fold increase of the mass (or volume) to obtain a single doubling of the radius.

To normalize the x value (ln 2/ln y) several percentages of the oxygen rate at line 10 were tested and summarized as follows (figure 24):

From figure 24, it appears the first doubling of the radius occurred between 430 MYA and 490 MYA but more likely between 455 MYA and 490 MYA since sulfur (2.9%) stopped growing 448.1.6 MYA. Table 4R utilizes 75% oxygen. Any such change in percentage only affects the data for times older than 220.3 MYA and the radius doubling 175 MYA would remain the same.

The red highlight in the last column (% heating) indicates an extensive heating period between 358.1 MYA and 241.0 MYA that materially intensified for the 25 MY period between 266.0 MYA and 241.0 MYA. In the light of today's global heating debate where a few degrees rise in temperature in a few decades (or centuries) is considered highly detrimental to life by many, envision 25 million years of increasing heat with very small incremental increases in temperatures (permitting some adaptation) and its affect upon all life on the planet. Coincidentally, the intensified heating culminated near the Permian-Triassic boundary (250 MYA); the geological time of the world's greatest extinction. Consequently, geologists may want to ponder excessive heating as a cause for that event.

The initial breakup of the continents likely started between 600 and 700 MYA, meaning the older mass data is probably less accurate. The unknown density due to compression before the breakup should have been much greater than after the mantle and crust was severely broken and the planet's integrity forever weakened to the point where the volume could expand more freely at the cracks with less compression. After the severe initial breakup, the density remained reasonably constant with very small incremental gravity/compression increases. As the radius increased, the cracks lengthened and widened becoming the continental shelves. Some of these shelves later cracked and opened to accommodate the floor of the oceans.

In Table 5R (figure 26), a shortcut to the procedure outlined in the IGE Lagging Radius paper is used. To obtain a 100-year lag, one merely adds 100 to the total "x" time from the sixth column of Table 2R (49,522,800 years + 100 years = 49,522,900 years). The present rate of growth for the radius in Table 5R is then 4.05378 ($0.4952290x\sqrt{2}$).

The left half of Table 5R (figure 26) is essentially Table 4R (figure 25). The right half results when the increasing radius (volume) follows the increasing mass by 100 years.

The above chart and its graph below indicate a surface gravity and a radius of 75% of present around 75 MYA, 50% around 175 MYA, and 25% around 470 MYA. It also indicates no change in density (mass/volume) with a 100-year lag of the radius.

The table also indicates the phenomenal amount of new mass added each year during the past 18.9MY of 7.31 E+16 kg/yr [(5.98 E+24 - 4.5987 E+24) / 18.9 E+6] with an average increase in radius of about 2.8 cm/yr [(6378.96-5844.22) / 18.9 E+6 = 2.829 E-5 km/yr]. In perspective, 7.31 E+16 kg/yr translates to adding about 2.5 million tons of new mass per second.

Figure 28 correlates the past 200 MY with the NOAA Age of the Ocean Floor map. Adding the radius/gravity curves now allows one to estimate the size and surface gravity as well as the mass in accord with the NOAA map colors. The present values are: Mass = 5.98 E+24 kg Radius = 6378 km Gravity = $9.8m/s^2$

When the time of the ionization energy levels (from Table 3R or figure 21) are plotted as shown in Figures 31 and 32, it is obvious the planet was primarily heating for the first 3,000-3,500 million years of its existence. Temperatures during that period were sufficient to melt the iron that gravitated to the core while the lighter elements rose to form the molten crust. After water arrived as a cooling agent 1200 or 1400 MYA, the molten crustal rock solidified.

Unfortunately, this limits radiometric dating of "ancient rock" to the time of solidification. The ionization time chart also indicates very little change in the size of the planet prior to 700-800 MYA when exponential growth essentially began.

3. Conclusion

Science is about numbers. The underlying data and methodology of an Ionic Growing Earth demonstrates the same eight basic elements that started the planet have been growing (and heating) and expanding Earth's radius in consonance with recorded geology. For most people, growing the elements (atoms) counters an assumed certainty in modern science that essentially states... atoms cannot change size...can never grow larger. Credo quia ab-

NEW TABLE 4 - VARIABLE EARTH MASS GROWTH RATES FROM IONIZATIONS of the 8 ELEMENTS										
MY	Duration t (CMY)	% total earth	Element	Rate/≈eV	y	Mass/y^t (kg)	% of Current	x (ln 2/ln y) MY	% growing	% heating
0	1	98.8%	0	0	4.05379	5.98000E+24	100.00%	49.5228	98.8%	0.0%
18.9	0.189	-1.5%	-Ca	-0.04018	4.01361	4.59868E+24	76.90%	49.8778	97.3%	1.5%
24.0	0.051	-13.1%	-Mg	-0.57862	3.43499	4.31818E+24	72.21%	56.1701	84.2%	14.6%
45.4	0.214	-1.4%	-Al	-0.05570	3.37929	3.32761E+24	55.65%	56.9243	82.8%	16.0%
72.0	0.266	-15.1%	-Si	-0.57722	2.80207	2.52990E+24	42.31%	67.2724	67.7%	31.1%
81.2	0.092	1.5%	+Ca	0.04018	2.84225	2.29808E+24	38.43%	66.3555	69.2%	29.6%
127.8	0.466	13.1%	+Mg	0.57862	3.42087	1.29556E+24	21.66%	56.3582	82.3%	16.5%
140.5	0.127	-2.9%	-S	-0.09710	3.32377	1.11227E+24	18.60%	57.7094	79.4%	19.4%
191.4	0.509	1.4%	+Al	0.05570	3.37947	5.98449E+23	10.01%	56.9218	80.8%	18.0%
220.3	0.289	-30.1%	-O x 100%	-2.01968	1.35979	5.47588E+23	9.16%	225.5386	50.7%	48.1%
241.0	0.207	-32.1%	-Fe	-0.61707	0.74272	5.82362E+23	9.74%	-233.0395	18.6%	80.2%
266.0	0.250	15.1%	+Si	0.57722	1.31994	5.43319E+23	9.09%	249.7078	33.7%	65.1%
337.0	0.710	-1.5%	-Ca	-0.04018	1.27976	4.56031E+23	7.63%	281.0025	32.2%	66.6%
358.1	0.211	-1.8%	-Ni	-0.03350	1.24626	4.35333E+23	7.28%	314.8610	30.4%	68.4%
374.9	0.168	32.1%	+Fe	0.61707	1.86333	3.92114E+23	6.56%	111.3734	62.5%	36.3%
448.1	0.732	2.9%	+S	0.09710	1.96043	2.39559E+23	4.01%	102.9686	65.4%	33.4%
512.4	0.643	1.8%	+Ni	0.03350	1.99393	1.53709E+23	2.57%	100.4405	67.2%	31.6%
586.3	0.739	-13.1%	-Mg	-0.57862	1.41531	1.18910E+23	1.99%	199.5545	54.1%	44.7%
705.2	1.189	-1.4%	-Al	-0.05570	1.35961	8.25259E+22	1.38%	225.6364	52.7%	46.1%
780.9	0.757	-32.1%	-Fe	-0.61707	0.74254	1.03385E+23	1.73%	-232.8485	20.6%	78.2%

Figure 22. Table 2R - Variable earth mass growth rates from ionizations of the 8 Elements

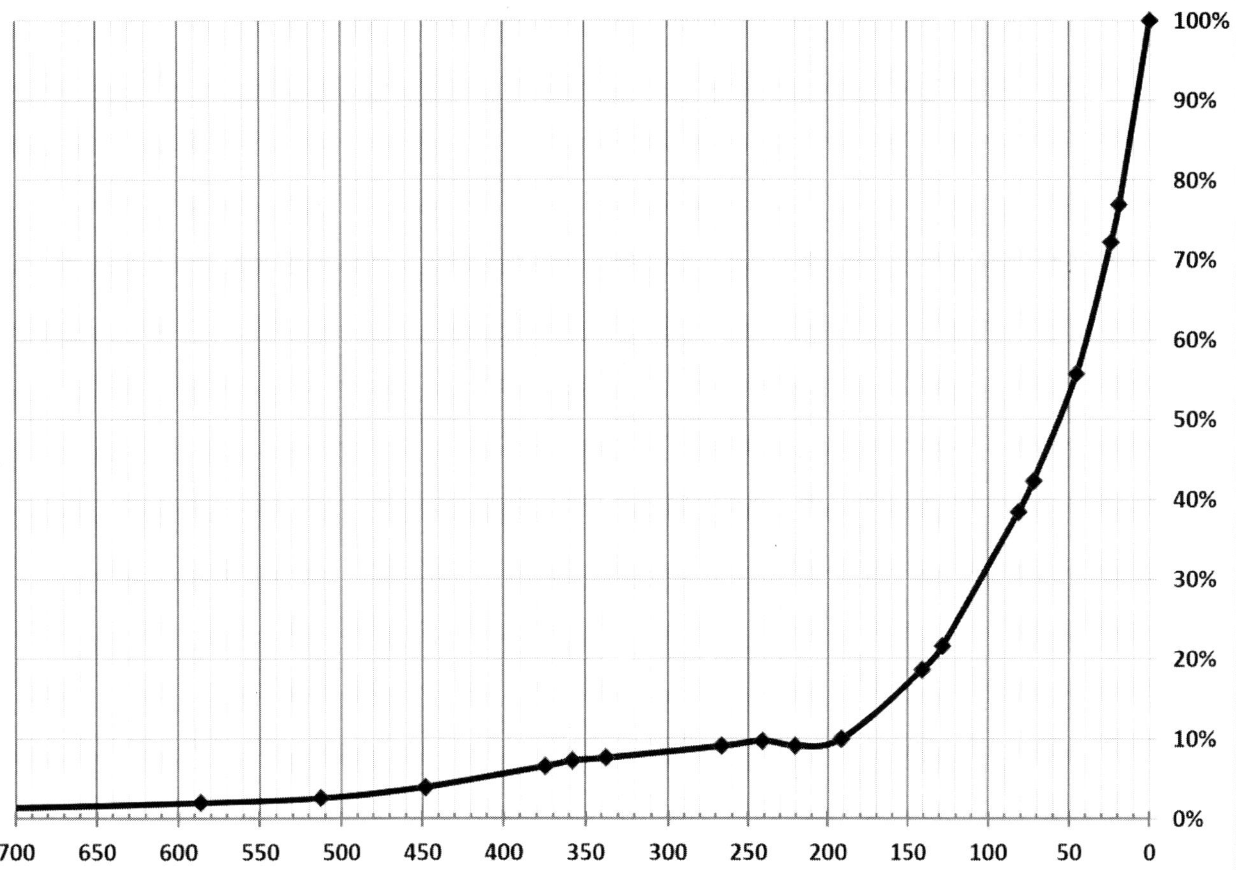

Figure 23. Graph of New Table 4

% Oxygen (line 10)	1.56% present mass ≅ 25% present radius	*x* at 243 MYA (line 11)
1.00 x 2.01968 = 2.01968	~700 MYA	-200.xxx
0.85 x 2.01968 = 1.71673	~510 MYA	6744.xxx
0.80 x 2.01968 = 1.61574	~490 MYA	656.xxx
0.75 x 2.01968 = 1.51476	~470 MYA	360.xxx
0.70 x 2.01968 = 1.41378	~450 MYA	254.xxx
0.60 x 2.01968 = 1.21181	~430 MYA	166.xxx

Figure 24. Oxygen rates tested and summarized

TABLE 4R - VARIABLE EARTH MASS GROWTH RATES FROM IONIZATIONS of the 8 ELEMENTS										
MY	Duration *t* (CMY)	% total earth	Element	Rate/≈eV	*y*	Mass/y^t (kg)	% of Current	*x* (ln 2/ln *y*) MY	% growing	% heating
0	1	98.8%	0	0	4.05379	5.98000E+24	100.00%	49.5228	98.8%	0.0%
18.9	0.189	-1.5%	-Ca	-0.04018	4.01361	4.59868E+24	76.90%	49.8778	97.3%	1.5%
24.0	0.051	-13.1%	-Mg	-0.57862	3.43499	4.31818E+24	72.21%	56.1701	84.2%	14.6%
45.4	0.214	-1.4%	-Al	-0.05570	3.37929	3.32761E+24	55.65%	56.9243	82.8%	16.0%
72.0	0.266	-15.1%	-Si	-0.57722	2.80207	2.52990E+24	42.31%	67.2724	67.7%	31.1%
81.2	0.092	1.5%	+Ca	0.04018	2.84225	2.29808E+24	38.43%	66.3555	69.2%	29.6%
127.8	0.466	13.1%	+Mg	0.57862	3.42087	1.29556E+24	21.66%	56.3582	82.3%	16.5%
140.5	0.127	-2.9%	-S	-0.09710	3.32377	1.11227E+24	18.60%	57.7094	79.4%	19.4%
191.4	0.509	1.4%	+Al	0.05570	3.37947	5.98449E+23	10.01%	56.9218	80.8%	18.0%
220.3	0.289	-30.1%	-O x 75%	-1.51476	1.86471	4.99828E+23	8.36%	111.2408	50.7%	48.1%
241.0	0.207	-32.1%	-Fe	-0.61707	1.24764	4.77452E+23	7.98%	313.2828	18.6%	80.2%
266.0	0.250	15.1%	+Si	0.57722	1.82486	4.10793E+23	6.87%	115.2362	33.7%	65.1%
337.0	0.710	-1.5%	-Ca	-0.04018	1.78468	2.72280E+23	4.55%	119.6656	32.2%	66.6%
358.1	0.211	-1.8%	-Ni	-0.03350	1.75118	2.41921E+23	4.05%	123.7128	30.4%	68.4%
374.9	0.168	32.1%	+Fe	0.61707	2.36825	2.09300E+23	3.50%	80.3975	62.5%	36.3%
448.1	0.732	2.9%	+S	0.09710	2.46535	1.08122E+23	1.81%	76.8172	65.4%	33.4%
512.4	0.643	1.8%	+Ni	0.03350	2.49885	6.00022E+22	1.00%	75.6851	67.2%	31.6%
586.3	0.739	-13.1%	-Mg	-0.57862	1.92023	3.70484E+22	0.62%	106.2386	54.1%	44.7%
705.2	1.189	-1.4%	-Al	-0.05570	1.86453	1.76629E+22	0.30%	111.2582	52.7%	46.1%
780.9	0.757	-32.1%	-Fe	-0.61707	1.24746	1.49407E+22	0.25%	313.4885	20.6%	78.2%

Figure 25. Variable earth mass growth rates

				(49.5228 MY)			(49.5229 MY)						
MY	X	Element	Rate/eV	Rate of Growth	Mass (kg)	Current Mass	Rate of Growth	Radius (km)	Current Radius	Density (g/cc)	Current Density	Gravity (m/sec^2)	Current Gravity
0	1	0	0	4.05379	5.98E+24	100.00%	4.05379	6378.96	100.00%	5.5000	100.00%	9.80	100.00%
18.9	0.189	-Ca	-0.04018	4.01361	4.59868E+24	76.90%	4.01361	5844.22	91.62%	5.5000	100.00%	8.98	91.62%
24.0	0.051	-Mg	-0.57862	3.43499	4.31818E+24	72.21%	3.43499	5722.90	89.72%	5.5000	100.00%	8.79	89.72%
45.4	0.214	-Al	-0.05570	3.37929	3.32761E+24	55.65%	3.37929	5246.79	82.25%	5.5000	100.00%	8.06	82.25%
72.0	0.266	-Si	-0.57722	2.80207	2.5299E+24	42.31%	2.80207	4788.69	75.07%	5.5000	100.00%	7.36	75.07%
81.2	0.092	+Ca	0.04018	2.84225	2.29808E+24	38.43%	2.84225	4637.72	72.70%	5.5000	100.00%	7.13	72.70%
127.8	0.466	+Mg	0.57862	3.42087	1.29556E+24	21.66%	3.42087	3831.20	60.06%	5.5000	100.00%	5.89	60.06%
140.5	0.127	-S	-0.09710	3.32377	1.11227E+24	18.60%	3.32377	3641.27	57.08%	5.5000	100.00%	5.60	57.08%
191.4	0.509	+Al	0.05570	3.37947	5.98449E+23	10.01%	3.37947	2961.59	46.43%	5.5000	100.00%	4.55	46.43%
220.3	0.289	-O x 75%	-1.51476	1.86471	4.99828E+23	8.36%	1.86471	2789.05	43.72%	5.5000	100.00%	4.29	43.72%
241.0	0.207	-Fe	-0.61707	1.24764	4.77452E+23	7.98%	1.24764	2746.79	43.06%	5.5000	100.00%	4.22	43.06%
266.0	0.250	+Si	0.57722	1.82486	4.10793E+23	6.87%	1.82486	2612.50	40.96%	5.5000	100.00%	4.01	40.96%
337.0	0.710	-Ca	-0.04018	1.78468	2.7228E+23	4.55%	1.78468	2277.83	35.71%	5.5000	100.00%	3.50	35.71%
358.1	0.211	-Ni	-0.03350	1.75118	2.41921E+23	4.05%	1.75118	2189.81	34.33%	5.5000	100.00%	3.37	34.33%
374.9	0.168	+Fe	0.61707	2.36825	2.093E+23	3.50%	2.36825	2086.60	32.71%	5.5000	100.00%	3.21	32.71%
448.1	0.732	+S	0.09710	2.46535	1.08122E+23	1.81%	2.46535	1674.25	26.25%	5.5000	100.00%	2.57	26.25%
512.4	0.643	+Ni	0.03350	2.49885	6.00022E+22	1.00%	2.49885	1375.85	21.57%	5.5000	100.00%	2.11	21.57%
586.3	0.739	-Mg	-0.57862	1.92023	3.70484E+22	0.62%	1.92023	1171.58	18.37%	5.5000	100.00%	1.80	18.37%
705.2	1.189	-Al	-0.05570	1.86453	1.76629E+22	0.30%	1.86453	915.24	14.35%	5.5000	100.00%	1.41	14.35%
780.9	0.757	-Fe	-0.61707	1.24746	1.49407E+22	0.25%	1.24746	865.50	13.57%	5.5000	100.00%	1.33	13.57%

Figure 26. TABLE 5R - Mass from table 4R with 100 year lagging radius

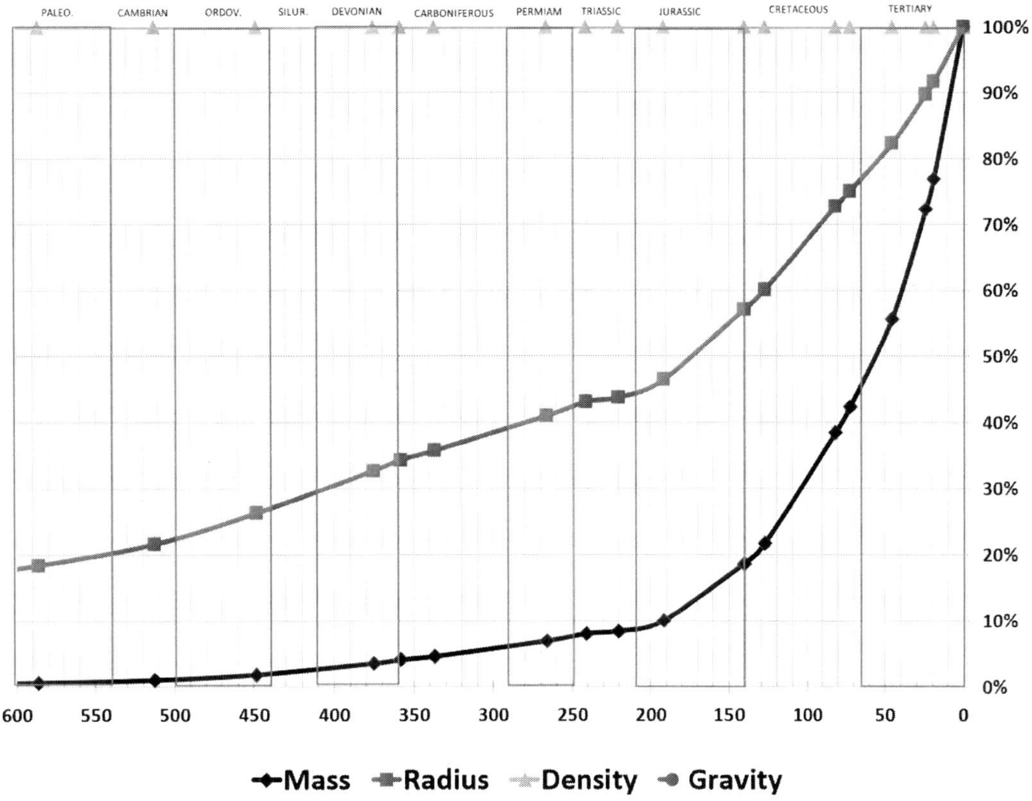

Figure 27. Graph of table 5R

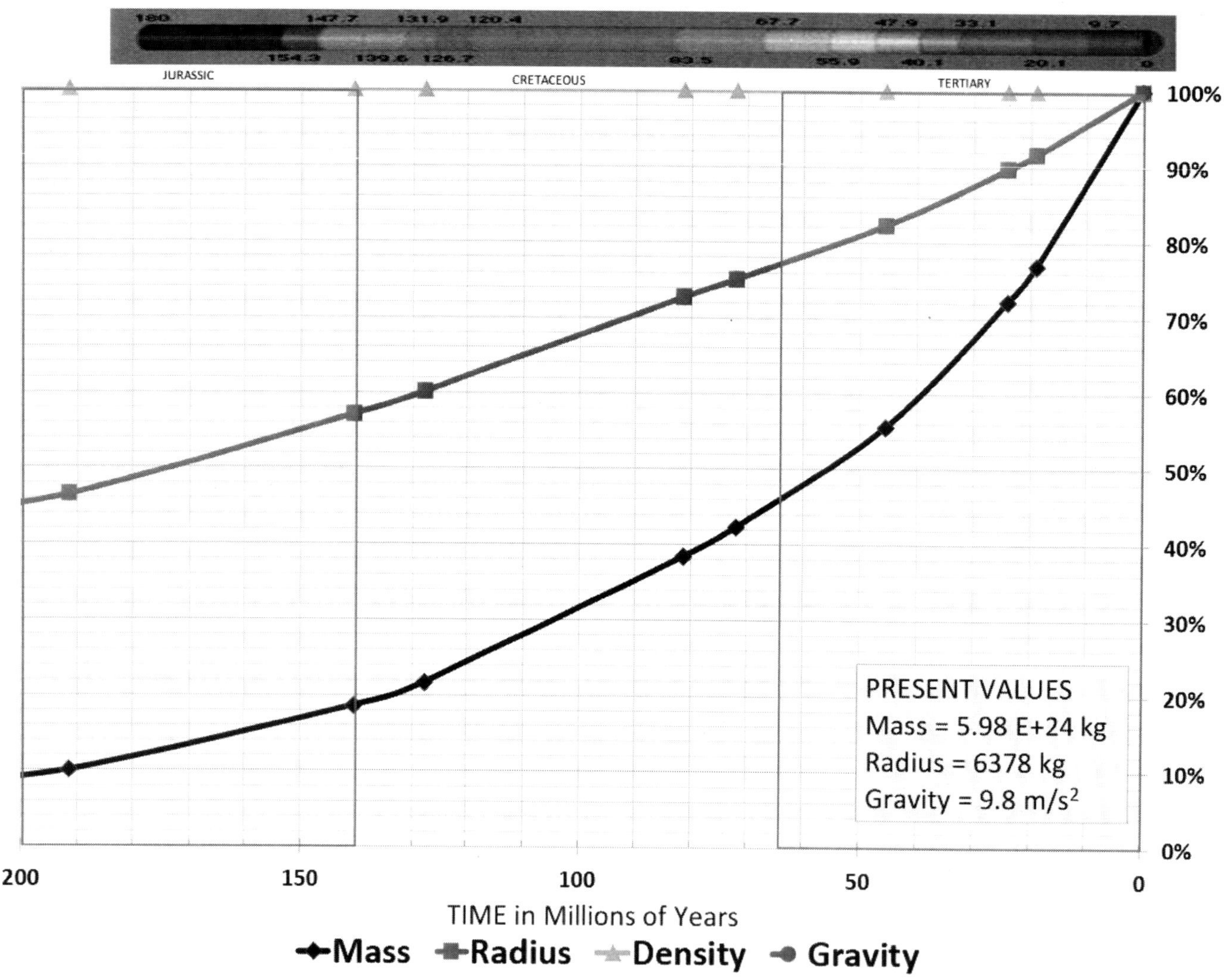

Figure 28. Mass, Radius, Gravity Correlated with NOAA Age of the Ocean Floor Map (http://www.ngdc.noaa.gov/mgg/image/crustageposter.gif)

TABLE 1R

NBS-34 Table 1, pages 2 and 3 -Ionization Potentials and Limits (in eV) (First 30 Elements only)

Z	Element	Spectrum																					Z
		I	II	III	IV	V	VI	VII	VIII	IX	X	XI	XII	XIII	XIV	XV	XVI	XVII	XVIII	XIX	XX	XXI	
1	H	13.598																					1
2	He	24.587	54.416																				2
3	Li	5.392	75.638	122.451																			3
4	Be	9.322	18.211	153.893	217.713																		4
5	B	8.298	25.154	37.93	259.368	340.217																	5
6	C	11.26	24.383	47.887	64.492	392.077	489.981																6
7	N	14.534	29.601	47.448	77.472	97.888	522.057	667.029															7
8	O	13.618	35.116	54.934	77.412	113.896	138.116	739.315	871.387														8
9	F	17.422	34.97	62.707	87.138	114.24	157.161	185.182	953.886	1103.09													9
10	Ne	21.564	40.962	63.45	97.11	126.21	157.93	207.27	239.09	1195.8	1362.16												10
11	Na	5.139	47.286	71.64	98.91	138.39	172.15	208.47	264.18	299.87	1465.09	1648.66											11
12	Mg	7.646	15.035	80.143	109.24	141.26	186.5	224.94	265.9	327.95	367.53	1761.8	1962.61										12
13	Al	5.986	18.828	28.447	119.99	153.71	190.47	241.43	284.59	330.21	398.57	442.07	2085.98	2304.08									13
14	Si	8.151	16.345	33.492	45.141	166.77	205.05	246.52	303.17	351.1	401.43	476.06	523.5	2437.68	2673.11								14
15	P	10.486	19.725	30.18	51.37	65.023	220.43	263.22	309.41	371.73	424.5	479.57	560.41	611.85	2816.94	3069.76							15
16	S	13.36	23.33	34.83	47.3	72.68	89.049	280.93	328.23	379.1	447.09	504.78	564.65	651.63	707.14	3223.84	3494.1						16
17	Cl	12.967	23.81	39.61	53.46	67.8	97.03	114.193	348.28	400.05	455.62	529.26	591.97	656.69	749.74	809.39	3658.43	3946.19					17
18	Ar	15.759	27.629	40.74	59.81	75.02	91.007	124.319	143.456	422.44	478.68	538.95	618.24	686.09	755.73	854.75	918	4120.78	4426.11				18
19	K	4.341	31.625	45.72	60.91	82.66	100	117.56	154.86	175.814	503.44	564.13	292.09	714.02	787.13	861.77	968	1034	4610.96	4933.93			19
20	Ca	6.113	11.871	50.908	67.1	84.41	108.78	127.7	147.24	188.54	211.27	591.25	656.39	726.03	816.61	895.12	947	1087	1157	5129.05	5469.74		20
21	Se	6.54	12.8	24.76	73.47	91.66	111.1	138	158.7	180.02	225.32	249.832	685.89	755.47	829.79	926							21
22	Ti	6.82	13.58	27.491	43.266	99.22	119.36	140.8	168.5	193.2	215.91	265.23	291.497	787.33	861.33	940.36							22
23	V	6.74	14.65	29.31	46.707	65.23	128.12	150.17	173.7	205.8	230.5	255.04	308.25	336.267	895.58	974.02							23
24	Cr	6.766	16.5	30.96	49.1	69.3	90.56	161.1	184.7	209.3	244.4	270.8	298	355	384.3	1010.64							24
25	Mn	7.435	15.64	33.667	51.2	72.4	95	119.27	196.46	221.8	243.3	286	314.4	343.6	404	435.3	1136.2						25
26	Fe	7.87	16.18	30.651	54.8	75	99	125	151.06	235.04	262.1	290.4	330.8	361	392.2	457	489.5	1266.1					26
27	Co	7.86	17.06	33.5	51.3	79.5	102	129	157	186.13	276	305	336	379	411	444	512	546.8	1403				27
28	Ni	7.635	18.168	34.17	54.9	75.5	108	133	162	193	224.5	321.2	352	384	430	464	499	571	607.2	1547			28
29	Cu	7.726	20.292	36.83	55.2	49.9	103	139	166	199	232	266	368.8	401	435	484	520	557	633	671	1698		29
30	Zn	9.394	17.964	39.722	59.4	82.6	108	134	174	203	238	274	310.8	491.7	454	490	542	579	619	698	738	1856	30

NOTES:

1) The ionization potentials are in electron volts (eV) for each spectrum.
2) The elements are arranged in order of increasing atomic numbers, Z.
3) The successive stages of ionization are indicated at the heading of each column: I, denoting the first spectra (neutral atoms); II, second spectra (single ionized atoms}, etc.
4) The amount of energy required to remove a single electron is based upon an ambient energy level the planet is experiencing at the present time. A billion years ago, that ambient level would have been very much higher.
5) Viewing the table, those higher energy levels would have been the time in the past the element ionizes. The highest limit, therefore would be the time an element first ionizes in a higher ambient.
6) Multiplying any level in Table 1R by 1.5952 produces the time of that level, e.g. oxygen was first able to bond at level VIII 1,390 MYA (1.5952 x
7) An anomaly surfaces when small incremental jumps of energy suddenly a become large jump as highlighted. See Table 3R and Figures 1R & 2R for the 8 elements of concern.

Figure 29. Graph of the mass

TIME TABLE 1R

TIME (in MY) of the Ionization Potentials (energy levels) listed in Table 1R

Z	Element	Spectrum																					Z
		I	II	III	IV	V	VI	VII	VIII	IX	X	XI	XII	XIII	XIV	XV	XVI	XVII	XVIII	XIX	XX	XXI	
1	H	21.6915																					1
2	He	39.2212	86.8044																				2
3	Li	8.60132	120.658	195.334																			3
4	Be	14.8705	29.0502	245.49	347.296																		4
5	B	13.237	40.1257	60.5059	413.744	542.714																	5
6	C	17.962	38.8958	76.3893	102.878	625.441	781.618																6
7	N	23.1846	47.2195	75.689	123.583	156.151	832.785	1064.04															7
8	O	21.7234	56.017	87.6307	123.488	181.687	220.323	1179.36	1390.04														8
9	F	27.7916	55.7841	100.03	139.003	182.236	250.703	295.402	1521.64	1759.65													9
10	Ne	34.3989	65.3426	101.215	154.91	201.33	251.93	330.637	381.396	1907.54	2172.92												10
11	Na	8.19773	75.4306	114.28	157.781	220.76	274.614	332.551	421.42	478.353	2337.11	2629.94											11
12	Mg	12.1969	23.9838	127.844	174.26	225.338	297.505	358.824	424.164	523.146	586.284	2810.43	3130.76										12
13	Al	9.54887	30.0344	45.3787	191.408	245.198	303.838	385.129	453.978	526.751	635.799	705.19	3327.56	3675.47									13
14	Si	13.0025	26.0735	53.4264	72.0089	266.032	327.096	393.249	483.617	560.075	640.361	759.411	835.087	3888.58	4264.14								14
15	P	16.7273	31.4653	48.1431	81.9454	103.725	351.63	419.889	493.571	592.984	677.162	765.01	893.966	976.023	4493.59	4896.88							15
16	S	21.3119	37.216	55.5608	75.453	115.939	142.051	448.14	523.592	604.74	713.198	805.225	900.73	1039.48	1128.03	5142.66	5573.79						16
17	Cl	20.685	37.9817	63.1859	85.2794	108.155	154.782	182.161	555.576	638.16	726.805	844.276	944.311	1047.55	1195.99	1291.14	5835.92	6294.97					17
18	Ar	25.1388	44.0738	64.9884	95.4089	119.672	145.174	198.314	228.841	673.876	763.59	859.733	986.216	1094.45	1205.54	1363.5	1464.39	6573.47	7060.54				18
19	K	6.92476	50.4482	72.9325	97.1636	131.859	159.52	187.532	247.033	280.458	803.087	899.9	465.942	1139	1255.63	1374.7	1544.15	1649.44	7355.4	7870.61			19
20	Ca	9.75146	18.9366	81.2084	107.038	134.651	173.526	203.707	234.877	300.759	337.018	943.162	1047.07	1158.16	1302.66	1427.9	1510.65	1733.98	1845.65	8181.85	8725.33		20
21	Se	10.4326	20.4186	39.4972	117.199	146.216	177.227	220.138	253.158	287.168	359.43	398.532	1094.13	1205.13	1323.68	1477.16							21
22	Ti	10.8793	21.6628	43.8536	69.0179	158.276	190.403	224.604	268.791	308.193	344.42	423.095	464.996	1255.95	1373.99	1500.06							22
23	V	10.7516	23.3697	46.7553	74.507	104.055	204.377	239.551	277.086	328.292	367.694	406.84	491.72	536.413	1428.63	1553.76							23
24	Cr	10.7931	26.3208	49.3874	78.3243	110.547	144.461	256.987	294.633	333.875	389.867	431.98	475.37	566.296	613.035	1612.17							24
25	Mn	11.8603	24.9489	53.7056	81.6742	115.492	151.544	190.26	313.393	353.815	388.112	456.227	501.531	548.111	644.461	694.391	1812.47						25
26	Fe	12.5542	25.8103	48.8945	87.417	119.64	157.925	199.4	240.971	374.936	418.102	463.246	527.692	575.867	625.637	729.006	780.85	2019.68					26
27	Co	12.5383	27.2141	53.4392	81.8338	126.818	162.71	205.781	250.446	296.915	440.275	486.536	535.987	604.581	655.627	708.269	816.742	872.255	2238.07				27
28	Ni	12.1794	28.9816	54.508	87.5765	120.438	172.282	212.162	258.422	307.874	358.122	512.378	561.51	612.557	685.936	740.173	796.005	910.859	968.605	2467.77			28
29	Cu	12.3245	32.3698	58.7512	88.055	79.6005	164.306	221.733	264.803	317.445	370.086	424.323	588.31	639.675	693.912	772.077	829.504	888.526	1009.76	1070.38	2708.65		29
30	Zn	14.9853	28.6562	63.3645	94.7549	131.764	172.282	213.757	277.565	323.826	379.658	437.085	495.788	784.36	724.221	781.648	864.598	923.621	987.429	1113.45	1177.26	2960.69	30

NOTE:

The energy decay rate (1ev/1.5952MY) is calculated from the Atomic Mass and the amounts of the 8 elements that comprise 98.8% of Earth's mass. Within each element, the decaying energy is converting to additional mass or to heat (entropy) when in the shaded areas of the chart.

Figure 30. Graph of the mass

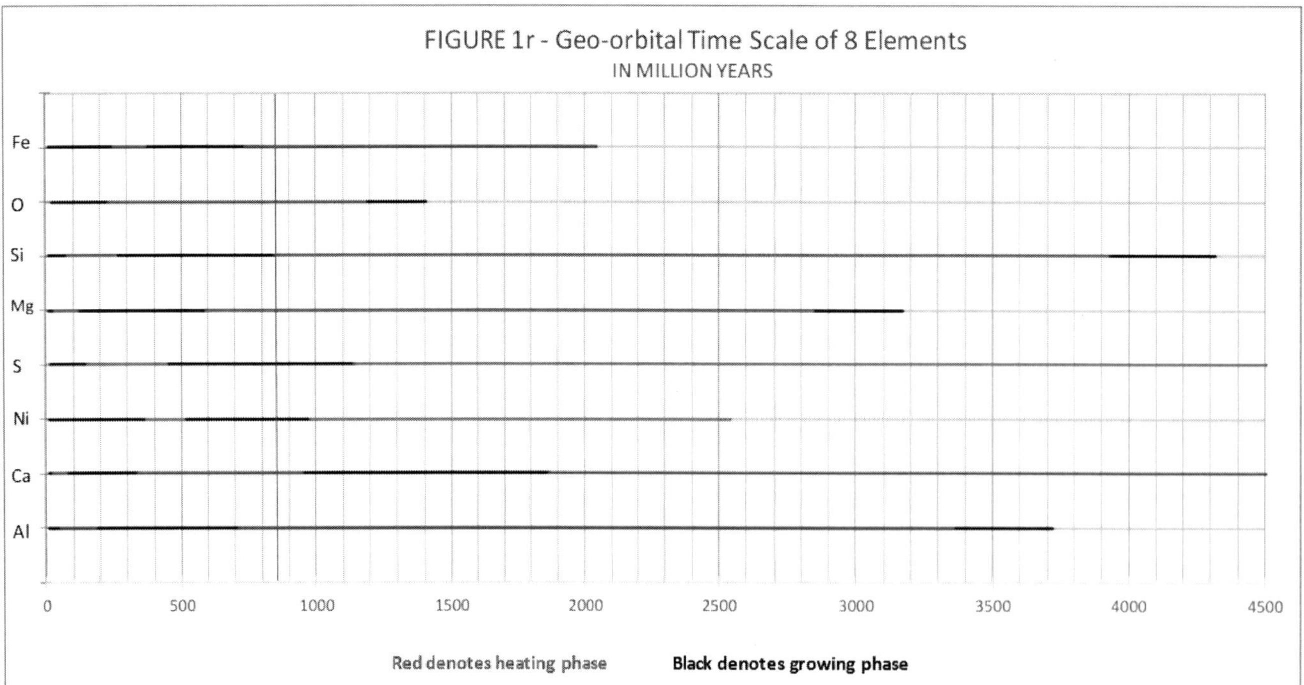

Figure 31. Graph of the mass

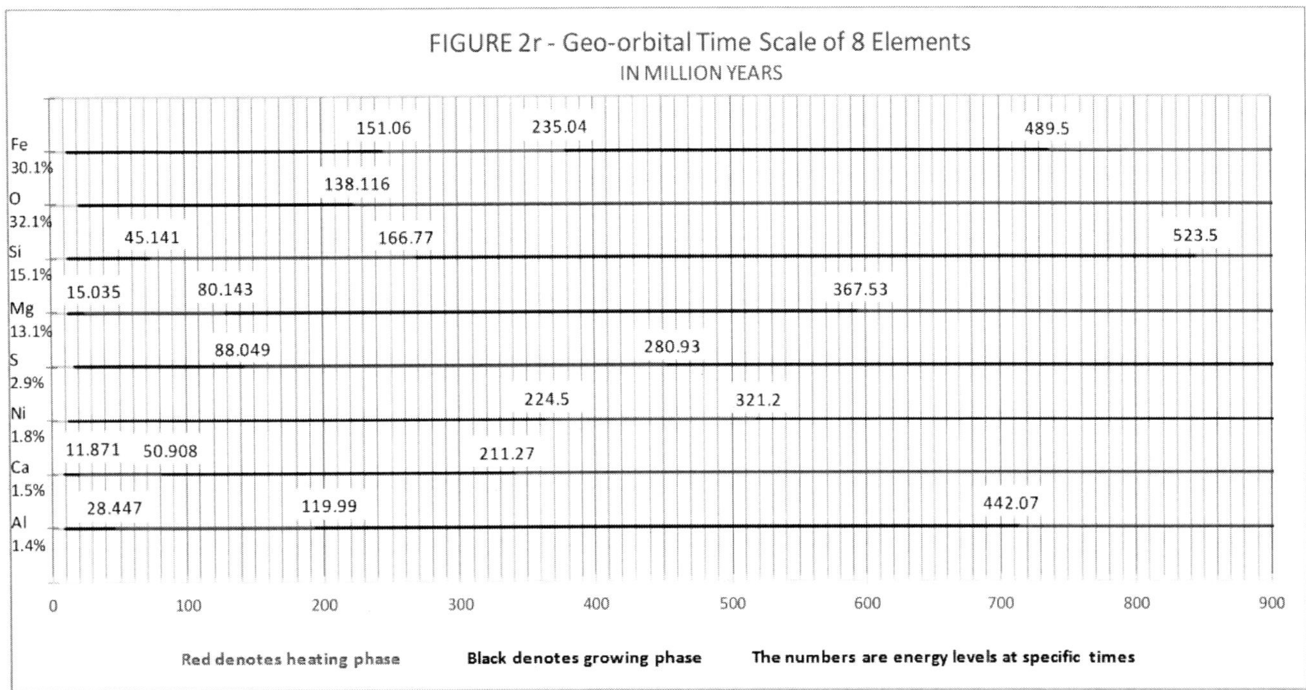

Figure 32. Graph of the mass

surdum...I believe because it is absurd. The entire universe is growing or expanding except the very elemental atoms of which it consists. A doubling of numbers herein reveals the opposite and questions this perceived and numerically unproven "certainty".

We are conditioned to believe the Earth formed with its present size; was born warm and was bathing in water. This is what one "sees" and "hears" today and thinks the world was always this way. We believe the impossible size of dinosaurs because we can see the largeness of their fossils, and yes, reduced gravity on a smaller planet would explain some, but not all, of the perceived largeness. We do not believe or even suspect that the elements of those petrified bones and fossils (Ca, Si, Mg, or Fe) could grow. We tend to believe water was always here or imported from space because we do not truly know when hydrogen joined oxygen for the first time to become a molecule of water. Would not the mechanism (ionization) that produces water be universal and be responsible for the water on comets, asteroids or other planets? Before ionization, the elements were unable to chemically bond and form molecules or compounds. With the ionization potential of an element defined as a measure of its ability to enter into chemical reactions, the timing of those potentials (and limits) as presented herein, tells us when water arrived. The enigma of having so much water on a smaller Earth is easily reconciled when one considers the oxygen in water growing along with the other seven elements.

We believe assumptions and accept them as authoritative. Perhaps we should question our beliefs by questioning the assumptions and follow Professor Samuel Warren Carey's advice ... "We are blinded by what we think we know, disbelieve if you can."

http://ionic-expanding-earth.Weebly.com

Who Needs Dark Matter? An Alternative Explanation for the Galactic Rotation Anomaly

Raymond HV Gallucci, PhD, PE

8956 Amelung St., Frederick, Maryland, 21704, gallucci@localnet.com, r_gallucci@verizon.net

Borrowing concepts from the Electric/Plasma Universe theories (*http://www.electricuniverse.info, www.plasma-universe.com*), I examine a possible explanation of at least part of the observed behavior for the galactic rotation anomaly for spiral galaxies by considering an idealized case where the combined magnetic fields from the galactic core (assumed to be a rotating charged sphere) and spiral arms (assumed to be a rotating charged disk) exhibit a trend toward the 'flatness' in these rotation curves as one proceeds outward radially from the galactic core to its edge. This hopefully is a plausible addition to the various alternate explanations for this anomaly that do not invoke the likely fiction of 'dark matter,' alleged to comprise roughly 85 percent of the total matter in the universe (and, with the other likely fiction 'dark energy,' alleged to comprise roughly 95 percent of the total mass-energy of the universe). In the process, I provide at least an introduction to some of these other alternative explanations for the galactic rotation anomaly.

Keywords: galactic rotation, electric universe, electromagnetism, gravity, globular cluster

1. Introduction

As discussed in [1]:

"Dark matter was postulated by Jan Oort in 1932 ... to account for the orbital velocities of stars in the Milky Way and by Fritz Zwicky in 1933 to account for evidence of 'missing mass' in the orbital velocities of galaxies in clusters. Adequate evidence from galaxy rotation curves was discovered by Horace W. Babcock in 1939, but was not attributed to dark matter. *The first to postulate dark matter based upon robust evidence was Vera Rubin in the 1960s through 1970s, using galaxy rotation curves* ... Together with fellow staff-member Kent Ford, Rubin announced at a 1975 meeting of the American Astronomical Society the discovery that most stars in spiral galaxies orbit at roughly the same speed, which implied that the mass densities of the galaxies were uniform well beyond the regions containing most of the stars (the galactic bulge), a result independently found in 1978 ... Rubin's observations and calculations showed that most galaxies must contain about six times as much 'dark' mass as can be accounted for by the visible stars ... Most galaxies were dominated by 'dark matter.' Starting with Rubin's findings for spiral galaxies, the robust observational evidence for dark matter has been collecting over the decades to the point that by the 1980s most astrophysicists accepted its existence."

Since dark matter has not actually been observed or detected, but only inferred by circumstantial evidence, primarily due to the alleged anomaly in galactic rotation curves (see Figure 1), dissident physicists have offered other explanations for the relative flatness of the rotational velocity of galaxies with increasing radius. That is, while the presumably densely packed galactic core (essentially a sphere of stars) rotates like a solid body (green, thick-dashed line in Figure 1), once into the disk region, galactic rotational speed flattens out, such that structures such as spiral arms continue to rotate as if 'fixed' like the spokes of a wheel (albeit 'bent backward' in a logarithmic spiral).

2. Some Explanations without Dark Matter

Review of some of these 'dissident' websites uncovers alternate (to dark matter) explanations, both gravitationally- and electromagnetically-based, such as the following.

"This theory attributes the anomaly in galactic rotation to the effects of time dilation on Newtonian speeds when making observations from the Earth's frame of reference ... The spherical time rate field around any mass is similar to a gravity well ... [F]or relatively short radii, we do not notice much physical effect from the time dilation diminishing with 'r' ... When we observe galaxies, we are taking a view over much, much larger distances than solar system scales. We might then envisage that the relentless continuation of this time rate increase (time dilation decay), from the galactic centre outwards, will accumulate over these immense distances and so become significant in terms of the red and blue shift of Newtonian rotation speeds ... The only radial position that shows us a REAL, unshifted Newtonian rotation speed is therefore at a radius similar to our own position in the Milky Way (for galaxies of similar mass and distribution) ... The Newton curve, therefore MUST pass through this point on the observed curve at a similar galactic radius as ours and which has the same time rate as we have ... [A]ll Newtonian speeds are redshifted and slowed down relative to our frame of reference, increasingly so, as you look closer toward the galactic centre ... The Newton curve inboard, therefore becomes increasingly lowered from the inverse square form. Outboard all Newtonian speeds are blueshifted relative to our frame and so appear increasingly faster than Newton

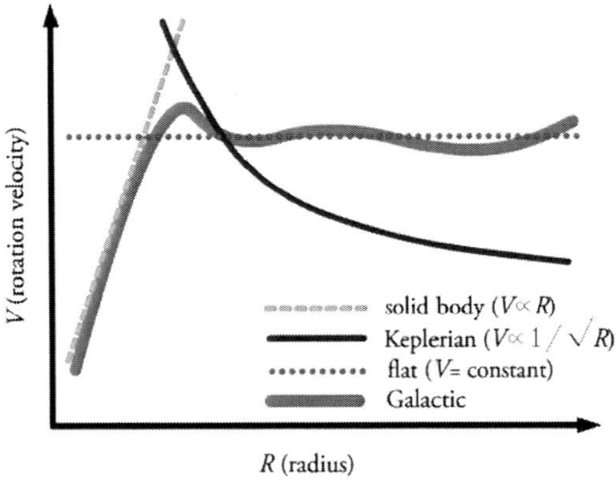

Figure 1. Rotational curves for a disk [2]

with increasing 'r.' The inverse square curve therefore becomes increasingly raised as you move outwards, bringing the Newton curve up to match the observed 'flattened' curve." [3]

"Electric Universe theory asserts that there is a model of spiral galaxy formation that has long been demonstrated by laboratory experiment and 'particle in cell' (PIC) simulations on a supercomputer ... [T]he particles are charged and respond to the laws of electromagnetism ... [W]e know know that more than 99.9 percent of the visible universe is in the form of plasma ... Plasma responds to electromagnetic forces that exceed the strength of gravity to the extent that gravity can usually be safely ignored. This simple fact alone suggests why gravitational models of galaxies must fail ... [C]omputer simulations have been backed up by experiments in the highest energy density laboratory electrical discharges–the Z-pinch machine ... This important work demonstrates that the beautiful spiral structure of galaxies is a natural form of plasma instability in a universe energized by electrical power. [4]

Continuing with the Electric Universe arguments:

"[O]ne of the reasons for the assumption of large amounts of Cryogenic (or Cold) Dark Matter (CDM) in the Gravity Model is to explain the observed rotation of galaxies ... However, there is another way stars could be made to orbit a galaxy in this fashion. Michael Faraday found ... that a metal disk rotating in a magnetic field aligned with the axis of the disk would cause an electric current to flow radially in the disk, so he invented the first generator, known as a Unipolar Inductor, or Faraday Generator ... Galaxies are known ... to possess magnetic fields aligned with their axes of rotation, and they also have conducting plasma among their stars ... [T]he conditions appear to be similar to that in a Unipolar Inductor or Faraday Motor ... [I]t is at least possible that it is these electrical effects that are causing the anomalous rotation that we see, not some huge quantity of invisible Dark Matter." [5]

One of the more unique explanations asserts that "The mutual perturbations among the component stars in a Spiral Arm can be shown to have far greater effects than previously noted. The inverse-square nature of gravitation causes the effect to be very strong at the relatively short distances within a Spiral Arm ... One interesting consequence of this research is the realization that the Sun and all other stars slowly weave back and forth across the Spiral Arm! ... The analysis [suggests that]: (1) A general tapering shape of an Arm is necessary to produce the effect described here. This suggests a reason for the common existence of spiral arms in galaxies. (2) A tapered Arm shape is a necessary resultant consequence of the metastable situation described here. These two statements suggest a mechanism for the genesis and persistence of spiral arms in many galaxies. (3) [T]he Sun and everything else in each Arm apparently laterally oscillate across the width of the Arm ... [T]his new premise suggests that within the Spiral Arms, a substantial previously undescribed conventional gravitational net force vector can be shown to also exist, primarily forward along the axis of the Arm ... This results in a meta-stable situation that establishes the stability and persistence of the Spiral Arm, including the circumstance where the Arm revolves in the observed non-Keplerian way ... This therefore explains the lasting integrity of the Arm structure, and also suggests a much less massive galaxy. It may remove the need for dark matter, exotic particles, materials, or objects to account for a lot of unseen distributed mass in the Galaxy." [6]

As can be seen, both gravitational (first and last) and electromagnetic (second and third) alternative explanations to dark matter as being responsible for anomalous galactic rotation have been proffered. While my hypothesis will align mainly with the electromagnetic explanation, I draw significantly from aspects of that developed by Johnson, albeit not its gravitational effects. The interested reader is directed to Johnson's website for the details of the simulations he performed to substantiate his hypothesis, too intricate and lengthy to be reproduced here.

3. Another Possible Explanation

My analysis begins with mathematically constructing a representative spiral galaxy, whose spherical, central core has a radius $R_s = 1$ and whose three, logarithmically spiraling, equi-spaced arms extend out from the core through the disk to radius $R_d = 5$ (Figure 2). (Logarithmic spirals, with an equation $r = exp[a\theta]$ in polar coordinates, reasonably approximate the arms of spiral galaxies, including our own Milky Way. [7]

Photographs indicate the number of spirals in galaxies which are reasonably symmetric range from the minimum of two to around five. Three are postulated for my representative analysis. The arms are shown as uniformly tapering, from a maximum width where they meet the core (black circle) of $\pi/3$ down to zero such that, if unwound and straightened spokes, each would comprise a triangle of base$\pi/3$ and height 16.12 (based on logarithmic spirals with the equation $r = exp(\theta/[2\pi/ln5])$ for three equally-spaced spirals).

3.1. Magnetic Effects

The equation for the component of the magnetic field B aligned with the axis of galactic rotation in the disk of the galaxy (ecliptic) outside a rotating charged sphere (the galactic core) at radius r is as follows [8]:

$B_s(r) = \mu_0 Q_s \omega R_s^2/12\pi r^3$ [Eq. 1]

where Q_s = total charge on the sphere (galactic core) and ω = rotational speed of the sphere (galaxy).

For the disk, the B field always aligns with the axis of rotation and has the following magnitude for a disk of radius r within the plane of the disk itself (also assumed to be rotating at ω):

$B_d(r) = \mu_0 \sigma \omega r/2$ [Eq. 2]

where σ = charge density = $q(r)/(\pi[r^2 - R_s^2])$ for $R_s < r \leq R_d$ and q(r) = total charge on disk from R_s through r (at R_d, $q[r] = Q_d$, the total charge of the disk).

Assume $q(r) = k(r)Q_s$, where k(r) = fraction of charge in disk relative to Q_s (for convenience, assume the disk charge Q_s cannot exceed that of the sphere, i.e., 0 < k(r) < 1). Within the plane of the disk itself,

$B(r) = (\mu_0\omega/2\pi)(k[r]Q_s r/[r^2 - R_s^2])$ [Eq. 3]

Combining Equations [1] and [3] yields

$B(r) = (\mu_0\omega Q_s/2\pi)(R_s^2/6r^3 + k[r]r/[r^2 - R_s^2])$ [Eq. 4]

With Q_s = 1 and R_s = 1 (such that all further calculations will be scaled to the sphere's charge and density), this simplifies to

$B(r) = (\mu_0\omega/2\pi)(1/6r^3 + k[r]r/[r^2 - 1])$ [Eq. 5]

where $R_s < r < R_d$, i.e., 1 < r < 5.

For subsequent analysis, define the following scaled value for the B field

$B'(r) = B(r)/(\mu_0\omega/2\pi) = 1/6r^3 + k(r)r/(r^2 - 1)$ [Eq. 6]

It is evident that, as one proceeds outward radially along the disk, the contribution from the sphere drops off as r^3 while that from the portion of the disk between the sphere and r only as 1/r, given the previous constraint on k(r).

When speaking of the 'disk,' I recognize that we really have three spiral arms lying within the galaxy's ecliptic. I will view this as if the charge (and mass, both of which I assume are directly proportional to each other) was uniformly distributed in the annulus between the sphere and radius r of the disk as one proceeds outward to $R_d = 5$. Thus, k(r) will increase from 0 at the sphere ($r = R_s = 1$, where the disk begins) to its maximum value of $Q_d/Q_s < 1$ at $R_d = 5$. How k(r) increases with r depends on the shape of the spiral arms. Figure 2 shows them as tapering. Another possibility is a uniform cross-section, i.e., no tapering (we will not consider the possibility of them widening as r increases as this is not evident from galactic photographs). Figure 3 shows this variation for the two 'extremes.'

3.2. Gravitational Effects

What about gravitational effects? Assuming the mass of the sphere (galactic core) = M_s (also assumed directly proportional to Q_s), the gravitational field G(r) solely from the sphere as a function of r is

$G(r) = \Gamma M_s/r^2, R_d < r$ (using Γ as the symbol for the gravitational constant). [Eq. 7]

Approximating the contribution from the disk mass as one proceeds outward ($R_s < r < R_d$), and assuming the same behavior of the mass fraction as for the charge fraction (i.e., again using k[r], now as $m[r]/M_s$), i.e., the ratio of the mass of the disk in the annulus from the sphere to r to the total sphere mass), we can modify Equation [7] as follows:

$G(r) = \Gamma M_s(1 + k[r])/r^2$, with 0 < k(r) < 1 as before. [Eq. 8]

Analogous to setting $Q_s = 1$, we now set $M_s = 1$ (such that all further calculations will be scaled to the sphere's mass), thereby simplifying this to

$G(r) = G(r)/\Gamma = (1 + k[r])/r^2$ [Eq. 9]

where $R_s < r < R_d$, i.e., 1 < r < 5.

For subsequent analysis, define the following scaled value for the G field

$G'(r) = \Gamma(1 + k[r])/r^2$ [Eq. 10]

It is evident that, as one proceeds outward radially along the disk, the contribution drops off as r^2, given the previous constraint on k(r).

4. Results

What we have shown so far is that the expected variation as one proceeds radially outward from the sphere along the disk for the B' field should be somewhat flatter (due to the 1/r variation becoming dominant over the $1/r^3$ variation) than that for the G' field, with its $1/r^2$ variation. Note that we are not comparing the relationship between the absolute strengths of the two types of field, magnetic vs. gravitational (the former is known to be much stronger), but only their variation relative to their maximum values (at the sphere). The results of the comparison are shown

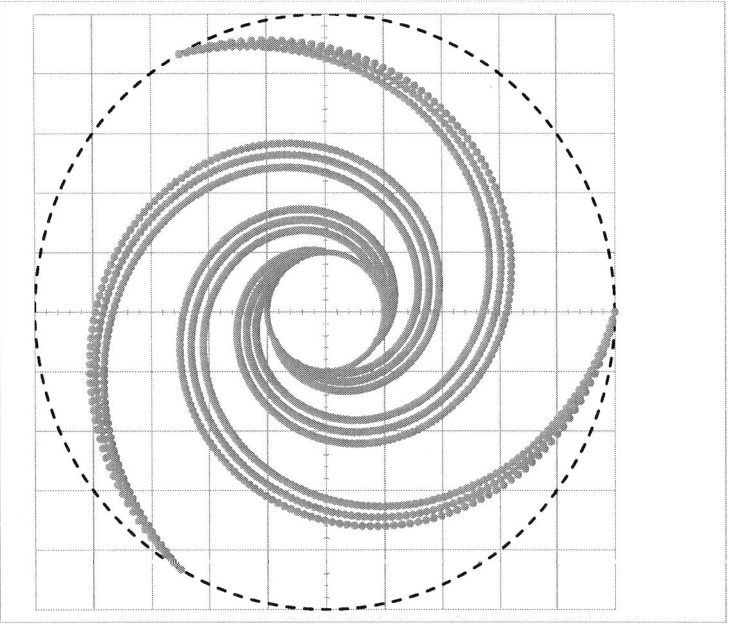

Figure 2. Representative Three-Armed, Logarithmic Spiral Galaxy

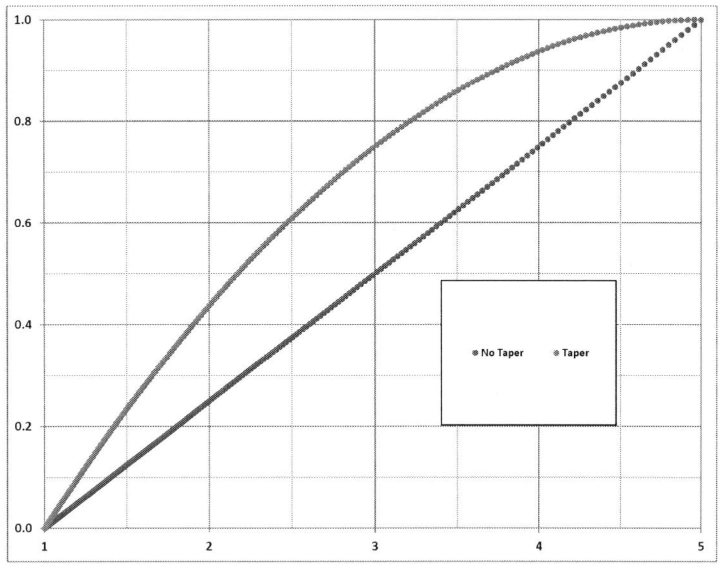

Figure 3. Variation in Disk Charge Fraction Based on Spiral Arm Tapering

in Figure 4 having averaged for both the tapering and non-tapering spiral arms, and indicate the expected trend toward 'flattening' of the B' field vs. the G' field.

Just to be clear, Figure 4 does not represent any relative strengths among the three charge (Q) ratios for the B' field, the three mass (M) ratios for the G' field, or between the two sets (B' and G'). Each specific case has been scaled to its maximum value (at the sphere) such that all curves have a value of 1.0 at R_s (or just infinitesimally farther out in the case of the B' fields since their maximum does not occur until at least an infinitesimal bit of the disk is included.) While one can readily surmise that the B' field increases with charge ratio, and the G' field increases with mass ratio, their strengths relative to each other are not represented in the Figure. The Figure solely illustrates the trend in each individual field's strength as one proceeds radially outward from the sphere along the disk solely for the purpose of illustrating the degree of 'flattening' in each particular case. (This caveat holds for Figure 5 as well.)

Comparing this with Figure 1, and assuming rotational velocity is reasonably proportional to field strength, one sees behavior closer to that of the flat or galactic curves for the B' field than for the G' field, at least beyond a radius of approximately 2. This is especially pronounced when the spiral arms are assumed not to taper. The average between the taper and no taper behavior is displayed in Figure 4 for an easier view, further illustrating the trend.

5. Conclusion

Hopefully I have at least made a plausible argument for one possible explanation for the galactic rotation anomaly, at least as one proceeds radially outward from the galactic core, for an idealized spiral galaxy to add to the lexicon of other such arguments that do not invoke the likely fiction of 'dark matter' (and its sibling 'dark energy'). Borrowing from the Electric/Plasma Universe theories, which assert that the much greater strength of electromagnetism vs. gravity may explain much of the observed behavior of the universe, I attempt to show mathematically that magnetic forces could account for at least some of the supposedly anomalous 'flattening' observed in rotational speed of a galaxy as one proceeds radially outward. It is by no means a rigorous treatment of the subject, but hopefully at least demonstrates that such an explanation merits further investigation.

6. Appendix: Possible Effect from a Globular Cluster Halo

As discussed in [9]:

"A globular cluster is a spherical collection of stars that orbits a galactic core as a satellite. Globular clusters are very tightly bound by gravity, which gives them their spherical shapes and relatively high stellar densities toward their centers ... Globular clusters ... contain considerably more stars and are much older than the less dense galactic, or open clusters, which are found in the disk ... These globular clusters orbit the galaxy at large radii of 40 kiloparsecs (approximately 131,000 light-years) or more ... Globular clusters are generally composed of hundreds of thousands of low-metal, old stars. The type[s] of stars found in a globular cluster are similar to those in the bulge of a spiral galaxy but confined to a volume of only a few million cubic parsecs ... Globular clusters can contain a high density of stars; on average about 0.4 stars per cubic parsec, increasing to 100 or 1000 stars per cubic parsec in the core of the cluster ... Some globular clusters ... are extraordinarily massive, with several million solar masses and multiple stellar populations."

To gauge the possible contribution from any magnetic field generated by a halo of globular clusters surrounding my representative spiral galaxy, I assume there is such a halo at a distance of $5R_d/2$ (i.e., r = 25/2), rotating with the galaxy at the same rotational speed ω as the disk so as to form a spherical shell of charge in which the galaxy resides. (This very crude approximation is based loosely on the estimated radius of the Milky Way galaxy [approximately 50,000-60,000 light-years] and the estimate that its halo of globular clusters is located at a radius of approximately 131,000 light years.) From [8], the B field inside such a sphere within the ecliptic plane is

$B_h = \mu_0 Q_h \omega / 6\pi r$ [Eq. 11]

where Q_h = charge on the spherical shell, i.e., the total charge of the halo).

As before, we can define $B'_h = B_h/(\mu_0\omega/2\pi) = Q_h/3r$ [Eq. 12]

Considering the same range on Q_h as for Q_d (i.e., from $Q_s/3$ to Q_s), and setting $Q_s = 1$ and $r = 5R_d/2 = 25/2$, we obtain

$B'_h = 2f/75$, where 1/3 < f < 1. [Eq. 13]

When this is added to the combined B field from the rotating sphere and disk, the total B field rises as much as approximately 8 percent, as shown in Figure 5 (plotted against the scaled averages as in Figure 4 for convenience of viewing).

REFERENCES

1. Wikipedia, *Dark Matter*, http://en.wikipedia.org/wiki/Dark_Matter
2. Wikipedia, *Rotation Curves*, http://upload.wikimedia.org/wikipedia/commons/d/dc
3. Ken Hughes, *Galactic Rotation Anomaly*, http://www.thenakedscientists.com/forum/index.php?topic=39624.0
4. Wallace Thornhill, *Electric Galaxies*, http://www.holoscience.com/wp/electric-galaxies/
5. David Talbott, *Essential Guide to the Electric Universe*, https://www.thunderbolts.info/wp/2012/02/29/essential-guide-to-the-eu-chapter-10/
6. Carl Johnson, *Gravitational Effects on Galactic Spiral Arms*, http://mb-soft.com/public/galaxyzz.html
7. Wikipedia, *Logarithmic Spiral*, http://en.wikipedia.org/wiki/Logarithmic_spiral
8. I. Vagner, *Electrodynamics of Magnetoactive Media*, Springer Series in Solid State Sciences, ISSN 0171-1873; 135 (2004)
9. Wikipedia, *Globular Cluster*, http://en.wikipedia.org/wiki/Globular_cluster

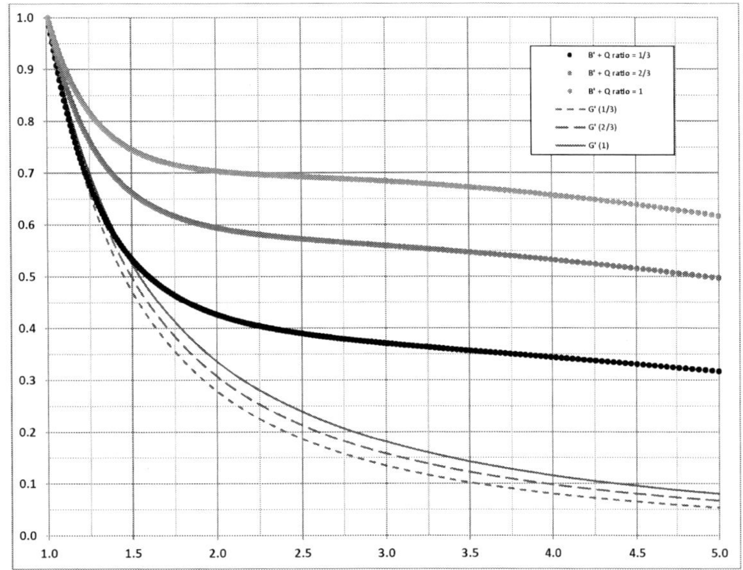

Figure 4. Comparison between B' and G' Field (Scaled) Variaton with Radius, Using Average between Taper and No Taper Results

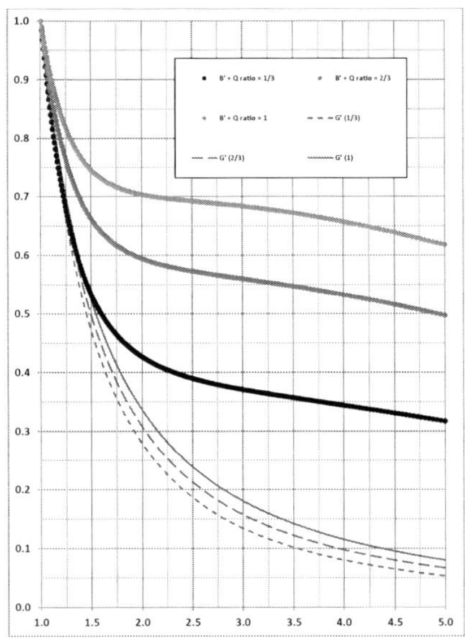

Figure 5. Scaled Average B' Fields between Taper and No Taper (with Halo of Globular Clusters)

Can Varying Light Speed Explain Photon-Particle Interactions?

Raymond HV Gallucci, PhD, PE

8956 Amelung St., Frederick, Maryland, 21704, gallucci@localnet.com, r_gallucci@verizon.net

Photon-particle interactions, both 'classical,' such as Compton Scattering, and 'speculative,' such as ones associated with 'tired light' theories of the cosmological red-shift, are explained with the assumption of the constancy of the speed of light. For classical interactions, reciprocal variations in light frequency and wavelength occur under the constraint that their product always equals constant speed 'c.' Proponents of a cosmological red-shift claim that the universe is expanding due to expansion of space (or space-time) itself as light, traveling at 'c,' is stretched as the distance between the source and observer increases due to this space (or space-time) expansion. Counter arguments to this interpretation often fall into the realm of 'tired light,' dismissed by mainstream physicists for various reasons, but still advocated by various 'dissident' physicists, since the term was first coined by Zwicky in 1929. In this paper, I examine a classical photon-particle interaction, Compton Scattering, and one of the more popular 'tired light' theories to show that the assumption of a constant speed of light is unnecessary, i.e., similar results evolve from assuming a variable light speed.

Keywords: light, Compton Scattering, 'tired light,' Lyndon Ashmore

1. Introduction

Classical Compton Scattering and the alleged cosmological red-shifting of light are based on the assumption that the light wave maintains a constant speed while the waveform is altered by reciprocal variations in frequency and wavelength. For the cosmological red-shift, it is space (or space-time) itself that expands, increasing the distance between the source and observer. In classical wave theory, the wave's behavior is determined by its medium of transmission. Since its speed is constant due to the medium itself (assuming the medium is not moving), either the waveform is stretched if receding from the observer or remains the same if stationary but the observer is receding from the wave, an analogous effect; or a combination of both effects if both source and observer are mutually receding. Unless you adhere to an aether theory or one such as Calkins' where the electromagnetic medium itself is light's medium that propagates with it [1], there is no *a priori* reason why the speed of light need be constant for a moving source or independent of a moving observer even if the light source remains stationary. This is an assumption based on Einstein's relativity or, in some cases, claimed to be required by Maxwell's equations. For the latter, I believe that the only requirement is that light speed be 'c' relative to its emission from a stationary source. If that source is moving, light acquires the source velocity as well. In this paper, I examine Compton Scattering and one of the more prevalent 'tired light' theories to show that the assumption of a constant speed of light is unnecessary for the phenomena, i.e., the phenomena will still occur with a variable light speed.

2. Re-examination of Compton Scattering

Classical Compton Scattering (including its low-energy limit where a photon's energy [frequency] is much less than the particle mass, known as Thomson Scattering [2]) evolved from "early 20th century research ... [where it] was observed that, when X-rays of a known wavelength interact with atoms, the X-rays are scattered through an angle θ and emerge at a different wavelength related to θ. Although classical electromagnetism predicted that the wavelength of scattered rays should be equal to the initial wavelength, multiple experiments had found that the wavelength of the scattered rays was longer (corresponding to lower energy) than the initial wavelength. In 1923, Compton published a paper in the Physical Review that explained the X-ray shift by attributing particle-like momentum to light quanta (Einstein had proposed light quanta in 1905 in explaining the photo-electric effect, but Compton did not build on Einstein's work.) [3] The energy of light quanta depends only on the frequency of the light. In his paper, Compton derived the mathematical relationship between the shift in wavelength and the scattering angle of the X-rays by assuming that each scattered X-ray photon interacted with only one electron. His paper concludes by reporting on experiments which verified his derived relation:

$$\lambda' - \lambda = h(1 - \cos\theta)/(m_e c)$$

where λ is the initial wavelength, λ' is the wavelength after scattering, h is the Planck constant, m_e is the electron rest mass, c is the speed of light, and θ is the scattering angle (Figure 1)." [4]

2.1. Derivation of Classical Compton Scattering

The derivation is reproduced below [4] so that I can follow it with my altered assumption of a variable speed of light where the waveform remains unchanged (i.e., λ remains constant) and the energy loss resulting from the

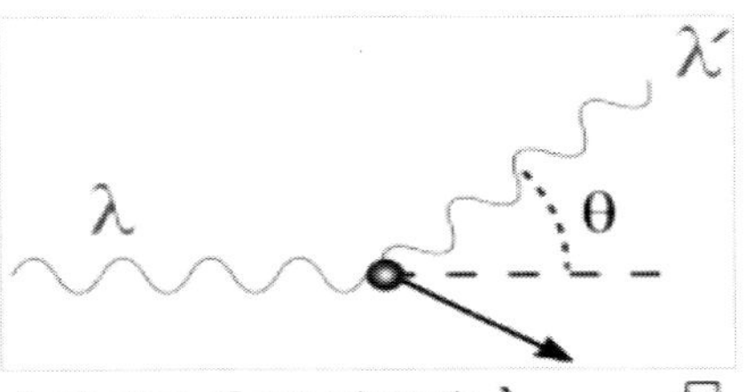

A photon of wavelength λ comes in from the left, collides with a target at rest, and a new photon of wavelength λ' emerges at an angle θ.

Figure 1. Classical Compton Scattering

reduced speed is characterized by a reduction in the frequency 'f.'

"A photon with wavelength λ collides with an electron in an atom, which is treated as being at rest. The collision causes the electron to recoil, and a new photon with wavelength *lambda*$'$ emerges at angle θ from the photon's incoming path ... Compton allowed for the possibility that the interaction would sometimes accelerate the electron to speeds sufficiently close to the velocity of light and would require the application of Einstein's special relativity theory to properly describe its energy and momentum.

"At the conclusion of Compton's 1923 paper, he reported results of experiments confirming the predictions of his scattering formula thus supporting the assumption that photons carry directed momentum as well as quantized energy. At the start of his derivation, he had postulated an expression for the momentum of a photon from equating Einstein's already established mass-energy relationship of $E = mc^2$ to the quantized photon energies of hf which Einstein has separately postulated. If $mc^2 = hf$, the equivalent photon mass must be hf/c^2. The photon's momentum is then simply this effective mass times the photon's frame-invariant velocity c. For a photon, its momentum p = hf/c, and thus hf can be substituted for pc for all photon momentum terms which arise in course of the derivation below. The derivation which appears in Compton's paper is terser, but follows the same logic in the same sequence as the following derivation.

"The conservation of energy E merely equates the sum of energies before and after scattering.

$$E_{photon-before} + E_{electron-before} = E_{photon-after} + E_{electron-after}$$

Compton postulated that photons carry momentum; thus from the conservation of momentum, the momenta of the particles should be similarly related by

$$P_{photon-before} = P_{photon-after} + P_{electron-after}$$

in which the electron's initial momentum is omitted on the assumption it is effectively zero. The photon energies are related to the frequencies by: $E_{photon-before} = hf$; $E_{photon-after} = hf'$. Before the scattering event, the electron is treated as sufficiently close to being at rest that its total energy consists entirely of the mass-energy equivalence of its rest mass: $E_{electron-before} = m_e c^2$. After scattering, the possibility that the electron might be accelerated to a significant fraction of the speed of light, requires that its total energy be represented using the relativistic energy-momentum relation:

$$E_{electron-after} = \sqrt{(P_{electron-after}c)^2 + (m_e c^2)^2}$$

Substituting these quantities into the expression for the conservation of energy gives,

$$hf + m_e c^2 = hf + \sqrt{[P_{electron-after}c]^2 + (m_e c^2)^2} \text{ [Eq. 1]}$$

This expression can be used to find the magnitude of the momentum of the scattered electron,

$$(P_{electron-after}c)^2 = (hf - hf' + m_e c^2)^2 - (m_e c^2)^2 \text{ [Eq. 2]}$$

"Equation [1] relates the various energies associated with the collision. The electron's momentum change includes a relativistic change in the mass of the electron so it is not simply related to the change in energy in the manner that occurs in classical physics. The change in the momentum of the photon is also not simply related to the difference in energy but involves a change in direction. Solving the conservation of momentum expression for the scattered electron's momentum gives,

$$P_{electron-after} = P_{photon-before} - P_{photon-after}$$

Then by making use of the scalar product,

$$P^2_{electron-after} = P_{electron-after} \text{ dot } P_{electron-after} = (P_{photon-before} - P_{photon-after}) \text{ dot } (P_{photon-before} - P_{photon-after}) = P^2_{photon-before} + P^2_{photon-after} - 2P_{photon-before}P_{photon-after}\cos\theta \text{ [Eq. 3]}$$

Anticipating that $P_{photon-before}c$ is replaceable with hf, multiply both sides by c^2 ... After replacing the photon momentum terms with hf/c, we get a second expression for the magnitude of the momentum of the scattered electron:

$(P_{electron-after}c)^2 = (hf)^2 + (hf')^2 - 2(hf)(hf')\cos\theta$ [Eq. 4]

Equating both expressions for this momentum gives

$(hf - hf + m_ec^2)^2 - (m_ec^2)^2 = (hf)^2 + (hf')^2 - 2(hf)(hf')\cos\theta$

which after evaluating the square and then canceling and rearranging terms gives

$2hfm_ec^2 - 2hf'm_ec^2 = 2h^2ff'(1-\cos\theta)$

Then dividing both sides by $2h^2ff'm_ec$ yields

$c/f' - c/f = h(1-\cos\theta)/(m_ec)$

Finally, since $f\lambda = f'\lambda' = c$,

$\lambda' - \lambda = h(1-\cos\theta)/(m_ec)$."

2.2. Derivation with Variable Light Speed

As discussed in my papers [5, 6, 7], I contend that light need not be constrained, unless there is an aether (or a medium that moves with light itself, as per Calkins [1]), to a constant speed. I postulate that it is light's waveform, not its speed, that remains invariant such that, in Compton Scattering, the reduction in energy translates into a reduction in speed (c becomes câĂŹ) of the 'scattered' photon (which, in 'tired light' theory, still proceeds in its incident direction via other phenomena), characterized solely by a reduction in its frequency, i.e., f becomes f'. Following the previous derivation, I show that a similar result can be obtained from this assumption.[4]

My approach follows the previous up through Equation [2], rewritten and expanded here:

$(P_{electron-after}c)^2 = (hf - hf' + m_ec^2)^2 - (m_ec^2)^2 = h^2(f-f')^2 + 2h(f-f')m_ec^2$ [Eq. 5]

Next I rewrite Equation [3], substituting hf/c and hf'/c' for the photon momenta before and after scattering:

$P^2_{electron-after} = P^2_{photon-before} + P^2_{photon-after} - 2P_{photon-before}P_{photon-after}\cos\theta = (hf/c)^2 + (hf'/c')^2 - 2(hf/c)(hf'/c')\cos\theta$.

Multiplying both sides by c^2 yields:

$(P_{electron-after}c)^2 = (hf)^2 + (hf'c/c')^2 - 2h^2ff'(c/c')\cos\theta$ [Eq. 6]

Equating Equations [5] and [6] produces:

$h^2(f^2 - 2ff' + f'^2) + 2hfm_ec^2 - 2hf'm_ec^2 = (hf)^2 + (hf')^2(c/c')^2 - 2h^2ff'(c/c')\cos\theta$

which reduces to

$2h^2ff'([c/c']\cos\theta - 1) + (hf')^2(1-[c/c']^2) + 2h(f-f')m_ec^2 = 0$.

Eliminating c and c' via the substitutions $c = f\lambda$ and $c' = f'\lambda$ transforms this into the following:

$2h^2f(f\cos\theta - f') - h^2(f+f')(f-f') + 2h(f-f')m_ec^2 = 0$.

Since the reduction in photon speed (and therefore energy and frequency) is essentially negligible, assume $f + f' \approx 2f$, thereby simplifying this equation as follows:

$2h^2f(f\cos\theta - f') - 2h^2f(f-f) + 2h(f-f')m_ec^2 = 0$.

Dividing by 2h and rearranging yields:

$f - f' = (h[1-\cos\theta]/m_e)(f/c)^2$

which, with $c = f\lambda$, reduces to:

$f - f' = h(1-\cos\theta)/(m_e\lambda^2)$.

This has the same form as the equation for classical Compton Scattering, but in terms of the reduction in frequency (vs. an increase in the wavelength) with the constant speed of light c now replaced by the square of the constant wavelength λ.[5]

3. Re-examination of One 'Tired Light' Theory

Claims that the universe is expanding due to expansion of space (or space-time) itself are based on the assumed cosmological red-shift in which light, traveling at constant speed 'c,' is stretched as the distance between the source and observer increases due to this space (or space-time) expansion. Counter arguments to this interpretation often fall into the realm of 'tired light,' dismissed by mainstream physicists for various reasons, but still advocated by various 'dissident' physicists, since the term was first coined by Zwicky in 1929.[8] Among the many of these, I particularly note those by the father and son pairing of Paul and Louis Marmet, and the popular 'New Tired Light' Theory of Lyndon Ashmore, which I examine further below.[9, 9, 11] These theories have in common phenomena whereby an interacting photon retains its incident direction so as not to 'blur' the source image, an alleged inevitable result of 'tired light' behavior by which mainstream physicists dismiss the theories since such blurring is not observed.

3.1. Ashmore's 'New Tired Light' Theory

"In this 'New Tired Light' theory, [Ashmore] explains the increase in wavelength as being due to photons of light interacting, or colliding, with the electrons in the plasma of inter-galactic [IG] space and thus losing energy. The more interactions they make, the more energy they lose and the lower their frequency becomes. As the frequency reduces the wavelength increases and thus the photons are red-shifted. Photons of light from galaxies twice as far away travel twice as far through the intergalactic medium, undergo twice as many collisions with the electrons, lose twice as much energy, have their frequency reduced by twice as much and their wavelength increased by twice as much. Hence galaxies twice as far away have twice the red-shift. Doesn't this make more sense than an expanding Universe stretching the photons?'[11]

The details of Ashmore's analysis are found in his paper on the "Recoil Between Photons and Electrons Leading to

[4] It is a common misconception that 'color' can be equivalently characterized by wavelength or frequency. The fact that there is no 'color' change during refraction demonstrates that 'color' is really a function solely of frequency. Therefore, there is no change in 'color' (using this term loosely to apply to non-visible light as well) unless there is a change in frequency.

[5] Using $c = f\lambda$ and $c' = f'\lambda$, this can also be expressed as $c - c' = h(1-\cos\theta)/(m_e\lambda)$.

the Hubble Constant and the CMB [Cosmic Microwave Background]." [12] They are summarized here, as with the analysis for classic Compton Scattering, to pave the way for my re-examination of the derivation with my assumption of a variable light speed with invariant waveform.

3.2. Derivation for Ashmore's 'New Tired Light'

Ashmore [12] contends that "[t]he plasma of intergalactic space acts as a transparent medium and photons of light, as they travel through space, will be absorbed and re-emitted by the electrons in this plasma. At each interaction where the momentum of the photon is transferred to the electrons, there will be a delay. So the electron will recoil both on absorption and re-emission - resulting in inelastic collisions. A double Mossbauer effect will occur during each interaction between photon and electron. Some of the energy of the photon will be transferred to the electron, and since the energy of the photon has been reduced, the frequency will reduce and the wavelength will increase. It will have 'undergone a red-shift'."

"Energy lost to an electron during emission or absorption is equal to $Q^2/2m_ec^2$, where Q is the energy of the incoming photon (hc/λ), m_e is the rest mass of the electron and c is the speed of light. This energy calculation must be applied twice for absorption and re-emission. Hence, total energy lost by a photon is $Q^2/m_ec^2 = h^2/\lambda^2 m_e$, [i.e.,] (energy before interaction) - (energy after) = $h^2/\lambda^2 m_e$,

$hc/\lambda - hc/\lambda' = h^2/\lambda^2 m_e$ [Eq. 7]

where λ is the initial wavelength of the photon and λ' is the wavelength of the re-emitted photon. Multiplying through by $\lambda^2\lambda' m_e$ and dividing by h gives:

$\lambda\lambda' m_e c - \lambda^2 m_e c = h\lambda'$.

Increase in wavelength is $\delta\lambda = \lambda' - \lambda$, so:

$\lambda(\delta\lambda + \lambda)m_e c - \lambda^2 m_e c = h(\delta\lambda + \lambda)$ which leads to $\lambda m_e c\delta\lambda + \lambda^2 m_e c - \lambda^2 m_e c = h\delta\lambda + h\lambda$ which finally yields $\delta\lambda(\lambda m_e c - h) = h\lambda$.

Then since h « $\lambda m_e c, \delta\lambda = h/m_e c$."

Ashmore [11] continues: "On their journey through IG space, photons will [experience] many such interactions where they are absorbed and re-emitted each time (photons of light make, on average, one collision every 70,000 light year[s]). Each time they will lose energy and be red-shifted a little more. Total shift in wavelength, $\Delta\lambda = N\delta\lambda$, [w]here, $\Delta\lambda$ is the total shift in wavelength, N is the total number of interaction[s] made by the photon on its journey and $\delta\lambda$ is the increase in wavelength at each interaction ... With red-shift, we find that the longer the wavelength, λ, the greater the shift in wavelength, $\Delta\lambda$. In fact, experiment tells us that the shift in wavelength, $\Delta\lambda$ is proportional to the wavelength,λ, i.e., ... $\Delta\lambda = z\lambda$, where z is a constant called the 'red-shift.' We usually write this as: $z = \Delta\lambda/\lambda$. For a particular galaxy, the red-shift, z, is a constant for all wavelengths.

"... In the 'New Tired Light' theory, the number of collisions made by each photon depends upon its collision cross-section, σ This represents the probability of a photon being absorbed by the electron. We know the photo-absorption collision cross-section for a photon - electron interaction from experiments carried out by the interaction of low energy X-rays with matter and it depends upon the radius of the electron and the wavelength of the photon:

collision cross-section, σ = 2 x (classical radius of electron, r) x (wavelength of photon, λ), or $\sigma = 2r\lambda$.

The number of collisions the photon makes on its journey depends both on the probability of the photon 'bumping' into an electron and upon how densely packed the electrons are in IG space. The greater either of these quantities are, then the more likely it is for a photon to bump into an electron and be absorbed and re-emitted. The average distance between collisions is called the 'mean free path' and this can be calculated [as] mean free path = $(n\sigma)^{-1}$, or $(2nr\lambda)^{-1}$, ... [w]here 'n' is the number of electrons in each cubic metre of IG space.

"... The number of collisions, N, made by the photon in travelling from a galaxy a distance 'd' away is simply the distance 'd' divided by the average distance between each collision (the mean free path), [i.e.,]

Number of collisions by photon, $N = d/(2nr\lambda)^{-1}$, or $N = 2nr\lambda d$.

As we have seen before, the shift in wavelength, $\delta\lambda$, at each interaction is the same for all wavelengths and equal to $h/(m_ec)$. The total shift in wavelength experienced by the photon during its entire journey is found by multiplying the total number of collisions, N, by the shift in wavelength at each collision.

Total shift in wavelength, $\Delta\lambda = N\delta\lambda$, or $\Delta\lambda = (2nr\lambda d)(h/[m_ec])$.

The red-shift z is defined as $z = \Delta\lambda/\lambda$. Rearranging ... gives:

$z = \Delta\lambda/\lambda = (2nhrd)/(m_ec)$."

3.3. Derivation with Variable Light Speed

I begin with Equation [7] for total energy lost by a photon, i.e.,

(energy before interaction) - (energy after) = $hc/\lambda - hc/\lambda' = h^2/\lambda^2 m_e$

but assume that the light speed (and therefore just the frequency, since I consider λ constant) is reduced, using the symbols from Section 2.2 to rewrite this as:

(energy before interaction) - (energy after) = $hc/\lambda - hc'/\lambda = hf - hf' = h^2/\lambda^2 m_e$.

Paralleling Ashmore, I define $\delta f = f - f'$, the decrease in frequency of the photon due to the interaction with the electron (unlike Ashmore's wavelength, the primed value here is the lower one). Then this easily rearranges into: $\delta f = f - f' = h/(m_e\lambda^2)$.

Continuing to parallel Ashmore, but with my variable light speed assumption (and changes in *italics*): "On their journey through IG space, photons will [experience] many such interactions where they are absorbed and re-emitted each time ... [to] lose energy and be red-shifted a little more. Total shift in *[frequency]*, $\Delta f = N\delta f$, [w]here, Δf is the total shift in *[frequency]*, N is the total number of interaction[s] made by the photon on its journey and δf is the *decrease in frequency* at each interaction ... With red-shift, we find that the *slower the light speed*, ... the greater the *shift in frequency,* Δf. In fact, *experiments could also be interpreted* to tell us *not* that the shift in wavelength, $\Delta\lambda$ is proportional to the wavelength, λ, i.e., ... $\Delta\lambda = z\lambda$, where z is a constant called the 'red-shift,' *but rather that the shift in frequency,* Δf, *is proportional to the frequency,* f, *i.e., ...* $\Delta f = zf$. We *can* write this as: $z = \Delta f/f$. For a particular galaxy, the red-shift, z, is a constant for all *frequencies.*"

As before, "... the [n]umber of collisions by [the] photon, $N = d/(2nr\lambda)^{-1}$, or $N = 2nr\lambda d$ ... [T]he shift in *[frequency],* δf, at each interaction is the same for all *[frequencies]* and equal to $[h/(m_e\lambda^2)]$. The total shift in *[frequency]* experienced by the photon during its entire journey is found by multiplying the total number of collisions, N, by the shift in *[frequency]* at each collision.

Total shift in *[frequency],* $\Delta f = N\delta f$, *or* $\Delta f = (2nr\lambda d)(h/[m_e\lambda^2]) = (2nhrd)/[m_e\lambda])$.

The red-shift z is defined as $z = \Delta f/f$. Rearranging with $c = f\lambda$ ... gives:

$z = \Delta f/f = \Delta f/(c/\lambda) = (2nhrd/[m_e\lambda])/(c/\lambda) = \underline{(2nhrd)/(m_e c)}$."

This matches Ashmore's red-shift formula.

4. Summary

My analyses sought to show that, for Compton Scattering and one of the more popular 'tired light' theories, Ashmore's 'New Tired Light,' the implicit assumption of constant light speed need not be retained to derive similar results. Light can be assumed to lose energy during Compton Scattering or a 'tired light' interaction via a decrease in speed, with a corresponding decrease in frequency, holding the wavelength constant. Note that this does not preclude the possibility that a decrease in light speed may be accompanied by both a decrease in frequency and increase in wavelength, provided the decrease in frequency more than counteracts the increase in wavelength so as to result in the lower speed.

5. Acknowledgment

I would like to thank both Lyndon Ashmore and Louis Marmet for their insightful reviews of my paper and recommended improvements. Note that this does not imply agreement with my views regarding variable light speed or the conclusions drawn.

REFERENCES

1. R. Calkins, *The Problem with Relativity: Maxwell was Right, Einstein was Wrong, and the Human Condition Prevailed*, http://www.calkinspublishing.com, 2015
2. Wikipedia, *Thomson Scattering*, https://en.wikipedia.org/wiki/Thomson_Scattering
3. A. Compton, *A Quantum Theory of the Scattering of X-Rays by Light Elements*, Physical Review 21(5), pp. 483-502, 1923
4. Wikipedia, *Compton Scattering*, https://en.wikipedia.org/wiki/Compton_Scattering
5. R. Gallucci, *Questioning the Cosmological Doppler Red-Shift*, Proceedings of the 1st Annual Chappell Natural Philosophy Society Conference, August 5-8, 2015, Florida Atlantic University, pp. 68-70 (also http://vixra.org/pdf/1601.0078v1.pdf)
6. R. Gallucci, *Does Light Travel with the Velocity of a Moving Source?*, Proceedings of the 2nd International Conference of the John Chappell Natural Philosophy Society, July 20-23, 2016, College Park, MD, pp. 94-99 (also http://vixra.org/pdf/1606.0127v1.pdf)
7. R. Gallucci, *The Speed of Light: Constant and Non-Constant*, Proceedings of the 2nd International Conference of the John Chappell Natural Philosophy Society, July 20-23, 2016, pp. 67-73 (also http://vixra.org/pdf/1606.0128v1.pdf
8. Wikipedia, *Tired Light*, https://en.wikipedia.org/wiki/Tired_Light
9. P. Marmet, *A New Non-Doppler Redshift*, http://newtonphysics.on.ca/hubble/index.html
10. L. Marmet, *Optical Forces as a Redshift Mechanism: The 'Spectral Transfer Redshift'*, 2nd Crisis in Cosmology Conference, CCC-2, ASP Conference Series, Volume 413, F. Potter, ed., 2009
11. L. Ashmore, *Ashmore's 'New Tired Light' Theory*, http://lyndonashmore.com/tired_light_front_page.htm (2006)
12. L. Ashmore, *Recoil Between Photons and Electrons Leading to the Hubble Constant and CMB*, Galilean Electrodynamics, Summer 2006, Volume 17, Special Issues No. 3, pp. 53-56

Alleged Extended Lifetimes of Atmospheric Muons – Does This Really Confirm Relativity?

Raymond HV Gallucci, PhD, PE

8956 Amelung St., Frederick, Maryland, 21704, gallucci@localnet.com, r_gallucci@verizon.net

One of the long-standing 'proofs' of Einstein's relativity is the alleged time dilation effect that muons created during cosmic ray collisions with particles in our upper atmosphere experience as they plummet downward at nearly the speed of light. Given the assumption that all are created at one high altitude, relativists see only a 'slowing' of their 'clocks' as the means by which their decay can be sufficiently delayed so that an unexpectedly (according to classical physics) large number reach sea level. One of the earliest experiments allegedly demonstrating this was by Frisch and Smith in 1963. Dissident physicists have offered non-relativistic explanations for the relatively high numbers of atmospheric muons reaching sea level, including the possibility that they are created by cosmic ray collisions with particles throughout our atmosphere, not just at a single altitude. The plausibility of this argument is examined here as an alternative explanation to relativistic time dilation as the only acceptable answer offered by mainstream physics today.

Keywords: atmospheric density, muon decay times, time dilation, relativity, cosmic rays

1. Introduction

Atmospheric muons are assumed to be created only in the upper atmosphere (at an altitude of approximately 15 km) when cosmic rays collide with particles. [1] If created only at these altitudes, and given their half-life of only 2.2 μ s, half should decay every $(2.2E-6s)(3E+8m/s) =$ 660 m if they are traveling at near the speed of light c. This would leave only $1/2^{15000/660} \approx 1/2^{23} \approx 1E-7$ (one ten-millionth) reaching sea level. Experiments such as that by Frisch and Smith in 1963 indicated that the number of muons reaching near sea level is much greater than would be expected from these standard assumptions, prompting them, and successive physicists, to conclude that the muon half-lives were significantly lengthened due to their near-c speeds as postulated by Einstein's relativity theories. [2] In fact, they measured a decrease from an altitude of approximately 2 km down to sea level of only 151 out of 563 muons, or approximately 27 percent. Even over this relatively short distance, a $2.2-\mu s$ half-life would suggest a decrease by $1-1/2^{2000/660} \approx 1-1/2^{3} \approx 88$ percent. Therefore, they concluded that relativistic time dilation had 'slowed' the internal decay 'clocks' by an average factor of approximately 8.4.

As with other 'proofs' of Einstein's relativity, dissident physicists have considered possible non-relativistic explanations for observed results, typically being dismissed by relativists by patching up 'The Standard Model' with fictions such as Dark Matter/Energy, Big Bang Inflation, etc. Specifically related to atmospheric muons is [3]:

... [W]hy are we adamant that we know everything about the muon and controlled all the factors which could affect its speed and life span? Relativists propose time dilation as if our knowledge about the life span and the speed of muons is perfect and absolute. Under certain conditions (gravity, energy state, environment, etc.) why not a muon [that can] travel faster or live longer before it decays into the smaller particles.

Muon's time dilation is only a calculated/predicted effect from the mathematics of relativity and hence can't be accepted as a proof of relativity. Muon's time dilation is what we would propose in the given scenario if the theory of relativity is correct. Relativists resort to circular logic here, i.e., they believe that relativity is true, so they imagine time dilation as really happening for the muons and then they claim their imagination of time dilation as proof of relativity - like this they keep going in circles in every scenario that they claim as proof of relativity.

Why not [suppose that] the muons produced in the laboratory experience the same time dilation and length contraction if their speed was same as that of the cosmic ray muons? And if they did, why haven't we seen the laboratory muons travel the same 16000 meters as their cosmic counter parts? And if they travelled 16000 meters distance in their life span of 2 microseconds, what would be their speed?

Since atmospheric muons apparently are created by particle collisions with cosmic rays, why should these collisions be limited only to the upper atmosphere when atmospheric density increases with decreasing altitude? If muons could be created throughout the atmosphere, what might be observed with decreasing altitude? Could observations similar to that by Frisch and Smith be explained by simply assuming muons are created throughout the atmosphere, not just in the upper atmosphere, thereby eliminating the need for 'time dilation' as a panacea?

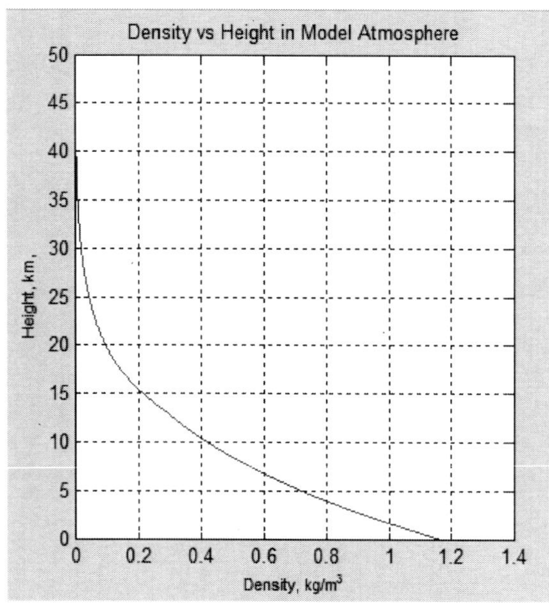

Figure 1. Atmospheric Density vs. Altitude

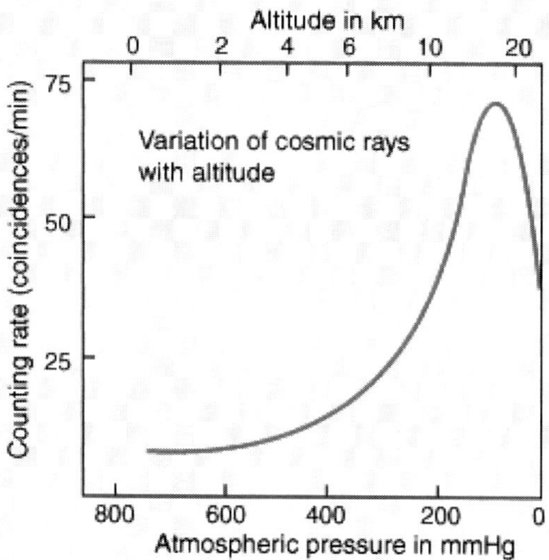

Figure 2. Cosmic Ray Intensity vs. Altitude

2. Creation of Muons as a Function of Atmospheric Density

From Reference [4], a plot of atmospheric density vs. altitude shows an exponential-like increase with decreasing altitude, from near-zero density at approximately 35 km to approximately 1.3 kg/m^3 at sea level (0 km), as shown in Figure 1. Where muons supposedly are created (approximately 15 km), the atmospheric density is only about 0.2 kg/m^3, or $< 1/6^{th}$ of the maximum. Would it not seem logical to assume cosmic rays create muons at altitudes less than 15 km where collisions with particles should be more likely, perhaps all the way down to sea level? Countering this to some extent (evaluated below) is the decrease in cosmic ray intensity with decreasing altitude, from a maximum at approximately 15 km (roughly 70/min according to [5]) to a minimum at sea level (about 8/min, from the same reference), as shown in Figure 2.

Let us assume that the creation of muons is directly proportional to the ratio of the atmospheric density at altitude y to that density at approximately 15 km = 15,000 m (here we use 15,180 m so that equal intervals of 660 m exist down to sea level, corresponding to the distance over which half of the muons created at altitude y decay) as well as to the ratio of the cosmic ray intensity at altitude y to that intensity also at approximately 15 km = 15,000 m (again using 15,180 m). Start with one muon created at 15,180 m and calculate the number created and remaining undecayed for every decrease in altitude by 660 m down to sea level. The net number of muons at each altitude decrement is shown in Table 1 and Figure 3.

3. Speculation

The trend shown in Figure 3 indicates the number of muons vs. altitude rises initially with decreasing altitude as the atmospheric density increases fairly steadily while the cosmic ray intensity decreases sharply but is still at its highest levels. Subsequently the number of muons decreases with decreasing altitude, leveling off when approaching sea level at around 1.4 as the steady increase in atmospheric density is countered by the leveling off of the decrease in cosmic ray intensity and continued decay of previously created muons. The trend over the same range measured by Frisch and Smith (approximately 2000 m to sea level) is slightly upward (1.342 to 1.393), an increase by approximately 4 percent vs. their observed decrease by approximately 27 percent. However, this does not even remotely approach the presumed non-relativistic decrease of approximately 88 percent over that same range that would be expected if all atmospheric muons were created at one altitude (around 15 km) then decayed with the $2.2 - \mu s$ half-life as they plummeted downward at near-c speed.

Therefore, while the relativists will contend that the Frisch-Smith observations are explained by relativistic time dilation, dissidents like myself might counter that other non-relativistic explanations are also plausible. Given the extreme simplicity of my model here (direct proportionalities to only the ratios of atmospheric density and cosmic ray intensity), it is easy to imagine other secondary effects that could change the slight increase over the Frisch-Smith range that I estimate to align with the decrease they observed without resorting to relativistic time dilation as a panacea.

REFERENCES

1. Hyperphysics, *Atmospheric Muons*, http://hyperphysics.phy-astr.gsu.edu/hbase/particles/muonatm.html
2. Wikipedia, *Time Dilation of Moving Particles*, http://en.wikipeida.org/wiki/Time_dilation_of_moving_particles

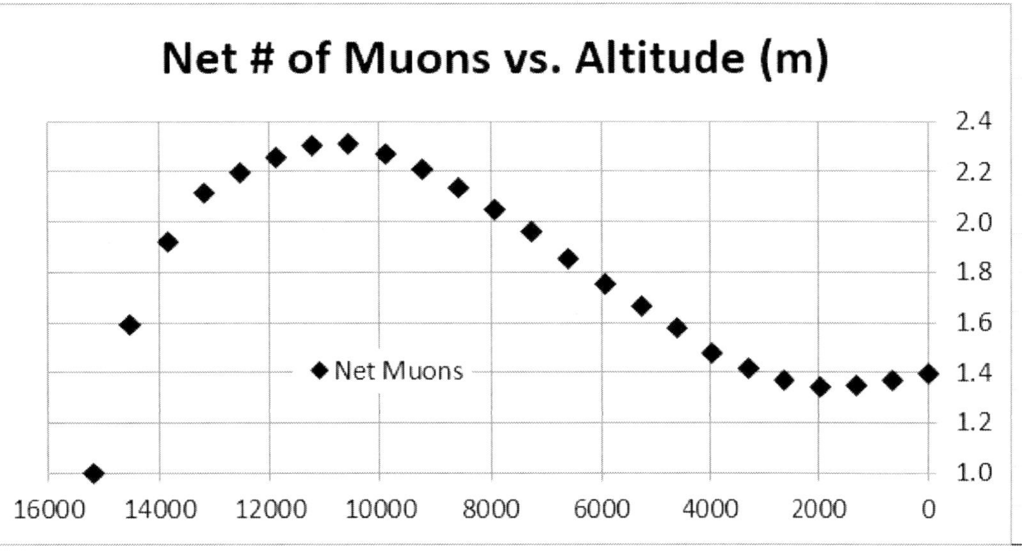

Figure 3. Net Number of Muons vs. Altitude (m)

TABLE 1. Table 1. Net Number of Muons vs. Altitude (Calculated in 660-m Decrements, but Shown in 1320-m Decrements Only)

Altitude (m)	Density (kg/m^3)	Intensity (1/min)	Muons Created	Muons Undecayed	Net Muons
15180	0.196	71.21	1.000	0.000	1.000
13680	0.238	65.91	1.124	0.795	1.919
12540	0.280	56.82	1.140	1.056	2.196
11220	0.340	48.19	1.174	1.127	2.301
9900	0.425	36.59	1.114	1.154	2.269
8580	0.480	30.07	1.034	1.104	2.139
7260	0.555	23.53	0.936	1.023	1.959
5940	0.665	17.28	0.823	0.927	1.750
4620	0.765	13.60	0.746	0.833	1.579
3300	0.890	10.66	0.680	0.738	1.418
1980	1.040	8.82	0.657	0.685	1.342
660	1.200	8.09	0.695	0.675	1.370
0	1.280	7.72	0.708	0.685	1.393

3. Debunking Relativity, *Time Dilation of Muons*, http://debunkingrelativity.com/muons-time-dilation/
4. Wikipedia, *US Standard Atmosphere 1962*, http://en.wikipedia.org/wiki/File:Comparison_US_ Standard_atmosphere_1962.svg.
5. Hyperphysics, *Cosmic Rays*, http://hyperphysics.phy-astr.gsu.edu/hbase/Astro/cosmic.html

The 'Ponderable' Aether

Raymond HV Gallucci, PhD, PE

8956 Amelung St., Frederick, Maryland, 21704, gallucci@localnet.com, r_gallucci@verizon.net

Despite the long-accepted claims by mainstream physicists that the 1887 Michelson-Morley interferometer experiment 'proved' that an aether did not exist, based on its alleged 'null result,' 'dissident' physicists have long contended that it proved the opposite, some citing the 'null result' as evidence of its existence due to 'aether drag,' others lending credence to the relevance of the alleged 'noise' that was dismissed when arriving at the 'null' conclusion. The latter group attest that the alleged null result was anything but, with an 'aether wind' on the order of 10 km/s detected but dismissed as 'noise,' thereby opening the door to Einstein's special relativity. Repeated interferometer experiments even more sensitive were performed by Dayton Miller, including several with Edward Morley, in the first part of the 20th century, allegedly confirming an 'aether wind,' again summarily dismissed as anomalous 'noise' to preserve Einstein's relativity. Now there may be as many aether theories as there are dissident physicists who postulate an aether, some believing it to be fixed against absolute space, others that it can be 'dragged' by massive bodies such as Earth (and hence the alleged 'null result'), and some that believe it flows between 'sources' and 'sinks' throughout the universe. Some believe it comprises all matter and energy, with light just being one of its various manifestations. I know not whether there is an aether. All evidence appears to be circumstantial, as nothing material has ever been detected (if that is even possible), and I do not begin to claim to even know how such would be possible. My goal here is to examine some phenomena for which an aether, if it exists, could offer an alternate explanation, neither confirming nor denying its existence. [6]

Keywords: aether, Michelson-Morley, 'aether drag/flow,' Dayton-Miller, relativistic effects

1. Introduction

There may be as many aether theories as there are 'dissident' physicists who believe in the aether. I have encountered some (for a synopsis of many of them see "Modern Scientific Theories of the Ancient Aether," *http://www.mountainman.com.au/aetherqr.htm*), with the more popular themes being that it is 'dragged' by massive bodies, such as the Earth (with or without corresponding rotation), thereby 'explaining' the 'null result' from the Michelson-Morley interferometer experiment of 1887, e.g., [1], or that it 'flows' from 'sources' throughout the universe (in some cases, such as Ref. [2], the 'cosmic voids' themselves) into 'sinks' (such as the Earth [2]). I refer to these as the 'dragged aether' and 'aether flow' models in subsequent discussion.

I do not know if there is an aether. Various 'relativistic' phenomena, e.g., time dilation, cosmological redshift, 'extended' muon lifetimes, can be and have been explained 'classically,' with or without any aether being considered or the need to restrict light speed to a constant, maximum universal limit (e.g., see [3, 4, 5, 6, 7, 8], which cite some of these sources). The purpose here is to examine three such phenomena, explained 'relativistically' by mainstream physics (and even some 'dissidents'), assuming the presence of an aether to determine if an alternate explanation is plausible.

2. Cosmological Redshift - Due to 'Aether Stretch?'

The mainstream physics explanation for the cosmological redshift is expansion of the four-dimensional space-time universe due to the original Big Bang, where an infinitely dense non-volume of 'whatever' exploded, and its momentum outward continues today, possibly unchecked. Many 'dissident' explanations cite various forms of 'tired light' theories (for a synopsis of many, see [9]), whereby light interacts with particles, fields, etc., during its long inter-galactic journey from source to Earth such that it loses energy and thereby 'reddens.' Aether is specifically excluded in the mainstream explanation; it may or may not be included in some of the 'tired light' explanations. Might 'aether stretch' be a plausible explanation for the cosmological redshift as well?

Assume a stationary, pulsing source that emits (light) waves toward a stationary receptor. If the medium of the waves (the aether) remains stationary with respect to the source and receptor, waves that are not Doppler-shifted are received by the receptor. However, if the medium itself is stretching, say at a velocity 33 percent that of the wave speed (constant) in the medium itself, the receptor will receive Doppler-shifted waves with a frequency 25 percent lower and a wavelength 33 percent longer (analogous to a 'red-shift' for light), as shown in Figure 1.

The 'aether stretch' explanation for this would be that

[6] The choice of 'ponderable' in the title is a play on words. It implies both something that is "capable of being weighted or measured" as well as the ability "to think about (something)." While I do not know if an aether can be weighed or measured, at least I can think about it.

Earth serves as a planetary 'receptor' toward which aether is stretched, such that all 'sources' are necessarily 'upstream' and, thus, light from these sources is red-shifted. Recognize that motion of the source relative to the medium can result in smaller red-shifts or even blue-shifts when the source approaches Earth ('with the stretch'), but larger red-shifts when it recedes from Earth ('against the stretch').

To elaborate a bit on this concept, consider a star that emits light with frequency, wavelength = ν_-,λ_+. Assuming the aether in the immediate vicinity of the star is somehow 'stretched' (e.g., gravity or some other phenomenon), the starlight would be perceived by an observer in the interstellar medium, assuming the observer has no 'aether-stretching' effect, as having frequency, wavelength = ν_0,λ_0, ostensibly 'blue-shifted' from the emission point but, in actuality, perceived as the 'true' frequency, wavelength, assuming no way to travel to the star to perceive the original ν_-,λ_+. Now insert an observer, e.g., a planet or even another star, that can also 'stretch' the aether in its vicinity. The 'true' frequency, wavelength of the starlight as perceived in interstellar space, ν_0,λ_0, is now perceived as ν^-,λ^+, likely different from the original ν_-,λ_+ as emitted from the star (i.e., $\nu_-,\lambda_+ \neq \nu^-,\lambda^+$), but still 'red-shifted' relative to the light perceived in the interstellar medium in the absence of the 'aether-stretching' observer. Effectively, the original starlight is 'doubly-stretched,' although there is no way of gauging the 'original' stretch as it leaves the star (unless one were to travel to that star). Thus, the 'effective' red-shift is the decrease in frequency from ν_0 to ν^- and increase in wavelength from λ_0 to λ^+.

3. 'Time Dilation' - Due to 'Aether Drag?'

'Aether drag,' as used here, must not be confused with 'dragged aether.' The latter is a fairly popular theory that the aether is 'dragged' along with Earth during its motion around the sun (and with the sun around the Milky Way, and the Milky Way relative to other galaxies, etc.), with or without accompanying rotation due to Earth's rotation. 'Aether drag' is used here in the classical sense of a resistive medium, such as air or water. Relativistic time dilation is often attributed to the mass increase of the particles that comprise a 'clock' (physical, atomic, etc.) as the clock approaches light speed, thereby slowing the motion of the particles due to increased inertia. As such, 'moving clocks always run slower' in the relativistic world. This does not necessarily imply any change in time itself (at least not to some dissident physicists), but is just a physical, or possibly only observational, phenomenon.

Most discussions of relativistic time dilation or mass increase focus on sub-atomic particles, such as those in particle accelerators or atomic clocks (e.g., Hafele-Keating experiment, Global Positioning System, 'extended' muon lifetimes). Although beyond the current capabilities of our technologies to accelerate macroscopic objects toward light speed, it might be instructive to imagine a physical, macroscopic clock at such high speeds, such as a water or pendulum clock, in the presence of air as an analogy with motion relative to an aether. Consider Figures 2 and 3.

As these two examples show (substitute a resistive aether for the air), motion can speed up or slow down (or leave unchanged) 'clock time,' depending not only on the direction by which the 'clock time' is measured (e.g., unidirectional [water clock] or oscillatory [bi-directional, pendulum clock]), but also on the direction of motion of the clock relative to the direction by which the 'clock time' is measured. Not shown, but apparent by analogy, if either clock moves in a direction perpendicular to the direction by which the 'clock time' is measured, there is no effect on the resistive drag, and the 'clock time' remains unchanged relative to the stationary case.

4. Maximum Speed - Due to 'Aether Drag?'

The speed of light is allegedly the maximum speed attainable by anything in the universe, be it matter or energy (some 'relaxation' is conveniently granted by mainstream physics to permit space-time itself to exceed this speed to preserve the current cosmological expansion model [as well as the occasional 'inflationary' period]). Does the concept of a limiting speed make sense in the absence of an aether? Does an aether imply a limiting speed?

Return to the 'water clock' example, where the net force was shown to be $\rho\pi r^2(4gr/3 - Dv^2/2)$, using 'v' instead of 'w' generically for speed. The first term is due to gravitational acceleration; the second due to air (aether) drag deceleration. Setting the constants = 1 for simplicity and using F = ma = a = dv/dt (set m = 1), we can write this general expression as $dv/dt = 1 - v^2$, where '1' is a unitized constant acceleration (analogous to gravity) and v^2 represents the drag. Solving this with initial condition (0,0) yields v = tanh(t). As shown in Figure 4, the answer is 'yes.'

5. Conclusion

The only conclusion I can draw from these simple investigations is that, if there is an aether (be it 'fixed,' 'dragged,' 'stretching,' etc.), it can provide alternate explanations to the allegedly relativistic phenomena examined here: 'cosmological redshift' (due to expanding space-time), 'time dilation' and limiting speed. While I do not specifically address the role of an aether in establishing a constant light speed (relative to an aether), I believe an aether would be necessary for such a constraint to exist. Otherwise, light speed should be variable with not only observer but also source velocity. Without 'aether drag,' what would limit the speed of matter or energy to the speed of light? But, my beliefs aside, it appears that at least these three phenomena, supposedly explained only by relativity and the current mainstream cosmological model, can have alternate explanations based on the existence of an aether.

6. Addendum - Mass Increase?

A classicist, relativist and 'aetherist' stop off at a bar after watching a baseball game. The classicist asks: "Did you notice they were using a specialized catcher's mitt that records the force 'F' with which the pitcher throws

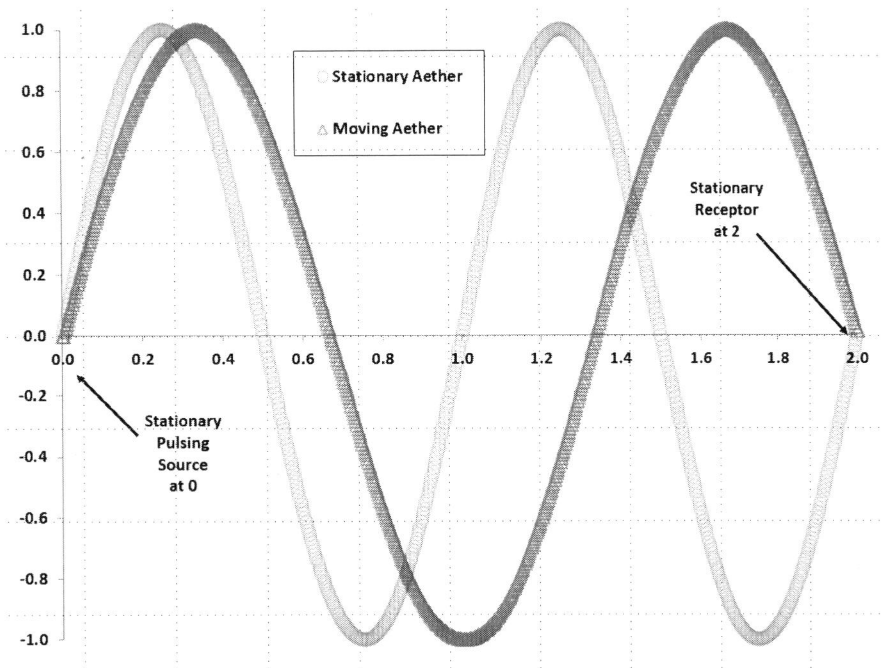

Figure 1. Red-Shift from Stationary Source due to Stretching Medium (Aether)

the baseball? It measures the impulse (change in momentum, $\Delta P = \Delta[mv]$) during the contact time (Δt), thereby providing the force ($F = \Delta P/\Delta t = \Delta[mv]/\Delta t$). During pregame warm-up, the pitcher threw with force F. However, during the game, he doubled this to 2F, meaning he threw twice as fast during the game vs. warm-up, since the mass of the baseball 'm' and the contact time remained unchanged, so he had to have doubled the speed 'v' to 2v." "Not so fast," countered the relativist. "Consider that the maximum speed at which a baseball can travel is not 2v but only $v\sqrt{3}(= 1.73v)$ according to relativity. Thus, the only way he could have doubled the force during the game would be if the mass of the baseball m itself increased to $2m/\sqrt{3}(= 1.15m)$ due to the now maximum speed of $v\sqrt{3}$, i.e., the mass of the baseball increased by 15 percent."

"But wait a minute," rebutted the classicist. "If the alleged maximum speed of a baseball were only $v\sqrt{2}(= 1.41v)$, then the alleged mass increase of the baseball would have been from m to $m\sqrt{2}(= 1.41m)$, or 41 percent. Thus, the mass would have increased even more for a lower maximum speed. Is this consistent with your theories?" "You both have a piece of it right," inserted the aetherist. "While it's true that there is a maximum speed at which a baseball can travel due to 'aether drag,' although my esteemed anti-aether relativist would not agree to this being the reason, there is no need to postulate a mass increase of the baseball due to increased speed. The baseballs used during the game were just heavier (more massive) than those used during pre-game. So, the pitcher threw a baseball of mass $2m/\sqrt{3}$ at speed $v\sqrt{3}$ during the game, vs. one of mass m at speed v during warm-up.

REFERENCES

1. R.W. Kehr, *The Detection of Ether*, available at http://www.teslaphysics.com (2002)
2. C. Ranzan, *The Dynamic Steady State Universe*, http://www.cellularuniverse.org/
3. R. Gallucci, *Time Dilation in Relativity*, Proceedings of the Natural Philosophy Alliance, 20th Annual Conference of the NPA, July 10-13, 2013, Volume 10, College Park, MD, pp. 84-86
4. R. Gallucci, *Questioning the Cosmological Doppler Red-Shift*, Proceedings of the First Annual Chappell Natural Philosophy Society Conference, August 6-8, 2015, Florida Atlantic University, pp. 68-70
5. R. Gallucci, *Michelson-Morley Interferometer Experiment of 1887: 'Null' Result*, Proceedings of the First Annual Chappell Natural Philosophy Society Conference, August 6-8, 2015, Florida Atlantic University, pp. 66-67
6. R. Gallucci, *Alleged Extended Lifetimes of Atmospheric Muons - Does This Really Confirm Relativity?*, Proceedings of the Third Annual Chappell Natural Philosophy Society Conference, 2017
7. R. Gallucci, *Does Light Travel with the Velocity of a Moving Source?*, Proceedings of the Second Annual Chappell Natural Philosophy Society Conference, July 20-23, 2016, College Park, Maryland, pp. 94-99
8. R. Gallucci, *The Speed of Light: Constant and Non-Constant*, Proceedings of the Second Annual Chappell Natural Philosophy Society Conference, July 20-23, 2016, College Park, Maryland, pp. 67-73
9. L. Marmet, *On the Interpretation of Red-Shifts: A Quantitative Comparison of Red-Shift Mechanisms II*, http://www.marmet.org/cosmology/redshift/mechanisms.

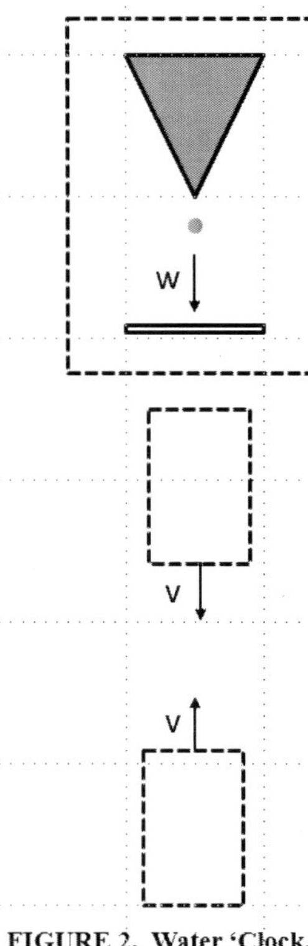

FIGURE 2. Water 'Clock,' Stationary and Moving

A stationary water clock (water-filled pail + plate) drops water uniformly as droplets of radius 'r' and speed 'w' onto a plate under a gravitational field in air (assume w = average speed of droplet during fall). The time interval between the droplet's emergence from the pail and striking the plate is the measured time unit. The net force on the droplet is Gravity minus Drag = $\rho g(4\pi r^3/3) - \rho w^2 D\pi r^2/2 = \rho\pi r^2(4gr/3 - Dw^2/2)$, where ρ = water density, g = gravitational acceleration and D = drag coefficient (air).

Now, move the water clock (pail + plate) downward (in direction of gravity) at uniform speed 'v,' such that the net speed of the droplet relative to the air is w + v. Since the distance between the pail and plate is unchanged, the gravity force is the same. However, the higher speed of the droplet relative to the air (w + v > w) translates into increased drag, slowing the speed at which the droplet falls to the plate relative to the water clock. The measured time interval is now longer, meaning the 'clock time' has slowed.

Finally, reverse the situation, moving the water clock upward (opposite to gravity) at v, such that the net speed of the droplet relative to the air is now w – v (which can be positive, negative or zero, depending on v [note that it enters the equation only as a squared term, so its squared value is always non-negative]). This lower speed of the droplet relative to the air (w – v < w) translates into decreased drag, increasing the speed at which the droplet falls to the plate relative to the water clock. The measured time interval is now shorter, meaning the 'clock time' has sped up.

Figure 2. Water 'Clock,' Stationary and Moving

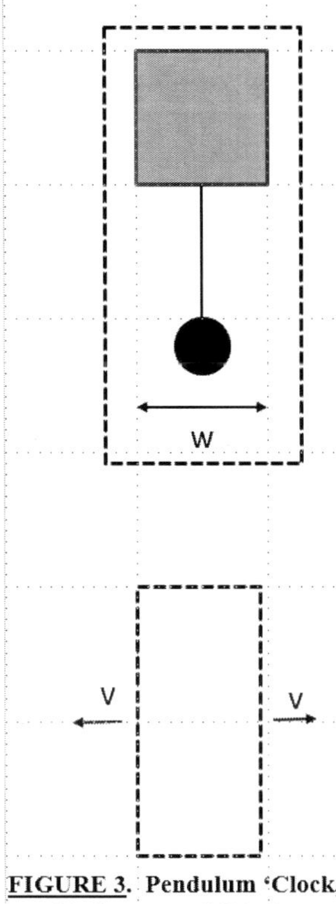

FIGURE 3. Pendulum 'Clock,' Stationary and Moving

A stationary pendulum clock with a pendulum of radius 'r' and thickness 'h' measures time by the interval over which the pendulum, swinging with average speed 'w,' returns to its original position. Ignoring gravity, which acts uniformly downward on the pendulum throughout its swing, the only force acting in the direction of swing is the resistive drag from air, i.e., $\rho w^2 D(2rh)/2 = \rho w^2 Drh$, where ρ = pendulum density and D = drag coefficient (air). Since the average speed of the pendulum (w) relative to the air is the same in each direction, the drag force is the same in each direction, such that each 'back' and 'forth' time interval is the same (the total is the measured 'pendulum time').

Now, place the pendulum clock in uniform motion either right or left with constant speed v. When the pendulum is swinging in the direction of v, its speed relative to the air is $w + v > w$, and the resistive drag force increases. The time interval for this 'back' (or 'forth') swing is thereby increased, i.e., the 'pendulum time' slows for this portion of the swing. On its return (the 'forth' or 'back' portion), the speed relative to the air is now $w - v < w$ and the resistive drag force decreases. The time interval for this 'forth' (or 'back') swing is thereby decreased, i.e., the 'pendulum time' speeds up for this portion of the swing. However, note that the speed enters the drag force as a squared term. As a result, the drag force increase when the pendulum swings in the direction of the moving pendulum clock $(w + v)^2 - w^2 = v(2w + v)$ exceeds drag force decrease when the pendulum swings against the direction of the moving pendulum clock $(w - v)^2 - w^2 = v(v - 2w)$ by $v(2w + v) - v(v - 2w) = 4vw$. The net effect for the overall 'back' and 'forth' swing is increased drag, thereby slowing the swing speed relative to the air and increasing the measured time interval, i.e., 'pendulum time' slows.

Figure 3. Pendulum 'Clock,' Stationary and Moving

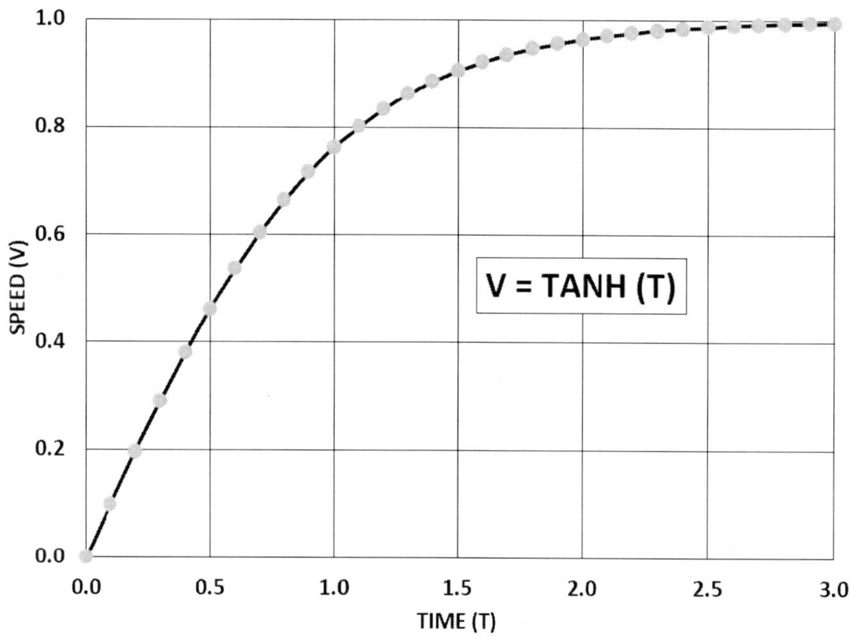

Figure 4. Effect of 'Aether Drag' on Maximum Speed

Another Role for Corpuscles in the Double-Slit Experiment?

Raymond HV Gallucci, PhD, PE

8956 Amelung St., Frederick, Maryland, 21704, gallucci@localnet.com, r_gallucci@verizon.net

The classic double-slit experiment, first performed by Young in 1801, is often cited as proving the dual wave-particle nature of light, with an emphasis on the wave aspect. In fact, when first conducted, the conclusion refuted Newton's postulate of a corpuscular nature to light in favor of light being purely a wave. Not until the discovery of the photoelectric effect did light's potential behavior as a particle become rejuvenated. This paper examines a possibly enhanced role for light's corpuscular nature beyond what is currently assigned as a result of the double-slit experimental results in hope of opening yet another avenue of exploration into the still mysterious nature of light.

Keywords: double-slit, wave-particle, light, photon, diffraction

1. Introduction

The double-slit experiment suggests the alleged wave-particle duality of light. First performed by Young in 1801, this experiment splits a light wave into two that later combine via a phase shift to create an interference pattern. Reputedly it is the wave nature of light that causes the interference, producing bright and dark bands on a screen - a result that would not be expected if light consisted of particles. However, the light is always absorbed at discrete points as individual particles (not waves). Furthermore, detectors at the slits find that each detected photon passes through one slit (as would a classical particle), and not through both slits (as would a wave), suggesting wave-particle duality. Electrons also exhibit the same behavior when fired toward a double slit. [1]

When the 'single-slit experiment' is conducted, the pattern is a diffraction pattern in which the light is spread out rather than one corresponding to the size and shape of the slit, expanding as the slit width decreases. When Young first demonstrated this phenomenon, it indicated that light consists of waves vs. Newton's corpuscular theory, later rejuvenated via the photoelectric effect. Today the double-slit experiment is used to support light having both wave and corpuscular properties, the former usually being easier to comprehend from the results than the latter. This paper attempts to offer one possible avenue of exploration to support the latter.

2. Light as Corpuscles

Assume that a photon can be represented by a ball bearing (incompressible), but that its collision with an impenetrable barrier in which there is a slit wide enough for the ball to pass through cleanly will be less than totally elastic. If the ball hits the barrier head-on (impact angle α of 0), it is stopped completely, implying that the 'reaction' vector is exactly equal to the 'impact' vector (assumed, for convenience, to have a magnitude [length] of unity). For less than head-on impacts (up to a 'just miss' at $\alpha = 90^o$), the reaction vector will have length < 1 at angle α, deflecting the ball while still allowing it to pass through the slit at an angle $\theta = 90^o - \alpha$). This is illustrated in Figures 1 and 2. The impact vector will always have length 1 downward vertically. The reaction vector will have length = $\cos\alpha$ with vertical and horizontal components of $(\cos\alpha)^2$ and $\sin\alpha\cos\alpha$. Therefore, the 'deflection' vector will be the vector sum of the impact and reaction vectors, with length = $\sqrt{(1-\cos\alpha^2)^2+(\sin\alpha)^2(\cos\alpha)^2}$ and direction $\theta = 90^o - \alpha$ relative to vertically downward.

Passing through a single slit, a symmetric pattern peaked at the center will result on a screen placed parallel to the barrier. As the balls travel past the screen (some deflected, most not), they will strike the screen at a horizontal location of $\cos\theta$. If we make a leap of faith and assume the intensity at each screen position is proportional to the length of the deflection vector, the pattern shown in Figure 3 results, based on the calculations derived from Figures 1 and 2. This leap of faith represents the assumption that most balls pass through the slit without deflection, leading to peak intensity toward the center, which is represented by the length of the deflection vector at an angle = 90°).

To expedite subsequent calculations using the screen pattern, a regression fit (representing the 'right side' of the curve in Figure 3, i.e., for horizontal position ≥ 0) yielded the following, also shown in Figure 3: [2]

$y = 1.701/(x+1.524), x \geq 0$

where y = length (of deflection vector) and x = horizontal position. The 'left side' of Figure 3 is just a mirror image of the right. The result somewhat resembles the typical pattern exhibited by single slit diffraction (Figure 4), albeit with a sharper peak.

Now consider the double slit counterpart where the ball bearings are shot through two slits a distance of 0.5 unit apart (relative to the horizontal scale on the screen). If there is no interaction among the balls after passing through the slits, the expected screen pattern would just be the summation of two single-slit patterns with center

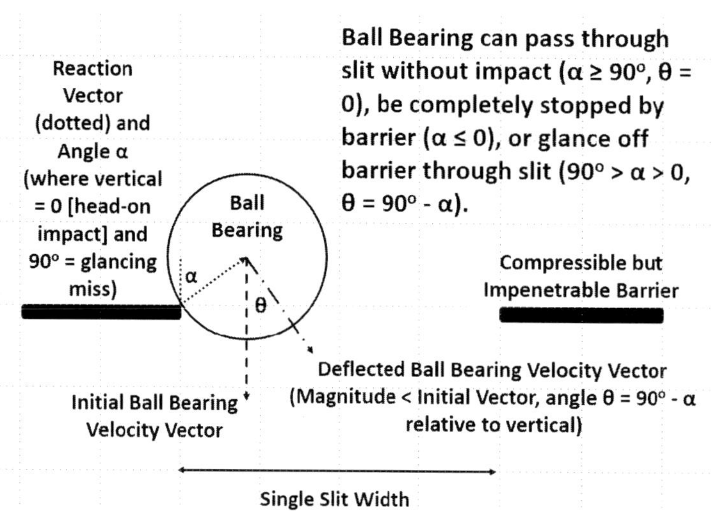

Figure 1. Geometry of Ball Bearing Impact with Slit Barrier

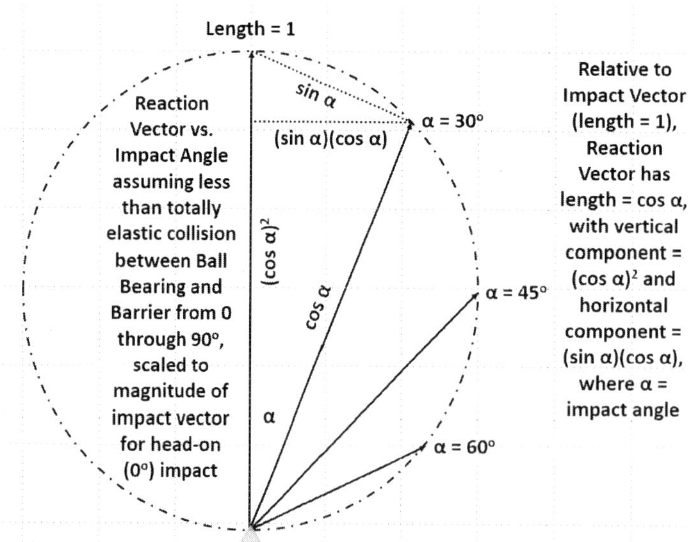

Figure 2. Schematic for Reaction Vector

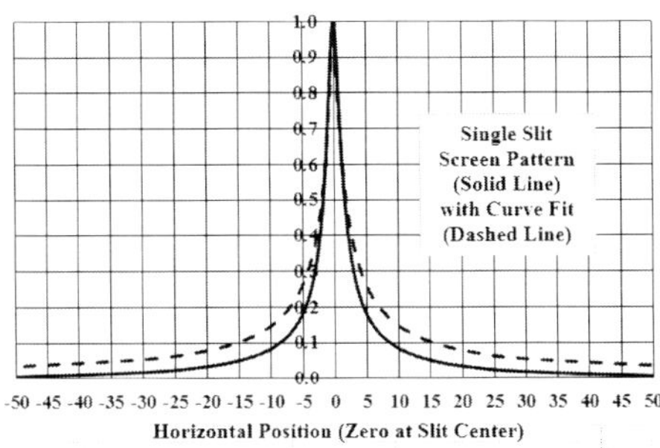

Figure 3. Single Slit Screen Pattern (Scaled)

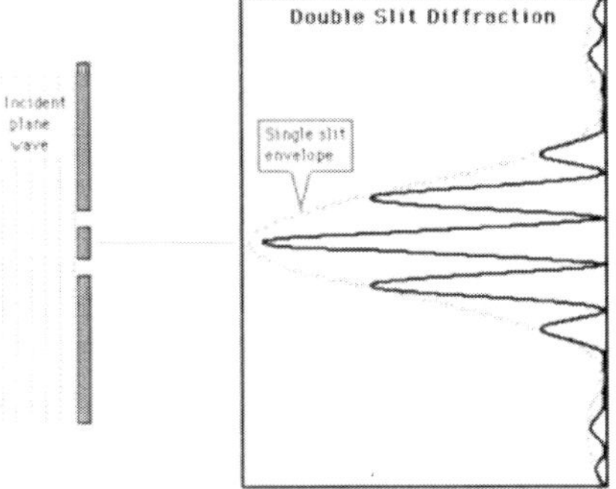

Figure 4. Diffraction Pattern for Single and Double Slit Experiment [3]

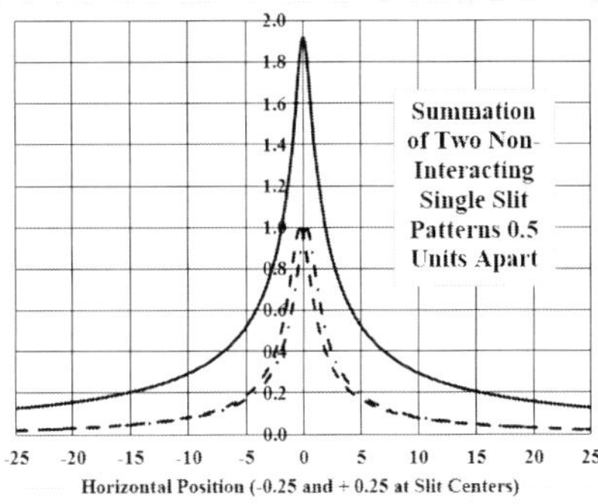

Figure 5. Non-Interacting Double Slit Screen Pattern (Scaled)

peaks 0.5 unit apart, as shown in Figure 5.

What if the ball bearings collide with one another after passing through the slits? This, is not expected to occur for the single slit arrangement, since each ball bearing, representing a photon, retains its initial speed even after impacting the barrier; so any two passing even very close, but still ever so slightly offset, in time will never collide even if their trajectories intersect. With the double slit arrangement, multiple balls can pass, some deflected, such that intersecting trajectories, with just the right time offset, can result in (assumedly) totally elastic collisions between a pair. These would rebound off one another and continue at their pre-collisional speed and reverse deflection angle. Figure 6 illustrates the presumed geometry.

While 'outward' collisions are possible, I assume the propensity for these to be much less than that for 'inward' collisions, so outward collisions are ignored. From Figures 1 and 2, with the results from Table 1, the deflection vectors length and direction, $V(\theta)$ and $W(\phi)$ in Figure 6, are known. Therefore, assuming D = 0.5 (distance between slits), the following transcendental equation can be solved to obtain the horizontal locations where the deflected balls strike the screen after collision:

$$V(\theta)^2 + W(\phi)^2 = (0.5)^2 + 2V(\theta)W(\phi)\cos(\theta+\phi)$$

An interesting property of the family of results is symmetry about impact angles for vector 1 of 15° and 75°, with no solution between 30° and 60°. For the lower range of impact angles, collisions satisfying the transcendental equation occur when the sum of the deflection angles $(\theta+\phi) = 150^o$, with each angle constrained to the range from 60 to 90°. Over this range, the pair of ball bearings strike the screen between horizontal locations -23.4 to -11.6 and 11.6 to 23.4. For the upper range of impact angles, collisions satisfying the transcendental equation occur when the sum of the deflection angles $(\theta+\phi) = 30^o$, with each angle constrained to the range from 0 to 30°. Over this range, the pair of ball bearings strike the screen between horizontal locations -0.20 to -0.08 and 0.08 to 0.20, essentially indistinguishable from the central peak and constrained within the distance between slits of 0.5 (-0.25 to 0.25).

To illustrate the possible effect of these 'preferred collisions' and their potential resultant 'buildup' at the horizontal locations on the screen, we arbitrarily double the length of the deflection vectors shown for the ranges of horizontal locations in Figure 3 for the lower range of impact angles for vector 1 (i.e., -23.4 to -11.6 and 11.6 to 23.4 for impact angles from 0 to 30°) for the summation shown in Figure 5. The result is Figure 7.

While this only crudely approximates just one pair of secondary peaks for the double slit pattern shown in Figure 4, it nonetheless offers a potential avenue of investigation toward the possibility that at least part of the explanation for the unique diffraction pattern for light in the double slit experiment could arise from light's corpuscular nature. One might imagine that with better modeling of the potential for collisions between photon corpuscles after passage

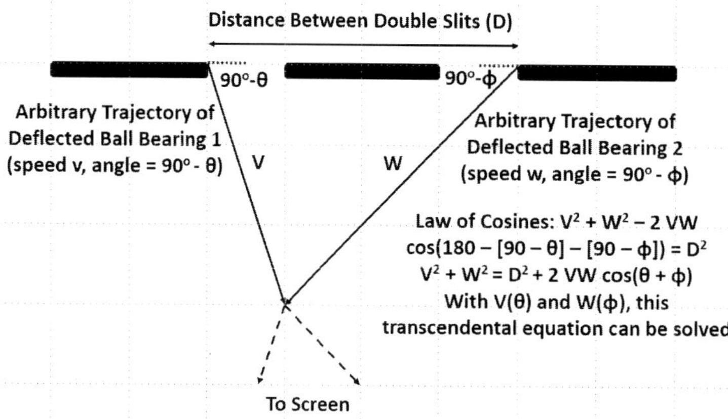

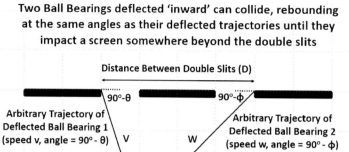

Figure 6. Assumed Geometry for Ball Bearing Collisions after Passing 'Inward' through Double Slits

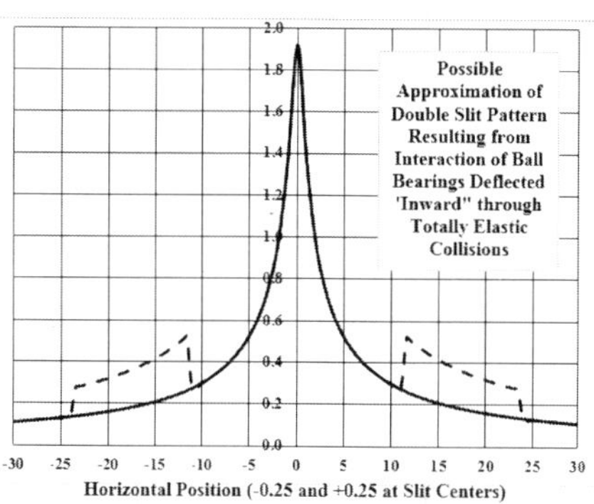

Figure 7. Interacting Double Slit Screen Pattern (Scaled)

through the double slit, peaks other than just the central might result, perhaps approaching the pattern currently attributed exclusively to the wave nature of light.

3. Summary

The double-slit experiment is often cited as indicating the dual wave-particle nature of light, with the emphasis on the wave aspect, which is usually easier to comprehend. Any corpuscular behavior by light is limited to absorption at discrete points as individual particles and detectors at the slits suggesting that a photon passes through one slit (as would a classical particle), and not through both slits (as would a wave). This paper attempts to offer one possible avenue of exploration to support an enhanced role for the corpuscular nature of light than has previously been attributed.

REFERENCES

1. Wikipedia, *Double-Slit Experiment*, https://en.wikipedia.org/wiki/Double-slit_experiment
2. Xuru.org, *Non-Linear Regression*, http://www.xuru.org/rt/NLR.asp#CopyPaste
3. Wikipedia, *Double-Slit Diffraction Pattern*, http://www.bing.com/images/search?q=double+slit+diffraction&qpvt=double+slit+diffraction&qpvt=double+slit+diffraction&FORM=IGRE

The Mandelbrot Set as a Quasi-Black Hole

Lori Gardi

lori.anne.gardi@gmail.com

Black holes, first identified by general relativity, are some of the most mysterious objects in the universe. Scientific consensus is that black holes do in fact exist in nature. Not only that, but they are considered as an important feature of our universe. The equally mysterious concept called fractal geometry, popularized by Benoit Mandelbrot, is also considered a very important feature of nature. Since fractals appear just about everywhere, it seemed reasonable to wonder if the geometry of the Mandelbrot set (M-Set) might also appear somewhere in nature. The main property that distinguishes fractal geometry from other geometries is the property of self-similarity. That said, it is well known that black holes come in many sizes. Stellar-mass black holes are typically in the range of 10 to 100 solar masses, while the super-massive black holes can be millions or billions of solar masses. The extreme scalability of black holes was the first clue that black holes may in fact have the property of self-similarity. This ultimately led to the quasi-black hole analogy presented in this essay. Here, the anatomy of the Schwarzschild black hole is used as a starting point for the analogy. All of the main features of black holes, including the singularity, the event horizon, the photon sphere and the black hole itself, are mapped to features of M-Set. The concepts of time, space-time curvature and black hole entropy are also addressed. The purpose of this research is to see how far this analogy can be taken. Consensus is that both black holes and fractals exist in nature. Could there be a mathematical fractal that describes black holes, and if so, do they also exist in nature? Can this approach make a prediction and if so, is it testable? It turns out that M-Set as a quasi-black hole does lead to some interesting predictions that differ from standard thinking. Given the evidence presented herein, further investigation is suggested.

Keywords: fractal geometry, Mandelbrot set, self-similarity, black hole, singularity, event horizon, photon sphere, iteration, time, entropy, relativity, space-time curvature, chiral symmetry, morphology

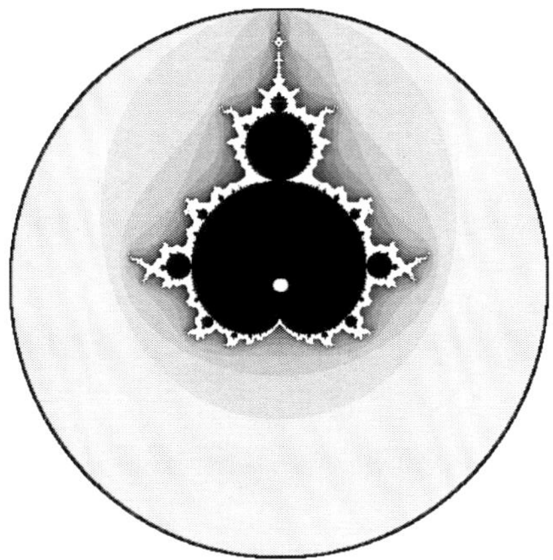

Figure 8. Mandelbrot set traditional rendering.

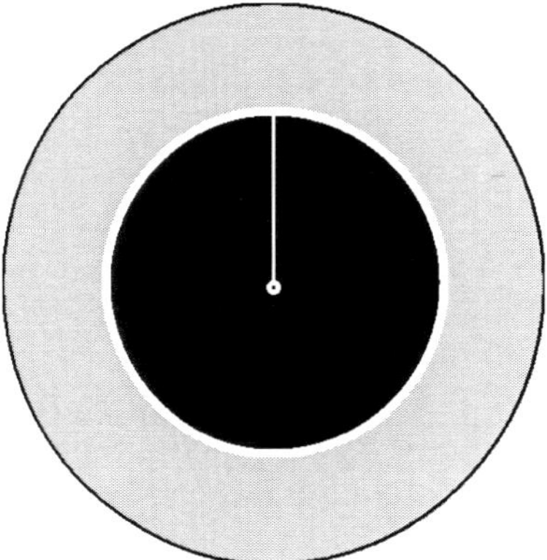

Figure 9. Schwarzschild black hole.

1. Prelude

Due to the controversial nature of this research, a few things need to be clarified. First, the author admits to the circumstantial and highly speculative nature of the "evidence" presented in this essay. This idea was developed independently by the author over many years of investigation. It began as a "thought experiment" and a few simple questions. What if relativity was never invented? What if the concept of fractal geometry predated relativity? Would we still have the concept of the black hole? Would we still be talking about event horizons and space-time curvature? This "thought experiment" is in no way, meant to replace any of the currently accepted theories of black holes. This is a philosophically different approach to cosmology that looks nothing like the the way it was done before.

2. Introduction

"*There is always another way to say the same thing that doesn't look at all like the way you said it before.*" Richard Feynman

The "Mandelbrot set" is one of the most recognizable mathematical fractals. The formula, $z := z^2 + c$, gives no clues as to the vast complexity and unending beauty hidden within this simple iterative system. At first glance, a connection between M-Set and black holes may seem improbable. For example, M-Set, as depicted in Figure 8, doesn't look anything like Figure 9, i.e., the Schwarzschild black hole. What does fractal geometry have to do with black holes? Recent research suggests that a relationship between black holes and fractal geometry does in fact exist. Using a mathematical duality between Einstein's relativity and fluid dynamics, simulations show that fractal patterns can form on the horizons of feeding black holes [1]. This important point shows that relativity and fractal geometry may be intimately linked.

One of the main objections to this body of work is that it does not reference the many successes of relativity. Aside from comparing M-Set to the Schwarzschild black hole, this research doesn't look anything like relativity. This is a completely different approach to cosmology that is founded on different principles. Whether relativity is successful (or not) does not affect this line of thinking. What if relativity was never invented? What if the discovery of fractal geometry (and M-Set) predated relativity? Would we still have intuited the existence of black holes? Can the geometry of M-Set tell us anything new about black holes that we didn't know before? Can it make any predictions and if so, are they testable? This essay is an attempt to address all these questions. If this "thought experiment" can give us insights into the inner workings of nature, then is it not philosophically worthy of further investigation?

This essay starts with the generalized methods used to generate the M-Set related images presented in this essay (Section 3), followed by a brief discussion (Section 4). The anatomy of the Schwarzschild black hole, Figure 9, is then compared to the anatomy of the M-Set as depicted in Figure 8 (Sections 5 - 9). Next, some discussions about dimensionality, black hole entropy and space-time curvature (Sections 10-12) are presented. This is followed by a controversial discourse on "the atom as a quasi-black hole" (Section 13) and a brief discussion about symmetry as it relates to the fractal geometry found within M-Set (Section 14). Finally, in Section 15, a prediction is made and some evidence presented that, if found to be true, would answer the question "do quasi-black holes exist in nature?".

3. Methods

The term M-Set refers to the complex plane as iterated through the following function:

$$z := z^2 + c \tag{1}$$

where, z and c are complex numbers. Because "z" is on both sides of the equation, the ":=" notation is used. Using this notation, equation (1) better reads, "z transforms into z squared plus c". Below is pseudo code for the generalized algorithm for M-Set. This algorithm applies to all the computer generated images presented in this essay:

```
1:  c = (a , bi)
2:  ClearPointList()
3:  z = c
4:  while (!done)
5:     z := z * z + c
6:     AddToPointList(z)
7:     if (StoppingCriteria == true) done = true
8:  AnalyzePointList()
9:  GoTo 1:
```

Explanation: 1) Select a test point c from the set of complex numbers. This corresponds to one pixel in Figure 8. 2) Clear the list. This list will be used to store the sequence of points generated by the iteration process for test point, c. 3) Initialize z to the test point c. 4) Begin the iteration loop. 5) Iterate the function (1). This generates a new complex point, z. 6) Add the new z to the list of complex points. 7) If the iteration process reaches some stopping criteria, then end the iteration loop. 8) Analyze the data from the list. Update the image accordingly. 9) If there are more test points, repeat steps 1 through 9.

It is found that each test point, c, from the complex plane generates a different trajectory and each trajectory has a different behaviour and/or structure. Put simply, no two points from the complex plane make the same picture. Note that in this model, we are only concerned with the complex points inside the 2.0 radius circle of the complex plane (outer circle in Figure 1). All points outside this boundary are outside of the scope of the M-Set model.

The trajectories are divided into three regions or domains. The first is referred to as the domain of convergence. This corresponds to the central black region of Figure 8. The second domain is referred to as the domain of divergence and corresponds to the outer grey-scale region of Figure 8. The third region is the domain of uncertainty. These are the points whose trajectories do not diverge nor converge, even after the maximum number of iterations. The uncertain region is depicted in Figure 8 as the bright halo surrounding the black region.

Below is a description of the three tests used to stop the iteration loop.

Divergence test: If the trajectory extends outside the 2.0 radius circle of the complex plane, then the iteration loop is stopped and the initial point is assigned to the diverging domain (grey-scale region of Figure 8).

Convergence test: If the trajectory contracts beyond the digits of precision of the computer, then the iteration loop is stopped and the initial point is assigned to the converging domain (black region of Figure 8).

Undecided test: If the maximum number of iterations is reached before convergence or divergence, then the iteration loop is stopped and the initial point is assigned to the domain of uncertainty (bright halo surrounding black region of Figure 8). Note that, given more iterations and more digits of precision, most of these points will eventually be resolved. However, since computers have limits, there will always be some uncertain points on this list.

4. Methods Discussion

The points from the diverging domain of M-Set are well studied since these points have a very clear stopping criteria. These are the points whose trajectories escape the 2.0 radius circle after a finite number of iterations. The non-escaping points (the black region) are a bit more illusive. It is commonly thought that the trajectories from the *black* region of M-Set fall into periodic orbits or cycles. This, however, is only partly true. It was found through experimentation that a majority of these cycles were merely an artifact of the limit to the digits of precision of the computer. When more digits of precision are added to the computer program, then the collapse can continue past the previous limit. In theory, given an infinite number of digits of precision (and an infinite number of iterations), the collapse could continue indefinitely.

In short, aside from some special complex points such as (0,0) and (-1,0), there are no stable periodic orbits in M-Set. This realization is the key to the quasi-black hole analogy presented in this essay.

5. Anatomy of the Schwarzschild Black hole

The simplest black hole described by general relativity is the Schwarzschild black hole (SBH). The anatomy of an SBH is depicted in Figure 9. It is characterized by a region of space referred to as a black hole (black region in Figure 9). At the center of the black hole is an infinitely dense, infinitely small volume of space-time called a singularity (white dot at the center of the black region in Figure 9).

The lesser known region just outside the black hole is referred to as the photon sphere (outer grey region in Figure 9). The photon sphere is a region of space just outside the black hole where photons are forced to travel in complex orbits due to the extreme curvature of space within this region [2]. According to relativity, there are no stable orbits within the photon sphere of an SBH.

Finally, the boundary that exactly separates the black hole from the photon sphere is referred to as the event horizon (white circle surrounding the black region in Figure 9). The distance from the central singularity to the event horizon is known as the Schwarzschild radius. According to relativity, nothing, including light, can escape the event horizon of a black hole. Put simply, "things" can fall into a relativistic black hole, but "things" can never come out.

6. M-Set as a Quasi-Black Hole

Figure 8 depicts three regions of M-Set that are analogous to the three regions of the SBH as described in the previous section. The black region of M-Set is analogous to the black hole of the SBH. These are the points whose trajectories collapse past the digits of precision of the computer after a finite number of iterations. The outer grey-scale region of Figure 8 is analogous to the photon sphere of the SBH. These are the points whose trajectories travel in (complex) orbits until they escape the 2.0 radius circle of the complex plane after a finite number of iterations. Finally, the region exactly separating the black region from the grey-scale region in Figure 8 is analogous to the event horizon of the SBH (the white fuzzy boundary just outside the black region). The white dot within the black region of Figure 8 is the (0,0) point of the complex plane. This is analogous to the zero point or singularity of the SBH model. Each of these concepts will be discussed in greater detain in the next sections.

7. Quasi-Singularities

The trajectories generated by the points inside the black hole region of M-Set (Figure 8) are referred to as quasi-singularities. These are the points whose trajectories collapse or converge toward infinitely small regions within the complex plane. Like the singularities of relativity, quasi-singularities never escape the boundary condition of the quasi-black hole. Unlike the singularities of relativity, quasi-singularities can collapse/converge toward more than one region in the complex plane. For example, the middle image in Figure 22 is a quasi-singularity that is converging toward 9 regions within the complex plane.

It was found, through experimentation, that the points closer to the event horizon of M-Set take more iterations to collapse past the digits of precision of the computer than the points closer to the origin (0,0). It was also found that the points nearest the event horizon generate quasi-singularities with extremely complex behaviours as depicted in Figure 22. As stated earlier, each point from the complex plane generates a different trajectory and each trajectory generates a different picture. The quasi-singularities depicted in Figure 22 are only a small sampling of the infinite number of unique and interesting "singularities" generated by M-Set.

8. Quasi-Photon Sphere

The grey-scale region just outside of the quasi-black hole of Figure 8 is referred to as a quasi-photon sphere. These are the points whose trajectories can and do reach the escape condition of M-Set after a finite number of iterations. These trajectories appear to travel in ever expanding "orbits" up until the point where they reach the escape condition, i.e., the 2.0 radius circle of the complex plane. The behaviours of these trajectories are quite interesting. Like the quasi-singularities from the previous section, it was found that the points close to the edge of the event horizon take the more iterations to reach the escape condition. The dynamics of these trajectories also appear to be more chaotic and exhibit complex morphologies when plotted directly. A hand full of these trajectories are depicted in Figure 4. The bottom row shows the computer generated trajectories and above each of these is a morphologically similar (self-similar) cosmological object. Figure 12 is an example of a complex trajectory that looks a lot like a galaxy cluster. On the left is the computer generated trajectory and on the right is the Virgo Cluster. Keep in mind that the figure on the left was generated using only one seed point from the complex plane, as with the all the other trajectories.

Also, it should be noted that all the cosmological objects depicted in Figures 4 and 5, which include planetary nebula, galaxies and galaxy clusters, are all thought to be associated with black holes. The most surprising quasi-photon trajectory in Figure 17 is the one that looks similar to Einstein's cross. In standard cosmology, the appearance Einstein's cross is thought to be caused by gravitational lensing, but what if gravitational lensing is not the only way to explain this object? If the discovery fractal geometry and M-Set predated relativity (and indirectly the concept of gravitational lensing) then M-Set as a quasi-black hole would have been able to predict the appearance of objects such as Einstein's cross along with the other objects depicted in Figures 4 and 5.

9. Quasi-Event Horizon

The event horizon from the standard model is described as a theoretical boundary surrounding a black hole beyond which nothing, including light, can escape. The photon sphere is rarely mentioned in the black hole discourse. Technically, the event horizon exactly separates the black hole from the photon sphere as depicted in Figure 9. The photon sphere will be described in more detail in the next section.

In a similar manner, the boundary that exactly separates the quasi-black hole of M-Set from the quasi-photon sphere is referred to as a quasi-event horizon. This is an event horizon in the truest sense as it exactly separates the escaping "events" from the non-escaping "events". But what is an event?

In a previous paper by the author [3], iteration is considered the mathematical analogy for time. Iteration generates change and change gives us the sensation of time. Here, one iteration generates one unit of change and one unit of change is one event. Thus, the complex plane as iterated through the function $z := z^2 + c$ can be considered as an event generator. When the sequence of events is plotted, it produces images like the ones in Figures 3, 4 and 5.

The M-Set event horizon (the fuzzy boundary in Figure 8), separates the collapsing events from the expanding events (the converging domain from the diverging domain). It was found, through experimentation that trajectories, whose seed points are close to the quasi-event horizon, require more iterations to reach the stopping criteria than the seed points farther away. This is true on both sides of the horizon. In other words, quasi-black holes exhibit asymptotic behaviour on both sides of the event horizon. This is a huge departure from standard black hole theory.

The implication here is that it is just as hard to get into a "black hole" as it is to get out of one. If this were true, then there should be some evidence of this in nature. Recent Chandra images of the black hole at the center of our galaxy, Sagittarius A*, indicate that only a fraction of a percent of the gas (if any) actually fall into the black hole. It appears that most of the material that approaches the black hole gets ejected before it reaches the event horizon [4] or "point of no return". Asymptotic behaviour on both sides of the event horizon may help explain this observation. This behaviour is further discussed in Section 13.

10. On Time and Dimensionality

The most common concern about M-Set as a quasi-black hole has to do with dimensionality. Before we can continue, the concept of dimensionality needs to be addressed. Since M-Set (as depicted in Figure 8) is a 2-dimensional static structure, how can it possibly tell us anything important about the 3-dimensional dynamic universe we observe? This is a good and important question.

In the standard model of cosmology, space and time are combined together into a 4-dimensional "space-time" manifold where time is treated as another spatial dimension. In order to understand M-Set as a quasi-black hole, we need to decouple the concept of time from the spatial manifold. In the cosmology outlined in this essay, time is an emergent property of change brought about by an iterative feedback process. In this manner, time is analogous to iteration, and vice verse. The other important point to make here is that the change associated with iterative time cannot be undone. As one cannot un-break a glass or unborn a baby, one cannot undo iteration. This is yet another way of looking at entropy. Quite simply, entropy means that change cannot be undone. "It is the unending, unknowable uniqueness of each moment that gives us the sensation of time and the arrow of time"[3]. Without unending, unknowable, irreversible change, there would we no sensation of time and no arrow of time. That said, the only math that can mimic this kind of unending, unknowable, unrepeatable, entropic change over time is iteration, especially as it relates to chaos theory and fractal geometry. This, of course, includes M-Set.

With time out of the way, we need to rectify the spatial dimension problem. M-Set clearly resides in a 2D complex plane. How can a 3D dynamical system be explained by a 2-dimensional (mathematical) structure? It is well known that 2D complex numbers (r,i) can be extended to 4D complex numbers using quaternions (r,i,j,k) [5]. Unfortunately, 4D complex structures are difficult to depict in a 2-dimensional format such as an article or paper. That said,

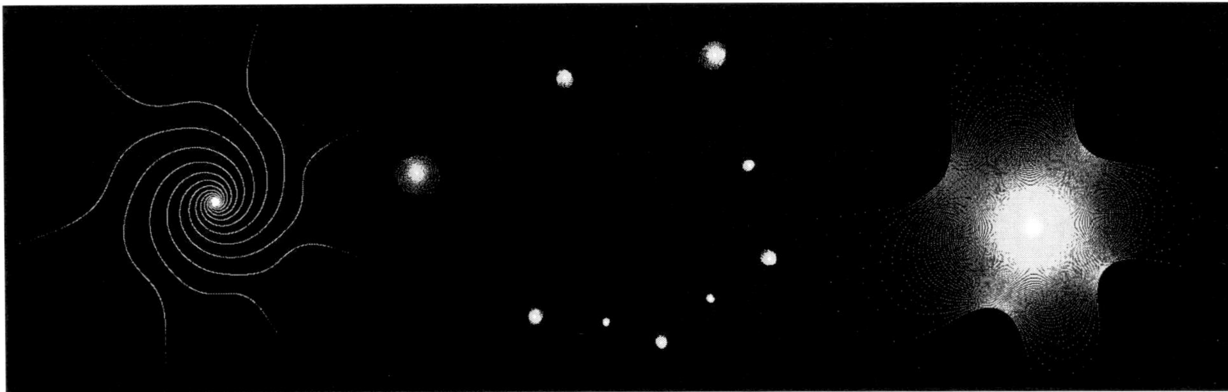

Figure 10. This figure depicts three distinct singularities from the quasi-black hole of M-Set. Each singularity, including the cluster, was generated from a single seed point (real, imaginary) from the complex plane. Left: (0.11421610355396709, 0.5957090739182781O); Middle: (0.33751130482196073, 0.41014244936187033); Right: (0.25161670227079957, 0.49833246356572231).

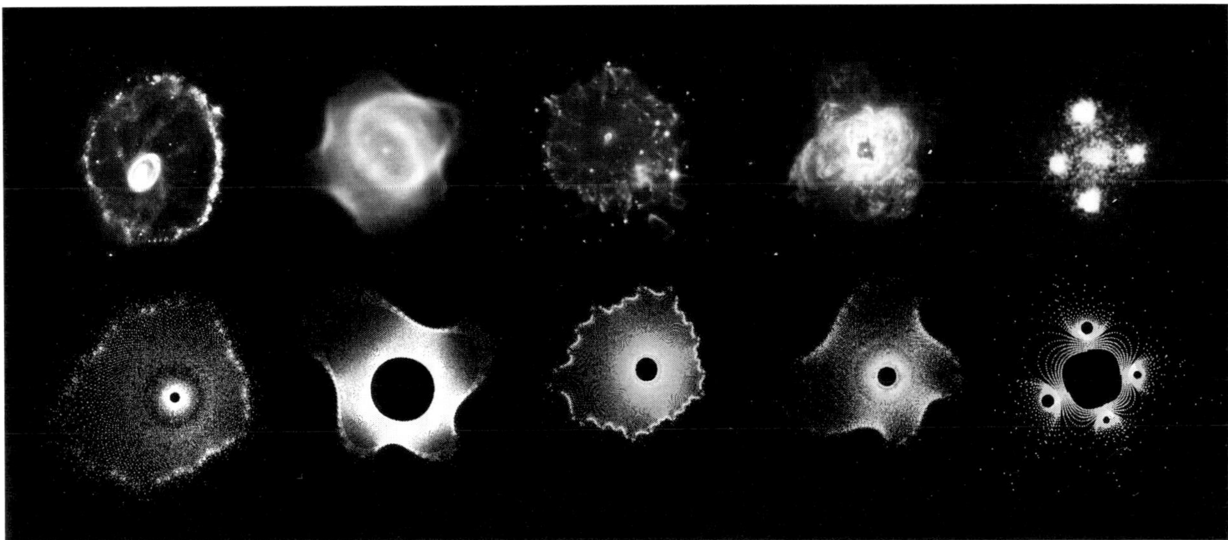

Figure 11. This figure depicts a handful of the trajectories from the quasi-photon sphere of M-Set together with some familiar cosmological objects (credit NASA). The top row from left to right: Cartwheel Galaxy, Stingray Nebula, CatâĂŹs Eye Nebula, NGC 5315, EinsteinâĂŹs cross. Below each of these is a computer generated (M-Set) trajectory with a similar morphology. Each trajectory depicted in this figure was generated using a single seed point from the complex plane as reported in Appendix A.

it is found that projecting a 4D M-Set onto a 2D plane gives us back M-Set. In other words, the "physics" of the 4D M-Set set is no different from the "physics" of the 2D M-Set. Thus, the 2D complex plane is used throughout this essay with the assumption that it can be extended to the higher spatial dimensions using quaternions, not unlike what is done in standard physics.

Logically, if space is 3-dimensional, as we perceive it to be, then the manifold housing 3D-space must be 4-dimensional. As it takes the 2-dimensional complex numbers to represent 1-dimensional angles and curves, it takes 4-dimensional complex numbers (quaternions) to represent 3-dimensional angles and curves. The complex curve depicted in Figure 1 (i.e. the quasi-event horizon) is technically a 1D fractal curve housed within a 2D complex space. Analogously, the curvature of space (previously curved space-time) could be modelled as a 3D fractal curve housed within a 4D complex space. This new concept of "curved" space is discussed further in Section 12.

11. On Black Hole Entropy and Evolution

The purpose of this research is to see how far we can take the black hole analogy. What can M-Set tell us about black hole entropy? Bekenstein was the first to make a connection between the area of a black hole horizon and entropy[6]. He concluded that the area of the event horizon of a black hole must continuously increase over time as expressed by the following equation:

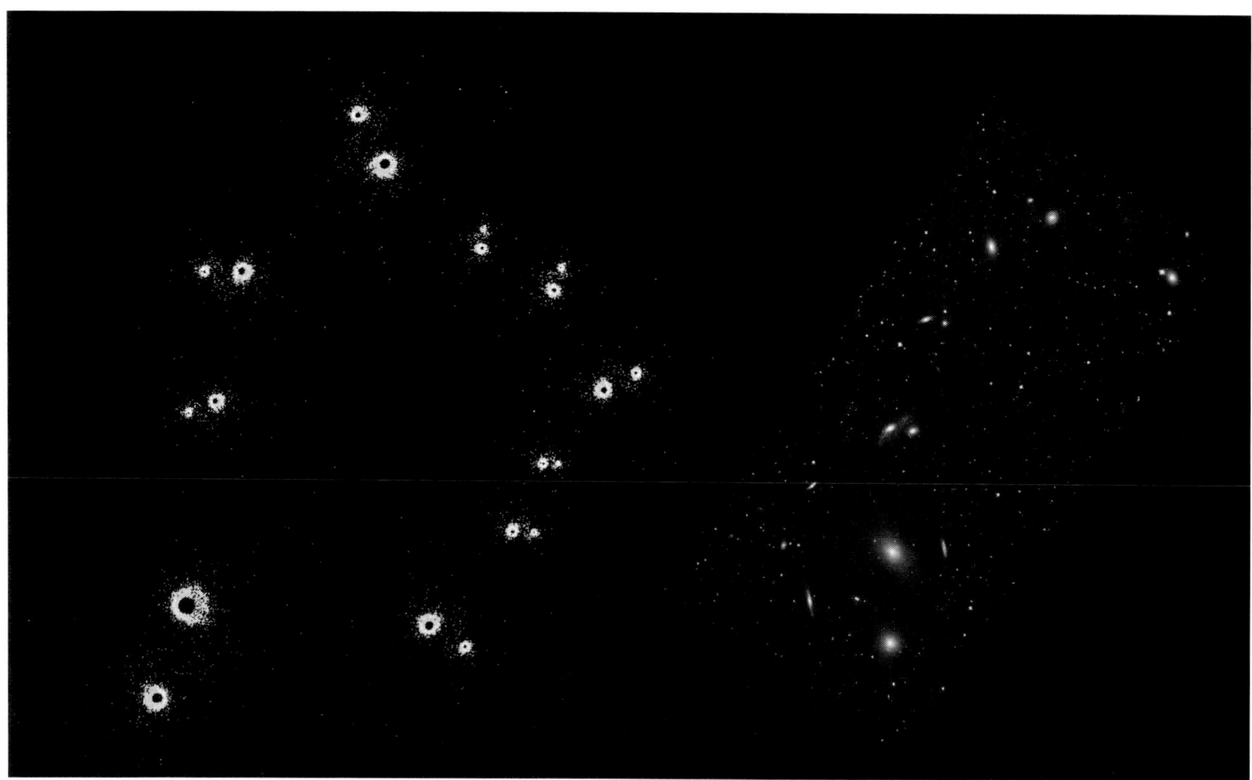

Figure 12. This figure depicts an M-Set cluster from the photon sphere of M-Set on the left and the Virgo Cluster on the right. Credit NASA. This cluster was generated using a single seed point from the complex plane: (real, imaginary) = (0.05103771361715907 , 0.64098319549560490)

$$S = \frac{A}{4} \quad (2)$$

Using Euclidean geometry, the only way that the surface area of a spherical object (such as the Schwarzschild black hole) can continuously increase over time is by increasing the radius of the object. Thus, to satisfy black hole entropy, black holes must get bigger over time. Black holes cannot shrink. Hawking later proposed that black holes might evaporate, but let's assume that the area of the horizon of a black hole must continuously increase over time as originally proposed. How does fractal geometry rectify this problem?

In 1967, B. Mandelbrot wrote a paper called "How long is the coastline of Britain?'[7] where he proposed that the measurement of a rough geometric shape such as a coastline would change depending on the size of the measuring stick used for the measurement. In short, the smaller the measuring stick, the longer the coastline. This turns out to be true of all fractal structures. Einstein also had something to say about measuring sticks by arguing that measuring sticks "shrink" as one get closer to the event horizon of a black hole. This is commonly referred to as length contraction.

What does this mean for the quasi-black hole? The event horizon of M-Set (the bright halo in Figure 8) is a rough geometric shape with the property of self-similarity, i.e., it is a fractal. Fractal geometry gives us another mechanism for continuous increase in the event horizon area over time. If the "measuring sticks" of the universe are allowed to "shrink" over time, then the surface area of quasi-event horizons (if they exist) would also increase over time. In this manner, black hole entropy would be valid for all black holes with fractal event horizons (i.e., quasi-black holes).

This of course is a huge departure from standard thinking about how the universe evolves. If the measuring sticks (i.e., pixels) are shrinking over time, then the "pixels" of the early universe must have been much "bigger". One way this could manifest is if the atoms from the past were "scaled bigger" than the atoms of today. This leads to the idea of "scale relativity" where the earlier universe, although scaled differently, could still experience the same laws of physics. Atoms of the earlier universe would emit light of a much longer wavelength, thus, this line of thinking gives us an alternate mechanism for observed cosmological red-shift. In this case, accelerated expansion is an optical illusion in that universal expansion only appears to be accelerating because the universal measuring stick is shrinking. This idea is difficult to visualize using the current paradigm but easy to visualize within the fractal paradigm. A recent paper by independent researcher Blair MacDonald (*Fractal Geometry a Possible Explanation to the Accelerating Expansion of the Universe and Other Standard ΛCDM Model Anomalies*) offers great support to this alternate line of thinking [8]. An ever shrinking measuring stick would allow ever increasing frequencies (of light) to appear over time. Ever increasing frequencies would guarantee the irreversibility of time (i.e., the arrow of time). This line of thinking may also explain why evolution always increases in complexity over time since, like the computer generated fractal, an increase in resolution would allow more details and thus, more complexity to be represented.

12. On Space-Time Curvature

According to Einstein's general relativity, the phenomenon of gravity is caused by the curvature of space-time. But what if relativity was never invented? What if fractal geometry proceeded general relativity? Would we still have the concept of space-time curvature? Let's begin by remembering that we previously decoupled the concept of time from the concept of space. In a fractal universe, time is merely an emergent property of change brought about by an iterative feedback process. Time is not a spatial dimension in that it does not include any coordinates or locations that we can physically return to. With time out of the picture, we need only be concerned with the curvature of space. What does it mean to *curve space*?

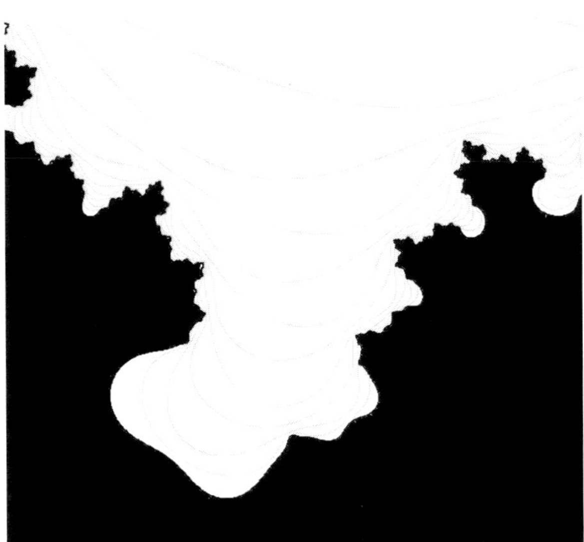

Figure 13. This figure is a zoomed in regions of the M-Set quasi-event horizon. An edge filter was applied to this image to highlight the topological gradient. Notice that the regions of complex curvature are also the regions with the steepest gradients.

If we simplify all forces, including gravity, to the concept of the gradient, then it is easy to visualize the curvature of a manifold of space. Think of a topographic map. When the lines are closer together, it means the slope of the gradient (and indirectly, the force) is greater. Technically, M-Set can be thought of as a gradient generator. Figure 13 depicts a zoomed in region of M-Set. An edge filter was used to make it look more like a topographic map.

Notice how the lines of the gradient get closer together as you look closer to the black region (the M-Set quasi-black hole). When one zooms into the M-Set fractal, what is happening is the slope of the gradient is ever increasing. In order to accommodate this, the computer must continuously decrease the measuring stick of the fractal generator. As the measuring stick (pixel dimension) decreases, the slope of the gradient increases.

Figure 14 depicts a sub-region of the complex plane along side a sub-region of space known as the Grand Spiral Galaxy, NGC 1232. Notice the morphological similarity between the way that M-Set "curves space" and the way nature "curves space". Hence, fractal geometry, in particular M-Set, gives us an analogy for the curvature of space that is similar to (self-similar to) the curvature of "space-time" that we observe in nature.

13. The Atom as a Quasi-Black Hole

A black hole with asymptotic behaviour on both sides of the event horizon leads to an interesting line of thinking. Since quasi-black holes have the property of self-similarity, and they exhibit asymptotic behaviour on both sides of the event horizon, then there is nothing preventing the atom from being a quasi-black hole. Self-similarity implies scale invariance and so why should the scale of the atom be an exception? In the atom as a quasi-black hole, the nucleus plays the role of the "black hole" and the electrons shells play the role of the "photon sphere". As quarks cannot and do not escape the nucleus of the atom, electrons cannot and do not fall into the nucleus of the atom. In other words, the atom exhibits asymptotic behaviour on both sides of the event horizon. But what is the event horizon of the atom? Here, the weak force plays the role of the event horizon.

Event horizons of the standard model are generally associated with strong gravity. As strong gravity can bring things together, it can also tear things apart. In a similar manner, the weak force is responsible for bringing things together (fusion) and tearing things apart (fission). In other words, the (poorly named) weak force at the atomic scale is self-similar to (the poorly named) strong gravity at the cosmic scale. The domain (range) of the weak force is quite small (10^{-18} meters) compared to the size of the atom (10^{-10} meters). The domain of the M-Set event horizon is also quite small compared to the escaping and non-escaping domains. Again, if quasi-black holes exist in nature, then there is nothing preventing the atom from being a "black hole". If these are the black holes that nature makes, then black hole theory will need to be revised to incorporate the property of self-similarity and account for the asymptotic behaviour on both sides of the event horizon.

14. On Chiral Symmetry

Another interesting feature of M-Set has to do with the various kinds of symmetries found within the standard M-

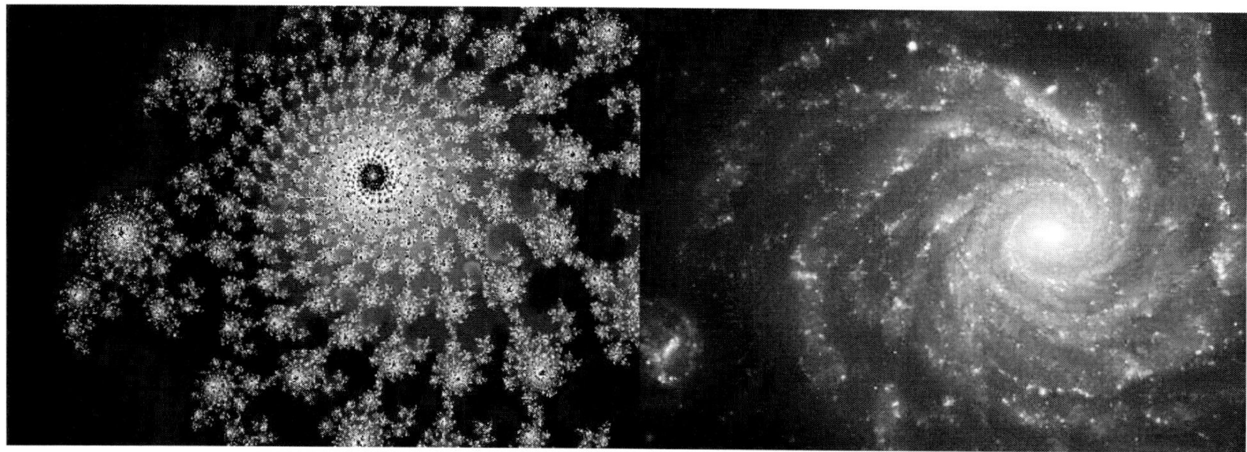

Figure 14. On the left is a region of M-Set depicting a fractal gradient analogous to "space-time curvature" of relativity. On the right is a region space showing the "space-time curvature" surrounding the Grand Spiral Galaxy, NGC 1232, (Credit: FORS1, 8.2-meter VLT Antu, ESO). In both images, the bright regions correspond to regions of high curvature and the dark region correspond to regions of low curvature. The morphological similarities between these images is of particular interest. (Real Center: 0.238291710520393 Imaginary Center: 0.38038103197243328 Real Extent: 0.00020176911157024794 Imaginary Extent: 0.00015132683367768596)

Set rendering. First, you will notice the obvious left-right symmetry of the quasi-black hole in Figure 8. This can be considered an axial symmetry since a rotation or flip about the vertical axis leaves the image unchanged. Another kind of symmetry can be found when you look closely at some of the smaller scale quasi-black holes buried deep within the event horizon of M-Set as seen in Figure 15. Notice that the black hole still has the left-right symmetry but the region far away from the black hole exhibits a different kind of symmetry known as chiral symmetry. In general, a chiral object is an object that is not superimposable on its mirror image. Chiral symmetry is commonly seen in the spiral arms of galaxies. In general, it is found that late-type spiral galaxies have a stronger chiral signal than the early-types as depicted in the Hubble tuning fork diagram or sequence[9].

Chrial symmetry breaking is an important phenomenon in theoretical physics; from quantum chromodynamics and the study of mesons [10] [11] to the study of nanoparticles in semiconductors [12]. According to standard cosmology, quantum fluctuations of the early universe were greatly expanded during the inflationary epoch. Thus, macroscopic chirality is thought to be caused by some primordial process shortly after the big bang. In the fractal cosmology (presented herein) any similarities between the quantum scale and the cosmic scale are thought to be due to the property of self-similarity.

What does this have to do with black holes? Spiral galaxies (with supermassive black holes at their centers) exhibit a strong chiral signal in their spiral arm structures. Lenticular galaxies also show the signature of spiral arms with a weak chiral symmetry, as recently detected by the *IRAC* instrument on the *Spitzer Space Telescope* [13]. It is also found that galaxies in galaxy clusters exhibit a strong chiral symmetry far away from the central black hole and weak chiral symmetry closer to the central black hole [14][15]. The M-Set model also exhibits strong chiral symmetry far away from the central black hole and a weak chiral symmetry close to the central black hole. As a side note, it turns out, chirality is also related to quaternions; the 4-dimensional extension of the 2-dimensional complex plane as discussed in Section 10 [16]. In short, a transition from chiral symmetry to axial symmetry is a signature of a quasi-black hole.

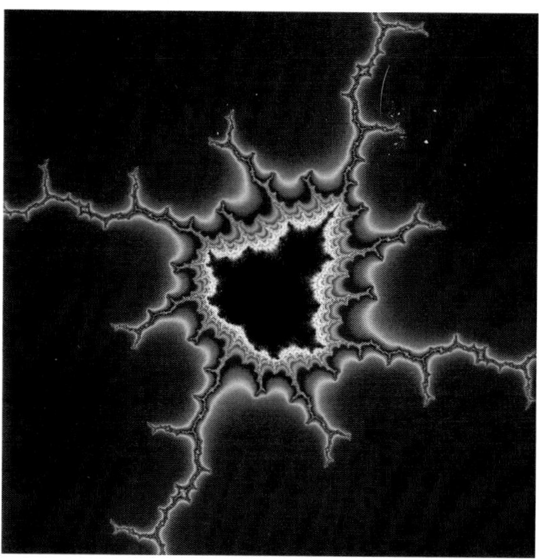

Figure 15. This figure depicts a quasi-black hole found deep within the quasi-event horizon of M-Set. Here we see that the region close to the black hole exhibits a left-right symmetry while the region far away from the black hole exhibits chiral symmetry. This is one of the signatures of a quasi-black hole.

15. Do Quasi-Black Holes Exist in Nature?

It is generally accepted that black holes exist in nature.

But what kind of black holes does nature actually make? There are currently two contenders: 1) The standard black holes that Relativity describes, and 2) the quasi-black holes as described in this essay. Do quasi-black holes exist in nature? In order to test this, we need to be able to make a prediction. What is the signature of a quasi-black hole? In the previous section, we saw that the transition from chiral symmetry to axial symmetry is a signature of a quasi-black hole.

General relativity also makes very specific predictions about the morphology of the region surrounding a black hole. The movie, Interstellar, used computer simulations to accurately depict the behaviour of a relativistic black hole. These simulations predict a bright ring of light surrounding a shadow cast by the black hole. It has been a long standing goal of astrophysics to directly observe the environment surrounding the event horizon of a black hole. The Event Horizon Telescope, a large telescope array consisting of a global network of radio telescopes, is uniquely suited to observe the black hole at the center the Milky Way (catalogued as Sagittarius A*). The data from the Event Horizon Telescope was collected in April 2017 and, as of the writing of this paper, the data has not yet been analyzed. It could be the end of 2017 or the beginning of 2018 before the results are released to the public.

The prediction made by M-Set as quasi-black hole is quite different. In this case, the prediction is based on the shape of the halo of the photon sphere. Here, the author speculates that the shape of the photon sphere surrounding the black hole will appear either oblate or slightly pear shaped depending on how far we can see into the photon sphere of the black hole, if at all. If we can see deep into the photon sphere, we should begin to see the shape of the quasi-black hole as depicted in Figure 8. If a pear-like shape is found, then a prediction can be made as to the exact location of the singularity in that region. In the case of the primordial quasi-black hole, singularity is at (0,0) of the complex plane (white dot in Figure 8).

Luckily, we don't have to wait until the results come in from the Event Horizon Telescope to test this prediction. Messier 87 is a super-giant elliptical galaxy in the constellation Virgo. It was recently discovered that the supermassive black hole at the center of M87 does not currently reside at the measured center the galaxy but instead, is 22 light years away [17]. Figure 16 is an image showing the region in question.

Notice that the shape of the bright region housing the black hole is slightly pear-shaped. Figure 17 shows a close up of the pear-shaped region (left) along side a rendering of M-Set after only two iterations (right). The image on the left of Figure 17 shows the pear-shaped region of M87 aligned to and alpha blended with the M-Set image on the right. When this was done, it was noticed that the location of black hole (singularity) of M87 overlays exactly with the (0,0) point of M-Set. In other words, the black SMBH of M87 is exactly where it is predicted to be by the M-Set model.

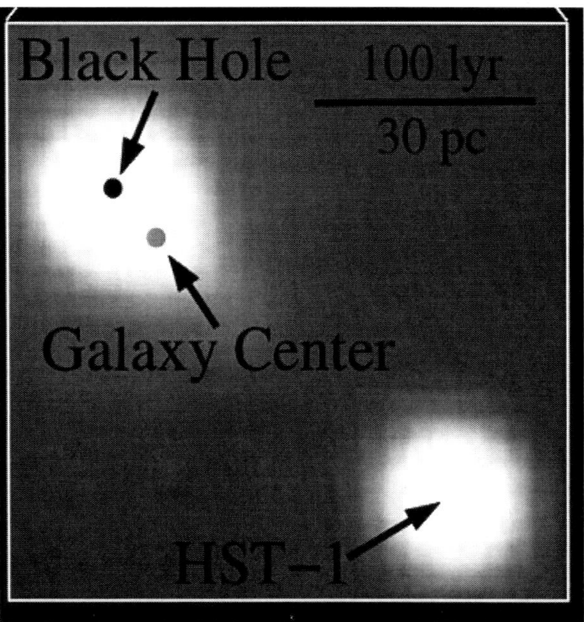

Figure 16. Astronomers found that the location of the black hole at the center of M87 is offset from the center of the galaxy by 22 light years. The light dot indicates the center of the galaxy's light distribution and the dark dot is the location of the black hole. Image credit Nasa.

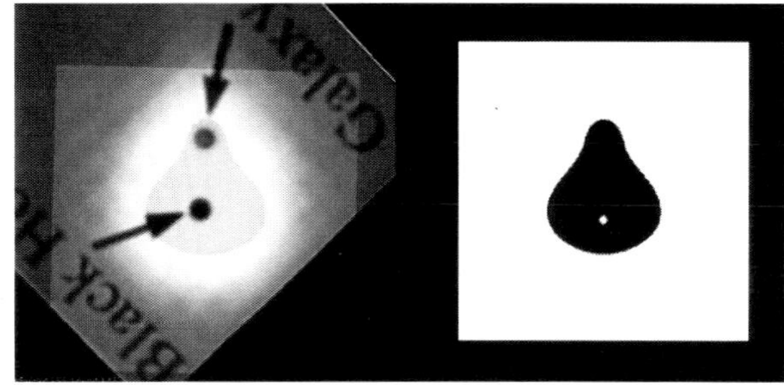

Figure 17. The image on the left shows the region surrounding the M87 black hole registered to and blended with the M-Set quasi-black hole on the right. The white dot in the M-Set model (0,0 of the complex plane) aligns precisely with the SMBH of M-87.

Quasar 3C-186 in an example of a quasar that is also offset from the center of gravity [18] as seen in Figure 18. Notice that the bright region in the vicinity of the quasar is slightly pear-shaped (as outlined in white) and the bright quasar itself is exactly where it is suppose to be according to the M-Set model.

The author agrees that this is highly speculative, however, if quasi-black holes do exist in nature, then all quasi-black holes, at all scales, should exhibit this signature. Interestingly, recent studies have shown that the nuclei of some atoms, such as Radium-224 and Barium-144, are found to be asymmetrical and pear-shaped [19]. This supports the idea that the atom is a quasi-black

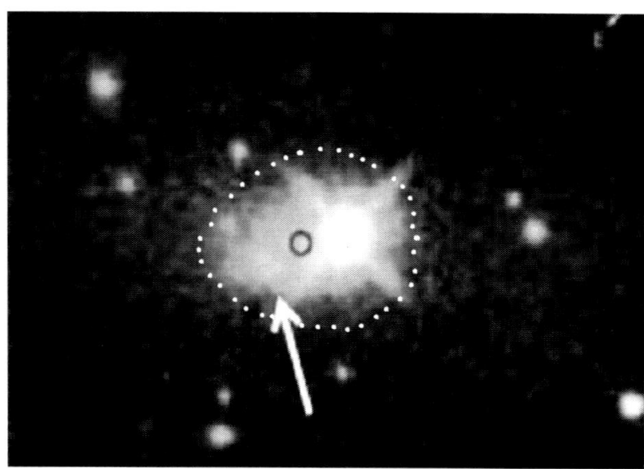

Figure 18. The bright source in this image, Quasar 3C 186, is shown displaced from the center of its host galaxy, indicated with a grey circle.The white arrow points to a blob like feature of unknown origin). Image: Hubble

hole, as suggested in Section 13. Before discounting the existence of quasi-black holes in nature, let's wait and see what the evidence shows us.

16. Conclusions and Future Work

It is well known that fractal geometry mimics nature very accurately. Benoit Mandelbrot wrote a book on this called "The Fractal Geometry of Nature"[20]. The evidence presented in this essay shows how Mandelbrot's signature fractal is able to mimic the morphological features of a multitude of cosmological objects which, coincidentally, also happen to be associated with black holes. Of course, this kind of mathematical model cannot tell you the exact trajectory of an actual gravitational body orbiting the black hole at the center of our galaxy. That said, dynamics like this are strangely encoded in the M-Set model as seen in Appendix A (Figure 19). It also may not be possible to predict exactly how a set of particles will interact with each other in a particle accelerator, however, dynamics like this are also strangely encoded into M-Set as seen in Appendix A, Figure 20. Future work will be to determine the correspondence (if any) between images such as these and physical reality.

Fractal geometry is illusive. Using extremely simple rules and a simple formula with no arbitrary constants, one is able to generate an endless set of "figures" that strikingly resemble familiar cosmological objects as depicted in Figures 3, 4, 5 and 7. At the very least, we have to admit that the universe is very "Mandelbrot-like". If fractal geometry did preceded relativity, the author suggests that we would have been able to intuit the existence of black holes using fractal geometry alone. Then the question becomes, "Could the laws of physics be emergent properties of fractal geometry?"

17. Appendix A

Parameters from Figure 4

Below are the seed points for the trajectories found in Figure 4. From left to right (a,b,c,d,e):

4a: (0.07023590960694610, 0.61486872535543668)
4b: (0.25520149659878483, 0.49473324077959746)
4c: (0.13811184749188554, 0.58354392530509225)
4d: (0.26464143869779005, 0.48473638288631671)
4e: (0.24725611046013074, 0.50292165702256331)

Orbital Dynamics

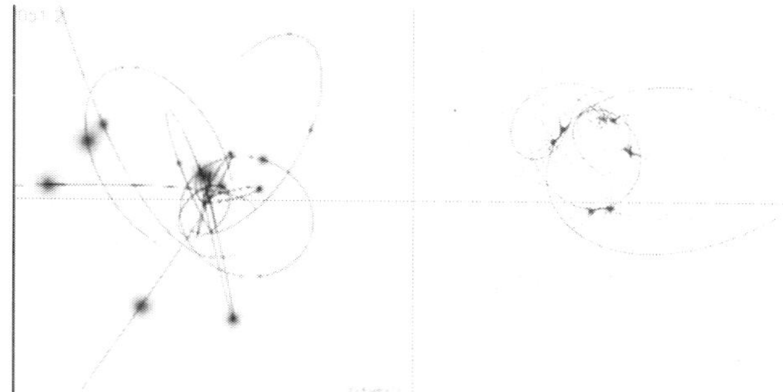

Figure 19. The image on the left represents 16 years of data consisting of the most detailed observations yet of the stars orbiting the centre of our galaxy [21]. On the right is an M-Set experiment that depicts similar dynamics. These are preliminary results that need to be investigated further.

Particle Dynamics

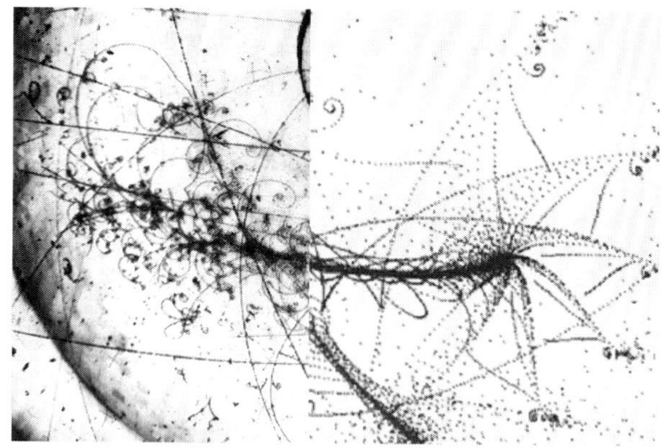

Figure 20. The left half of this image comes from an actual bubble chamber experiment depicting particle collisions. Source: Fermilab. The right half of this image is an M-Set experiment that shows similar dynamics. These are preliminary results that need to be investigated further.

REFERENCES

1. Adams, Allan, Paul M. Chesler, and Hong Liu. "Holographic turbulence." Physical review letters 112.15 (2014): 151602.
2. Cvetic, M., Gary W. Gibbons, and Christopher N. Pope. "Photon spheres and sonic horizons in black holes from supergravity and other theories." Physical Review D 94.10 (2016): 106005.
3. Gardi, L. "The Mandelbrot set and the fractal nature of light, the Universe, and everything." SPIE Optical Engineering+

Applications. International Society for Optics and Photonics, 2013.

4. Wang, Q. D., et al. "Dissecting X-ray-emitting gas around the center of our galaxy." Science 341.6149 (2013): 981-983.
5. Klitzner, Herb. "1 What Are Quaternions and." Multisensor Attitude Estimation: Fundamental Concepts and Applications (2016): 1.
6. Bekenstein, Jacob D. "Black holes and entropy." Physical Review D 7.8 (1973): 2333.
7. Mandelbrot, Benoit B. "How long is the coast of Britain." Science 156.3775 (1967): 636-638.
8. Macdonald, Blair D. "Fractal Geometry a Possible Explanation to the Accelerating Expansion of the Universe and Other Standard ΛCDM Model Anomalies." Update (2014).
9. Aryal, B., R. Pandey, and W. Saurer. "A Study of chiral property of field galaxies." arXiv preprint arXiv:1307.1830 (2013).
10. Acharya, R., and P. Narayana Swamy. "Patterns of Broken Chiral Symmetry in Quantum Chromodynamics." arXiv preprint hep-th/0010157 (2000).
11. Aryal, B., R. Pandey, and W. Saurer. "A Study of chiral property of field galaxies." arXiv preprint arXiv:1307.1830 (2013).
12. Kumar, Jatish, K. George Thomas, and Luis M. Liz-Marzan. "Nanoscale chirality in metal and semiconductor nanoparticles." Chemical Communications 52.85 (2016): 12555-12569.
13. Pahre, Michael A., et al. "Spatial Distribution of Warm Dust in Early-Type Galaxies." The Astrophysical Journal Supplement Series 154.1 (2004): 229.
14. Capozziello, Salvatore, and Alessandra Lattanzi. "Spiral galaxies as chiral objects?." Astrophysics and Space Science 301.1-4 (2006): 189-193.
15. Capozziello, Salvatore, and Alessandra Lattanzi. "Spiral galaxies as enantiomers: chirality, an underlying feature in chemistry and astrophysics." arXiv preprint physics/0509144 (2005).
16. Capozziello, Salvatore, and Alessandra Lattanzi. "Chiral tetrahedrons as unitary quaternions: Molecules and particles under the same standard?." International journal of quantum chemistry 104.6 (2005): 885-893.
17. Batcheldor, Daniel, et al. "A displaced supermassive black hole in M87." The Astrophysical Journal Letters 717.1 (2010): L6.
18. Chiaberge, M., et al. "The puzzling case of the radio-loud QSO 3C 186: a gravitational wave recoiling black hole in a young radio source?." Astronomy & Astrophysics 600 (2017): A57. 17
19. Bucher, B., et al. "Direct Evidence of Octupole Deformation in Neutron-Rich Ba 144." Physical review letters 116.11 (2016): 112503.
20. Mandelbrot, Benoit B., and Roberto Pignoni. The fractal geometry of nature. Vol. 1. New York: WH freeman, 1983.
21. Gillessen, Stefan, et al. "Monitoring stellar orbits around the Massive Black Hole in the Galactic Center." The Astrophysical Journal 692.2 (2009): 1075.

A Medium for the Propagation of Light Revisited

Lori Gardi

lori.anne.gardi@gmail.com

Although it is well known that mechanical waves require the presence of a medium for wave propagation, it is commonly thought that electromagnetic waves do not require a medium. The purpose of this essay is to demonstrate, using logic and common sense, that electromagnetic waves (i.e., light) also requires the presence of a medium for propagation. Using the analogy of wave propagation in a material medium, the composition of the medium for the propagation of light (the aether) is deduced, the null result of the Michelson-Morley experiment is explained, and an alternate experiment to detect the luminiferous aether is proposed.

Keywords: aether, light, sound, propagation, waves, medium, Michelson-Morley, gravity waves, LIGO, virtual particles

1. Introduction

The luminiferous aether has been hotly debated topic for more than 100 years. Although it is commonly thought that light does not require a medium for propagation, the debate is all but over. First, we must all agree that waves do not *travel* in the traditional sense as a car travelling down a highway or a particle travelling through a particle accelerator. Waves *propagate*, i.e., the mechanism for travelling waves is much different than the mechanism for travelling particles. This is an important point.

It is well known that a sound that you hear propagates through the medium called air. When I speak a word, I am not *emitting* a sound. A sound is not leaving my mouth and travelling to your ear. What I am doing is I am setting up a perturbation in the medium called air. The perturbation generates a wave pattern which then propagates through the air, at a constant velocity (the speed of sound in air), until it reaches the detector, in this case, the ear. Here is another example. I am sitting in a pool of water. When I sit still, nothing happens. When I start waving my arms in the water, then you will see some waves. Am I emitting these waves? Obviously not. I am perturbing the medium called water which manifests as a wave that then propagates through said medium. In other words, something must be *waving* in order for a wave to appear. The act of waving perturbs the medium.

Here, I argue a similar thing for light. When you turn on a light, what is actually happening? Does the light bulb emit particles of light or photons that then travel through space to a detector? Does the detector then catch the photons? Doesn't it make more sense that the light bulb is setting up a perturbation in a medium? Why should light waves behave so much differently than all other waves? Short answer; they don't. In this essay, it is argued that light and sound are exactly the same, only propagating in different media. This has been argued many times in the past [1] [2] [3], but most physicists still believe that light propagation does not require a medium. The null result of the Michelson-Morley experiment is usually sited as support for this belief system, however, there may be another explanation for this null result that wasn't considered historically. This will be the subject of this essay.

Claims:

1. All waves are caused by perturbations (waving). In order for a wave to form, "something" must be waving.
2. All wave propagation requires a medium. There are no exceptions.

2. On the Speed of Sound

The equation used to calculate the speed of sound through a material medium is as follows:

$$v = \sqrt{\frac{K_s}{p}} \tag{3}$$

Here, K_s is the stiffness coefficient (or the modulus of bulk elasticity for gases), and p is the density coefficient. Stiffness is the resistance of an elastic body to deformation by an external force, and density is mass per unit volume. In general, a material with a large mass per unit volume (density) will tend to exhibit a slower speed of sound, and a material with a large stiffness coefficient will tend to exhibit a faster speed of sound. (The opposite is true of low density and less elastic materials.) In reality, it is much more complicated than that. A rarefied medium, e.g., rarefied air, which has a lower mass per volume, will also have a lower stiffness coefficient. In this case, the speed of propagation in rarefied air is much slower than in non-rarefied air, even though the density coefficient is lower. In general, rarefied materials exhibit a slower speed of propagation than the non-rarefied materials. This is an important point that we will come back to later.

3. On the Speed of Light

One of the equations used to calculate the speed of light is as follows:

$$c = \sqrt{\frac{1}{\varepsilon_0\,\mu_0}} \tag{4}$$

Here, ε_0 corresponds to permittivity (of free space) and μ_0 corresponds to permeability (of free space). With a little adjustment, we can make this equation look exactly like the speed of sound equation (1):

$$c = \sqrt{\frac{\mu_0^{-1}}{\varepsilon_0}} \tag{5}$$

Here, inverse permeability, μ_0^{-1}, plays the role of the stiffness coefficient. This makes logical sense since materials that are more permeable (like a sponge) tend to be less stiff than materials with a lower permeability, and vice verse. Analogously, the ε_0 parameter plays the role of the density coefficient, K_s. This also makes logical sense since permittivity is directly proportional to dielectric polarization density (polarized particles per unit volume). In this manner, the equation to calculate the speed of light in the vacuum of space (using vacuum permittivity and permeability) can be made to look exactly like the equation used to calculate the speed of sound in a material medium. Although this does not prove that there is a medium for the propagation of light, it does imply that a medium could exist. If there is a medium, then what is its composition?

Logically speaking, if empty space is a medium, then that medium cannot be made of ponderable matter (particles with mass), since the *vacuum of space* is by definition, empty of matter. If the vacuum of space is not ponderable matter, then what is it? Well, it must be made of something other than ponderable matter. But if the vacuum of space is not made of ponderable matter, then it doesn't exist, right? This is not necessarily true. We currently cannot directly observe dark matter, but we can infer its existence by the behaviours of the galaxies and galaxy clusters. We also cannot directly observe dark energy, but its existence can be inferred by the apparent accelerated expansion of the universe. By analogy, just because we cannot directly observe the medium for the propagation of light doesn't mean that it does not exist. The fact that light propagates at a finite velocity implies that a medium should exists. That said, if the medium is not made of ponderable matter, then what could it be possibly made of? Can we intuit the medium for the propagation of light by studying the propagation of sound waves through a "ponderable matter" medium?

4. On the Speed of Sound in NaCl

In this section, we will analyze the behaviour of a ponderable material medium called sodium chloride, NaCl, commonly known as salt. These experiments were done by Menahem Simhony at the Hebrew University in Israel [5] [6]. In his experiments, Simhony noticed that the clear salt crystal, NaCl, becomes cloudy and electrically conducting when exposed to UV light of around 8 eV. With this exposure, Na and Cl ion pairs are released from the crystal lattice medium and are free to wander (conduct) within the medium. When the UV energy is removed, the ions fall back into the lattice and the 8 eV energy (used to free the ions) is released, after which the crystal becomes clear again.

Using equation (1), the speed of sound within the NaCl lattice can be calculated by replacing the stiffness coefficient , K_s, with the binding energy of NaCl within the lattice, and the density coefficient, p, with the mass per unit volume of the NaCl medium. The assumption here is that the binding energy of a material determines its stiffness (and indirectly the elastic properties) of the medium. For these calculations, the unit volume of a single NaCl pair was chosen.

$$v = \sqrt{\frac{K_s}{p}} = \sqrt{\frac{A}{B+C}} = 3700\,[m/s] \tag{6}$$

Here, $A = 1.3052 \times 10^{-18}$ is the binding energy of the NaCl bond, $B = 3.818 \times 10^{-26}$ is the mass of the sodium ion, and $C = 5.720 \times 10^{-26}$ is the mass of the chlorine ion. This equates to 3700 [m/s] which is in fact the speed of sound within the NaCl medium.

Using the logic of this example, we can now speculate as to the makeup of the luminiferous aether. First, we make a guess that it is made up of "particle pairs" of some sort, however, it cannot be made up of "atomic" particle pairs (like NaCl) because the vacuum of space is by definition empty of ponderable matter. Here, it is assumed that the vacuum of space is made of and/or filled with *something*, but what could this *something* be?

5. On the Medium for the Propagation of Light

In physics, there is a phenomenon referred to as electron-positron annihilation. This occurs when electrons and positrons get close together and collide. The result of one collision is the annihilation of an electron and a positron with a release of two gamma ray photons, each with an energy of 0.511 MeV or 1.022 MeV in total. In the NaCl experiment, the free roaming Na and Cl ions fell back into the lattice with the release of the 8 eV of energy that was used to extract the ions from the lattice in the first place. What if the same thing is happening with electrons and positrons? What if the electrons and positrons are not annihilating, but instead, are merely falling back into a lattice or medium of some kind? If this is the case, then the 1.022 MeV energy release (after collision) can be considered as the binding energy of an electron-positron pair in a medium consisting of bound electron-positron pairs. Using the NaCl analogy, the speed of propagation of such a medium can be calculated as follows:

$$v = \sqrt{\frac{A}{B+C}} = 299792458.0\,[m/s] \qquad (7)$$

Here, A is the binding energy of the electron-positron pair in the medium ($A = 1.637421 \times 10^{-13}$ [J]) and $B+C$ is the mass per unit volume of the electron-positron pair ($B+C = 1.821876582 \times 10^{-30}$ [kg]). Notice that this evaluates to exactly the speed of light. This suggests that the vacuum of space consists of a medium of bound electron-positron pairs. This is, for all intents and purposes, Dirac's sea [7]. Although these electron-positron pairs are not ponderable in of themselves (since they are charge condensed and mass condensed), they do become apparent when unpaired (ponderable) atoms and ions enter the medium. Figure 1 is a 2D schematic of how a sea of electron-positron pairs might self-organize in the presence unpaired charges.

From Figure 1, it is clear to see that the sensation we experience as charge could very well come from a field or medium consisting of a sea of bound particle-antiparticle pairs. This may explain why both electrons and protons "have" the same charge even though they have different masses and are of different sizes. It is possible that particles do not have the property of charge in of themselves, but instead, they experience charge the same way, via the particle-antiparticle medium. It should also be noted that equation (5) apples to all particle-antiparticle pairs, not just electron-position pairs. For example, if we insert the binding energy and mass per unit volume for a proton-antiproton pair into equation (5), we will still get the speed of light. We could use quark-antiquark pairs as well and get the same answer. Thus, a medium of particle-antiparticle pairs would explain where all the virtual particle-antiparticle pairs come from in quantum field theory.

6. On the Detection of the Aether: Part I

The null result of the Michelson-Morley experiment is often sited as evidence that the aether does not exist. The MM experiment measures the speed of light in two perpendicular directions as the earth orbits around the sun. The hypothesis is as follows: If the aether exists, then the measured speed of light should be different in the direction of motion through the aether as compared to a direction at right angles. This experiment has been done many times with increasing sensitivity over the years [4], and a difference has never been detected. Given this null result, the consensus is that the aether does not exist. This hypothesis, however, is merely an assumption. A literature search will show that an acoustic Michelson-Morley experiment has never been officially performed. Unofficially (independently) however, a Michelson-Morley type experiment has been performed in air using an ultrasonic range finder [8]. Interestingly, this experiment also produces a null result. Given these results and the logic of the MM experiment, we must conclude that air does not exist. Obviously, this is not the case. It seems that direct detection of the aether is not be possible using the MM experimental setup. Using light emitters and detectors to detect the medium for the propagation of light may be akin to circular reasoning. In other words, the logic of the MM-experiment may be inherently flawed.

7. Similarities Between Sound and Light

There are many similarities between sound and light. For example, both sound and light carry energy from one place to another. Both sound waves and light waves experience wave interference. They both exhibit Doppler shift. Both experience reflection, refraction and diffraction. Refraction is the bending of a wave when it moves between media with different propagation speeds. Both sound and light refract toward the normal of the gradient when moving from a fast medium to a slow medium.

Another similarity has to do with the speed of sound in a rarefied medium. Earlier, it was noted that the speed of sound actually slows down in rarefied air even though the density is lower than the non-rarefied air. Rarefied mediums actually reduce the stiffness constant of the medium which also affects the speed of sound in said medium. If light propagates in a medium, then the speed of light should also slow down when the medium is rarefied.

As sound waves propagate in matter, light waves propagate in aether. This is the hypothesis. Here it is argued that when matter is present, then aether is rarefied and when aether is present, then matter is rarefied. When matter is rarefied, sound slows down and when aether is rarefied, then light slows down. In materials that transmit both light and sound, for example NaCl, aether is rarefied AND matter is rarefied. The vacuum of space is not empty, it is just empty of matter, but full of aether. In a similar manner, an opaque material medium is empty of aether but full of matter. When matter is present, aether is rarefied and vice verse. Without recognizing the existence of the aether, this reciprocal nature of matter and aether cannot be realized.

Now, the only difference between sound and light appears to be that sound is a longitudinal wave and light is a transverse wave. Therefore, instead of saying that light and sound are exactly the same, only propagating in different media, we are going to say that *photons* and *phonons* are exactly the same (only propagating in different media). Phonons are the sound equivalent to photons (ie. they oscillate transverse to the direction of motion), only they propagate in solid media. Technically, solids support the propagation of both transverse waves and longitudinal waves. In seismology, longitudinal waves are referred to as pressure waves or P-waves and transverse waves are referred to as shear waves or S-waves. This line of thinking also suggests that there may be a (previously undiscovered) longitudinal component to light propagation. Longitudinal electromagnetic waves would be very difficult to detect since the displacement, perpendicular to the direction of motion would be very small. That said, there may be an experiment that is well suited to the

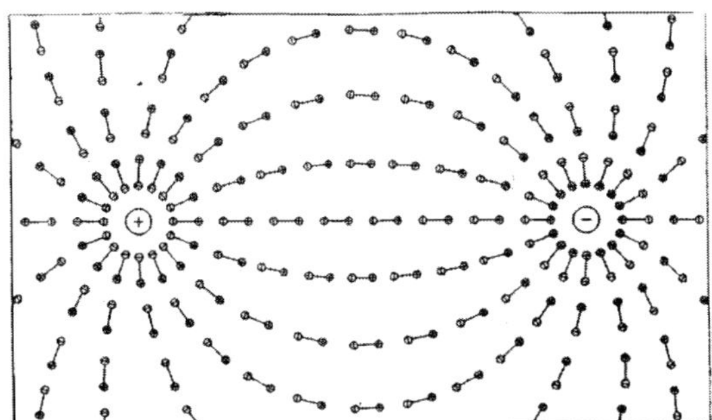

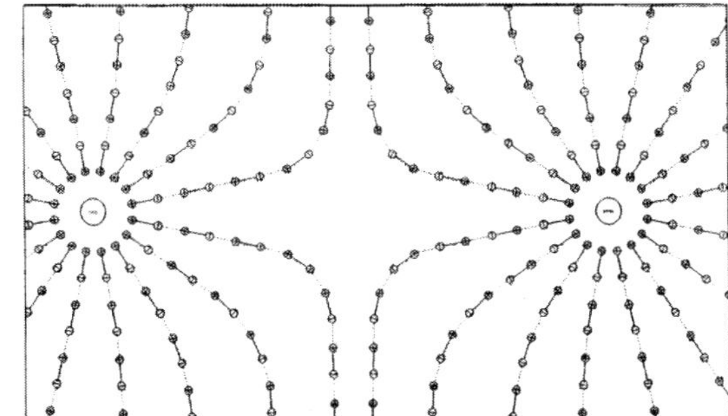

Figure 21. This figure depicts how a medium of electron-positron pairs might self-organize in the presence of ions or charges within the medium. The image on the left shows unlike charges in the medium and the image on the right shows like charges in the medium. Image source: "Diracs equation and the sea of negative energy" by Don Hotson

detection of such waves as explained in the next section.

8. On Detection of the Aether: Part II

The Michelson-Morley experiment failed to detect the aether. Earlier, we suggested that the logic supporting this experiment may be inherently flawed since it uses light emitters and detectors to detect the light medium. There is, however, another experiment that might be better suited to detecting the medium for the propagation of light that does not rely on light emitters and detectors. To explain this, we are going to use the analogy of wave propagation in ponderable matter. As mentioned in the previous section, earthquakes generate both P-waves and S-waves. P-waves are compression waves that propagate in the direction of the compression. These waves are very subtle and therefore, much more difficult to detect. S-waves move particles perpendicular to the direction of travel and thus propagate slower than P-waves. S-waves are much easier to detect as they create more of a disturbance. In the analogy presented herein, S-waves are analogous to transverse electromagnetic waves and P-waves are analogous to longitudinal electromagnetic waves which, according to the standard model of electromagnetism, do not exist. Without a medium, it is difficult to reconcile the existence of longitudinal waves in the vacuum of space.

If longitudinal electromagnetic waves do exist, 1) they will be very subtle and difficult to detect and 2) they will travel faster than the transverse electromagnetic component (aether S-wave). That said, according to relativity, no-thing can travel faster than the speed of light, however, waves are not things and they do not travel, they propagate. The argument here is that the subtle longitudinal waves of the aether can and do propagate slightly faster than the speed of light, analogous to the P-waves of seismic theory. Although the Michelson-Morley experiment was ill suited to detect longitudinal electromagnetic waves, there is another experiment that may be much better suited to detect these waves. This experiment is called LIGO.

On September 14, 2015, such a signal was detected by LIGO, allegedly caused by the collision of two black holes 1.3 billion light years from Earth. According to the above analogy, what was detected was, for all intents and purposes, the P-wave of an earthquake in the aether (an aether-quake if you may) likely caused by the black hole collision. According to the earth quake analogy, this P-wave should have been followed by an S-wave (transverse electromagnetic wave), and it was. A transient gamma ray signal was detected approximately 0.4 seconds after the detection of the so called gravitational wave [11] [12]. Of particular interest is the fact that the signal detected by LIGO is morphologically very similar to a seismic P-wave (see Figure 2). It should also be noted that relativity does not predict that a gamma ray signal should necessarily follow a gravitational wave. That said, if all future "gravitational waves" are followed by a gamma ray signal, then the idea of a medium for the propagation of light (as outlined in this essay) should be revisited.

9. Discussion

Using the analogy of waves propagating in a solid medium, it could be argued that the aether is solid of some kind, since solids can and do transmit transverse waves. There are, however, other possibilities. It has recently been discovered that superfluids behave somewhat like a solid in their ability to conduct transverse (shear) waves, contrary to what was previously thought. A group of physicists at Northwestern University have shown that at sufficiently low temperatures, superfluid helium-3 exhibits a collective behaviour that supports the propagation of shear waves [9]. Another possibility lies in the research associated with Bose-Einstein condensates (BEC). It is found that (transverse) electromagnetic waves can propagate in a BEC when it consists of atoms with dipole moments [10]. Therefore, it is possible that a medium made of (polarizable) electron-positron pairs might behave as Bose-Einstein condensate. The author is leaning toward a BEC consisting of particle-antiparticle pairs (generalized as vortex-antivortex pairs [13]) as the medium for the propagation of light.

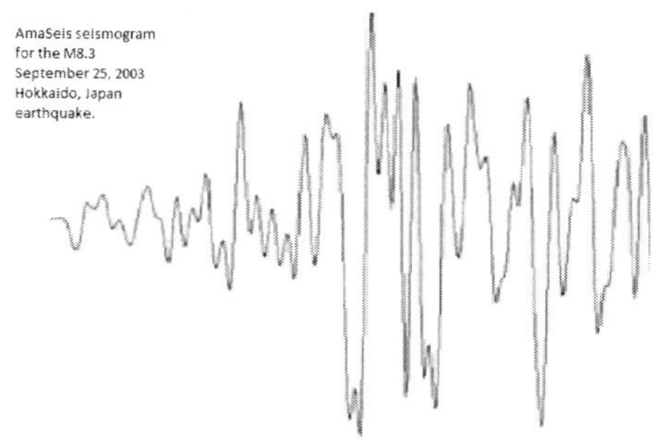

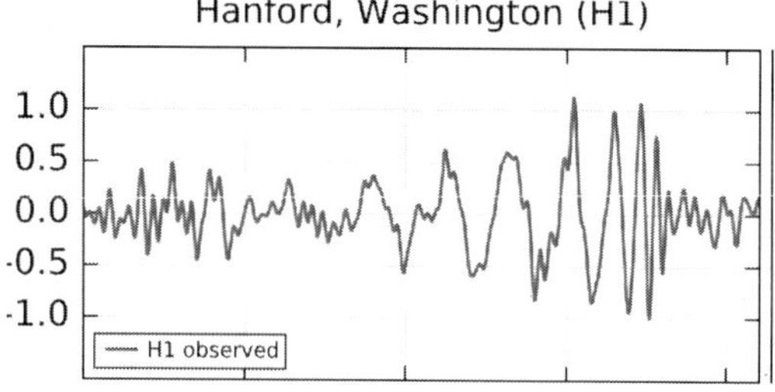

Figure 22. On the top is a close up of the P-wave of the M8.3 September 25, 2003 Hokkaido, Japan earthquake recorded at West Lafaytte, Indiana. Below that is a graph of the gravity wave detected on September 14, 2015 at 09:50:45 UTC, by LIGO in Hanford, WA

10. Conclusion

A change in perspective shows that light may in fact propagate in a medium, contrary to common thinking. Using the analogy of calculating the speed of sound in NaCl (i.e., salt), the medium that supports the propagation of light waves is deduced to be a medium of bound particle-antiparticle pairs. It was shown how the logic of the Michelson-Morley experiment may be inherently flawed and that the null result reported by these experiments does not preclude the existence of a medium. It was also shown how another experiment, called LIGO, may be better suited to directly detect the luminous aether medium. Here, the gravitational wave detected by LIGO in 2015 is thought to be analogous to the detection of the P-wave of an earthquake in the aether. Of course, there does exist another aether detector that has been around for much longer than LIGO or any other experiment that man has dreamed up. They are called "eyes".

REFERENCES

1. Petroni, Nicola Cufaro, and Jean Pierre Vigier. "Dirac's aether in relativistic quantum mechanics." Foundations of Physics 13.2 (1983): 253-286.
2. Whittaker, Edmund. "A History of the Theories of Aether and Electricity. The Modern Theories, 1900-1926." (1954).
3. Eling, Christopher, Ted Jacobson, and David Mattingly. "Einstein-aether theory." arXiv preprint gr-qc/0410001 (2004).
4. MÃijller, Holger, et al. "Modern Michelson-Morley experiment using cryogenic optical resonators." Physical review letters 91.2 (2003): 020401.
5. Simhony, Menahem. The electron-positron lattice space: cause of relativity and quantum effects. Physics Section 5, Hebrew University, 1990.
6. Simhony, Menahem. "Velocity of Elastic Waves in NaCl Crystals, in the Electron Positron Lattice (Epola) Space, and their Phonons/Photons." APS Meeting Abstracts. 2003.
7. Hotson, Donald L. "DiracâĂŹs equation and the sea of negative energy." Infinite Energy 43 (2002): 2002.
8. Feist, Norbert. "Acoustic Michelson-Morley Experiment with an Ultrasonic Range Finder." Proc. NPA (2010): 1-4.
9. Northwestern University. "Superfluid Is Shown To Have Property Of A Solid." ScienceDaily. ScienceDaily, 30 July 1999.
10. Poluektov, Yu M., and I. V. Tanatarov. "Propagation of electromagnetic waves in Bose-Einstein condensate of atoms with dipole moments." arXiv preprint arXiv:1408.1526 (2014).
11. Connaughton, V., et al. "Fermi GBM observations of LIGO gravitational-wave event GW150914." The Astrophysical Journal Letters 826.1 (2016): L6.
12. Loeb, Abraham. "Electromagnetic counterparts to black hole mergers detected by LIGO." The Astrophysical Journal Letters 819.2 (2016): L21.
13. Schweikhard, Volker. Ultracold Bose gases under rotation, in lattice potentials, and both. Diss. University of Colorado at Boulder, 2009.

Implosion of Aether and Universal Energy Theorem

David Garroway Jr.

United Kingdom, phiman888@yahoo.co.uk

On the West Coast of the United States there are two separate gravitational anomalies. One outside of Santa Cruz called the "Mystery Spot" and the other "Oregon Vortex." After visiting such unusual places, it became obvious to me the current Estonian view of gravity (mandate no anti-gravity) must be completely wrong or at least incomplete. A correct theory does not allow for such anomalies, and furthermore, a correct theory would be able to describe the behavior (or non-behavior) of something.

Most of the time, a valid theory does not make the cut. Indeed, Einstein was wrong. The aether does exist all around us and its complex behavior is what causes gravity. Gravity is an effect rather than an invisible force reaching through nothingness which grabs onto objects or things. We are courtesy of the de- astro fractating implosive force of the inward flow of aether being pushed down to the Earth, not pulled.

The same force and movement of the spiraling aether, also known as the Golden Mean, and the consequent spiraling waves occurring within it are responsible for all of the "forces" of nature. From the orbit of Jupiter to the orbit of the electron, attraction and repulsion, and even anti-gravity and the reversal of the Coriolis effect are all the result of the aether; its constantly accelerating movement as well as the right and the left spiraling wave inside it. This abstract describes how this force arises and how it can be manipulated.

Keywords: aether, vortex

1. Introduction

The Importance of Gravitational Anomalies Around the world, many gravitational anomalies exist. In recent years, I have had the pleasure of visiting two of these in western North America. One anomaly dubbed "The mystery spot" in Santa Cruz, CA, as well as the "Oregon Vortex" on the border between Oregon and California. Both of these surreal places truly defy the laws of conventional physics. According to Einstein, anti-gravity cannot exist, yet I have seen such a force at work in both of these places on Earth. In both Oregon and Santa Cruz, golf balls not only fall but accelerate uphill along a plank determined to be level by government appointed measurement as demonstrated by the guide. Another phenomenon seen here is conducted by a person who stands at the end of a level beam, eye to eye with another person standing opposite of him (on the other side of the plank) at the length of 5 ft. Upon changing places and while looking over the other person's head, space and time compress as they get closer to the center of this 300 ft. diameter circular spot. One could go on all day about the many anomalies, but the one effect that clued me in to the nature of time-space is the phenomenon that the Corriolis effect is actually reversed. In one particular instance, water swirls down the drain the "wrong way" from the northern hemisphere; this proved to me that anti-gravity has torque associated with it. This became especially apparent as we'd push standing at the center of the spot. It is in this very spot that you can lean so far forward you cannot see past your own feet.

If a theory does not support observational phenomena, the theory must be wrong. There can be no exceptions or anomalies. This is why I have come up with the imploding aether theory. "... When you eliminate the impossible, whatever remains, however improbable, must be the truth" to quote the doctor Spock school of logic. So is the case here. This universe is made up of left-handed, inward-flowing aether. It is connected to 3 others: leftward-outwards, rightward-inward, righthanded outward, and left-handed outward (counter-clockwise relative to the direction of flow). What makes it so fantastic is that these universe might be this exact one we are currently in, perhaps at another time, but they exist because of a universe behavior theory I wish to present today; this theory proves that other universes must exist in order for the others to function. Within my prospectus, the aether implodes in a spiraling vortex along the lines of the golden mean; This explains why this ratio of PHI 1.6181 permeates nature from the curve of a chamber nautilus to the curve of a ram's horn.

2. Imploding Aether and Astro-Defractation

Aether implodes downward into the atom and pushes the nucleus of this universe leaving behind a black hole. Place half the time at about 60 billion times per second, per second, until the nucleus reappears and cycles again. First, I would like to mention two historical hypotheses for explaining the failure of the Michaelson-Morley experiment: (1) the length contraction hypothesis of Fitzgerald and Lorentz, and (2) the other in the constancy of light velocity hypothesis of Einstein. In my findings, both of these theories are wrong.

The real reason the MMX failed is because of the astro-defractating inward following the path of gravity down and in toward the local matter, furthermore, the experiment failed because the experiment itself was surrounded by

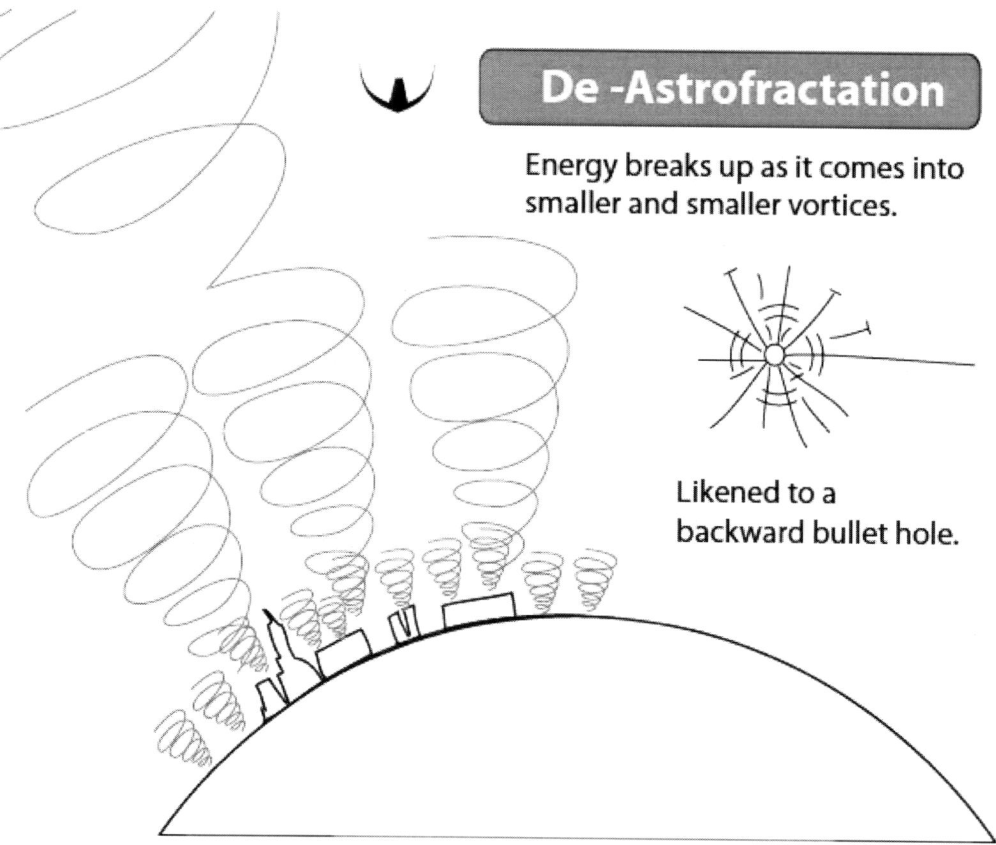

Figure 1. De-Astroficataion

a vortex aether field that moves with, and in essence, is attached to it. This way, only light motion in (or close to) the apparatus will be detected as at light speed. Every thing in existence has this conglomerate of a dodecahedron of gravitational vortexes around it.

This brings me to my next point regarding the ever-accelerating speed of light. In traditional schools, we are taught that light travels a 186,000 per second in a straight line. The problem with that is nowhere in our universe does a straight line exist. Why? Because there is no place without gravity. Experiments have proven that gravity bends light, and if this is true, a beam passing Earth not only travels at 186,000 per second but also "falls" at 32ftÂš per second, per second âĂŞ and lesser as it pulls away from Earth. Now deceleration is the same as acceleration in terms of change of velocity.

First, a light beam falling toward Earth bends more and more, then, becomes less bent (but never 100expanding or shrinking aether; it is being pushed sideways to and fro by other aether waves. I believe that the speed of acceleration due to gravity is dependent on the density of local aether waves and not their velocity. The denser the aether, like air flow, the more it will affect matter and light around it. However, the speed of the aether movement itself is 186,000 miles per second, that is the speed at which the universe is imploding in our own neighborhood.

This means that light is actually always under constant acceleration and its speed is 186,000 miles per second, per second. The reason it appears constant is because of the secondary acceleration of the light wave, due to the aether that allowed time itself to take place. Indeed, if high-speed was continuous and not an ongoing series of accelerations, time itself would not occur. The semantics of time flow become complicated because we use time (or aether flow) on an everyday level, moving things at the same rates which we are aware of. Through experimentation, we mathematically know different gravity fields produce different rates of time flow, not aether flow which is almost constant everywhere except time flow.

Einstein was correct in some ways, but not aether. The actual speed of light, electricity, etc. is not just 186,000 miles per second but rather 186,000 miles per second, per second.

Like the orbit of electron or a planet, the speed of light is also under constant acceleration. Newton stated that an object in orbit is under constant acceleration, and in my theory so is a light beam being bent by gravity. Straight lines do not exist nor does a constant velocity. This is because gravity exists everywhere albeit in different increments.

3. Irrational Universe

Zero vs. Infinity: Real Measurements are irrational. Practically no thing is consistent or constant in our universe, but numbers are. Just because a number is bigger than we can imagine does not necessarily mean it goes on infinitely. This is why zero and infinity are mathematical jokes, or approximations at best. All real things have a fractal edge to them. The closer you look, the more of it you see. However, even if we can't see it, we must assume some ascertainable amount is present which we cannot detect. Therefore all measurements of real things have to be a rational number and fractal in nature, simply because everything in nature is.

Certainly, our universe once exploded during the Big Bang âĂŞ however, it occurred about twice as long ago as believed in popular science. That is because in the initial expansion phase there was only darkness and chaotic, agitated aether. The aether remained until our universe started to condense about 14 billion years ago, that is, when particles and photons began coalescing and participating outside of the aether. Hydrogen atoms spontaneously began to form as our condensing, crystallizing aether formed into what we call matter. The more connections to the aether itself, the higher on the atomic scale in particles. The aether now only supports a certain number of elements, but as it grows more will be added, becoming stable. This is proved by the slowing rate of atomic decay since the 1950s when measuring began. Only a change of aether density could explain this. As we pass through the galactic plane, the aether has also. Initially, the implosive matter of aether that formed and began shrinking were sinister, i.e. lefthanded.

in and counterclockwise. Then atoms began to appear, first as simple light then more complex. They all had one thing in common: a nuclear ("new clear") center. The clear half, right-handed time (a black hole) behaved in a way that "soaked up" incoming aether which then eliminated a clockwise auto gain, expanding the wave of energy up and out again through the opposite incoming wave.

Friction occurs, but not much. Aether is thin but out against in, up against down, and right against left. The outgoing, right-handed energy then becomes polished and smooth rubbing against the flow of incoming aether. This secondary wave rebounds vortex matter to become a right-handed inward vortex, again reaching down to the nuclear level where the aether is absorbed half the time, and shifted around three adjunct universes only to return as a left-out wave fighting the incoming aether.

4. The Four Types of Waves and Twelve Spirals

These four types of waves attempt to make up what we call flat space: 12 waves in all, 3 sets of each, and a bonus 13th synergistic wave which is known as gravity. To capture energy from these waves and focus them, we must resonate with their structure âĂŞ just like sympathetic resonance with guitar strings only in more complex dimensions. To do this, we must compound accelerations. Newton stated that an object in orbit is under constant acceleration due to gravity being the active direction changer; Compound the east-west trajectory and add a north-to-south orbit. Finally, twist all this into a figure eight clockwise orbit changing to a counter-clockwise orbit.

Counter-clockwise orbit and track becomes another constant change acceleration. Bend the figure eight 72 degrees up and down; repeat another. Finally, add more figure eights underneath diminishing 3 which are expanding upwards. Geometrically, this structure will sync up the 12 waves and an electron in it will get an extra push riding from one 3.0 golden mean spiral section to the next. Each of the figure eight types of spiral accelerate. The structure will harvest gravity, turning it into other forms of energy, heat, EMF, etc. (It should be superconducting for best results.) It will also speed up time locally just a little, as gravity is lessened and turned into usable energy. The figure eights lock together like a triple-decker four leaf clover with the biggest clover on top, smallest on bottom.

This happens three times each figure diminishes in size and length, forcing the electron to travel a more curved path, adding acceleration, then decreasing in it's spiraling, adding more acceleration as it moves âĂŞ much like a surfer riding an incoming wave, mounting it, then jumping to an outward barrel wave (rebounding) first traveling in and north, then out and north. That is just one side of the Figure eight. Next it repeats on the other side of the eight, only this time going in south and down, then out south and up. This will have happened three times as the surfer speeds up going downward and inward more each Figure eight, taking advantage of three sets of waves. Waves traveling down the y-axis travel fastest because they have gravity assisting them; naturally, upward being slowest as it fights gravity. East to west are different rates; north and south aether waves travel at different rates due to the rotation of the earth and magnetic fields affecting travel time of waves.

As the surfer descends those of the three diminishing figure eights, he is changing his position in the gravitational field, then back again as he travels the ascending figure eights out of page. The ascending eights are bent upward another acceleration 90 degrees out of phase, then decelerate and travel upward out of the gravitational field.

Electrons or photons traveling this convoluted geometry will gain only momentum, but also more spin as the particle spins near the speed of light. The particle must then become smaller to avoid a paradox, so it shrinks down to plank length then disappears from our universe as it transitions to three others before returning as radiating-out energy. This happens naturally with all nuclei, but the coil makes it happen a bit faster than normal, harvesting gravity and turning it into heat, torque, EMF, etc.

Another example of the spiraling aether (and how it can be used to resonate with and harvest in experimentation or application) is the fact that it moves in around and around, but it also bunches up and smooths out. As it does so, it rotates even faster on its way down like my previous

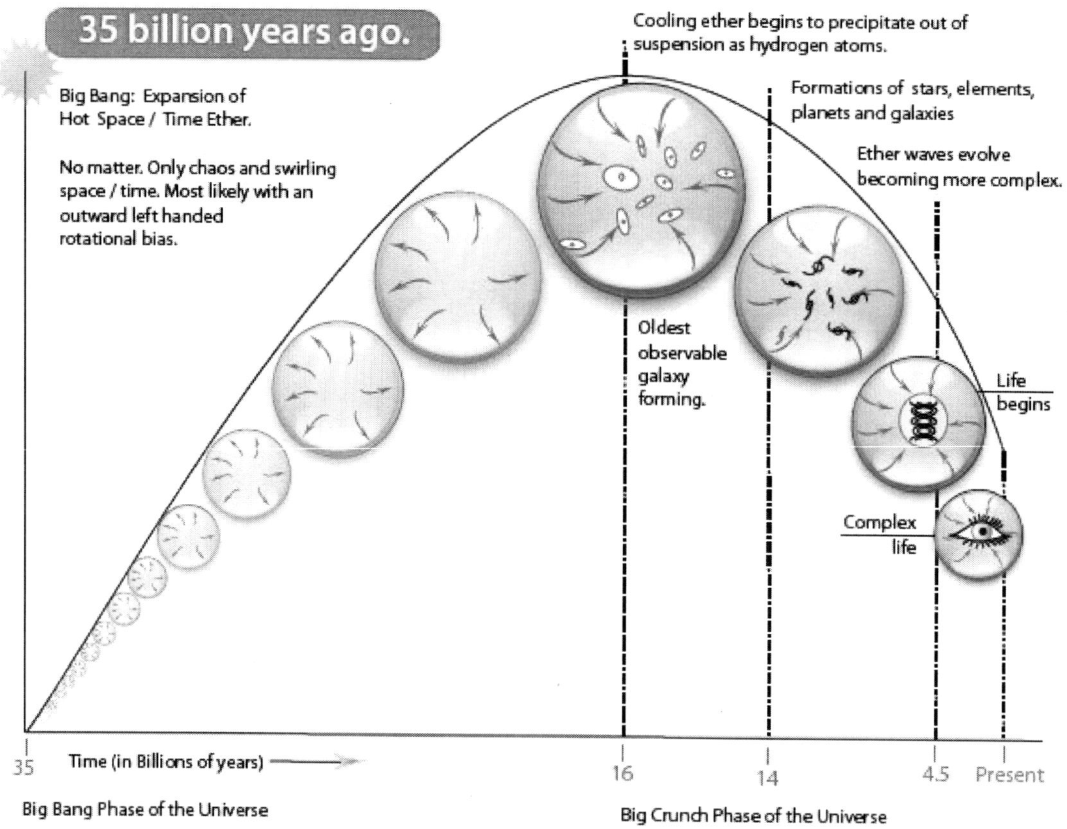
35 billion years ago.
Big Bang: Expansion of Hot Space / Time Ether.
No matter. Only chaos and swirling space / time. Most likely with an outward left handed rotational bias.
Cooling ether begins to precipitate out of suspension as hydrogen atoms.
Formations of stars, elements, planets and galaxies
Ether waves evolve becoming more complex.
Oldest observable galaxy forming.
Life begins
Complex life
35
Time (in Billions of years)
16
14
4.5
Present
Big Bang Phase of the Universe
Big Crunch Phase of the Universe

Figure 2. Big Bang, Big Crunch

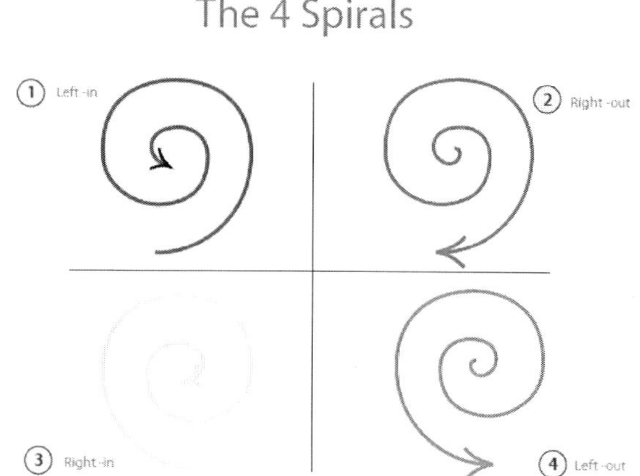
The 4 Spirals
1 Left-in
2 Right-out
3 Right-in
4 Left-out

Figure 3. Four types of spirals

example of water going down the shower drain. Water "spikes" you sometimes notice radiating out from the drain is where the flow gets ahead of itself and bunches up. It is just after this bottleneck when it starts accelerating again, and that energy can be caught. Part IV: Mathematical Formula

The aether accelerates around according to the Fibonacci series; first 1 then 2, 3, 5, 8, 13 units of space are covered per second. 72 degrees of a circle, in this case, because every vortex has 5 sides. Mathematically, it would look something like PHIÂš divided by secondsÂš over seconds. At the beginning of a second, it can be intersected by matching the direction of the flow at that point every time the spiral goes around once. The math gets complex, so for this paper I will say that if you resonate with these patterns that have been derived, you can glean energy. It is essentially the combination to a fractal lock.

In essence, the wheel spins faster according to the golden mean. And in simpler terms, this is to say for the first 3 seconds the aether is accelerating more than usual. The next second a little less, then a little more the next second, then for the next 5 seconds you can catch it going a little less at the beginning of each of those 5 seconds.

It is possible to build energy attractors with these geometries and rational patterns. They are pulling in a bit more energy than the surrounding matter, ambient light increases, reflection gets more intense, and temperature rises. I have sanded metallic surfaces, I made wind chimes and made music with this technology, and repeatedly attracted energy of the focal aether flow. Part V: Conclusion: Practical Use and Application

There is a reason all DNA on Earth is right-handed. The initial, inward aether direction is leftin, that is, counterclockwise shrinking inward toward the matter. The clockwise-outward expanding wave must fight against these on their way out and up from matter becoming smoother and more compacted. The reason has been said that we are born in sin is because "sinister" equates to left-handed movement, but the struggle of life is righteous.

A clockwise spiral has more information carrying capacity and more actual rotation in it. Righthanded energy tends to pull matter together, crystallize, and cool, while left-handed energy is responsible for chaos, separation, and melting or morphing things. The yin and yang energies do exist and now we know why they do.

5. Conclusion

This theory is ripe for commercial development and application pending further research and the writer of this paper is currently seeking financial backing to continue such research. Experiments have been done with the tensor coil and two jars of organic lentils which were prepared identical in all ways except that one of the jars had a coil hanging over it. When water was added, the lentils germinated. In only a couple of days it was plain to see that the jar with lentils underneath the coil was far richer and thicker with sprouts than the other jar. This is because the coil was able to focus the life force itself using right-handed waves into the lentils which helped them to grow.

These coils will grow food faster and may perhaps even be useful in healing wounds or assisting recovery in surgery. Great potential exists when we can separate and utilize different types of waves for different applications in science and technology.

How to Win the Nobel Prize by Finding the Mysterious and Much Maligned Aether

Franklin Hu

19166 130th Ct. NE Bothell, WA, USA, franklinhu@yahoo.com

The easiest way to a Nobel Prize is to find a new fundamental particle. What better particle to find than the particle that makes up space? This paper explores the idea that this particle that has eluded detection can be found and that the Nobel Prize will be yours.

Keywords: aether, aether particle, Nobel Prize

1. Introduction

Who wants to win a Nobel Prize? That is the dream of many scientists, but how do you do it? Usually, you have to invent or discover some revolutionary process like LED lights to be recognized. But one of the most surefire ways to win a Nobel Prize is by discovering a new fundamental particle. Several Nobel Prizes have been awarded for things such as finding the Higgs Boson, the J/Psi particle, and W and Z particles and neutrinos. It wouldn't seem like such a big deal to find some particle, but you are virtually guaranteed to be awarded a Nobel Prize for it.

2. What's Left to Find?

You would think that every fundamental particle that is going to be found has been found. In the search for the Higgs Boson, they have scanned just about every possible place that a particle could be hiding and the chances of you building some machine bigger than CERN to find even more massive particles is hardly practical. I would suggest you look at the opposite end of the scale to find a much lighter particle. The lightest particle we have is the electron, so could there be something just a bit bigger than an electron? Such a light particle would be accessible to relatively modest experimental setup.

3. What About the Aether?

In the history of physics, the aether was the medium that the electromagnetic wave propagated in. The trouble is, nobody has been able to find it - Yet. So, here is the golden opportunity to find a brand new particle. So, what should we be looking for? First, we should be looking for something that can actually be found. By this, I mean that whatever we think the aether particle is, it should be able to show up in our experiments. If we postulate that the aether particle is some totally different kind of matter that is different from any known particle and can't possibly be detected (like the strings in string theory), then it is generally hopeless. So, ideally, the new particle should be made out of things we know about like electrons, muons, protons, quarks, etc. and should not rely upon the invention of some new particle like a Spheriton, Circulon, FP, Fiber, or whatever. Second, if the particle is the medium of the EM wave, then it should be completely stable and be everywhere. If your particle just falls apart in a microsecond like the Higgs Boson, that is hardly a candidate for the aether. So, we are looking for a lightweight particle that is everywhere, but hasn't been detected yet.

4. What Could it Be?

So, we are looking for a lightweight particle made out of known matter particles which is stable and everywhere, but yet hasn't been detected. That's a tall order. Some might say this is impossible, but if it exists, it is probably just hiding under our noses and the only reason we don't see it is because we deliberately choose to ignore it. However, there is a particle that could theoretically fit the bill. That particle is a positron/electron dipole particle which I will dub the 'poselectron'. Now I know what you're thinking - positrons and electrons annihilate each other leaving nothing so that can't possibly be a particle. However, that is exactly, the choice to deliberately ignore the particle which has kept the particle hidden for the past 100 years.

5. Poselectrons Fit the Problem

Assuming that positrons and electrons do not annihilate, then what do they do? I suggest that when they collide, the energy of their collision is released as gamma rays and the particles combine into a newly formed poselectron particle. It is a true dipole combination and not positronium or some version of hydrogen. This combination of would very light, about the mass of 2 electrons, making it the 2nd lightest particle in the universe. In order to hide after the reaction, it would have to look exactly like empty space - which if it were filled with poselectrons would make it indistinguishable from the background. So, we would have a particle which is categorically denied by the mainstream (which prevents its discovery), it is made out of ordinary positron/electron matter which can be easily detected, and it is extremely light weight and completely stable.

6. Finding the Poselectron

One of the main problems with finding the aether particle is that nobody has provided a model for what that particle is made out of. You can't find something if you don't know what you're looking for. With this paper, I have given you a plausible suggestion for what to look for. It will then take clever experimentalists to devise a unique and convincing experiment to prove beyond and doubt that this particle exists. Look for it and you will find it and garner yourself a Nobel Prize in the process.

Space Lattice Theory

Bruce Nappi

16 Spinnaker Hill, Hull MA 02045, bnappi@A3RI.org

Space Lattice Theory is a study of the fundamental structure of the universe. The study asks what that structure might be like if, instead of being mostly an empty void, space is a densely packed, crystal-like Lattice, and the existence and interaction of what we call matter is due to movable defects or dislocations in the Lattice. This theoretical study found that a dislocation model could produce a comprehensive set of simple, visualizable explanations for most of the concepts of physics, including many that are currently unanswered. It explains matter, time, cause and effect, energy, and how energy converts to matter. It explains gravity and electric and magnetic fields; how they can be physical realities, and how they could work.

Space Lattice Theory supports a "big bang-like" beginning for a 3-D "visible" universe, explaining how it could easily emerge from what appears to be the nothingness of space, but without having to change any laws of physics. Puzzles like the particle-wave nature of photons are explained. Problems with current theories for subatomic particles, cosmology and Special Relativity are discussed. New models are suggested.

Most significantly, Space Lattice Theory presents a model for a comprehensive Grand Unification of all forces and matter in the universe.

Keywords: Structure, Matter, Energy, Gravity, Electro-magnetism, photon dualism, singularity, big bang, relativity

1. The Inspiration

In 2004, the 100th anniversary of Einstein's Special Relativity paper, I was reading an article by Dr. Lee Smolen that reviewed Einstein's idea that gravity could be visualized as a fabric in space. Einstein, as we know, suggested that a mass in space could be visualized as a "knot" in the fabric. This has always been unsettling for me because knots in a fabric don't move. An alternate concept appeared in my mind based on my experience with electric current flow and metals. This concept led to Space Lattice Theory. [1]

Electric current is well established as the "flow" of electrons. But on the atomic scale, in order for electrons to move through a conductor, a number of intermediate steps must occur.

First, the structure of the conductor must have atoms with electrons that can be easily removed from the atomic structure leaving an atom with a missing electron (valence). Second, an electric field must be established to apply a force on the electrons. Once the field exists, an electron in one atom, which is adjacent to an atom that is missing an electron, can jump out of its current location to fill the adjacent valence. This, of course, just creates a new valence in the atom it came from. Another adjacent atom, with an available electron, can then supply an electron to fill that valence. To create a current, this process continues throughout the conductor essentially filling available valence "holes" and opening up other ones. From a distance, it would look like a bucket brigade.

For example, upon applying a voltage to a one meter horizontal copper wire, with the (+) terminal on the right, an estimated $4.4x10^9$ electrons have each moved a **single** atomic step right to release a single electron into the (+) terminal. From the standpoint of the "conductor" as a whole, however, it appears that a single electron jumped in from the left terminal (-) of the conductor and came out at the right end (+). Alternatively, however, the result can also be "interpreted" as a **single positive charge** jumping in from the right (+) and moving the **entire length** of the conductor to emerge at the left (-). In electronics, this "virtual" positive charge is called a "hole".

While this seems like a trivial mechanism, it presents some very important observations:

1. To free up just one single electron at the end of the conductor, the process requires that a huge number of electrons along a continuous path through the entire conductor, each move just one atomic spacing.
2. The jumps do not occur simultaneously. As in a bucket brigade, a valence opening must occur first in an atom, setting up a local field condition, before an adjacent electron can respond and move into the valence (hole).
3. From the standpoint of the overall conductor, (say 1 meter long), when one electron exits the wire into the (+) terminal, $4.4x10^9$ electrons each make a one atom jump toward the (+) terminal. **However**, in the same time period, it appears that one single **"virtual positive charge"** (a hole), moves the entire length of the conductor to the (-) terminal.
4. The average speed of electrons through a wire is actually quite slow - on the order of micro-meters per second. They jump quickly, but then stay bound to atoms for a long time before being involved in another jump. The virtual charge, however, moves very fast, as it passes along a continuous path from one jumping electron to another. In copper, this speed is about 52% of the speed of light.
5. Since electrons have mass, an electric current in a

metal conductor actually transfers mass through a solid in response to the presence of an **electric field**.

Materials, generally, also experience a similar "hole propagation" phenomenon at the molecular scale. In materials, the "holes" are referred to as "dislocations". They are created by misalignments of the material molecular and crystalline structures of adjacent crystals or polymers. The moving dislocations act like a lubricant between crystals and polymer molecules making the materials much weaker than single crystals or molecules. The dislocations are the enablers of crack propagation. Most important for SLT, the dislocations can be observed to move through the material in response to **physical stress fields**. What occurred to me that started this entire study was that Einstein's "knots" in the **fabric** of gravity, might in fact be "holes" or "dislocations", because they can move. The question was, could they also create the property we call mass. Without knowing where this would lead, I started to explore how such dislocations would have to work to explain each basic function of physics. Some concepts, like subatomic particles moving in a lattice initially seemed quite simple. But addressing specifics like photons and charges introduced very challenging complications. The dynamics and geometric constraints, however, turned out to be pretty narrowly bounded. Unlike complex principles such as string theory, the constraints were a benefit because they limit the alternatives needing analysis. The solutions required a lot of geometric modeling. The reason I continued was that, upon solving each difficult relationship, **new** and **simple** concepts emerged which explained some tough age-old questions in physics - like photons. This carrot-on-a-stick kept me going for over two years. The result was breathtaking.

2. The Discoveries

In summary, the reasons I now continue to share the discoveries are:

1. they provide **so many** new explanations for **major** enduring questions of physics
2. The are consistent with many well accepted conventional experimental and theoretical observations
3. They are all simple to visualize; and, most important,
4. The theory, as a whole, provides a **simple but comprehensive example of Grand Unification**. One single component, the Aa, assembles into a structure, that can produce the functionality we observe as mass, energy, all the fields, inertia, and explanations for how all of these interact.

3. The Aa

- The basic constituent of the universe is a very small object which I call an Aa. I have no observational evidence for the specific shape of an Aa. But after attempting to physically construct model lattices from many different Aa forms, taking into account both static and dynamic properties, one simple geometry, with precise proportions, appeared to work. It may be visualized as a simple dumbbell with two contacting equal spherical ends.
- The Aas are **unique**. No other objects or fields exist. They only occur in one form. Every property we observe in the universe is explained by them.
- Space is completely and densely filled with Aas. Unlike atoms and molecules, the Aas are in direct contact. They act as if they are under great compression, like a fluid pressure.
- The Aas contact each other at their ends. Due to their dumbbell shape, they self organize to create a "lattice" that fills the entirety of a conventional 3-dimensional space.
- The space lattice has local structure that appears like a single crystal. The Aas, however, are only held together by the pervasive cosmic pressure - like a liquid under pressure.
- There are NO attractive forces of any kind in the universe. On the scale we associate with visible mass (grains of sand, planets, stars, galaxies), the lattice appears amorphous. But the alignment of Aas in the structure are continuous over infinitely large ranges.
- An Aa does not exhibit **directly observable** properties because of its small size. However, it has mechanical properties similar to solids including elasticity and ballistic inertia. The Aas interact completely without friction.

4. Matter and Mass

Matter, or more specifically, any fundamental particle we observe, is **created** in space by an organized collection of dislocations or "holes" in the space lattice. Specifically, the property we call **mass is caused by a local grouping of dislocations in the framework of space**.

5. Matter Creation and Destruction

- The **creation of matter out of nothing** (the big bang) is easily handled by SLT. A buildup of stress in the space lattice, due to colliding waves in the lattice, can open a huge void in the lattice - a universal **space quake**. That would create an equivalent to the big bang. Without the prevailing lattice pressure, Aas would fall off the inner walls into the void. Matter would be created randomly as the void collapsed and Aas were trapped in distorted arrangements leaving many **dislocations**.
- SLT answers in simple form, a serious big bang question: how can matter expand out of a big bang singularity, which is essentially a major black hole? SLT suggests that the creation of matter occurred during the collapse of a large space void. It was never a singularity. As the void closed up, the inertia of the lattice imploding around the void, would cause an overpressure where the void occurred. This high pressure volume in the lattice, which actually defines the shape

of gravity, would appear as a huge antigravity field. This would propel the newly formed mass outward.

- The destruction of matter into nothing is also explained by SLT. This is the role and fate of **Black Holes**. As particles of mass, which are collections of "holes", fall into a Black Hole, the extreme gravity disassociates atoms to fundamental particles and then pushes the particles together. As the holes, which form the particles, are pushed together, they simple merge. The Aas from one particle also combine to fill the voids in other particles. The result is simply pure lattice. The reduction of the bending in the lattice due to the elimination of the holes reduces the effective gravity of the Black Hole.
  Ironically, while initially forming as an inescapable concentration of mass, at some limit, additional mass will just be "dissolved". In this SLT model, a Black Hole could become just a mass-limited steady state mass eater, balancing the effects of universal space quakes.
- **Particles** are formed by the stable associations of groups of dislocations. An infinite number of particle types can be created by varying the arrangements of dislocations. This would explain why we keep getting more particle types with stronger particle accelerators. Only specific arrangements, however, are stable due to the joining angle restrictions of the Aa. The physics of how the Aas can be captured in non-aligning patterns governs particle stability.
- Particles move by the propagation of stable collections of dislocations through the lattice.
- Particles can change form by rearranging their dislocations.
- **Atoms** are collections of particles.

6. Gravity - Force at a Distance

GRAVITY

The lattice is under a universal pressure. As mass is created by dislocations, the shape of the lattice in the area around the mass changes. As masses come together, a large distortion of the lattice shape occurs. The distortion is accompanied by a conventional, mechanical stress-strain "field" in the Lattice. This stress-strain pattern is what we interpret as gravity.

If two collections of mass are brought together, as they approach, the **field structures** of their lattice distortions interact. The distortion around a dislocation has **less** stress than undisturbed lattice. The interaction of the fields from two masses causes the lattice field **between** the structures to become the sum of the two fields, thereby exhibiting less strain than the volume of the lattice beyond the masses. This non-spherical imbalance causes a force that **pushes** the masses together.

That is, masses are pushed together by the imbalanced pressure of a mass-warped lattice; they are not pulled together by some attractive means. This supports Einstein's view of gravitation as a warped field in space.

Unlike General Relativity, however, SLT also suggests that the value of gravity is limited, both at its upper level and at low levels. The upper limit is caused by the limited ability to geometrically distort the Lattice. This happens at the very small dislocation level. It therefore denies the existence of gravitational singularities. The lower limit occurs at great range due to the ability of events to disrupt lattice continuity. SLT also suggests that gravity can be manipulated by artificially introducing or eliminating voids (mass).

FORCE AT A DISTANCE

One of the greatest puzzles in all of physics, is explained in a simple way by SLT.

A **vacuum**, on the macro scale, does not actually produce a suction force. The force we observe is caused by a **pressure** which is not equally opposed. SLT suggests that the same concept in the universe explains **all** forces at a distance. Force occurs at a distance because the lattice structure is continuous. The effect of lattice bending at any point extends to infinity in all directions. The force decreases as the **square of the distance**, simply because the strain of the bending is expanding into the "far field" as a volume with spherical geometry.

7. Antimatter

In SLT, the term "anti-matter" means **true** "anti-**matter**". It is not the same as the conventional concept of similarly structured particles with opposite polarity electric charge (which should more accurately be referred to as anti charge). While an Aa missing from the lattice causes a pushing-in of the lattice to fill the missing space, a case may also occur where an additional Aa gets forced into the lattice. This would push the lattice outward around the extra Aa. This would produce the property we would call **anti-gravity** (not anti-charge).

Interesting dynamics result. In the formula $Fg = -Gm1 * m2/r^2$, conventional masses m1 (+mass) and m2 (+mass) attract. But, mass (+) and antimass (-) would repel. Ironically, we then find that antimass (-) and antimass (-) also attract! This suggests that space might contain substantial size antimatter objects. Their interaction with mass would be to repel it! So, there might exist entire antimass galaxies. The problem is, they would be very hard to see because if light is thought to exhibit mass (+) properties, it would be deflected from the antimatter. Instead of antimatter "black holes", the same geometric object made of antimatter would be an antimatter MIRROR!

If we could somehow force matter and antimatter to collide, the excess Aas in the antimatter might fill in the holes of the matter. The result would be the complete annihilation of both particles, with the production of substantial energy. But ONLY energy. This would be entirely distinct from the standard model anti-charge annihilations observed.

Ironically, during an SLT "big bang", there would **not** have to be the creation of an equal amount of SLT antimatter, because the collapsing void could preferentially trap "hole" dislocations independent of "inclusion" dislocations. (which is what we observe in the universe).

8. Photons and Nuclear Energy Transformation

PHOTONS in SLT are independent single dislocations in the lattice. They are typically created by a change in the internal structure of a particle which ejects a single dislocation from the structure. The dislocation is ejected with an associated energy package that may possibly be in the form of an enclosing rolling toroid (smoke ring). In SLT, the property of a photon that discriminates it from a bulk wave (radio wave) in the Lattice is its **ability to transfer mass**.

This model has a number of consequences. Being a dislocation, a photon has inherent mass. Having mass, it reacts as mass in a gravity field. An ejected photon removes mass from the ejecting particle. The photon travels without expanding because it is a single dislocation. Typically, it travels through the lattice until it interacts with another particle in a way that it can add a single element dislocation to the other particle. When that happens, the photon disappears, and **mass** is added to the encountered particle.

The SLT model, however, suggests many new properties for the photon. The photon is not a wave. It does not have a wavelength. Wave like behavior only occurs when it interacts with matter or other photons. What appears as a wave property is actually an energy transfer behavior related to its energy packet. The photon does not lose energy as a $1/r^2$ loss because of the toroidal shape of its propelling energy packet. It does lose energy, however, due to the interaction of the energy packet and the lattice. This, SLT suggests, is the primary cause of the linear component of the Hubble Constant. The loss of energy to the lattice is a primary contributor to the Cosmic Microwave Background. But, most unexpectedly, SLT suggests that the photon can slow to zero speed. At that speed, it's energy packet has been exhausted. It no longer has sufficient energy to interact with atoms or fundamental particles. And since it is so small, it can't be detected using conventional techniques. It does, however, still have mass, and may exist in great quantity in the universe. This makes it a prime candidate for dark matter and scavenging by black holes. Photons explain the transition mechanism from mass to energy and $E = mc^2$. Photon E actually has 2 components: the energy of a photon's propelling energy packet plus the energy of the photon's rest mass moving at the speed "c". Mass converts to energy by ejecting a dislocation as a photon. Photon energy converts to mass when a particle captures a photons energy packet and dislocation mass.

9. Electric Charge

Electric charge is a component that is added on to particles. It is an arrangement of dislocations that cause a **pancake twisting distortion** of the lattice. The twist can appear in two forms: + and - . The twist does not introduce a density change in the lattice, so it does not appear as mass. The twist only affects other particles that also introduce a twist. This property allows electric charge and gravity to overlap in the lattice without affecting each other to the first order.

10. Electro-Magnetics (E-M)

- SLT provides very descriptive models for how both electric charge and magnetism work. All magnetic effects are due to moving charges, and the magnitude of the effects are relative to motion with respect to the Lattice.
- The phenomenon classical electrodynamics refer to as ELECTROMAGNETIC WAVES, are actually multiple distinct phenomenon. Unlike photons, E-M waves are not able to transfer mass. Ultra-violet light may mark the crossover from radio waves to photons. The property referred to as **light**, is primarily E-M waves.
- E-M waves are simple **twisting** vibrations of the lattice caused by the motion of electric charges. E-M waves spread geometrically, are subject to $1/r^2$ loss, and can dissipate to zero amplitude.
- Refractive Index: The lattice fills the intervening volume between the fundamental particles in the atom and between atoms. The structure of the lattice is "regularly amorphous". This means it has a structure that is intimately dependent on the atoms surrounding it. The increased disorder of the lattice requires light waves to take circuitous paths through materials, decreasing propagation speeds. This also explains how light waves can resume their speed as they emerge from matter. They just enter less disturbed lattice.
- E-M Induction: Lattice elements must move in response to electric charge motion. All lattice motions are dynamically (time) regulated by the Lattice Relaxation Response (LRR). The LRR measures the rate that a pattern of compressed Aas will return to their normal state. This is due to the ratio of elasticity to inertia of the Aa in compression. The inherent impedance of space to radio wave generation is a measure of the LRR for forced twisting. The speed of E-M waves (including light) is a measure of the LRR for compression recovery. The magnetic induction and capacitive constants are based on the same mechanism.
- E-M waves follow gravitational bending in the lattice. This is due to refractive effects in a distorted Lattice, however, not gravitational effects.

11. The Aether

The Space Lattice is the aether. The shape of the Space Lattice produces gravity. But the shape of the Lattice is dynamically dependent on the collection of mass in it. As the earth moves through the Lattice, the Lattice inside and around the earth interacts with the earth. The earth has sufficient mass to drag the Lattice. The drag near the planet surface is significant. (Michelson - Morley measured an aether speed of about 76,600 km/hr. which is lower than the earth orbital velocity of 108,000 km/hr.) Measurements using the Michelson - Morley approach show higher aether speeds with increased distance above sea level (Dayton Miller).

- SLT accepts and explains the Lorentz effects on dimensional lengths due to motion with respect to the aether. These effects are caused by the Lattice Relaxation Response.
- A re-evaluation of the Hafele - Keating data shows agreement with SLT to less than 3% error.

12. Grand Unification

SLT is a mechanical aether model. SLT suggests that the universe is entirely composed of tightly packed mechanical elements, referred to as Aas, that form a structured infinite universal Lattice. It is the ability of the Lattice, by itself, to simultaneously create the phenomena we call mass, energy, gravity, electro-magnetism, electro-statics, and the weak and strong nuclear forces that finally produces an opportunity for developing a Grand Unification theory for existance.

REFERENCES

1. Bruce Nappi, *Space Lattice Theory*, complete paper, www.a3society.org/Documents/Space_Lattice_Theory_Nappi_2015.pdf ■

Improving CNPS Effectiveness Through Structured Communication: Year 2

Bruce Nappi

16 Spinnaker Hill, Hull MA 02045, bnappi@A3RI.org

The internet is well accepted by society as a great technical milestone in human communication. In many ways, it is. But, as critical thinkers understand, this is just one more misleading mainstream generalization. When humans become a component of a communication system, information handling performance is severely limited. This is due to limits of human brains to manage large amounts of information, flaws in how society uses language, and serious emotional obstacles.

Modern science requires humans to analyze extremely complex information. Human brains have good capabilities to do that in quiet, undisturbed, unrushed environments. Evolved language skills, however, are best adapted to person-to-person dialog and single person oration. Unfortunately, the internet has focused on these "stream of consciousness" styles with formats like email, articles, article and commentary, blogs, and discussion forums. All of these are poor when communicating complex issues that require logical reasoning and exploration of novelty and hidden meanings.

At the 2016 CNPS conference, a presentation was made discussing the detailed limitations of conventional internet communication for scientific discussions. After the conference, some basic outlining tools were applied to an ongoing email discussion among some CNPS members. The goal was to verify and measure the extent of how the limitations were present in that discussion. This presentation explores the results of that study and describes new tools and approaches now being applied using the CNPS Forum to greatly improve cooperative analysis.

Keywords: analysis, communication, effectiveness, language, internet, science papers

1. Introduction

The internet is well accepted by society as a great technical milestone in human communication. In many ways, it is. But, as critical thinkers understand, this is just one more misleading mainstream generalization.

When humans become a component of a communication system, information handling performance is severely limited. This is due to limits of human brains to manage large amounts of information, flaws in how society uses language, and serious emotional obstacles.

Modern science requires humans to analyze extremely complex information. Human brains have good capabilities to do that in quiet, undisturbed, unrushed environments. Evolved language skills, however, are best adapted to person-to-person dialog and single person oration. Unfortunately, the internet has focused on these "stream of consciousness" styles almost exclusively with formats like email, articles, article and commentary, blogs, and discussion forums. All of these are poor when communicating complex issues that require logical reasoning and exploration of novelty and hidden meanings.

At the 2016 CNPS conference, a presentation was made discussing the detailed limitations of conventional internet communication for scientific discussions.[1] [2] [3] The annual CNPS conference is not the only time society members discuss issues. There are multiple methods for ongoing discussion and information sharing throughout the year. These include: Articles, Blogs, Books, Facebook, Testimonials, Video Podcasts, member videos, a Forum, Critical Wiki pages, and a number of email strings. The problem my paper raised was that the effectiveness of all of these approaches are severely limited by the issues discussed in the paper. I wanted to investigate this and see if there were ways our effectiveness could be improved.

The process I chose to investigate was the email discussions, because email is so popular and notoriously ineffective. The approach I planned to use included the following steps:

1. I was already included in a number of email groups. So, they would become the focus.
2. I would capture all the emails sent in these discussions as the subject of the study.
3. The baseline for effectiveness was pretty simple. No one involved in the discussions could point to documented results achieved by the discussions. So the study had two objectives. One was to explore how the discussions were falling apart. The second was to try to guide the discussion to some effective conclusions that would lead to publications.
4. I was offered the use of software from Professor Mark Klein at MIT that I had used successfully with other groups. The software was designed to facilitate discussions by organizing them as debates. The software was customizable. So this allowed including methods that were directly aimed at the material under discussion.

This paper explores the results of that study and describes how the results are now being applied using the new CNPS Forum to improve the cooperative efforts of the members.

2. Conclusions

The main conclusions of the study were:

1. Participants put a lot of time into these discussions. Over the 338 day sample period, 63 participants sent 6968 emails. This is an average of 20.6 emails per day.
2. It is hard to accurately measure the effort that was expended because the emails vary so widely in amount of content. The amount varies from single phrases to dozens of pages with analysis, graphs and references. Based on the estimating method discussed below, I estimated that the group of participants on the email discussion expended 15,887 hours of effort over the 338 day period. This is a rate of 17,156 hours or 7.8 effort years per year.
3. Because there was no organized way to capture the thinking that was being generated, except for a few insights that were achieved by a few members, the knowledge produced in this process has all been lost to the Internet Landfill!

3. Basic Statistics

The email discussion is an un-moderated interchange of views of CNPS members supposedly aimed at exploring issues in mainstream science that members don't believe are accurate descriptions of nature. The discussions are open to anyone who is recommended to participate by any current member of the discussion. So this includes both CNPS members and non members. There are no "rules" that participants must agree to for participation. Tolerance is quite high, which makes both "lively" discussions at times, but also, a tolerant environment for participants to push all the edges of current scientific belief. This, thus fulfills one of CNPS's major goals.

Here are some basic variables for the study:

- Duration: 338 days - July 7, 2016 through June 9, 2017.
- The number of email addresses with To: addresses: 43 to 77 (readers)
- Maximum number of participants listed with From: addresses: 63 (posters)
- The participants were involved almost every day, especially on weekends, and posted at all hours of the day from countries around the world.
- Total emails captured: 6968
- Average post rate: 20.6 emails per day!
- Number of distinct Subject: titles: 194
- Maximum number of attachments: 14
- Total number of emails with attachments: 2196
- Total number of attachments: 5113
- Size of messages: smallest 1.1K; largest 29.1M

4. Analysis

Calculation of basic statistics

The basic statistics allow making multiple observations. The observations become more meaningful when seen on a graph.

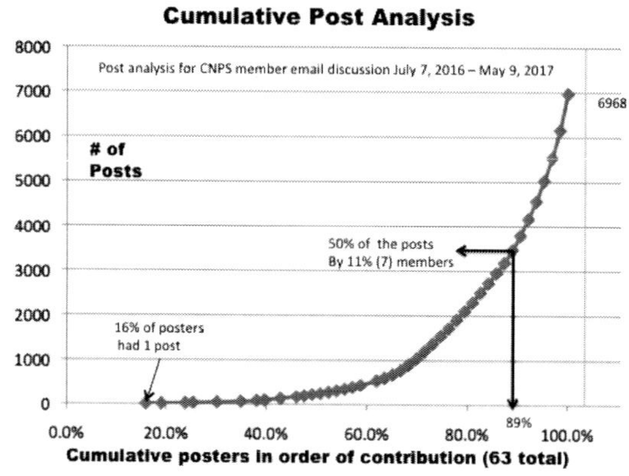

Figure 4. Cumulative # of posts vs % of posters

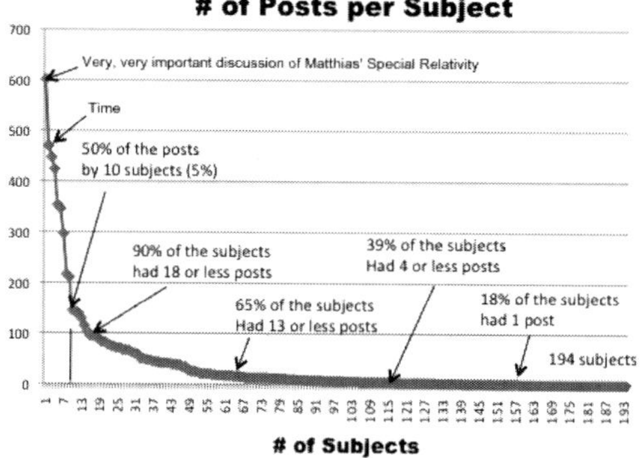

Figure 5. Number of posts for each subject discussed

1. Participants put a lot of time into these discussions. Over the 338 day sample period, there were 6968 emails. This is an average of 20.6 emails per day.
2. Based on the effort analysis shown below, the participants, as a group, expended 15,887 hours of effort over the 338 day period. This is a rate of 17,156 hours or 7.8 effort years per year.
3. There were 77 distinct email addresses (the To: address list) that showed up over the time period. Of these, 63 participants posted comments or initiated subjects. As a point of reference, the new CNPS Forum, which has now been alive for 5 months has a member list with 42 names.
4. The graph titled Cumulative Post Analysis shows the distribution of number of posts per participant. Par-

ticipants contributed from 0 to 813 emails each. Most participants only posted a few times. Each data point on the graph represents a cohort of participants that posted the same number of posts. 18% of those on distribution were only readers. They do not show up on the graph. The first data point at lower left is for the cohort making a single post. 16% of the posters (10 posters) only posted a single time. The next data point is for the cohort making 2 posts (2 posters). Each point after that represents a cohort making a higher number of posts. Each of these cohorts had from 1 to 3 people. The x-scale plots the percent of posters

5. The number of posts in the first 10 cohorts were: 1,2,3,4,5,6,11,12,19,21, each indicated by a data point. The number of posts for the last 7 cohorts (each single members) were: 324, 379, 398, 459, 505, 625, 813.
6. While the posted content of many emails are very short (only one line, for example) many are also very long, going on for many pages. Simple message sizing is not helpful to analyze this for two reasons: a. the inclusion of attachments, and b. the inclusion of prior posts when members hit "reply".

Effort estimate

Making an estimate of the amount of time participants have put into the email effort is very time consuming. Each email is so different. To get a gross number, I used the emails for the subject "Atomic Clocks At Sea Level". I chose a short 3 day run near the middle of the discussion (from May 1 to May 3, 2017) which included 24 emails. I extracted the content.

The text of the posts varied from 3 lines to 112 lines with the average being 22 lines. To get an effort estimate, we have to take into account the amount of time taken to create each email, but also the amount of time it took other participants to read it. Reading habits are very erratic. Some people read everything. Others only read topics they are interested in. Some are on travel and just delete blocks of posts when the get back.

Reading a line of text takes about 6 seconds for a short comment. As the email grows longer, reading gets more complicated. It takes time to understand equations. It takes time to relate concepts from one paragraph to the next. The same principle applies to both reading and writing. Including the literature research needed to produce a long email, along with associated graphics and attachments, the process can take many hours. To model this process, I used the following assumptions from timing myself going through the process:

- Short, simple sentences take about 6 seconds to read. This same value applies for small paragraphs of up to about 10 lines, which takes about 1 minute to read.
- A long post, of about 100 lines takes about 4 times as long per line, including repeat readings, side calculations and outside reading.
- While there is only one email creator, there are many readers. I scanned the entire 424 emails to find everyone who posted to the subject and counted them as readers. In this case, there were 18.

I produced the following simple equations by curve fitting a number of selected cases: (n = the number of text lines in an email)

- The time to read an email in minutes = 6 x $(LOG(n))^2\ x\ (n)/60\ \{1\}$
- The time to write an email in minutes = 6 x $(LOG(n))^{3.4}))\ x\ (n)/60\ \{2\}$
- Attachments were evaluated on a case by case basis. Graphics take a long time; pasting reference documents only around 5 minutes. {3}
- Total time per email = {1} x (# of readers- 18 in this case) + {2} + {3}

The results for these 24 emails, including all participants reading the posts, were:

- The shortest email: 19 minute.
- The longest email: 17 hours
- The average time: 2.28 hours
- The total effort for the group to write and read these 24 emails: 54.7 hours!

Discipline of staying on topic

The ability email discussions to stay on topic is very weak. My participation as mostly an observer in the discussions confirmed this. As an example, I will again use the popular subject: "Atomic Clocks At Sea Level", that had a long run from March 26 to June 1, including 424 emails. This subject heading first appeared on March 26 when one member quoted a February 26 post by Ron Hatch, one of the CNPS experts on atomic clocks and GPS.

Post 1 described the intent of the new subject, but also created a lynch-pin for staying on topic right from the beginning: poor title. Atomic Clocks are complex instruments. When a subject for discussion is too general, the stage is set to subdivide it. In the very first post, the poster did just that with 5 sub-topics 1. What is the basic clock mechanism that causes clock rate variation? 2. How do environmental factors affect clock rate? 3. Are atomic clocks primarily sensitive to velocity and gravitation? 4. If clock rates are affected by velocity and gravity, how can you say they run the same rate everywhere at sea level? 5. Can you explain how the earth flattens at the poles due to earth's spin?

Post 2, while mentioning the sub-topics of the first post, also had its own axe to grind. The poster picked up on a statement in Ron's source document which claimed that the poster was, "unable to recognize that scalar measurements can be measured in different sized units." The problem with this was that it triggered an old rivalry between aether and relativity adherents. The poster responded, "Even high school students know that what distinguishes scalar measurements IS NOT different sized units, but IS the frame of motion (v) of the measurer." While I took that as typical humorous rivalry, others took it as a call to arms. Adding another complication, the poster also copied his post to the CNPS Forum, thus launching a second discussion path.

Post 3 focused on keeping the discussion focused, not on any scientific question.

Post 4 did not appear for 2 weeks. It was from the author of post 1. It tried to narrow the discussion around his issue 5, but further expanded that asking why the bulge of water at the equator is counter acted by the change of gravity in a way that Atomic Clock rates do not vary. He then introduced an observation from some other discussion, that I was not on distribution for, which stated that "forces are not involved". Instead there is an "equipotential surface" at sea level. The poster replied this cannot be true because the "gravitational potentials" must be different - not realizing that the "equipotential" statement from the other discussion was not claimed to be just from gravity. He also didn't realize that the "equipotential surface" was not a real physical construct, but merely a mathematical convenience.

Post 5 headed off on a different concern. The poster, an ardent relativist, did not want someone slipping a "speculative aether" into the discussion, suggesting that quantum mechanics must be included.

Post 6 and 7 jumped in supporting Ron's statements and asked why the author of post 1 doesn't understand them.

Post 8 dug into the fine structure of the equations for both gravity and earth bulge and said the math does not precisely add up to cancel out. This began a long series of arguments about what equations are correct.

Post 19 tried to turn the focus to the physics of the atom that is being changed by outside forces.

Post 20 raised the issue that Newton only assumed that inertial and gravitational mass are the same. The post claimed they aren't.

The discussion then see-sawed back and forth about every one of these issues, eventually pulling in things like black holes. And, as a whole, this discussion was much more focused than most. In the end, however, the better observations were still lost to the Internet Landfill.

Tools applied to the discussion

After the 2016 CNPS Conference, some basic outlining tools were applied to the ongoing email discussion about subjects related to relativity. This discussion was also wandering far afield. It started on Aug 28, 2016 and ran until November 2, 2016 with 602 emails. In an attempt to focus the discussion, I brought in an outline mapping tool provided by MIT professor Mark Klein called the Deliberatorium. Here is a list of key subtopics that came up during that discussion that were significant enough to merit their own branch on the MAP.

- Definitions: There was not agreement on the following definitions
  - Aether
  - Clock
  - ECI Earth-centered inertial frame
  - Frame of Reference
  - Frame Equivalence
  - Frames - Inertial, Lorentz, Special Relativity, Starting, Stay-at-home, Zero Momentum
  - GPS Global Positioning System
  - Gravity
  - Gravitational warping
  - Light
  - Lorentz Relativity
  - Net Proper Time Dilation
  - Relative motion (relative velocity)
  - Simultaneity
  - Space-Time curvature
  - Special Relativity
  - Stellar aberation
  - Time dilation clock retardation
  - Twin Paradox
  - Twin Paradox - classic
  - Twin - Stay-at-home
  - Twin - traveling
- The relevance of math vs physics
- Theory Validation requires empirical validation
- Does science understand the physical universe?
- How can CNPS approach clarifying problems with SR?
- How does relativity address that reality requires absolute existence and motion
- Specific Special Relativity (SR) Issues
  - SR is measurement error, not absolute physical reality. (The Twin Paradox, The Fast Light Paradox)
  - Empirical evidence exists that disputes SR (The GPS problem)
  - Moving Observer Paradoxes (The Twin Paradox, The Triplet Paradox)
  - SR misunderstanding: Einstein presented SR, not as a principle, but to discredit the concept of light speed being relative to all observers
  - Over 1300 papers have been published disproving SR (The Sapere Aude Study)
  - Every entry in the definitions list above

These subtopics from the discussion were made available to the discussion members in a user interactive online graphic format shown in the following figures. What the interactive format provides is a way for members to view a high level index of what has been discussed. They can then drill down on any heading by just clicking on the black circles with a (+) sign. When they open, subheadings appear. The black circles with (-) signs close that branch.

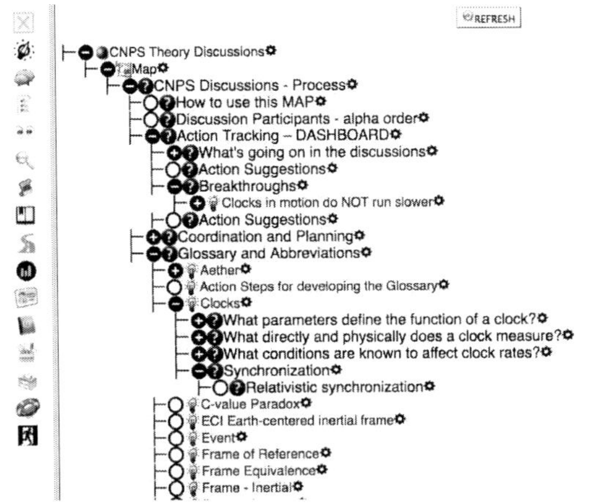

Figure 6. Section of expanded MIT Deliberatorium MAP

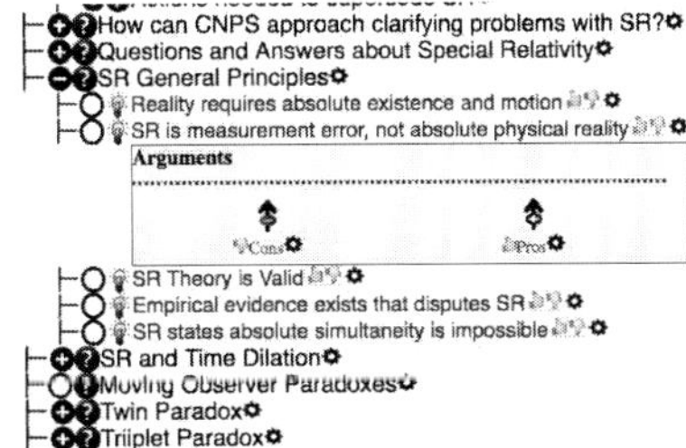

Figure 7. Expanded MIT MAP with pros and cons

This MAP was invaluable to new people joining the discussion because the prior emails for all the discussions had been captured and summarized in an organized index. It was valuable to discussion veterans because it provided a map of what they had discussed.

The tragedy of this email discussion, like most other email discussions, was that, before implementing the MAP, the knowledge and wisdom uncovered during the discussion was lost to the Internet Landfill. In this case, the insights I was able to capture are all still available in the MAP. A process, however, will be needed to move that information into a more permanent repository.

Carrying the MIT MAP tools forward into the CNPS Forum

A discussion held in Forum format provides better features for the organization and retention of knowledge. CNPS had a forum application before. A major attraction of email over a forum is the simple convenience of a post intrusively showing up in a person's in-box. The old forum software did not have an option for that. New forum software was enabled in January 2017 primarily to provide automatic notification to participants that a new post had been made to topics they were following. But, I also had another goal: to implement the MIT outline model right in the forum. The forum software did not support that. It only had 3 levels of outlining. I developed a "virtual nesting" approach, which allows unlimited outline levels to overcome this obstacle. The Forum is now operational with the virtual nesting process to implement the key elements of "structured discussion", specifically: 1. A fully indexed subject list; 2. Coordination; 3. Tracking; 4. References; and 5. Indexed storage of discussions.

Where should the process go from here For the process to work, facilitators, paper writers and reference researchers are needed. The next step will be to recruit these resources.[4]

REFERENCES

1. Bruce Nappi, *The Internet Landfill*, Medium, Sept 21 2016, http://bit.ly/A3Society-The-Internet-Landfill
2. Bruce Nappi *Improving CNPS Effectiveness, 2016 CNPS Conference, Power Point Presentation*, http://www.a3society.org/Documents/CNPS-structured-communication.pdf
3. Bruce Nappi, *Improving CNPS Effectiveness*, 2016 CNPS Conference, Video, http://bit.ly/A3Society-Structured-Com-video
4. Bruce Nappi, *Overview of CNPS Structured Forums*, John Chappell Natural Philosophy Society, 2016. http://bit.ly/CNPS-Overview-Structured-Forums

The Highly Collimated Jet Streams of Quasars

2017 © Cameron Rebigsol

P.O. Box 872282, Vancouver, WA 98687, crebigsol@gmail.com

Basic facts common to quasars [1]:

1. Highly compact both in mass and energy [2],
2. Having a super massive material center,
3. Excluding the material center, the general existence of mass is in a state of plasma,
4. Rapidly spinning,
5. Periodical variation in luminosity,
6. Highly remotely located from Earth with high value of red shift.

In addition to the above common facts, a high percentage of quasars are also found containing jet streams [3]. The strange thing is that the jet always comes in a set, with one from the set pointing in the opposite direction of the other, and both jets are highly collimated.

As far as we know on Earth, to create highly collimated beams of light or particles, technology must rely on lenses; be they optical, mechanical, or electrostatic. Beams that can travel even in the order of millions of light years and still retain their high collimation in many cases should be beyond what artificial lens can handle, let alone that the lens must be able to withstand the destructively high energy that the lens must let through.

As a thumb of rule, the higher the energy content is found in any physical entity, the higher chance of randomness is associated with this entity. Special filtering mechanism must be present for orderly output of anything to come out of this entity. Without a lens-like arrangement, how would the jet stream of a quasar stay highly collimated and remain in pair? Could this pairing have anything to do with the quality of collimation in our interest? In other words, must the collimation rely on some mechanism that produces the pairing? Or, if no pairing were to be present, would the jet stream not be formed at all? In nature, action and reaction always coexist, so do matter and anti-matter, as well as electric and magnetic poles. How should we relate the phenomenon shown by the jet pair of opposite directions from the philosophical aspect in terms of physical interaction?

In modern science, when high energy and high speed are involved, it has been so natural for a big number of science workers to apply Einstein's Theory of Relativity [1] to explain many puzzles about which classic physics seems lead them to no solution. What is odd is that the jet streams from blazars, a special group of quasars, boldly present superluminal movement in our observation [5]. To those who trust relativity, they say superluminal movement so detected is only a mirage, an illusion. Obviously, quasars, with their extraordinarily high energy content, have challenged us with this dilemma: Should this superluminal movement serve as physical evidence to topple the validity of relativity, or should we once again allow our mental work to contort what we observe as illusion? Are we sure we should forever let our mental work overpower the physical world?

Keywords: plasma, spinning, electric field, magnetic field, neutron core, superluminal movement, relativity

1. Material Distribution in a Quasar Disk

The typical characteristics of a quasar include huge quantity of mass, extraordinary high rate of self-spinning, intensive heat and illumination, and having jet streams pointing away from it along the spinning axis of the quasar. The intensity of the heat and illumination alternates periodically. The heat and illumination from them can be so intense that, for example, a quasar named 3C 273 is said to shine in the sky as brightly as our Sun if it is placed at 33 light-years from us.

It may be considered controversial as to how the quasars to have obtained their power, both kinetic and electromagnetic, to begin each of their lives, nonetheless scientists all accept that the major substance state within the quasar is of hot plasma.

Rapid self-spinning is an inevitable consideration if no one can reject that the birth of a quasar is a result of some off-center collision between some huge quantities of mass. To give support to this speculation, many theories suggest that the Andromeda Galaxy and our own Milky Way Galaxy could collide and form a quasar someday in the remote future. If this becomes fact, a new and huge material formation inheriting a formidable residual angular momentum must be the result; its self-spinning shall be extraordinary. Let's simply imagine what amount of gravitational energy these two galaxies could contribute to the collision when their rectilinear movement must subsequently end at said collision; if the materials from both galaxies contract into a small conglomeration due to the overall elevation of gravitational force after the collision, the new formation so raised must spin at high angular velocity.

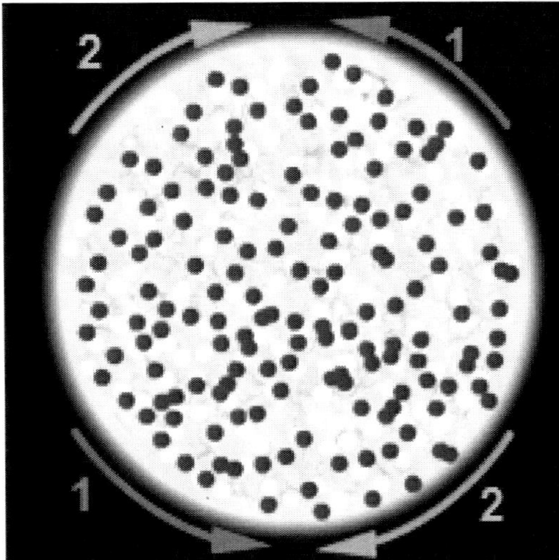

The disk could have spun in the red direction (1) or the green direction (2)

White Particles = Protons;
Dark Particles = Neutrons

Figure 8. A quasar disk at its early stage

In a plasma, all subatomic elementary particles, being in a charge state or neutral, just move in a "lawless" manner, declining any summoning for forming steady association from any others (Fig. 8). As to protons, with their pronounced mass as well as positive charge, they are potentially designated to concentrate at the outskirts of the spinning bulk as much as possible by two forces: Force one is the centrifugal force produced out of the spinning; force two is their own electrical repelling force they exert on each other. However, whether or not they would finally occupy that area would also be determined by another force: magnetic force. We will elaborate this further a little later.

Lacking the electrical repelling force, but with mass compatible to that of protons, neutrons stealthily move toward the central region of the spinning bulk. The sinking movement may be slow at the beginning, but gravitational principle would sooner or later accelerate this process, because a few of them have an opportunity to get closer than others and to come together forming small gatherings here and there. As such, tiny gathering of neutrons gradually increases its population across the entire plasma. Some gravitational predators would eventually come into shape and accelerate the aggregation processing until only one can exist and rein itself at the center of the plasma, or the quasar disk.

Lacking a repelling force between each neutron member, which grants the gravitational force an opportunity to dominate, is not the only reason for the neutron aggregate to become highly compact. Observation tells us that all neutron stars carry strong magnetism. Although the reason why neutron stars carry strong magnetism is not yet clear, the magnetism so unexceptionally carried by all of them, however, would tell us that any formation rich of neurons must be some potential candidate of magnetic body. Driven by the magnetic force, all the members in the aggregate must clench each other as much as possible. At the very early age of the quasar, when both the protons and the neutrons are spread across and thus share the same area, the bulk of protons and the bulk of the neutrons must also share about the same magnitude of angular momentum of the entire quasar. However, gradually the bulk of neutrons sinks into a small aggregate and become a core body at the center of the quasar. The original momentum possessed by the entire neutron bulk must now enable the small core to spin at a rate far above that of the bulk of the protons, which is the major material occupier of the far spread disk. In other words, the spinning revolution rate between the neutron core and the material bulk spreading away from the core are contrastingly different from each other.

Electrons, as an entire bulk of substance, may have two ranges in the disk for them to reside. If, as we mentioned above, the dynamic situation of the quasar disk happens to have the protons occupy the outskirt of the disk, the electrons will be located in and around the central region of the disk. If the dynamic situation of the quasar disk had designated the protons to stay about the central region, the electrons will take the outskirt. Which of these two types of mass distribution would prevail is solely determined by one dynamic factor: The spinning direction of the neutron core that is a strong magnetic body.

With all that is illustrated above, an observer stationary to the outskirt of the quasar disk can have two different dynamical views in his observation, depending on which spinning direction of the neutron core appears in his detection. Fig. 9 would tell him that he may have detected either clockwise or counterclockwise direction for the neutron core if he takes a bird's eye-view on the disk while facing the north magnetic pole of the neutron core. If, for example, the neutron core spins in a counterclockwise direction, as shown in the left diagram in Fig. 9, the magnetic flux from the core will herd all the positive charge particles, majorly protons, to go far away from the core and thus stay at the outskirt of the quasar disk. Likewise, electrons are herded to stay in the central region about the core by the same flux. If the core is found to spin in opposite direction, the protons and electrons will change their residing locations.

2. Formation of the Jet Streams

In the upcoming paragraphs, the illustration focuses on one dynamical situation: The spinning of the core has caused the central region to be the place where the major bulk of protons is found, while the electrons stay at the outskirt of the disk. So, naturally in such situation, the central region of the quasar can only be an electrical field of exceedingly strong positive potential. Any positively charged

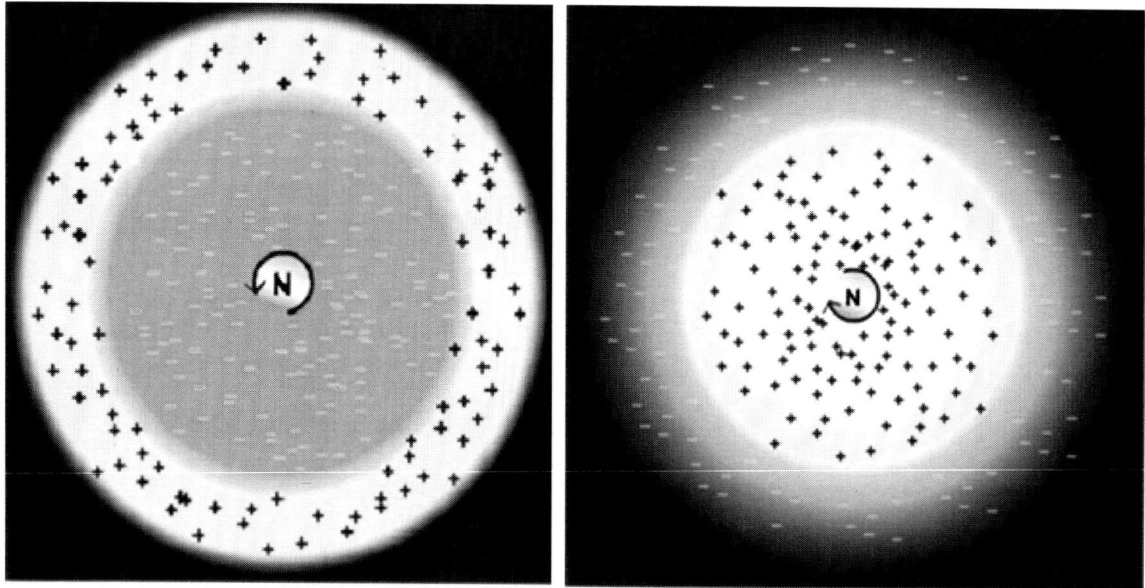

"+" = Protons; "–" = Electrons; "N" = Neutron Core. Viewer is stationary with the outskirt of the disk but directly faces the North pole of the magnetic field generated by the neutron core.
!!! Different rotation direction of the core causes different distribution of the charge particles !!!

Figure 9. Bird's Eyeview on a Quasar Disk

particle entering this region would be compelled to move along a designated direction by two forces: (1) electrical repelling force and (2) electromagnetic force. While force (1) should result in an isotropic scattering movement, force (2) would decline any scattering movement but confine all particles to move along the axis of the magnetic field as much as possible. Both forces working together then compel the particle to leave the disk with high speed but at a definite direction; a jet stream is thus constructed. The force for the positive particles to leave the disk is so strong that no gravitational force can ever hinder their movement. Force (2), being produced by a spinning magnetic field, causes a helix path to appear in the jet for the movement of the protons. With the same reason that one jet stream can be constructed on one side of the disk, another jet must also be constructed on another side of the disk. This is why jet streams always appear in pair for the quasars.

With more protons or other positive particles having departed from the quasar, nothing else can play the role to retain the excessive electrons to continue staying with the disk; they must evaporate from the quasar under their own mutual repelling force in addition to the expelling force generated by the spinning magnetic field. The more positive particles that have left through the jet, the more electrons will subsequently vaporize. Gradually, more and more loss of mass will bring the quasar to meet its day of disappearance, leaving only its neutron core, namely, a neutron star, to witness the historical location of the bygone quasar (if its red shift receding movement from us is not taken into consideration).

In a likewise manner, but with opposite spinning direction of a quasar's core with respect to an observer stationary to the outskirt, it would be the electrons that have been "jailed" in the central region of the quasar disk and to form the jet stream as shown in the diagram on the right of Fig. 10; protons are now located at the outskirt.

3. Alternating Luminosity

As the plasma rapidly spins, the protons, or other positive particles, must oscillate between two distances with respect to the neutron core. They are either moving closer and closer to the core or farther and farther away from it. Generally, they tend to move toward the core because of the overall gravitational pull of the entire quasar; the neutron core always exerts its pronounced gravitational influence on all materials at its vicinity as well. When the protons are too close, however, the electrical repelling force between each of them increases, and the centrifugal force on them also increases due to excessive angular momentum for an ever shortening spinning radius. When these two forces reach certain magnitude, the bulk of protons must begin to push all elementary members to get away from each other; the bulk then expands its territory. When the members get too far away, their rotation about the core slows down and the distance between each particle increases. Subsequently, the centrifugal force is reduced and their mutual electrical repelling force is weakened. Then the gravitational force once again dominates their movement, pulling them back toward the center. This back and forth moving pattern of protons must be persistent and will

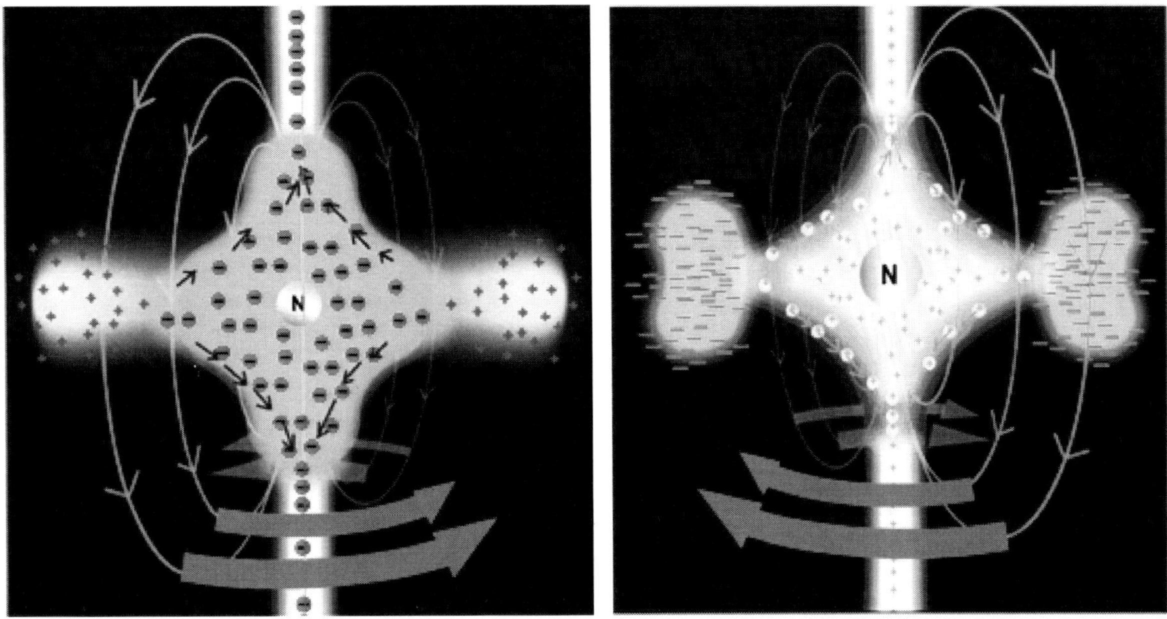

The direction of a spinning magnetic field has not only caused different material distribution in a quasar disk, but it has also inevitably caused different substance to form the jet streams

Figure 10. The Formation of Jet Streams

not lose itself no matter whether the protons have occupied the outskirt or the central region of the quasar disk to start the oscillation. Of course, whether the protons have occupied the central region or the outskirt to begin the oscillation will cause a different amplitude as well as different extremes of the amplitude with respect to the center of the quasar for the oscillation. The aforementioned oscillation causes the periodical alternation of a quasar's brightness. The closer the material members of the plasma get to each other, the more illumination of the quasar is concentrated at a smaller area, making the quasar appear brighter, and conversely, dimmer during the period of expansion as the same amount of illumination being diluted in a bigger area.

As of today, about 200,000 quasars are detected at distance of billions of light-years from us. Given the remote distance they are from us, the reason they can show up in our observation is because of their extraordinary power output. The power of some of them, called blazars, are so strong that superluminal motions of the jet materials are seemingly displayed in our observation. It is due to relativity that such superluminal motion is declined to be accepted as a reality, but instead, explained as an illusion. Should the science world rely more heavily on the observation, or more on a theory? How could we trust that relativity is able to seamlessly bridge us between reality and human being's mental work? What if relativity is found having unsalvageable mistake in its mathematical derivation such as that it must lead itself to end up with speed of light $c=0$?

4. Relativity's inability in dealing with speed

Unfortunately to the theory of relativity, its mathematical derivation does display lacking proper credibility in explaining movement; with its own mathematical derivation, relativity must end up with a conclusion showing speed of light being nothing else but $c=0$. This conclusion so arrived is because relativity relies on an equation set that is implicitly conditioned to be solved with speed $v=0$.

Any reader interested in pursuing this issue is cordially invited to refer to the article **Relativity Is Self-defeated** (1 of 3) by *Cameron Rebigsol*, which can be found in the 2016 Proceedings of John Chappell Natural Philosophy Society (http://www.naturalphilosophy.org/site/), or at Rebigsol's website *www.huntune.net*.

With $v=0$ so preconditioned for the relativity's equation set, another serious mathematical consequence must present itself troubling relativity's validity. The consequence is that, because of the permanent condition $v=0$, no nonzero differential operator dx or ∂x can be established, where x represents the numerical coordinates on a linear spacial dimension, along which movement is supposed to be found. Immediately following this outcome is that all calculus operations in relativity relying on the variation of x must find no legitimacy to exist.

If relativity cannot dissociate itself from the two consequences mentioned above, i.e, (1) $c=0$ and (2) no calculus operation being possible, it can hardly convince us how to follow it to visualize the superluminal movements as illusions.

If relativity must disable itself, no other existing theory else is found to stand in the way obstructing us from accepting superluminal movement out of blazars in our observation as being factual.

5. Energy Source of Superluminal Movement

According to documents, quasars usually appear not much bigger in volume than the solar system, which can have a radius as large as 30 AU (Neptune's mean orbital radius). It then means that some electrical charge in the quasar disk can have an opportunity of being at a distance of 30 AU away from the neutron core. When it is swept toward the neutron core by the spinning magnetic field, it has a path of 30 AU to gain and accumulate kinetic energy during the movement toward the axial line of the ever escalating magnetic field. This field is not only a strong one by any measure, but also rapidly spins with a rate, the spinning rate of the neutron core, in the order of several hundred turns per second for many of the quasars. When this particle is finally delivered near the axial line of the magnetic field and then expelled as part of the jet stream, the huge energy it has ever so accumulated must now propel this charge particle to move with extraordinary speed.

Let's qualitatively examine some moving potentials that observations have been offering us so far. The energy $\boldsymbol{E}$ that a charge particle $\boldsymbol{q}$ can acquire from the movement of a magnetic field of strength $\boldsymbol{B}$ is

$$\begin{aligned} E &= \int_a^b F \cdot dR \\ &= \int_a^b qvB \cdot dR \end{aligned} \tag{1}$$

In Eq. (9), dR is the distance element of the entire moving path R of the charge. R covers a distance from point a to point b, where a can be as large as 30 AU suggested by observation and b can be any infinitesimally small value. Besides 30 AU being a formidable distance in the equation for a charge to be accelerated, speed v in the equation can be another astounding figure. This speed v, which is tangential to R, is the relative speed between the moving magnetic flux and the charge particle q. Let's assume the relative difference of the angular velocity between the neutron core and the material bulk of the disk to be 400 revolutions/second. At 30 AU, the linear speed v matching this angular velocity will be $1.13x10^{13}$ km/second, a value in front of which the speed of light is absolutely dwarfed. When E is obtained with all these extraordinary figures and converted to kinetic energy according to $E = 1/2mV^2$, where V is the velocity for the charge particle pointing directly at the center of the quasar, can we imagine what value V can reach? It is equipped with this energy that the charge particle is found riding on the jet and leaving the quasar disk! It is with the speed enabled by this magnitude of energy that a jet stream takes good care of its collimation because particles of the same electrical charge moving in the same direction must keep their traveling path staying together; the higher the speed, the longer the parallelism will survive. This is why blazars can shows collimated jets of millions of light years long.

Of course, the understanding of Eq. (9) actually needs to be restricted by two more considerations. (1) We cannot be certain whether the assumed figure of 30AU is the dimension covering the area including even the most outskirt of the disk or just the "ball" of the same charge hovering about the neutron core. But even if 30 AU is for the entire quasar disk while only 20 AU is for the ball of the same charge, such huge ball of the same charge is an astonishing phenomenon to be comprehended with our daily experience obtained on Earth. (2) The relative tangential speed $1.13x10^{13}$ km/second between the magnetic flux and the charge particle at 30 AU should not be a value obtained as straightforwardly as we have shown. Because of the manner of propagation of electromagnetic waves, the angular speed of the flux corresponding to the revolution rate of the neutron core but at a distance 30 AU away from the core must be substantially lagging behind, and the corresponding linear speed is then substantially lower than $1.13x10^{13}$ km/second. However, further discussion on the nature of propagation of electromagnetic waves is not in the scope of this paper. Therefore the quantitative discussion on Eq. 9 with precise detail is unable to be explored in this paper. However, the qualitative conjecture based on all these possibilities presented so far should have made us feel difficult not to accept the superluminal movements as a material fact; neither can any theory prevent us from accepting it as material fact.

REFERENCES

1. wikipedia, ***Quasar*** Publisher: https://en.wikipedia.org/wiki/Quasar,
2. Egret team, ***Gamma-Ray Quasar*** Publisher: https://apod.nasa.gov/apod/ap981226.html
3. Giles Sparrow and Dava Sobel, ***Cosmos,*** *a Field Guide* Publisher: Quercus, UK 2016
4. Albert Einstein, ***On the Electrodynamics of Moving Bodies,*** in **The Principle of Relativity**, published by Dover Publications, Inc. USA, 1923
5. Robert Naeye, ***Blazars and Active Galaxies,*** Publisher: https://www.nasa.gov/mission_pages/GLAST/science/blazers.html

The Solar System Resulted by Random Collision

2017 © Cameron Rebigsol

P.O. Box 872282, Vancouver, WA 98687, crebigsol@gmail.com

Hubble's Law is conventionally expressed with $v = H_0 D$, where v is the recessional speed of a celestial object, usually a galaxy, D is the distance between an observer and the recessing object, and H_0 is the so called Hubble's constant. However, while this equation does give a straight line diagram between v and D , no publication is found to have given convincing argument regarding what has led H_0 to be resulted. In other words, $v = H_0 D$ is only a convenient summary of phenomenon, but hardly an equation led to by genuine physical analysis.

However, work relying on genuine physical analysis does lead us to have one set of mathematical expression that can show a straight line relationship between recessional speed of heavenly bodies and their distance with respect to certain point in space. Such a mathematical expression set is listed below:

$$v_{n,i} = \frac{1}{1+1.5\alpha} v_i - \frac{\sqrt{2}\alpha}{\sqrt{(4+\alpha)(4+2\alpha)}} v_c \tag{2}$$

$$v_{n,o} = \frac{1}{1+1.5\alpha} v_i + \sqrt{\frac{4+\alpha}{2+\alpha}}\, v_c \tag{3}$$

where $\alpha = \frac{3n^2+3n+1}{n^3}$, and $v_i = v_{(n-1),o}$, while $\boldsymbol{n}$, representing distance, can be any positive integer, from 1 to infinity. It is the value of v_c embedded in these two equations that enables them to show how nature works out for the linear relationship between speed and distance to be established. Speed v_c herein involved is obtained according to $E = \frac{1}{2} m v_c^2$, where E is the energy released per unit mass m that takes part in a hydrogen fusion reaction. Obviously, v_c is the spine in the above two equations. It is so not only because each equation must have it but also because each $v_{n,o}$ can be determined only after $v_{(n-1),o}$ at a distance $(n-1)$ prior to $\boldsymbol{n}$ has been determined, where $v_{(n-1),o}$ is obtained according to the above two equations but with value of $(n-1)$.

A computer diagram charted according to the above equations will show a straight line of increasing speed $v_{n,o}$ *vs* distance $\boldsymbol{n}$, which is represented by the ordinate in the diagram while speed is represented by the abscissa. Distance $\boldsymbol{n}$ can carry any length unit, such as kilometer, light year, parsec, kilo parsec, and the straightness of the resulted line universally holds. In the computer charting, v_c is normalized as unit 1.

The computer charting done by this author according to the above equations is presented in Fig. 11 in the main text.

That Eq. 9 and Eq. 10 can be so developed and resulted is based on a hypothesis that the increasing speed of heavenly objects is a consequence of momentum accumulation of numerous fusion explosions of hydrogen of countless generations. The reactions are relayed and propagate through chain reaction in an isotropic manner starting from one point in every direction in the space. Letter $\boldsymbol{n}$ in the above equations not only represents distance, but it can also represent generations, with the higher number to mean younger generation. Of course, then, all these would further mean as well as require that, before the first explosion and light ever appeared in the universe, hydrogen as an "innocently" idle material would have been stocked all over in the boundless space. So stocked, the hydrogen can be homogeneously found everywhere with inevitable local irregularity, and such irregularity would not alter the appearance of Eq. 9 and Eq. 10. As to how the first ever explosion was ignited, it is also presented in the article **How Nature Has Formulated the Hubble's Law** at *www.huntune.net*. The key for such ignition is the persistent gravitation between any materials.

Explosions must result in chaos. More and more explosions can only generate wilder and wilder chaos. If the aforementioned hypothesis is ever factual, the Milky Way galaxy and subsequently the solar system would have been impossible not to be the products put up by such chaos. Above all, the Milky Way is found to be a salad bowl containing heavenly bodies as old as 13.5 billion years in age and something like our solar system that is believed to be about 4.6 billion of years young, not to mention that something far younger is also found. It is from such chaos we see the consistent reasons that can explain the wide variety of characteristics of the solar system listed in the following introduction.

Keywords: chaos, Sun, inner planets, tectonic plates, asteroid belt, Jupiter siblings, orbital plane

1. Introduction

1. The solar system's spinning direction about the Sun is opposite to the spinning direction of the Milky Way about its galactic center[1][2][1].
2. Most planets including the Earth's Moon and the asteroid belt as an entire group, must have their spinning direction the same as their orbital moving direction, a counterclockwise direction if looked from the north side of the ecliptic.
3. While the orbital plane of each of the above heavenly body lies closely about the ecliptic, their spinning axes can tilt widely different from each other. Two of them like Venus and Uranus even have retrograde spinning [1][2][1].
4. Separated by the asteroid belt[2], on one side of this belt is a group of planets whose material composition and appearance are widely different from that are found on the other side. Why must they be so separated by a loose ring of rocky powder?
5. Both the Sun and Earth show phenomenon of magnetic polarity reversal. However, the Earth's reversal never shows with ridged period and the "period" may take from many thousands to many hundred thousands of years, while the Sun's reversal appears highly regulated and the period is far shorter, about 23 years for one complete recovery [5][6] .
6. While the Venus and Earths are compatibly resemble to each other in many ways, the terrestrial crust of Venus is dominated by profuse volcanoes while the crust of Earth is divided by "rings of fire".
7. Surrounded by all the rings of fire are land mass called tectonic plates. How have the embryos of these plates been brought into shape?
8. The Earth's Moon must faithfully face Earth with one side, which shows high area of maria[7]. The slowly drifting away of the Moon from Earth must mean it had a history of very close to Earth in distance. As a matter of fact, it inevitably did!
9. The phenomena mentioned in 8 above is a by-product of a historical event that has resulted in the highest mass density for Earth among all the planets.
10. All atmospheric blanket of the gaseous planets show bands of different shades in color, while these bands are usually dominated with features of violent cyclones.
11. The Jupiter is found with a feature of Great Red Spot, which seems gliding back and forth at the same latitude in our view.
12. Apparently a spinning fluidic body, the Sun presents to us as one perfect spherical volume with differential rotation.

(Note this **only** exception: When doing computer charting according to the equations in the abstract, the value $v_i = v_{(n-1),o}$ for $n = 1$ should use 1.34715. As to why this value of 1.34715 needs to be so introduce for $n = 1$, some extra detailed derivation is involved. For detailed derivation of the above equations, a reader is cordially invited to visit the PDF copy of the article **How Nature Has Formulated the Hubble's Law** at *www.huntune.net*)

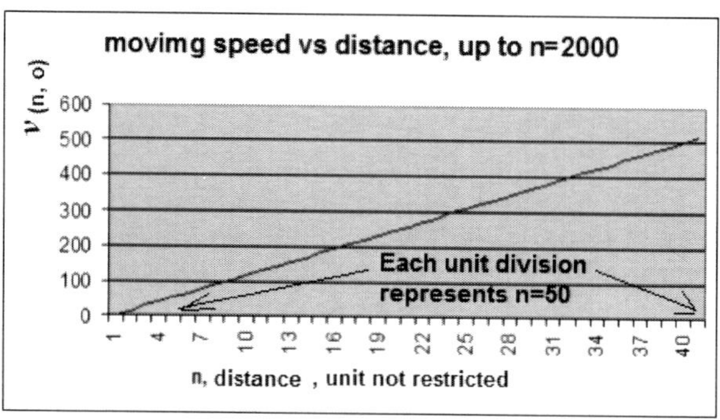

Moving Speed of Celestial Objects VS. Distance (Charted by Computer Simulation accordig to Equations Given in above Text)

Figure 11. The straight line shown in this diagram strongly suggests that the following two reality and theoretical analysis support each other: (1) reality: Hubble's law, (2) analysis: celestial movements as an entirety is a result of momentum accumulation of an exceedingly long history in the boundless universe caused by hydrogen fusion reactions. Any length unit can be used for n.

2. How They Found Each Other

2.1. The Chaos, a Brief Prelude

As those burning fragments of various sizes sent out by numerous random explosions were flying, materials of different ages (since their burning began) traveling at different speeds from different birthplaces along different direction could have all random chances tossing themselves at each other at any location. To those burning fragments that had missed any opportunity to meet others, they must continue their random flying in the space and finally become a cool body. But no one can guarantee their permanent lonesomeness. In some of the uncertain days, they may be captured by some large material organization. We need only one word to describe the state inside the realm consisting of all these burning and flying materials: ***chaos***. Therefore, we can further imagine that a material organization resulted through the chaotic combination must have members possessing properties widely different from each other in physical and chemical nature (Fig. 12). While Fig. 12 is only an imaginary picture from this author, reality does offer some example suggesting how heavenly object could have been flying in every possible direction resulted by explosion like what is shown in Fig. 13 and 14. While the example shown here suggests a style of converging flying, nature certainly also enables diverging flying in even unlimited cases.

As a sizable material organization, the Milky Way, must have also been baptized by such chaos, although many bil-

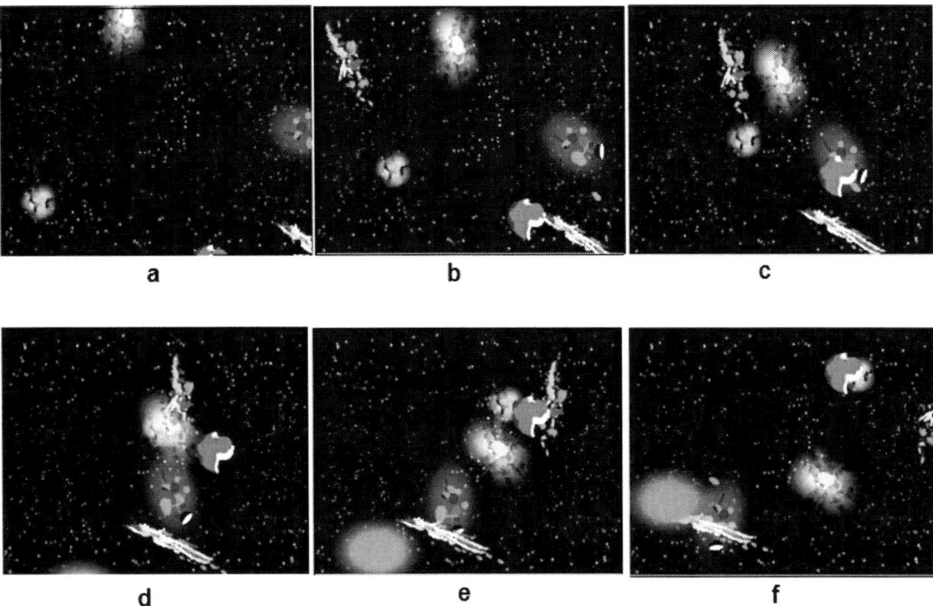

Figure 12. An imaginary view of chaotic material groups flying after a few initial explosions in the early universe (picture sequence from a to f)

lion years ago. The baptizing lasted a prolonged period of time that easily having spanned for billion years. At the location where the Milky Way was later to be given birth, there could have been huge amount of gelid hydrogen clouds idly hanging around. Then, all of a sudden, some uncertain number of gangs of burning invaders from any possible direction rushed to this area where many gelid hydrogen clouds were sleeping. In responding to the awakening by the invaders, a big portion of these clouds joined the explosion and burning.

During the ancient major period of firing and explosion launched by the foreign visitors, the Milky Way galaxy may have also ejected countless burning fragments leaving the Milky Way, too. No one would ever know where they eventually ended up to. However, with their long lasting burning, some of them may well ignite explosions out of some clouds at some formidable distance away from "home", repeating what those violent visitors had done to their parent cloud that had provided the material base for Milky Way's birth.

The so called Milky Way in those early days may have far less mass than it has today. The total amount of mass that we see from the Milky Way today is a result of billions of years of material accumulation. Today, such mass accumulation is still going on. The accumulation can be suggested, but not limited, by all these facts: the prediction that the Andromeda galaxy are steadfastly approaching the Milky Way; some globular clusters are found continuing their contribution from somewhere to the Milky Way; the movement of Magellanic clouds found in the close neighborhood of the Milky Way...

Hurled along with the materials so joining may include some substance in various nature and size that were not necessarily in burning state, such as gases of different compositions, steam, iceberg, grains of sand, rock, boulders, asteroids, but may well also include numerous burning fragments, in each of which one or a few of burning cores could be found; those burning cores were huge volume of mixture in which nuclear burning and synthetic reaction were fiery in process.

Eventually, at some undetermined epoch during the growth of the prototype Milky Way, it came such a day that some burning fragments of distinctive characteristics were tossed over here.

The birth location of all these materials, fiercely hot or gelidly cold, would forever be unknown to us. They may well be gangsters emerging from different locations, within or outside the Milky Way, but just have picked each other up at various spots along each of their own long journey of flying. Crossing each other's way, these rushing gangsters were accidentally put into one tentative gang of materials. About the time these gangsters were mingling as one bigger gang, their seemingly unbound journey was also ended when they happened to move into the vicinity of a giant burning fluidic gathering, whose total mass was more than a thousand times of what all these flying pieces put together. The gravitational attraction from this giant ball should have been a fatal grip for the continuous independent existence of this gang of materials, those burning as well as those not burning. Fortunately, their linear moving momentum with respect to this giant, in terms of the total consideration including speed, direction and distance, was formidable enough for them to resist such grip. Other than directly plunging toward this giant, the gang compromised with a movement of curving trajectory around the giant. It was possible that some gang mem-

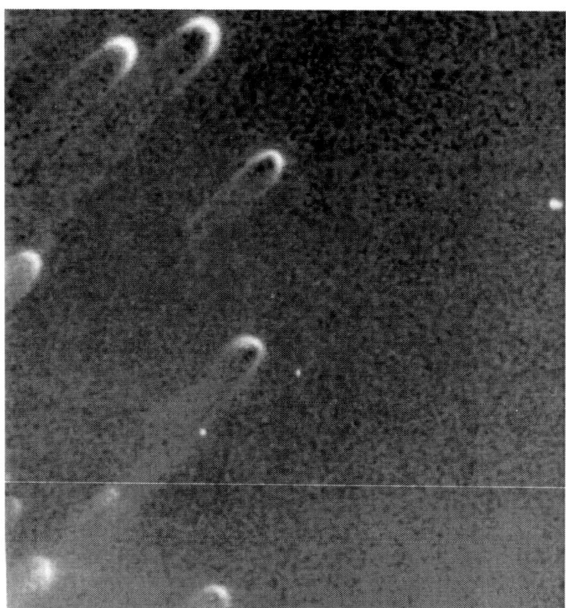

A portion of the inside lip of the Helix Nebular

Picture Credit: *Robert O'Dell* and *Kerry P. Handron* of *Rice University*

Source Credit: ***A Photographic Tour of the Universe,*** *Gabriele Vanin,* Firefly Books LTD

Figure 13. This is a partial view of the inside lip of the Helix Nebula (See Fig. 14). There are thousands of globular objects like these shown here but flying in every direction toward one point. The head of each of these globules is at least twice the size of the solar system, and the tail is about 1000 AU.

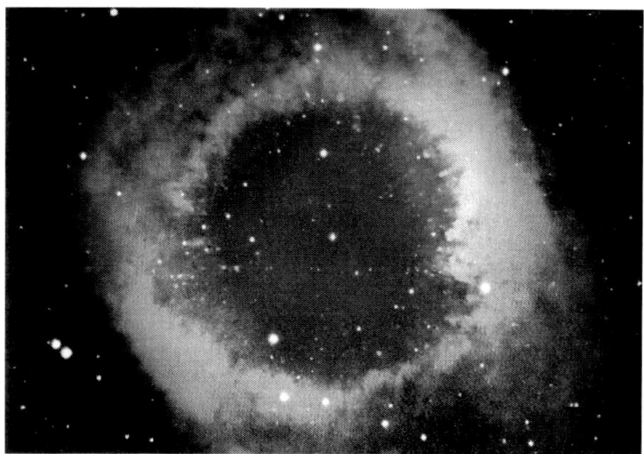

The Helix Nebula, NGC 7293 in Aquarius

Picture Credit: D. Malin

Source Credit: ***A Photographic Tour of the Universe,*** *Gabriele Vanin,* Firefly Books LTD

Figure 14. This picture and Fig. 13 just present as an example suggesting the possible flying of every random direction made by heavenly objects.

bers did lose themselves to the giant's gravitational pull before the close orbits for those survival ones finally took shape. With the direction of movement the gang happened to move before the giant's grip was sensed, the survival materials now continued their close orbits with a direction so predetermined that they moved in a way opposite to the Milky Way's self-spinning. Their direction of movement was by no means the result of any self-generated action out of an isolate cloud.

It was possible that the aforementioned giant was also ejected over here from somewhere else, but it was also highly possible that this giant had always been "Made in Milky Way" out of some smaller local hydrogen clouds because of the incessant accretion caused by the persistence of gravitation. So we even could not exclude such a possibility: This giant had never been burning but a gelid cloud. Its burning was only ignited by some burning gang members mentioned in the above paragraph when they plunged into it. This giant may have spent some billion years of a lonely hermit life before it finally had a chance to collect its harems. Together with its harems, because of various reason we can no longer trace back, it finally settled at the minor rotation arm Orion Spur in the Milky Way Galaxy.

2.2. There came the belt shape clouds

The gang members that were arrested by the giant potentially belonged to two clans that were from two different hometowns. One of the clans was more gaseous than the other, while both having been cloud bodies stretched like ribbons of extensive length before they met. Each ribbon was consisted of many fragments of different sizes; a bigger fragments usually contained a dense core, burning or not. The formation of such core is a natural gravitational consequence of a huge mass gathering. However, the less gaseous ribbon could be found with many sections whose cores were in far more active burning condition than the more gaseous belt. Longer history of burning had converted the less gaseous belt into a material ribbon being more terrestrial in nature.

Random movement brought these two material clans crossing each other's way and they collided. Sensing the giant's gravitational pull, the gaseous one was in the journey of alternating its moving loci. With the momentum it carried with respect to the giant, it may have been powerful enough to escape this giant's permanent grip, had the more terrestrial one never happened to have come to knock it out of its path. It looked like that the terrestrial belt had been on a way of head-on plunging into the giant. As much as the more terrestrial belt had curbed the gaseous belt from running away from the giant, the gaseous belt also pushed the terrestrial belt away from its suicidal plunging toward the giant. In this process of clashing, both material clans temporarily formed a gang in which certain materials mingling and momentum recombination inevitably happened (Fig. 15). A big part of the terrestrial belt turned out being amputated by the gaseous ribbon.

From the above description about the giant and gang joined by two clans in belt shape, the readers may well feel what is implied here as the giant; it could well be the Sun. That is right! It is what this article intends to present. This

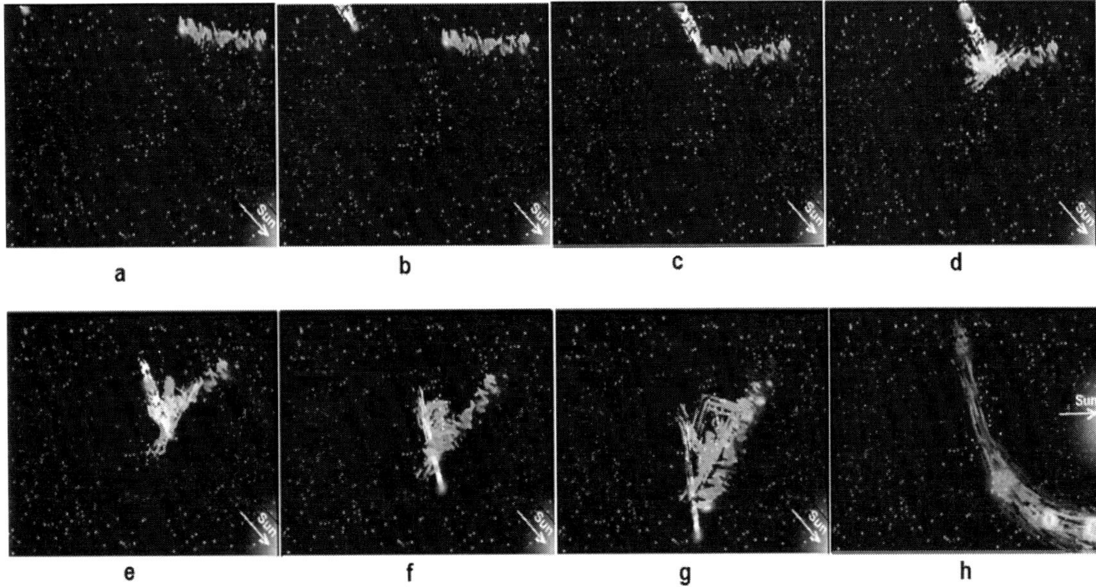

Figure 15. Collision of two ribbons of cloud bodies. Blue ribbon: the more gaseous belt; orange ribbon: the more terrestrial belt

giant and the material gang with its continuous movement were about to determine a geometrical plane in the heavens that is called gravitational platform in this article. The ecliptic and the invariable plane of the solar system have high approximation with it.

2.3. The fate of the surviving few

After being severely amputated by the gaseous clan, the survival part of the terrestrial clan continued on the journey towards the Sun, carrying along with it some gaseous materials snatched from the gaseous group. Meanwhile, the gaseous ribbon had been more concentrated into a few fragments, with one of them being outstandingly bigger than any others because it retained the major part of what was amputated from the original terrestrial ribbon. This biggest fragment was eventually evolving into what is called Jupiter today. The other major fragments also eventually became other gaseous planets revolving about the Sun. For convenience, we will call them all the Jupiter siblings. In orchestrating the movement of the survival portion of the survived terrestrial fragments, the Jupiter siblings had the advantage in distance to begin with, but the Sun had the eventual advantage in mass. The gravitational pull from them but in opposite direction steadfastly worked out to stretch the surviving portion more and more into a narrow streak, which was not one homogeneous piece but consisted of quite a few segments. Each of these segments contained a dense burning core. Between these segments were clouds of dust of various thickness and of different materials. We will call this streak the **Transition Streak**.

The momentum guiding the movement of the survival terrestrial Transition Streak was the residual momentum resulted by the sideway knocking of the gaseous ribbon as well as the original terrestrial belt's direct plunging toward the Sun. It was extremely possible that some part pioneering the Transition Streak did not received enough sideway knocking from the gaseous ribbon, the original plunging momentum still led this part to plunge into the Sun. The later part of the Transition Streak, having had its plunging movement grated a little longer by the gaseous ribbon as well as received longer time of sideway knocking, had the chance of avoiding the plunging. Avoiding the plunging, however, the Transition Streak could not get away from the Sun's pull either. Then, revolving about the Sun was the only settlement it could get into. In so doing, this Transition Streak further broke itself into a few more obviously separated entities with stable close orbits. However, orbits initiated with this kind of momentum as mentioned here could hardly end up with a near perfect circular shape, but instead, some very elongated shape.

Separate elongated orbits about one common focus could only mean that their orientation must trespassing each other. The orbital period of each of these entities traveling on them must be different from each other, too. So, orbital collision between these entities was only a matter of time, and inevitable. As collisions occurred, momentum recombination and substance regrouping will happen, new heavenly object would emerge. We will leave the further discussion on corresponding development in some later chapters.

As of now, let's use the term Jupiter Clash to call the collision presented by Fig. 15. We also use Jupiter-Sun transition to call the entire journey that the Transition Streak went through after the Jupiter Clash all the way up to the appearance of the several elongated orbits about the Sun (Fig. 16). We could easily imagine that accompanied with the development of these few entities was a space

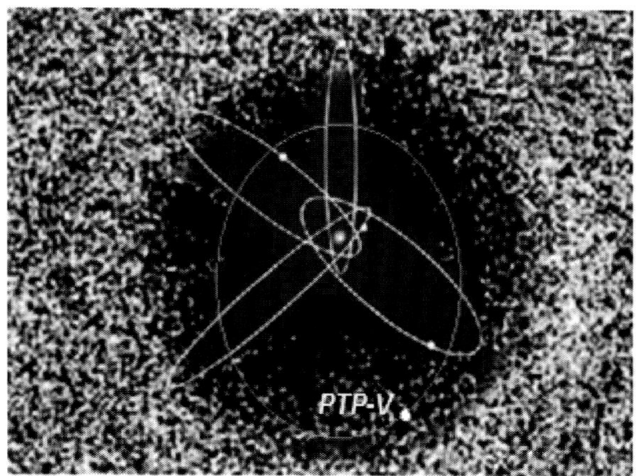

Figure 16. Some lanky orbits about the Sun before the birth of the current inner planets. The body on the least lanky orbit is marked as PTP-V for illustration purpose.

filled with dust of particles in size as small as steam mist or as big as those pieces we can find from the asteroid belt. In the areas commonly shared as inside space by all these orbits, the space was clear of such dust particles, but these kind of particles did embrace all the orbits from outside for a long time. It was the persistent work of the few terrestrial entities traveling on these few lanky orbits that had finally made the space squeaky clean all the way up to where we see as asteroid belt today. Besides lanky, each orbit also had certain orbital precession. The precession helped further sweep cleaning a bigger area.

2.4. The Massive Giant Has the Least Angular Momentum, but a Dwarf Few Takes the Lion's Share, Why?

With all the discussion presented so far, we could have partly contributed an answer regarding the disproportional sharing of angular momentum between the Sun, a mass giant, as one group and all the planets together as another group, but a dwarf group. However, the answer so come up could only offer the explanation about the part of angular momentum possessed by the planets with their orbital movement. What about the part produced by the planets' self-spinning?

Right after the Jupiter Clash, the gaseous gathering that eventually grew into Jupiter was very puffy and occupied a far bigger space than we know of Jupiter today. As the primordial puffy Jupiter moved on a tangential direction with respect to the Sun, while widely spreading, each of its particles received a different gravitational pulling force from the Sun. Subsequently this resulted in different angular momentum between all the particles with respect to the Sun. Generally the particle farthest from the Sun had the biggest momentum, while the closest one but of the same mass had the smallest with respect to the same center of the Sun. This inequality in angular momentum was retained but with a different magnitude if the comparison was made with respect to the mass center of Jupiter. The different angular momentum between the farthest and the closest particles must initiate speed difference between them with respect to the same mass center. The speed difference between them would further escalate into some ever more rapid rotational movement about the mass center if they are bound by gravitational pulling force (Fig.17). The speed may not be obvious to start with. However, the primordial gas gathering gradually shrank. Had the primordial Jupiter's flat gaseous disk started its existence in the same vicinity of the Sun with a radius of 1,000 times (1/20 of an astronomical unit) of its current equator's radius, Jupiter's current spinning rate would have been 1 million folds of that of the old days.

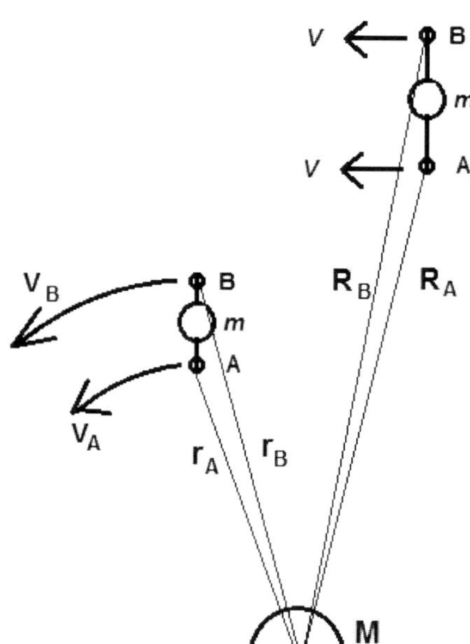

Figure 17. Spinning of object AmB is initiated as it gravitationally falls toward M. A and B of the same mass at the the same linear speed V started the falling with $R_B > R_A$. So A has bigger angular momentum than B to start with. As R_B and R_A get shortened, it ends up with $V_B > V_A$ dominating the spinning direction. During the falling, length AB further shrinks and thus enables a permanent counterclockwise spinning about mass center m of AmB. Passing the gravitational field of M, V can be considered as the initial orbital speed of AmB around M. Now, the spinning direction takes the same direction of what the initial orbital direction shows.

Although initially both the farthest particle and closest particle from the Sun moved in the same tangential direction about the Sun, the ultimate spinning direction resulted from them must be dominated by the bigger initial momentum, which was possessed by the one further away from the Sun. In other words, the rotational direction of the outer edge of a spinning entity took the same direction as the orbital direction of this entity if this entity's self-spinning was developed with mechanism we mentioned above. This mechanism resulting in the outer edge of a spinning entity to take the same moving direction as its orbital movement should be applicable to all other planets, inner or outer.

Gravitational interaction is reciprocal between two massive bodies in a distance. As much as self-spinning can be resulted on planets because they moved in the Sun's gravity field, the planets could have so caused self-spinning on the Sun, too. The direction of the spinning so caused should be the same as that of the planets as well. However, the angular momentum difference between the farthest and the closed parts on the Sun so caused by a planet is too little, the spinning so agitated on the Sun therefore can never be prominent, although unable to be zero. Furthermore, in the entire history of self-spinning being induced on the Sun, the Sun had never strikingly shrunk. In our retrospective reasoning above regarding Jupiter, we assumed a primordial disk for Jupiter to begin its history with a radius of 1,000 times of its current radius. Had the Sun also had such a primordial radius of 1,000 times of its current equatorial radius, the Sun would have occupied a space almost up to where the Jupiter is today. The existence of all the inner planets and the asteroid belt must reject such a speculation.

3. Terrestrial Planets

3.1. The Prototype Inner Planets and the Asteroid Belt

Upon ending the Jupiter-Sun transition, only those few pieces approaching the Sun carrying enough tangential momentum with respect to the Sun could finally survive and settle on some closed orbits. These few survivors should have been some trailing segments of the Transition Streak aforementioned, which had chance receiving more sideways pushing from the Jupiter siblings, either through physical contact during the Jupiter Clash or a while afterwards through gravitational dragging in a distance during the Jupiter-Sun Transition.

The long journey of the Jupiter–Sun Transitions let the few survival segments elevate their radial momentum toward the Sun strikingly stronger than the tangential components. Only by "luck", the proportion between these two momentum components were in the "right" magnitude for each of the survival pieces so that they could avoid directly plunging into the Sun; each of them ended their journey with a close orbit about the Sun. However, each of such closed orbits so resulted by two momentum contrastingly different in magnitude could only be some ellipse that was strikingly elongated in shape. When the elliptical orbits finally settled down , there were five significant major surviving segments moving around the Sun. They were not the nowadays inner planets, but they provided the materials base for the birth of the nowadays terrestrial planets, which eventually appeared after some historical accidents explained later. For illustration purpose, they were regarded as prototype terrestrial planets (PTP) and be named as PTP-I, PTP-II, PTP-III, PTP-IV, and PTP-V for a total of five.

Among the five PTP's, PTP-V was a piece that had been trailing behind everyone else in the Transition Streak during the Jupiter-Sun Transition and thus kept being the furthest object away from the Sun than the other PTP's. Therefore it had its orbit resulted in with the least radial momentum with respect to the Sun and, subsequently, its orbit was the least elongated one. Fig. 18(a) is a duplication of Fig.16, but with the name added to each PTP. The name in number for each of them was not designated according to any reasoning or rule but just for the need of illustration.

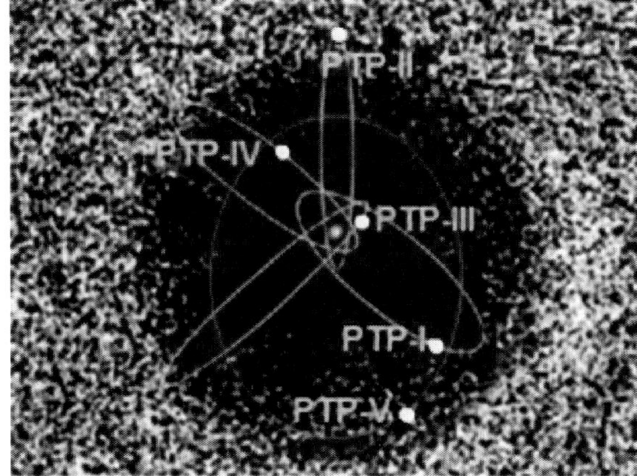

(a) Some lanky orbits about the Sun in a dusty environment

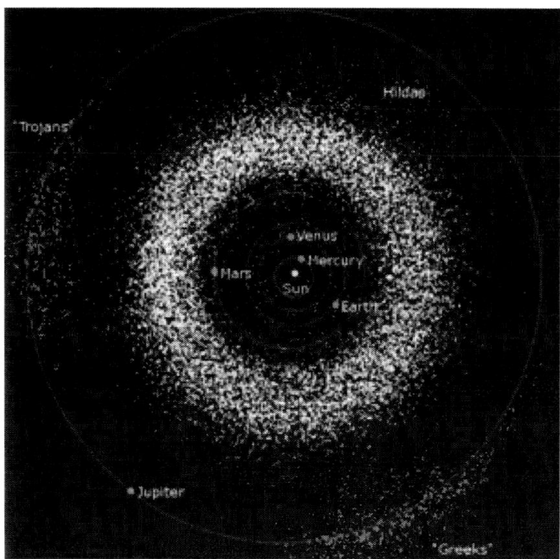

(b) Trimmed from outside by Jupiter, being gnawed a hole by the PTP's from inside, the asteroid belt settled with a donut shape before the inner planets were given birth

Picture credit of (b):
https://en.wikipedia.org/wiki/Asteroid_belt

Figure 18. Asteroid belt shown in (b) is a ramnant of the predator work of Jupiter and the PTP's, which were traveling on various elongated orbits shown in (a) about the Sun

As mentioned before, the five PTP's settled themselves

in a very dusty environment. Since all the objects swarmed over here as dusts with the same reasons that had impelled the appearance of the PTP's, they all shared a general trend of movement with the same counterclockwise material flow about the Sun if viewed from the north side of the ecliptic. It can be easily imagined that, when the PTP's patrolled on their orbits, they must sweep clean all the dust droplets in the vicinity of their paths via gravitational gobbling. The dusty area so cleaned could extend as far as the major axis of the ellipse could reach and little beyond—gravitation collection always worked with efficiency through a certain distance. Since each of the orbit must show precession with its focus being anchored at the Sun, each of them gradually increased the angular area with ever escalated cleanliness about the Sun. Four of them arduously worked together through a long history finally poked a hole out of the dusty "carpet" around the Sun. Working hard to clean such carpet were not just the PTP's; Jupiter also trimmed it in a distance away from the PTP's. Instead of poking hole, however, Jupiter tried to trim a circular piece out of the carpet. The result of them working together finally left a carpet with a shape of a donut. This donut in space but with all the loose dust droplets is what human beings today called the asteroid belt. Given how and where the asteroid belt had obtained the material source for its formation in history, the collection of members of the asteroid belt should have carried the most genuine record of birthday of the solar system not including the Sun. The majority of dust particles found at the Lagrangian points dominated by Jupiter should also be from the same source forming the asteroid belt.

Cutting a hole out of the dusty carpet was not the only feat the four PTP's contributed. Through orbital precession of a long history, their gravitational influence also modified the orbit of the PTP-V into a more and more circular path around the Sun. Of course, it was only by chance that they did not collide at PTP-V. The same luck did not exist among the PTP-I, -II, -III, and IV themselves. Given that the orbital shape of these four PTP's were so elongated but also crossing each other, collision between them was only a matter of time.

3.2. The Mercury-Venus Pair

So, one day, collision did happen between two of the five PTP's. Let's call these two PTP-I and PTP -II. Around the time the collision happened, all PTP's should still be quite "puffy". As such, the diameter for each of these spinning PTP disks was far larger than what we see from any inner planets today. Each PTP had two essential parts of substances: at the center was a dense burning core, and surrounding this burning core was a thick but puffy jacket consisting of all kind of loose materials, both volatile and rock hard solid.

Refer to location A in Fig. 19a. This is a hypothetical point where dynamic status can be found leading to collision between PTP-I and PTP-II. Let's suppose an event sequence like what Fig. 19b shows: Just at the moment PTP-I was leaving A, PTP-II plunged into the same location. A hair of difference on timing between the leaving and the plunging-into made their two cores miss each other. With the major portion of the linear momentum concentrated with a core, the PTP-II's core just simply penetrated through the puffy jacket of PTP-I without too much trouble. Indeed, this linear momentum was even further escalated prior to the collision by the mutual gravitational

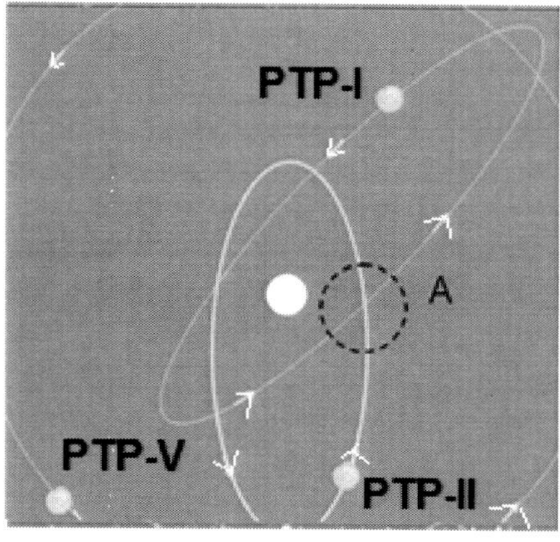

a

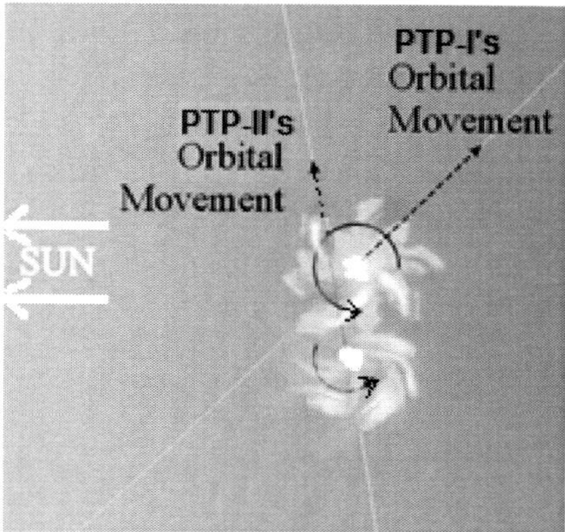

b

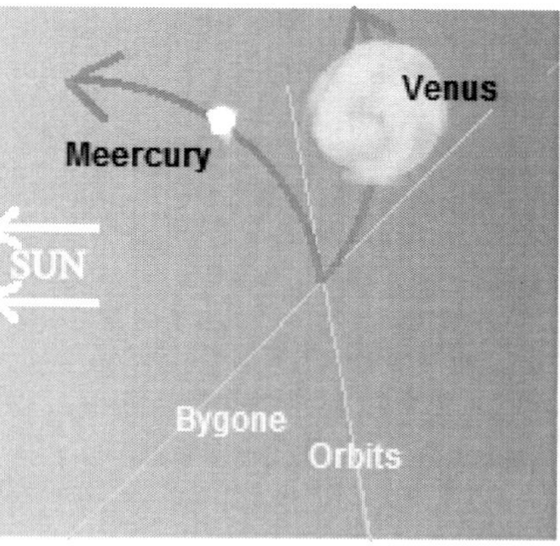

c

Figure 19. Collision sequence resulting in Mercury and Venus

interaction between the two PTP's.

The trespassing made by PTP-II was done on the side of the spinning disk of PTP-I that was closer to the Sun. When the trespassing completed, the spinning direction of the loose jacket of PTP-I was able to block the trespassing of the loose jacket of PTP-II, allowing only the core of PTP-II, the major carrier of linear momentum, to egress. So, although having successfully escaped from the collision scene, the core of PTP-II came out naked, with only little trace of loose materials trailing behind it. Besides, while being the major carrier of linear momentum, the core sure carried only a trivial part of the angular momentum of the original spinning disk of the PTP-II. Such a trivial angular momentum was even further dissipated by friction during the penetration of its own jacket and the jacket of the PTP-I; the naked core then only ended up with some extremely low self-spinning rate in its future movement.

Lighter in mass after the trespassing, this naked core still turned out to be fortunate enough to have retained adequate momentum to resist the deadly gravitational summon from the Sun, able to establish a new, smaller, and more circular orbit about the Sun. Surviving, the movement of this naked core has to inherit the same angular orbital direction of the parental PTP-II. This naked core of PTP II finally earns the name Mercury from the human beings.

After getting out of the collision scene, the naked core that later gained the name Mercury still retained its thermal energy for a while but rapidly lost it to the space. During the process of heat loss, its materials state evolved from a plasma to boiling lava, then to some "muddy" paste, then finally rock solid. During this process of material consistence change, some liqueur hot materials continued to ooze and bubble out from within, and left behind plenty of bumps when the materials got out to the surface and condensed and solidified. On the other hand, the trace of loose materials following the core's escape eventually accredited on the surface of Mercury before this crust completely solidified, leaving on it a blanket of craters (Fig. 20).

As to PTP-I, the collision caused it to spin in a reversed direction ever since. The reason is simply that not only the penetration of PTP-II was done in a direction opposing to its original spinning direction, but also the momentum dumped on it by the puffy jacket from PTP-II had been too large for the original angular momentum of PTP-I to overcome. Of course, the new spinning rate so resulted must be very low because the residual momentum was left behind by momentum subtraction between two spinning disks. The collision also redrew the orbit of PTP-I, from a lanky ellipse to a near perfect circle, because now PTP-II needed to haul a new burden to move along, and this new burden also had its original orbital momentum added to the new movement, too.

The collision had not only dramatically modified the moving state of PTP-I, but also abruptly altered its physical characteristics. The retaining of an extra puffy jacket increased its atmospheric pressure, and built up an efficient insulator for this newly appearing planet to retain the heat from its thermal core. The prolonged process of heat escaping to the space extended the time for the crust of the new planet to solidify. Because of the crust in a long lasted soft condition, the volcanoes motivated by the thermal core's exploding force could find abundant chances to form and spew all over in the planet's history. This is the landscape we found with Planet Venus. Compared to Earth, Venus has far more volcanoes and its volcanoes are far bigger, although these two planets, among all planets, are the most compatible two both in size and distance from the Sun. The extra puffy jacket also lowered Venus's mass density to 5.24 gm/cm^3 while the loss of the same elevated Mercury's mass density to 5.43 gm/cm^3.

Before the debut of Mercury and Venus, the orbital plane of PTP-I and PTP-II should not have well coincided with the nowadays ecliptic. An inclination of 10 or 15 degrees or even more for their orbits should not be a surprise. A reasonable inference of such inclination may be led to by the "thickness" of the asteroid belt, which are between 10 to 15 degrees about the ecliptic, and some of the member asteroids may reach as much as 35 degrees (with the Sun being at the apex of the angle measurement). In the old time that the PTP-I and PTP-II were still mingling with these scattered dust particles before the asteroid belt taking any obvious shape, both may be in some position that was quite deviated from the final ecliptic. They kept the deviation during the Jupiter-Sun transition. Had the collision bringing Mercury and Venus to exist never happened, these two primordial terrestrial planets may continue to possess orbits with high inclination. After the collision, their momentum component that was vertical to the ecliptic was nullified, resulting in their orbital plane with a trivial inclination.

Table 1 in Fig. 21 lists some data that can serve to support the above conjecture about the formation history of Mercury and Venus. The data about Mercury and Venus in this table show good coherence with the physical characteristics we derive about them so far.

3.3. Earth-Moon Pair

The struggle for space also happened between PTP-III and PTP-IV. Instead of a near head-on collision like the one leading to the birth of Mercury and Venus, PTP-III and PTP-IV came together at a manner that looked more or less like a merger. Merger meant no one body pronouncedly penetrating through another. The merger could have a higher chance to happen if the trajectories of two moving bodies were about the same in direction while crossing each other.

Before the merger, both PTP-III and PTP-IV should have traveled about the Sun innumerous times. During such traveling, their orbits were gradually modified to less elliptical because of two major reasons: (1) gravitationally gobbling up smaller objects in the process of shaping up the asteroid belt as well as cleaning up the area in the vicinity of their orbits, (2) the abundant opportunities for the two PTP's to line up with the Sun in a straight line.

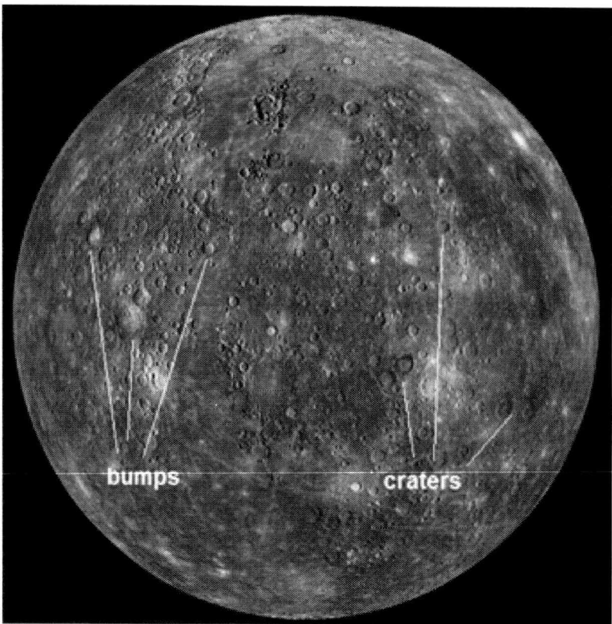

Coexistence of bumps and craters on Mercury's surface
Image credit: NASA

Figure 20. Landscape of Mercury

	Mercury	Venus	Earth	Mars	Jupiter	Saturn	Uranus	Neptune
M, Mass (10^{23} *kg*)	3.3	48.69	59.74	6.4	18992	5687	868.5	1023.5
R_p, *Semi-major axis of orbit* (10^5 *km*)	57.9	108.2	149.6	227.9	778.3	1427	2870	4497
Mean Density (*gm/cm*^{3})	5.43	5.25	5.52	3.93	1.33	0.71	1.24	1.67
Orbital Period (Earth Years)	0.24	0.62	1	1.88	11.86	29.46	84.01	164.79
Gravitational Influence on the Sun, ($G*M/R_p^2$) *Relativie Unit Only*	2.003	9.306	6.048	0.276	70.15	6.246	0.233	0.133
Magnetic Moment (gauss R^3_p*)*	0.0035	<0.0003	0.31	<0.0006	4.3	0.21	0.23	n/a

Table 1 Main characters of the planets

Figure 21.

Just like PTP-I and PTP-II, both PTP-III and PTP-IV were also consisted of one dense thermal core with a rapidly spinning disk of puffy jacket.

We previously mentioned that, prior to the Jupiter Clash, the long axial line of the cloud ribbon that contributed the material base for the future PTP's as well as the asteroid belt may have a tilting angle of 10° or 15° with respect to the future ecliptic. After the Jupiter Clash as well as during the Jupiter-Sun Transition, if no forceful interference from other moving material gathering, this angle will be inherited by the Transition Streak of cloud that eventually led to the settlement of the asteroid belt and all the PTP's. The speculation on such an angle can be reasonably inferred by drawing a triangle with the Sun in its apex and the linear dimension of the belt's thickness to be placed at the side opposite to the apex (Fig. 22).

With the angle so inherited by the Transition Streak, the orbital plane for each PTP so eventually developed into must potentially form a nonzero angle with the future ecliptic. The reason is like this: The ecliptic plane is a plane that has high approximation with the gravitational platform of the solar system; the high approximation is resulted because the momentum component vertical to the gravitational platform is nullified upon the collision between some heavenly objects that move in this platform. The gravitational platform is decided by the mass center

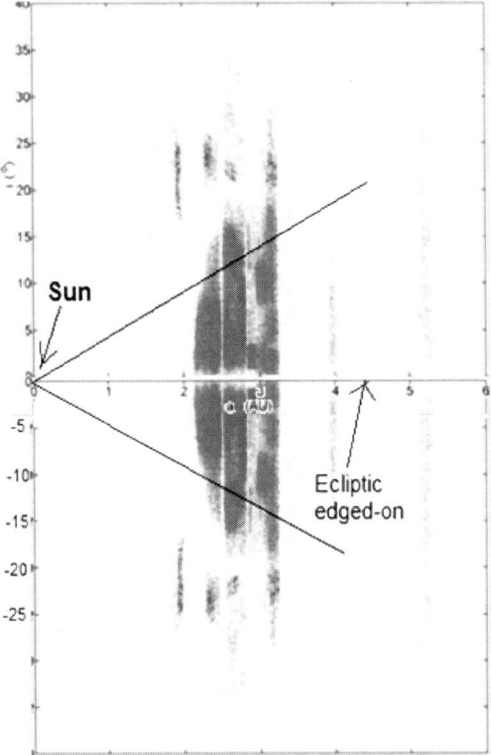

The asteroid belt showing the orbital inclinations versus distances from the Sun, with asteroids in the core region of the asteroid belt in red and other asteroids in blue

credit:http://en.wikipedia.org/wiki/Image:Main_belt_i_v s_a.png

Note: The original diagram contains only the upper portion up to and include the horizontal axis suggesting the elicptic. The lower part is added by this author. It is added only for illustration purpose with an assumption that a portion of the belt statistically mirroring the upper portion may also exist below the ecliptic. The two slanted angle lines and words inside the diagram are also added by this author. Profound gratefulness from this author, Cameron Rebigsol, to the original author Deuar Piotr .

Figure 22. The angle "thickness" of the asteroid belt

of the Sun, the mass center of the Jupiter siblings, and the mid-point of the amplitude fluctuation made by the mass center of the entire Transition Streak. However, the mass center of each material fragment in the streak was not necessarily coincided with such a plane to begin their transition journey. Instead, they all were more likely "bobbing" above and below this plane in the journey. The residual momentum the fragment so inherited after the Jupiter Clash with respect to the gravitational platform destined a nonzero angle to be preserved by the orbital plane of those final material fragments, i.e., the asteroid belt and the PTP's with respect to the gravitational platform. The angle should not deviate much from the value of 10° or 15° mentioned above. However, with the geometrical focus at the Sun, the major axis of each elliptical orbit were oriented in very different direction. So, the orbital plane of one PTP may have chance to intersect with the orbital plane of another PTP with an angle as wide as 30°. With similar reasoning, the plane of the spinning disk of each PTP may not necessarily be the same as the orbital plane of that particular PTP. Instead, the disk may incline by a nonzero angle with respect to its orbital plane.

Given that the spinning disk of each PTP may tilt by an angle with respect to its own orbital plane, and that the orbital plane of one PTP may intersect with another orbital plane with a quite prominent angle, when these two PTP's merged, no merger could possibly be gentle by any measure. The materials from two spinning edges just struck at each other from absolutely opposite direction, just like two improperly aligned gigantic cogwheels at high spinning speed crossing and thus grinding at each other. Each of them needed to knock away part of the other's for its own movement (Fig. 23).

While the PTP-II's core missed the Venus's core and was able to get away to become Mercury, the gentler merging of PTP-III and PTP-IV was unable to offer enough momentum for either core to escape from the arrest of the other. As the merging was further completed, the cores of these two PTP's were wedded together into a new core because of the gravitational effect. The new core so appeared naturally took over the reign as the mass center of the new but more massive gravity body. The uncompromising striking between the two spinning disks violently disrupted their spinning. The majority of the materials from both puffy jackets would then find themselves no choice but to collapse and pile up rapidly over each other as well as over the new core.

Possessing loose materials as the puffy jacket, each PTP had developed into a spinning body with some rotation arms before the merger. Some arms were so long from the central dense core that the tip part of the arm were far enough from either of the original cores. With the extra length, these few tips happened to have enough angular momentum to resist to join the collapse. Instead of collapsing toward the new core, they flew away.

After the merging happened, these tips so freed from the merging scene continued their angular movement about the same previous cores, which, however, had joined with another one becoming a more massive core. The collapse of other materials that were in shorter distance from the original core caused no effect in alternating these few freed tips' angular momentum. Therefore, after the disengagement from the original PTP's, the tips must continue to face the same old cores as if they had still been on the same spinning disk. This meant that the few tips must permanently be "cheated" to stare at the parent cores (but now a single fatter one) with the same face. However, the collapse of the rotation arms did remove the material bridge between them and the other materials. The gravitational force between the tips and the core were reduced. The same an-

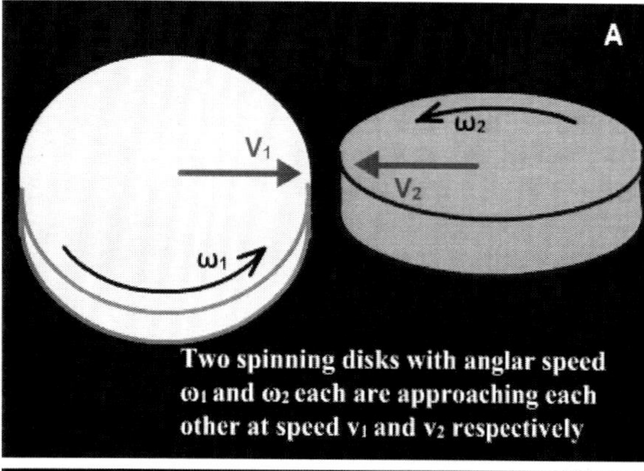

A
ω2
V1
V2
ω1
Two spinning disks with anglar speed ω1 and ω2 each are approaching each other at speed v1 and v2 respectively

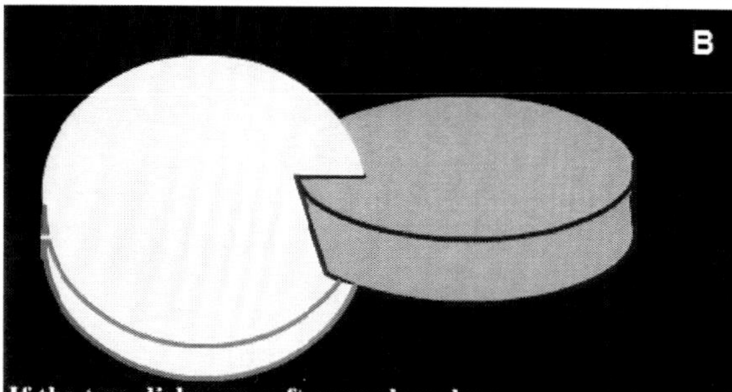

B
If the two disks are soft enough and possess no movement of any kind , the above geometrical result should be the outcome after they are made intruding each other.

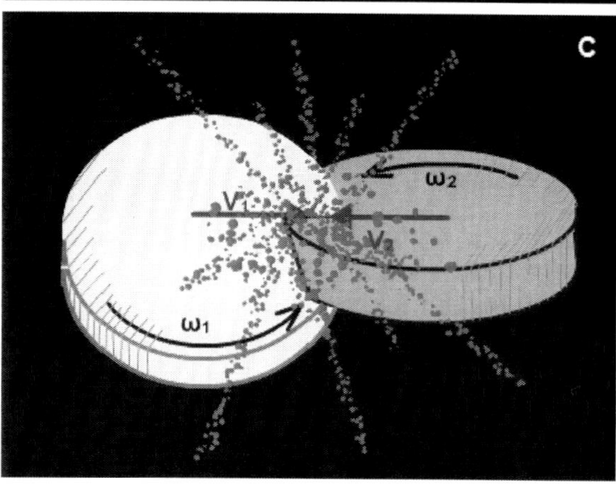

Figure 23. Two spinning disks with different spinning orientation intrude into each other. Shown in **C**, at where they come in contact, materials collide, crush at each other and fly allover. Loose materials at the areas shaded with grey lines will fly away from the disks upon the abrupt disruption of the spinning of the disks.

gular momentum possessed by the tips now became excessive in retaining the same radius of rotation about the core. If nothing else would interfere, they would all gradually drift further and further away from the new core that serves as the common body of the two old cores.

All those disengaged material tips should have different linear velocities between each other but all in the same direction circulating about the same core. Different linear velocity but with different distance from the core meant different angular velocity. Sooner or later, they would catch each other up. Some catching may be gentle, some may be quite violent. The catching would be potentially violent if the two tips catching each other were originated from the two different PTP's, because these two disks had intersected each other with a wide angle before the merging. Before they all caught up each other, they all were satellites to the new core. But time eventually gave these satellites enough chance to join as one and become a single moon to the new heavenly body containing the two cores of the old PTP's. The materials so mutually catching each other up would not alter their dynamic status of the same center facing.

The new heavenly body having collected most of the merging materials, including the new core, is what we call Earth, and subsequently, the moon formed with those loose satellites gets its name as Moon. The merging brought out the existence of Earth and Moon is termed as Grand Merger in this article (Fig. 24) .

Fig. 25 are two photos serving as evidence how materials had collected each other in the history of Moon formation. Photo B shows that a big collection of material flow forcefully invaded the host body, which was then still not yet solidified but quite pasty. The speed of the invasion was so formidable that the host body could not completely stop the invaders' penetration. Entering from the south side, some invaders managed to get out from the north side of the host body. Having successfully escaped or not, the invaders left numerous bumps around the area of the lunar north pole, witnessing the history of material invading.

Craters left at the entrance and bumps left at the exit by the invaders could only mean some highly pasty consistence of the host body. Given that the major material constituents of the Moon being silicate minerals, when the invasion happened, the host body was in a state of high temperature. Entering from the south, exiting in the north, this route of movement made itself a clue suggesting that the host body and the invaders were disengaged from two spinning disks that had a wide angle between their axes of spin orientation.

Each spinning PTP was not a homogeneous disk of mass. The general tendency of material distribution was that the closer to the center of the disk the denser and hotter materials were found, or that the closer to the disk's edge, the lighter and colder materials were found. As the Grand Merger took place, a great deal of materials collided, and a widely spread material band of "dust" containing material droplets in various sizes was immediately agitated, filling up the vicinity embracing the newly born Moon and Earth. It had not taken too long for the droplets on the band to be collected by Earth and the Moon. For the powdery materials scattered between Earth and the Moon's orbit, Earth may have taken most of them; for those scattering outside of the Moon's orbit, the Moon should have the lion's share. This was potentially the reason why the far side of the Moon is found with more craters than the near

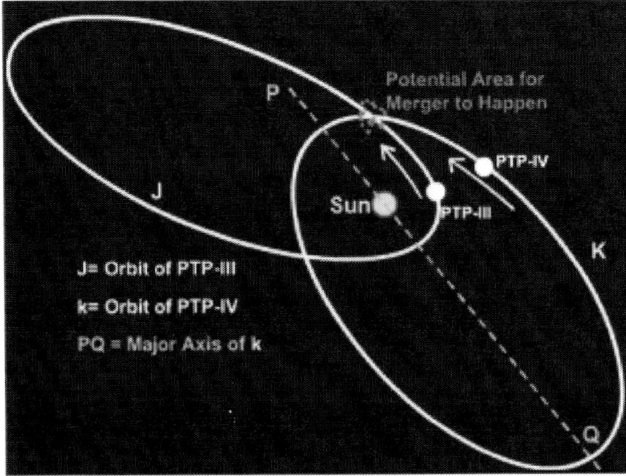

(a) Conventional Bird's Eye View

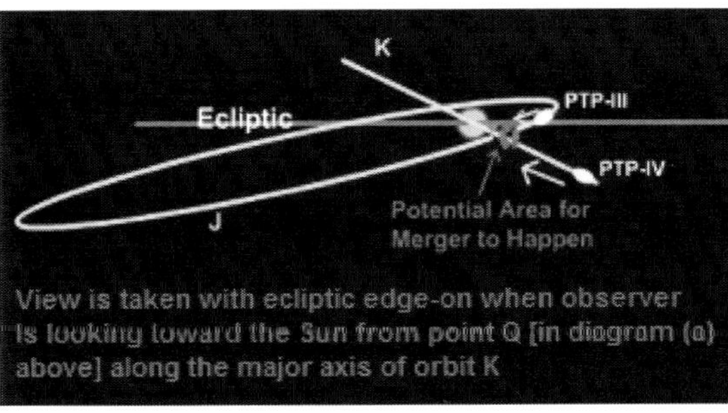

b

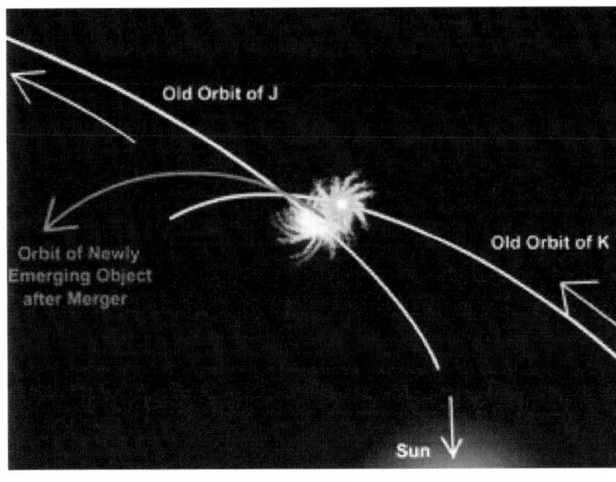

c

Diagram (C) is a magnified scene of the potential area of merger between two spinning bodies

Figure 24. The happening of Grand Merger

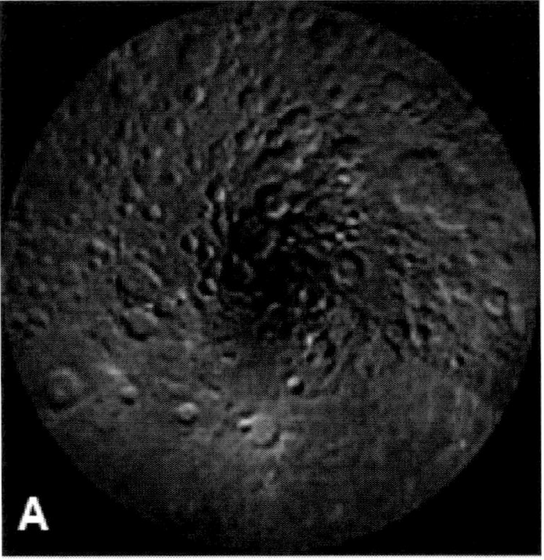

Lunar north pole

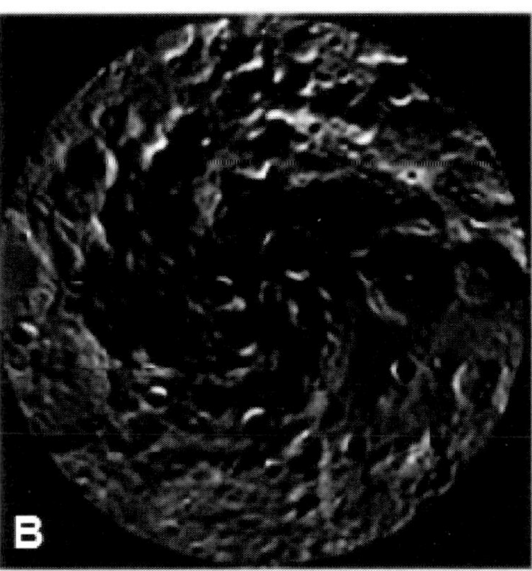

Lunar south pole

Photo credit from Wikipedia: Moon

Figure 25. Topograph of the two poles of the Moon

side (Fig. 26).

Whatever materials the Moon could have collected, they were majorly from the spinning edge of the original two PTP's, and therefore lighter. The inability to retain the dense core further led the Moon to end up having the lower mass density of 3.344 gm/cm^3. Conversely, having gobbling up two cores did elevate the mass density of Earth to 5.514 gm/cm^3, the highest among all the planets.

Since Earth continuous to spin with an appreciable frequency regardless of how the Grand Merger may have dissipated the spinning energy, this allows us to assume that, before PTP-III and PTP-IV merged, one of them must have spread significantly wider than the other. After the Grand Merger, the new body pronouncedly inherited the original spinning direction of the larger one although the spinning rate was substantially lowered afterwards and with certain deviation in angle from the original one, too. The unusual

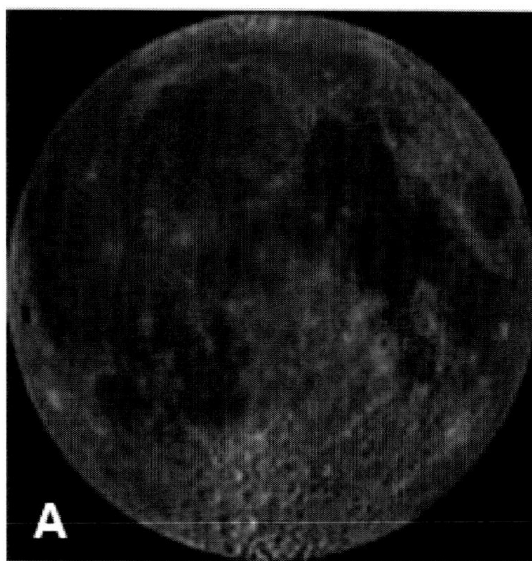

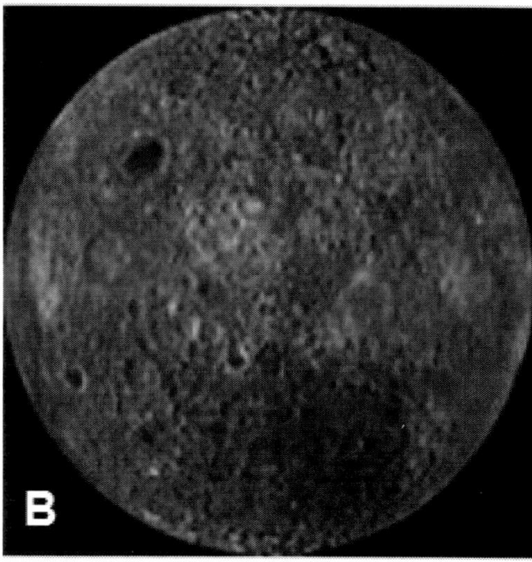

Figure 26. Topograph of the two sides of the Moon

tilting angle of the Earth's spinning axis (Fig. 27) compared to that of other planets could be potentially resulted by reasoning presented above. It could be well reasonable to imagine that it was also the larger one that had robbed away the core of the smaller one.

3.4. The Lonely Mars

As PTP-I, PTP-II, PTP-III and PTP-IV all have been converted into something else with new names, what about PTP-V?

Being in the same gang with PTP-I, PTP-II, PTP-III and PTP-IV as the survivors out of the Jupiter Clash, PTP-V was trailing behind them with a significantly large distance, or conversely, a relatively smaller distance from Jupiter. As such, it received enough gravitational pull from Jupiter to settle relatively quickly into an elliptical orbit. This orbit was not as lanky as that of the other PTP's; its average distance from the Sun was always far larger than the minor axis of each of the other orbits. During the Jupiter-Sun Transition, the reluctant movement of PTP-V would make it somebody more mingling with those droplets that formed the future asteroid belt other than a dasher toward the Sun like the other PTP's.

Staying as the biggest object in a space overcrowded by all kinds of dust and droplets, PTP-V became a local gravitational predator, although its appetite was not as viscous as the other PTP's showed when they patrolled here visiting their aphelion point. Little by little, the eccentricity of the elliptical orbit of the PTP-V gradually reduced due to its consistent material collection from the inner edge of the asteroid belt like what the other PTP's were also doing. In the beginning days of its trimming work, PTP-V may have its orbit intersect the orbits of the other PTP's. However, given that the orbital period of each of the PTP's were so different, and the distances between them were so formidable, the probability of collision between PTP-V and the others was very low. The chance of their collision even became zero after the other PTP's converted themselves into Mercury, Venus, Earth, and the Moon. Of course, then, we have only one more planet left inside the asteroid belt to be identified for PTP-V. This is Mars. Given that the mass of Mars is only 10% of Earth's, PTP-V should have been even lighter before it collected more mass from the asteroid belt. Relying on robbing mass from those that were otherwise part of the asteroid belt, Mars does not have high mass density but a figure of 3.935 gm/cm^3 today. Even if it may have started as an object of high mass density, greedy robbery eventually lowered its overall density.

The biggest object in the Asteroid belt is Ceres. It has only 0.15% of the mass of that of Mars. Had it ever had a mass compatible to what Mars has, the astronomical academy may have had to deal with a sixth inner planet today, and a completely different view of the asteroid belt as well.

4. The Moon

The Moon has long bothered us with several mysteries. Among them are:

1. It is gradually drifting away from Earth. Retrospective reasoning may easily lead us to speculate how it could not have been once a part of Earth. But, then,
2. Why does it have lower mass density than Earth?
3. It has kept the same face towards Earth.
4. The quantity of volcanic maria on the near side and the far side are incomparable; the far side is practically deficient of maria (Fig. 26).

The first three mysteries have been explored in the previous chapter. Born in the process so presented in that chapter, the seniority of the Moon's materials in the solar sys-

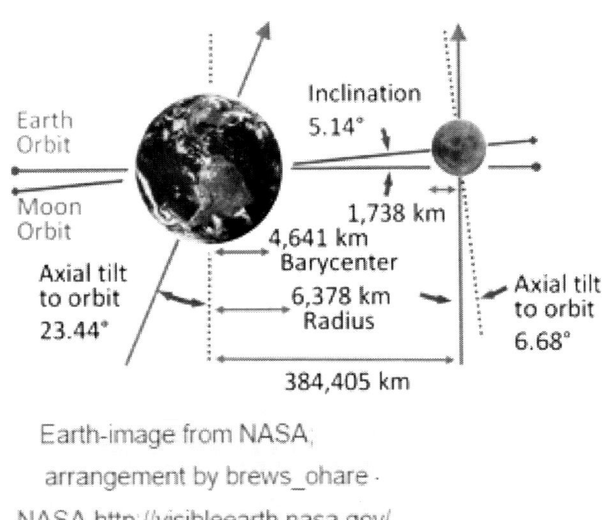

Figure 27. Earth's axis tilts by a prominent angle with respect to the Earth's orbital plane,i.e., the ecliptic. The tilting angle should be the residual combination of angular momentum of the materials flying above and below a certain plane before the Grand Merger. Said plane is gravitationally determined by the Sun, the Jupiter Siblings, and the mass center of the Transition Streak. The ecliptic just coincidentally has high coincidence with this plane. Fig. 23 and Fig. 24 would further suggest the process causing the tilting.

tem is no lower than that of the other inner planets.

The solution to the first three mysteries should offer us a clue leading to the solution of the fourth mystery. In the days of PTP's, each of them was some spinning disk dominated by violently burning materials at the central region. Therefore, in general, materials closer to the center of each spinning disk appeared more in the form of volcanic lava or even in a state of plasma if too close to the center where the burning core was. Contrasting to the hot materials closer to the center, materials near the edge of the spinning disk would appear more in the form of solid cold pieces in all kind of size and chemical nature. So, as the Grand Merger happened, materials joining to form the Moon would continue showing the same gradient pattern of physical states in substance distribution: with higher chance, the materials originally closer to each of the burning cores would join as some boiling lava. After the lava cooled off, rocky maria was what was left showing, continuing its old day tendency of staying closer to the old day core. Conversely, materials piling up at the far side of the Moon would have been those colder ones, and therefore appearing far less rocky.

5. Earth

5.1. Infant Tectonic Plates

The abundantly collapsing materials enveloping the new core were of various chemical natures. Among them, water was one of the major components. Not only did such a material piling up stifle the violent thermal activity of the new core, but the water also efficiently quenched these materials, which otherwise must stay in liqueur or even gaseous state for an extensively long period of time under the violent heat from the burning new core. Promoted by the incessant quenching action of the water as well as its arduous heat delivery to the outer space through steam, a rocky crust wouldn't have taken too long to appear on Earth. The turbulent heat exchange between the rocky crust and the volatile materials soon "filtered" all these materials into three major mass components for Earth's exterior appearance: atmosphere, ocean, and a solid shell, deep at the center of which was the thermal core (Fig. 28).

No one can expect that the initial violent material collapse happened in a homogeneous manner. Instead, some materials randomly piled up as bigger chunks than some others. Between the chunks, which were still so hot, there must be gaps. The quenching action closely following the piling up must harden the surface of these chunks, preventing the gaps from being "welded" smooth and disappearing.

Now, between the gaps and against the hardened surface of these chunks, two action from the nature competed each other: The relentless heat from the thermal core must melt the surfaces and weld the chunks, but the water's constant quenching must solidify the surface and keep the independence of each chunk. Random chance gradually allowed some chunks to melt into some bigger one, but some gaps stubbornly persisted and may even connect with other gaps to form a longer gap. Surrounded by some big long gaps, through which heat from the thermal core continued to egress, were some chunks persistently lasting. All these chunks coming together formed a solid spherical shell of extremely uneven thickness wrapping around the thermal core. So wrapping, each of them constantly shifted with respect to each other at the unyielding high pressure of lava and gas that must find exit between the gaps. The shifting was further enhanced because the melting and quench also constantly changed the shape of the chunks' edges. Tectonic plates were then a born-with feature of

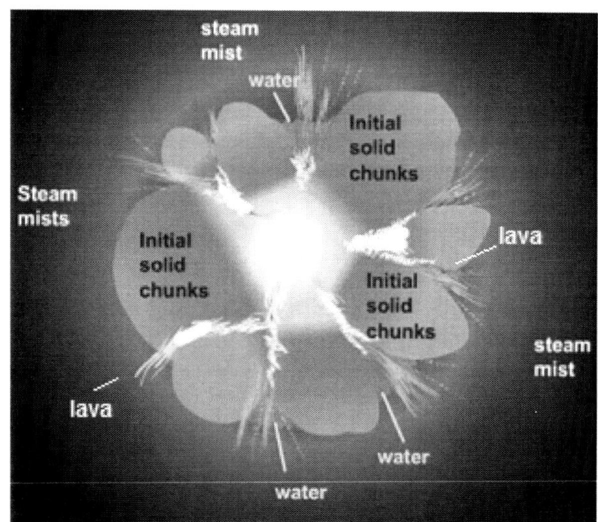

Figure 28. Three major structure components for the early Earth: atmosphere (with saturated steam), ocean, "solid" crust, under which was the thermonuclear inferno

Earth. They were there as a phenomenon ever since the Grand merger, although the size of the nowadays plates and those in the Earth's infant period have no comparison. It should be natural that in the old days these tectonic plates were smaller in sizes and moved and thus quaked more violently and more often. The shape change of the tectonic plates with mechanism so mentioned above resulted in continental drifting and ocean reshaping in Earth's history, although the pace of such drifting and reshaping can be regarded as nothing today compared in what happened in the remotely old days.

In the beginning days of Earth, the oceans may be in a constant boiling state, unable to hold a sizable volume of a water body like what we see today. The water was too busy presenting itself as steam circulating between the sky and Earth's solid surface that was yet far from being prominently settled. In comparison, lacking water to quench, Venus in its evolution progress appeared with a procedure more like a prolonged annealing. This was the result of Venus's robbery of someone else's puffy jacket in starting her life. The hot jacket was a good agent to keep water from condensing but then to push the water in steam form to get out to the outer space.

5.2. Magnetic Poles Drifting, Polarity Reversal

A thermal entity overwhelmingly relying on nuclear reaction to sustain its energy output usually produces abundant neutrons [4] [9]. A material collection that is rich of neutrons like neutron stars usually carries strong magnetism. This is not to claim that neutron is the source of magnetism, but just to say that a sizable volume consisted of high proportion of neutrons has inseparable association with magnetism. Is the magnetism caused by neutrons themselves or by a substance that is not yet identified by scientists but must follow the whereabouts of neutrons like the pilot fish following the sharks? We have no evidence to give solid answer to this question. But this article certainly would like to exploit the high degree affinity we find in nature between a collection of neutrons and magnetism to explain the magnetic phenomenon existing in the solar system. Since we are unable to determine whether neutron or just a separated substance does the job of magnetic field generation, this article would use the term *magnetic material* (abbreviated as magmat) for such a substance causing magnetism. A sizable body formed by such material and carrying magnetism is called a *magmat bearing chunk* (MBC). Whether a magnetic elementary particle is virtually the same as a neutron or something independent but highly associated with neutron is not the concern of this article.

In the upcoming text, we will see that allowing the existence of MBC will enable us to have high satisfaction in explaining the magnetic pole reversal in the Earth's history as well as the sunspot periodical magnetic polarity flipping. We know that the Earth's magnetic pole reversal happened with very irregular duration, ranging from thousands of years to hundred thousand or even millions of years. In comparison, the sunspots reverse their polarity in every 11 years or so. Why? The obvious physical character between the Sun and Earth is that the Sun's surface is extremely fluidic but the Earth's surface is rock solid. The behavior of the Sun's magnetic field is manifested through the activity pattern of sunspots, some material gathering of high mass density flying on the surface of the Sun with high degree of freedom in a fluidic environment. What if the same material gatherings are also found with the Earth? The core of the Earth is where a violent nuclear reactor is. Why material gathering rich in neutrons cannot be produced from it? If we could not exclude such production, and therefore we allow the existence of two sunspots existing in the lava fluid inside the Earth's crust, we will find why the Earth's magnetic field must flip, and flip with highly irregular "period".

If the MBC is something consisted of materials rich in neutron, we would naturally designate it as something of high mass density, the high mass density is further escalated since their magnetism must encourage each of such elementary particle to tightly clench each other. Judging from how a sunspot can defy the destructive temperature in the Sun, the MBC's material integrity should be independent of temperature. In other words, with all this description, the MBC we speculate existing inside the cage of the Earth's crust and the sunspot should be highly identical in material nature. A more detailed analysis on this regard can be found in the article **Sunspot cycle, gravity, and magnetism** in the 2017 Proceedings of John Chappell Natural Philosophy Society by this author or at the website *www.huntune.net* .

Because of its incessant and strong nuclear activity, the

thermal core of Earth must continuously spray neutrons onto the inner wall, or the mantle, of Earth. Once they get there, they would potentially collect each other at their own magnetic influence and form an MBC. The isotropic spraying with respect to the center of the thermal core would result in one of such MBC symmetrically to appear at each end of an Earth's inside diameter, which in absolutely most of the time is oriented in a direction different from the Earth's spinning axis. The reason of such orientation is given later. Some magmat happened to receive less power when sprayed. For them, they would fall to the center of the core and form another MBC. So, inside the shell of Earth, there are totally three absolutely major bodies of MBC: one at each end of the inside diameter and one at the center of such diameter. These three MBC's all line up their magnetic polarity with the same orientation, and therefore they act together as if each of them is part of one long magnet bar.

The two MBCs at the end of the inside diameter are pressured and anchored on the inside wall of the Earth's crust by at least two forces: the thermal core's exploding force and the centrifugal force caused by Earth's self-spinning. The Earth's inside shell wall should be something in a state from liquid lava to pasty hot "mud", which gradually solidified to more rocky materials at distance further away from the core. Because of the "muddy" condition, each MBC cannot find too much freedom to move if it must be motivated to move; its movement, if any, can only be slow sliding and wading on such a wall of high consistence. However, besides the two forces just mentioned, some other forces do also constantly influence the movement of the two MBC's so anchored on the muddy wall. Among these forces, the following major ones are found: (1) the centrifugal force produced by Earth's orbital rotation with respect to the Sun, (2) the gravitational force from the Sun and other planets, (3) the gravitational force from the Moon. While force (1) and (2) intend to confine the two MBC's to lie flat in the ecliptic, the centrifugal force from the Earth's self-spinning force tries to confine them on the Earth's equatorial plane, which forms an angle of 23.4^o with the ecliptic. In addition to all these, force (3) would intend to drag an MBC to another plane, which is the orbital plane of the Moon about Earth. There are more other forces, but they are far trivial than what have been mentioned, and we neglect them in our illustration.

The struggle between all these forces in the competition of relocating the two MBC's incessantly continues daily, monthly, and yearly. Indeed, in every six months, the two MBC's even take turn to get closer to the Sun or farther away from it. Had the Earth's interior wall and the MBC's been rock solid, we can imagine how the two MBC's would fiercely roll and tumple inside the Earth's shell. However, the thick lava mud hinder their tumbling movement into slow sliding or drifting. After a long history of drifting, a term called geomagnetic excursion can be applied to their trail of movement. If the excursion happens to have the two MBC's migrate across the equator, reversal of magnetic poles of Earth occurs (Fig. 29 , Fig. 30).

Not every excursion necessarily ends up with a magnetic pole reversal, unless equator migration does have happened. Although all forces influencing the MBC seems predictable individually, the vector sum of all them always changes in a nearly unpredictable manner; the unpredictable vector sum of these forces naturally makes the period of pole reversal hard to predict. Indeed, at some point of the excursion, whether Earth happens to be at its perihelion or aphelion gives a critical influence in tipping the happening or not happening of the equator migration of the MBC's. At certain point of time, even the whereabouts of the Moon may play a critical role whether to lure the equator migration to happen or not.

The idea of using MBC to explain the magnetic pole reversal in the Earth's history can render us good consistence in explaining the cycling rhythm that the sunspot activity shows. But we first need to look at the Sun's basic structure in more details to see the critical reasons.

6. The Sun

6.1. Basic Structure

If the Sun is homogeneous or isotropic in material distribution within its body, it would be inevitably oblate when spinning. The nearly zero oblateness at its "waist" must require of the existence of a force that is able to counteract the spinning centrifugal force, which will cause any spinning fluid body to appear oblate. The logical candidate that can produce such a force is some gravitational force from inside the Sun, provided that this force can be the strongest in the Sun's equatorial plane, but gradually weakening at higher and higher latitudes. A massive homogeneous body of high mass density in a spheroid shape could certainly function in this way if its largest circle is coincided with the equatorial plane of the Sun. So, conversely speaking, the near perfect but spinning fluidic body of the Sun strongly suggests the existence of such a spheroidal body deep below the surface of the Sun (Fig. 31). Of course, for this spheroidal body to counteract effectively the centrifugal force received by the materials on the Sun's surface, the mass density of this spheroidal volume must be far higher than that of the surface materials, too.

The Sun's apparent surface characteristics could not provide enough temperature and pressure for the thermonuclear reaction to be hosted at its surface. Therefore, a zone for such reactions to be continuously in process must be far below the material surface found in our direct view. It is commonly published that the core part of the Sun has a mass density of 150 gm/cm^3. Naturally, such mass density cannot exist in the zone of thermal nuclear reaction. All these must further suggest that such mass density can be found only in the space enwrapped by both the materials surface and the nuclear zone. Therefore, the Sun is fundamentally consisted of the following three layers:

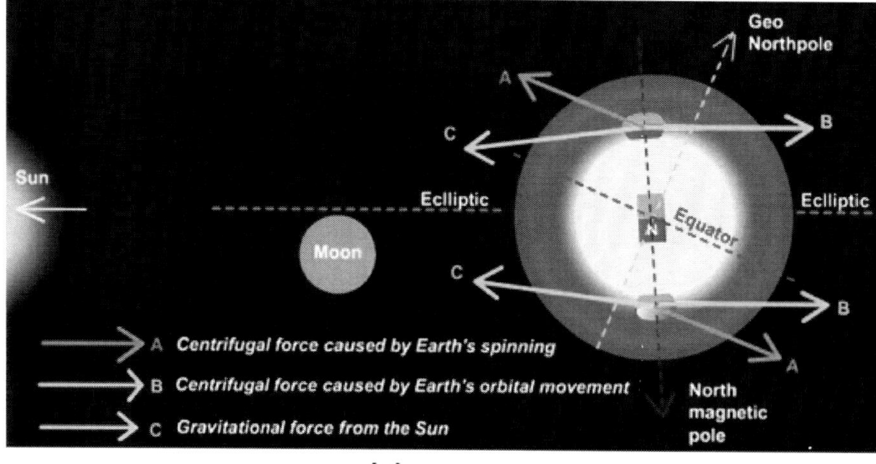

(a)

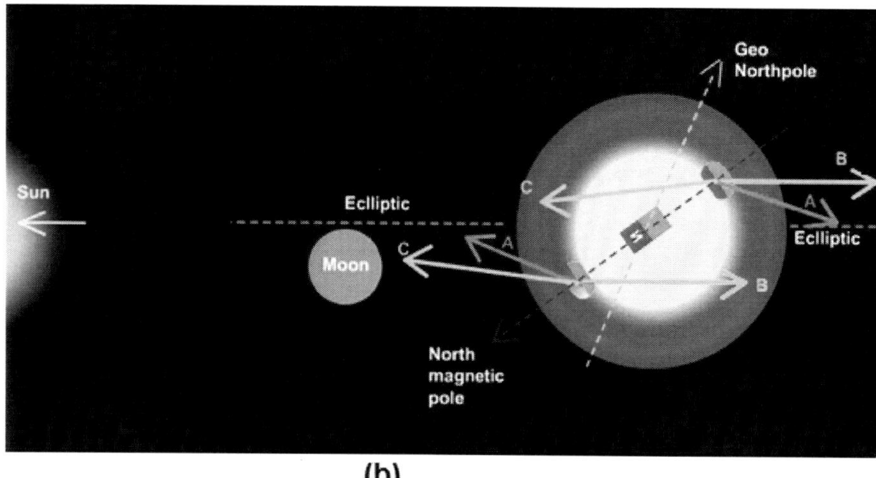

(b)

Major force line arrangement on the MBCs changes from (a) to (b) in 12 hours (Moon's force not shown)

Figure 29.

1. The outmost layer, which is called the fluidic "crust" of the Sun in this article; it is this crust that appears in our daily view about the Sun.
2. The nuclear furnace layer, which is below the crust mentioned above;
3. The Sun's core volume that monopolizes the Sun's absolute high mass density, which is called the Sun's yolk in this article (Fig. 32).

Given that the temperature must be inevitably outstandingly high in the inner part of the Sun, the Sun's yolk must be in a state with certain fluidity. This fluidic yolk cannot escape from self-spinning unless the Sun is not found spinning. Being in self-spinning, the Sun's fluidic yolk must shape itself into a spheroidal volume, with its biggest dimension coinciding with the Sun's equator. With this biggest dimension but of high mass density, the yolk naturally creates the strongest gravitational force measured on the Sun's equator, and the gravitational force from the Sun's center becomes the weakest at the pole. The strongest gravitational force lying in the equatorial plane then corrects the Sun's tendency of bulging at its "waist" due to self-spinning. We subsequently see the Sun in a shape of near perfect sphere.

The Sun's differential rotation can further serve as evidence suggesting the existence of a spheroidal yolk inside the Sun if the yolk can be further regarded as the storage tank of hydrogen fuel for all the major nuclear reaction in the Sun. Let's suppose on the surface of the yolk one nuclear reaction happens on the equator and another one happens near the pole area. Reaction product produced at the equator will find a shorter distance to reach the surface

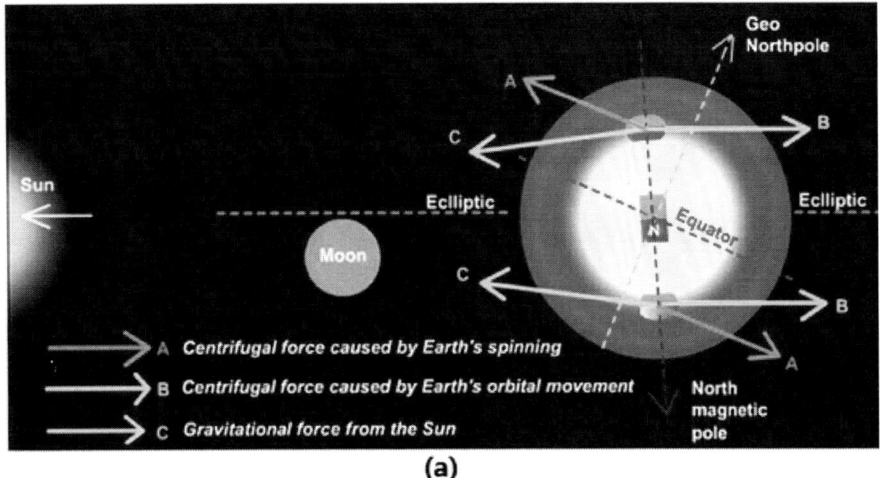

(a)

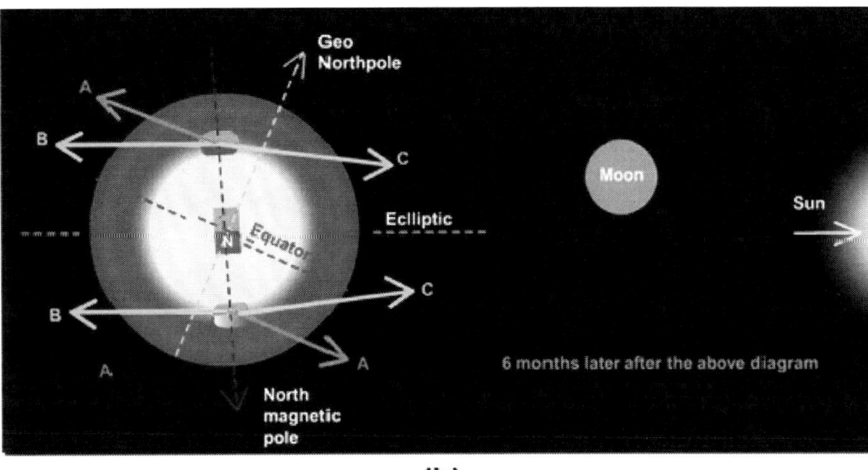

(b)

Major force line arrangement on the MBCs changes from (a) to (b) in 6 months (Moon's force not shown)

Figure 30.

of the Sun compared to those produced near the pole. Besides, those materials produced at the equator of the yolk are also born with bigger angular momentum and subsequently higher tangential velocity with respect to the center of the Sun. Both factors of shorter radial distance to the surface of the Sun and higher tangential velocity at the equator will result in the Sun's differential rotation.

That the yolk of the Sun can stay in shape is because of the packing action exerted on by the nuclear explosions, which happen in an isotropic manner with respect to the center of the Sun allover in the entire vicinity of this yolk. It is also such packing action that has forced the volume of fluidic state to stay in shape with high mass density. With a mass density of 150 gm/cm^3 for this fluid yolk, even osmium can float on it like a feather.

We have previously reasoned that the material forming the sunspots should be some substance gathering that is rich of neutrons. If the material forming the sunspots can be found in the fluidic crust above the fusion reaction zone, the same should have equal chance to be found at the bottom of this zone. At the bottom of the reaction zone, or on the surface of the yolk, material floating there should have far less area to spread out than those in the fluidic crust, and would thus easily collect each other and clench into a big material body under their own mutual magnetic influence. We will call this body floating on the surface of the yolk the migrating magnetic body (MMB). Why "migrating"? The reason is to be given soon. To imagine how big this MMB could be, let's at least put together all those sunspots found in our direct view. This is only natural. Sprayed out equally in all directions by each nuclear reaction, riding on the free movement thus gained, the newly born materials

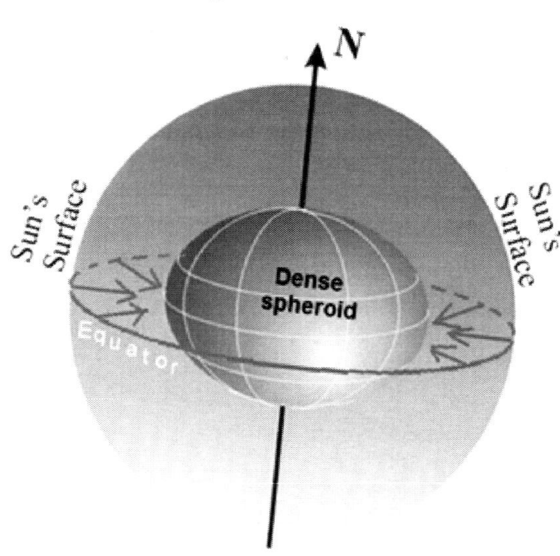
N
Sun's Surface
Sun's Surface
Dense spheroid
Equator
A dense sphroid's strongest inward pullining gravitational force at the equator corrects the Sun's oblateness at its "waist".

Figure 31. Dense core of the Sun

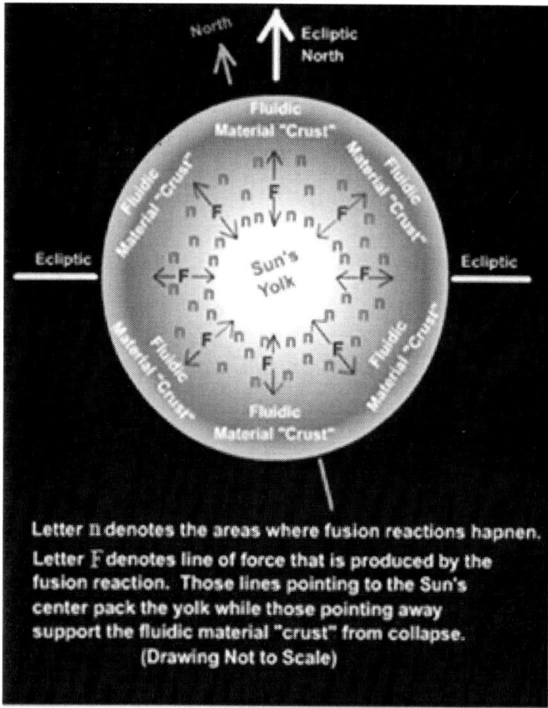
North
Ecliptic North
Fluidic Material "Crust"
Ecliptic
Ecliptic
Sun's Yolk
Letter n denotes the areas where fusion reactions hapnen.
Letter F denotes line of force that is produced by the fusion reaction. Those lines pointing to the Sun's center pack the yolk while those pointing away support the fluidic material "crust" from collapse.
(Drawing Not to Scale)

Figure 32. Three fundamental layers of the Sun's material structure: Fluidic crust, thermonuclear burning zone, the yolk

would have far higher chance to fly toward the source of gravity other than away. The MMB floating on the surface of the yolk and the two MBC's residing inside the Earth's terrestrial cage in our previous reasoning and the sunspots should all be essentially consisted of the same materials. However, we continue to call sunspots as sunspots, following the customary calling.

With the Sun's yolk so structured, even if the MMB has higher mass density than the yolk, but the MMB is said still to be able to float on the surface of the yolk. Isn't this reasoning violating Archimedes' principle concerning hydrostatics? The paragraphs below present the reasons to solve this mystery. The solutions should also serve as the key to unlock the riddle about the appearance of prominence and solar flare.

Among all forces that can happen in the Sun, no force can be more violent than the explosive force resulted from hydrogen fusion. Violent as it is, however, the hydrogen fusion cannot have happened inside the yolk. If it ever has, the yolk would have been disintegrated, and no perfectly round Sun can ever appear in our observation. In other words, a hydrogen bulk can join the fusion reaction only if the source material of fuel from it can "slowly" infiltrate into the region outside of the yolk but through a process of gradual shedding. This further means that at where there is less hydrogen infiltrating, there is less fusion reaction and thus less strong explosive force. So natural, then, at where the MMB covers, hydrogen cannot directly infiltrate to the reaction region. This immediately means less inward packing force is received by the yolk at where the MMB resides and covers. The shielding provided by the MMB creates inevitable chance for virgin hydrogen as a huge bulk to leak from the yolk beneath the MMB. The leaking cannot be a gentle process but some violent jet squirting because of the exceedingly high pressure received anywhere else by the yolk. The violent jet squirting forcefully supports the MMB from sinking to the inside of the yolk.

With the MMB in the Sun being so resulted and with its mass density so high, it must have its own conspicuous response to the gravitational summon from all the planets. We know that the Sun's equator has a 7.5^o inclination with respect to the ecliptic, in which lie all the planets' orbit. Therefore, the planets must have their force combined in one single vector sum in one plane and herd this MMB's movement. Because this vector sum of force must rotate as the planets rotate, from time to time this force vector inevitably drags the MMB to migrate across the equator of the yolk; the MMB permanently faces one direction with its magnetic orientation with respect to the center of the Sun. As this MMB moves, it must in turn orchestrate the swarm of all the sunspots to follow via the magnetic force between them. To give detailed description how the swarm of sunspots dances following this MMB's conducting, it deserves one single topic by itself. In order not to disturb the coherence of a discussion on how the solar system is given birth, which is the main focus of this article, this author decide to separate the detailed elaboration on the sunspot activity from this article and present it in another article titled as **Sunspot Cycles, Gravity, and Magnetism**. This article can be found in the 2017

Proceedings of Chappell Natural Philosophy Society via www.naturalphilosophy.org. The same article can also be found at this author's website *www.huntune.net.*

Before we end this topic, this author would like to say that between the MMB and each sunspot, there is a magnetic "tube" formed by them. It is this magnetic tube that links the appearance of solar flare and prominence. Details concerning their appearance can also be found in the article mentioned above.

7. Jupiter's Red Spot

Jupiter is a powerful radiator of thermal energy. A long history ago in its evolution, Jupiter's thermal core must have been far more powerful, and the nearly entirely gaseous Jupiter must be occupying far more volume as well. However, this gaseous conglomeration but in rotating state could only be fundamentally a flat disk except in area around its core. Because of the stronger gravity of the core, it collected more materials around it and resulted in a bulged volume at the central region of the flat disk. The edge-on view of the Milky Way could well render us an imagination how a spinning disk should look like (Fig. 33). In comparison, the primordial Jupiter was a huge spinning disk comprising loose materials as its absolutely majority of components. The materials that this spinning disk consisted of must be constantly compelled to move by these three forces: (1) the exploding force of the thermal core, (2) centrifugal force resulted by the spinning of the disk, (3) gravitational force. Force (1) and (2) must throw materials away from the center of disk, but force (2) being the strongest at the equatorial plane of the disk, while force (3) always contracts materials toward the core.

Figure 33. Edge-on view of the Milky Way Galaxy. PIcture credit: ESO/NASAJPL-Caltech/M.Kornmesser/R.Hurt

While the materials were so violently shuffled by all these three forces, when they got to the outer edge of the spinning body where coldness dominated, they cool down and potentially solidified. When they were pulled back toward the center by gravity, the thermal core would have them melted again. The countless trips of these materials between the gelid outer edge and near the thermal core caused immeasurable amount of heat loss of the core. Gradually, solidified materials must get closer and closer to the core to get melted again. This closeness about the core also increased the chance for each solid chunk to meet and be fused with another solid chunk neighbor. As bigger and bigger chunks gradually formed, they gained more and more potential to defy the explosive force of the thermal core, which was inevitably getting weaker and weaker as time progressed because of heat loss. Finally, there came the day that even the final gap between the chunks got sealed up. A ring thus took shape and continued to rotate about the core because of the residue angular momentum that the ring inherited from those ancestral flying chunks. Of course, only materials of high melting point could have the chance to form such a ring (Fig. 34).

(i) After the Jupiter Clash, loose materials flew around a dense core

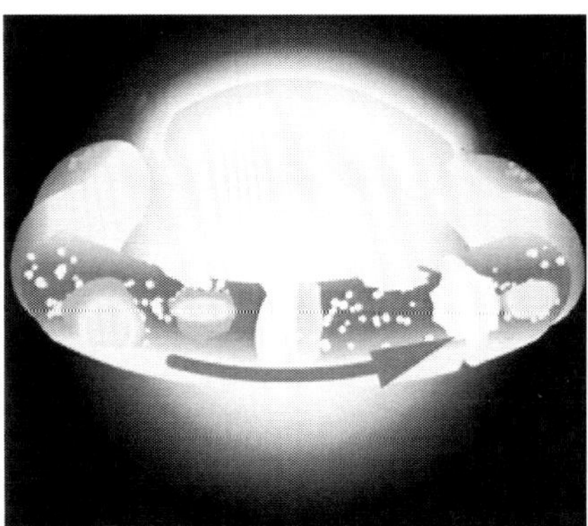

(ii) Gradually, the loose materials fused with each other to form bigger and bigger chunks to continue flying about the core

Figure 34. A solid ring gradually grew out of the loose materials around the thermal core

The dynamical nature leading to the birth of the ring should make this ring most potentially seat flat in the Jupiter's equatorial plane. Its birth shielded up a great deal of the core's heat radiation in that plane. Therefore, more materials flying at the outer edge would speed up their pace to get solidified. Most of these solid materials, unable to overcome the escape velocity destined by Jupiter's gravity, lost the flying power and then plunged and piled up at the outer surface of the ring. Their piling up at a distance closer to the center naturally escalated the self-spinning rate of Jupiter. As to those solid chunks with momentum that was slightly higher than what the escape velocity allows, they may stay at the outer edge to become one of the sources of Jupiter's satellites.

As to the materials supposedly contributing to the source of Jupiter's satellites, had their natural conditions happened to be proper, they may have left behind a ring other than some satellites around Jupiter. The natural conditions mentioned here included their physical property, such as melting point, the distance from the core, the size of each individual chunk... They were so left behind as a ring just like the ring that was formed closer to the core in the previous reasoning, but to form a ring closer to the core the materials must be of higher mass density and higher melting point. This mechanism how a ring can form should be well applicable to explain how Saturn got its multiple icy rings of different diameters.

The materials on the inner wall of the ring, being closer to the thermal core, kept being liquefied or even vaporized. The materials so liquefied must be swung out by the Jupiter's centrifugal force as well as blown out by the core's nuclear exploding force. Blocked by the thick wall of the ring, the fluidic materials can only find the upper rim and the lower rim of the ring as their exit. However, once they exited, they entered an environment where temperature abruptly plummeted. Those materials of high melting point would easily got solidified again. So solidified, they soon formed a new ring packed on top or below the first ring (Fig. 35). The newly formed rings was at higher latitudes, south as well as north, where centrifugal force is weaker, and therefore must be in smaller diameter than the first one. The same action of nature just repeated itself, and soon a third tier of ring but in even smaller diameters appeared.

Figure 35. New ring was in the process of forming above (and below) the existing old ring.

More tiers of rings continued forming. However, time eventually brought this process to a point of balance, which was mainly determined by the following factors: the "left over" of the thermal power of the core, the overall thickness of the rings, the height of the shaft embraced by the rings from top to bottom, the self-spinning angular velocity of Jupiter, the melting point of the various materials consisting of the rings. When this balance point arrived, no more prominent ring appeared.

Would the opening at top or bottom of the shaft be eventually sealed up? Not if the thermal core is still powerful enough! However, both of the openings must be in a process of diminishing. Possibly nowadays they have been very small, and so small that they can practically be considered as the conduit and vent of two volcanoes, with one on each of the spinning poles of Jupiter. But they are certainly the most powerful volcanoes on that planet.

With the way how the tiers of ring have been resulted, we can be certain that the wall, or crust, encircling the shaft cannot be a dead solid blind wall. But instead, countless openings can be found and profuse materials of various chemical nature in high temperature are gusted out from them by the thermal core. These openings are then the innumerous volcanoes in Jupiter. Now, the countless powerful volcanoes, the ridge and valleys that are formed by the piling up of rings and parallel to the equator, and the abundant materials of various properties all come together covering Jupiter giving us a view like this: Incessant cyclonic storms of high magnitude of power are relentlessly whirling all over because the volcanoes appear in both the ridges and valleys; the atmosphere so agitated by these storms shows different bands of alternated brightness and colors because at where a valley is found the vertical dimension of the atmosphere is bigger than that is over the ridges on both sides of this valley. At very high latitudes, the rings are formed under weaker magnitude of centrifugal force and the contrast of height between the ridges and valleys is less prominent. So the gaseous blanket at higher latitudes appears with less distinctive bands (Fig. 36).

The immense heat of the core makes the rings' materials under a constant recycling process. The inside surface of the shaft is continuously melted by the core; the melted materials then are thrown out as steam, ashes or lava through all the volcanoes. Once they get to the outside world, they solidify and redeposit on the outer surface of the rings, renewing the landscape of the ridges and valleys. This unstoppable recycling makes the structure of the crust very unstable, and therefore "earthquake" (Should we call it Jupiter-quake?) happens on Jupiter with high frequency. The highly unstable crust would always shift the location of various volcanoes, too. In other words, some active ones may be suddenly "plugged" for some reason, but some new one may suddenly emerge somewhere else, too.

There may be three material sources contributing to form Jupiter's moons: (1) those that were hurled together by Jupiter's main cloud body even before the Jupiter Clash while the appearance of the solar system was still in the unknown future, (2) those that were later fly-by and gravitationally captured by Jupiter, (3) those that were left behind during the formation process of the rings near the core because these left-outs had possessed enough angular momentum to resist falling onto Jupiter's solid surface. However, in contrast to those successfully staying as moons of Jupiter, there was also the failure of many other materials.

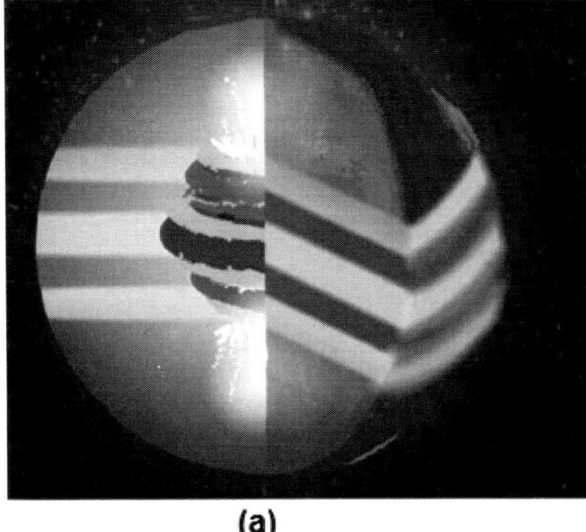

(a)

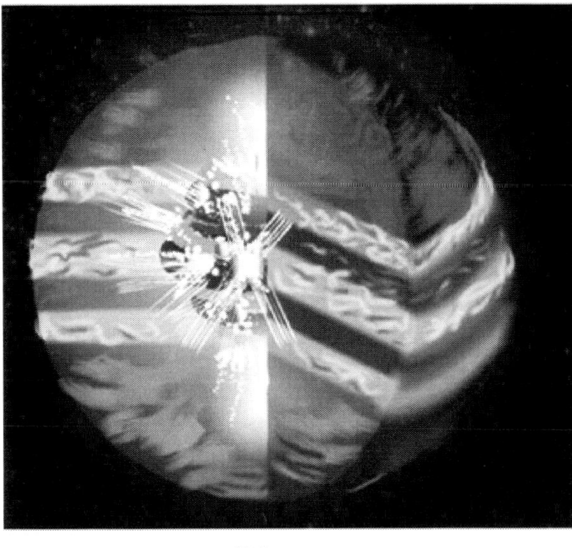

(b)

Reasons for bands and gas turbulence in our view about Jupiter

In both view (a) and (b) the front left part of gas is removed, revealing a solid shell enwrapping the burning core in its central shaft.

The shell is formed of a pile of rings, which cause the shell to have different thickness as the latitudes variate. The different thickness of the shell allows different intensity of energy output from the burning core and results in feature of bands of color.

The way the shell being formed could not have left behind a solid shell as shown in (a), but left behind with the shell numerous holes, or volcanos, as shown in (b).

Incessant powerful energy output of the Jupiter's burning core through all those volcanos of various sizes is the reason why Jupiter displays all those relentlessly violent cyclones.

Figure 36. Atmospheric bands appearing in other gaseous planets should also be able to explain with reasoning shown in this picture

As we mentioned before, some of these failing to stay up high joined to form Jupiter's solid crust that looked like a pile of rings near the core; some others also so failing joined the rings at a later time but then just landed as a separate piece on the outer surface of these rings.

Naturally, after landing as a separate piece, the trough, or valley, between two rings would be the place most probably for this landing piece to stay as a result worked out by both probability and gravity together. If this landing piece was a huge object, the surface underneath where it stayed would always be a number of volcanoes. Several reasons may cause this loose object to slide back and forth along the trough that fostered this loose piece: (1) the self-spinning of Jupiter; (2) the blowing force from the volcanoes, whose venting opening may have size and direction different from each other; (3) the materials of various melting point may sometimes act as solid glue or sometimes as lubricant at where the ground and the loose object came in contact, depending on the instantaneous environmental temperature, which was constantly changing. The cloud features of the Great Red Spot (Fig. 37) and several smaller spots shown in our observation gave us good inference to the existence of such loose objects on Jupiter.

It is possible that Jupiter's solid crust is largely composed of terrestrial materials. But under the formidable atmospheric pressure, they may act somewhat differently from what we know about terrestrial materials on Earth. Nevertheless, consisting of several tiers of rings in the way we conjecture, Jupiter's terrestrial crust should be the thickest near the equator and gradually getting thinner at higher and higher latitude. Ignoring the rippling outline between consecutive rings, the overall shape of this crust is

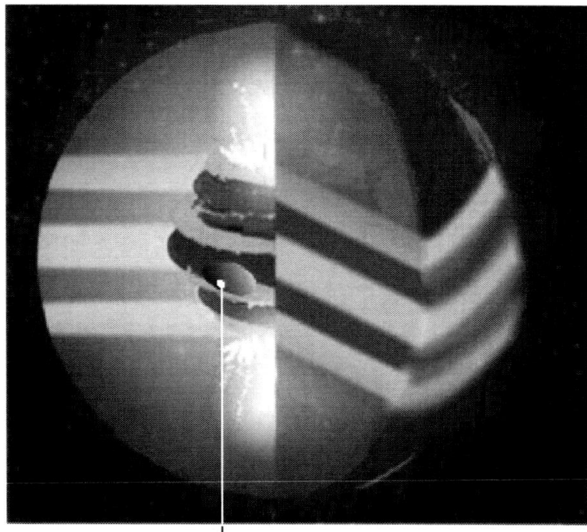
An indepentent object
causing the view of the
"Great Red Spot"

Figure 37. The Great Red spot can slide back and forth in a trough resulted by to adjcent rings

Saturn in natural color approaching equinox, photographed by *Cassini* in July 2008.

From: https://en.wikipedia.org/wiki/Saturn

Figure 38. Saturn

a spheroid, with its biggest dimension coinciding with the equator. With the dense crust having collected more mass at the equator, Jupiter's gaseous blanket at the equator is pulled toward the center of Jupiter; Jupiter's spinning is unable to shape this blanket into an oblate object in our view.

The above description regarding the formation of ridges and valleys of Jupiter's solid crust, if factual, should give us explanation why the gaseous surface of other outer planets are also found divided into many parallel belts and zones (Fig. 38, 39, and 40).

Fig. 33 and 34 together may also render us a clue how the ring system of ice of Saturn has been formed. While some heavier materials could only have stayed so far away from the burning core and danced back and forth about

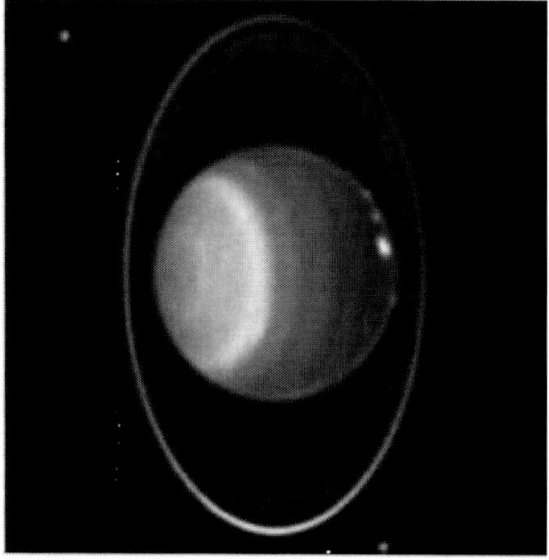

A 1998 false-colour near-infrared image of Uranus showing cloud bands, rings, and moons obtained by the Hubble Space Telescope's NICMOS camera.

From: https://en.wikipedia.org/wiki/Uranus

Figure 39. Uranus

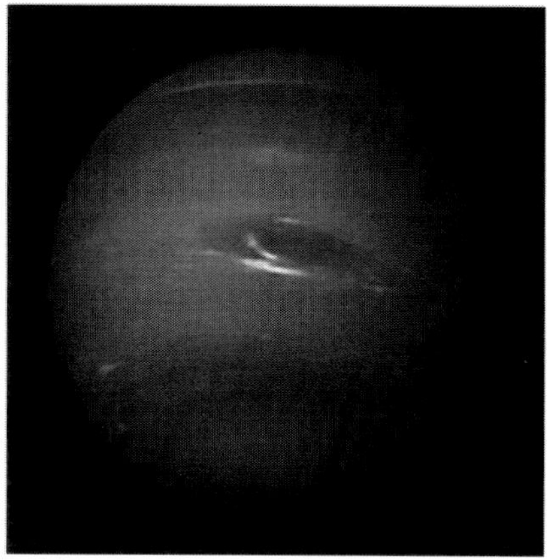

From: https://en.wikipedia.org/wiki/Neptune

Figure 40. Neptune

a certain distance from the dense core before forming the solid crust, some lighter materials could stay farther away from the same core. Eventually, centrifugal force, gravitational force, exploding force, melting temperature all work out "right" to have filtered those powdery chunks of ice intact at where they are found today. Had they not been in such powdery size, they may have been at lower altitude as steamy droplets joining as part of the atmospheric blanket of Saturn. Or, had its size been big enough, also been able to keep enough distance from the core, it may be joining other bigger chunks as part of the Saturn's satellite. However, so formed, the ice ring status could have been acquired only at the very early history when the cloud fragment of the entire future Saturn was still in a flatter shape and spread far widely than we see Saturn today.

Like Venus, Uranus also has retrograde spinning; its axial tilt is 97.9^o to the orbit's. We previously mentioned that Jupiter Clash had brought the opportunity for the inner planets to form. It was highly possible that, about the time the Jupiter Clash happened, the belt shape cloud contributing the major quantity of substance for the outer planets to form was also struck by a comparatively minor size of gas cloud. The minor gas cloud happened to strike at the end part of the belt where the future Uranus and Neptune were to appear. In Fig. 41, the host body H was spinning with its disk highly coinciding with its orbital plane. However, if a visitor like M with proper mass passed in a direction penetrating H's orbital plane at the right speed at a right distance from H, M and H would eventually mingle together under their mutual gravitational influence. The new body so formed by H and M together would have a high chance to end up with a spinning axis essentially parallel to the orbital plane. Visitor P or Q could do the same job as what M did. But, of course, what the diagram shows would mean that all these visitor had come from different sources.

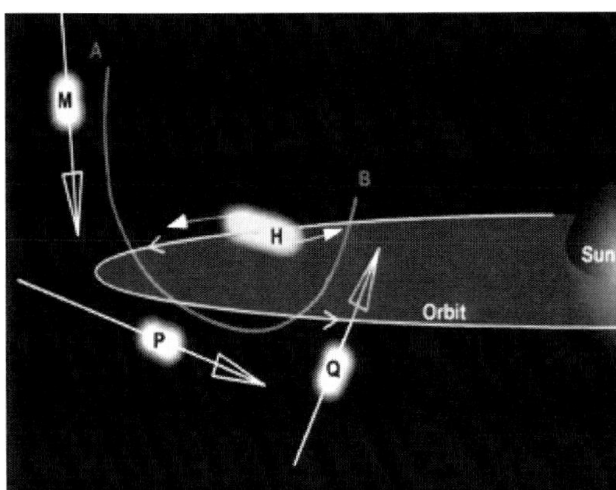

Shown in picture, H's spinning axis should be perpendicular to its orbital plane. The Invasion of a gas cloud M, or P, or Q can offer a potential causing H's spinning axis to lie flat within its orbital plane if the invasion happens in the following environment: (1) H is not too widely spread, (2) M, P, or Q is far enough not touching H, but (3) not far enough to escape from the eventual gravitational arrest of H, (4) the cloud has enough mass.

Curve AB is to show the possible trajectory of M circulating around H.

Figure 41. Possible reason for the direction of Uranus's spinning axis with respect to its orbital plane

8. More on magnetism of the planets

A typical characteristic of the Sun's magnetism is that it is accompanied with a high temperatures environment. Such an environment is also well accompanied with the sustenance of the Earth's magnetic field. There seems existing other evidence in the solar system associating the MBC's as well as the sunspots with exceedingly high temperature environment. Jupiter, the one planet that radiates the most thermal energy among all planets, has the strongest magnetic moment of $1.56x10^{20}$ Tm^3 (Table 2 in Fig. 42). All these let us cast serious doubt on that the magnetic behaves of the Sun and the planets have anything to do with iron, which must dissociate itself with magnetism above the temperature of 770° C; the theory of dynamo requires the existence of iron or iron alloy to support the magnetic activity found in the Sun and planets, and even other celestial bodies.

As to the inner planets, we would compare among three groups to see how magnetism and thermal activity corelate. One group is Mercury and Venus, the other group is Earth and the Moon, and the last group is Mars itself.

Mercury came to exist after one of the PTP's lost its puffy "jacket" of light materials. The jacket so lost resulted in a permanent exposure of Mercury's dense core and the consequential rapid loss of heat energy. As if by a coincidence, Mercury has a much weaker magnetic moment than that of Earth's, which has a solid crust to have its own dense core well wrapped.

Because of Mercury's penetration, Venus had its lighter materials swept to one side of its own future globe for a while. This created a chance for the Venus's denser thermal core exposed on another side of the globe for some time. This action certainly opened a big window for Venus to lose a tremendous amount of thermal energy. However, this was almost nothing compared to the second reason that led to Venus's thermal loss. When the gas jacket returned to a more normal state and had the entire Venus globe evenly robed around, the extremely poor thermal conductivity of the jacket prevented a hard outer crust from forming. For a long time, the crust-to-be for Venus was actually thin flakes of solidified lava floating over an ocean of yet fluidic lava. Gradually, when the flakes gained both in numbers and sizes, numerous volcanoes were formed and hot materials relentlessly continued squirting out through them. In other words, in its entire history of evolving, Venus retained the most generous vents for its thermal energy profusely escaping. The result co-related to this excessive loss of thermal energy is the weak magnetic field of Venus. Interestingly, Venus is by far the hottest planets in the solar system with a surface temperature of 462°[10], a temperature still favoring iron to carry magnetism, if iron is needed to explain the existence of magnetism as what dynamo requires.

Possibly, the reason that Mercury had been able to keep a little stronger magnetic field than Venus was its sudden quick loss of thermal energy right after its thermal core became naked and fully exposed to the space. Following the

Table 2 PLANETARY MAGNETIC FIELDS

	Rotation Period (days)	Magnetic Moment (Earth=1)[a]	Field at Equator (gauss)	Field Ratio[b] Maximum / Minimum	Tilt of Dipole[c] (degrees)	Typical Magnetopause Distance (Rplanet)	Typical Magnetopause Distance (km)	Plasma Sources[d]
Mercury	59	0.0007	0.003	2	+14°	1.5	0.04 x 105	W
Venus	243 (R)[e]	<0.0004	<0.0003	?	-	-	-	A, W
Earth	1.00	1	0.305	2.8	+10.8°	11	0.7 x 105	W,A
Mars	1.03	<2.5 x 10^{-5} [f]	<5 x 10^{-5} [f]	?	-	-	-	A, W
Jupiter	0.41	20,000	4.2	4.5	-9.6°	80	60 x 105	S, A, W
Saturn	0.44	600	0.20	4.6	-<1°	20	12 x 105	S, A, W
Uranus	0.72 (R)[e]	50	0.23	12	-59°	20	5 x 105	A, W
Neptune	0.74	25	0.14	9	-47°	25	6 x 105	S, A, W

[a] Earth's dipole moment = 7.906 x 10^{25} Gauss cm^3 = 7.906 x 10^{15} Tesla m^3

[b] Ratio of maximum surface field to minimum equals 2 for centered dipole field

[c] Angle between the magnetic and rotation axes

[d] W = solar wind, A = atmosphere, S = satellite(s) or rings

[e] (R) = retrograde

[f] These values are upper limits on a global magnetic field. The Mars Global Surveyor has shown Mars to have 2000 km x 200 km regions of strong, local magnetization, presumed to be remnant magnetization produced by an ancient (now inactive) dynamo.

Credit: lasp.colorado.edu/~bagenal/3750/ClassNotes/Class13/Class13.html

Figure 42. Data comparison for magnetic characteristics of the planets

dramatic pace of heat loss was also the less dramatic loss of magnetic moment, because some strong MBC produced in its early history was rapidly frozen and then better preserved inside its body.

Compared to Mercury and Venus, Earth had a much more pronounced thermal core. Not only had this core been the combination of two from the original PTP's, its thermal energy was also well preserved by a thick and hard crust of poor conductivity, which also has far less volcanoes. Accompanied with the effectively retained thermal energy is seen the strongest magnetic field for Earth among all inner planets. On the other hand, lacking the thermal core materials, the Moon not only has kept the lowest mass density compared to other inner planets but it also shows almost zero magnetic moment.

The physical properties of Mars almost fell into the same suit as the Moon: low mass density, no radiation of heat energy, and almost no magnetic moment. This in turn tells us that, lacking the core materials like that of Earth, Mars is unable to establish an apparent magnetic field. Although the reddish color of Mars may have been an indication that Mars was an iron-abundant planet, the element iron obviously has no help for the Mar's magnetic strength. In other words, all planets and the Sun seem coming together telling us that heat, instead of iron, is indispensable for celestial objects to carry a magnetic field, at least so as far as the solar system is concerned.

Must iron in liquid state be an indispensable candidate to help establishing the geomagnetic field? Neutron stars seem rejecting this concept. Not only neutron stars showing strong magnetism radiate high temperature, but their dead solid structure must decline the existence of any fluidic movement like what dynamo requires. It is said that the solar dynamo relies on ionized gas and the geodynamo relies on liquid iron for their operation[11]. Given the environmental temperature that the supposed gas and liquid are in, we must first feel skeptical why the same substances have not been existing in a state of plasma but gas or liquid. Second, for a fluid body to form an electrical current carrying a single charge, it must have to dispose of the other part that carries opposite charge. How will this part of opposite charge exist and work out to maintain the neutrality of the entire fluid body? Just to disappear without producing any electrical and magnetic effect? Ultimately, how will the dynamo theory give a consistent explanation about the difference between the 23 year rhythm shown by the solar magnetic field and the wildly fluctuating "rhythm" of the geomagnetic field?

9. Conclusion

The celestial array displayed in the heavens is showcased by hydrogen thermonuclear reactions sustained through a chain reaction of many billions of years, starting from one point, spreading in an isotropic manner in the unlimited space, generation after generation. This chain reaction of extensively long history then agitated and accumulated all kinds of wild randomness of material combination and material movement. However, wild and uncontrollable as the randomness may appear, any material forming part of it must gradually be grouped, filtered, governed, and settled by some simple laws of nature, among which Newton's laws in mechanics and gravitation play the main role in conducting their behaviors. Among all these settlements, Hubble's Law can be said the best overall rhythmic description about the celestial array so orchestrated by these laws. The appearance of the Solar system is only one of the numerous auxiliary music notes in the grand composition of such rhythmic description. In this system, so many possibilities of combination brought up by wild randomness agitate by awesome magnitude of power have been preserved yet also so systematically arranged, controlled and managed. The seeds of all these arrangements can be so naturally sown by randomness, relying on no precise opportunistic accidents or incidence. However, precise opportunistic accidental occasion seems the dominating theme in the conventional explanation concerning the formation of the solar system. Simply, for example, how could the great varieties of dynamic behaviors found among the Sun and the planets have been self-generated from a cloud of a single state at the absolute absence of foreign interference? The other example is the Moon's staring at Earth with one face. The happening for the staring requires an accident that must happen precisely to the point in every aspect in dynamics. The sad part about the conventional explanation is that when it explains one phenomenon with "satisfaction", it easily fails the explanation on the other phenomenon that requires the explanation of the same nature.

10. Glossary, acronym, abbreviation

Fluidic crust (of the Sun)—the outmost material layer of the Sun in our direct view, which is in a state of plasma.

Grand Merger—a remotely ancient abrupt process of intruding into and mingling with each other made by two heavenly bodies; at the completion of this process appeared our Earth and its annex, the Moon.

Gravitational Platform—a geometrical plane determined by the following three points: (1) the mass center of the Sun, (2) the mass center of the entire collection of the outer planets, (3) the mid-point of the amplitude fluctuation made by the mass center of the Transition Streak (See corresponding term referred below)

Jupiter Clash—a remotely ancient clash made by two major separate cloud bodies in addition to some minor ones. At the completion of this clash came out the primordial group of Jupiter siblings and the Transition Streak (See corresponding term referred below), which provided the material basis for the final appearance of the asteroid belt and all the inner planets.

Jupiter siblings—all gaseous outer planets

Jupiter-Sun Transition—the entire journey made by the Transition Streak (See corresponding term referred below), from the time of its initial appearance to the time it broke and settled as the dust "carpet" that finally evolved into the asteroid belt and a few of pre-terrestrial planets (See corresponding term referred below) revolving about the Sun.

Magmat—magnetic material

MBC—magmat bearing chunks

Migrating magnetic body, abbreviated as MMB —a theoretically derived magnetic body that should be of the same material nature as that of the sunspots but with a mass quantity that is no less than all the sunspots put together. It is a body floating on the surface of the Sun's yolk (See corresponding term referred below) and cruising on it in response to the combined influence from all the planets. Its whereabouts determines where the swarm of sunspots to show up.

MMB—migrating magnetic body in the Sun

Pre-terrestrial planet, abreviated as PTP—a heavenly body revolving about the Sun in time before the appearance of the nowadays inner planets. In the speculation of this article, there should be five of such major bodies, and from them were born the inner planets we see today after some astronomical accidents.

PTP—Pre-terrestrial planets

Rotate—a word in this article most of the time used to describe the revolution movement of an object about an axis that is outside of this object.

Spin—a word in this article most of the time used to

describe the revolution movement of an object about an axis that passes through this object itself.

Terrestrial—used as a noun or adjective in this article to refer to various materials with which the crust of Earth is composed of even if such materials are found in other heavenly objects.

Transition Streak—the material streak formed after the Jupiter Clash and existing during the Jupiter-Sun transition. It is the parental material basis out of which the inner planets and the asteroid belt are finally settled with.

Yolk of the Sun—a theoretically derived material body in fluidic state existing deep inside the Sun. It has extraordinarily high mass density, should be the storage tank of all virgin hydrogen as fuel supply supporting the nuclear burning of the Sun. Due to self-spinning of the Sun, this yolk takes the shape of a spheroid, with its equator and the Sun's equator coinciding in the same plane.

REFERENCES

1. Gabriele Vanin ***A photographic Tour of the Universe***, Firefly Books LTD. 1999
2. Giles Sparrow ***Cosmos, a Filed Gide***, Quercus Publishing Ltd, UK., 2007
3. wikipedia, ***Solar System*** URL: *https://en.wikipedia.org/wiki/Solar_System*
4. wikipedia, ***Asteroid Belt*** URL: *https://en.wikipedia.org/wiki/Asteroid_belt*
5. wikipedia, ***Sun*** URL: *https://en.wikipedia.org/wiki/Sun*
6. wikipedia, ***Sunspot*** URL: *https://en.wikipedia.org/wiki/Sunspot*
7. wikipedia, ***Moon*** URL: *https://en.wikipedia.org/wiki/Moon*
8. The Columbia Electronic Encyclopedia, 6th ed. 2012 ***Nucleosynthesis,*** Publisher:Columbia University Press.
9. wikipedia, ***Proton-Proton Chain Reaction,*** URL: https://en.wikipedia.org/wiki/Proton-proton_ chain_ reaction.
10. wikipedia, ***Venus,*** URL: https://en.wikipedia.org/wiki/Venus.
11. wikipedia, ***Dynamo Theory,*** URL: https://en.wikipedia.org/wiki/Dynamo_theory.

Sunspot Cycle, Gravity, and Magnetism

2017 © Cameron Rebigsol

P.O. Box 872282, Vancouver, WA 98687, crebigsol@gmail.com

No material we know of on Earth can withstand the temperature of nearly 6,000 ^oK found on the surface of the Sun and still stay in one stable structure as how the sunspots show [1] [2]. The heaviest element Osmium has a mass density of $22.6g/cm^3$ with a boiling point of 5285 ^oK, above which no one stable piece of osmium can be found. The next material found with higher mass density is neutron stars. All these potentially lead us to believe that sunspots are composed of material of mass density far higher than osmium. But what is its material nature?

With volumes that can reach even 1,000 times of that of the Earth, together with the unusually high mass density, the sunspots must have response to the gravitational influence from all the planets conspicuously different from the fluidic materials in their environment. The gravitational influence from the planets on the Sun is just an inescapable reciprocal response to the gravitational force from the Sun onto the planets. Therefore, as part of the Sun, the sunspots must be responsible of the exertion of the influence as well as sharing the corresponding reciprocal response from the planets.

When the size of the sunspot is mentioned in our study, we have been getting used to a concept that is portrayed by terms like contract, expand, and decay. If gravitational influence from the planets cannot be excluded in a reasonable speculation, we may have to include one more concept that is portrayed by the term "buoyancy". As such, the visual effect of contracting in our view happens when a sunspot sinks deeper and deeper below the Sun's surface, whereas the visual effect of expanding happens when the sunspot resurfaces and exposes itself more and more in our view. So, given the unusually high mass density of the sunspots, true decaying of them in the sense of material integrity may not be a reality that our study can pursue.

Looking at whether the sunspots should have response to the gravitational influence from the planets, we cannot escape from the awareness of two numbers that are very close in value. One of them is the more or less than 11 year beat of the rhythm shown by the maximum and minimum of the sunspot population; the other is the 11.86 year period of Jupiter's orbital movement. In case the gravity of Jupiter does have influence on the cycle of sunspots, what about other planets? Further, we must be aware of that the Sun's spinning axis tilts by an angle of 7.5^o with respect to the ecliptic, but when a solar maximum begins, the initial few spots always show up near the 45° latitude, north or south. Will the Sun's axial tilt also play a role in affecting the sunspot cycle?

Documents show that the Sun's magnetic field strength distributes itself differently across the surface of the Sun. At its polar field, the strength is found to be 1-2 gauss, whereas it is typically 3,000 gauss in areas where sunspots populate, and 10–100 gauss in solar prominences [1]. Such field strength distribution thus reveals to us the following typical features: (1) the field strength at areas near the equator is far stronger than that near the polar area; (2) while the field is strong near the equator, it is further concentrated at where the sunspots show up; (3) number of the sunspots in our vision displays no direct proportional relationship with the overall strength at where they show up; (4) that 10–100 gauss is found in solar prominences conversely means that the field strength of each sunspot is comparatively weak until some chance is introduced together with a prominence.

Features (1) and (2) can be hypothetically realized by such an arrangement: A strong magnetic bar is placed deep below the surface of the Sun and this bar always has its pole pointing at about the equator, but never at either of the Sun's poles. Feature (3) removes the possibility that the strong magnetic strength near the equator is solely contributed by the sunspots; therefore this reasoning further emboldens a believing that a separate magnetic source other than the sunspots owns this strong field. Being not the source, however, the sunspots' appearance can serve as an index to help tracing how this source has been moving. Is it only coincidence that sunspot never appears at the pole where the magnetic strength is so weak? Feature (4) further witnesses that each sunspot is a weak magnet compared to the one hypothetically assumed existing far below the Sun's surface.

Reasoning in this article based on observation leads to a believing that the Sun is consisted of three basic material layers: (1) the out-most layer, which, in a state of plasma, is the layer in our daily view, and shall be called the **fluidic crust** of the Sun in this article; (2) deep below this crust is a zone that hosts the absolute major thermonuclear reactions of the Sun; (3) further below the nuclear reaction zone is the core body of the Sun, a spheroidal volume of exceedingly high mass density. This spheroidal dense volume shall be called the **yolk of the Sun** in this article. This yolk is embraced by numerous nuclear reactions, which happen all over on the yolk's surface in an isotropic manner with respect to the center of the Sun. Floating on this dense massive yolk is a gigantic magnetic material body (**MMB**), which should have contained no less mass than all the sunspots put together, and its material nature should be essentially the same as that of the sunspots.

Floating on the yolk with mass far exceeding what our Earth has, this MMB cannot escape from the governing action exerted on it by the gravitational force from the planets, particularly Jupiter. Being a gigantic magnetic carrier, its whereabouts must in turn orchestrate the debuting and hibernation of the population of those magnetic sunspots through magnetic reaction. In comparison to this giant MMB, each sunspot is merely a magnet droplet, even if such droplet may reach a volume as big as 1000 times of the Earth. From this thread of reasoning, let's further pursue how the MMB and each sunspot are to form various magnetic "tube" that guides the appearance of prominence, solar flare, and subsequently the coronal mass ejection.

Keywords: magnetism, thermonuclear reaction, equator crossing, ecliptic, centrifugal force

1. Three Fundamental Layers for the Sun

The Sun's apparent surface characteristics could not provide enough temperature and pressure for the thermonuclear reaction to be hosted at the Sun's surface. Therefore, a zone for such reactions to be continuously in process must far below this material surface. It is commonly published that the core part of the Sun has a mass density of 150 gm/cm^3[1]. Naturally, such mass density cannot exist in the zone of thermal nuclear reaction. All these must further suggest that such mass density can be found only in the space enwrapped by both the materials surface and the nuclear zone. Therefore, material-wise, the Sun is fundamentally consisted of the following three layers:

1.) The out-most layer, which is called the fluidic "crust" of the Sun in this article;
2.) The nuclear furnace layer, which is below the crust mentioned in 1);
3.) The Sun's core volume that monopolizes the Sun's absolute high mass density, which is called the Sun's yolk in this article (Fig. 43).

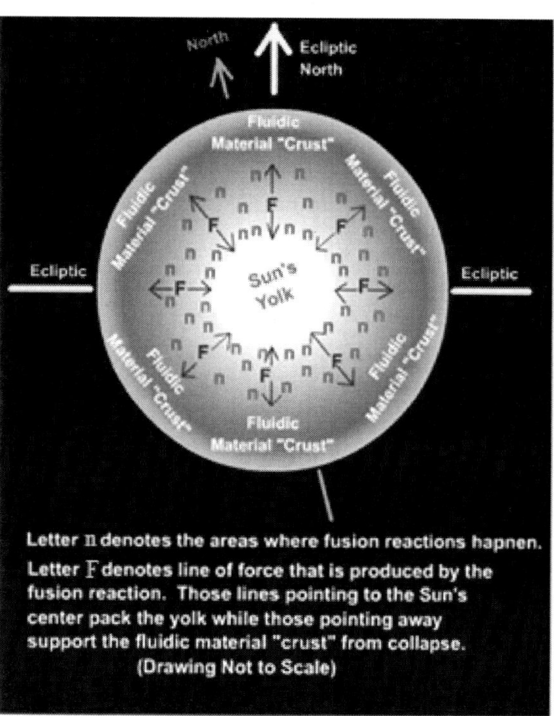
North
Ecliptic North
Fluidic Material "Crust"
Ecliptic
Ecliptic
Sun's Yolk
Letter n denotes the areas where fusion reactions hapnen.
Letter F denotes line of force that is produced by the fusion reaction. Those lines pointing to the Sun's center pack the yolk while those pointing away support the fluidic material "crust" from collapse.
(Drawing Not to Scale)
Basic Structure of the Sun
Fig. 01

Figure 43. Basic Structure of the Sun

Given that the temperature must be inevitably outstandingly high in the inner part of the Sun, the Sun's yolk must be in a state with certain fluidity. This fluidic yolk cannot escape from self-spinning unless the Sun is not found spinning. Being in self-spinning, the Sun's fluidic yolk must shape itself into a spheroidal volume, with its biggest dimension coinciding with the Sun's equator. With this biggest dimension but of high mass density, the yolk naturally generates the strongest gravitational force on the Sun's equator, and correspondingly the weakest gravitational force at the poles. Because of the biggest gravitational force from the center of the Sun found at the equator, the Sun's tendency of bulging at its "waist" due to self-spinning is corrected and we see the Sun with a near perfect sphere. Conversely, the Sun's differential rotation can serve as evidence suggesting the existence of a spheroidal yolk of high mass density inside the Sun. Let's suppose on the surface of the yolk one nuclear reaction happens at its equator and another one happens near the pole area. Reaction product produced at the equator will find a shorter distance to reach the surface of the Sun compared those produced near the yolk's pole. Besides, those materials produced at the equator of the yolk are also born with bigger angular momentum. Both factors of distance and angular momentum will result in the sun's differential rotation, with materials at the Sun's equator moving faster than those near the Sun's pole.

That the yolk of the Sun can stay in shape is because of the packing action exerted on by the nuclear explosions, which happen in an isotropic manner with respect to the center of the Sun allover in the entire vicinity of this yolk. It is also such packing action that creates the volume of fluidic state in high mass density. With a mass density of 150 gm/cm3 for this fluid, even osmium can float on it like a feather. However, that the MMB can float on this dense yolk cannot rely on the floating force described according to Archimedes' principle in hydrostatics, because the MMB should have far higher mass density than the yolk. More details concerning such a "floating" force is given near the end of this article.

We have reason to believe that material forming the sunspots should be the inevitable materials left behind by fusion reactions. Although the nature of such material is hard to verify, its high mass density should make it reasonable to believe that sunspots are something rich of neutrons. If the material forming the magnetic sunspots can be found in the fluidic crust above the fusion reaction zone, the same should have equal chance to be found at the bottom of this zone. At the bottom of the reaction zone, or on the surface of the yolk, material floating there should have far less area to spread out than those in the fluidic crust, and would thus easily collect each other and clench into a big material body under their own mutual magnetic influence. We will call this body so floating on the surface of the yolk the magnetic material body (MMB). To imagine how big this MMB could be, let's at least put together all those sunspots found in our direct view. This is only natural. Sprayed out equally in all directions by each nuclear reaction, riding on the free movement thus gained, the newly born materials would have far higher chance to fly toward the source of gravity other than away.

2. Resultant Gravitational Force of the Planets

With the MMB that is imagined to have collected a total mass no less than all the sunspots put together, we must allow it to have strong response to the gravitational influence from the planets. To analyze such gravitational action, let's first have one inertial system **X-Y-Z** to describe the orbital movement for each planet so that we can later combine all their influence on the Sun as one. This system has its origin coincide with the mass center of the Sun, and its **X-Y** plane coincides with the ecliptic. The orbit of each planet would be regarded as having zero eccentricity and zero inclination to simplify our analysis. The positive direction of the **Z** axis takes the same side with the north geographical pole of the Earth but perpendicular to the ecliptic. The **X** axis has its positive direction points through the Jupiter's orbital position found on Jan 5, 1987. With a day so chosen, we can find the official data about the planets' angular position on that day according to the Astronomical Almanac of 1987, section E, printed by the U.S. government. The positive direction of the **Y** axis is determined by the right hand rule formed by the **Z** and **X** axes.

The angular velocity of all the planets in the **X-Y** plane is taken as shown by their sidereal period. The angle associated with such angular velocity is taken as zero when a planet's orbital radius coincides with the **X** axis. According to all these, we can come to a general vector expression for the gravitational force between the Sun and each planet:

$$\vec{F}_{sp} = GM\frac{m_{sp}}{R_{sp}^2}[\cos(\omega_{sp}t+\theta_{sp})+i\sin(\omega_{sp}t+\theta_{sp})] \quad (4)$$

where M is the mass of the Sun; m_{sp} is the mass of a planet; R_{sp} is the magnitude of the mean radius of the orbit of a planet; ω_{sp} is the angular speed of R_{sp} ; t is the time (Unit of time is to be explained later but will further have $t = m\Delta t$); θ_{sp} is the initial phase angle between the **X** axis and R_{sp} of each planet found on Jan 5, 1987. A picrorial list of θ_{sp} for all the planets fitting Eq.4 is shown in Fig. 44.

For computer calculation, GMm_{sp}/R_{sp}^2 is normalized as unit 1 for the relative magnitude of gravitational influence on the Sun from each planet. All these parameters are listed in the table shown in Fig. 45. With these data, as an example, Eq. 4 can lead us to have the vector equation of gravitational force for Mercury as shown below:

$$\begin{aligned}\vec{F}_{MC} =& 2.003[\cos(4.152m\Delta t+275.97)\\ &+i\sin(4.152m\Delta t+275.97)]\end{aligned} \quad (5)$$

In similar way, the readers can easily figure out the vector equation for each planet. In all these equations, we standardize the time advancement Δt across all the equations according to the following stipulation: Let Δt be the time duration that Jupiter needs to advance by 3 degrees on its

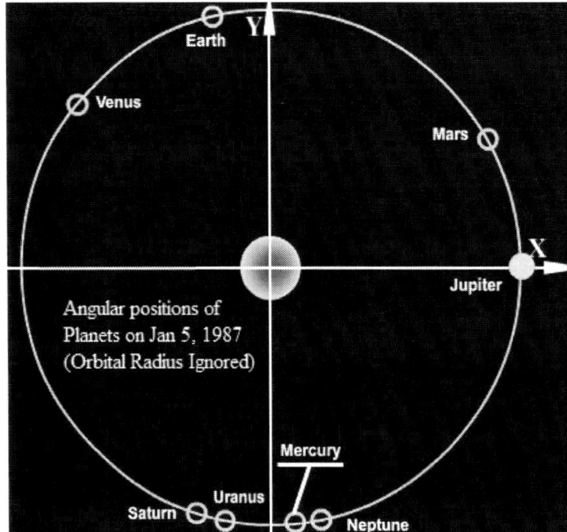

Figure 44. Phase angle of each planet's orbital radius on Jan 5, 1987

orbit. As such, we would have $\Delta t = \frac{3^o/360^o}{11.86} years$ (11.86 years=Jupiter's orbital period), or 0.0988 years. Integer m in these equations stands for the number of increments of Δt, and can be any number including zero. A zero value of m represents the precise day of Jan 5, 1987. If m advances in the positive direction, it means time advances towards the future after Jan 5, 1987; if in the negative direction, it means the time retrogrades towards the past before Jan 5, 1987.

All the force vectors of the planets modeled by Eq.4 can be summed up to one resultant force vector as:

$$\begin{aligned}\sum\vec{F}_{sp} = \vec{F}_{Mc}+\vec{F}_{Vn}+\vec{F}_{Er}+\vec{F}_{Ma}+\vec{F}_{Jp}+\\ \vec{F}_{Sa}+\vec{F}_{Ur}+\vec{F}_{Np}\end{aligned} \quad (6)$$

The magnitude of the resultant force and its corresponding angle ϕ that $\vec{F}_{sp}$ forms with the **X** axis can be calculated according to Eq. 7 and Eq. 8 respectively:

$$F_T = \sqrt{A^2+B^2} \quad (7)$$

$$\sin\phi = \frac{B}{\sqrt{A^2+B^2}} \quad (8)$$

where in both of the above equations
$A = \sum\vec{F}_{sp}\cos(\omega_{sp}t+\theta_{sp})$,
and
$B = \sum\vec{F}_{sp}\sin(\omega_{sp}t+\theta_{sp})$.

Starting from $m = 0$, computer simulation helps to plot F_T and ϕ verses the time for about 30 years after Jan 5, 1987 as well as 100 years prior to that date. The plotting result is shown by the light blue dots in Fig.46. The dots on the top part of Fig. 46 represent angle $(\omega_{sp}t+\theta_{sp})$ and the dots at the bottom represent the magnitude F_T of the

Table I Data for Planets								
	Mercury $= Mc$	Venus $= Vn$	Earth + Moon $= Er$	Mars $= Ma$	Jupiter $= Jp$	Saturn $= Sa$	Uranus $= Ur$	Neptune $= Np$
Mass, M_{sp}, x 10^23 kg	3.3	48.69	60.46	6.4	18992	5867	868.5	1023.5
Orbital Radius, R_{sp}, x 10^6 km	57.9	108.2	149.6	227.9	778.3	1427	2870	4497
Orbital Period, Actual Years	0.24	0.62	1.00	1.88	11.86	29.46	84.01	164.79
Orbital Period, Times of Jupiter's	49.25	19.28	11.86	6.307	1.00	0.403	0.142	0.072
Angular Speed, ω_{sp}, Periods/(Earth year)	4.152	1.6255	1	0.5317	0.0843	0.03395	0.0119	0.006069
Gravitational Influence on Sun, Relative Ratio Value of $M_{sp}/(R_{sp})^2$ between planets	2.003	9.306	6.048	0.276	70.15	6.246	0.233	0.133

Figure 45. Parameters for numerical set up of Eq. 4 for each planet

vector sum of the total gravitational force from all planets (VSGP). In the middle part of Fig. 46 is a diagram from NASA showing the daily sunspot population for a 130 year time span. The bottom curve of Fig.46 shows that the resultant force can fluctuate between a relative magnitude of value 93 at the peak and 46 at the bottom.

In Fig. 46, some lines are drawn "punching" vertically through all three diagrams in the top, middle and bottom parts, matching the time advancement between each of these three diagrams according to the solar maximum and solar minimum. These lines are so named: When a line is through the solar minimum, it is named with a lower case letter, such as ***a***, ***b***, ***c***... When it is through a solar maximum for a group showing one magnetic polarity, it is named with an odd Roman number, such as I, III, V... but for the group showing opposite polarity, it is named with an even Roman number, such as II, IV, VI...

With the zero reference time set on Jan 5, 1987, called the *zero day* in this article, Fig. 46 coves all Jupiter's periods listed in the next paragraph on all days that the NASA diagram covers. To avoid visual confusion, these periods are not specifically marked in the diagram. Each of the period covers 4333 Earth days, but for convenience of illustration each of these periods shown below may have few days earlier or later than actual day.

Period **A-B** starts on (A), Apr 5, 1880, 9 Jupiter periods before the zero day, ending on (B) Feb 15, 1892; Period **B-C** starts on (B) Feb 16, 1892, 8 Jupiter periods before the zero day, ending on (C) Dec 25, 1903 In a similarly manner, we have Period **C-D**, **D-E**, **E-F**, **F-G**, **G-H**, **H-J**, **J-K** (where **K** marks the zero day), **K-L**, **L-M**, then, the most current period, **M**, which starts on Sep 25, 2010 and continues at the present time. A reader shall find that more detailed dates for each period are shown in all corresponding diagrams for the sunspot movement that will be given in upcoming illustration.

We will soon see that the pointing direction of the spinning axis of the Sun is a critically important factor affecting the location appearance of the MMB. With a big volume of mass floating on the yolk and the magnetism the MMB is supposed to have carried, the whereabouts of this MMB must play an imperative role in determining how the magnetic sunspots should show up in the Sun.

Viewed by an observer moving on the Earth's orbit, the north pole of the Sun's spinning axis would be seen as tipping toward him the most on the day about 20 days before the autumnal equinox in the entire year. If we have a bird's eye view on the ecliptic from its north side, the projection of the Sun's spinning axis on the ecliptic should form an angle of $28.37^o (= -8.64^o - 20 \times 360^o/365)$ dragging behind the **X** axis, which has been chosen as the zero time reference (Fig. 47). The reason why angle (-8.64^o) shows

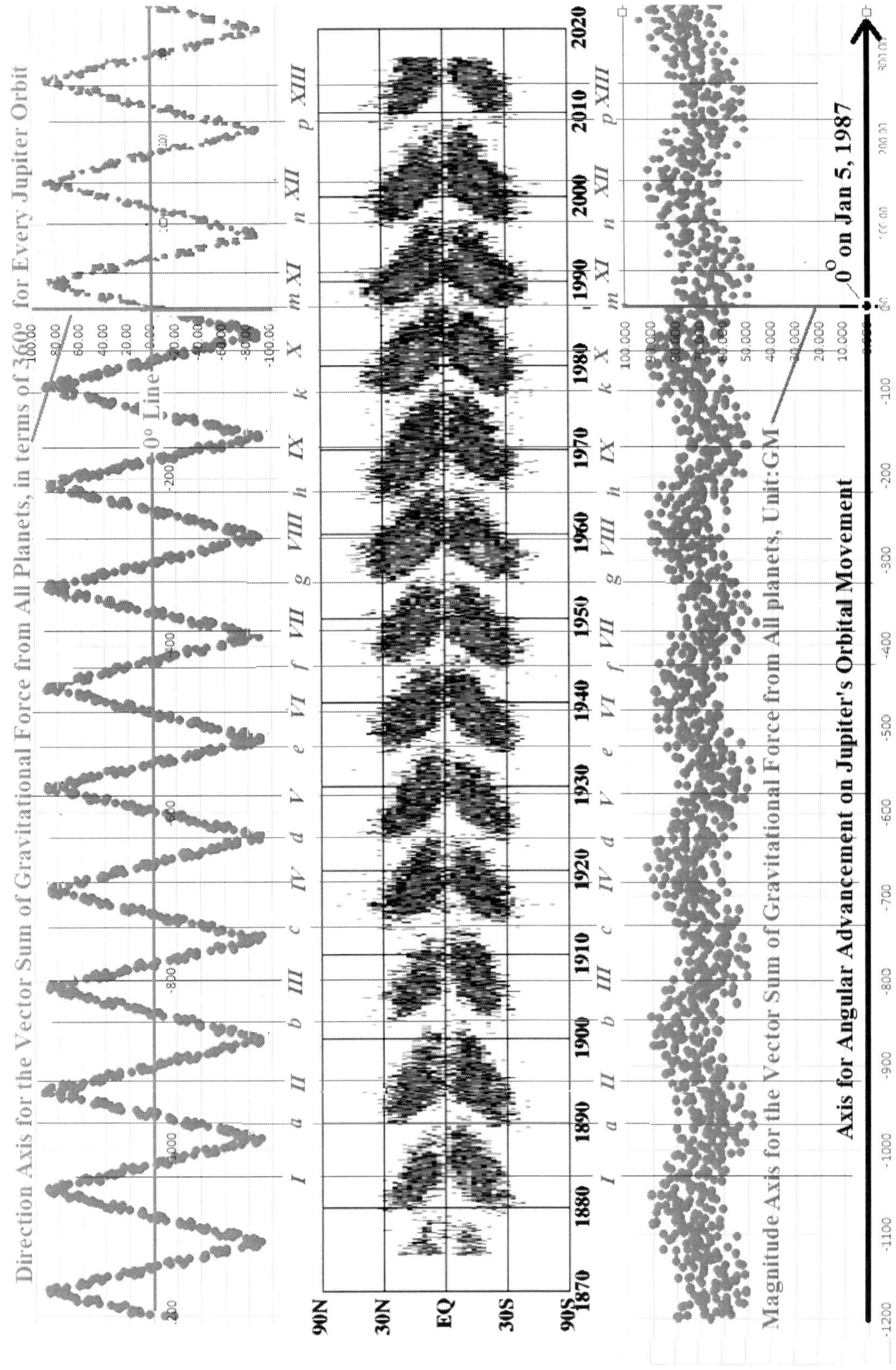

Figure 46. (1) Blue curve on left–angle variation of VSGP; (2) blue curve on right–magnitude variation of VSGP; (3) plot in middle –daily population of sunspots shown by NASA

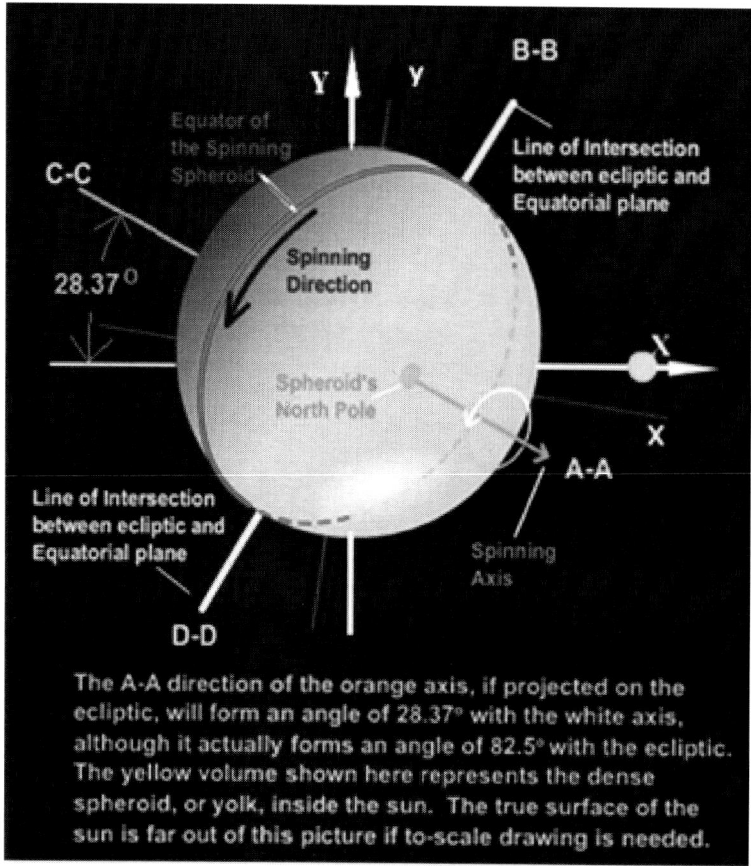

Note: the x-axis passes the autumnal equinox, so the angle between the x axis and X-axis is -8.64°

Projection of the Sun's tilting axis (A-A-C-C) on the ecliptic

Figure 47. The tilting of the spinning axis of the Sun. The yellow yolk is a spheroid. Solid curve of the equator is above the ecliptic; the broken curve of the equator is below the ecliptic.

up is shown in Fig. 47.

3. Time Progression of the Gravitational Influence

Suppose an observer at the location where the Earth's orbit intersects the C-C line, which is the projection of the Sun's tilting axis on the ecliptic (Refer to Fig. 47 and Fig. 48, but Earth's orbit is omitted here), found the MMB floating at position 1 of the Sun's yolk, as indicated by the little blue star behind the yolk in Fig 49. Besides the MMB, he also found that the vector sum of gravitational force from all planets (VSGP), shown as force I with a pink vertical bar in Fig. 49, is moving to the right in his view. (Note: all the light blue balls in both Fig. 48 and Fig. 49 and many upcoming figures represent Jupiter. Jupiter in Fig. 48, in many other diagrams as well, is supposed to be far behind the Earth observer and therefore should not be in his view. The force line and Jupiter so shown in these pictures are to help the viewer to correlate the angle position of the force and Jupiter in his view with the same angles that are suggested in corresponding diagrams.)

Besides the pulling force from the VSGP, shown as force I, the centrifugal force due to the yolk's spinning would also bring the MMB at position 1 to move toward the equator of the yolk. In Fig. 49 and Fig. 50, the MMB shown at position 1 are the same material body. When near the equator, the MMB should have a strong tendency to be pulled across the equator by the VSGP, a force coincides with the ecliptic.

If the MMB does so migrate across, further development guided by the VSGP will bring the MMB to raise to higher and higher latitude in the south hemisphere, as suggested by position 2, 3, 4 and 5 in Fig. 49. During the course of the latitude ascending of the MMB the instantaneous VSGP represented by line I also gradually becomes weaker and weaker besides moving to the right of the picture (actually toward line D-D). During such development, the reducing strength of force I concedes to the centrifugal force a big dominant part of the role in guiding the MMB's movement. Centrifugal force herds the MMB to move toward the equator, resulted in the MMB's movement to be represented by positions 6, 7, 8, 9 in Fig. 49. However, as explained in upcoming paragraphs, between each two consecutive positions, the MMB may have actually rotated about the Sun's spinning axis quite a few times. 49, 48

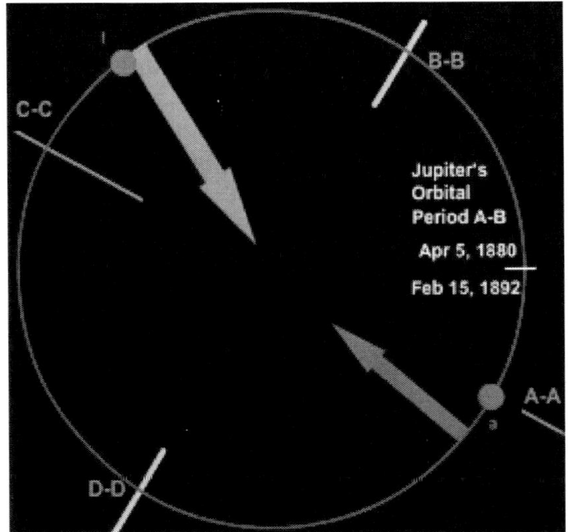

High/low VSGP during period A-B (Apr 5, 1880 to Feb 15, 1892)

Figure 48. High and Low of VSGP during Jupiter's orbital period AB

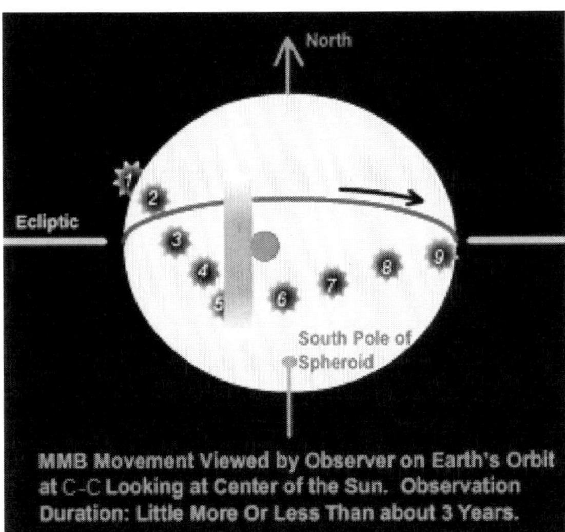

MMB moving to different positions in a 3 year duration in period A-B

Figure 49. Movement of the MMB from position 1 (behind the yolk) to 5 (high south latitude) to 9 (near equator)

Disregarding the differential rotation of the Sun, to make explanation simpler, we can safely assume that the Sun finishes one period of spinning per Earth month. For quick reference, we can also say that Jupiter completes about 30° of movement on its orbit in one Earth year. Therefore, when the MMB completes one rotation about the Sun's axis, Jupiter would have moved only 2.5^o on its own orbit. For practical reason in our illustration, we could sometimes temporarily regard the direction and magnitude of the VSGP to have stayed unchanged when one rotation of the MMB about the spinning axis completes. Therefore, we can imagine that an Earth observer at B-B cannot see the MMB to have completed its relocation from position 3 to 4 in Fig. 49 in one uninterrupted view. But instead, between positions 3 and 4, the MMB would have traveled and gotten behind the dense spheroid and away from his view several times.

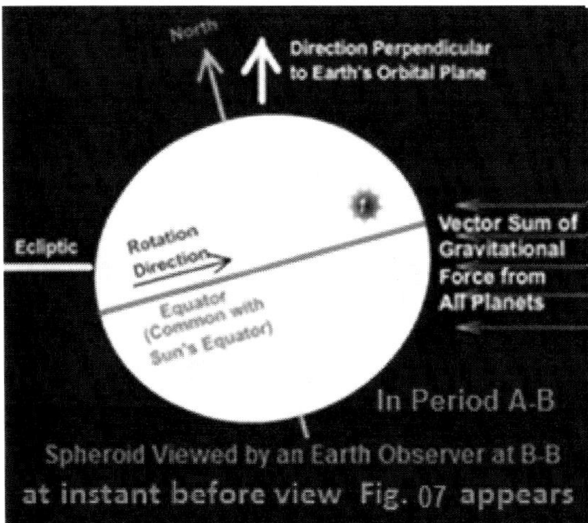

- **MMB at position 1 is found by the Earth observer at the B-B location**

Figure 50.

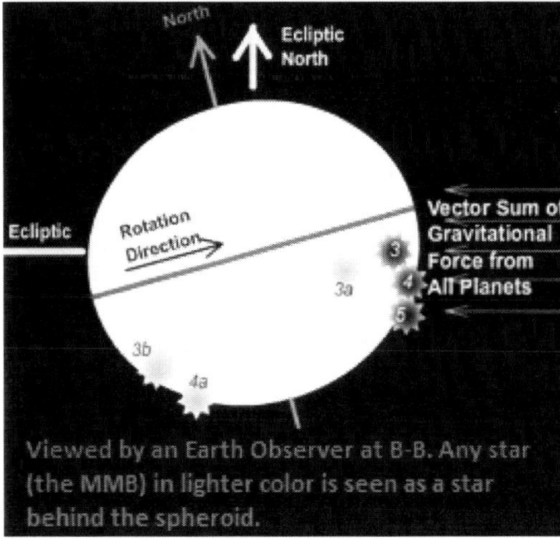

Figure 51. The MMB may get behind the yolk several times between any two apparent positions shown in the diagram.

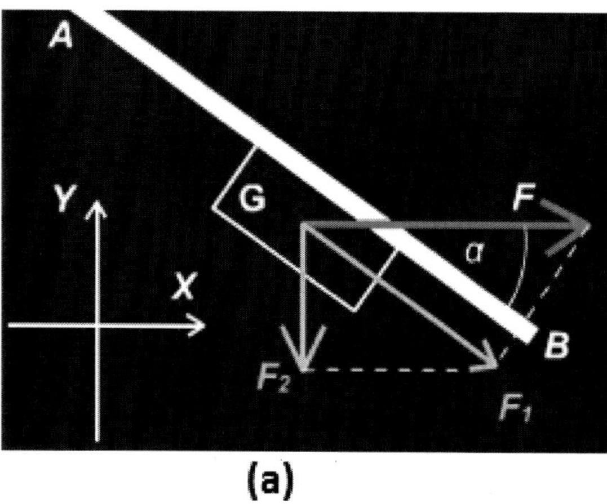

(a)

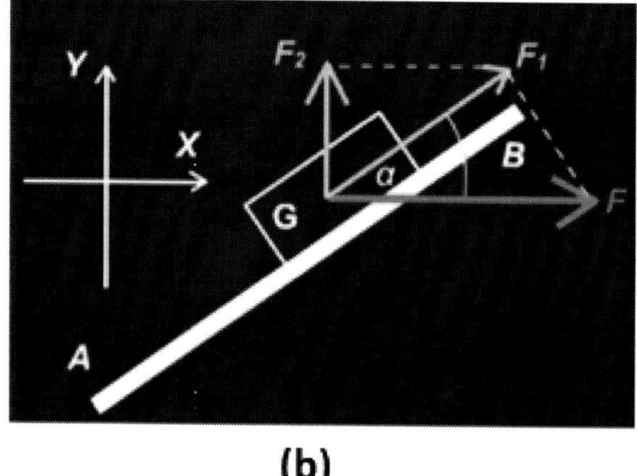

(b)

Figure 52. Pulling force on a block on a slanted surface resolved along the X and Y direction.

Now, let's examine more in detail the movement of the MMB during the time from position 3 to 5 in Fig. 49 in the view of the Earth observer at the B-B location; his view is portrayed with more supplemental details shown in Fig. 51. Once the MMB gets behind the spheroid in this view, as indicated by position 3a, the mass flow of the spheroid and the pulling from the VSGP are in opposite direction, and weaker centrifugal force exerted on the MMB is resulted. Subsequently the MMB has less potential to approach the equator but is more likely to be brought further southward away from the ecliptic. The huge distance of the source of the pulling force acting on the MMB allows it to be considered as being parallel to the ecliptic most of the time. In reaching closer and closer to position 3b, the latitude climbing becomes more and more dramatic. The mathematical reason for this movement becoming more dramatic will be explained in the paragraph after the next.

After position 3b, the spinning of the yolk brings the MMB to reappear in the observer's direct view. Now, because of the mass flow of the yolk, the MMB is in a course moving toward position 4, which is closer to the ecliptic. After passing 4, the MMB would go behind the spheroid again, moving along a route toward 4a. In this route, the MMB fundamentally repeats the same moving style as showed from 3a to 3b but at higher southern latitude. After 4a, the MMB moves toward position 5, which is closer to the ecliptic than 4a. By the time the MMB reaches position 5, the VSGP would have faded behind the page quite a bit, and with a different magnitude, too.

Suppose in the free space, with respect to the coordinate system X-Y (not the same X-Y set by the Sun and Jupiter), there exists one slanted surface AB, against which a block called G is pulled by a force F parallel to the X axis [Fig. 52(a)]. Because of the slanting of AB, F so acting can produce a force F_2 that points at due (-Y) direction with a magnitude $F_2 = F_1 \sin\alpha = (F\cos\alpha)\sin\alpha = (1/2)\sin 2\alpha$. F_2 will reach maximum at $\alpha = 45^o$. Similarly, in Fig. 52(b), we can also find a force F_2 in due (+Y) direction with a magnitude $F_2 = (1/2)\sin 2\alpha$, which also reaches maximum at $\alpha = 45^o$.

Angle $\alpha = 45^o$ leading to a maximum F_2 would lead us to a very reasonable speculation that the MMB, an object floating on a fluidic body, once having migrated across the equator and begun its latitude climbing, should most likely choose the 45° latitude to stay if the VSGP never changes its magnitude and direction. We will call this 45° latitude the most favorable latitude (MFL). However, this MFL is measured with respected to the ecliptic. If we take the Sun's axial tilting of 7.5^o into consideration, the MFL for the MMB to reach should be 37.5^o in the south and 52.5^o in the north with respect to the equator shown in Fig. 53. A similar view is also presented in Fig. 54 with the VSPG having moved to the other side of the picture.

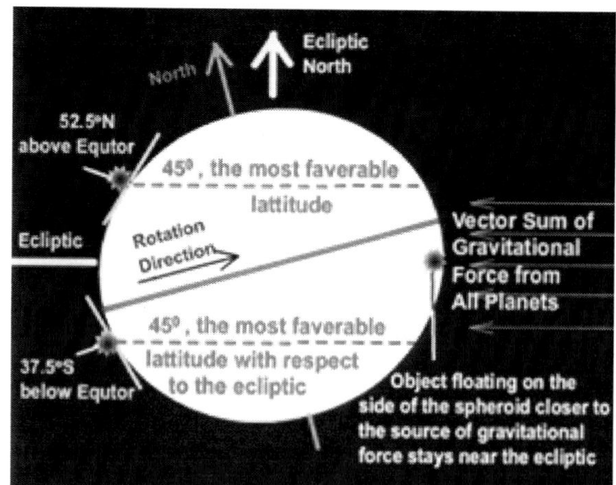

Figure 53.

However, the MFL may not necessarily be exactly where the MMB must choose to reside during each of its moving course of latitude climbing. The following dynamic elements can have a combined effect to disable the MMB from climbing further but to force it to descent toward the equator again: the direction and magnitude of the

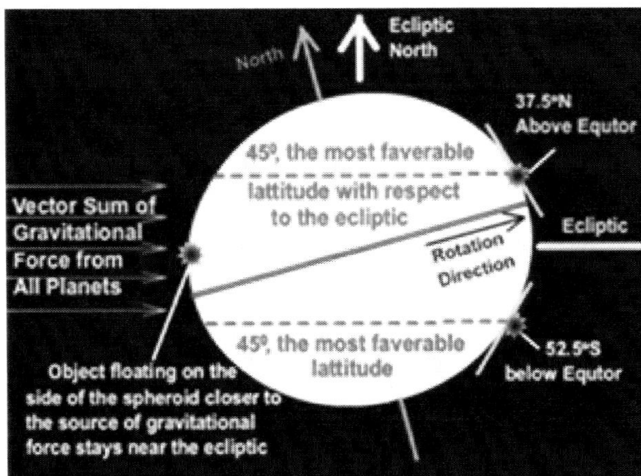

The most favorable latitude (VSGP from left)

Figure 54.

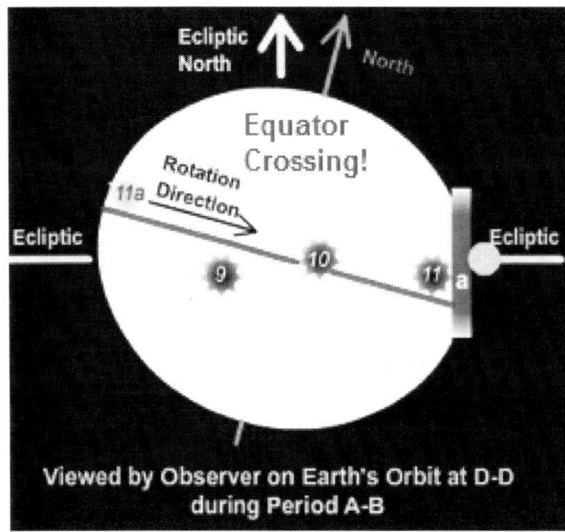

Figure 56. MMB position progression viewed from D-D in Period AB

VSPG at the instant where the MMB has reached, such as the height of the latitude, its angular position on the yolk with respect to the VSPG. Nevertheless, this MFL speculation should serve as a strong clue why a sunspot period usually starts with their initial appearance near the 45° latitude. Of course, more works need to be done for further confirmation.

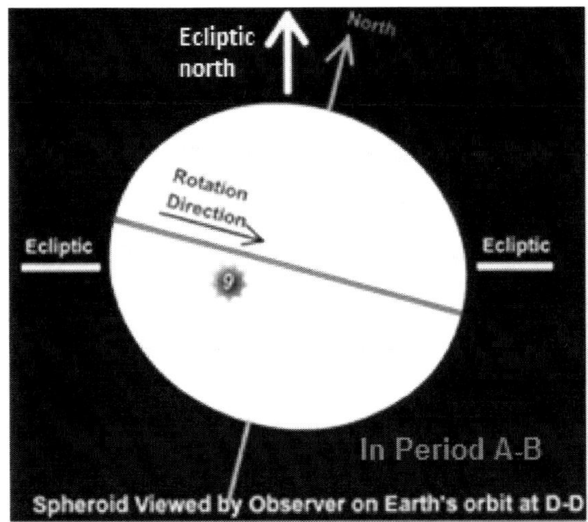

Figure 55. MMB position viewed from D-D in Period AB

In Fig. 49, when the MMB reaches near the MFL, the VSGP and the centrifugal force would have worked together to gradually lower the latitude location of the MMB. So, at some point of time in the course, the Earth observer at the D-D location would see this: The MMB shown in position 9 in Fig 49 and Fig. 55 reaches the equator. At such location, due to the angle position of the VSGP, which is developed into line ***a*** as shown in Fig. 48 and Fig. 56, the MMB is naturally pulled migrating across the equator and reaches position 10 in Fig. 56.

Once the MMB having migrated across, the principle of MFL begins to show effect. Now, it is the 45^oN (with respect to the ecliptic) that the MMB is approaching. Before it can steadily approach the northern MFL, the self-spinning of the spheroid would still lead the MMB to "bob" above and below the ecliptic quite a few times, as what position 11 in Fig. 56 may potentially suggest. After position 11, Jupiter soon enters its B-C period (Fig. 57), and the MMB continues its north MFL approaching under the influence of the VSGP that is gradually shows up as force line II.

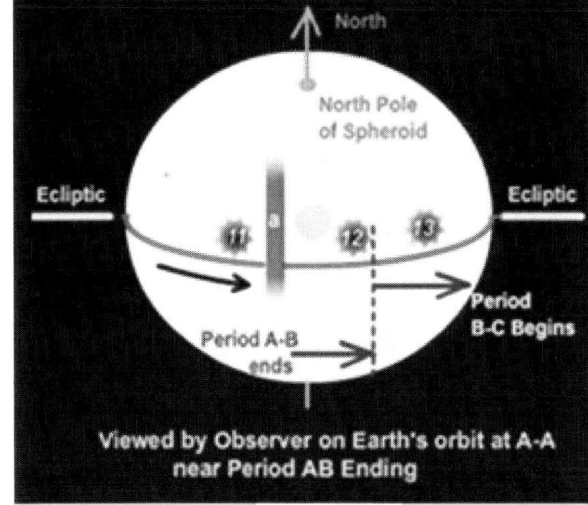

Figure 57. MMB migrated across the equator and about to enter period B-C

This time, with the angle position that force line II shows, the MMB may not really be able to reach the MFL but begins its latitude descending earlier. As the VSGP moving toward the D-D line, it allows the MMB to come back near the equator. However, the force line ***b*** following this situation helps the MMB to stay at the north hemisphere longer until force III appears in Jupiter's C-D period (Fig. 59) and then the MMB is herded migrating

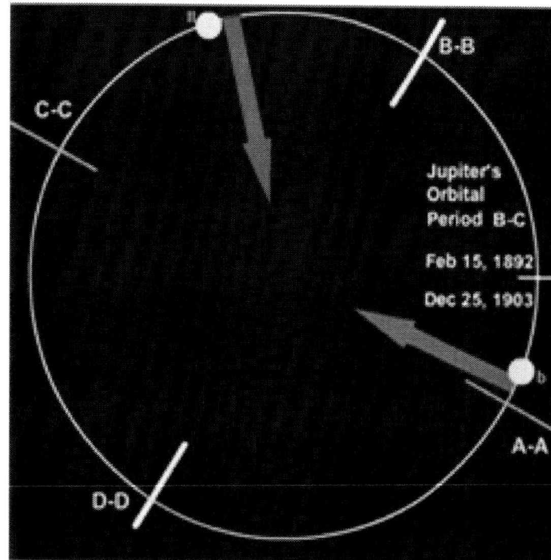

Figure 58. Time progression of VSGP, from line II (maximum) to line b (minimum), in period BC (Feb 15, 1892 to Dec 25, 1903

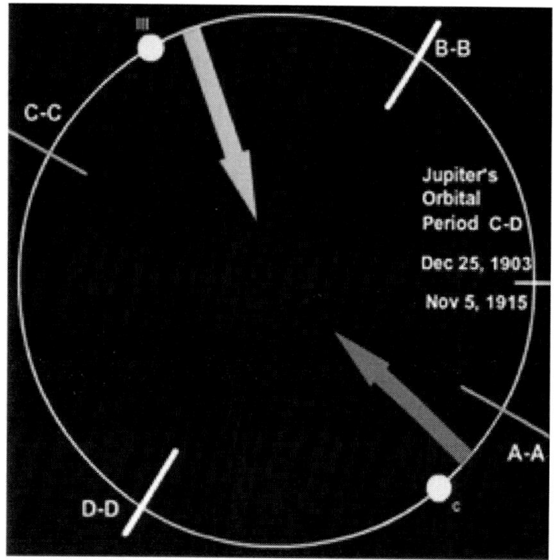

Figure 59. Time progression of VSGP, from line III (maximum) to line c (minimum), in period CD (Feb 15, 1892 to Dec 25, 1903

into the yolk's south.

The aforementioned equator crossing and subsequent MFL approaching repeat for the MMB in about every 11 years. The 11 year rhythm is moderated sometimes longer and sometimes shorter. One of the prominent elements that would moderate this rhythm is that the magnitude and direction of the VSGP moving in the ecliptic could not show ridged time period. Similar to Fig.48 and Fig. 58, this author also draws the force line of the VSGP for each Jupiter's period and "compress" them all in one diagram as shown in Fig. 60.

One immediate impression from Fig. 60 is that the majority of the force lines show up in the two angular areas fanned with yellow color. Both areas are not much away from the intersecting line B-B/D-D. This should be a strong indication to us that the whereabouts of the MMB, and subsequently where the sunspots would swarm, can be decisively affected by the tilting angle of the Sun' axis in relation to the direction as well as magnitude of the force line of the VSPG.

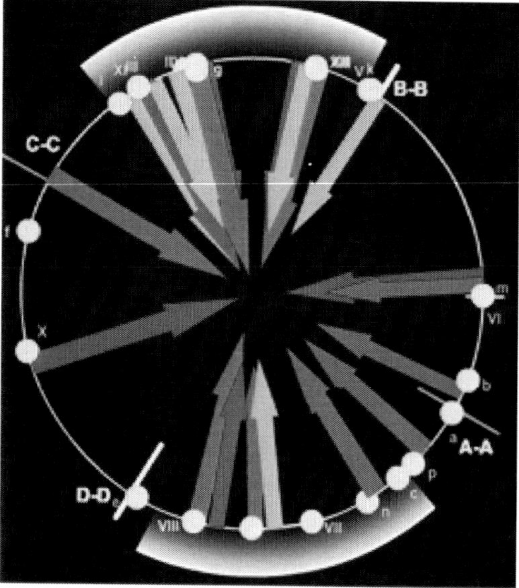

Figure 60. Maximum and minimum VSGP lines of all periods are printed in one diagram to help visualizing where they appear the most often

If a reader is interested in the detailed progression of the VSPG in each Jupiter's orbital period that has been "compressed" in Fig. 60 , he can find them in the section "More Diagrams" toward the end of this paper.

4. The Stable Orientation of Magnetic Polarity

Given that neutron stars usually carry strong magnetism, it becomes a reasonable speculation for us to associate the strong magnetism and high mass density of the sunspots with a conjecture that the sunspots are composed of material rich in neutrons. No evidence has been found that the spinning rate of a neutron star and this star's magnetic field strength have inseparable mathematical relationship. In other words, no one can exclude that a neutron star, even not spinning, may still carry strong magnetic strength. Therefore, just being rich in neutrons could be enough reason for the sunspot to be born of a magnetic body. As to why a material body rich in neutrons is a natural magnetic body, it is not what impels the elaboration of this article. But instead, this article just tries to exploit what observation from neutron stars can offer us to lay a reasonable background for our exploration on sunspots.

The above assumption would give us the following convenience in our theoretical exploration regarding sunspots:

(1) Sunspots have the highest mass density than any material we know of on Earth, although we cannot confirm such mass density is compatible to that of a neutron star, a celestial body containing high purity of neutrons; (2) they are indestructible even in extraordinarily high temperature; (3) they are the inevitable products of nuclear fusion reaction. That neutrons can be copiously produced in nuclear reaction is a well-known fact [4][5]. When they are introduced to exist in a plasma as independent particles, besides the chance of forming material combination with protons, each of them should also have chance to be associated with another neutron. The impossibility of a neutron-neuron formation is at least potentially denied by the existence of neutron stars. In an environment of plasma of extraordinarily high temperature, if a neutron itself is a magnet carrier, it should even have higher potential to be associated with another neutron other than a proton that also flies freely but carries no magnet. The potential of such an association is even further escalated by gravitational influence because neutrons are slightly more massive than protons.

If the MMB is a steady object carrying magnetism and never flips with respect to the center of the Sun, each time it migrates across the equator of the yolk and gets to the other hemisphere, it must accordingly have its same magnetic pole pointing to an opposite side of the Sun's equatorial plane (Fig. 61). To an observer on Earth, being able to detect the side exchanging of the polarity with respect to the equatorial plane but unable to see a magnetic body cruising from one hemisphere to another, he would naturally conclude the side exchanging of polarity with the word "reversal". He would even more firmly visualize the side exchange of the polarity as a reversal when comparing the manifestation of magnetism that the MMB enables near the MFL; there is a difference of 90° in latitude between the northern MFL and the southern MFL. The 90° difference in latitude can so easily lead to an imagination that the magnetic polarity reversal is caused by some acrobatic flipping of a certain magnetic entity, either a liquid collection or a solid body (Fig. 61).

When products of a nuclear reaction are sprayed out from the nuclear reaction zone in an isotropic manner, they fundamentally have three major directions to move along: (1) directly away from the Sun's center i.e., directly toward the Sun's surface, (2) directly pointing toward the Sun's center, (3) anywhere in between. Materials that would form something like sunspots of course would move in these three directions, too. Those moving along direction (1) would form sunspots in our observation as we have repetitively mentioned. Those moving along direction (2) would have been equipped with enough thrusting power to overcome the floating force of the yolk and sink into the very center of the Sun. Those moving in direction mentioned in (3) above may either go to the surface or the center, depending upon their initial angle of movement with respect to the radial line of the Sun. However, statistically, because of gravitation from the Sun's center, more of them would be showered toward the yolk than

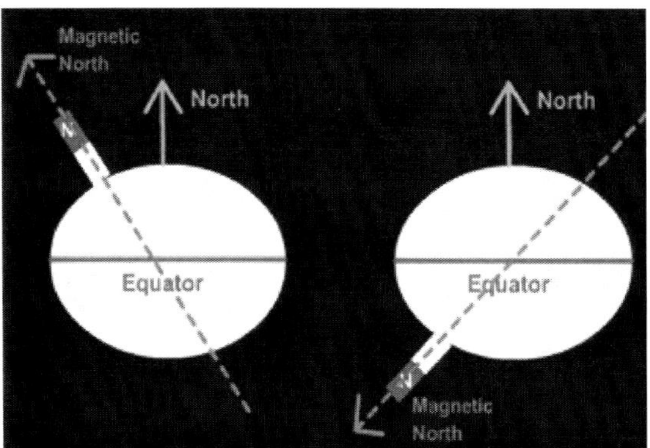

Magnetic polarity of the entire spheroid is seen as having reversed if the magnetic bar migrates across the equator while keeping the same pole facing the center of the spheroid.

Figure 61. MMB migration across the equator

toward the surface of the Sun. This gravitational reason enables the statement that "(the MMB) should have contained no less mass than all the sunspots put together" in the abstract. With less momentum to pierce into the yolk like those mentioned in (2) above, they stay as something floating on the surface of the yolk and collect each other to form the MMB via magnetism.

To those that are injected straightforwardly toward the center of the Sun, they would penetrated the surface of the yolk and sink to the center of the yolk. Indeed, at certain depth below the surface of the yolk, they do not need any extra propelling force; further sinking becomes natural to them. Once they get to the center, their magnetic nature of course would cause them to clench on each other and form one single magnetic body. This single magnetic body should be the core of the core for the Sun, and is called the **core magnet** in this article.

So, two huge magnetic bodies are found associated with the Sun's yolk: (1) the MMB, which is shown as a lump but pictorially presented as a small bar floating on the yolk in Fig. 62 and Fig. 63; and (2) the core magnet, which is a core piece inside the yolk, shown as the ball in the same diagrams. Besides the MMB and the core magnet, we would not exclude that some sunspot-like pieces in far smaller size can be constantly found sporadically spread across the surface of the yolk; the incessant fusion reactions continuously produce more and more of them. Given some extra time, they would sooner or later be collected by the MMB.

Although at this point, we are unable to determine the actual polarity orientation of these two bodies, it can be certain that both would force each other to follow the same orientation. This permanent alignment practically makes them to act as one single magnet piece with the same pole, north or south, staying closer to the center of the Sun. Under the control of the stubborn magnetic force, the nuclear explosions are unable to flip the MMB into any random orientation. For the time being and for purpose

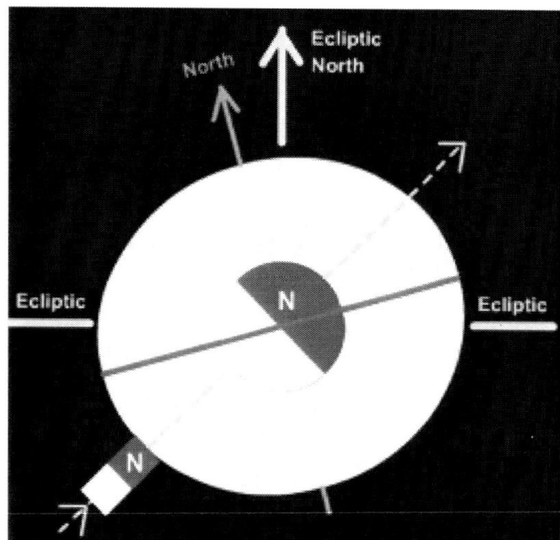

The MMB (in bar shape) and the magnetic core effectively form one single huge magnet bar inside the Sun (with north pole pointing up)

Figure 62. With MMB residing in the south hemisphere

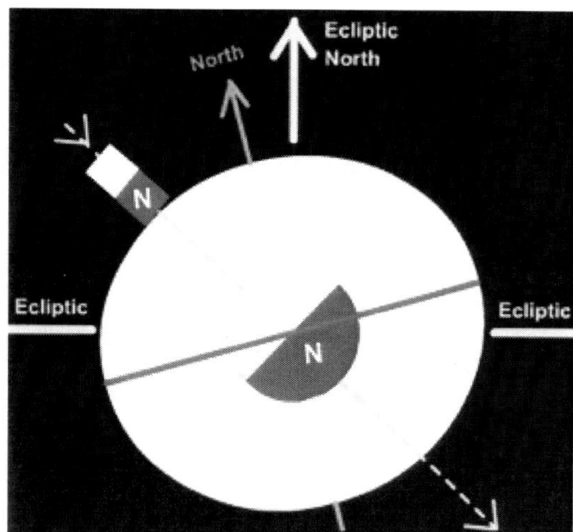

The MMB (in bar shape) and the magnetic core effectively form one single huge magnet bar inside the Sun (with north pole pointing down)

Figure 63. MMB migratingn across the equator and residing in the north hemisphere

of illustration, let's assume the MMB facing the center of the Sun with its north pole. Later we'll also cover the illustration regarding the situation that the MMB happens to face the Sun's center with its south pole. We will find that the actual orientation will not affect the behavior of the array of the sunspots. Nevertheless, the magnetic orientation of the MMB and the core magnet together will enable us to visualize that there is only one magnetic bar in the Sun; at one end of this bar is the MMB and at the other end is the core magnet.

5. Swarm of the Sunspots

It is only naturally that, with the magnetism they are born to carry, the sunspots in our observation must swarm where magnetism is found strongest on the surface of the Sun. Our reasoning so far has been suggesting that this surface area for the sunspot to swarm is found nowhere but on the spot below which the MMB could reside. A similar scene can be imagined if some iron chip is spread on a piece of cardboard and below it a magnet bar is placed. On the opposite side of the dense spheroid where the MMB is not found, the appearance of the sunspots should be close to impossible.

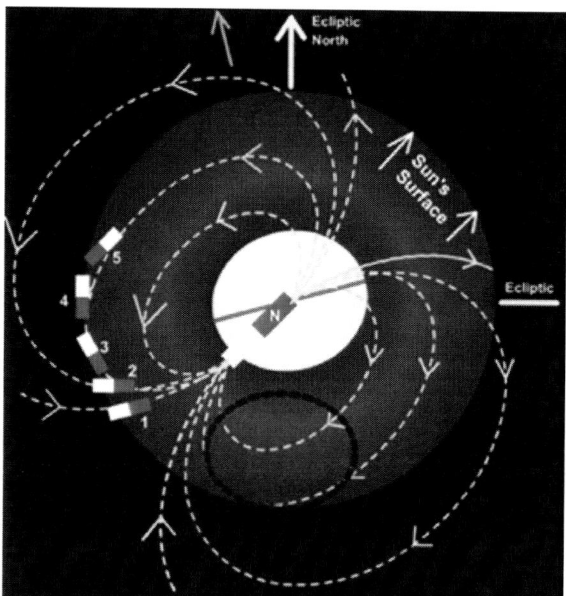

Sunspots dispaly their array on the surface of the Sun in alignment with magnetic flux

Figure 64. The swarming of sunspots

Swarming at area closer to the MMB, the array of the magnetic members, i.e., the sunspots, must always obey the alignment commanded by the lines of magnetic flux generated by the bar that contains both the MMB and the magnetic core. This is illustrated in Fig. 64. In this diagram, we can regard the portion of the magnet bar protruding out of the yolk as the MMB. The smaller magnet 1, 2, 3, 4 and 5 each represents a sunspot. Sunspot 1 would appear as a unipolar in the observer's view when showing up; spot 3 would appear as a bipolar, while spot 2 should be in a transition from unipolar to a bipolar. Spot 1, 2, 3 all show up in the south hemisphere. Sunspot 4 and 5 are in the north hemisphere while 5 shows with stronger unipolar appearance than 4. It is not very likely that a sunspot would appear right at the axis of the magnetic bar, where the magnetic force is the strongest. There, a sunspot would be "sucked" deep below the surface of the Sun. In fact, we can also imagine that all three sunspots 1, 2, and 3 are actually the same one but has been drifting to different locations because of the constant compelling magnetic force from the MMB as well as the centrifugal force from the Sun's spinning. Besides, at the position as shown by the large bar in Fig. 64, the MMB may likely have been having a movement leaving the MFL and cruising toward the equator. Such a movement of the MMB certainly guides the same sunspot shown at 1 to drift gradually to 3. The description in the above two paragraphs closely match a typical fact that we obtain from observation: In the beginning of each cycle of the sunspot activity, some few sunspots would show up as a unipolar near the 45° latitude, north or south, and gradually drift down toward the equator with higher and higher population. On the way drifting down, their bipolar appearance is more and more obviously unveiled. The 45° latitude so mentioned is what the MFL is supposed to be and derived in our previous reasoning.

When all the sunspots in the south drift to the position of spot 3, and those in the north to position like spot 5, it would mean that the MMB has been very close to the equator. Now, the sunspots are arrested near the bar's magnetic axis, where the magnetic force is the strongest. Being "sucked" by the strongest magnetic force and the strongest gravitational force on the equatorial plane, no more than natural, the sunspots are all made vanished from the Sun's surface. The Earth observer sees a solar minimum now.

Solar minimum should provide good opportunity for us to verify whether or not the MMB in our speculation does exist because this minimum helps to eliminate the interference of the sunspots swarm in our direct view. If the MMB does exist, at the absence of the sunspots, a magnetism detecting equipment circulating about the Sun on its equatorial plane should still be able to find some particular longitudinal areas on the Sun showing magnetic field strength conspicuously stronger than any other areas.

So in reality, the number of sunspots have never been reduced in the duration of the solar minimum; they just "hibernate" deeper below the surface. Probably it could be more appropriate for us to adopt a new concept that solar minimum and solar maximum may not have too much to do with the up and down trend of the Sun's overall thermonuclear activity. The maximum or minimum are just more of some seasonal debut or hibernation of the same population of the sunspots, and therefore unable to serve as any clue suggesting whether the thermonuclear reaction in the Sun has had periodical variation. (*In a long run, however, the population of the sunspots must slowly increase!*)

In Fig 64, we cannot find sunspots in the area of the lower butterfly wing formed by the lines of magnetic flux and circled by broken purple line, which is symmetrically the same as the corresponding area in the upper wing where sunspots swarm. For the sunspot to surface up, strong enough centrifugal force is needed in addition to the thrown-out force enabled by the nuclear explosion. However, the more toward the pole of the spinning axis, the weaker the centrifugal force becomes. No sunspot can receive enough momentum to choose there to swarm.

6. A "Perforated" Surface for Coronal Mass Ejection

If we claim that the increasing or decreasing population of the sunspots in our observation does not necessary indicate the up or down trend of the Sun's overall thermonuclear activity, how do we explain why the frequency of prominence and solar flare do seem following the increasing or decreasing of the sunspot population [6][7]? The prominence and solar flare, with their violent power in energy spewing and high affinity with the location where the sunspots appear, do seem able to serve as some index for us to conjecture that the up and down of the sunspot population and the Sun's overall activity closely relate to each other.

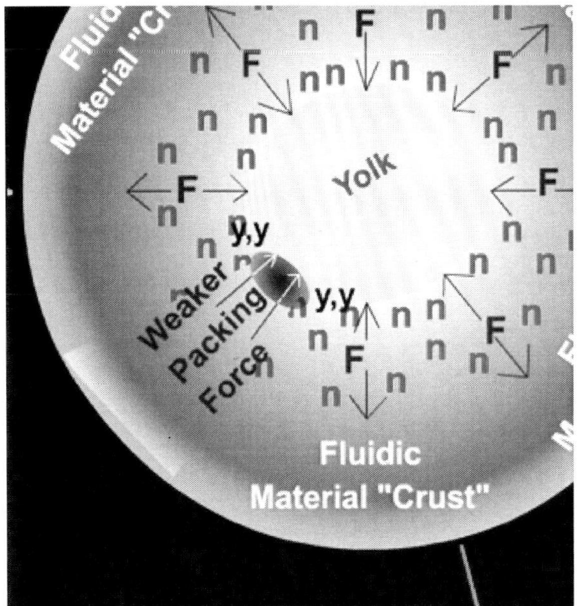

Figure 65. At where the MMB covers, the yolk should have received less packing force than that is received by any other area of its surface

In Fig. 65, we enlarge a portion of Fig. 43 but with the MMB (the purple lump) being added to it. In the area of the yolk that is shielded by the MMB, the packing force received by the yolk from the nuclear fusion reaction should be statistically weaker than in any other areas of the yolk that are not so shielded. (A detailed reasoning why the shielded area shows up with weaker fusion explosion is given later.) Not only that, the nuclear exploding forces near the areas marked with (Y,Y) do have tendency to yank the MMB from the yolk. Both of these acts create a weak spot that becomes a vent for the yolk's materials profusely jetting out. An unstoppable "underground" geyser but of hydrogen streams is permanently maintained (Fig. 66).

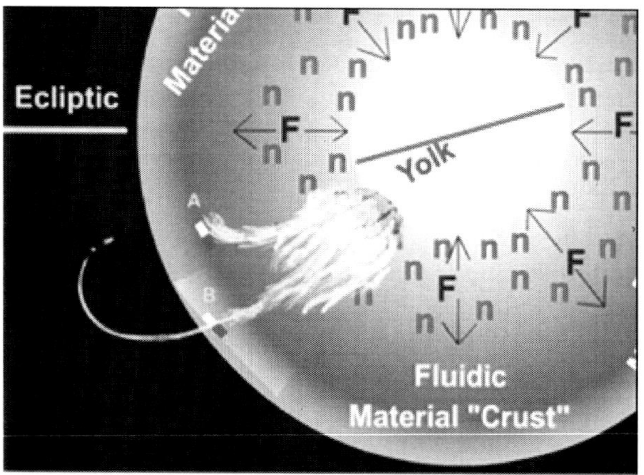

Figure 66. A hydrogen geyser leading to (1) Solar flare at spot A, (2) prominence at spot B

When the hydrogen streams get out, they of course show no hesitation to join the fiery process of fusion reactions that have been going on. However, some of the streams contains so much materials that not the entire bulk jetted out in that geyser stream get enough time to join the reaction. Then, riding on the exceedingly strong momentum, the extra bulk finds chance to get exemplified from the reaction and dash penetrating through the nuclear reaction zone. In so dashing out, the extra bulk inevitably drags along with itself some materials that have been in the process of nuclear burning. When the flaming trail comes near the surface, where the pressure and the temperature dramatically drop lower and therefore unfavorable for nuclear reaction to continue, the last flame riding with the bulk necessarily extinguishes. If the momentum and material quantity of the bulk endowed at the time of being jetted out have too much surplus, it would go all the way piercing through the Sun's surface, presenting a prominence in our observation (the jet near spot B in Fig. 66). However, some of the jets are unable to do so. The last flame carried by a weaker jet must extinguish beneath the Sun's surface while no extra material can reach the surface. While the material cannot come out, however, the thermal energy and optical energy so spewed with the extinguished jets can still burst out to show up in space outside of the Sun. This jet with weaker momentum thus creates solar flare in our view, as shown near spot A in Fig. 66.

Whether those geyser materials would end themselves with a solar flare or as a prominence, they are in a state of plasma and are thus some collections of charge particles in their entire journey. Being charge particles, their movement must show response to magnetic guidance. Because all sunspots are magnetism carriers, a line connecting any of them and the MMB would naturally concentrate more magnetic flux and form a more conspicuous magnetic "tube" for those charge particles. In their journey as a jet, the charge particles of the geysers would naturally find those tubes restricting their movement. For those happen to have moved along the axial direction of such a tube, they would go straight forward along the tube's axis. For those happen to be in a direction perpendicular to the tube axis when their journey starts, they would continue their outgoing journey along some helix lines. All this should explain to us why the appearance of solar flare and prominence has high affinity with the location of the sunspots. This also conversely reveals to us why we have such an observation mentioned in the abstract that magnetic strength near prominence shows comparatively higher magnitude: "10–100 gauss in solar prominences".

The prominence and solar flare following the magnetic tubes guided by the sunspots just have created "perforation" on the Sun's surface for coronal mass ejection to find convenient outlets. Otherwise the same materials constituting the ejection will continue to be locked under by the thick fluidic crust of the Sun. Therefore, it is questionable whether the prominence and solar flare can serve as the key for us to conjecture the up and down of the thermonuclear activity inside the sun.

7. Array of Sunspots

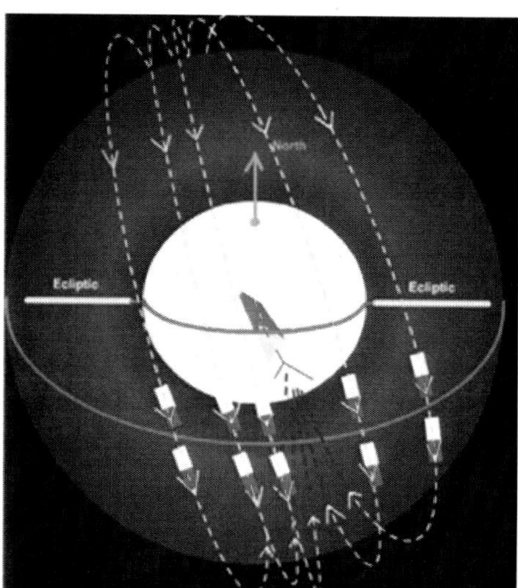

Sunspot alignment without taking into consideration of the Sun's self-spinning

Figure 67. Flux lines come out of the back of the Sun, loop around on the front of the Sun, and return to the south pole of the big magnetic bar below the surface of the Sun.

As shown in Fig. 67, if the sunspots are free floating objects on the Sun's surface, the sunspots should show opposite poles toward the Sun's equator on each side of the equator. This is a natural arrangement as the sunspots must be responding to the flux of the big magnetic bar. However, the spinning of the Sun will force them to deviate from such a floating orientation with a resultant array as shown in Fig. 68. This is because the Sun's surface has higher linear speed than the surface of the yolk if they both have the same angular velocity. The sunspots' orientation

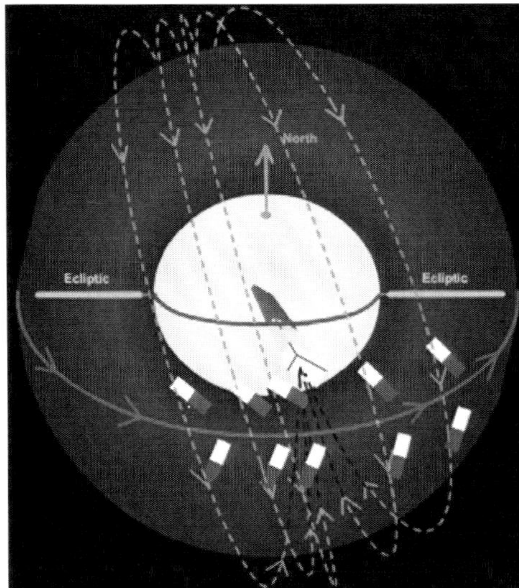

Figure 68. Mass flow of the highest speed at the equator knocks the sunspot alignment off line.

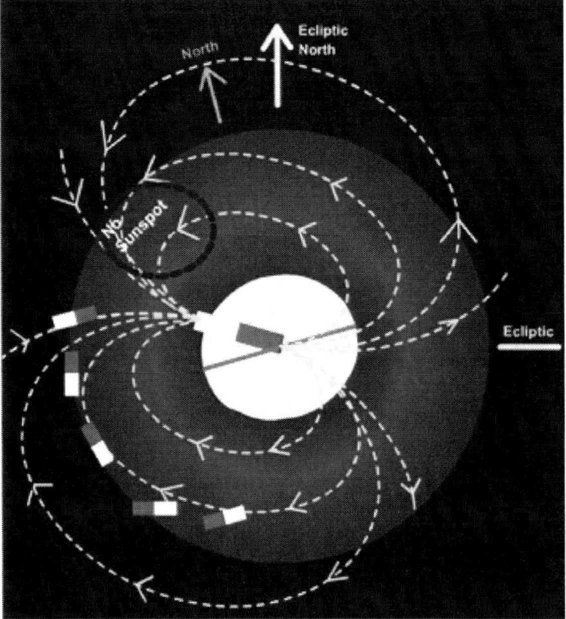

Figure 69. Mass flow of the highest speed at the equator knocks the sunspot alignment off line.

must obey two forces now: the magnetic force exerted on them through the flux from the big bar and the mechanic force exerted on them by the mass flow of the fluid in their vicinity. While the magnetic force is a backward dragging force on them because of the lower linear speed of the MMB, the mechanical force is a forward pushing force on them because of the higher linear speed of the mass flow.

If, instead of pointing to the Sun's south, the south pole of the big bar in Fig. 64 points to the north side of the equatorial plane, as shown in Fig. 69, the sunspot will spread at the lower half of the butterfly wing formed by the magnetic flux. Corresponding to such spreading, and equivalent to what is shown in Fig. 68, the sunspot array will spread on the Sun's surface like what is shown in Fig. 70. If we judge the magnetic field orientation of the Sun only by what is portrayed by the array of the sunspots, the comparison between Fig. 68 and Fig. 70 naturally leads someone to say that the Sun has had its magnetic poles reversed between these two pictures. But the more factual reality is that the Sun only has the same magnetic pole migrate from the south hemisphere to the north hemisphere.

Lacking enough information, this author cannot exclude the possibility that the MMB, if exists, is indeed pointing its south pole toward the center of the Sun, a situation opposite to what is presented by Fig. 68 and Fig.70. To match this second possibility, Fig. 71 and Fig. 72 are presented as the MMB is having its north pole point to the south side of the Sun's equatorial plane. When the MMB has its north pole point to the north side of the Sun, Fig. 73 and Fig. 74 are presented accordingly. Now, the array of the sunspots explains to us (1) why the sunspots always

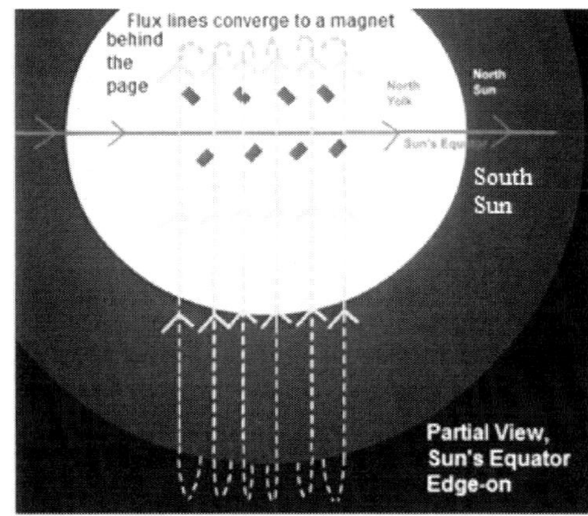

Figure 70. Sunspots reverse their polarity alignment compared to what is shown in Fig. 68

have one pole leading and the leading pole is also closer to the equator in approaching the equator, and (2) why such leading alters in 11 years or so and repeat in 22 years or so.

Now, let's come back to explore what supports the aforementioned speculation that the area of the yolk shielded by the MMB is a weak spot receiving less packing force than other surface area of the yolk.

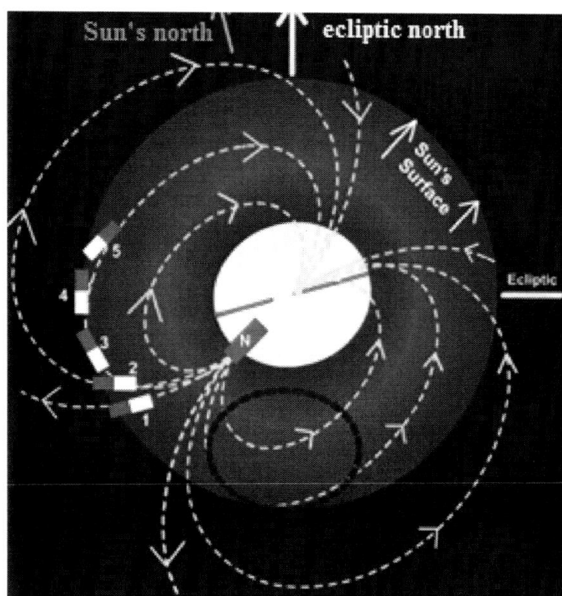

Sunspots aligned by the "butterfly wing" as the MMB points its north pole to the south side of the Sun

Figure 71.

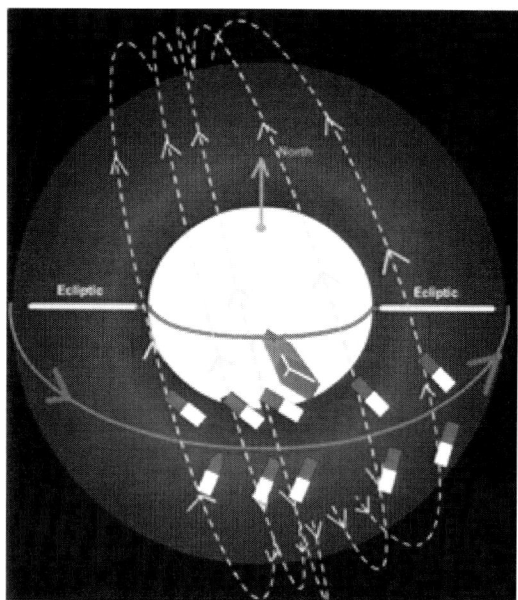

Sunspots alignment on the Sun's surface as the MMB has its north pole point to the south side of the Sun

Figure 72. Magnetic flux lines come out of the north pole of the big bar, loop in front of the Sun, and diverge behind the Sun then back to the south pole of the bar

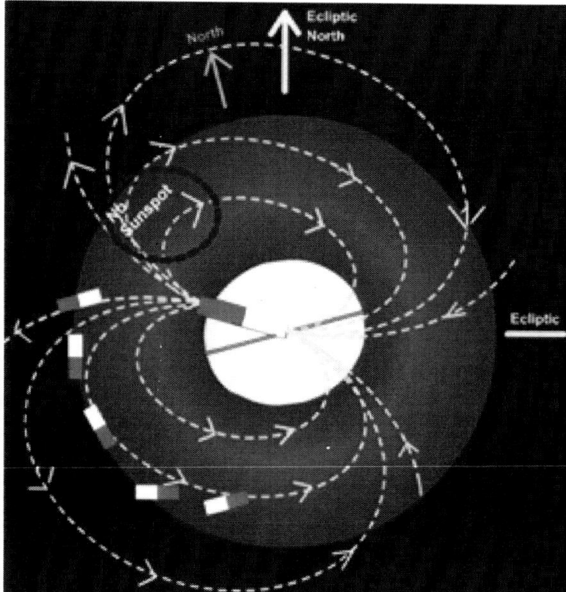

Sunspots aligned by the "butterfly wing" when the MMB has its north pole point to the north side of the Sun

Figure 73.

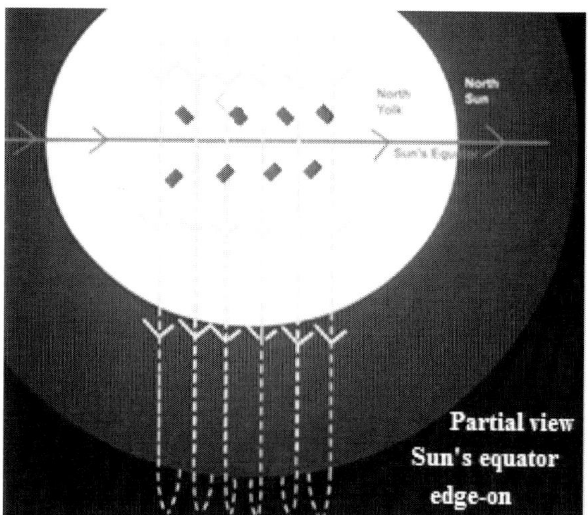

Sunspots alignment when the MMB (not shown) has its north pole point to the north side of the Sun

Figure 74. Magnetic flux lines come out of the north pole of the big bar (above the equator and below the surface of the Sun), loop in front of the Sun, and diverge behind the Sun then back to the south pole of the bar

It is said that hydrogen burning in the Sun is at the rate of 4.26 million metric tons per second. It is also said that the Sun will remain fairly stable for at least another five billion more years. Both statements would lead us to believe that the Sun now should still have at least 6.72×10^{23} tons of hydrogen for the Sun's future "fairly stable" consumption. If all this amount of hydrogen supply is stored in the yolk of mass density of 150 ton/m^3, and if the yolk is assumed to be a sphere for simple calculation, this yolk would have a volume of $4.48 \times 10^{21} m^3$, which gives this spherical volume a radius of $1.02 \times 10^7 m$. The total surface area for such a spherical volume would be $1.31 \times 10^{15} m^2$. The thickness of the shell covering this surface area with 4.26 million metric tons of material in a density of 150 ton/m^3 would be $21.62 \times 10^{-12} m$. In comparison to this dimension, the Van der Waals radius of a hydrogen atom is $120 \times 10^{-12} m$. This close to zero "skin" thickness of $21.62 \times 10^{-12} m$ thus allows only such a manner in the hydrogen consumption: directly coming in contact with the thermonuclear reaction zone by the most virginal hydrogen supply is the necessary and sufficient condition for the highest hierarchy of a cascade of nuclear reactions to happen. The highest hierarchy in the cascade of nuclear reaction is where the most powerful reaction takes place.

So, hydrogen supply in the area of the yolk shielded by the MMB cannot come in direct contact with the nuclear reaction zone, and therefore no reaction of the highest hierarchy can happen here. Now, on one side of the skin of the yolk, nuclear reaction madly goes on, but wrapped inside of this skin, virgin hydrogen supplies have to peacefully wait for their turn. So peaceful, however, these supplies receive tremendous packing pressure from the skin, just like the air inside a fully blown balloon. Any opening found in the balloon is an immediate choice for the air to pop out. In comparison, the area shielded by the MMB naturally creates a vent for the hydrogen supply to jet out at no time.

The aforementioned phrase "fairly stable" should have allowed the skin to be even thinner if we take into consideration that the yolk must also contain extra supplies that are to be wasted beyond the stable period. The extra content thus brings in bigger volume and thus bigger surface area for the yolk. Bigger surface area would in turn mean thinner skin for the same volume of material shedding—4.26 million metric tons per second.

With good consistence, the repeating magnetic field reversal in the Earth's history can be explained with all the foregoing ideas regarding the sunspot activity. However, being severely restricted by the mantle wall of the Earth, the material gathering that possesses the similar nature of the sunspots cannot have movement as free as those near the surface of the Sun. This is substantially the reason why the magnetic pole reversal of the Earth takes hundreds or even thousands of centuries to display one. Besides, the forces influencing the movement of the "sunspots" inside the Earth's mantle cage must include (1) the friction between the spot and the mantle wall, (2) the centrifugal force produced by the Earth's orbital traveling, (3) the centrifugal force produced by the Earth's self-spinning, and (4) the Moon's gravitational force. (The readers are cordially invited to visit the article **The Formation of the Solar System**, which can be found in both the 2017 Proceedings of John Chappell Natural Philosophy Society (*http://naturalphilosophy.org/site*) and at this author's website *http://www.huntune.net*.

8. More diagrams

In this section are listed the diagrams illustrating the maximum and minimum VSGP variation in each period of the Jupiter orbital movement, exceppt period A-B, B-C and C-D, which have been previously presented. All diagrams in this section are fundamentally presented in a time sequence following the order of names of period. Then, following each period of the VSGP variation are diagrams suggesting views showing how the MMB moving on the surface of the yolk in the order of (1) viewed at location B-B on the Earth's orbit, (2) location C-C of the same orbit, (3) D-D, and (4) A-A, where new period starts. In viewing the diagrams of MMB movement, always keep in mind that between two locations that are marked with consecutive numbers the MMB may have gotten behind the direct view of the observer several times.

(Diagram series Continued from Fig. 58.)

(For VSGP variation in period C-D, see Fig. 59)

9. Glossary abbreviation, Acronym

Magmat—an abbreviation for magnetic material

Magnetic core —a big material gathering at the center of the Sun assumed having the material nature that is the same as those that the sunspots are consisted of.

MBC—magmat bearing chunks

MFL —the most favorable latitude

Migrating magnetic body, abbreviated as MMB —a theoretically derived magnetic body that should be of the same material nature as that of the sunspots but with a mass quantity that is no less than all the sunspots put together. It is a body floating on the surface of the Sun's yolk (See corresponding term referred below) and cruising on it in response to the combined influence from all the planets. Its whereabouts determines where the swarm of sunspots to show up.

MMB—migrating magnetic body in the Sun

Most favorable latitude, abbreviated as MFL—it is the

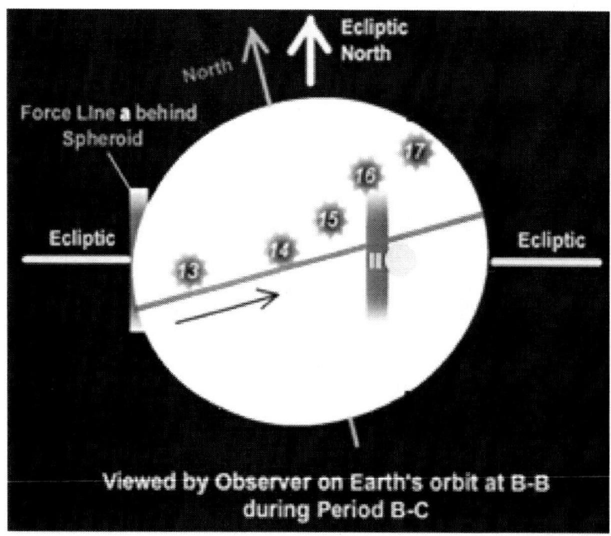

Figure 75.

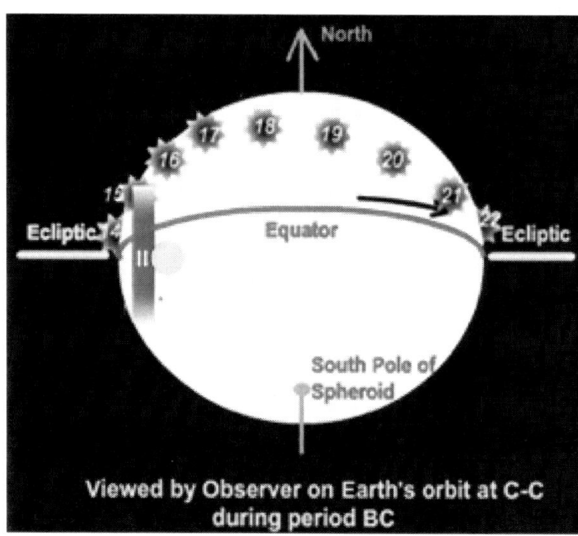

Figure 76.

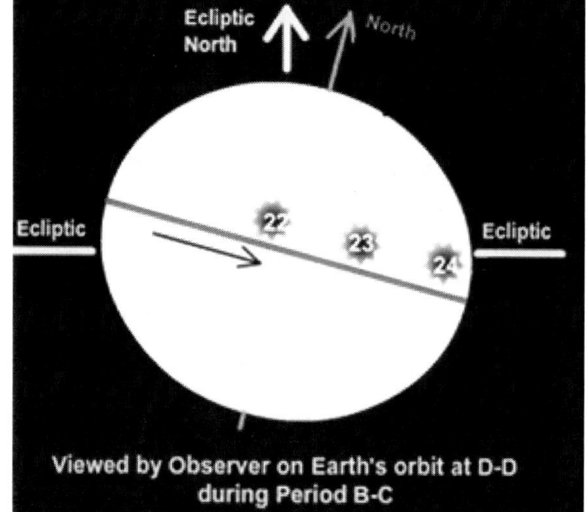

Figure 77.

45° latitude above or below the ecliptic on the Sun for the MMB to climb to under the influence of the combined gravitational force from all planets. Mapped on the Sun, this MFL would mean 52.5^{o}N/37.5^{o}S and 52.5^{o}S/37.5^{o}N with respect to the Sun's equator.

Rotate—a word in this article most of the time used to describe the revolution movement of an object about an axis that is outside of this object.

Spin—a word in this article most of the time used to describe the revolution movement of an object about an axis that passes through this object itself.

VSGP—an acronym of (**V**ector **S**um of **G**ravitational force from all the **P**lanets

Yolk (of the Sun)—a theoretically derived material body in fluidic state existing deep inside the Sun. It has extraordinarily high mass density, should be the storage tank of all virgin hydrogen as fuel supporting the nuclear burning of the Sun. Due to self-spinning of the Sun, this yolk takes the shape of a spheroid, with its equator and the Sun's equator coinciding in the same plane.

Zero Day—the zero reference time marked as Jan 5, 1987.

REFERENCES

1. wikipedia, ***Sun*** URL: https://en.wikipedia.org/wiki/Sun,
2. wikipedia, ***Sunspot*** URL: https://en.wikipedia.org/wiki/Sunspot,
3. Holly Zell, ***What Is a Solar Prominence*** URL: https://www.nasa.gov/content/goddard/what-is-a-solar-prominence
4. The Columbia Electronic Encyclopedia, 6th ed. 2012 ***Nucleosynthesis,*** Publisher: Columbia University Press.

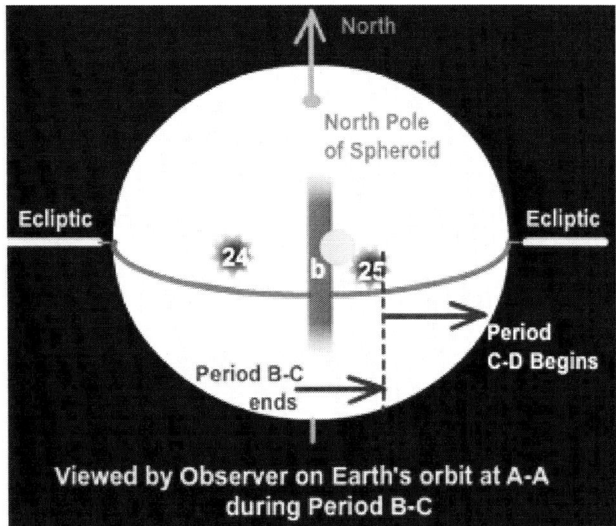

Figure 78.

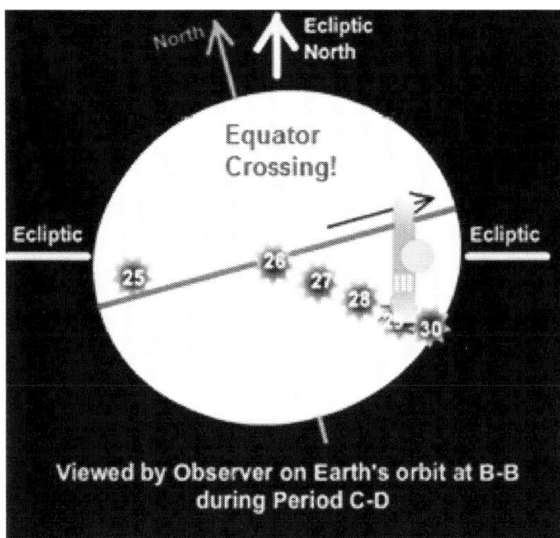

Figure 79.

5. wikipedia, ***Proton-Proton Chain Reaction,*** URL: https://en.wikipedia.org/wiki/Proton-proton_ chain_ reaction,
6. Robert Naeye, ***What Is a Coronal Mass Ejection?*** URL: https://www.spaceweatherlive.com/en/help/what-is-a-coronal-mass-ejection-cme
7. NASA Administrator, ***Sunspots and Solar Flares,*** URL: www.nasa.gov/multimedia/imagegallery/image_feature_2201.html█

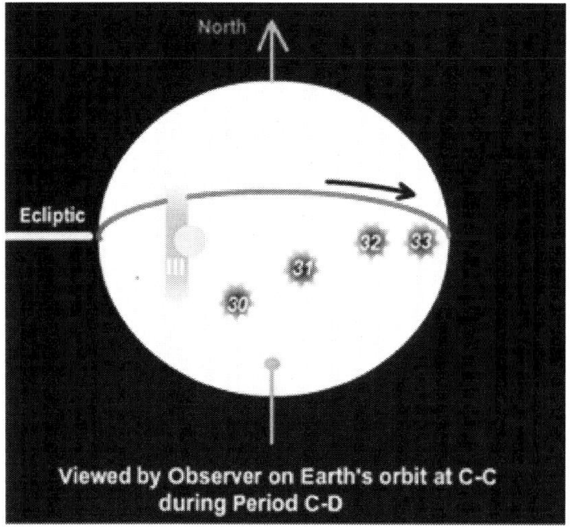

Figure 80.

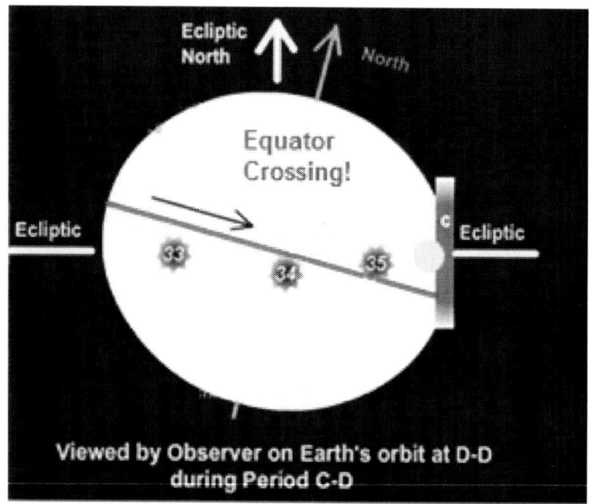

Figure 81.

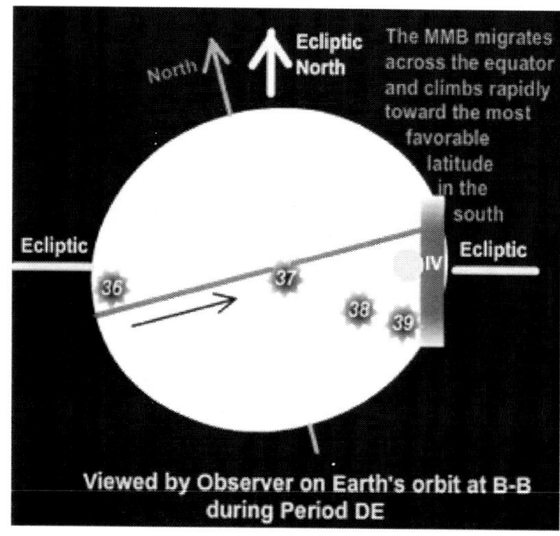

Figure 84.

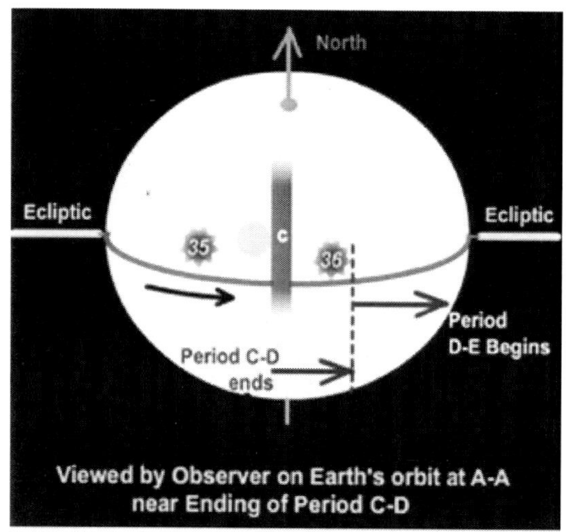

Figure 82.

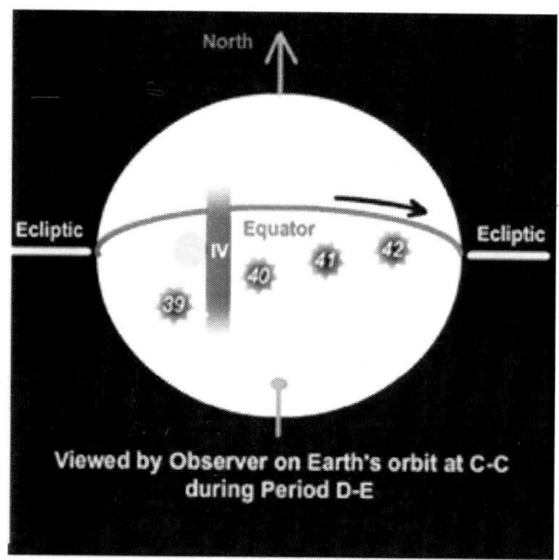

Figure 85.

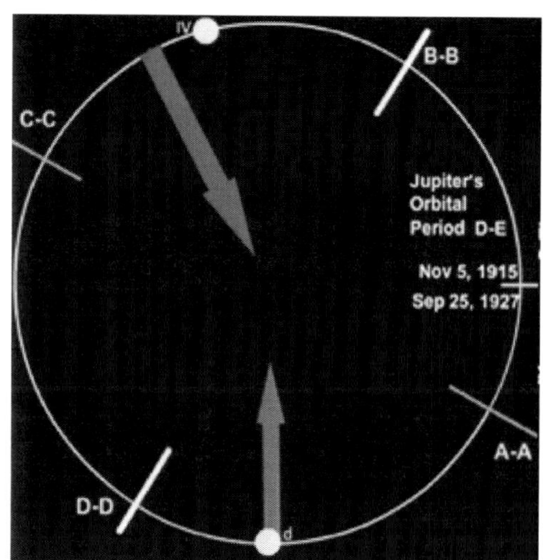

Figure 83.

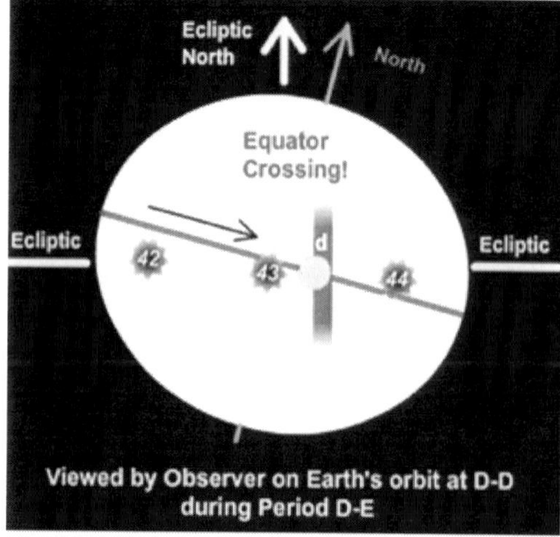

Figure 86.

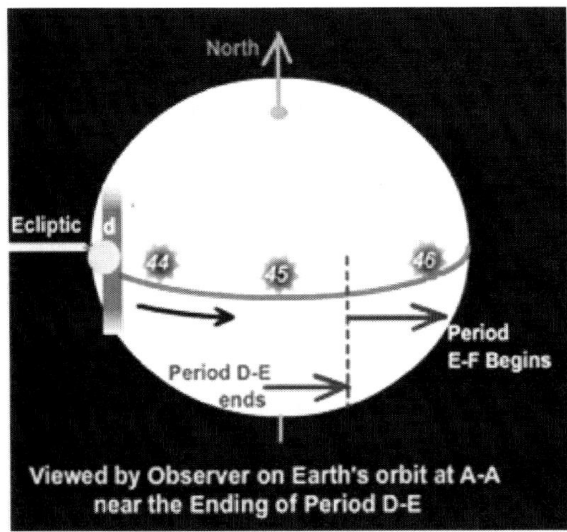

Figure 87.

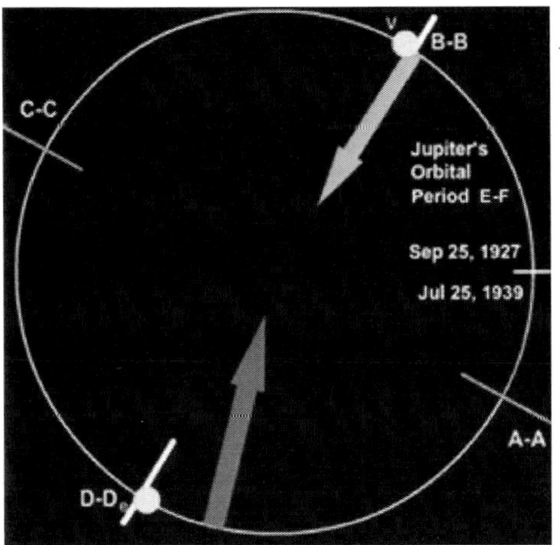

Figure 88.

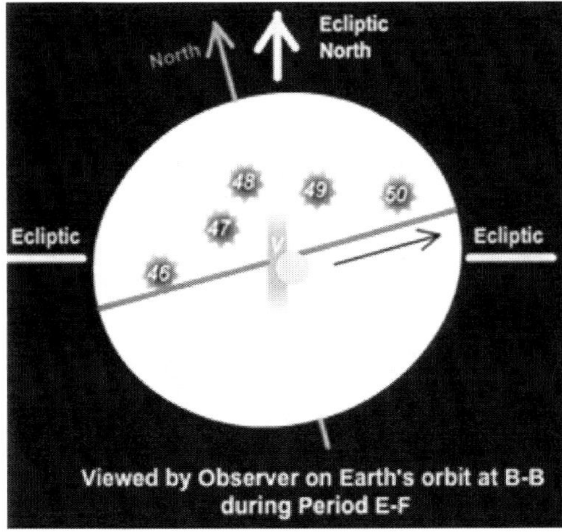

Figure 89.

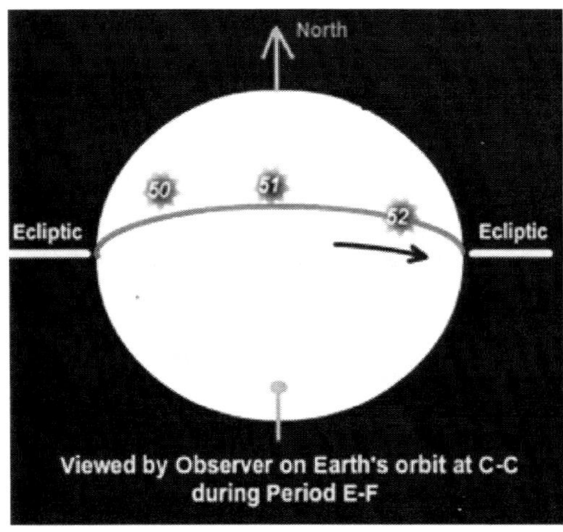

Figure 90.

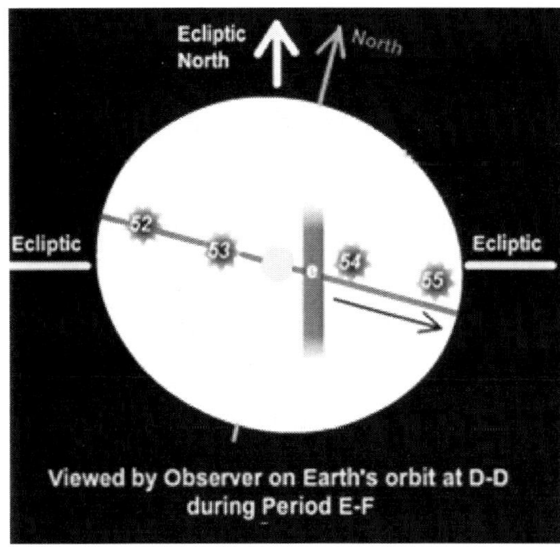

Figure 91.

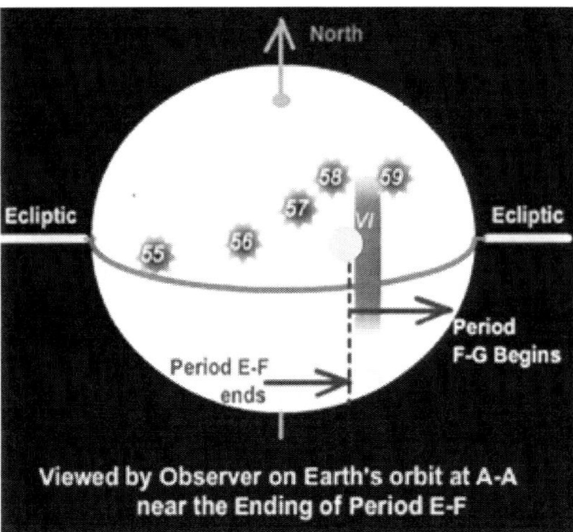

Figure 92.

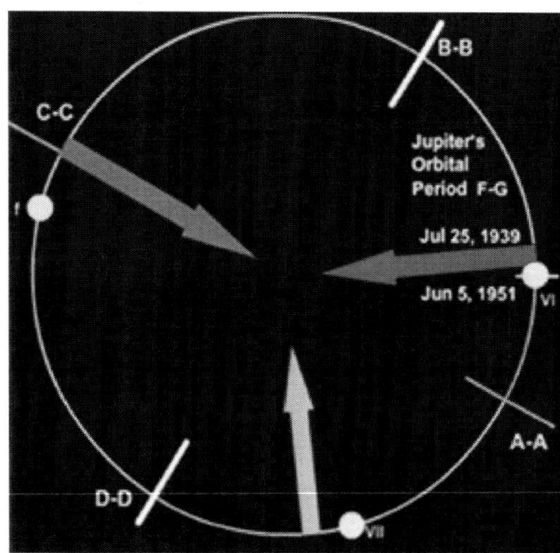

Figure 93.

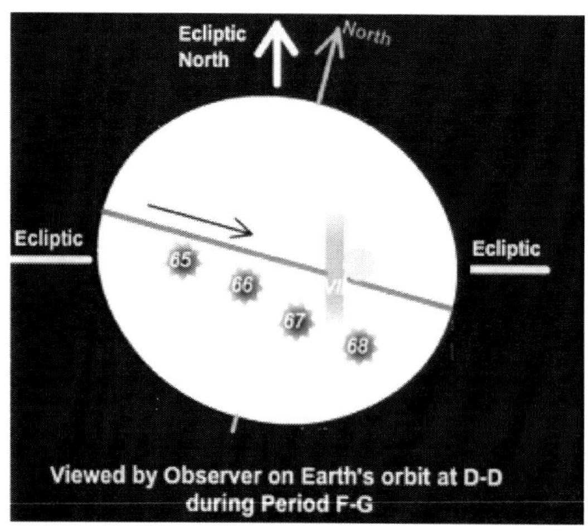

Figure 96.

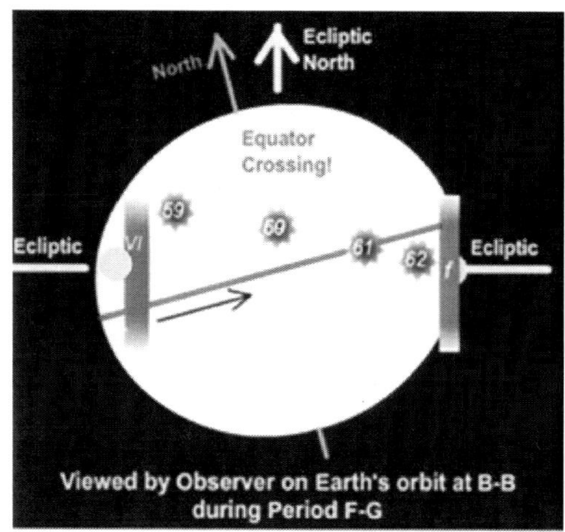

Figure 94.

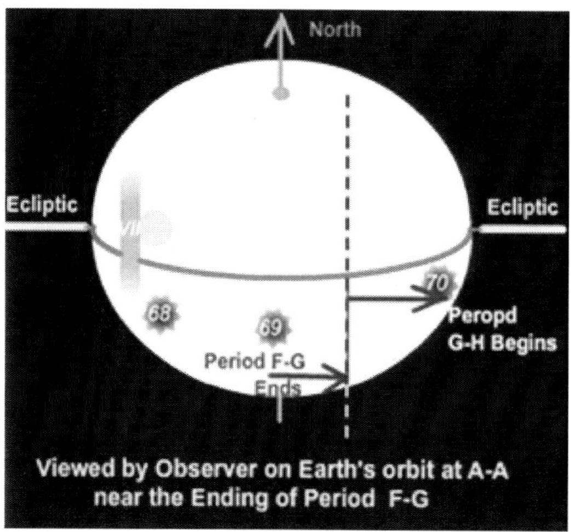

Figure 97.

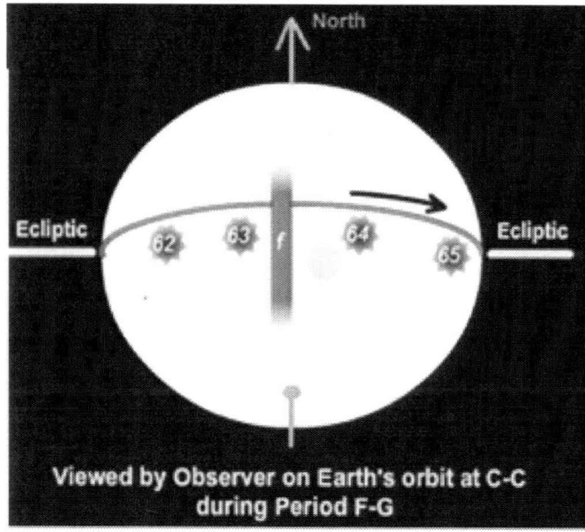

Figure 95.

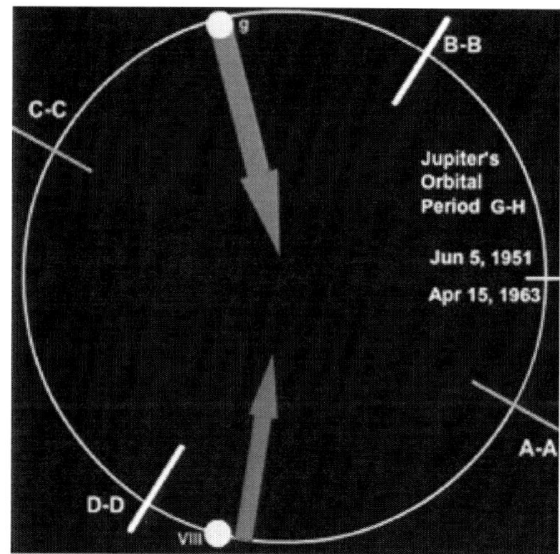

Figure 98.

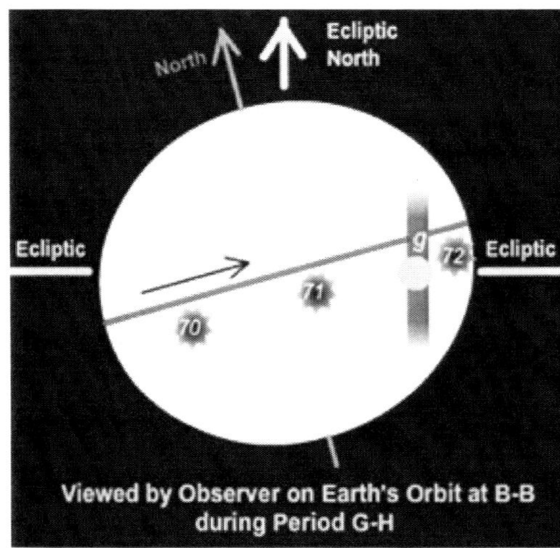

Figure 99.

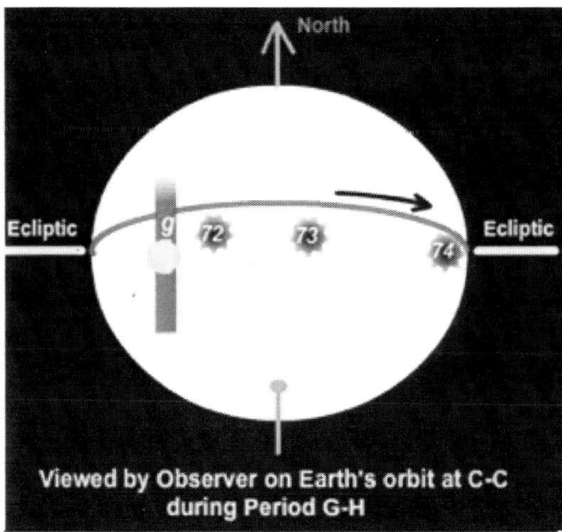

Figure 100.

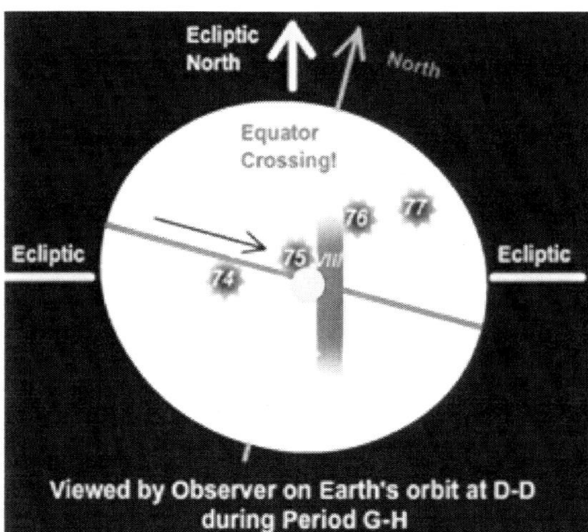

Figure 101.

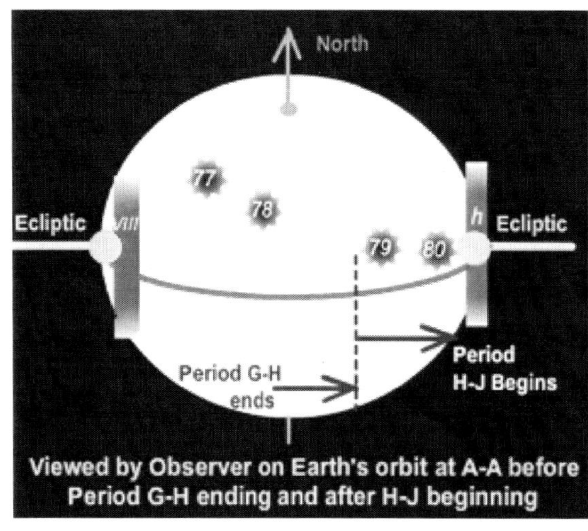

Figure 102.

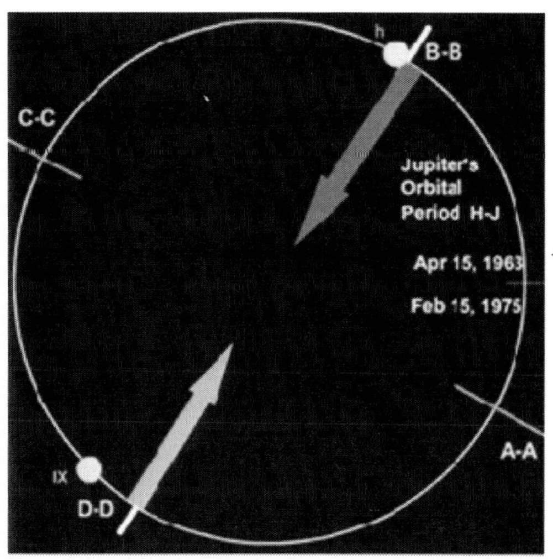

Figure 103.

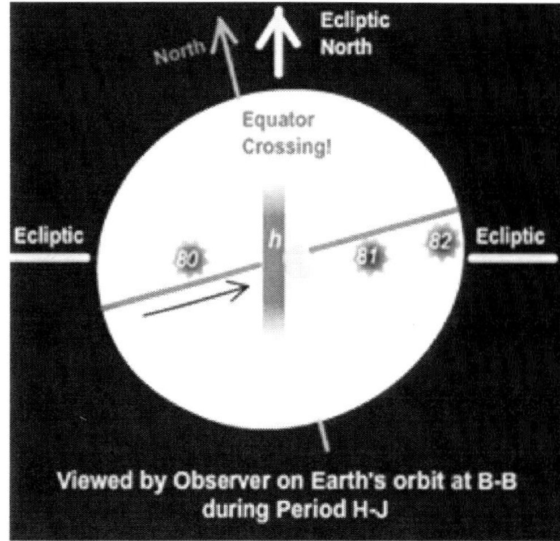

Figure 104.

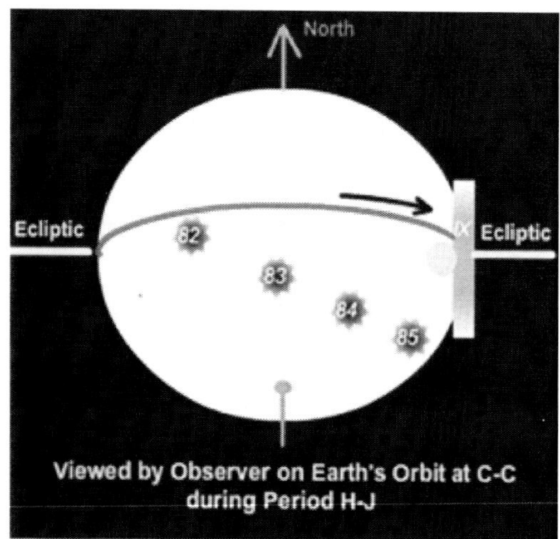

Figure 105.

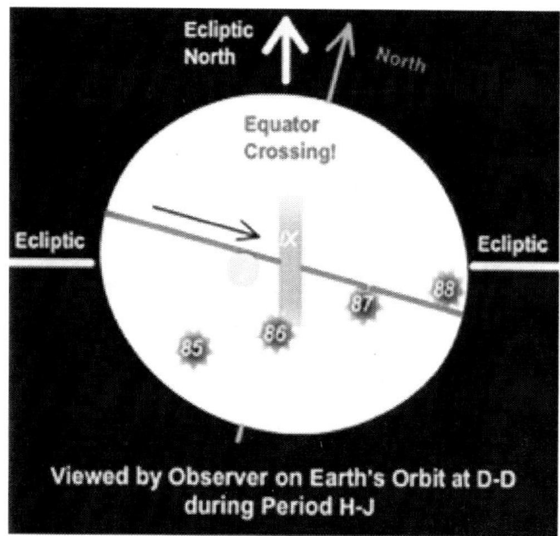

Figure 106.

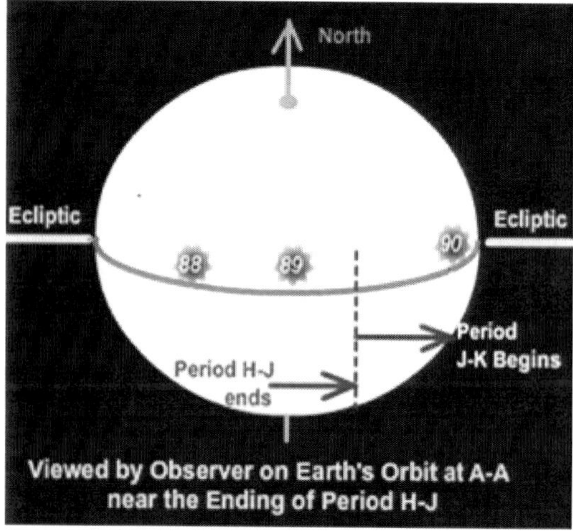

Figure 107.

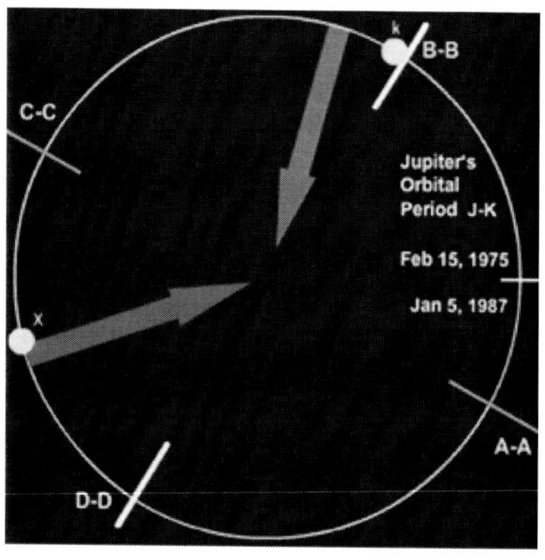

Figure 108.

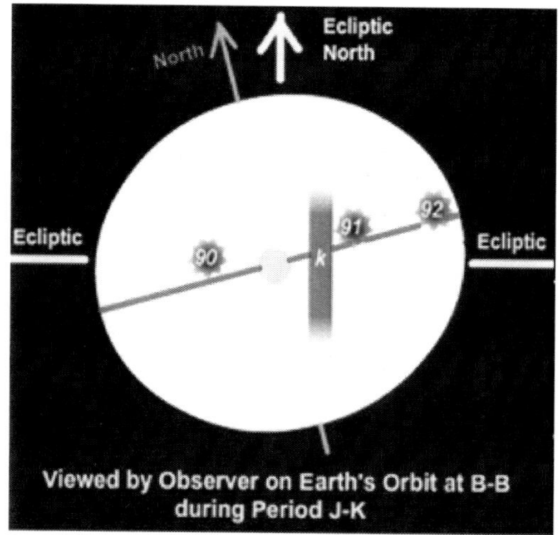

Figure 109.

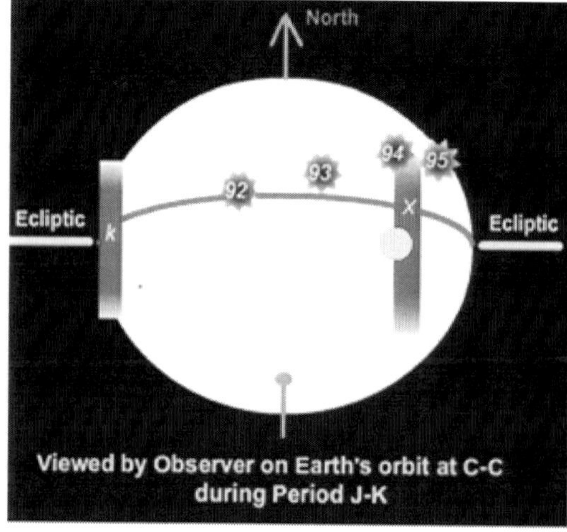

Figure 110.

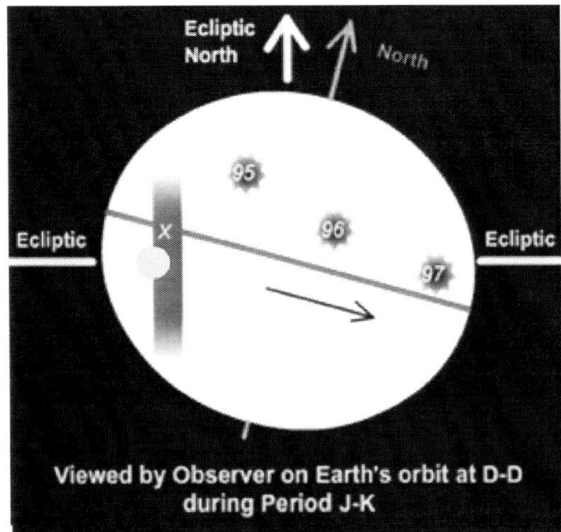

Figure 111.

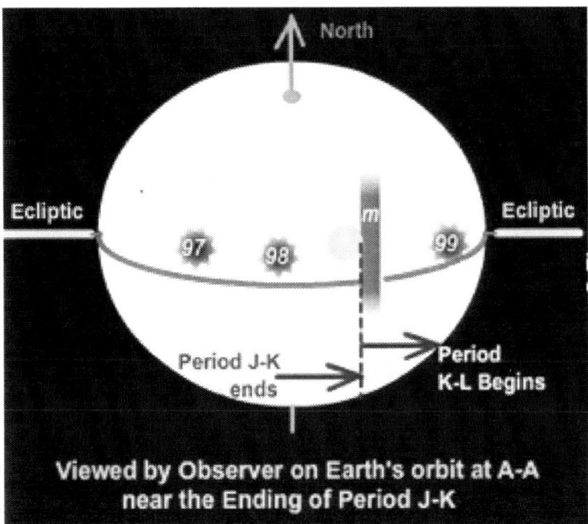

Figure 112.

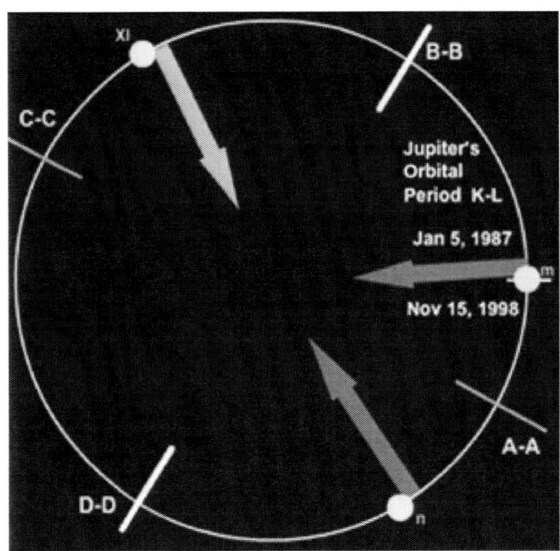

Figure 113.

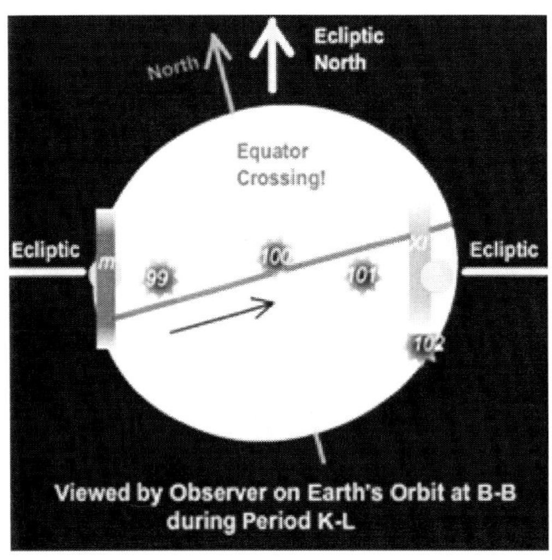

Figure 114.

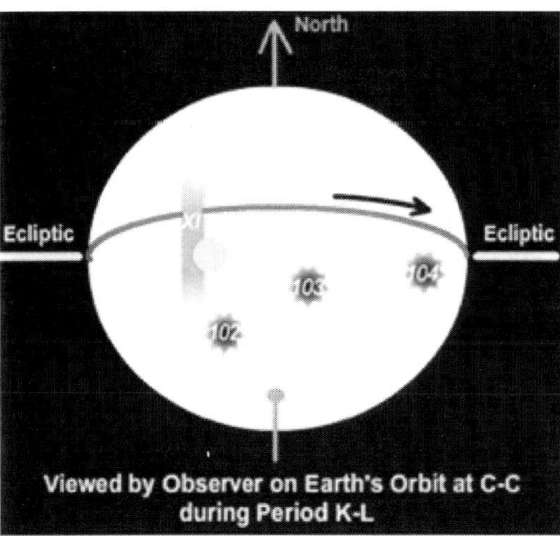

Figure 115.

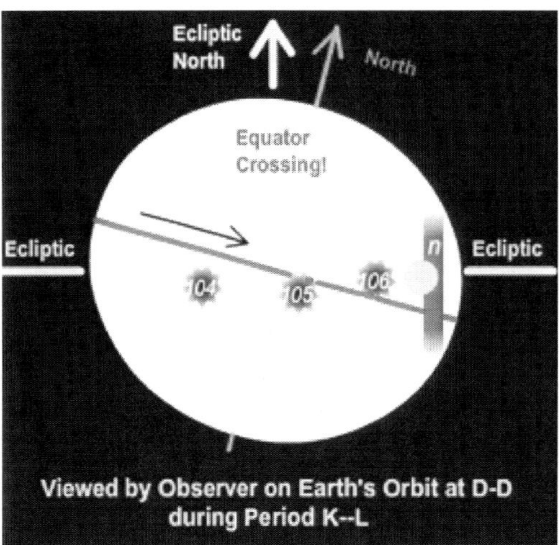

Figure 116.

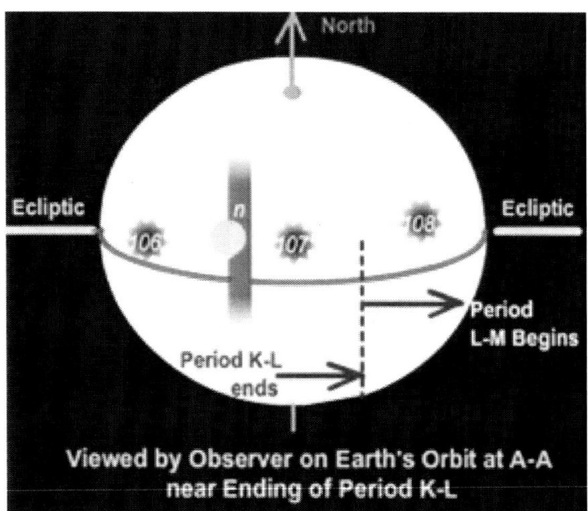

Figure 117.

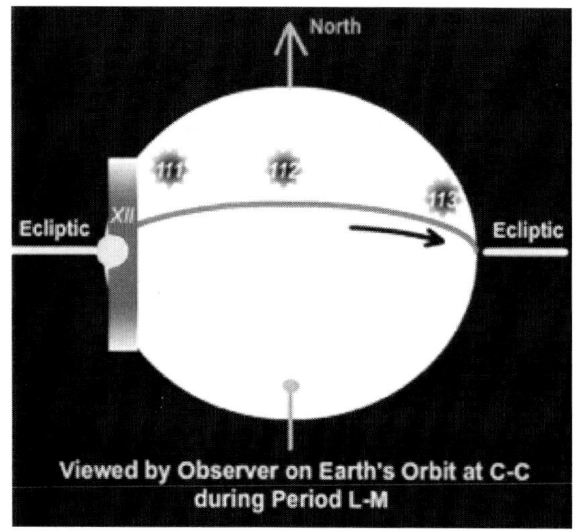

Figure 120.

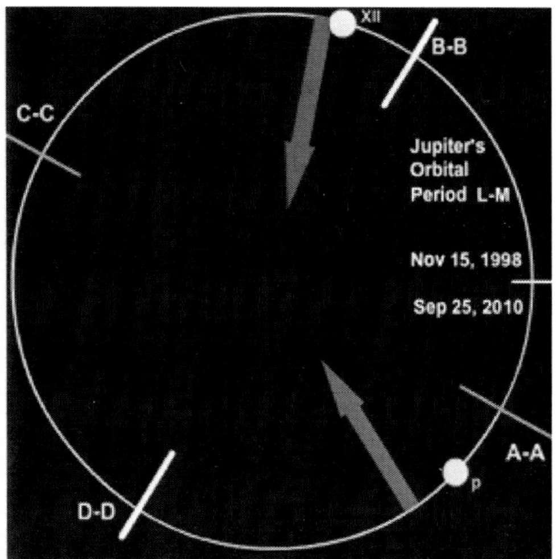

Figure 118.

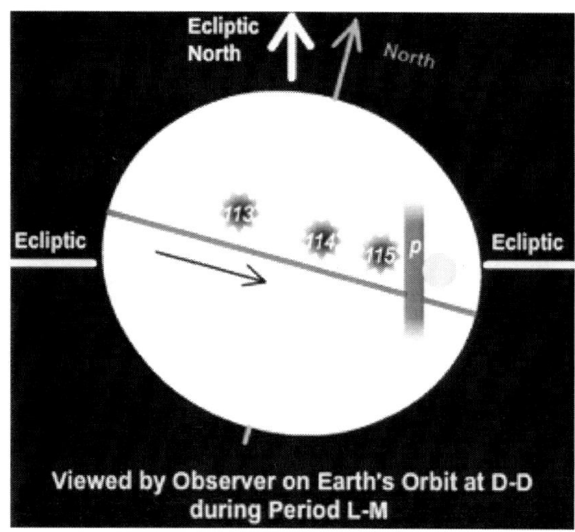

Figure 121.

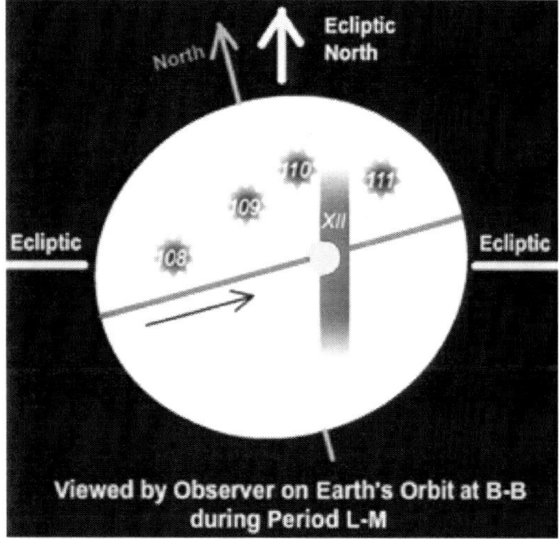

Figure 119.

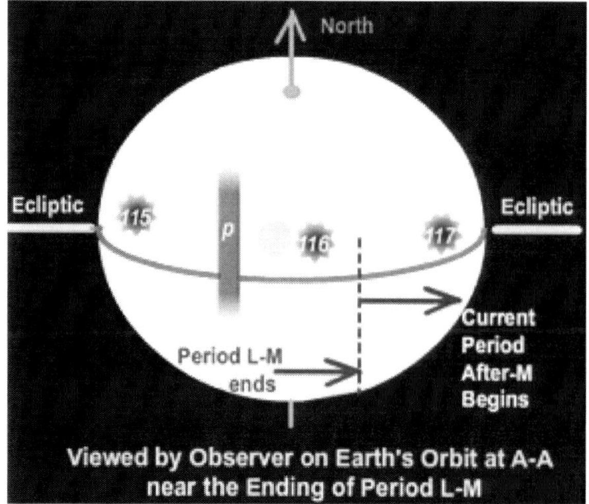

Figure 122.

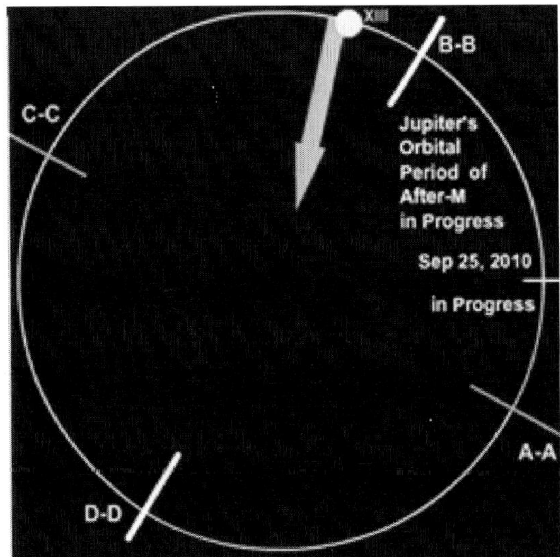

Figure 123.

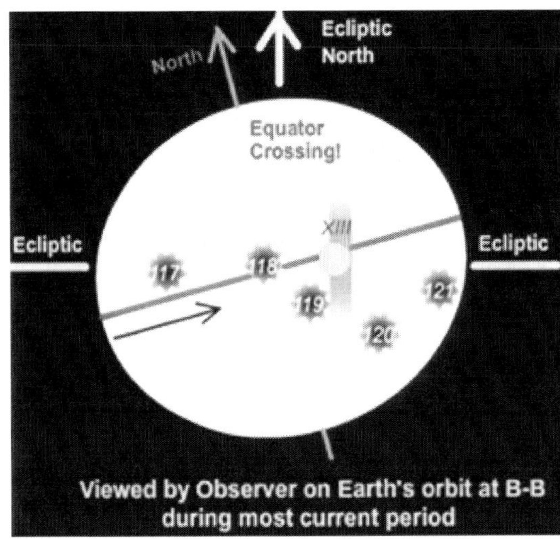

Figure 124.

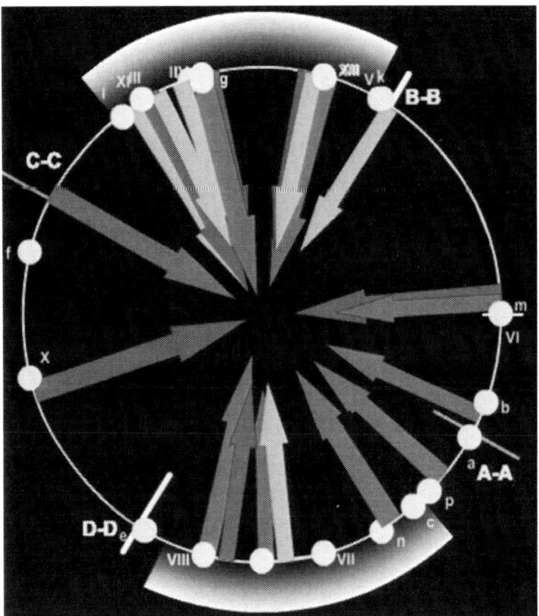

Figure 125.

Newton's Gravitational Law over Dark Matter

P.O. Box 872282, Vancouver, WA 98687, crebigsol@gmail.com

Observation of stellar movement of the Milky Way galaxy shows that celestial objects at distance beyond 10 kpcs from the galactic center appear to move at speed higher than what Newtonian gravitational law predicts and that celestial objects in the inner range at distance between 1 and 8 kpcs from the center appear to move at speed lower than predicted (Please refer to figure 126 in the main text). It appears to a group of people that this phenomenon is suggesting certain failure of the Newtonian gravitational law and that remedy to repair the failure is therefore needed. They mainly propose two ideas as the remedy: (1) dark matter, (2) to modify Newton's gravitational law.

To promote the acceptance of dark matter, it has been popularly advocated that the validity of relativity has enabled the dark matter to exist with unchallengeable legitimacy. A term called space-time fantasized out of relativity plays a key role for dark matter to enjoy a niche where verification never seems able to reach. To reject the existence of dark matter, someone needs first to have relativity refuted. It is so unfortunate to dark matter, however, relativity is exactly a theory that defeats itself, both in terms of mathematical derivation as well as in terms of physical explanation***. Space-time as an independent fourth dimension in the universe does not exist, but space and time as two separate physical elements being absolute can be proven***. If relativity cannot even defend itself, it can only be obvious that it is unable to support the existence of dark matter. Subsequently, the concept of dark matter is refutable.

Finding no support from dark matter, this article can only go by the restricted application of the Newton's gravitational law in exploring the reason governing the speed distribution displayed in Fig. A. However, then, we must encounter the argument that Newton's law needs to be modified. But how? We will soon find that Newton's gravitational law can lead someone to have unlimited quantity of dark matter —if it is misapplied.

Allowing Newton's gravitational law to be modified in the science world, we just end up placing ourselves to confront with a school principle that is as ancient as human beings ever have schools: Should a student taking a test be given the flexibility to modify a rule or law from a textbook only because he found this rule or law fails him from arriving at an answer at his satisfaction? In the auditorium of science, we all are students of Mother Nature. Never has she given us the privilege of arrogance with which we can claim that "I have no fault in study. If no answer can be arrived at my satisfaction, it is the fault of the law that I am taught to follow." Nevertheless, Newton's laws in mechanics study are put up by great minds of many generations including those well respected pioneers like Copernicus, Galileo, Kepler...besides Newton. It is for sure that we need to have an open mind toward all natural laws that are summarized by human. However, to anyone attempting the modification of a natural law that has been confirmed by numerous practice, he must present the following two indispensable elements before so attempting: (1) miscalculation or mistreatment in the derivation of the law in concern is found, (2) some part of the derivation is found having been decisively misled by irrelevant facts, or inadequate facts, or improperly explained facts. Plunging into modification without presenting these two gravely critical elements is only an excellent expression defining the word recklessness. Frankly, no such attitude should be accepted in any serious business.

This article presents several cases needing the scrutiny guided by Newtons gravitational law. After the examination of these few cases, a reader can easily arrive at a conclusion regarding whether the science world has come to a need to modify Newton's law or a need to modify some people's attitude of attempting the modification of Newton's law. Through applying Newton's law, it also appears to us that the Magellanic Clouds [2] cannot be expected to have been traveling on a close orbit about the Milky Way, but instead, they are only one time visitors to our galaxy. No close orbit means no satellite. It therefore means that the Magellanic Clouds are of no satellite to the Milky Way. Newton's gravitational law also gives us explanation why two-rotational-arms is a prominently popular phenomenon among rotating galaxies.

Please refer to the following three articles: ***Relativity is Self-defeated (1 of 3)–*in terms of Mathematics*; ***Relativity is Self-defeated (2 of 3)***–*in terms of physics*; ***Relativity is Self-defeated (3 of 3)***–*Lorentz factor, Aberration, and Ether*. All these three articles by *Cameron Rebigsol* can be found in the 2016 Proceedings of John Chappell Natural Philosophy Society (CNPS).

Keywords: on-axis effect, off-axis effect, dark matter, the Milky Way

10. Introduction

Through studying several special cases on the relationship between shape and gravitation, we will explore how some flying materials at a certain distance from the center of the Milky Way galaxy would show up with speeds higher or lower than "normal". The so called "normal" speed referred to in this article is the speed conventionally believed to be possessed by an object that is moving

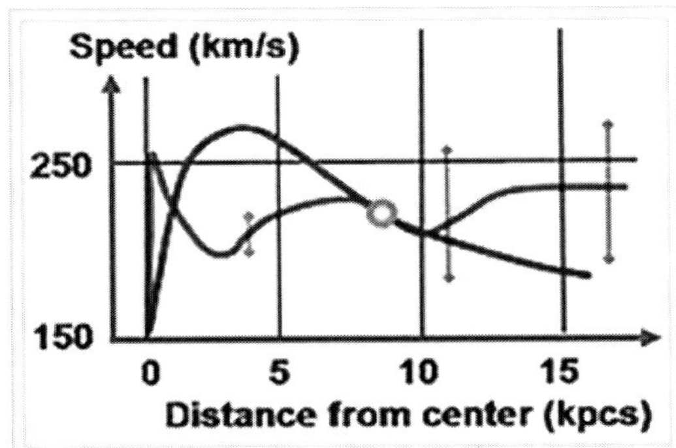

Figure 126. Galaxy rotation curve for the Milky Way. Vertical axis is speed of rotation about the Galactic Center. Horizontal aix is distance form the Galactic Center in kpcs. The Sun is marked with a yellow ball. The observed curve of speed of rotation is blue. The predicted curve based upon stellar mass and gas in the Milky Way is red. Scatter in observations roughly indicated by gray bars. (Wikipedia)

around a point mass at a distance far larger than the dimension of the point mass. The speed so obtained is derived according to the Newtonian gravitational law.

Since the situation involving such conventional treat ment repeats many times in this article, the term "normal" speed or "normal" force will be used here with the inseparable quotation marks. Almost all cases presented here are hypothetically assumed in geometry, but they sure would lead us to have a peek at how the shape of a gravity body can lever the movement of some objects that appear in its vicinity of close range. Being so levered, though, all these movements cannot get away from the governing of Newton's gravitational law.

11. Consideration on Some Special Cases

11.1. Case 1: The On-Axis Effect

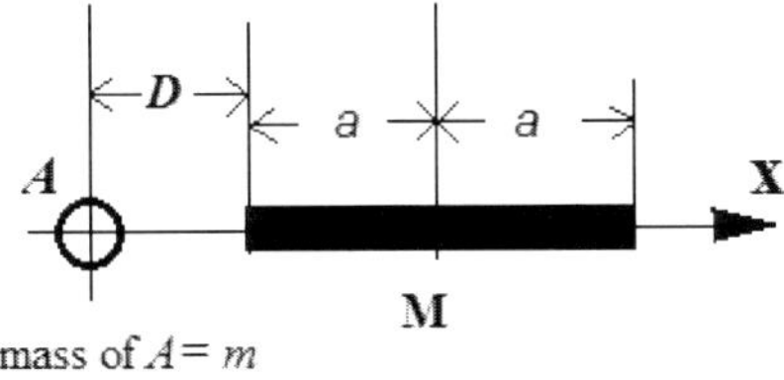

Figure 127. Object A of mass m is on the axis of a homogeneous bar with a distance D

In figure 127, object A of mass m is on the axis of a homogeneous bar with a distance D from one end of this bar. The bar of mass M has a length of L(=2a) . The gravitational force between A and each differential mass element dm of the bar is

$$df = G\frac{m \cdot dM}{x^2} \tag{9}$$

where G is the universal gravitational constant.

Since $dM = (M/L)dx$, we get

$$df = G\frac{mM}{Lx^2}dx \tag{10}$$

Thus the total force $F_{1/1}$ between A and the bar is

$$\begin{aligned} F_{1/1} &= \int_D^{D+2a} G\frac{mM}{Lx^2}dx \\ &= G\frac{mM}{D(D+2a)} \end{aligned} \tag{11}$$

The tangential speed $v_{1/1}$ that is large enough for A to resist the bar's gravitational pull will lead to:

$$m\frac{v_{1/1}^2}{(D+a)} = G\frac{mM}{D(D+2a)} \tag{12}$$

and therefore

$$v_{1/1}^2 = \frac{GM(D+a)}{D(D+2a)} \tag{13}$$

Had the bar become a point mass and stayed at where its original mass center is, the gravitational force $F_{1/2}$ between it and A should be

$$F_{1/2} = G\frac{mM}{(D+a)^2} \tag{14}$$

The tangential speed corresponding to $F_{1/2}$ for A to resist the pull of the point mass is

$$v_{1/2}^2 = \frac{GM}{D+a} \tag{15}$$

The comparison between $v_{1/1}$ and $v_{1/2}$ would lead to

$$\frac{v_{1/1}^2}{v_{1/2}^2} = \frac{D^2+2aD+a^2}{D^2+2Da} \tag{16}$$

In order to make $v_{1/1} \approx v_{1/2}$, we need $D >> a$ so that length a becomes trivial in equation (11) and the bar can then be regarded as a point mass. The smaller the distance D is, the higher the magnitude $v_{1/1}$ becomes if A is to survive the gravitational pull of the bar. Once A survives the pull at this point, it will retain this higher than "normal" (moving about a point mass at large distance) momentum forever until something else brakes on it.

We use the term **on-axis effect** to name the effect that leads to $F_{1/1} > F_{1/2}$ and thus also leads to $v_{1/1} > v_{1/2}$, where $F_{1/2}$ is the "normal" force and $v_{1/2}$ is the "normal" speed.

Now, we have come to a point that a big question demands answer:

Do we need "dark matter" or to "modify" Newton's law to explain the on-axis effect based on $v_{1/1} > v_{1/2}$ that is correspondingly caused by $F_{1/1} > F_{1/2}$???

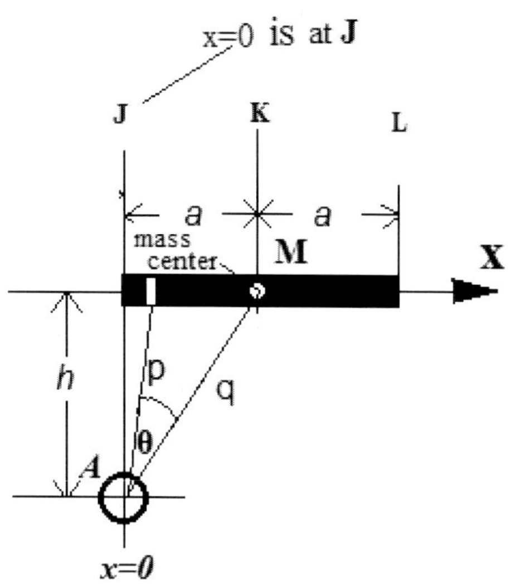

Figure 128. q is the distance between the two mass centers

11.2. Case 2: Gravity off the Axis of a Bar, Situation 1

STEP (A)

The same two gravity bodies in figure 127 are rearranged so that **A** is located a distance of h away directly below the end point J of the bar. (figure 128)

In figure 128, q is the distance between the two mass centers, and thus

$$q^2 = a^2 + h^2 \tag{17}$$

Line p represents the distance between the mass center of **A** and the differential element dx of the bar. Therefore,

$$p^2 = x^2 + h^2 \tag{18}$$

The gravitational force df_1 between dx and **A** is

$$\begin{aligned} df_1 &= \frac{Gm}{p^2} dM \\ &= \frac{Gm}{x^2+h^2} dM \\ &= \frac{Gm}{x^2+h^2} \cdot \frac{M}{2a} dx \end{aligned} \tag{19}$$

If df_1 is projected on q, we get df_1' , which is

$$\begin{aligned} df_1' &= df_1 \cos\theta \\ &= \frac{Gm}{x^2+h^2} \cdot \frac{M}{2a} dx \cdot \frac{p^2+q^2-(a-x)^2}{2pg} \end{aligned} \tag{20}$$

and thus further becomes

$$df_1' = \frac{Gm}{x^2+h^2} \cdot \frac{M}{2a} dx \cdot \frac{(x^2+h^2)+(a^2+h^2)-(a-x)^2}{2\sqrt{x^2+h^2} \cdot \sqrt{a^2+h^2}} \tag{21}$$

The total force between **A** and the segment JK of the bar is $F_{2/1} = \int_0^a df_1'$ and thus further becomes

$$F_{2/1} = \frac{GmM}{2h\sqrt{a^2+h^2}} \tag{22}$$

STEP (B)

Figure 129 is a duplicate of figure 128 but point $x = 0$ is located at K for calculation convenience.

In figure 129, s represents the distance between the mass center of **A** and the differential element dx on the bar. Therefore,

$$s^2 = h^2 + (a+x)^2 \tag{23}$$

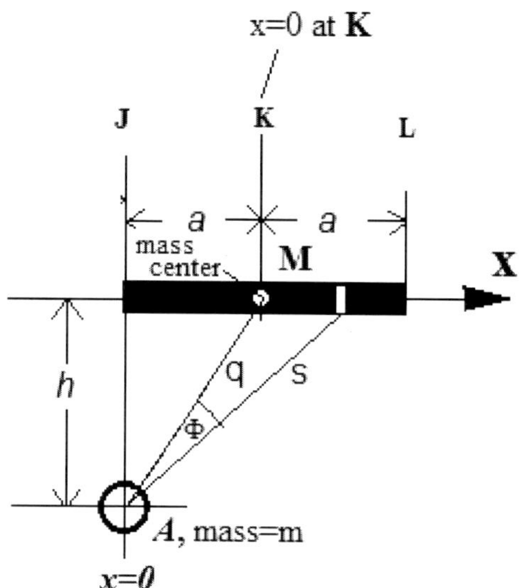

Figure 129. q is the distance between the two mass centers

The gravitational force df_2 between dx and **A** is

$$\begin{aligned} df_2 &= \frac{Gm}{s^2} dM \\ &= \frac{Gm}{(a+x)^2+h^2} dM \\ &= \frac{Gm}{(a+x)^2+h^2} \cdot \frac{M}{2a} dx \end{aligned} \tag{24}$$

When df_2 is projected on line q, we have $df_2' = df_2 \cos\phi$, and with $x^2 = s^2 + q^2 - 2sq\cos\phi$, we further have

$$df_2' = df_2 \cdot \frac{h^2+(a+x)^2+(a^2+h^2)-x^2}{2\sqrt{(h^2+(a+x)^2} \cdot \sqrt{a^2+h^2}} \tag{25}$$

The total force between A and the segment KL of the bar is $F_{2/2} = \int_0^a df_2'$, which, following equation (refeq:16), would then further develop into

$$F_{2/2} = \frac{GmM}{2\sqrt{a^2+h^2}\cdot\sqrt{4a^2+h^2}} \tag{26}$$

STEP (c)

The total force between A and the mass center of the entire bar is $F_{2/3} = F_{2/1} + F_{2/2}$ and thus

$$F_{2/3} = \frac{GmM}{2h\sqrt{a^2+h^2}} + \frac{GmM}{2\sqrt{a^2+h^2}\cdot\sqrt{4a^2+h^2}} \tag{27}$$

If **A** happens to move at speed $v_{2/3}$ in a direction perpendicular to line q, the centrifugal force thus needed to resist the bar's gravitational pull will lead to

$$\frac{mv_{2/3}^2}{\sqrt{a^2+h^2}} = \frac{GmM}{2h\sqrt{a^2+h^2}} + \frac{GmM}{2\sqrt{a^2+h^2}\cdot\sqrt{4a^2+h^2}} \tag{28}$$

Had the bar become a point mass and stayed at where its original mass center is, the "normal" gravitational force between A and this point mass will be

$$F_{2/4} = \frac{GmM}{a^2+h^2} \tag{29}$$

The "normal" centrifugal force for **A** corresponding to $v_{2/4}$ would lead to

$$\frac{mv_{2/4}^2}{\sqrt{a^2+h^2}} = \frac{GmM}{a^2+h^2} \tag{30}$$

Thus, we can have the comparison between $v_{2/3}$ and $v_{2/4}$ as

$$\frac{v_{2/3}^2}{v_{2/4}^2} = \frac{\sqrt{a^2+h^2}}{2h} + \frac{\sqrt{a^2+h^2}}{2\sqrt{4a^2+h^2}} \tag{31}$$

Let $h = na$, where $n \neq 0$, equation (31) leads to

$$\frac{v_{2/3}^2}{v_{2/4}^2} = \frac{\sqrt{1+n^2}}{2n} + \frac{\sqrt{1+n^2}}{2\sqrt{4+n^2}} \tag{32}$$

If $n = 1$, for example, we have

$$\frac{v_{2/3}^2}{v_{2/4}^2} = 1.8 \tag{33}$$

If n=3, however, we will have

$$\frac{v_{2/3}^2}{v_{2/4}^2} = 0.96 \tag{34}$$

If we must introduce dark matter to explain the phenomenon brought up by equation (33), how do we explain the phenomenon brought up by equation (34)?

Of course, when $n \to \infty$, we no longer need to be concerned with dark matter, as equation (32) would give us a value very close to 1, fitting our conventional concept that the bar can be viewed as a point mass.

If $F_{2/3}$ is to be resolved on the line connecting **A** and J, we have $F_{2/5}$, where

$$\begin{aligned} F_{2/5} &= \frac{F_{2/3}\cdot h}{\sqrt{a^2+h^2}} \\ &= \frac{GmM}{2(a^2+h^2)}\cdot\left(1+\frac{h}{\sqrt{4a^2+h^2}}\right) \end{aligned} \tag{35}$$

11.3. Case 3a: Gravity off the Axis of a Bar, Situation 2

In figure 130, we duplicate the bar in figure 128, or figure 129, and "weld" it with the original bar end to end and thus form a new bar.

On each side of the mass center of this longer homogeneous bar, the half bar has a length of 2a (therefore the total length is 4a). The gravitational force $F_{3/1}$ between **A** and the full length new bar is two times of $F_{2/5}$ found in equation (35) and therefore

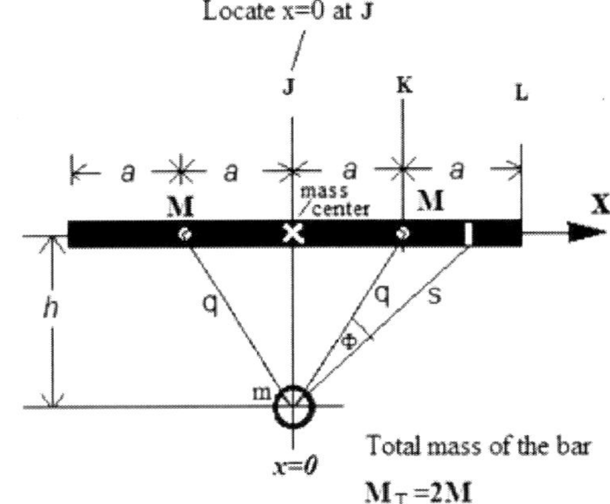

Figure 130. Two of the same bars "welded" together

$$\begin{aligned} F_{3/1} &= 2F_{2/5} \\ &= \frac{GmM}{(a^2+h^2)}\cdot\left(1+\frac{h}{\sqrt{4a^2+h^2}}\right) \end{aligned} \tag{36}$$

The tangential speed $v_{3/1}$ that is large enough for **A** to resist the bar's gravitational pull will lead to

$$\frac{mv_{3/1}^2}{h} = \frac{GmM}{a^2+h^2}\cdot\left(1+\frac{h}{\sqrt{4a^2+h^2}}\right) \tag{37}$$

Had the bar become a point mass and stayed at where its mass center has been, the "normal" gravitational force $F_{3/2}$ between **A** and the bar will be

$$F_{3/2} = G\frac{m\cdot 2M}{h^2} \tag{38}$$

The "normal" centrifugal force corresponding to $F_{3/2}$ would lead to

$$m\frac{v_{3/2}^2}{h^2} = G\frac{m\cdot 2M}{h^2} \tag{39}$$

Thus, we can have the comparison between $v_{3/1}$ and $v_{3/2}$ as

$$\frac{v_{3/1}^2}{v_{3/2}^2} = \frac{h^2(h+\sqrt{4a^2+h^2})}{2(a^2+h^2)\sqrt{4a^2+h^2}} \tag{40}$$

Let $h = na$, where $n \neq 0$, we have

$$\frac{v_{3/1}^2}{v_{3/2}^2} = \frac{n^3}{2(1+n^2)\sqrt{4+n^2}} + \frac{n^2}{2(1+n^2)} \tag{41}$$

Each term on the right side of equation (41) is smaller than 0.5. Therefore, $v_{3/1}$ is forever smaller than $v_{3/2}$ for any value of n. **Dark matter must fail** in explaining the phenomenon brought up by equation (41).

11.4. Case 3b: Off-axis Effect

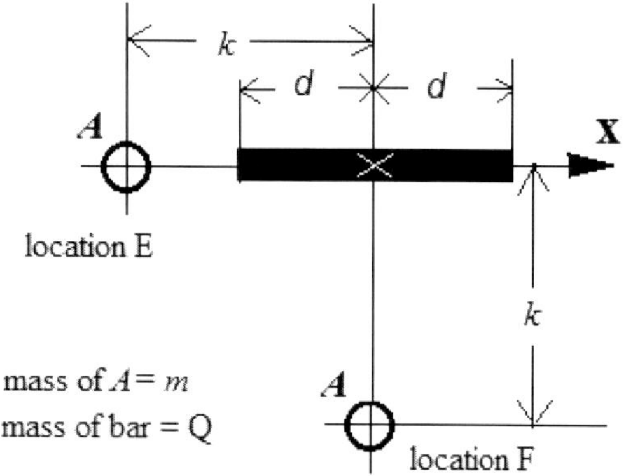

Figure 131. Off-axis Effect

In figure 131, we are going to compare the dynamic status of **A** between location E and F.

At location E, the reasoning of equation (11) gives us the gravitational force received by **A** as

$$F_{3b/1} = G\frac{mQ}{(k-d)^2+2d(k-d)} \tag{42}$$

The speed $v_{3b/1}$ matching the corresponding centrifugal force for **A** to survive the pull from the bar leads to

$$v_{3b/1}^2 = \frac{GQk}{(k-d)^2+2d(k-d)} \tag{43}$$

At location F, the reasoning of equation (36) gives us the gravitational force received by A as

$$F_{3b/2} = \frac{Gm(Q/2)}{(d/2)^2+k^2}\cdot\left(1+\frac{k}{\sqrt{4(d/2)^2+k^2}}\right) \tag{44}$$

The speed $v_{3b/2}$ matching the corresponding centrifugal force for A to survive the pull from the bar at F leads to

$$v_{3b/2}^2 = \frac{G(Q/2)k}{(d/2)^2+k^2}\cdot\left(1+\frac{k}{\sqrt{4(d/2)^2+k^2}}\right) \tag{45}$$

Therefore we can further have

$$\frac{v_{3b/1}^2}{v_{3b/2}^2} = \frac{(d^2+4k^2)\sqrt{d^2+k^2}}{2(k^2-d^2)\sqrt{d^2+k^2}+k} \tag{46}$$

Letting $k = nd$, where $n \neq 0$, we have

$$\frac{v_{3b/1}^2}{v_{3b/2}^2} = \frac{(1+4n^2)\sqrt{1+n^2}}{2(n^2-1)(n+\sqrt{1+n^2})} \tag{47}$$

If $n+e > 1$, but with $e \to 0$, equation (47), easily leads us to have higher and higher value for the ratio of the two speeds.

So, if we must regard the bar as a point mass in explaining the speed of **A**, then, at location E we must face inexplicable reason for **A**'s higher than "normal" speed. When **A** moves to area near location F, we may perplex even more, because, carrying the momentum equipped at E, **A** now is encountered weaker and weaker than "normal" gravitational pull at F. Indeed, we can expect that A is going to fly away from the bar. For example, if $n = 2$, the ratio in equation (47) is 1.49, or $v_{3b/1} = 1.22v_{3b/2}$. The bar definitely can no longer bind **A** with gravitation at F. From the behavior of **A** at location F, should we conclude that some apparent mass from the bar must have lost its gravity? Or, should we propose that Newton's gravitational law needs to be modified?

We use the term **off-axis effect** to name the effect that leads **A** to receive weaker than "normal" gravitational force $F_{3b/2}$ at F. Equation (47) tells us that the off-axis effect will diminish as $n \to \infty$ and the bar can be regarded as a point mass at a remote distance.

We have come to a point to propose a serious question: If the concept of dark matter can "help" to explain some phenomena similar to the on-axis effect, how would the same concept now help to explain the off-axis effect, which seems showing some mass otherwise having disappeared with no good reason? Or should we begin to propose a new idea to explain where some of the apparent mass has been made lost and how? Or should we again begin to suspect the validity of Newton's law?

11.5. Case 4: Gravity in the Vicinity of a Cross

In figure 132, two bars of length $2a$ and mass M each are placed perpendicularly crossing each other at their dead centers. Body **A** is a distance a from each bar, and therefore it is a distance q away from the mass center of the cross, where $q = \sqrt{2}a$. Taking advantage of the analysis shown with figure 128 and 129, replacing h in equation (27) with a, we can have the gravitational force $F_{4/1}$ between **A** and the mass center of the cross as

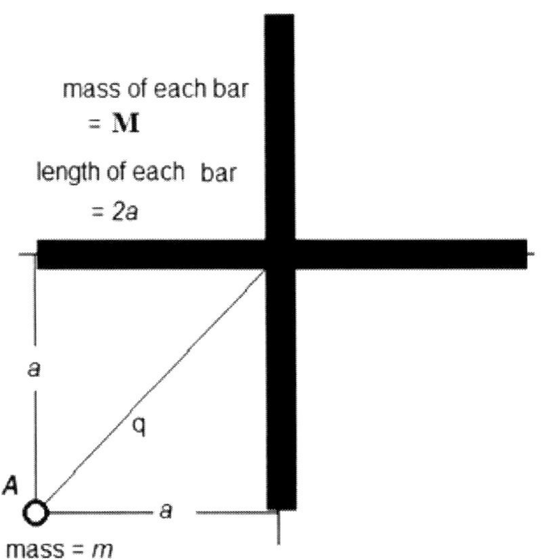

Figure 132. gravity in the vicinity of a cross

$$F_{4/1} = 2\left(\frac{GmM}{2a\sqrt{a^2+a^2}} + \frac{GmM}{(2a\sqrt{a^2+a^2}\sqrt{4a^2+a^2}}\right) = GmM\left(\frac{\sqrt{5}+1}{a^2\sqrt{10}}\right) \tag{48}$$

The tangential speed $v_{4/1}$ that is large enough for **A** to resist the cross's gravitational pull will lead to:

$$m\frac{v_{4/1}^2}{\sqrt{2}a} = \frac{GmM(\sqrt{5}+1)}{a^2\sqrt{10}} \tag{49}$$

Had the cross become a point mass and stayed at where its mass center has been, the "normal" gravitational force $F_{4/2}$ between A and the cross will be

$$F_{4/2} = G\frac{m(2M)}{(\sqrt{2}a)^2} = \frac{GmM}{a^2} \tag{50}$$

The "normal" centrifugal force for **A** corresponding to $F_{4/2}$ thus leads to a "normal" tangential speed $v_{4/2}$ as shown below

$$m\frac{v_{4/2}^2}{\sqrt{2}a} = G\frac{m(2M)}{(\sqrt{2}a)^2} \tag{51}$$

Thus, we can have the comparison between $v_{4/1}$ and $v_{4/2}$ as

$$\frac{v_{4/1}^2}{v_{4/2}^2} = \frac{(\sqrt{5}+1)/a^2\sqrt{10}}{1/a^2} \approx 1.023 \tag{52}$$

Equation (52) thus shows that, at the location as shown in figure 132, the tangential velocity for **A** to survive the pull will not change much whether the gravitational influence is from a cross or a point mass of the same mass.

11.6. Case 5a: Gravity at the Tip of a Cross

In figure 133, the gravitational force $F_{5/1}$ between **A** and the vertical bar can be calculated according to equation (11). In so doing, D in equation (11) is replaced with $D = q - a$. Therefore, we have

$$F_{5/1} = \frac{GmM}{(q-a)^2 + 2a(q-a)} = \frac{GmM}{q^2 - a^2} \tag{53}$$

The gravitational force $F_{5/2}$ between **A** and the horizontal bar can be calculated according to equation (36). In doing so, M in equation (36) is replaced with $M/2$, a is replaced with $a/2$, h is replaced with q. Then,

$$F_{5/2} = \frac{Gm(M/2)}{(a/2)^2 + (\sqrt{2}a)^2} \cdot \left(1 + \frac{\sqrt{2}a}{\sqrt{4(a/2)^2 + (\sqrt{2}a)^2}}\right) \approx 0.403\frac{GmM}{a^2} \tag{54}$$

The total gravitational force $F_{5/3}$ between **A** and both bars together is then

$$F_{5/3} = F_{5/1} + F_{5/2} = 1.403\frac{GmM}{a^2} = 1.403\ F_{4/2} \tag{55}$$

where $F_{4/2}$ is the gravitational force that **A** would have received if the cross had been a point mass at the mass center of the cross [See equation (50)].

The tangential speed $F_{5/3}$ that can equip **A** with enough centrifugal force against the cross's gravitational pull will lead to:

$$m\frac{v_{5/3}^2}{\sqrt{2}a} = 1.403\left(\frac{GmM}{a^2}\right) \tag{56}$$

Applying equation (50) in comparing the centrifugal force displayed in equation (47), we have $\frac{v_{5/3}^2}{v_{4/2}^2} = 1.403$ or

$$v_{5/3} = 1.184v_{4/2} \tag{57}$$

In figure 134, let's imagine that the tangential momentum of each of objects **A**, **B**, and **C** has enabled them to survive the gravitational pull of the cross.

To any object in a situation similar to that of **A**, **B**, and **C**, the general expression for the gravitational force $F_{5/4}$ it receives from the cross can be written as (Refer to equation (36) , (44) and (53), with proper replacement of corresponding quantities) $(F_{5/4}) = forcefromverticalbar$ + force from horizontal bar

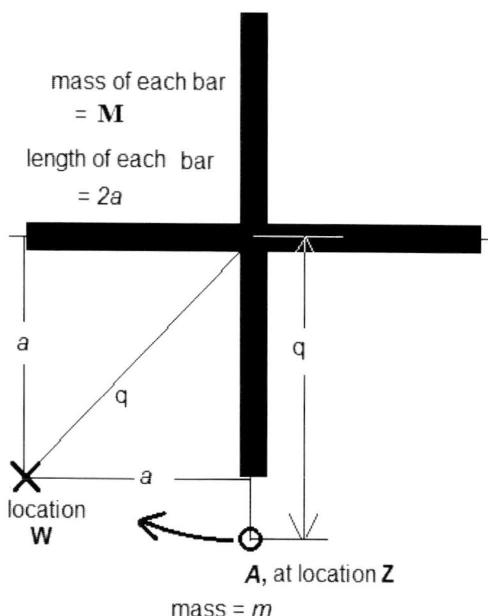

Figure 133. Gravity at the tip of the cross

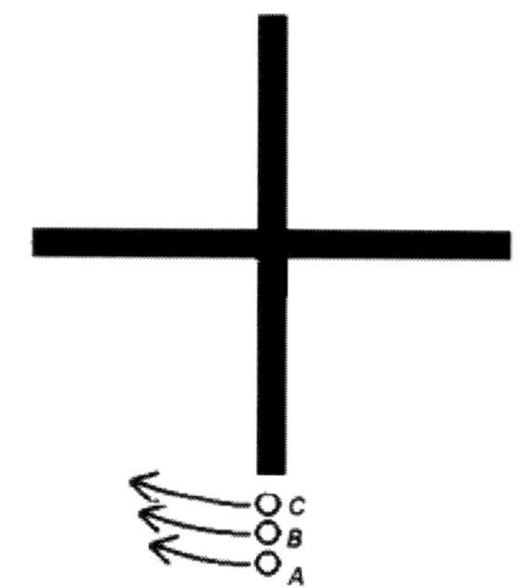

Figure 134. Three objects flying at the tip of the cross

or

$$F_{5/4} = \frac{GmM}{q^2 - a^2} + \frac{Gm(M/2)}{(a/2)^2 + q^2} \cdot \left(1 + \frac{q}{\sqrt{(4(a/2)^2 + q^2}}\right)$$
$$= GmM\left[\frac{1}{q^2 - a^2} + \frac{2\sqrt{q^2 + a^2} + 2q}{(4q^2 + a^2)\sqrt{q^2 + a^2}}\right] \quad (58)$$

The tangential speed $v_{5/4}$ corresponding to $F_{5/4}$ would show

$$v_{5/4}^2 = GMq\left[\frac{1}{q^2 - a^2} + \frac{2\sqrt{q^2 + a^2} + 2q}{(4q^2 + a^2)\sqrt{q^2 + a^2}}\right] \quad (59)$$

Let $q = na$, where $n \neq 0$, correspondingly, equation (49) and (50) will become

$$F_{5/4} = \frac{GmM}{a^2}\left[\frac{1}{n^2 - 1} + \frac{2\sqrt{n^2 + 1} + 2n}{(4n^2 + 1)\sqrt{n^2 + 1}}\right] \quad (60)$$

and

$$v_{5/4}^2 = GMa \cdot n[\frac{1}{n^2 - 1} + \frac{2\sqrt{n^2 + 1} + 2n}{(4n^2 + 1)\sqrt{n^2 + 1}}] \quad (61)$$

Figure 135 is a chart showing how $F_{5/4}$ and the ratio $v_{5/4}/v_{4/2}$ change in accordance with $n = 1.05$, $n = 1.1$, $n = 1.2$, $n = 1.3$, $n = 1.4$, $n = 2$, and $n = 5$.

Note 1: The so called F_{normal} in the chart is the gravitational force that a moving object receives from the cross but the cross has been shrunk into a point mass of the same mass quantity at its mass center.

Note 2: a is the arm length of the cross, q is the distance between the moving object and the mass center of the cross.

11.7. Case 5b On the Gravity of a Softened Cross and on the Rotation Arms of the Milky Way

If the lower arm of the cross is: (1) a rotating body with respect to the mass center of the entire cross and (2) composed of loose materials, all the materials in this arm must display the same movement pattern as what A, B, and C are showing in figure 136.

The same reasoning must equally apply to other arms of the cross, if all other arms also possess the same nature as that of the lower arm. (figure 137)

However, as our inspection moves closer and closer to the center of the cross, we must notice that the arm length of the cross is getting shorter and shorter. The ever shortened arms of the cross must lead two things to happen: (1) The contrast between the on-axis effect and off-axis effect gradually diminishes; (2) movement of the objects about the mass center should show more and more obviously a pattern that is gravitationally governed by a point mass. When this happening is in progress, we cannot ignore one fact that the angular velocity of the moving objects near the center is higher than that of those farther away from the center. The higher and higher angular velocities of the materials toward the center gradually blur out any distinctive feature of a cross. Instead, they just come together and present a rapidly spinning cloud. (figure 138)

The problem is that, unless the cloud is absolutely homogeneous, given enough time, the spinning cloud will sooner or later evolve into a rotating bar. The reason for the appearance of such a bar, ironically, is exactly because the gravity in this range is more and more dominantly governed by a point mass. This point mass must be an extremely compacted and massive one if it is to stabilize the movement of so many objects traveling in orbits of short radius around it.

Let's suppose that some objects of more prominent mass inside a spinning and inhomogeneous cloud happen to

n=q/a	a	q	F_{5-3} , set as S $value \times \frac{GmM}{a^2}$	F_{4-2} , set as T $value \times \frac{Gm(2M)}{a^2}$	S/T	v_{5-3}/v_{4-2}
1.05	1a	1.05a	10.39	1.81	5.74	2.4
1.1	1a	1.1a	5.39	1.65	3.26	1.81
1.2	1a	1.2a	2.8	1.39	2.02	1.42
1.3	1a	1.3a	1.91	1.18	1.61	1.27
1.4	1a	1.4a	1.45	1.02	1.42	1.19
$\sqrt{2}$	1a	1.414a	1.403	1	1.39	1.18
2	1a	2a	0.556	0.556	1.12	1.06
5	1a	5a	0.81	0.08	1.01	1

The ratio v_{5-3}/v_{4-2} strongly suggests that stellar rotating speed to be observed can be dramatically different whether or not the shape of a dominating gravity body has been taken into consideration when applying Newton's gravitational law in close distance.

In comparison, v_{5-3} are speeds compatible to the speeds shown by the blue line in **Fig. 1** and v_{4-2} are speeds compatible to the speeds shown by the red line in the same diagram.

Data here are only for some suggestion of clues for some qualitative understanding. They

Figure 135. Data comparison showing how Newton's gravitational law can be "failed", if the shape of a gravity body is not taken into consideration. The shorter the distance is between the gravity body and the flying object, the more serious attention should be paid to the shape of the gravity body. It seems to us that on the line of n=q/a=1.05 in the above table, the end figure 2.4 appears being a value hungry of waiting for the makeup of "dark matter".

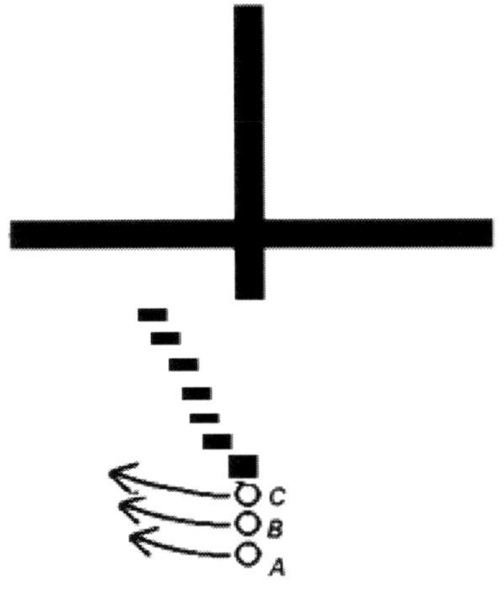

Figure 136. One arm of the cross is consisted of loose materials

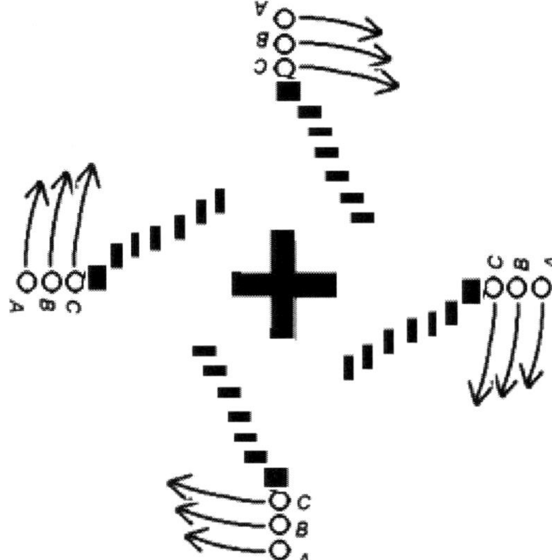

Figure 137. All arms of the cross consist of loose materials

have concentrated along a certain radial direction with respect to the mass center of the cloud, such as those shown along line OJ and OK in figure 139. Having so joined by a random chance, these groups would act together like certain bars to a certain extend. So the newly formed bar, although a broken one, would exert their gravitational influence through the *on—axis* effect onto those materials flying near the end of such bar. Highly potentially, the flying objects are recruited by the bar. Once so recruited, the newly joining material would contribute to beef up the gravity strength of the materials gathering of the bar and further escalated the bar's on-axis gravitational strength. For those material groups like L and R, they are located at the area that the *off—axis* effect of the bar is more obvious. Depending on the angular velocity they already pos-

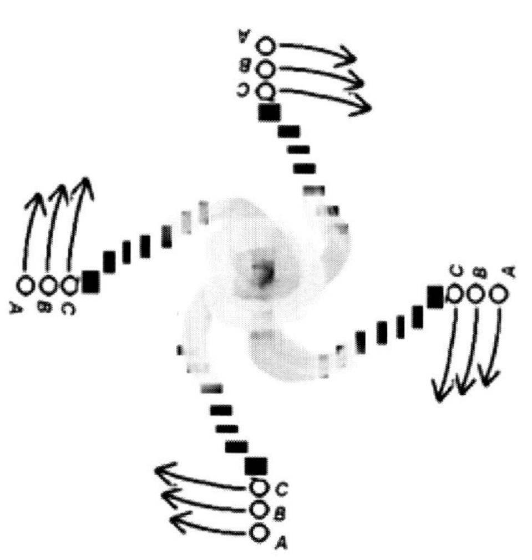

Figure 138. A rotating body consisting of rotation arms of loose materials

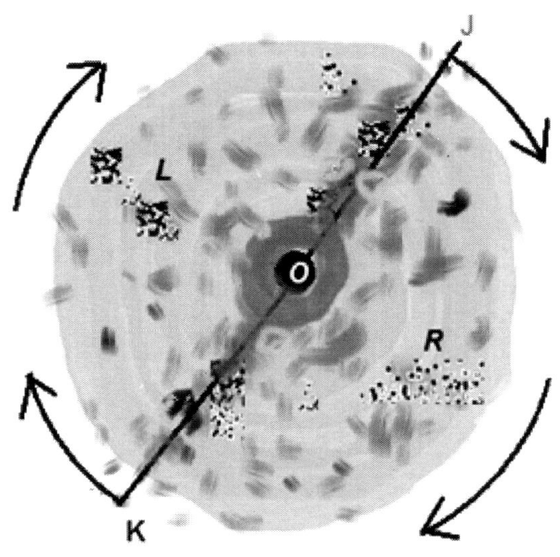

Figure 139. Higher concentration of materials on each side of the mass center may form a bar of more pronounced gravity in its environment

sess, they may slowly drift (with rotation movement about the cloud's center) either toward the center or away from the center. To those drifting toward the center, their ever shortened rotation radius may accelerate them to plunge into the bar. To those drifting away from the center, their ever lengthening rotating radius and thus decreasing angular velocity may just make them sooner or later be arrested by the bar's sweeping. Either way, the bar is an unstoppable gravitational predator once so formed. As to the bars OJ and OK, once they stabilize their predator position, the centrifugal force and their own on-axis effect exerted on each other will line them up on one straight line across the cloud's center.

When materials of a huge quantity were tossed together in the remotely old days, no one can ever expect that a solid gravity body with a shape of high regularity could have formed itself like what is presented as the cross in this article. When the materials of various sizes were so randomly thrown at each other, the momentum between them is impossible to be exactly canceling each other out. The vector sum of all the off-center residual momentum contributed by each material chunk then forces the entire gathering to rotate about the center of the overall material formation.

The same randomness must also prevent the appearance of absolute homogeneity of material distribution across the entire formation. At areas where more materials have come together, the seed of a future rotation arm is planted. As shown in figure 140, blobs E, F, and G can all lure the formation of some rotation arms inside the big rotating formation.

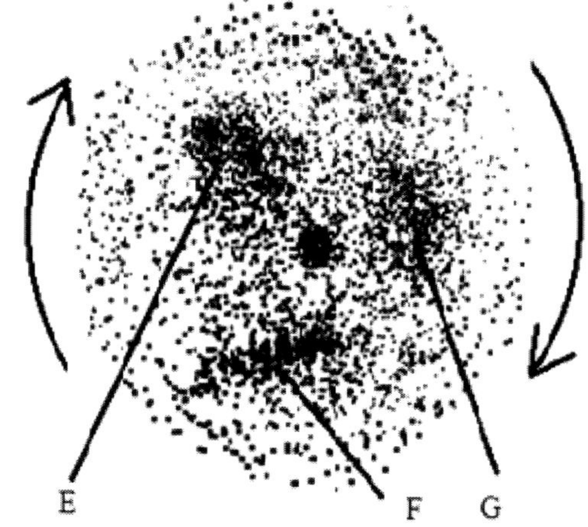

Figure 140. Inhomogeneous mass distribution sows the seed for rotation arms to gradually get into shape

From a state shown in figure 140 to a state shown in figure 141 for the nowadays galaxy of Milky Way, there is a long history of transition similar to what is illustrated in figure 138 and figure 139. Today, after the long history of transition, with a stable rotation that the Milky Way has evolved into, we can say that the Milky Way has two types of rotation arms: the straight arms, such as what is shown as the Galactic Bar at the galaxy center, and the spiral arms, such as what are shown in areas outside where the Galactic Bar is sweeping. Those objects get recruited as one of the members in the Bar may move with all kinds of orbit in different shape with respect to the dead center of the Bar, from lanky ellipses to near perfect circles. Their orbital planes may even intersect at any angle with the galactic plane, from lying perfectly within the plane to being perpendicular to it.

The analysis of figure 133, figure 138 and figure 141 would easily suggest to us that the spiral rotation arms may not be an unchanged establishment over time. Somewhere

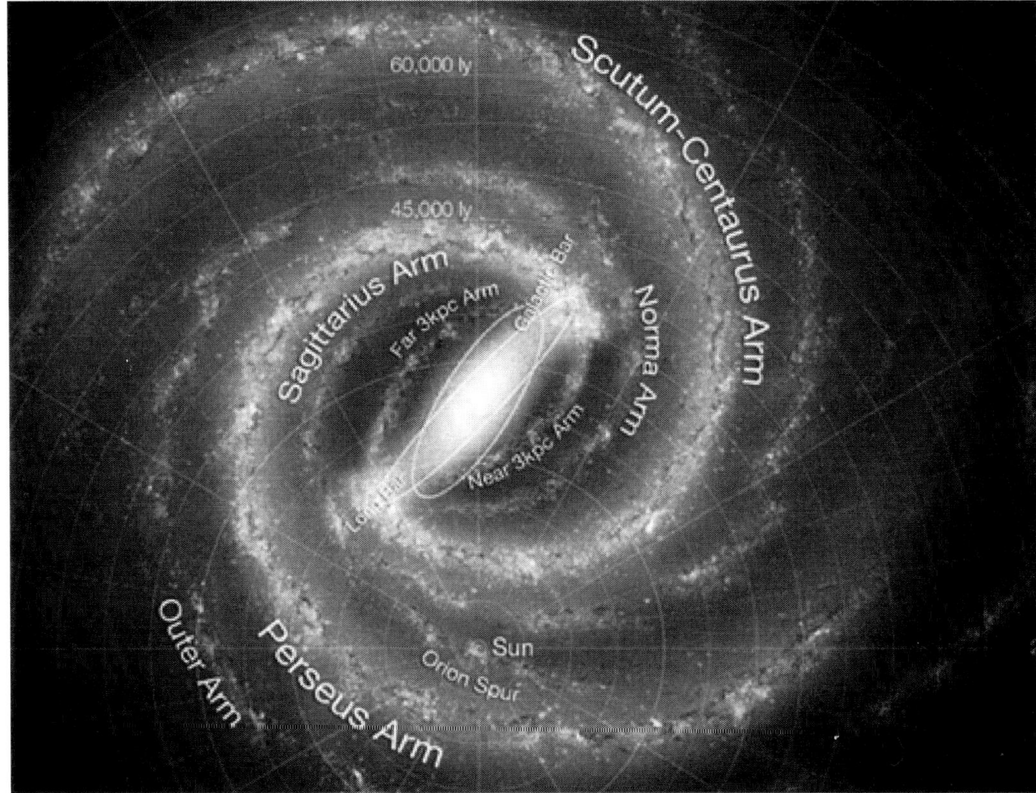

Figure 141. All arms of the cross consist of loose materials

there may be some material chunk that finds itself having entered a region with speed higher than necessary to balance the gravity field there and thus advanced to join the next arm. On the contrary, some may find itself not flying with enough angular momentum to keep up with the peers around it and gradually lag behind and eventually fall into the arm that is coming after. However, given the movement stability of the formation that has been established today, all these migrations can only happen in an extremely slow process. It is this slow process that has introduced the formation of some minor spiral rotation arms in the Milky Way's rotation disk found in figure 141.

Figure 141 shows two major spiral arms for the entire Milky Way, one flowing out from each end of the rotating Galactic Bar. Although two distinct bars are identified in the photo at the central region of the Milky Way, the close proximity between them allows us to consider them working as one. It seems common among rotating galaxies that fundamentally two spiral arms are found for the entire galaxy, with one spiral to be dragged following each end of the rotation bar (figures 142, 143, 144, 145). In astronomical study, we may have also encountered many photos about rotating galaxy in which the feature of only two major spiral arms are not obvious although a single core is prominent. Given enough time, they will eventually evolved into a galaxy that would have two major spiral arms with one bar connecting in between.

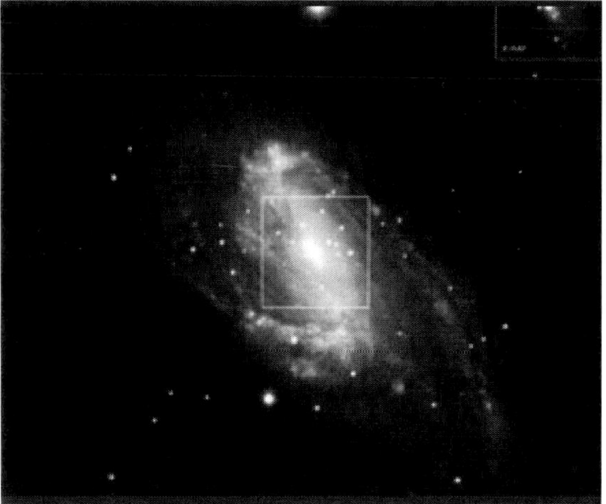

Figure 142. Photo credit: NASA.Gov

If we consider the on-axis effect, the phenomenon that one major spiral arm follows at each end of the rotation bar should appear highly natural. As the bar rotates, somewhere along its long axis but farther away from the center there must begin to appear some location where materials chunks, such as object A in figure 146, cannot have enough angular momentum to catch up with the bar's an-

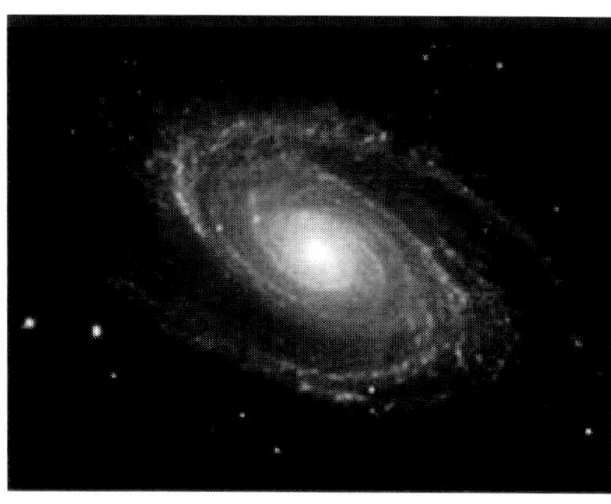

Figure 143. Photo Credit: NASA.Gov

Figure 144. Photo Credit:content.time.com

Figure 145. Typical feature of two rotation arms

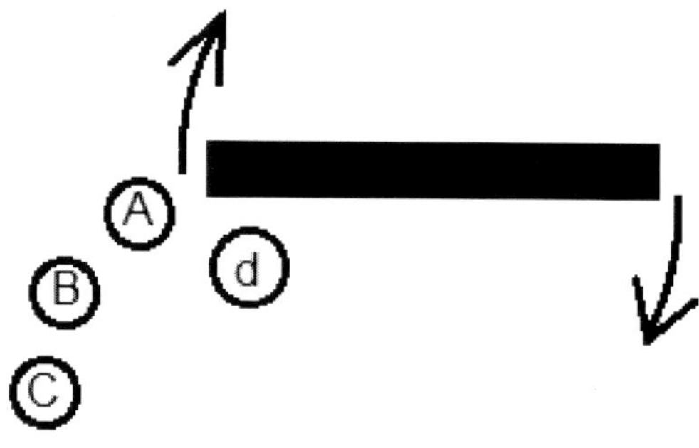

Figure 146. Object A, B and C provide materials to extend a rotation arm; bodies similar to object d is the source for the formation of the Far 3KPC Arm and Near 3KPC Arm to form in the Milky Way

gular advancement. The centrifugal force disengages it a little from the bar. As this happens, its angular movement must somewhat lag behind the bar's. However, the strong "extra" gravitational force because of the on-axis effect must continue to bind object A in a "controllable" distance. In some sense, object A taking its position is just as natural as some celestial body taking the Lagrangian point in some other gravitational system, although the cause is different. Staying away from the bar with the same reason like A's, object B lags behind even more. The more being away from the region of the on-axis effect for B means the more for it to be in the region where off-axis effect is pronounced. However, the gravitational pull from A will not let go of B freely. Object A and B would also work together to drag C along while C has been even further away from the end of the rotation bar. This reaction continues so that a ribbon of materials are joining together to form a spiral formation following at the end of the bar. The same also happens at the other end of the bar.

To the material chunks happening not at a close vicinity of the bar end, they would move away, waiting to be caught by the upcoming but extensively long spiral arms that is led by the other end of the bar, or just directly absorbed by the bar if its angular momentum is really so weak. Therefore, we cannot expect to have a spiral arms flowing out at the middle of the bar. Clearly shown in figure 141, and similarly suggested in figures 142, 143, 144, 145, no spiral arm stems from the middle of the Bar of each picture. The Far 3kpc Arm and the Near 3kkpc Arm in figure 141 are formed by materials not having enough angular momentum and thus entering the off-axis effect region. Object *d* shown in figure 146 is an example for an object of such a group. After entering the region where the off-axis effect dominants, object *d* seems to have moved about a point mass but of less massive in substance. If the bar's rotation period happens to synchronize well with the rotation period of *d*, *d* will not sink into the bar. The synchronization makes *d* appear retaining an unvaried

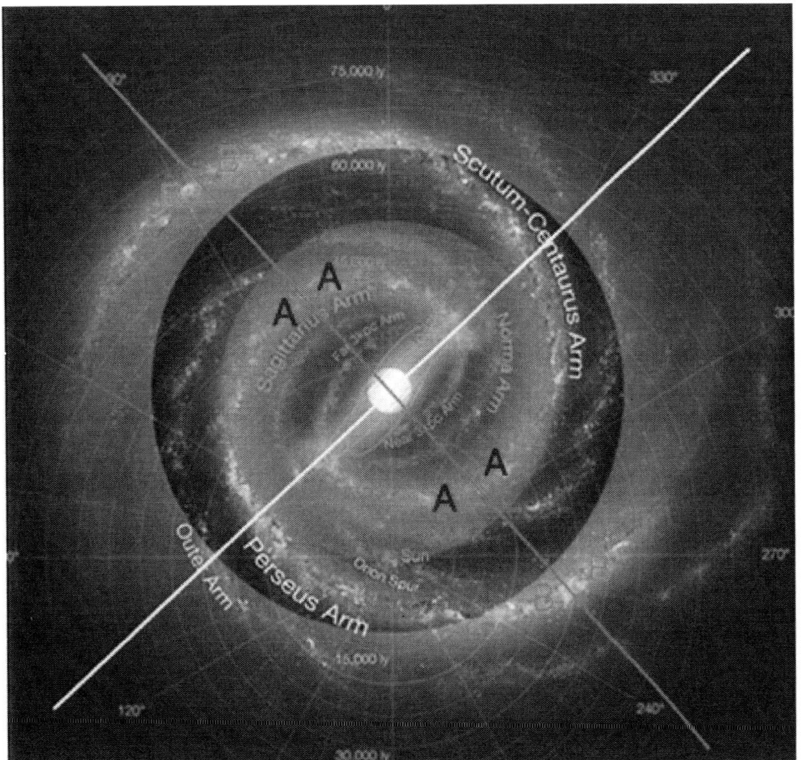

Figure 147. Two perpendicular lines showing the running directions of the on-axis effect and off-axis effect across the Milky Way plane

distance from the Bar. Many objects with moving status like that of *d* but slightly different from each other will form a ribbon spanning from end to end of the Bar just like what the Far 3kpc Arm and the Near 3kpc Arm show. Since there is an off-axis effect region on each side of the Galactic Bar, it is why the Far 3kpc Arm and the Near 3kpc Arm must appear as a pair. On the other hand, figure 141 does show that the on-axis effect has captured higher concentration of materials at each end of the Galactic Bar.

Figure 147 is a duplicate of figure 141 but with the following modification: (1) the area between the 1 kpcs and 8 kpcs from the Galactic center is shaded green, while the area with a distance bigger than 10 kpcs is shaded yellow; (2) a yellow line is drawn along the long axis of the Galactic Bar, indicating the running direction of the strongest on-axis effect, while a purple line is drawn perpendicular to the Galactic Bar, indicating the running direction of the strongest off-axis effect. In the unshaded area between the yellow and green areas are materials moving with "normal" speeds. In the picture, given that materials near A-A are in an area where the off-axis effect dominates, they would have flown away if they had not carried a speed lower than "normal". The reason that they did not fly away is because (1) their speed has been filtered to synchronize well with the rotation of the Galactic Bar during the long history of establishment of a rotating organization and (2) the gravitational interaction between chunks in the same arm just keeps extending their pulling on the materials further lagging behind, as shown in figure 146. On the other hand, the materials near A-A, with their lower than "normal" speed but higher population there, compensate somewhat the loss of gravitational pull to a certain extend along the purple line. This compensation enables a stronger gravitational pull on the materials near the area of B-B, which otherwise may have flown away because of their higher than "normal" speed. Their higher than "normal" speed is not something produced by the galaxy itself, but is a residual speed with which these materials survived the galaxy's overall pull in the old days. All these give us a reason why the blue line in figure 126 shows speeds lower than what the red line (prediction by Newton's law) shows before the distance marked by the Sun but higher beginning from certain distance beyond the Sun.

11.8. Case 6: The Theoretical Impossibility for the Magellanic Clouds to Move on a Close Orbit about the Milky Way

Had the Magellanic Clouds ever been some satellites of the Milky Way, their current location and movement would only indicate that they have now been far away from the point called periapsis, which is the point for them to be the closest from the mass center of the Milky Way if they ever owned an elliptical orbit about the Milky Way.

The Milky Way disk can be considered as being composed of many bars like what is shown in figure 148. When a massive body, called A, moves near the bars, it must receive certain on-axis effect of gravitation from each bar. If A ever moves along an elliptical orbit about one bar, and the axis of the bar lies in the orbital plane, we have several situations as shown in figure 150, 151 and 152.

Comparison between figure 150, 151 and 152 should lead us to visualize that figure 150 is the most probable situation to happen. In Fig figure 150, body A will receive the strongest gravitational force around the bar because of the on-axis effect when it migrates crossing the bar's axis, or at the point of periapsis. Subsequently, body A has the highest speed here in the entire orbit.

The problem is that, when body A leaves the periapsis, it would enter a region where the off-axis is getting more and more prominent, thus the gravitational pull from the bar reduces more and more. However, the angular momentum with which A survives the gravitational pull at the periapsis remains the same. In other words, body A has more and more excessive momentum in responding to the gravitational pull of the bar after it leaves the periapsis. Any excessive momentum thus resulted must derail A from the supposed close orbit; any moving object considered to be a satellite of something else must have a close orbit about this something else.

The Milky Way as an entirety can be regarded as a collection of bars laid side by side but within the galactic plane. The on-axis effect of gravitational influence from each bar on the Magellanic Clouds is fundamentally the same, although the farther away a bar is from the galaxy center, the less prominent the on-axis effect would be. As the Magellanic Clouds move to a location like what position F indicates in figure 148, the off-axis effect between it and each bar would have been quite pronounced, or the gravitational pull from the Milky Way would have been quite weak. Then the only destination for the Clouds is to fly away from the Milky Way with their momentum that must become more and more excessive.

Therefore, we can claim with confidence that the Magellanic Clouds are visitors to the Milky Way only once in the Milky Way's life time, and in the Clouds' life time as well. Given that the current speed of the Large Magellenic Cloud is $378 km/sec$ and the speed of the Small Cloud is $302 km/sec$, if the universe (! its visible portion only!) has an age of 13.5 billion years, their birth place should have been no more than 17 million light years away from the current position, and about 100 times of the current distance between them and the Milky Way, provided that nothing has ever altered their movement during their entire journey, and that their journey had been a straight line. (A side-line question: Will the Big Bang theory accept a universe with a radius as small as what is suggested by "100 times of the current distance between them and the Milky Way"? But then the far younger age of the Large Cloud [about 1.6 billion years according to http://iopscience.iop.org/article/10.1086/310727/pdf] must come out to even defy this conclusion on the total distance that they could have traveled.)

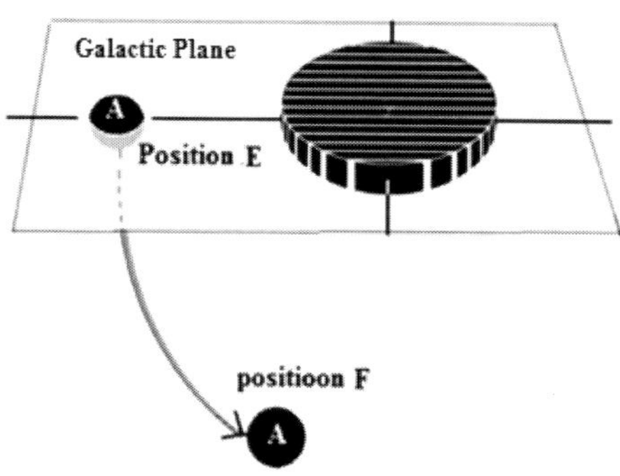

Figure 148. At position E, object A receives on-axis gravitational effect from the Milky Way disk, while at position F, off-axis effect.

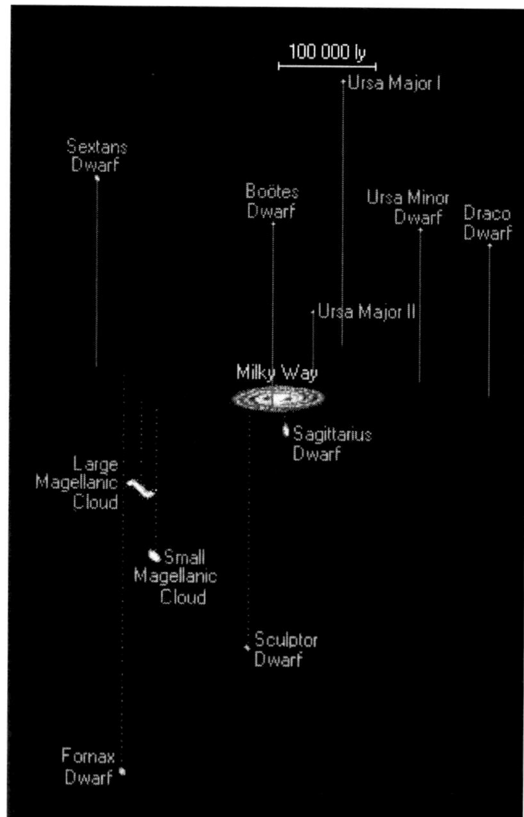

Figure 149. With respect to the Milky Way disk, the Magellanic Clouds are now at the off-axis position similar to what object A shows at F in figure 148. Therefore, flying away from the Milky Way seems their inevitable ultimate fate. Picture credit: Richard Powell - http://www.atlasoftheuniverse.com per Wikipedia

REFERENCES

1. Isaac Newton, *MATHEMATICAL PRINCIPLES OF NATURAL PHILOSOPHY*

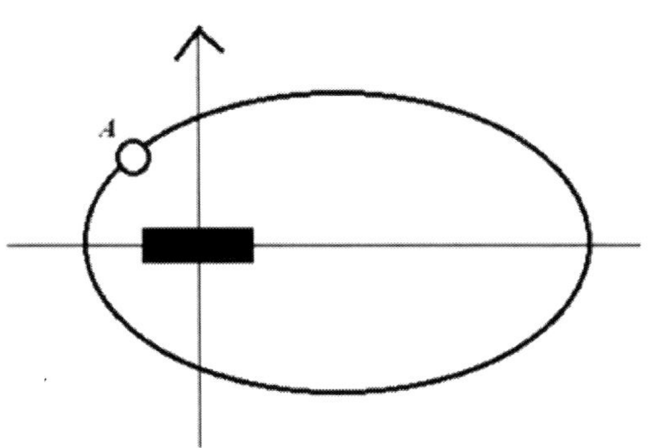
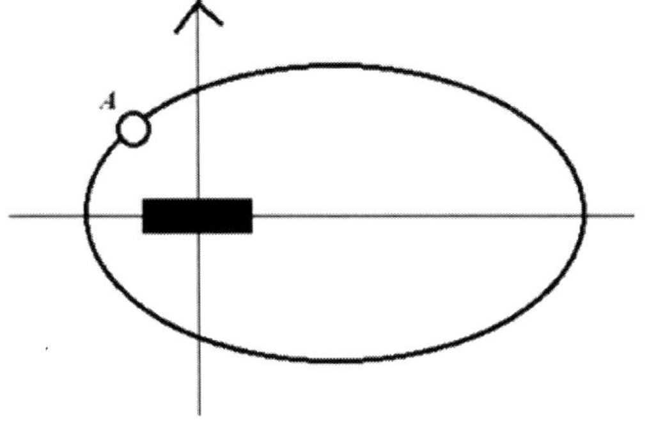

Figure 150. Instead of a single bar, the bar in this picture can also represent the collection of bars shown in figure 148 if the galactic plane there is viewed edge-on

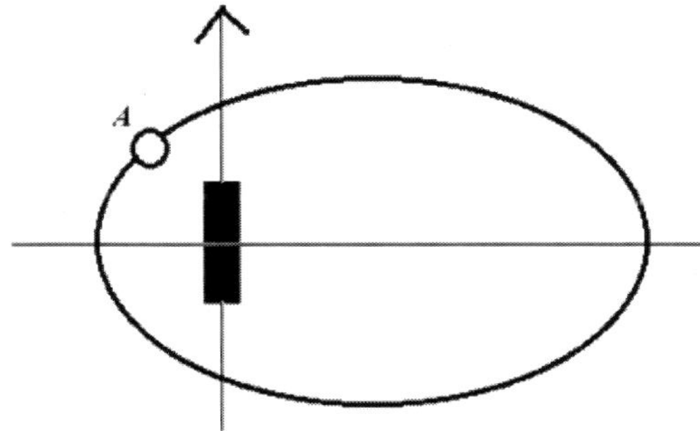

Figure 151. An orbit can hardly happen as shown because the periapsis is not found on the long axis of the ellipse

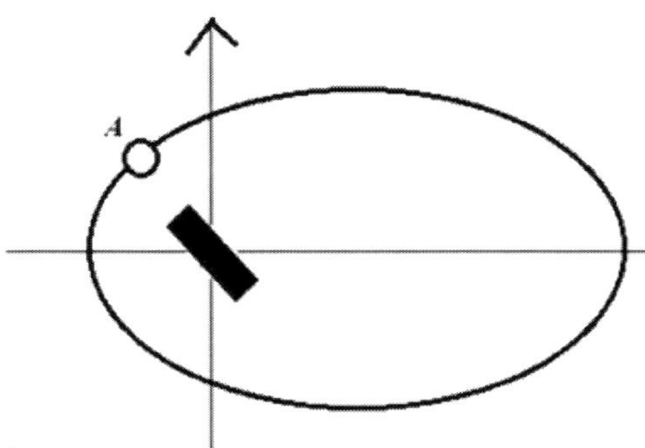

Figure 152. This picture is highly improbable for the same reason presented in figure 151

2. URL, *http://phys.org/news/2007-01-magellanic-clouds.html* 2016

3. *DARK MATTER*, Wikipedia, the Free Encyclopedia, 2016

4. *MILKY WAY*, Wikipedia, the Free Encyclopedia, 2016.

5. *RELATIVITY IS SELF-DEFEATED (1 of 3) —In terms of Mathematics*, Presented in the CNPS Conference of 2016 by *Cameron Rebigsol*

6. *RELATIVITY IS SELF-DEFEATED (2 of 3) —In terms of Physics*, Presented in the CNPS Conference of 2016 by *Cameron Rebigsol*

7. *RELATIVITY IS SELF-DEFEATED (3 of 3) —Lorentz Factor, Aberration, and Ether*, Presented in the CNPS Conference of 2016 by *Cameron Rebigsol*

Experiment and Theory Removing all that Quantum Photon Wave-particle-Duality Entanglement Nonsense

Eric S Reiter

251 Nelson Avenue, Pacifica CA 94044, unquant@yahoo.com

Definitions of particle and wave in the classical sense, and quantum mechanical sense, are very different. Let us define a classical particle as anything that holds itself together, and understand that a classical wave does not. They are opposite concepts. However, a quantum-particle has those two opposite classical concepts inexplicably mixed together. A quantum-wave can spread across the whole universe, then collapse to a minuscule quantum-particle. A quantum-wave is a non-physical wave of probability that goes everywhere. This kind of probability is not like throwing dice, because dice go somewhere, and that quantum-wave is everywhere. To resolve the problem requires revisiting experiments that are famous for their particle-like interpretation. Here, we show how a new Threshold Model can work for both our wave-like and particle-like experiments. Two sets of experiments have been performed to substantiate our Threshold Model: with light using gamma-rays, and with matter using alpha-rays. They are both beam-split coincidence experiments that reveal a two-for-one effect. It only looks like two-for-one if you are sold on quantum mechanics. We do not obtain something from nothing. The Threshold Model embraces a pre-loaded sub-quantum state, called for in our new experiments.

Keywords: photon, wave-particle duality, quantum mechanics, entanglement

1. Introduction

It is well known that Einstein and Schrödinger argued against quantum mechanics (QM). Schrödinger's skepticism is well documented:

"Let me say at the outset, that in this discourse, I am opposing not a few special statements of quantum mechanics held today, I am opposing as it were the whole of it, I am opposing its basic views that have been shaped 25 years ago, when Max Born put forward his probability interpretation, which was accepted by almost everybody" [1, his 1952 Dublin Seminar].

Schrödinger's works coining entanglement [2] and his cat [3] followed the so-called EPR paper [4], and followed his discussion with Einstein on that paper. Therefore papers [2, 3] can be understood to say that the world-view delivered by QM is far too incomprehensible to take seriously. Arguments have raged. Most famously, QM entanglement is said to be upheld by so-called two-"particle" experiments performed by Aspect and team [5]. In such a test, a probabilistic wave-function spreads from a central point, then detectors on opposite sides can click in either of two states as read by a coincidence circuit. When clicks happen in coincidence the wave-function is thought to collapse, and state correlations are recognized. However, a much simpler single-"particle" test will address this issue of wave-function collapse. Either test, the single or two-"particle," is most easily done with visible light, with what they call singly emitted "photons" [6]. Our examination of these fundamentals calls for careful language. There is a "tell." When you see a paper written in terms of photons, even if it is intended to question if photons exist, the result will always lead to photons. There is a way to avoid the photon model, yet embrace $h\nu$ (Planck's constant times frequency) in our equations, and that is what this essay is about. We need a new word. I use $h\nu$, pronounced h-new. An $h\nu$ is a quantity of energy, but here it is not about the energy of a light-particle. It is about a threshold-energy in matter.

Wave-particle duality, wave-function collapse, entanglement, and quantum mechanics, are all the same thing: a non-explainable model. Showing how entanglement is an illusion, is what this essay is about.

Here is the experiment: A source of electromagnetic radiation is tested to see if it emits only one $h\nu$ at a time, except by chance. Two detectors will surround our source in what is called a true-coincidence test. Then with that same source, we re-position the same detectors to do a beam-split coincidence test. This test will monitor singly emitted $h\nu$ energy encountering a wave-front-like split, to see how it interacts with our two detectors in coincidence. The coincidence circuit tests to see if one detection excludes the other detector from clicking, except by chance, as expected by QM. These "clicks" are microsecond pulses we see on an oscilloscope. The coincidence circuit will reveal: (1) if light somehow holds itself together so as to only deliver coincident clicks at a chance rate, or (2) if light can spread classically to deliver coincident click rates exceeding chance. Such beam-split-coincidence tests performed in the past [5] have upheld result (1), as predicted by QM. Literature asserts, if this one-way-or-another property of quantum particles were to be refuted, it would call for a major revision of QM [6 Brannen and Ferguson]. Previous to my work, no one performed this test with gamma-rays, perhaps because gamma-rays are thought to be the most particle-like form of light. Here we report that a gamma-ray beam-split-coincidence test can contradict the quantum mechanical chance prediction. When the chance rate is exceeded, we call it the unquantum effect.

Our true-coincidence test uses the same circuit and detectors as the beam-split coincidence test, except the geometry is different. A true-coincidence test for gamma-rays will sandwich an isotope between two detectors to see if it emits two $h\nu$ in a single decay [7]. Similarly these tests can be performed upon other... phenomena. I write other "phenomena" because we are tempted to say particles. This linguistics problem is part of our 100 year-old physics problem.

Nuclear physicists have a long history of deciphering decay schemes by comparing to chance rates. But for safe keeping, this true-coincidence test has been performed in-house on our isotopes sources: 109Cd and 57Co, well known to emit only one gamma-ray at a time. With these isotopes we detect an x-ray in coincidence with the gamma, but those x-rays are filtered out and not counted.

One might expect we are seeing two "half-photons," or a Compton effect split. We use pulse-height filters to count only full-height pulses, in a manner that delivers a two-for-one effect. The same filter and coincidence circuit we used to test for one-at-a-time emission, are then used again to test for two-at-a-time, but now our detectors are arranged like a beam-splitter. From other experiments, we know that pulse-height is proportional to electromagnetic frequency.

Many tests performed at our laboratory since 2001 show that this unquantum effect is not some artifact, it is not a special case, and it is not some experimental error. Also, the reason why it works, and not-works, is revealed in our test variants. Details of one gamma-ray unquantum test are in Appendix I [8, 9]. That test exceeded QM chance by 35.

To transcend wave-particle duality requires removing this duality from both matter and light. We have performed many beam-split coincidence tests, now here with alpha-rays, to demonstrate the unquantum effect for the matter-wave. We split the atom like a wave. The word "atom" sounds like a particle, but think of splitting a helium-nuclear-matter-wave. We are not splitting helium atoms into two deuterons. The binding-energy of helium is 7 MeV per nucleon, so it would take 14 MeV to split the alpha. We employ 241Am, known to emit alpha at only 5.5 MeV. When we direct alphas toward a gold foil, the bulk of these wave-packets will usually either go through the foil or are reflected, like a particle. Usually, but not always. When we measure detection pulses in-coincidence, we conclude the alpha matter-wave must have split. Most of these coincident pulses are half-height, and this measurement repeatedly exceeds chance by 100 times. This is not two-for-one, but it violates particle-binding theory. Now, if we measure only the full-height pulses in-coincidence we do see a two-for-one effect, and exceed chance by four. I performed many variants and control tests to remove doubt. Details of an alpha-ray unquantum test are in Appendix II [8, 10].

These tests compel us to re-interpret past experiments. Our non-dualistic model explains the relevant experiments.

Now, thinking of the gamma-ray unquantum effect, two-for-one implies energy must be pre-loaded in either the detector or the scatterer, preceding the detection event. Otherwise we violate energy conservation. We uphold energy conservation. Therefore we are forced to consider an accumulation hypothesis, also known as the loading theory. We say we are violating particle-energy conservation. This is similar to the Bohr-Kramers-Slater [11] idea, whereby energy conservation did not require particle-per-particle accounting. Arguments on this issue were poor [see 9 or 12]. Accumulation ideas are old, with many variants [13, 14, 15]. In Millikan's book of 1947 [16] he correctly considers a pre-loaded state in the photoelectric effect. However, he did not understand how it could be true. Since then, the element of time in the photoelectric effect is routinely considered as starting from empty. A way to visualize the loading theory is by figure 161.

A few definitions are overdue. First, particle and wave. A particle will hold itself together. A particle can be anything from a dimensionless point to a galaxy. A wave does not hold itself together and spreads. We just need that distinction. Particle and wave are opposite ideas. For the definition of the photon, N Bohr paraphrases Einstein:

"If a semireflecting mirror is placed in the way of a photon, leaving two possibilities for its direction of propagation, the photon would be recorded on one, and only one, of the two photographic plates situated at great distances in the two directions in question, or else we may, by replacing the plates by mirrors, observe these effects exhibiting an interference between the two reflected wave-trains [17]."

This way of combining classical concepts and using the same words for quantum concepts causes confusion. Many physicists assert this confusing combination is an inescapable response to experiment. There is a way out, but first please understand that a quantum particle is an incomprehensible model, not a thing. A photon has never been a thing, and it should not be spoken of that way.

To explain our wave effects and our new experiments, I propose a two-state solution. Consider that a quantum-particle, such as an atom, can hold itself together but can also "lose-it." Please examine the equations famous for "particle-wave" experiments in Table 1. These equations have ratios of e, h and m. Let us look at electron mass m. If we think of m as the mass of a particle, we will forever be stuck in wave-particle duality. Now realize that these equations have ratios like e/m. Please consider our constants in terms of thresholds; consider that our constants are maxima.

Consider an arbitrarily small cubic volume of a charge-wave. Imagine charge in this cube to be some sub-threshold value of e. Then think similarly for action and mass. The simplest relationship would be linear such that the e/m ratio in this cube will be conserved. Now realize similarly for our h/m and e/h ratios. In this scenario our experiments could not make the distinction between this

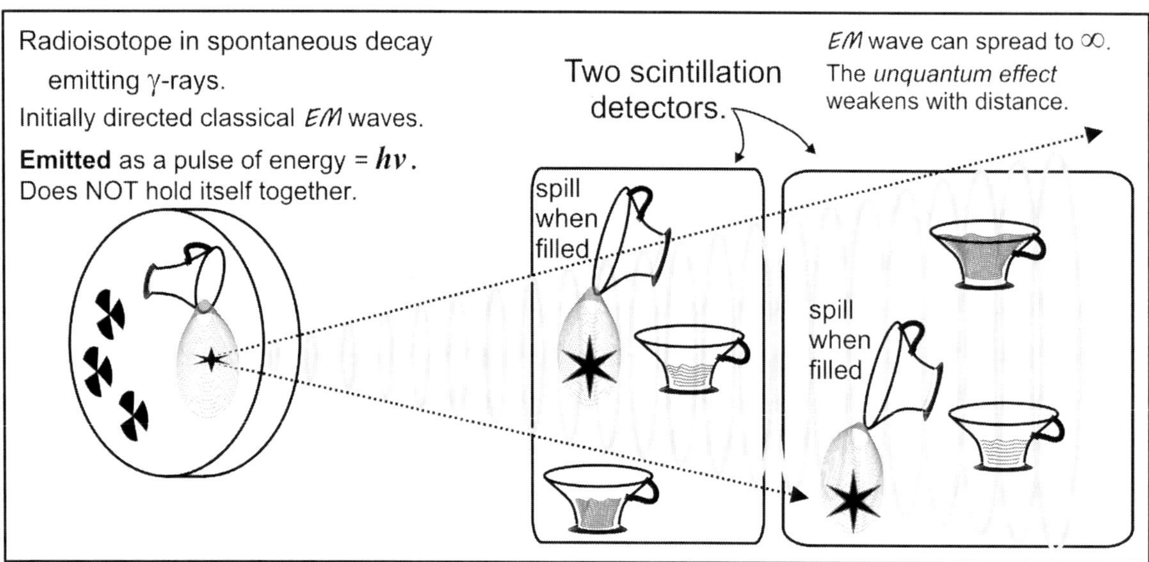

Figure 153. A way to visualize the loading theory in the gamma-ray test.

new threshold-ratio model and QM. The way to tell the difference between those models is our beam-split coincidence test.

What about experiments reporting quantized charge? Measurements of e are performed upon ensembles of many atoms, such as in the Millikan oil drop experiment (and earlier by J. J. Thompson). It is a false assumption to say that quantization seen in an ensemble will carry over to free charge. From evidence of charge-diffraction alone, it is a false assumption to think charge is always quantized at e. In our new model, if charge were to spread like a wave, maintain a fixed e/m ratio for any unit of volume, load-up upon absorption, and be detected at threshold e, it would remain consistent with observations. An electron's worth of charge need not be spatially small. Chemists performing Electron Spin Resonance (ESR) often model an electron as large as a benzine ring. A point-like electron would predict a smeared-out ESR spectrum. Carver Mead argued for an extended electron [18]. Many famous experiments become free of wave-particle duality by this threshold/ratio interpretation.

Our Threshold Model, supported by the unquantum effect easily resolves the enigma of the double-slit experiment. For light, its kinetic energy would load up in the charge-wave. For matter, we say matter actually loads up. Much detail can be encoded in a spreading matter-wave to equal an identifiable element (atom). However, it is beyond reason to expect a complicated molecule to load up. We stand with convincing experiments on the wave nature of atoms, charge, and neutron matter-waves (neutrons) [19, 20].

Consistent with the threshold model is a recent helium diffraction experiment that revealed both particle and wave signatures in a helium diffraction pattern [21]. The matter-wave behaves like a solution; it can either hold itself together in a particle state, or spread in a wave state. This is subtly different from complementary, whereby the distinction between a wave or particle state depends on how one looks at it.

2. Flaws in Recent Experiments of Others

To challenge QM is to show how its key experiments are flawed. Here I handle two key tests, one using light and one using matter.

Recall the popular work by Aspect and team [5] that convinced mainstream publishers the world is made of spooks. They used an atomic beam, stimulated by a laser, to emit pairs of "photons." Correlated clicks behind polarizers are reported to defy classical interpretation. Take notice: they failed to tell you their laser delivers polarized light. The atoms in the beam are known to emit in a two-$h\nu$ cascade. Therefore we can expect the atomic beam to emit polarization-correlated $h\nu$ pairs. By $h\nu$, I mean that this energy was emitted in an initially-quantized and initially-directed burst. Thereafter this energy can spread classically. Their data is in figure 2. This graph is just what is expected from Malus's law and classical polarized light as a function of angle. Indeed, I am not the only one saying this; see figures 3 and 4.

An article in Nature received much attention for claiming that giant molecules emitted one-at-a-time, could somehow project an interference pattern [24]. It is a far stretch to imagine how such a thing can be true, by either QM or the loading theory. They argue that their diffraction fits the de Broglie equation 62:

TABLE 2. Table 1. Equations of wave-like experiments expressed by quantum mechanics, and those equations re-written by our new Threshold Model.

	Quantum Mechanics	Loading Theory
Matter wavelength	$\lambda_{\text{phase}} = \dfrac{h}{m\upsilon}$	$\lambda_{\text{group}} = \dfrac{Q_{h/m}}{\upsilon_{\text{group}}}$
Photoelectric	$h\nu_L - h\nu_0 = \dfrac{m\upsilon^2}{2} = eV_0$	$Q_{h/m}(\nu - \nu_0) = \dfrac{\upsilon^2_{\text{group}}}{2} = Q_{e/m}V_0$
Compton	$\Delta\lambda = \dfrac{h\,(1-\cos\theta)}{mc}$	$\Delta\lambda_{\text{group}} = Q_{h/m}\dfrac{1-\cos\theta}{c}$
Lorentz force	$F = ma = e\,(\upsilon \times \boldsymbol{B})$	$a = Q_{e/m}(\upsilon_{\text{group}} \times \boldsymbol{B})$
Aharonov-Bohm	$\Delta x = \dfrac{e\,L\lambda Bw}{h}$	$\Delta x = Q_{e/h}\,L\lambda_{\text{group}}Bw$

$$\lambda = d\sin\theta = \frac{h}{mv} \tag{62}$$

It is more reasonable to expect these molecules are casting mere shadow patterns, and that the pattern is magnified by an electric field. Electric field effects are the most obvious source of artifact and were not addressed. I have identified and posted four striking anomalies (see appendix) that require explanation: (1) there is insufficient velocity resolution in their model to prevent their fringe widths from being blurred-out to twice as wide, (2) fringe orders have the wrong relative intensities, (3) there is a large mismatch upon applying $d = (gt^2)/2$ = (dist of particle fall) = one half (acceleration of gravity)$(distanceparticletravels/velocity)^2$ to their data, and (4) their movie-data shows a sharp-edge fringe intensity profile that is characteristic of a shadow pattern. Crucial control tests addressing electric fields are required before taking their message seriously. A graphic from this Nature article, detailed calculations in a letter to its author, and his response are in Appendix III.

3. Conclusion

Entanglement is an illusion of the threshold and ratio properties of charge, action, and mass. Much elaboration upon experiment and theory outlined here has been developed; please see http://www.thresholdmodel.com. We welcome visitors to Unquantum Laboratory in Pacifica CA to witness or adjust our experiments.

4. APPENDIX I, The Gamma-ray Unquantum Experiment [8, 9]

After spontaneous decay by electron capture, 109Cd becomes stable 109Ag. 109Cd also emits an x-ray, far below the lower level of our discriminator (LL). Chance is immediately recognized by a flat band of noise on a time-difference histogram Δt, and can be measured by 63:

$$R_c = R_1 R_2 \tau \tag{63}$$

where R_1 and R_2 are the singles rates from each detector, and τ is the chosen time window within which coincident events are counted from the Δt histogram. Later we will compare this to the experimental chance rate Re to see how they differ.

Recent tests were performed with two detectors, each consisting of a NaI(Tl) scintillator crystal coupled to a PMT. Detector 1 was a custom-made thin detector, at 4 mm thick, and is shown in figure 157. Behind the thin detector was thick detector 2, a 1.5" Bicron. We call this thin-thick detector arrangement tandem geometry. The thin detector serves to randomly absorb a fraction of an emitted gamma-ray. Two 10 μCi check-sources of 109Cd were inside a Pb box of 1/4" walls with a 1/4" diameter hole and a 1/8" square tungsten aperture. The aperture was designed to optimize how the cone of emitted gamma fits the larger detector 2. Poor collimator design can just deliver chance. The test was performed inside a lead shield lined with tin and copper; this lowered singles background rate 1/31. Coincidence background rates are manageable fractions to be subtracted. To assure that the unquantum effect was not generated by background, several all-night and all-day tests, with and without the source, were examined.

Referring to figure 158, components for each of the two detector channels are an Ortec 471 amplifier, an Ortec 551 SCA, and an HP 5334 counter for singles rates (not shown). A four channel LeCroy LT264 digital storage oscilloscope (DSO) with histogram software, monitored the analog pulses from each amplifier on DSO chan-

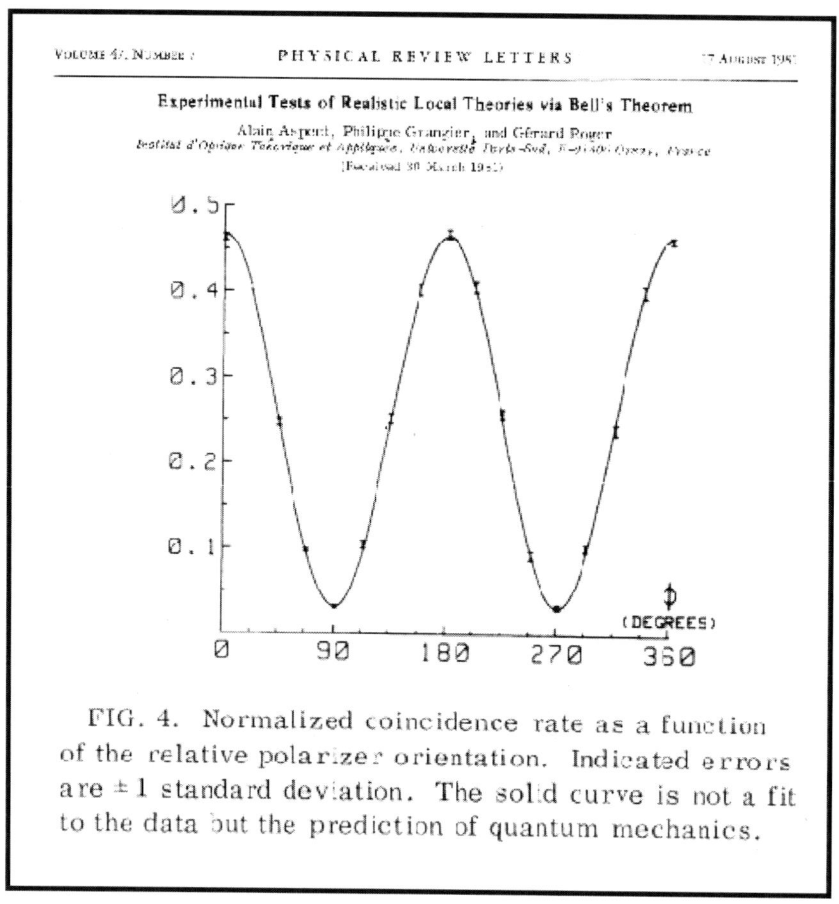

PHYSICAL REVIEW LETTERS

Experimental Tests of Realistic Local Theories via Bell's Theorem

Alain Aspect, Philippe Grangier, and Gérard Roger

FIG. 4. Normalized coincidence rate as a function of the relative polarizer orientation. Indicated errors are ±1 standard deviation. The solid curve is not a fit to the data but the prediction of quantum mechanics.

Figure 154. Data from [5] PRL 47, pg 460 (1981), Aspect, "Experimental Tests of Realistic Local Theories via Bell's Theorem."

nels (1) and (2). DSO also monitored SCA timing pulses at channels (3) and (4). The stored image of each triggered pulse show well behaved pulses to assure that noise and pulse-overlap were not a factor. This DSO can update pulse-heights, (A)(B), and time difference Δt (C) histograms after each "qualified"-triggered sweep. To assure exceeding particle-energy conservation, LL on each SCA window was set to at least 2/3 of the 109Cd 88 keV gamma characteristic pulse-height.

A coincidence background test with no source present had 304 counts/49.4 ks = 0.00615/s, a rate to be subtracted. Within the same time window τ taken as 200 ns, the chance rate from Eq. 1 was R_c = (8.21/s)(269/s)(200 ns) = 0.000442/s. The experimental coincidence rate within tau was R_e = (101/4.59ks) - (0.00615/s) = 0.0158/s. The unquantum effect was R_e/R_c = 0.0158/0.000442 = 35.7 times greater than chance.

5. APPENDIX II. The alpha-ray unquantum experiment [8, 10]

Americium-241 in spontaneous decay emits a single 5.5 MeV alpha-ray and a 59.6 keV gamma. An alpha is known as a helium nucleus. Two silicon Ortec surface barrier detectors with adequate pulse-height resolution were employed in a circuit nearly identical to that used in figure 158. Figure 159 shows the detectors and pre-amplifiers in a vacuum chamber. These tests were performed under computer (CPU) control by a program written in QUICK-BASIC to interact with the DSO through a GPIB interface. Here, both SCA LL settings were set to only 1/3 the characteristic a pulse-height because it was found that an alpha-split usually, but not always, maintains particle-energy conservation. By this we mean the "energy" read from the two detectors in coincidence usually adds to the emitted 5.5 MeV. The coincidence time-window was τ = 100 ns. The Δt histograms of figure 8 were from DSO screen captures.

Data of figure 8-a was a two hour true-coincidence control test with the two detectors at right angles to each other and with the 241Am centrally located. Only the chance rate was measured, assuring that only one alpha was emitted at a time. 4π solid angle capture was not attempted because it requires a specially made thin source. However, the right angle arrangement is adequate, and it is well known how 241Am decays. Any sign of a peak is a quick way to see if chance is exceeded. A background coincidence test of 48 hours with no source present gave a zero count. Data of figure 8-b taken Nov. 13, 2006 was from the arrangement of figure 7 using two layers of 24 carat gold leaf suspended over the front of detector 1.

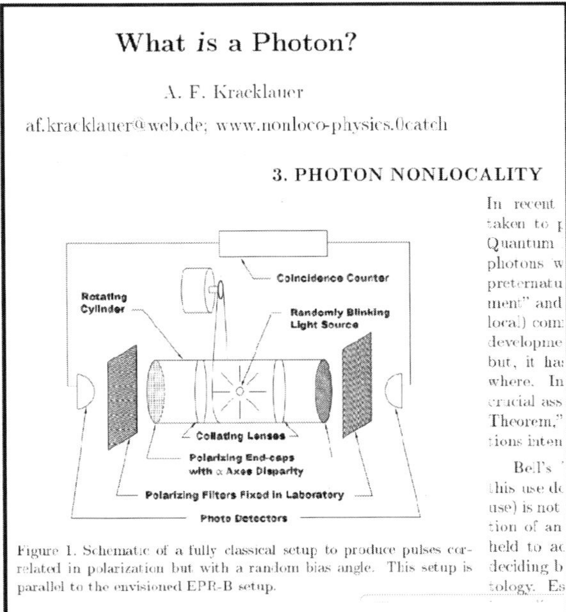

What is a Photon?

A. F. Kracklauer

af.kracklauer@web.de; www.nonloco-physics.0catch

3. PHOTON NONLOCALITY

Figure 1. Schematic of a fully classical setup to produce pulses correlated in polarization but with a random bias angle. This setup is parallel to the envisioned EPR-B setup.

In recent
taken to p
Quantum
photons w
preternatu
ment" and
local) com
developme
but, it ha
where. In
crucial ass
Theorem,"
tions inten
Bell's
this use d
use) is not
tion of an
held to ac
deciding b
tology. Es

Figure 155. Excerpt from Kracklauer, SPIE paper [22].

Einstein-Podolsky-Rosen-Bohm correlation for light polarization

Int. J. Modern Phys. B. 7, 1321 (1993) (9 pages)
S. S. Mizrahi, and M. H. Y. Moussa

Abstract

Considering a classical source of light (macroscopic), we propose an experiment, based on the principles of the Einstein-Podolsky-Rosen-Bohm correlation, for which one expects to obtain the same polarization correlation coefficient as the one predicted by the quantum theory, when photons are counted in coincidence. The results of a numerical simulation give good ground to believe that the conjectured experiment is reasonable. So, one may argue that the property of light called polarization, that is manifest at any level - microscopic and macroscopic - and which has a precise description in both, the quantum and the classical theories, leads to coincident results under correspondingly similar experimental procedures. Therefore the EPRB correlation is a consequence of that property of light, independently whether it is viewed as constituted by photons or by electromagnetic waves.

Therefore the EPRB correlation is a consequence of that property of light, independently whether it is viewed as constituted by photons or by electromagnetic waves.

Figure 156. The experiment quoted in Kracklauer [23].

Mounted at the rim of detector 2 were six 1μCi 241Am sources facing detector 1 and shaded from detector 2. Every coincident pulse pair was perfectly shaped. $R_c = 9.8x10^{-6}/s$, and $R_e/R_c = 105$ times greater than chance.

From the CPU program and data used in the test of figure 8-b, data is re-plotted in figure 9. Figure 9 depicts each pulse-height as a dot on a two dimensional graph to show coincident pulse-heights from both detectors. The transmitted and reflected pulse-height singles spectra were carefully pasted into the figure. We can see that most of

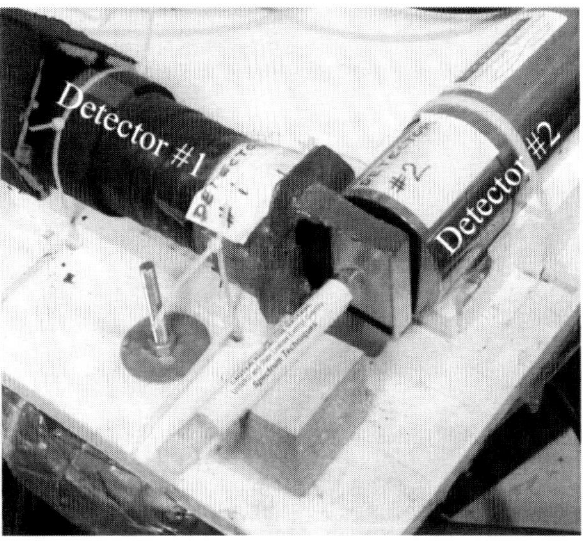

Figure 157. Two sodium iodide gamma-ray detectors in tandem geometry. Detector 1 is a custom-made 4 mm thick slab.

the alpha pulses (dots) are near the half-height marks, demonstrating particle-energy conservation. However, the six dots circled clearly exceed particle-energy conservation. Counting just these 6, we still exceed chance: R_e/R_c = 3.97. This is a sensational contradiction of QM because it circumvents the argument that a particle-like split, such as splitting into two deuterons, is somehow still at play. Several other materials were tested in transmission and reflection geometries to reveal the usefulness of this matter-wave unquantum effect in material science. It is not necessary to use gold to exceed chance. However, many materials tested just gave chance.

6. APPENDIX III

On, 22.05.2012, 01:54, Eric Reiter wrote: Dear Dr Juffmann Regarding your recent article, "Real-time single-molecule imaging of quantum interference," I have performed calculations on your data that do not make sense to me.

1. Let's calculate the fall of a particle. We can use $(1/2)gt^2$, where t = time = distance/velocity. For a fast particle (eq 64):

$$H = \left(\frac{9.8}{2}\right)\sqrt{\left(\frac{2m}{340m/s}\right)} = 169x10^{-6}m \quad (64)$$

For a slow particle (eq 65):

$$H_{slow} = \left(\frac{9.8}{2}\right)\sqrt{\left(\frac{2m}{440m/s}\right)} = 1x10^{-3}m \quad (65)$$

Hslow - Hfast = 830 micrometers. But you show only 240 micrometers. Therefore the difference in falls should be 3.4 times larger than you show.

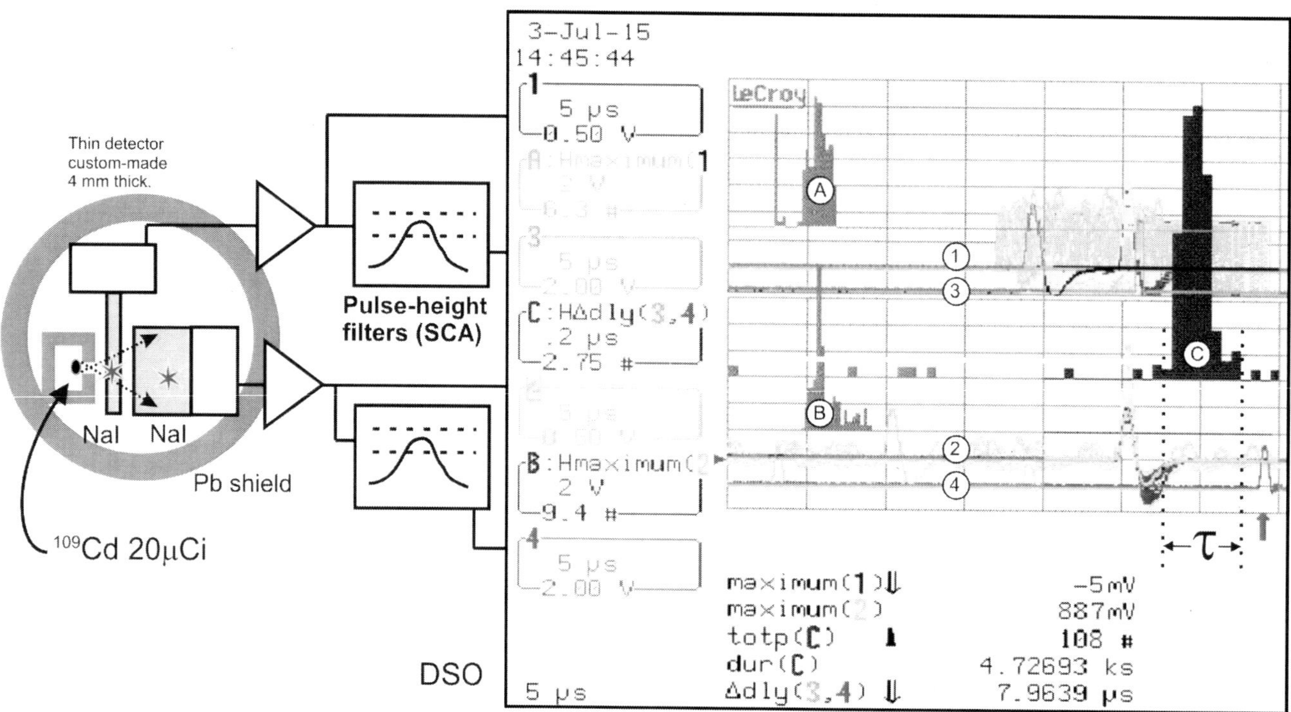

Figure 158. Gamma-ray experiment in tandem geometry using 109Cd. Counters and computer interfaces are not shown. DSO screen is annotated.

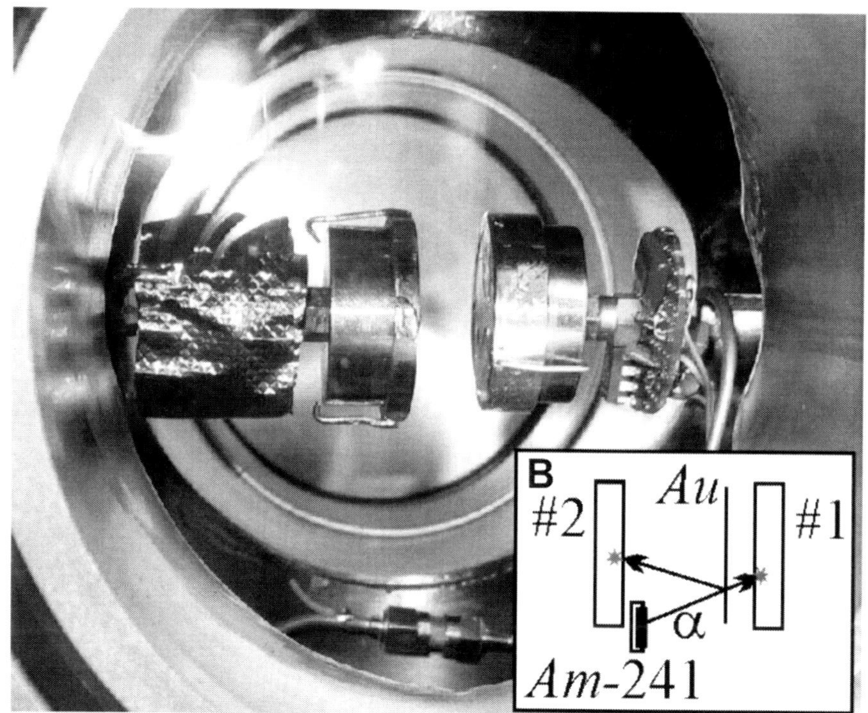

Figure 159. Alpha Ray Experiment

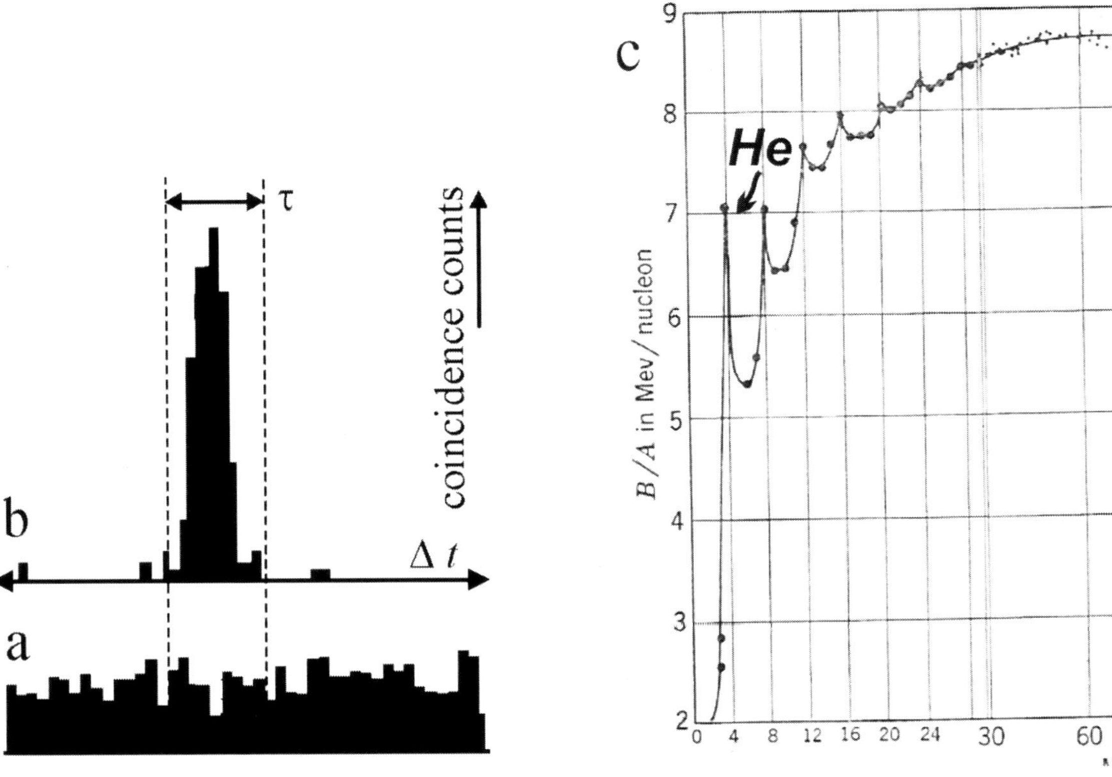

Figure 160. a: true-coincidence "sandwich test" histogram. b: alpha-ray coincidence histogram. c: binding-energy per nucleon [25].

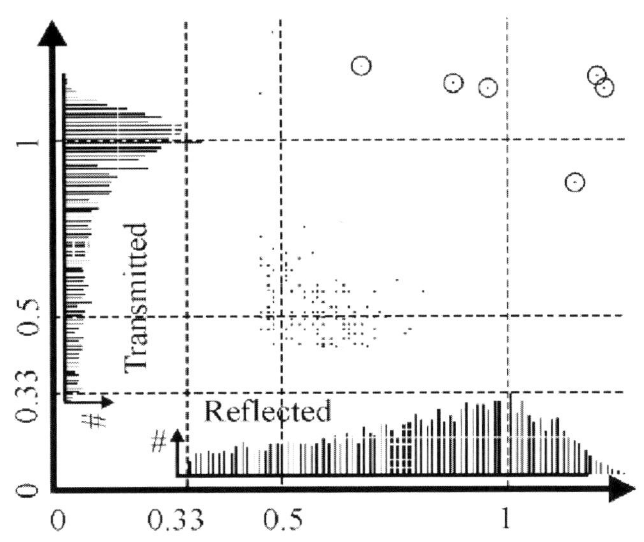

Figure 161. The computer controlled experiment of figure 8 with pulse-height pairs on each detector plotted X-Y.

2. I used a multiple slit diffraction simulation tool to test what the intensity profiles should be. I found your first order fringes were a few times brighter than they should be for the given wavelength/slit-width and wavelength/slit-spacing ratios. The tool I used is http://wyant.optics.arizona.edu/multipleSlits/multipleSlits.htm. Though this tool has fewer slits than yours, I found this did not change the intensity ratios.
3. Given the dimensions of your instrument, the velocity resolution should cover 0.43 of the sensor plane by the following calculation: The slit height is 100 micrometers, and the projection to the sensor plane should make this $2/(2-0.56)$ larger, that is 138 micrometers at the sensor plane. But the sensor plane is 320 micrometers high. Since $138/320 = 0.43$, a particle of any given velocity could land anywhere in a vertical segment of height that is 0.43 of the screen height. So the first order fringes should have been very noticeably widened as the fringes descend, by this apparently poor velocity resolution.
4. In the published movies of the detector plane, the intensity profiles of the fringes have edges that seem to rise and fall too abruptly. Also, the intensity profile of each fringe, especially the central fringe, in the movie looks flat. Fringes should have peak-like profiles.
   Unless I have made several silly errors, there is something going on other than quantum interference. Please consider a control test to eliminate the possibility that you are looking at a shadow pattern that has been magnified by a charge deflection effect at the slits. It would be very easy for the slits to become charged to deflect dye particles in a manner similar to a cylindrical lens. A simple test would be to introduce a voltage control wire to the slits. An even simpler test would be to shade half of the slit array to see if a half side of the fringe pattern disappears. Whether or not a focus effect was like a positive or negative lens, half of the fringe pattern would disappear. A focused shadow would explain the anomalies I point out. Thank you for your consideration and I hope to hear from you. Eric S Reiter, Unquantum Laboratory

Dear Mr. Reiter, concerning your considerations:

1. The equations are of course right, but our source emits molecules in all directions. Thus a flight parabola is defined by three source, the grating (which is only written onto a $100\mu m$ high window) and the height on the detection plane. Thus it is wrong to simply enter the distance source-detection plane into the calculations, since in the plane of the grating all molecules pass at the same height.
2. Your observation is right. The high intensity of the higher interference orders is due to the van der Waals interaction between the molecules and the grating wall. This is mentioned several times in our paper.
3. Please don't forget, that also the grating is only $100\mu m$ high and that, especially for the slow molecule, the projection is a non valid approximation.
4. I don't agree. Regarding the high transversal coherence in our experiment the shape of the fringes is in agreement with the theoretical predictions.

Best regards, Thomas Juffmann

REFERENCES

1. Schrödinger E, [The Interpretation of Quantum Mechanics] Ox Bow Press, Woodbridge, CN (1995).
2. Schrödinger E, "Discussion of Probability Relations between Separated Systems," Mathematical Proceedings of the Cambridge Philosophical Society, Volume 31, Issue 04, October 1935, pp 555-563
3. Schrödinger E., "The Present Situation in Quantum Mechanics" (Schrödinger's cat paper), Proceedings of the American Philosophical Society, 124, 323-338 (1980)
4. Einstein, Podolsky Rosen, "Can Quantum Mechanical Description of Reality be Considered Complete?" Phys Rev 47, 777-780 (1935).
5. Aspect A., "Experimental Tests of Realistic Local Theories via Bell's Theorm," Physical Review Letters 47 pg 460-463 (1981).
6. Brannen E., Ferguson H., "The question of correlation between photons in coherent light rays," Nature, 4531, 481-482 (1956). Clauser J. F., "Experimental distinction between the quantum and classical field theoretic predictions for the photoelectric effect," Physical Review, D9, 853-860 (1974). Grainger P., Roger G., Aspect A., "A new light on single photon interferences." Annals of the New York Academy of Sciences, 480, 98-107 (1986). This test was done with x-rays: Givens M.P., "An experimental study of the quantum nature of x-rays," Philosophical Magazine, 37, 335-346 (1946).
7. Knoll G., [Radiation Detection and Measurement], (1979). Also, for the chance equation see Melissinos, [Experiments in Modern Physics] (1966) Pg 407.
8. Reiter, E., "New Experiments call for a Continuous Absorption Alternative to the Photon Model," Proceedings of the SPIE 2015 What are Photons?, available on http://www.unquantum.org.
9. Reiter, E., "Photon Violation Spectroscopy," available on http://www.unquantum.org.
10. Reiter, E., "Particle Violation Spectroscopy," available on http://www.unquantum.org.
11. N. Bohr, H. A. Kramers, J. C. Slater, "The Quantum Theory of Radiation", in Sources of Quantum Mechanics, B. L. Van Der Waerden, ed. (Dover, New York, 1967); Phil. Mag. 47, 785 (1924); Zeits. f. Phys. 24, 69 (1924).
12. Reiter, E, "An Understanding of the Particle-Like Property of Light and Charge," available on http://www.unquantum.org.
13. Kuhn T. S., [Black-Body Theory and the Quantum Discontinuity 1894-1912], Oxford University Press, 235-264 (1978).
14. Whittaker E., [History of Theories of Aether and Electricity 1900-1926], 103 (1953).
15. Wheaton B. R., [The Tiger and the Shark] (1983).
16. Millikan R.A., [Electrons (+ and -) Protons Photons Neutrons Mesotrons and Cosmic Rays], University of Chicago Press, revised edition, 253 (1947).

17. Bohr N., [Atomic Physics and Human Knowledge], John Wiley and Sons Inc, New York, pg 50-51 (1958).
18. Carver Mead SPIE keynote talk 2013, http://natureoflight.org/?mpage=conf&spage=conf-2013#keynote
19. Estermann I., Frisch R., Stern O., "Monochromasierung der de Broglie-Wellen von Molekularstrahlen," Zeitschrift fur Physik, A73, 348-365 (1932).
20. Berman P. R., [Atom Interferometry], Academic Press (1997).
21. Doak R. et al, "Towards realization of an atomic de Broglie microscope: helium atom focusing using Fresnel zone plates," Phys. Rev. Letters, 83 (21), 4229-4232 (1999).
22. Kracklauer A. F., "What are Photons," Proc. of SPIE vol 9570 (2015). Available at www.nonloco.com
23. Mizrahi S. S, Moussa H. Y., "Einstein-Rosen-Pedolsky-Bohm Correlation for Light Polarization," Intl J Modern Physics B, pg 1321 (1993).
24. Juffmann T., "Real-time single-molecule imaging of quantum interference," Nature Nanotechnology, 7, pg 297-300 (2012).
25. Evans R., [The Atomic Nucleus], 717 (1955).

Aether Concept of Gravity

Duncan Shaw

1517 Angus Drive, Vancouver, BC, Canada, V6J 4H2, duncanshaw@shaw.ca

The author has proposed a conceptual model of the cause of gravity. The concept is set out in a trilogy of articles, *The Cause of Gravity: A Concept* [1], *Flowing Aether: A Concept* [2], and *Outflowing Aether* [3].

The three cited articles propose a model of a mechanical cause of gravity. The process is cyclic, much like the rain cycle we experience on Earth. Aether cells evaporate from cosmic bodies, migrate into space, condense into groups (droplets) of cells, and condensed-state aether flows back into cosmic bodies. Inflowing aether exerts ram pressure on the atomic matter of cosmic bodies. Outflowing aether also exerts ram pressure on atomic matter, but to a lesser extent. The net difference is the force of gravity.

The gravity process involves numerous elements that operate in conjunction with each other. This article considers these elements and describes their roles in terms of physical cause and effect.

Keywords: aether, gravity

1. Introduction

Isaac Newton gave us the inverse square rule that provides the mathematics to calculate the forces of gravity between bodies. Albert Einstein added mathematics that takes relative speeds of cosmic bodies into account. However the underlying physical cause of gravity is another matter. As yet there is still no generally accepted theory of the mechanics of gravity. As Richard Feynman observed in *The Feynman Lectures on Physics* [4]:

> "**What is gravity?**
> "But is this such a simple law? What about the machinery of it? All we have done is to describe *how* the earth moves around the sun, but we have not said *what makes it go*. Newton made no hypotheses about this; he was satisfied to find out what it did without getting into the machinery of it. *No one has since given any machinery*."

The three articles cited in the Abstract propose gravity as a cyclic process. The process is based upon the premise that a sub-atomic substance called aether permeates space and cosmic bodies. The postulated aether has separate and distinct states or phases: a gaseous state and a condensed state. In its gaseous state, aether consists of separated aether cells. In its condensed state, aether is comprised of groups or droplets of aether cells. Aether in its condensed state flows into cosmic bodies and exerts ram pressure on all atomic matter if its path. The ram pressure is the direct cause of gravity. Heat generated by inflow causes the condensed-state aether to evaporate into its gaseous state. Gaseous aether flows back into space by way of diffusion and convection and condenses back into its state of groups or droplets of aether cells. The cycle continues with aether in its condensed state flowing back into cosmic bodies.

The cells of evaporating aether are tiny compared to the size of groups or droplets of condensed aether. Gravitational force is the net linear momentum exerted on atomic matter by inflowing aether less that exerted by outflowing aether.

It will be seen under the various headings below that there are numerous essential elements. The gravity proposal is the combination of the various elements working together as a system.

This article focuses upon various facets of the gravity proposal and provides explanations for each element. The explanations are based upon known phenomena.

It is helpful to consider Figure 162 below. It shows the Earth orbiting around the Sun and depicts aether flowing from space into the Sun and into the Earth.

2. Elements of the Cause of Gravity Concept

The observations below are mainly drawn from the three articles cited in the abstract. Notable additions are under the headings **Equivalence Principle** and **Black Holes**.

2.1. Atomic Matter

Throughout this article, the words "atomic matter" and "atom" are used as including atoms, molecules, ions and similar structured entities.

It is well established that atoms are mostly empty space. The particles that form an atom's structure occupy only a minute volume of space compared to the actual volume of the atom. This is significant in regard to interactions between flowing aether and atoms.

2.2. Aether

It is postulated that aether consists of subatomic cells that have the property of elasticity, the capacity to vibrate, and the ability to attach to and detach from each other and atomic matter. The postulated aether exists in gaseous form as separated cells, and in condensed form as groups of cells in the form of droplets. Aether cells are tiny compared to aether droplets, and both are small compared to atoms. Aether cells can easily pass through the empty space of

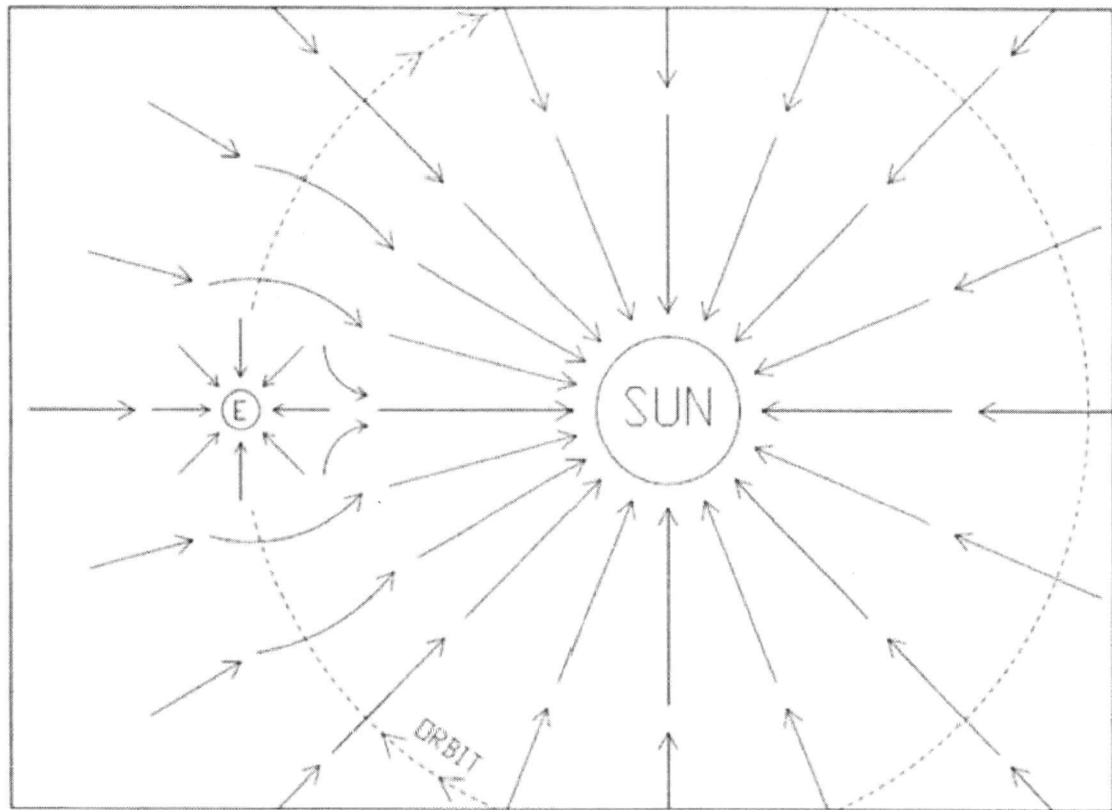

Figure 162. Inflowing Aether

atoms, whereas aether droplets are more likely to collide with the structure of atoms.

2.3. Gravity as a Pushing Force

The gravity proposal is built upon the assumption that gravity as a pushing force rather than a pulling force.

Most people think of gravity as an attracting force. We naturally assume that a falling object is pulled toward the Earth by a force that emanates from the Earth. However, there is a problem with this assumption. Common knowledge tells us that in order to pull an object there must be an attachment through which the pull can take place. One cannot pull with a broken chain. The problem is that there are no apparent attachments between the Earth and falling objects. Nor are there apparent attachments between the Sun and the planets.

What about gravity being a pushing force? We know that pushing does not require attachments. It only requires something physical to do the pushing. Consider, for example, the fact that flowing streams push on whatever objects they encounter. Now, visualize condensed aether droplets flowing into cosmic bodies and pushing on atomic matter that they encounter. It is that ram force – otherwise called transmission of linear momentum – otherwise called a pushing force – that this article poses as the cause of gravity.

Consider the operation of an ordinary vacuum cleaner. It appears to attract the air that flows into its intake. However, what actually occurs is a push, not a pull. The vacuum cleaner expels air and thereby creates a partial vacuum and this permits the surrounding air to push itself into the partial vacuum.

2.4. Cause of Inflow

Note that the word "pressure" as used in this section means the internal pressure of a fluid, as distinct from its ram pressure.

The gravity proposal contends that inflow is caused by the pressure of aether in cosmic bodies being lower than the pressure of aether in space. Pressure in cosmic bodies is lowered by the emission of aether from cosmic bodies. The resulting pressure differential causes aether in space to flow toward the partial vacuum – much like the emission of air from a household vacuum cleaner creates a partial vacuum into which surrounding air flows. Pressure in cosmic bodies is also lowered by the acceleration of inflowing aether from space to the relatively narrow targets of cosmic bodies. This is an application of Bernouilli's principle pursuant to which the pressure of a fluid that is flowing in a narrowing channel reduces as the speed of the fluid accelerates.

As a rough analog, recall that flows in our atmosphere proceed from higher-pressure areas toward lower-pressure areas.

2.5. Direction of Flows of Incoming Aether

As noted in the **Cause of Inflow** section above, lower pressure aether in cosmic bodies cause aether is space to flow into cosmic bodies. This pressure imbalance not only initiates the flow of aether from space, it also causes the direction of the flow to be toward cosmic bodies.

2.6. Energy Supply for Inflow

Cosmic microwave background and the 2.7 degrees Celsius temperature of space provide evidence that there is energy in space. On the assumption that aether permeates space, it may be inferred that aether is the principle repository of energy in space, with the energy being stored by vibrations of the aether cells and by their mutual collisions and rebounding. It may also be inferred that this is the energy that is harnessed by pressure differentials to propel inflows of aether into cosmic bodies. It is also a fair inference that the principal source of replenishment of this energy is the energy that evaporating aether cells remove from cosmic bodies and carry back into space.

2.7. Transmission of Gravitational Force Inside Cosmic Bodies

While the pushing effect of incoming aether is postulated to be caused by inflowing aether colliding with and exerting ram force on the atomic matter of cosmic bodies, it is likely that much of the ram force is transmitted throughout cosmic bodies by way of mutual collisions between the atoms and the aether that constitute and permeate cosmic bodies.

Think of a cue ball striking the lead ball of a rack of pool balls, with some of the momentum that is absorbed by the lead ball being transmitted to the other balls by collisions between them. This process may be called a form of scattering.

2.8. Heat Generated by Inflow

Scientists, such as Maxwell and Poincaré, have calculated that the energy that would be transferred to the Earth pursuant to a pushing theory of gravity (the Le Sage theory) would be so great as to quickly cause the Earth to incinerate. Might this assertion falsify the proposed concept of gravity? The answer is no. An essential aspect of the proposed gravity model is that aether cells emanate from cosmic bodies and transport heat into space. This is part of the cyclic system of gravity and it provides equilibrium between incoming and outgoing heat.

An analog is a body of water absorbing heat and then emitting heat by evaporation of water molecules.

2.9. Outflowing Aether

An essential part of the gravity concept is the outflow of aether into space. Outflow is essential because: (1) it replenishes the supply of aether in space required for continuous inflow; and (2) it provides a mechanism to dissipate into space the heat that is transferred to cosmic bodies by the ram force of inflowing aether.

The gravity proposal contends that heat generated by the ram force of inflow causes inflowing condensed aether to vaporize or evaporate into its gaseous state and flow back into space by way of diffusion and convection. When gaseous aether is back in space, it condenses into droplets of liquid aether.

To visualize the outflow of aether cells, consider the evaporation and rain cycle of water. When liquid water absorbs heat, water molecules break away from the liquid and evaporate or vaporize into the gaseous state of water. Evaporating water molecules migrate into the atmosphere by way of diffusion and convection. When the conditions are appropriate at altitude, the molecules condense into water droplets and return to the Earth as rain.

2.10. Condensation of Aether in Space

As aether cells proceed into space, they gradually come into contact with other aether cells and with droplets of condensed aether. These interactions, in combination with the low temperature of space, cause the cells to condense into the liquid state of aether. By this means the supply of condensed aether in space is replenished.

2.11. Gravity as a One-way Force

One of the most striking characteristics of gravity is that it is a one-way force. The phenomenon of one-way force can be explained in terms of mechanical cause and effect. The explanation is based upon the difference between inflowing and outflowing aether: in particular, their distinct states as condensed aether and gaseous aether. This difference permits inflow to exert greater ram force on atomic matter than outflow.

Recall that inflowing condensed aether is comprised of groups or droplets of aether cells, whereas outflowing gaseous aether consists of separate cells.

Each droplet consists of numerous cells that are joined together. Each droplet is therefore considerably larger than each individual cell. Recall now the fact that atoms are structures that consist mostly empty space. It stands to reason that inflowing aether droplets have a much greater probability than outflowing aether cells of striking the structure of atoms. Likewise, it stands to reason that outflowing aether cells have a greater probability of flowing right on through the structure of atoms.

Think of a fishnet the structure of which allows minnows almost free passage but impedes larger fish. This is the key to gravity being a one-way force.

This reasoning involves the concept of "collision cross-section". As described by Feynman [5]:

> "The effective "size" of a target in a collision we
> usually describe by a "collision cross section,"
> the same idea that is used in nuclear physics, or
> in light-scattering problems."

The collision cross-sections of droplets of condensed aether are much larger than the collision cross-sections of individual cells of gaseous aether.

It is fair to infer that there must be some measure of ram force on atomic matter exerted by outgoing gaseous aether. But the question is how much? Does it equal that of inflowing condensed aether? Given that individual aether cells are so small that most of them likely travel right on through the structure of atoms, and given that incoming condensed aether droplets likely have much greater collision cross-sections than outgoing aether cells, one may fairly contend that ram force exerted by outflow is minuscule compared to ram force exerted by inflow, and that inflow is therefore substantially the sole cause of gravity.

2.12. Equality of Momentum

Does the proposition that inflow produces higher ram pressure on atomic matter of cosmic bodies than outflow violate the law of equality of momentum? No, it does not. There is no law that says that incoming and outgoing momentum have to be exercised at the same time and at the same place. Equality of momentum is maintained by outflowing aether cells colliding in space with droplets of condensed aether and condensing into liquid aether.

2.13. Acceleration

Another notable characteristic of gravity is that it is an accelerating force. What causes the acceleration?

The flowing-aether approach to gravity provides an explanation of why gravity is an accelerating force. It is well established that when a fluid flows in a narrowing channel, the flow accelerates. Picture a wide river flowing into a narrow canyon – one can see the flow accelerate. An example with particular application to the proposed gravity model is the household vacuum cleaner. The air in the vicinity of a vacuum cleaner accelerates as it approaches the vacuum cleaner's intake. Place your hand in the vicinity of the intake and you can feel the air accelerate as it gets closer and closer to the intake.

The gravity proposal posits that as aether flows from space toward cosmic bodies it is subject to the same acceleration phenomenon. The flow from the wide expanse of space into the relatively small area occupied by a cosmic body is an ever-narrowing flow. Acceleration of the flow is the inevitable result.

Thus, the inflowing-aether proposal explains the acceleration aspect of gravity. In addition, the fact of acceleration itself is compelling evidence that gravity is likely caused by an inflowing substance.

2.14. Speeds of Gravity

In accordance with the proposed gravity concept, inflowing aether carries with it any unrestrained objects that it encounters. A tossed ball falling back to the ground is an example.

A more interesting example is a spaceship returning to the Earth from the moon. In the portion of the return trajectory that is within the Earth's sphere of gravity and through to the point where the friction of the Earth's atmosphere commences, the spacecraft uses only gravity for propulsion. It uses no means of self-propulsion. The spaceship is in a state of free-fall as it travels toward the Earth.

The speeds of spacecraft returning from the moon are well documented [6]. The speeds are no more than a tiny fraction of the speed of light. They vary from about 0.8 km per second at the point where the spacecraft enters into the Earth's area of gravitation, and rise to about 11.0 km per second where the craft starts to encounter the braking effect of the Earth's atmosphere.

Assuming that the spaceships are carried toward the Earth by inflowing aether, these data provide compelling evidence of the speeds of gravity.

2.15. Equivalence Principle

One of the fundamental aspects of gravity is that it acts equally on all objects, no matter what their respective masses may be. One might think that a heavier mass object should fall faster than a lighter mass object, but this is a misconception that was laid to rest a long time ago by dropping objects of different masses from the leaning tower of Pisa and seeing them arrive at the surface at the same time.

The flowing aether concept is consistent with the equivalence principle. The speeds of inflowing aether govern the speeds of falling objects, not their respective masses.

An apt analog is a flowing river that carries floating objects of differing masses. One will note that the speeds of the river, not the masses of the objects, govern the speeds of the objects.

2.16. Instantaneous Gravity between the Sun and the Earth

According to Isaac Newton, gravitational force between the Sun and the Earth points directly on the line that intersects the Sun and the Earth. See: Newton's Principia, Proposition LXV, Theorem XXV [7]. This fact has been taken to imply instant communication of gravitational force between the Sun and the Earth. Contrast this with the transmission of light from the Sun to the Earth. The travel time is about eight minutes and the trajectory therefore deviates from the line that intersects the Sun and the Earth.

There is a fundamental problem with the inference of instantaneous communication of gravitational force between the Sun and the Earth. Instantaneous action-at-a-distance is rejected by most scientists as being patently impossible.

There is a rational explanation for the appearance of instantaneous gravitational force between the Sun and the Earth. The explanation is that gravitation is caused by aether that flows from space toward the Sun, and does not involve communication of gravitational force between the Sun and the Earth. Pursuant to the inflow model, aether that is flowing toward the Sun exerts ram pressure on the Earth, and does so at the instant that the flow interacts with the Earth. The direction of the flow - directly at the Sun - sets the direction of the gravity force, and does so on the line that intersects the Sun and the Earth. Because this model does not involve communication between the Sun and the Earth, there is no "action-at-a-distance". Rather, gravity is caused by direct contact between the aether flow and the Earth.

Consider the diagram (Figure 1) that depicts aether flowing from space toward the Sun. Note the direction of aether flowing from space as it interacts with the Earth. It is directly at the Sun. Note as well that the ram force exercised by the inflowing aether must be instantaneous because it occurs at the instant of the flowing aether's encounter with the Earth.

In summary, it may be reasoned from the direct alignment of gravitational force between the Sun and the Earth and its implication of instantaneous action-at-a-distance, that communication between the Sun and the Earth is not the cause of gravity. It may also be reasoned that the cause of gravity is a pushing force caused by aether flowing from space into cosmic bodies.

2.17. Michelson-Morley Experiments and Cocooning

In 1887, Michelson and Morley conducted an experiment designed to determine whether the Earth in its orbit around the Sun is encountering aether. That experiment and numerous similar experiments that have been conducted since that time have produced results that have far lower than would have been expected if the Earth were in fact encountering aether. In result, probably a majority of scientists are of the view that the marginal results prove that aether does not exist.

However, many prominent scientists are of the contrary view. They contend that the results prove that aether does in fact exist. They rely upon the results of numerous experiments that show marginal, but none-the-less positive, indications that the Earth in its orbit is in fact encountering aether.

What can logically be drawn from the test results? This question raises the concept of cocooning. The idea of cocooning is that the Earth is surrounded by an envelope of aether that travels with the Earth is its orbital path, and this envelope of aether absorbs a large part of the ram pressure exerted by the aether that the Earth encounters in its orbital path.

Does a form of cocooning exist? Visualize inflowing condensed aether and outflowing aether cells as material substances that surround the Earth. Picture the flows being tied to the Earth in the sense that one is being continuously drawn into the Earth and the other is being continuously emitted from the Earth. It appears to be a rational assumption that much of this aether must move with the Earth in its orbital path around the Sun.

The significance of cocooning is the fact that the Michelson-Morley type experiments have taken place on the Earth's surface, well shielded by the aether envelope from the aether the Earth encounters in its orbit. Thus, the concept of cocooning provides an explanation of why the Michelson-Morley test results have been minimal but none-the-less positive. The aether envelope absorbs most of the orbital ram pressure and planet Earth itself absorbs only a minimal portion.

A simple analog: A passenger enclosed in an automobile travelling at 100 km per hour feels essentially none of the force of the air through which the car is travelling. The passenger is "cocooned" by the automobile's body.

Coming back to the question, what can logically be drawn from the test results? Given the likelihood of some form of cocooning, the inference that aether does not exist cannot be logically drawn. In addition, the positive but minimal test results support the proposition that the Earth in its orbit encounters a substance, presumably a form of aether.

2.18. Incremental Growth of Cosmic Bodies

While the process of incoming and outgoing aether is essentially cyclic, it may be that a portion of incoming aether is absorbed by cosmic bodies. While outflow is continuous and is necessary to replenish the aether supply in space, absorption of a portion of incoming aether is a credible source of supply of the building blocks of matter used for the growth and evolution of the Earth and our Solar system.

Might the absorption of aether that is used for incremental growth cause the ultimate depletion of aether in space? Likely not. The life cycles of stars, including their ultimate explosions into supernovae, are likely sources of replenishment of the aether that may be used in the growth of cosmic bodies.

2.19. Dark Matter and Dark Energy

Scientists hypothesize the existence of dark matter (matter we cannot see) and dark energy (energy that permeates space). Assuming they exist - and it is likely that they do – it is estimated that together they constitute about 95% of the mass-energy content of the universe.

Cosmic microwave background and the calculated temperature of space (2.7 degrees Celsius) provide evidence of a vast repository of matter and energy that occupy space. One may fairly speculate that this matter and energy are dark matter and dark energy and that they consist of aether that permeates space.

2.20. Black Holes

Black holes are said to be places, sometimes central to a galaxy, where gravity is so intense that matter is drawn in and caused to collapse. Black holes get their name because the speed of incoming gravity is so fast that it exceeds the speed of light, thus preventing light from escaping. Assuming that black holes in fact exist (some say they do not), is the proposed cause-of-gravity concept consistent with the force of gravity associated with black holes?

The answer is yes. Recall that the cause of aether inflow is posited as a differential between the pressure of aether in cosmic bodies and the pressure of aether in space. With this in mind, consider the implications of the collapse of atomic matter and aether cells as they enter a black hole. The volumes of space they occupied before their collapse are reduced by their collapse into miniscule volumes. In result, the volumes the atoms and aether cells formerly occupied become almost total vacuums. This creates pressure differentials that are so immense as to cause gravitational speeds being driven to levels that approach or exceed the speed of light – sufficient to prevent the escape of light.

3. Summary and Conclusions

There are certain elements of evidence that provide strong support for the proposition that gravity is caused by the flow of aether from space into cosmic bodies. The fact of instantaneous gravity between the Sun and the Earth only makes sense if one assumes inflow from space. Further, the fact of instantaneous gravity negates the commonly held idea that gravity is caused by something communicated between the Sun and the Earth. The fact of gravitational acceleration also supports the inflow concept. It is well established that when flow paths are narrowed, as they are from the expanse of space to the relatively narrow destinations of cosmic bodies, the result is that a flowing fluid accelerates. Thus, the fact that gravity is an accelerating force supports the proposition that gravity is caused by inflow from space to cosmic bodies. Consider next the principle of equivalence. The fact that objects that are carried in an accelerating river travel at equal speeds, no matter their respective masses, is further evidence that supports the proposition that gravity is caused by flows in the direction of cosmic bodies. In addition, the vacuum cleaner analog supports the contentions that gravity is not only a pushing force, but is also an accelerating force.

Other elements are more speculative, but none-the-less significant. Evaporation and condensation of aether into separate states or phases, gaseous and liquid, explains why gravity is a one-way force. The cyclic approach provides for replenishment of aether in space and disbursement of heat from cosmic bodies. Cosmic microwave background and the temperature of space provide evidence of energy that propels inflow. Pressure differences between aether in space and aether in cosmic bodies explain why inflow occurs. The evaporation of water molecules and their rise into the atmosphere by diffusion and convection provide an analog for the evaporation of aether cells and their migration into space. The cocooning effect of aether explains the marginal but positive results of the Michelson-Morley experiments and supports the proposition that aether in fact exists.

The above elements of the aether concept of gravity are based upon known phenomena. Each element bears upon the others. Each aspect alone provides evidence that supports the overall concept of gravity. The pieces fit together and describe an operating system that is a rational model of the cause of gravity.

REFERENCES

1. D. W. Shaw, Phys. Essays 25, 66 2012.
2. D. W. Shaw, Phys. Essays 26, 523, 2013.
3. D. W. Shaw, Phys. Essays 29, 485, 2016.
4. R. Feynman, The Feynman Lectures on Physics, The Definitive Edition, Vol. I (Addison Wesley, Reading, MA, pp. 7-9. 2006.
5. R. Feynman, The Feynman Lectures on Physics, The Definitive Edition, Vol. I (Addison Wesley, Reading MA, p. 43-3, 2006.
6. R. A. Braeunig, Circumlunar free return trajectory (2008), www.braeunig.us/apollo/free-return.htm; Hybrid Lunar Profile with LOI and TEI, www.braeunig.us/apollo/hybrid-profile.htm. 2008.
7. I. Newton, Principia, edited by Stephen Hawking, text by Daniel Adee, 1848 (Running Press Book Publishers, Philadelphia, PA), Proposition LXV, Theorem XXV. 2002.

Einstein's Repudiation of His Own Theory of Relativity

Peter Sujak, RNDr

Hradesinska 60, 10100 Prague, Czech Republic, peter.sujak@email.cz

Einstein in his works from 1905 till 1907 discarded the ether from physics but his more than 5 papers from 1920 to 1934 deal with the ether as an unexceptionable physical reality. In these papers Einstein becomes more an enthusiastic advocate of the testification of the ether than supporters of the ether before the year 1905. In this paper we show that Einstein by his own declarations after 1920 about testified existence of the ether himself openly repudiated his Special and General theories of relativity.

Keywords: Special relativity, General relativity, Einstein, Ether

1. Introduction

The conviction of physicists to the end of the 19th-century of the full existence of ether can best be seen in the search work of H.A. Lorentz - Ether theories and eather models (1901-1902), examining the work of many distinguished physicists of the 19th century on ether (Stokes, Planck, Fresnel, Maxwell, Kelvin, Neumann). In the beginning of the 20th century the properties of the ether was the prominent subjects of dissertations for a doctoral degree at the most Universities in Europe. In introduction to more excellent physical textbook from the beginning of the 20th century it can be repeatedly traced sentence like - 'The opinion on the existence of ether match certainty'.

Proclamations of most outstanding physicists on the testificatopn of the ether:

R. Descartes (1596-1650), the father of modern western philosophy, who had the most influence on Newton, considered the space to be entirely filled with matter. The formation of visual matter, planets, by Descartes, happens from vortexes of ether. Descartes' vacuum of space is not empty but composed of huge swirling whirlpools of ethereal or fine matter, producing what would later be called gravitational effects [9].

Newton in Letter to Robert Boyle in 1678-9 "I suppose, that there is diffused through all places an etherial substance, capable of contraction and dilatation, strongly elastic, and, in a word, much like air in all respects, but far more subtle". Newton's letter to Bentley 1692 : "Gravity so that one body may act upon another at a distance thro' a Vacuum, without the Mediation of anything else, by and through which their Action and Force may be conveyed from one to another, is to me so great an Absurdity that I believe no Man who has in philosophical Matters a competent Faculty of thinking can ever fall into it. Gravity must be caused by an Agent acting constantly and according to certain laws".

Newton in 1708: "Perhaps the whole frame of nature may be nothing but various contextures of some certain ethereal spirits or vapors, condensed, as it were, by precipitation; and after condensation wrought into various forms, at first by the immediate hand of the Creator, and ever after by the power of nature" [9]. Newton claimed that ether's adapted aethereal spirits produce the phenomena of electricity, magnetism, and gravitation. Newton's principia - gravity is "as a certain power or energy diffused from the center to all places around to move the bodies that are in them".

Maxwell in very last clause of his Treaties (1873): "In fact, whenever energy is transmitted from one body to another, there must be a medium or substance in which the energy exists. . . . all theories lead to the conception of a medium in which that propagation takes place. . . and this has been my constant aim in this treatise".

Riemann asserts us that "space in itself is nothing more than a three-dimensional manifold devoid of all form ; it acquires a definite form only through the advent of the material content filling it and determining its metric relations"[9].

Tesla in his works claimed that Einstein's relativity, which discards the ether, is entirely wrong and he proved that no vacuum (void space) exists. He asserts that all attempts to explain the workings of the universe without recognizing the existence of ether and the indispensable function it plays in phenomena are futile. He asserts that there is no energy in matter other than that received from the environment.

Hubble for a more likely explanation than explaining the red shift spectra by mutual receding of galaxies, considered the explanation of this shift by the loss of light energy passing through the medium of interstellar space. Hubble (1937): "The cautious observer naturally examines other possibilities before accepting the proposition, even as a working hypothesis. He (Hubble) recalls the alternative formulation of the law of red-shifts - light loses energy in proportion to the distance it travels through space. The law, in this form, sounds quite plausible. Interior nebular space, we believe, cannot be entirely empty" [9].

Einstein in 1924..." we are not going to be able to dispense with the ether in theoretical physics , that is, with continuum furnished with physical properties; ...every theory of contact action presupposes continuous fields, hence also the existence of an ether" [9].

2. Einstein's development of opinion on the ether

The regular controversial procedure, when Einstein declared both two of the opposite mutually excluding claim was also the case in question of the existence of the ether.

Einstein discarded the existence of the ether in 1905 but yet in 1916 paper he regretted that he rejected existence of the ether and he speaks about introduction of medium filing the space and assume that electromagnetic fields are ether states "metric facts can no longer be separated from true physical facts; the concepts of space and ether merge together. It would have been more correct if I had limited myself, in my earlier publications, to emphasizing only the non-existence of an ether velocity, instead of arguing the total non-existence of the ether" [2].

Einstein after 1916 came in with his rediscovery of the ether and he subsequently becomes more an enthusiastic advocate of the proven existence of the ether than supporters of the ether before the year 1905. In his papers (e.g. 1916, 1920, 1924 discussed more below) Einstein claimed:

"According to the general theory of relativity space without ether is unthinkable. The mechanical ether, designated by Newton as 'absolute space', must therefore be considered by us as a physical reality. In Newton's theory of motion, space has physical reality - in contrast to the case of geometry and kinematics. We are not going to be able to dispense with the ether in theoretical physics. According to our present conceptions the elementary particles of matter are also, in their essence, nothing else than condensations of the electromagnetic field".

But this Einstein's final cognition is concealed to us and gravity as the mystery of non-material space time curvature of GTR is daily forced upon public and wider physical community.

As is shown below in this paper all STR claims from 1905 resp. 1907 were recalled by Einstein in epoch from 1911 till 1934.

Einstein in his works from 1905 till 1907 discarded the ether from physics but his more than 5 papers from 1920 to 1934 deal with the ether as an unexceptionable physical reality. In his published lecture at a conference held in Leiden in 1920 [3], in his another paper published in his 1920 [1, V7, D31], and foremost especially in his work 'On the ether' from 1924 [1, V14, D332] Einstein comes with the opposite claim that without the ether it is not possible to explain the physical world around us.

Einstein concluded in his lecture in 1920 [3] - "Thus we may also say, I think, that the ether of the general theory of relativity is the outcome of the Lorentzian ether, through relativation. According to our present conceptions the elementary particles of matter are also, in their essence, nothing else than condensations of the electromagnetic field. According to the general theory of relativity space without ether is unthinkable. ...ether has to serve as medium for the effects of inertia. Recapitulating, we may say that according to the general theory of relativity space is endowed with physical qualities; in this sense, therefore, there exists an ether."

Einstein's in 36 pages 1920 paper 'Fundamental ideas and methods of the Theory of relativity, presented in their development'[1, V7, D31], containing no single one citation, declared his errant in rejecting ether in 1905 -

" My opinion in 1905 was that one should no longer talk about the ether in physics. But this judgment was too radical. Rather it is still permissible to assume a space-filling medium whose states may be imagined as electromagnetic fields. Therefore, one can say the ether has been resurrected in the theory of general relativity...space and ether flows into each other...The theory of space (geometry) and time no longer represent intrinsic physics propounded independently of mechanics and gravitation ".

This declaration meant in fact cancelation of STR and GTR by Einstein himself.

In conclusions of Einstein's 1920 papers [1, V7, D31] Einstein rediscovered the ether. In conclusions of this 1920 paper he newly discovered the ether as the direct consequence of 'his' GTR field equations although full assurance of the ether by physicists and hundreds of papers in topics of ether from Aristotle ages till 1905 existed.

In 1924 paper [1, V14, D332] (when continuous Millers experiments was keep confirming ether) Einstein becomes more an enthusiastic advocate of the existence of the ether than supporters of the ether before the year 1905. In his 1924 paper Einstein 'discovered':

- "The mechanical ether, designated by Newton as 'absolute space', must therefore be considered by us as a physical reality".

- "In Newton's theory of motion, space has physical reality- in contrast to the case of geometry and kinematics".

- "GTR adds characteristics to the ether that are variable from point to point and determine the metric and the dynamic behavior of material points".

- "The ether of the GTR, consequently, differs from the one of classical mechanics, i.e. the special theory of relativity, in that it is not 'absolute'; its local variable properties are rather determined by the ponderable matter".

- " we are not going to be able to dispense with the ether in theoretical physics , that is, with continuum furnished with physical properties; because GTR excludes any unmediated action-at-a-distance. However, every theory of contact action presupposes continuous fields, hence also the existence of an ether".

But after these Einstein's declaration in his 1924 paper and according Einstein's own affirmation in 1925 his STR and GTR become invalid. "My opinion about Miller's experiments is the following. Should the positive result (ether) be confirmed, then the special theory of relativity and with it the general theory of relativity, in its current form, would be invalid".

In Einstein's 1913 paper [1, V4, D13, p.153] 'Outline of the generalized theory' we can read -

"I have shown in previous papers that the equivalence hypotheses leads to the consequence that in a static gravitational field the velocity of light c depends on the gravitational potential. This led me to the view that special theory of relativity provides only an approximation to reality; it should apply only in the limit case where differences in the gravitational potential in the space-time region under consideration are not too great".

As the gravitational potential is changing in space from a star to a star, from a galaxy to a galaxy so according to the 1913 paper velocity of light in vacuum is no longer the constant and is changing (standard supposition of physicist before 1905). This means in fact an abolition of the first principle of STR which is based on firm proclamation that the velocity of light is the ultimate and constant velocity in the vacuum of the void space, that no carrying substance of the light propagation exists and that nothing can influence on the ultimate velocity of the light in the vacuum.

In his work from 1920 [4] Einstein declared: "If we had based our considerations on the Galilei transformation we should not have obtained a contraction of the rod as a consequence of its motion. The theory of space (geometry) and time no longer represent intrinsic physics propounded independently of mechanics and gravitation. In Newton's theory of motion, space has physical reality- in contrast to the case of geometry and kinematics".

This in closer context means also refusal of his energy momentum system.

It is necessary to stressed that Michelson-Morley's experiment in 1887 (and all others later) never provided zero results but results which was by Michelson and Morley considered as negligibly small in light of their early physical assumption of their experiment.

This mean that STR never become valid because its validity requires zero results.

This is clear also according affirmation of the Einstein himself detailed in chapter "Should the positive result be confirmed, then the special theory of relativity and with it the general theory of relativity, would be invalid".

Negligibly small results of M-M experiment Einstein enunciated as the zero result and on this never measured zero result he based his STR.

As the zero result is M-M experiment presented in all textbook of physics till today. The fact that the result obtained by Michelson and Morley in 1887 was not negligibly small was very fully set forth by Professor Hicks of University College Sheffield, yet in 1902, in his important theoretical examination of the original experiment [12].

3. Conclusion

As was shown above, Einstein by his own declaration in 1920 or 1924 papers about existence of the ether as an unexceptionable physical reality himself openly canceled his Special and General theories of relativity.

In spite of this fact, up to day, during next 90 years to students and general public it was claimed by ideological power structures, academics and main stream physics that STR proved non-existence of ether and that GTR in new understanding of space and time discovered the biggest achievement in history of mankind.

In these claims just the M-M experiment from1887 is referred to although in next forty years continuing M-M experiments confirmed the ether end motion of the earth determined by the ether-drift (detailed below).

In these claims just the Einstein's STR paper form 1905 is referred to although Einstein himself, as is documented in this paper, later canceled basic principles of STR from 1905. In these claims just the Einstein's GTR paper form 1915 is referred to although Einstein soon concluded that his Field equations resulted in rapid gravitationally collapsing universe and was not utilizable to Universe.

In these claims of discovery of new understanding of space and time just the Einstein's GTR paper form 1915 is referred to although Einstein after 1920 fully rejected his space-time concept and fully returned to ether concept.

Although Dayton Miller after 30 years of conducting Michelson-Morley interferometric experiments at least in 1933 fully determined the absolute motion and the speed of earth in surrounding ether [12] and although Einstein in 1913 came to the declaration that "special theory of relativity is only approximation to reality of changing light velocity" this facts are concealed next 100 years and validity of STR is forced upon public and students referring just to Einstein's 1905 paper and just to purported null result of Michelson-Morley's experiment from 1887.

Although Einstein after 1916 becomes more an enthusiastic advocate of the proven existence of the ether than supporters of the ether before the year 1905 and although he proclaimed in 1924 that "The mechanical ether, designated by Newton as 'absolute space', must therefore be considered by us as a physical reality" this fact is concealed by ideological power structures of the world next 100 years. Contrary alleged Einstein's mystery of nonmaterial space time is daily forced upon public and wider physical community referring just to Einstein's paper from 1915 in which no physical reasoning of Field equations was given.

Einstein after 1920 fully rejected his void space-time conception in General relativity, rejected his STR, fully accepted that the mechanical ether must be considered by us as a physical reality and explicitly declared inability to dispense with the ether in theoretical physics. But next 90 years just the space time conception from 1905 and 1915 are presented to general public as allegedly the Einstein's conception which he later rejected.

So the situation with Einstein is the same as in Hubble's case. Although Hubble remained cautiously against the Big bang theory [9] until the end of his life Hubble is by ideological power structures declared as the discoverer who proved the Big Bang theory. Einstein after 1920 admitted his fault from 1905 till 1915 and declared that his "theory of space and time no longer represents intrinsic physics". So although Einstein's himself after 1920 rejected space time conceptions from 1905 and 1915 next 90 years up today these rejected conception from 1905 and 1915 are lastly forced by mass suggestion of ideological power structures on general public as Einstein's ingenious new understanding of space - time and gravity as his ingenious conception of space - time curvature.

Of the hundreds of documentary films about the physical image of the universe produced in last thirty years not a single one mentions the biggest experimental discovery of our civilization about the creation and the annihilation of particles from and into the electromagnetic radiation so from and into the ether.

After 1920 Einstein openly admits his youngster thoughtlessness in his 25 to his 35 epoch from 1905 till 1916 when he formulated his relativity - "My opinion in 1905 was that one should no longer talk about the ether in physics. But this judgment was too radical".

As was shown above he fully rejected his physically incompetent approach based on kinematics of Galilei transformation so linear ratios of space and time. This means Einstein's confession of his non perception of basic physical principles of Dynamics of Nature so non-linear ratios of space and time (expressing change in densities of mater in space described by gradients of fields or by changes of the pressures or by accelerations or by changes of velocities).

Although Einstein after 1920 in his 40 fully understood the absurdity of his theories he had produced in previous 15 years, for the next 35 years of his life he as well did not produced no meaningful theory.

The reason for this professional disaster was that Einstein until the end of his life never understood the largest physical mistake of his scientific career which resides in his understanding of the unit of time as the independent physical quantity instead of a proper understanding of the unit of time in mechanics as the identical quantity with the quantity of the unit of velocity [12].

But power ideological structures quickly seized new opportunities to return the physical picture of the world with the help of these Einstein's incompetent mysterious theories of relativity from 1905 and 1915 back into line with their ideologies.

In 20th century continues the state of the destruction of physics during previous 2000 years. This destruction was caused by installation of the Ptolemy geocentric image of universe consistent with the idea of the principles of creation as the only tolerable image of the universe for 1500 years till 16th century. This destruction was caused during 17th, 18th and 19th century by the ban of the books of the most outstanding physicists as heretical (including Newton, Galilleo, Tycho Brahe, Kepler and Copernicus) on Index Librorum Prohibitorum (along with the restrictions on printing in Europe) [12]. But this ban becomes less and less effective from the second half of the 19th century especially after democratic revolutions in Europe in 1848 since civil rights became more and more a reality.

So power ideological structures come up with the proven procedure at Ptolemy model and violently installed Einstein's incompetent mysterious theories of relativity from 1905 and 1915 as the only one tolerable imagine of the universe to return the physical picture of the world back into line with their ideologies. On top of it (as the revenge to banned mis-believers) all previously banned most outstanding physicists including Maxwell as a bonus were in these theories of relativity refuted in substantial part. All previous physics was thus in fact impeached without looking for solutions in the physical reality instead of provided solutions in a mystery of the relativity and quantum mechanics.

During next hundred years after 1915 generations of students of physics are brainwashed with relativity and quantum mechanics although this theories are not understandable to nobody including academics who lecture them [12]. The mass-media suggestion on general public is performed with proclamation about Einstein's super geniality and with proclamation about his theories of space and time form 1905 and 1915 as the greatest achievement of human spirit in all history of mankind. This all despite the fact that Einstein himself after 1920 rejected these his own theories - "The theory of space (geometry) and time no longer represent intrinsic physics". The same mass-media suggestion is performed in proclamation Schrodinger's equations (in fact Einstein's bases) [12] of the quantum mechanics as the second greatest achievement of human spirit in all history of mankind despite Feynman, the Nobel Prize laureate for quantum physics in 1966 proclaimed "I think I can safely say that nobody understands quantum mechanics. We have always had a great deal of difficulty understanding the world view that quantum mechanics represents" [12].

Question is - what is the sense to teach such theory at universities moreover as the most important and most time consuming part of the physical education which even creators of these theories themselves, most genial physicists and lecturers do not understand? Answer is - the sense is destruction of physics (in which no consonant picture of the physical world exists and everybody can have its own true) in order to install and sustain predetermined dogmas of ideological political power structures.

But the larger sense are power and money. Political parties on religious bases are still the most powerful and ruling political parties in the countries of the world. Voters of these political parties vote them also for the reason that ideology of these parties provided to voters is allegedly confirmed as valid, because it is consonant with science. This consonance of religion with science (Big bang, mystery of space time, god's particles) is frequently and massively instilled to the mind of these voters at every occasion by every possible manner. Vice versa these ruling ideological political parties of countries support such scientific projects which offer the consonant order of the universe with their ideology.

It was documented in this work that Einstein's theories need not to be uprooted or refuted because by his declaration in his papers after 1920 Einstein refuted them himself. Just a familiarization of general public about this fact is necessary.

REFERENCES

1. *The Collected Papers of Albert Einstein*, Princeton University Press, open-access website
2. L. Kostro, *Einstein and the Ether*, Apeiron, Indiana University, 2000
3. A. Einstein, *Ether and the Theory of Relativity*, Methuen and Co. Ltd, London, 1922
4. A. Einstein, *Relativity*, 1920, Henry Holt and Company, New York
5. P. Sujak, *Big Crash of Basic Concepts of Physics of the 20th Century?*, Proceedings of the Natural Philosophy Alliance, 20th Annual Conference of the NPA, Maryland, 2013, http://vixra.org/abs/1108.0017
6. P. Sujak, *On the General Reality of Gravity, as Well as Other Forces in Nature and the Creation of Material Particles and Force Fields in the Universe*, Proceedings of the Natural Philosophy Alliance, 20th Annual Conference of the NPA, Maryland, 2013 http://vixra.org/abs/1304.0046
7. P. Sujak, *On Energy and Momentum in Contemporary Physics*, American Physical Society Meeting, Denver, March 2014, Y33, 3
8. P. Sujak, *On gravity, other forces in nature and the creation of mass particles and force fields in the universe*, Bulletin of the American Physical Society Meeting, Savannah, April 2014, T1, 56
9. P. Sujak, *Call to Repel the Physical Theories of the 20th Century*, 2016, J Phys Math 7: 202. doi: 10.4172/2090-0902.1000202
10. P. Sujak, *Historical, Philosophical and Physical Reasons for Denial of the Main Physical Theories of the 20th Century*, Proceedings of the Annual International Congress on Fundamental problems of science and technology, July, 2016, St. Petersburg
11. P. Sujak, *Call to Repel the Physical Theories of the 20th Century*, Proceedings of the John Chappell Natural Philosophy Society, Second Annual Conference, July 2016, University of Maryland
12. P. Sujak, *Extended Call to Repel the Physical Theories of the 20th Century*, The General Science Journal, 16. January 2017, http://www.gsjournal.net/Science-Journals/Research/20Papers/View/6753

The Ether

Ramsey

The intent of this article is to revise the assumptions associated with Einstein's relativity theories, thereby postulating an alternate theory, somewhat analogous to Einstein's concepts; however, now compatible with the existence of the ether. Therefore, as will be revealed, relativity and quantum mechanics, rather than being disconnected, are then a part of one overall unified theory.

Note: This paper contains chapter 1 and the first part of chapter 3 of a larger article. The second part of chapter 3, as well as chapters 2, 4, and 5 are not included.

Keywords: Ether, MMX, PFSRT, PFGRT

PREFACE

Einstein's relativity theories (SRT, GRT), as well as quantum mechanics (QM) are extremely difficult to fully grasp without the use of intricate mathematics. For instance, four-dimensional space-time is not easily visualized. In addition, quantum mechanics utilizes mathematical relationships that correctly predict outcomes, even though the theory makes no visual common sense. As a result, it is very difficult for the average person to appreciate them, let alone understand them. Here is a quote by the famous physicist Werner Heisenberg, a founder of QM supporting this belief, "If you think you understand QM, then you don't understand QM."

In contrast, this article uses three-dimensional space, logic, and a few equations to postulate a new alternative theory that encompasses, moreover, interconnects SRT, GRT, and QM. It is the author's conviction that modern-day physics [regarding relativity and QM] has lost sight of reality by using complex mathematical equations to produce correct outcomes. Nevertheless, the math employed does not characterize the actual and true universe. This paradox is apparent with present-day high school/college physics courses, whereby students often manipulate equations with no basic understanding as to how the math actually represents reality.

For instance, to clarify this divergence of mathematics versus reality, follow this logic. There are several methods by which math [and geometry] can portray the physics of the solar system, such as the Ptolemaic versus Copernican theories, as pictured in Figures 163 and 164. [Wikipedia] Note: with the use mathematics, both theories accurately predict the orbital mechanics of the solar system, but one represents reality while the other does not.

Now it is generally accepted that the best theory is the simplest (Copernican and Kepler), or in other words, Occam's razor, that theory closest to what makes common sense [Copernican and Kepler]. In essence, determining the best theory should be pursued first, then followed by the mathematics. The point being, the focus should be on the theory representing reality rather than just mathematics.

Ptolemaic Model of the Solar System

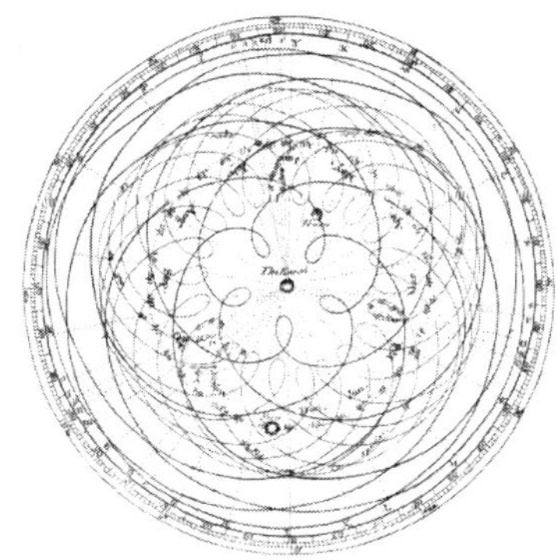

Figure 163. Ptolemaic Model

Source: Wikipedia

Copernican Model of Solar System

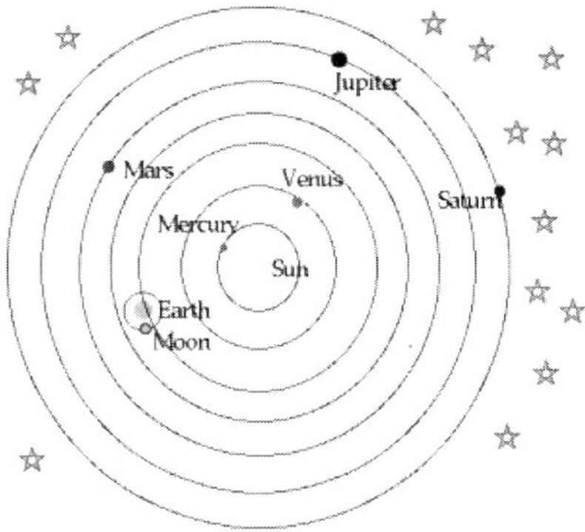

Figure 164. Copernican Model

Source: Wikipedia

Having stated all this, math is absolutely crucial for a rigorous proof of any given reality theory. So one should not demean math, only place it in its proper perspective. For this reason, one primary goal of this paper is: the average non-scientific individual should be able to read, moreover easily comprehend, this paper and its concepts, without the use of math.

The Michelson Morley experiment (MMX) is the main foundational block used as a validation for Einstein's relativity theories. Its null outcome implies there is no ether. Consequently, another basic goal of this paper is to demonstrate that the "null result" is, in fact, also compatible with the ether existence, rather than only a proof of its absence.

In essence, this new pictorial theory, defined in Chapter 1 of this article as the Preferred Frame Special Relativity Theory [PFSRT], combines Galilean transformation theory and Newton's theories [three dimensional space] with Maxwell's EM theory (velocity of light of c relative to the observer) to propose a new relativity theory somewhat equivalent to SRT, but now, in this case, the speed of light (c) is a function of an ether [PFSRT] not the observer.

In order to accomplish this objective, one needs to read, grasp, and accept the theories and assumptions presented in this paper. They are extremely logical. As a result, it will eventually become crystal clear as to why the MMX always demonstrates isotropy, specifically when performed on the rotating surface of the Earth, even in the presence of the ether wind. If correct, Einstein's SRT main foundation block validating the MMX is eliminated, and his relativity theories then collapse. As a result, a new groundwork of physics is required: **THE ETHER**.

CHAPTER 1 - SRT/PFSRT

1. Introduction

For an overall review of Einstein's relativity theories, the book *Relativity For The Layman, a Simplifies Account of History, Theory and Proofs of Relativity* by James Coleman, The New American Library of World Literature Inc, is recommended, since in order to comprehend this paper, one must have at least some rudimentary knowledge of both Einstein's Special Relativity Theory (SRT) and General Relativity Theory (GRT).

In addition, before evaluating Chapter 1, for those individuals who have little experience with SRT, it would be very beneficial to peruse Appendix 1 of this article, which explains the reasoning behind Einstein's (SRT). Furthermore, the websites listed below would also be highly helpful.

"Understanding Einstein's Special Theory of Relativity." [1]

"Special Relativity Explained In Under Three Minutes." [2]

"Theory Of Relativity Explained In Seven Minutes." [3]

A brief section of Appendix 1 is now presented below:

- *"Einstein's theory of special relativity created a fundamental link between space and time. The universe can be viewed as having three-space dimensions - up/down, left/right, forward/ backward - and one-time dimension. This four-dimensional space is referred to as the space-time continuum."*
- *"If you move fast enough through space, the observations that you make about space and time differ somewhat from the observations of other people who are moving at different speeds."*

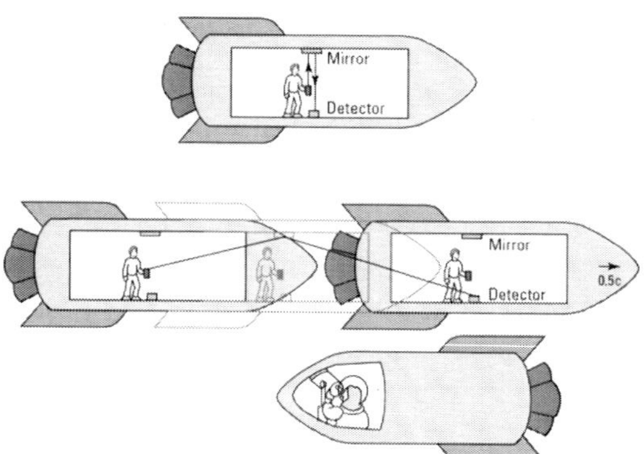

Figure 165. Spaceship Model for SRT

- *"You can picture this for yourself by understanding the thought experiment depicted in this figure. Imagine that you're on a spaceship and holding a laser so it shoots a beam of light directly up, striking a mirror you've placed on the ceiling. The light beam then comes back down and strikes a detector."*
- *"(Top) You see a beam of light go up, bounce off the mirror, and come straight down. (Bottom) Amber sees the beam travel along a diagonal path."*
- *"However, the spaceship is traveling at a constant speed of half the speed of light (0.5c, as physicists would write it). According to Einstein, this makes no difference to you - you can't even tell that you're moving. However, if astronaut Amber were spying on you, as in the bottom of the figure, it would be a different story."*
- *"Amber would see your beam of light travel upward along a diagonal path, strike the mirror, and then travel downward along a diagonal path before striking the detector. In other words, you and Amber would see different paths for the light and, more importantly, those paths aren't even the same length. This means that the time the beam takes to go from the laser to the mirror to the detector must also be different for you and Amber, so that you both agree on the speed of light."*

With reference to the above excerpt, [4] if the speed of light is c for both observers, then time and distance must differ with respect to you and Amber in order to maintain the speed of light at c. c = distance/time. So if c remains constant, then distance/time must change proportionally. Notice, referring to this example, the definition of c, as well as the concept of distance, are both a function of "time". And other than a mathematical equation, no rational reason or physical process is given as for why relative to the observer both distance and time change as a function of a constant c, essentially, no underlying cause and effect is presented. Please commit this example to memory, for it will be referred to at the end of this chapter from a different perspective.

The postulates of Einstein's SRT are, first, that with respect to inertial motion, all is relative. Therefore, the laws of physics are the same in all inertial reference frames. And second, the velocity of light is always c relative to only the observer. From these postulates, Einstein then deduced that with respect to the observer, as an object increases its velocity, its inertial mass increases, its "rate of time" slows down, and distance in the direction of motion decreases (including the physical length of the object in the direction of motion). In addition, Einstein assumed the ether as non-existent.

In contrast, this alternative SRT, now defined as the Preferred Frame Special Relativity Theory (PFSRT), posits the presumption of the ether, the preferred frame for the speed of light of (c), with very similar, although not identical, outcomes. Listed below are the four basic assumptions (2,3,4, and 5) of PFSRT.

2. Assumption of the Structure of the Universe

Please refer to Figure 166 below and the following discussion. Figure 166 depicts the expansion of the universe over time. This is a 2 D representation of a 3 D universe.

Left Right

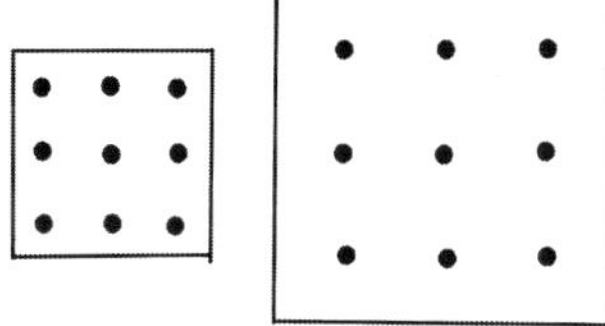

Figure 166. Expansion of the Universe

- *The ether (box) of the universe expands from left to the right. As a result, the galaxies (black dots) located within the box then separate from one another. However, the galaxies (dots) still remain at rest with the ether (box). Take note with reference to Figure 166 that the gravitational fields of the galaxies are ignored. This will be dealt with later on in Chapter 2 (GRT).*

The box on the left is smaller compared to the box on the right. The boxes represent the space (ether) of the universe. As shown above, the change in size from left to right represents the expansion of the universe over time. The black dots located within the box portray individual galaxies. They are all at rest with space, or by the terminology used in this paper, the ether. For now, assume the galaxies are not associated with their own gravitational fields. This will be discussed later on in this article in Chapter 2.

Notice, regarding Figure 166, as the ether or space expands in the areas between the galaxies, the universe also expands. Nevertheless, the galaxies still remain at rest with the ether. With reference to this expanding ether frame, the velocity of light is fixed at c. This basic model is the preferred frame of the universe, again for future reference, defined as the **Preferred Frame Special Relativity Theory (PFSRT)**.

Notice, too, as the universe expands, then from the prospective of an observer, located within each galaxy at rest with the ether, the further a galaxy is initially from the observer, then the faster is its movement from that observer. This applies to any observer associated with any galaxy; so each observer perceives the same effect. In addition, as the ether expands (space of universe expands), it then stretches the wavelength of the light traveling within it at c.

Consequently, the further a galaxy is from an observer, then for that observer, the greater the redshift of light from that galaxy. This matches the redshift of galaxies observed by astronomers; the greater the redshift, then the greater its distance with respect to the observer on Earth.

For further clarification, here is another analogy. See Figure 167. [5]

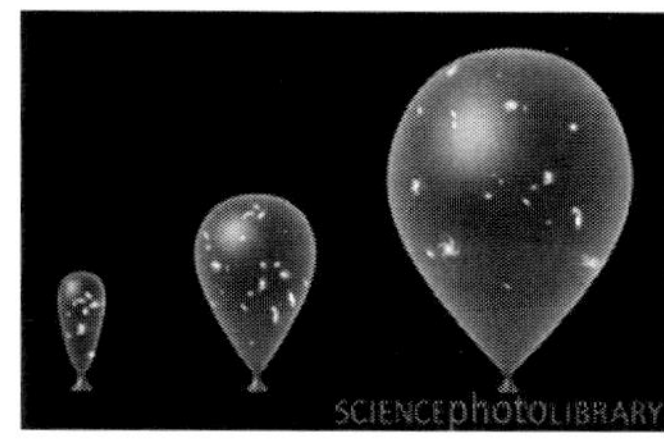

Figure 167. Balloon Expansion

- *This is analogous to Figure 166 but now with reference to the surface of a balloon.*

This example is the classic illustration, whereby the universe is depicted as limited to the surface of a balloon, with the galaxies represented by dots painted on its surface (2D illustration representing a 3D universe).

As the balloon is blown up, it therefore expands; the dots spread further and further apart from one another; nevertheless, the dots still remain at rest with the balloon's surface. In other words, as space or the ether expands (the surface of the balloon), the universe also expands; but the galaxies (dots) remain at rest with space/ether (surface of the balloon).

In essence, the fundamental distinction between PFSRT versus SRT is that this new theory posits that space is the ether, where light travels within it at a constant c. In contrast, SRT denies it exists; moreover, c is relative to only the observer.

3. Assumption of Inertial Mass

This is a classical definition of inertia: "*Inertia is the resistance of any physical object to any change in its state of motion, including changes to its speed and direction."* In other words, it is the tendency of objects to keep moving in a straight line at constant linear velocity. *"The principle of inertia is one of the fundamental principles of classic physics that are used to describe the motion of objects and how they are affected by applied force. Inertia comes from the Latin word, iners, meaning idle or sluggish. Inertia is one of the primary manifestations of mass, which is a quantitative property of physical systems. Isaac Newton defined inertia as his first law in his Phillosophiae Naturalis Principia Mathematica which states: The vis insita, or innate force of matter, is a power of resisting by which everybody, as much as in it lies, endeavour to preserve its present state, whether it be of rest or of moving uniformly forward in a straight line."* In common usage the term "inertia" may refer to an object's "amount of resistance to change in velocity" (which is quantified by its mass), or sometimes to its momentum, depending on the context. [6]

Einstein's SRT presumes that the inertial mass of an object, which is a group of associated atoms, is the intrinsic property of the object. What is more, no other factor is involved.

Alternatively, PFSRT differs considerably. It postulates that the ether is the entity, which resists an object's acceleration, although not its velocity. In addition, each of the elements elicits a different degree of resistance. In other words, an object's degree of resistance to its acceleration, from the ether, is defined as its inertial mass.

This new theory also posits: the greater an object's velocity has with respect to the ether of PFSRT, the greater, then, is the resistance to its further acceleration derived from that ether (Lorentz Transformation equation). This is to some extent, at least superficially, analogous to an exponential function. However, one important different aspect to acknowledge is that the velocity of the object cannot exceed the speed of light.

The mathematical equations that expresses this concept is called the Lorentz transformation, which is depicted below followed by a graph of that equation.

Lorentz Transformations

See Lorentz equations below and the following discussion.

Lorentz transformation equations

$$x' = \frac{x - vt}{\sqrt{1 - \frac{v^2}{c^2}}} \tag{66}$$

$$y' = y \tag{67}$$

$$z' = z \tag{68}$$

$$t' = \frac{t - \frac{v}{c^2}vx}{\sqrt{1 - \frac{v^2}{c^2}}} \tag{69}$$

- *It is not necessary for the novice to understand the actual equations. But it is essential to comprehend the graph of the equation as shown below.* [7]

A graph of the Lorentz transformation equation for mass vs velocity is shown in Figure 170 below. The inertial mass is represented by vertical axis and the velocity, from left to right, up to the speed of light is depicted by the horizontal axis. Notice the increased relativistic mass as a function of velocity is much more pronounced as the object approaches the speed of light [graph is skewed to the right]. Furthermore, the object's velocity cannot exceed the speed of light because of infinite relativistic mass.

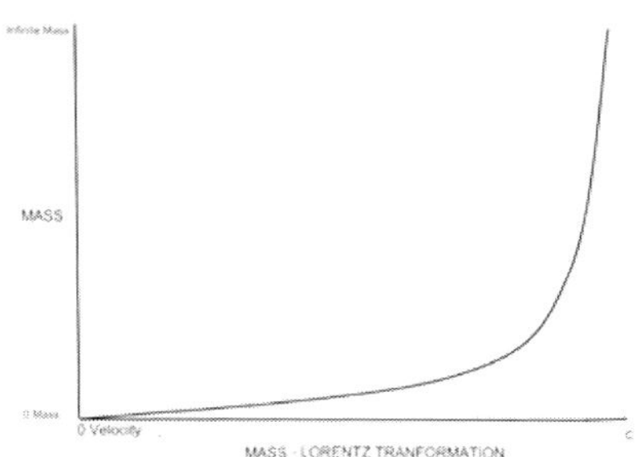

Figure 168. Mass vs Velocity

For future reference, the concept depicted by this graph will be defined as the **Lorentz Transformation Function [LTF]**. Again, the graph is skewed and only superficially similar to but, in fact not an exponential function, the latter of which doubles at a set constant rate.

Nevertheless, for the benefit of the novice and for simplicity of visualization, the author has decided to define/picture it this way. This is because in the author's opinion, the novice will understand exponential function better than Lorenz transformation function, even though exponential function is technically not correct. So for future reference, the letters **LTF** refers to the Lorentz Transformation Function concept including the LT curve as depicted in Figure 170.

For example, compared to an observer at rest with the PFSRT, an object at a high velocity relative to the PFSRT, exhibits increased inertial mass. In addition, as illustrated in the above graph, when the object's velocity increases linearly, again relative to the PFSRT, its inertial mass increases by an LTF. Additionally, the velocity of the object cannot exceed the speed of light as a consequence of infinite relativistic inertial mass. Notice regarding the new PFSRT all is not from the observer's reference frame [SRT], rather from the frame of the ether at rest [PFSRT].

This is *somewhat, and I emphasize somewhat*, analogous to a boat being propelled in water: the greater the velocity of the boat in the water, the more force needed to further increase its velocity (acceleration), in this case, as an exponential function. Nevertheless, there is a difference: water resists both the velocity and acceleration of the boat, whereas the ether only resists the acceleration of the object but not its velocity.

For review see Figure 169 below and the following caption.

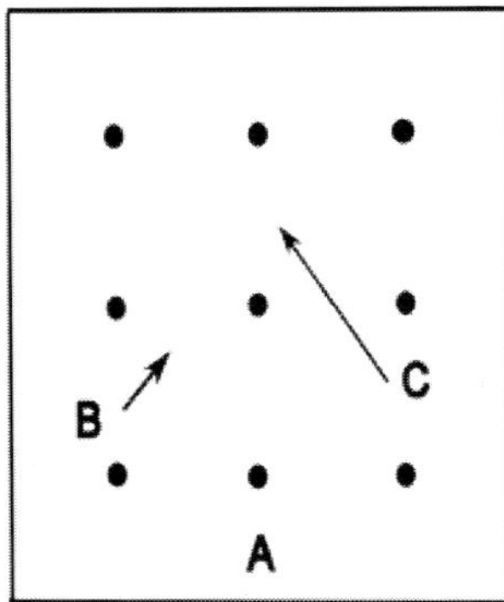

Figure 169. Rest Mass, Inertial Mass, and Relativistic Inertial Mass

- *Assume A, B, C are identical objects. The box represents the ether of the universe (PFSRT). The dots portray individual galaxies. The lengths of the arrows depict the relative velocities of objects B and C, (the longer the arrow the greater the velocity), whereas object A is at rest, all relative to the PFSRT. An object at rest with the PFSRT (A) resists acceleration derived from the ether. This is defined as the object's rest inertial mass.*
- *Alternatively, if an object (B or C) possesses a velocity (arrows) relative to the PFSRT (B < C), then, as its velocity increases linearly (C > B), the resistance to its acceleration increases by an LT function. This is defined as the object's relativistic inertial mass (B or C).*
- *Note again, the velocity of the object is limited by the speed of light.*

4. Assumption of the "Rate of Time"

What is time? Time, for Aristotle, is fundamentally linked to change and movement. "**Where there is alteration or movement, there is time, for everything that comes to be and ceases to be are in time.**"[8]

In essence, time is the motion of matter through space; the latter word defined within this article as the ether. You cannot describe time without motion, whether a clock, a pendulum, or an atomic clock (vibrations). In fact, all descriptions of time portray motion of matter through space, whether inertial or accelerated. Therefore, if the ether slows the acceleration of matter, then it also slows the ensuing velocities derived from those accelerations. Thus, it determines the overall rate of motion, within a given inertial reference frame, or in other words, the "rate of time". Fundamentally, "*time is just our counting of motion by comparing all motion to some repetitive motion, like the vibrating atoms of an atomic clock.*" (Lindner) So without motion, there is no time.

Note then, an atomic clock placed with B or C will have a slowing in the rate of its vibrating (acceleration) atoms compared to one positioned with A. This is because with respect to B and C, there is more resistance from the ether (C > B). In other words, from the perspective of A, the preferred frame, the atomic clocks placed with B or C, then will "tic" slower (C slower than B). This example illustrates the slowing in the "rate of time" from the frame of PFSRT.

As another example, assume you are absolutely alone in empty space (ether) where nothing else exists. One would assume that you would have the "notion of time" just by "thinking". But if all the chemical reactions (accelerations), as well as the vibrations (accelerations) of the atoms and molecules in your body slowed, including your brain molecules and chemical reactions, then all movement in your frame slows down, including you "rate of thinking". You would not perceive this effect, as you exist within this slowing frame. In contrast, someone else in a non-slowing frame, observing you, would notice it. In addition, if all motion in your inertial frame suddenly ceased, then for you, time stops. No motion. No time. For instance, regarding Hollywood science fiction movies, when time is portrayed to stop, then all motion stops.

Now, given all of the above, as shown in Figure 169, when B or C travels at a high velocity relative to the PFSRT, its relativistic mass increases, and its "rate of time" decreases. In addition, as the object's velocity increases linearly, the inertial mass increases by a LTF. And as the inverse, as the velocity increases linearly, because accelerations slow, the "rate of time" decreases (time dilation) by a LTF. This last conception is shown and described below in Figure 170 .

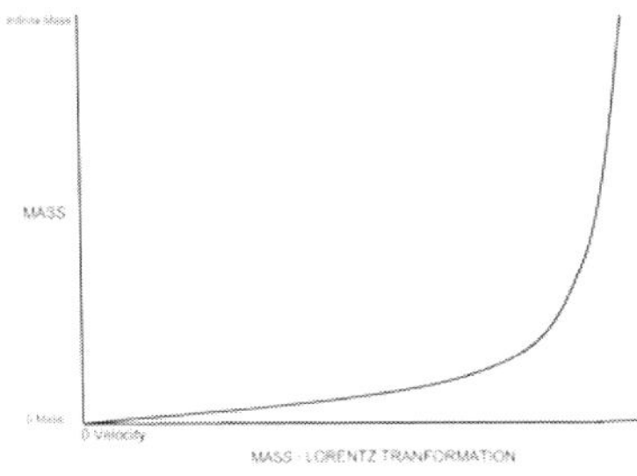

Figure 170. Rest Inertial Mass and Relativistic Inertial Mass

- *The horizontal axis represents the velocity of the object as a percentage of speed of light relative to the PFSRT.*

- *The Verticle axis depicts "time dialation"or the slowing in the "rate of time"as a function of velocity.*
- *This is a Lorentz Transformation curve, defined in this chapter as a LT function. However, in this instance, rather than relativistic inertial mass as just described, it is relavent to "time dialation"or "rate of time."*
- *Take note: the graph shown above is not really an exponetial curve, which doubles at a constant set rate. However, it is presented by the author in this way so that the average individual can easily visualize and understand the basic idea.*
- *It is not necessary for the novice to understand the Lorentz Transformation equation, but it is necessary for him/her to know the meaning of the graph.*

Take note; this inverse mathematical relationship occurs because both are a function of the increased resistance to matter's acceleration derived from the ether. Obviously then, they are intertwined by that ether. This is the visual reasoning for why inertial mass and the "rate of time" are always inversely proportional to one another.

Return to Figure 171 below.

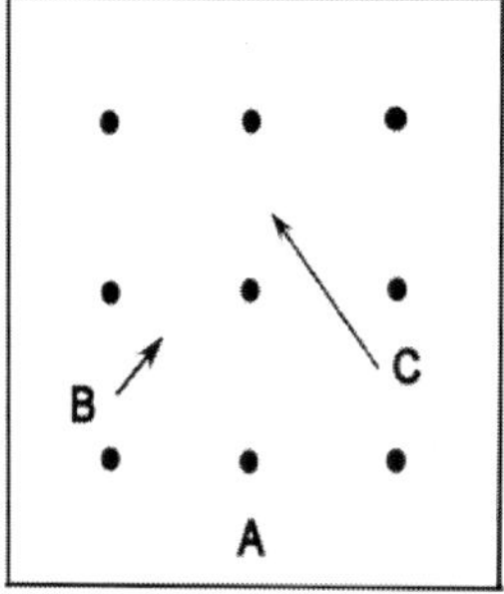

Figure 171. Rest Mass, Inertial Mass, and Relativistic Inertial Mass

For reinforcement compared to A located at rest with the PFSRT, both objects B and C possess increased relativistic inertial mass, [as a function of their velocity relative to the ether of PFSRT] moreover C > B (C velocity>B). Furthermore, our measuring sticks for evaluating time all involve repetitive motions, such as an atomic clock, and those repetitive motions are accelerations. Therefore, again, as a function of the ether, an atomic clock placed with object B/C will have increased resistance to the acceleration of its vibrating atoms; therefore, it slows down. For that reason, an observer placed at B/C will experience a slowing of all of his/her bodily chemical reactions including thinking. So compared to the frame of A (PFSRT), then B and C possess not only increased relativistic inertial masses but also a slowing of their "rates of time" in the mathematical LTF as just presented.

5. Assumption of the Perception of Distance and The Perception of the Velocity of Light as Function of the Observer's "Rate of Time"

Distance = rate x time. Essentially, distance is a direct function of time. Likewise, with reference to PFSRT, the rate of time is also assumed to be directly proportional to distance. Now, refer to Figure 172 below, moreover the following discussion.

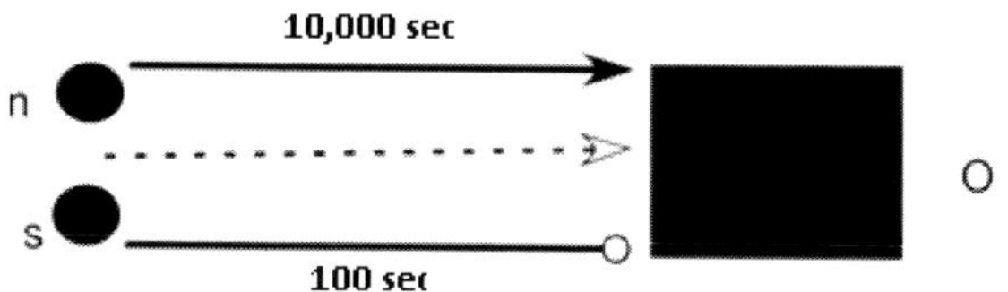

Figure 172. Two Astronauts, Different rates of time but with the same motion.

- *(Black box O) = object.*
- *(Upper black circle) = Astronaut (n), our local time frame.*
- *(Lower black circle) = astronaut (s) slow time frame compared to n.*
- *Time = solid lines labeled in seconds.*
- *Dotted line represents equal velocity of (n) and (s) towards O. Dotted line actually represents equal motion, since the concept of velocity has a component of time and [n] and [s] have different "rates of time". Essentially, the term motion has no time element.*
- *One-way of perceiving this concept of equal motion is this: The same velocity from the frame of [n], but [s] exists in a slower time frame. Therefore D = r x t or the idea of velocity [v = d/t] does not adequately define this example.*

In order to give explanation to this concept, imagine two astronauts, named (n) and the other (s), located side by side, moreover, at rest within the assumed ether of the universe (PFSRT). In addition, envision an object (o) positioned at a given interval of the ether from (n) and (s), moreover, also at rest with the PFSRT. Furthermore, visualize there are no other objects in this hypothetical universe.

Assume astronaut (n) exists in our local time frame. In contrast, compared to ours, the time frame of (s) is extremely slow. Subsequently, presume they both move towards object o (black square = o) at precisely the same velocity, actually motion (single dotted line). Both astronauts count seconds. Now n counts 10,000 seconds before he/she arrives at o.

Alternatively, s counts only 100 seconds before arrival, since he/she exists in a slower time frame compared to n. So from the perspective of n, he/she assumes a long distance to the object, because it took a considerable length of time to get there – 10,000 seconds. In contrast, s presumes a short distance to the object, since he/she got there right away – 100 seconds. In other words, the definition of distance in this instance is the time interval between two events or the **perception** of the amount of space between two objects [in this case the starting point and object o].

In this example, **time** is directly proportional to **perceived distance through space (ether), moreover, in the direction of motion.** As a result, they are intertwined with one another, defined within this paper as **space-time.**

This distance concept is exceedingly abstract, therefore, confusing. In addition, in the author's opinion, the classic equation of D = r x t and the idea of velocity [v = distance/time] cannot adequately define/describe this concept.

For instance, relevant to our own local rate of time reference frame, everything is logical, moreover, makes common sense [D = r x t] [v = d/t]. Alternatively, for an observer existing within a reference frame of a different "rate of time," when comparing the two different frames, it becomes confusing since for both scenarios, the two equations listed above, involve the mathematical symbol t [**time**]. Essentially, if an observer's "time frame changes," then between those two frames, his/her perception of D and v also change. For this reason, relative to the observer, when equating different "frames of time," by using [D = r x t] [v = d/t], the explanations are not only very difficult to describe, but perplexing. The author finds it very challenging to define this complex and abstract topic.

Therefore, this distance concept will now be re-explained from multiple different perspectives or reference frames, moreover, mainly involving mental imagery. However, before proceeding, take note that the velocity of light of c is a function of distance and time [C = d/**time**]. So an apples-to-apples comparison for the definition of distance should also be a function of motion through space/ether, again, a function of time [D = r x **time**].

1. Regarding astronomy, recall the distance to the stars is measured in light years. Distance = (speed of light, c) x (light years, which is a function time). Or speed [velocity c] = distance/time. So, if the observer's "rate of time" affects the *perceived* distance to a star through space/ether in the direction of motion (object in Figure 172). And, more importantly, if they are directly proportional to one another [t/d], then the speed [velocity] of light remains at a constant c for all inertial observers. This concept is abstract but will be clarified in the following passages.

2. Take note, the above concept depends upon the definition of rate of time as just elucidated [Section 4] and how that time frame relates to an observer's *perceived* distance through space in the direction of motion [Section 5] vis-a-vis *specifically* the *speed/velocity* of light. So as a consequence, then, with reference to all inertial motion, producing a constant value of c for all observers, irrespective of their different time frames, which is one of the two basic assumptions of Einstein's SRT, but now a function of the ether not the observer [See examples below].

3. For instance, assume an individual on Earth is observing reflected sunlight from Jupiter. That light is traveling towards that person at a velocity of 186,000 MPS, through a given distance x. Now, if the observer's rate of time slows down by one-half and if nothing else changes, the light is then traveling towards him/her at [186,000 x 2] MPS. But that observer's perception of the traveling distance to Jupiter is cut by one-half as well, since at the same given motion it only takes one-half the time to get there from Earth [D = r x t]. Taking into account both of these factors, then no matter what the observer's rate of time, the perceived velocity of light through space/ether, specifically in the direction of motion, remains at c. So relative to the later example [186,000 x 2] MPS x [one half the distance] = 186,000 MPS.

Notice, regarding this example, it is fairly easy to envision from the observer's reference frame, the first part, as to how his/her "time rate" relates to his/her *perception* of the velocity of light through space as just described.

- C = d/[rate of time] So if the time frame of the observer slows, then, for him/her, the velocity of light increases. This is an inverse proportional function. However, it is more difficult to imagine the second part, as to how the observer's time rate: effects his/her *perception* of distance through space in the direction of motion. Nevertheless, both are function of the observer's "rate of time".
- D = c x [rate of time]. So if the time frame of the observer slows, then for him/her, distance decreases. This is a direct proportional function.

Observe the two perceptions depicted above [direct/inverse] counteract one another. So, *for the observer*, the speed of light remains constant at c.

The author again denotes that the mathematical equations of D = r x t and velocity = d/t cannot be readily applied to give explanation to this hypothesis. In essence, the math used and the definitions of the words [e.g., velocity and distance] do not adequately define this abstract conception.

4. With respect to this theory, distance as measured by a physical ruler, now defined as a measuring stick distance, is a different concept compared to distance as a perception of movement through space [ether] which involves the "rate of time" [D = r x t]. Let's call this latter concept the motion distance.

For example, assume an object emits light directly towards an observer on Earth, moreover, is located 300,000,000 [x] distance away from Earth as physically measured by a given length of matter [x] – a measuring stick distance. This definition of distance does not involve the rate of time.

Scenario 1: Now if the light travels through this given measuring stick distance [space/ether] in one second, its velocity with respect to that observer is then 300,000,000 [x] per second. Furthermore, if the same observer moves from Earth towards that object at 1 [x] per second, it will then take a person 300,000,000 seconds to get there [D = r x t].

Scenario 2: Now if the observer's rate of time slows by one-half, the light then travels that same measuring stick distance in one-half second or 600,000,000 [x] per second. Additionally, if that observer travels to that object with the same motion as compared to Scenario 1, then he/she will be moving towards that object at 2]x] per second; moreover, it takes 150,000,000 seconds to get there. Furthermore, he/she will perceive the distance to that object as one-half the distance compared to Scenario 1 [D = r x t] for the same observer with different rates of time.

Scenario 1: [300,000,000 [x] per second] equated to [1 [x] per second].

Scenario 2: [300,000,000 [x] per half-second] equated to [1 [x] per half-second] .

Pertaining to the reference frame of Scenario 2, as above, for both the light and the traveling observer, then per unit of time of 1 second, they move at twice the physical measuring stick distance when compared to Scenario 1. Take note, the ratio remains constant. So, if the ratio remains constant, then from the observer's reference frame the *perception* of the velocity of light remains unchanged for both scenarios 1 and 2.

In other words, relative to this example, the perception of the velocity of the light and the perception of the motion distance are both a function of the observer's rate of time. Furthermore, they are proportional [direct and inverse] to one another, moreover, counteract one another. As a result, the velocity of light remains constant for both scenarios 1 and 2 – in this example, 300,000,000 [x] per second. The author once again denotes that the mathematical equations of D = r x t and velocity = d/t cannot be readily applied to explain this concept.

5. So distance as calculated by a physical measuring stick is a different concept when compared to the **perception** of distance as a function of motion [time] through space/ether [D = r x t]. Observe the latter concept involves the rate of time, whereas the first concept does not.

6. The measuring stick distance is the absolute frame. But the motion distance [D = r x t] is a function of the observer's "rate of time" while moving through that absolute frame. Now, in our local rate of time reference frame the two different distance concepts are mathematically equal to each other [defined that way]. On the other hand, with reference to a traveling observer with a different time frame compared to ours, they are unequal/different.

7. In other words, from our own perspective [observer at rest with the PFSRT] both the velocity of light and the motion distance are an effect of our own local "time frame." This is due to the fact that the concepts of both motion distance and the perception of velocity are a function of the observer's [our] "reference frame of time" [D = r x t] [V = d/t].

In addition, the classic interconnection between the motion distance and the measuring stick distance is also defined within our own [observer's] "time frame" [PFSRT].

For reinforcement, both light and the observer's movements are in fact motion through the *measuring stick distance*. However, only in conjunction with an observer's rate of time reference frame is there, in that setting, his/her perception of the concept of velocity and the idea of *motion* distance. This is because *relative to the observer*, both of these concepts involve his/her rate of time V = D/[rate of time] and D= [V] x [rate of time].

So the same observer in inertial motion, instantaneously transferring from one time frame into another, then perceives both the movement of light and the *motion* distance as different [changed]. In addition, for that observer those two changing perceptions counteract one another in such a way that the velocity of light remains at c. Yet again, the author denotes that the mathematical equations of D = r x t and velocity = d/t cannot be readily applied to explain this concept.

Once more; relevant to the PFSRT, both light and the observer possess movement through the measuring stick distance, but the perception of velocity and the perception of *motion* distance are a function of the observer's time frame. In addition, in the scenario whereby the observer changes his/her rate of time [increased/decreased velocity relative to the PFSRT], then the new altered perception of velocity and the new altered perception of motion distance always counteract one another, so, *for that observer* maintaining the perceived velocity of light as c..

8. For the reader, here is a key query: regarding the equations of Einstein's SRT, is the *mathematical* distance symbol used equivalent to the motion distance, the measuring stick distance or both? In the author's opinion, Einstein incorrectly intermingled the two distinct concepts/definitions.

Now, referring back to our "n" and "s" astronaut example. When n and s travel to object o, both travel through the same measuring stick distance, moreover, with identical motion. However, n and s possess different rates of time. Their **perception** of that same measuring stick distance then differs. So s perceives a shorter motion distance than n. Nevertheless, the physical measuring stick length/distance relevant to the astronaut's physical bodies [n and s] remains constant, independent of their individual rates of time.

In summary, only the **perception** of distance [the motion distance] changes as a function of the astronauts differing rates of time. In contrast, given the same scenario, the measuring stick length/distance of their physical bodies in the direction of motion does not change/contract.

What is more, if object o admits light, at a given frequency, then s perceives a shorter wavelength compared to n, because the number of light waves observed per second by (s) > (n). In other words, each of the astronauts observes the exact same total number of light waves, but s observes more per second than n, because for s, the "time frame" is slower.

PFSRT differs considerably compared to the above example, wherein both astronauts possess equal velocities [motion], although different time rates. That example was only used to simplify how the rate of time correlates to motion distance through space (space-time).

In contrast with reference to PFSRT, given that both B and C possess different velocities relative to the PF-SRT, they then possess different relativistic inertial masses [C>B], moreover different rates of time [C slower than B]; thus different perceptions of motion distance [C distance < than B], all as a function of their different velocities with respect to the ether (PFSRT).

In summary and for reinforcement once again, please refer to Figure 173 below and the following captions and paragraphs.

So given the existence of the ether (box), now shift the focus away from observer A to observers B and C (refer to repeat Figure 173 below).

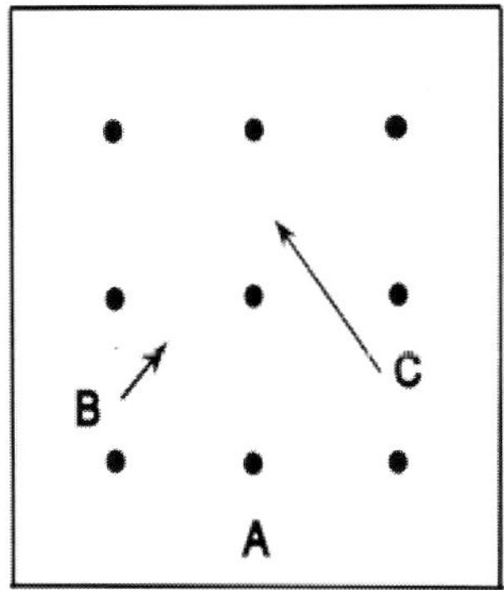

Figure 173. Rest Mass, Inertial Mass, and Relativistic Inertial Mass

- *Recall, B/C have increased velocity relative to the ether of PFSRT (C velocity > B = length of arrows); therefore increased relativistic mass (C > B), what's more, a slowing in the "rate of time"(C "time frame" slower than B).*

Therefore, from the reference frames of B or C, **which is from the reference frame of a velocity relative to the ether (PFSRT), moreover, not the observer**, the perceived motion distance to any given object at rest with the PFSRT is directly proportional to their respective rates of time (C motion distance < B).

So, as a result of this proportional inter-relationship, [t/d] then for all observers, regarding all inertial frames, notwithstanding of their different rates of time, the velocity of light remains at c. This is a function of v [c] = d/t and if t/d remains proportional, then c is constant.

In addition, assuming that the PFSRT is the preferred frame for light, then for C and B as the perceived motion distance to any object decreases (C < B), relative to A, then the observed wavelength of light emitted from that object to C and B also decreases proportionally (C wavelength <B wavelength < A).

In summary, here is a crucial concept, for all inertial observers, irrespective of their different rates of time, the speed of light remains at c, and the laws of physics are identical within all inertial reference frames, just like Einstein's SRT –except now, as a function of THE ETHER.

Take notice, a major distinction between the two theories [SRT, PFSRT] is that regarding SRT, by definition, the main focus is the assumption that the velocity of light is c relative to the observer. Whereas, with PFSRT, the key concept is the observer's rate of time as a function of his/her velocity with respect to the ETHER of PFSRT, which in turn again produces c relative to the observer. See Figure 174 below for a summary.

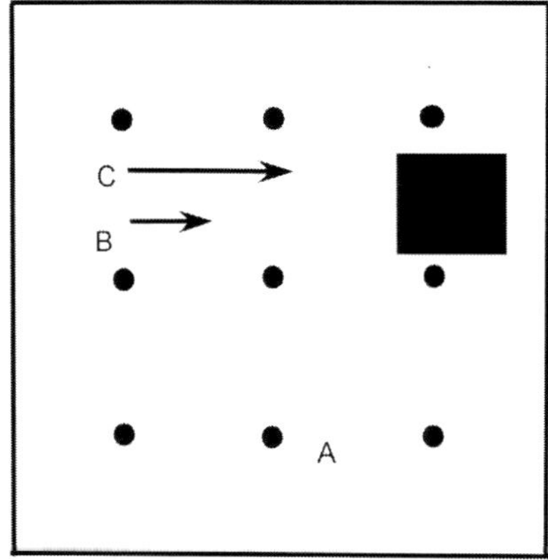

Figure 174. Summary

- *Length of arrows depicts velocity relative to the ether of PFSRT.*
- *Black box = an object at rest with the ether.*
- *B and C both exist at a high velocity relative to the PFSRT, with C > B.*
- *Given the new model, then B and C, as a function of the ether, also possess higher relativistic inertial masses (C > B) compared to the rest mass of A.*
- *In addition, B and C, again as a function of the ether. manifest a slower "rate of time"(C slower than B) compared to A.*
- *Given that the rate of time and motion distance are directly proportional (D = r x t), then for any single given object in the universe (black box), B and C then perceive less motion distance (C <B) compared to A.*
- *Furthermore, the observed wavelength of light from an object (black box) can change for (A, B, C).*
- *However, because the rate of time and motion distance are directly proportional, [t/d] the velocity of light remains a constant c for all inertial observers (A, B, C), irrespective of their different rates of time, and the laws of physics remain the same within all inertial reference frames (A, B, C).*
- *This new model (PFSRT) demonstrates most of the outcomes of Einstein's SRT; however, now there is the ether.*

- *In the author's opinion, there must be some sort of mathematical constant [like the gravitational constant G] related to the perceived motion of light through the PFSRT as a function of the observer's rate of time frame, thus producing a constant velocity of c for that observer, regardless of his/her time frame.*
- *This mathematical constant should involve c but also the observer's rate of time.*
- *This is the reason why whenever two atomic clocks are utilized to calculate the velocity of light on the surface of the Earth, the perceived result is always c. See Appendix 11 for a full explanation.*

6. Visualizing SRT vs. PFSRT

See Figure 175 below. SRT's four–dimensional space-time is a mathematical construct; therefore, one cannot readily visualize it with reference to three-dimensional space. Alternatively, using PFSRT, it is comparatively easy to do so. For instance, picture in your mind a cube with the inner part representing all of space/ether/universe/PFSRT. For purposes of this illustration, this cube represents the three-dimensions of the universe [PFSRT], but in the real universe without walls.

Fundamentally in the real universe, the dimensions are up-down, left-right, and forward-backward. Next, imagine an observer possessing a velocity relative to and within the cube depicted by the arrow. Recall the faster his/her velocity, the slower the observer's rate of time In other words, the velocity of the observer determines his/her "reference frame of time." So the arrow then represents the temporal fourth dimension [time].

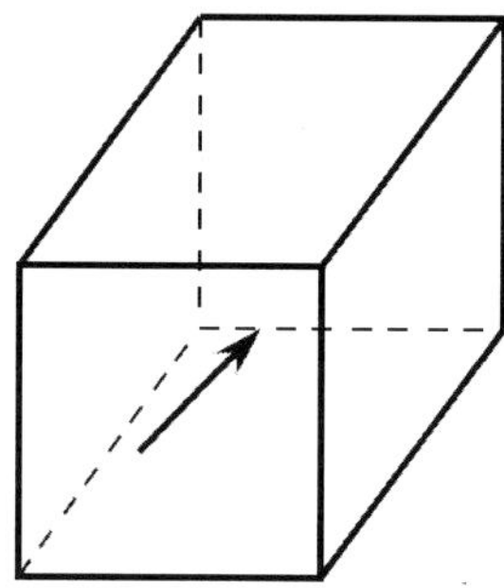

Figure 175. Three Dimensional Space and Time

- *The cube has three dimensions. The arrow is the fourth dimension.*

Now with reference Einstein's SRT, is the fourth dimension mathematically perpendicular/ orthogonal to the other three dimensions as shown above? That is the mathematics of SRT.

Depicted in Figure 176 is another 3-D presentation of 4-D space-time as downloaded from the Internet.

- *"Einstein's theory of special relativity postulates that space and time are related to each other in forming a space–time continuum of three spatial dimensions and one temporal dimension. While it is possible to visualize space-time simply by treating time as "time"and examining "snapshots"."*[12]

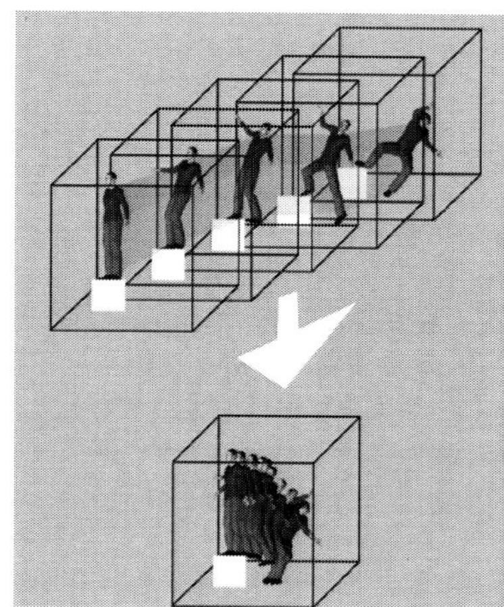

Figure 176. Einstein's Snapshot

Observe: the series of snapshots in Figure 176 is analogous to the arrow in Figure 175.

7. The Real Universe

Please, now refer to Figure 177 below and the following discussion. However, all is not that simple. The cosmic microwave background radiation (CWBR) observed from Earth has an anisotropy of approximately 378 km/sec in the direction of the constellation Leo.

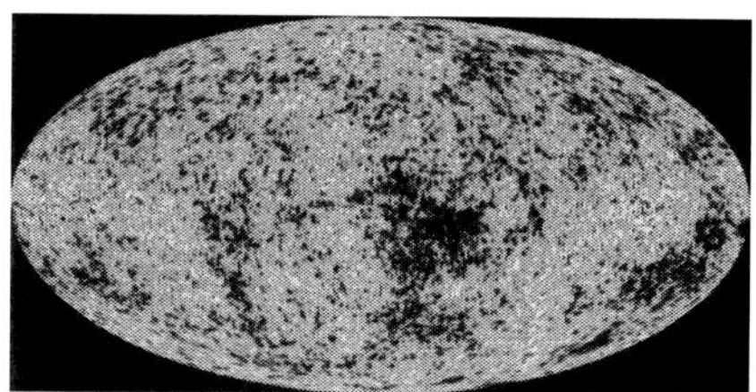

Figure 177. Cosmic Microwave Background

- *This image shows the Cosmic Microwave Background Radiation [9], which is almost, although not completely, uniform. The difference in color is equal to about 1 in 100,000.This radiation is at rest with the PFSRT.* [9]

This radiation permeates uniformly all of the ether (PF-SRT), or in classic terminology, all of the space of the universe. In addition, it is assumed to be at rest with respect to the PFSRT. Furthermore, it expands symmetrically along with the expansion of the universe (ether). Nonetheless, there are some minimal fluctuations; although they are evenly distributed as portrayed in Figure 177 by the different colors/shades.

Now, please refer to Figure 178 below and the following discussion.

Therefore, the redshift of the CWBR, as observed from Earth, represents our velocity relative to the PFSRT. This is due to the fact that the CWBR is at rest with the PFSRT. This observed redshift from Earth is the summation of the velocity of the galaxy, velocity of sun around the galaxy, and the velocity of the Earth around the sun, all relative to the PFSRT (Figure 178). Recall again, this chapter ignores gravitational fields, which will be discussed in Chapter 2.

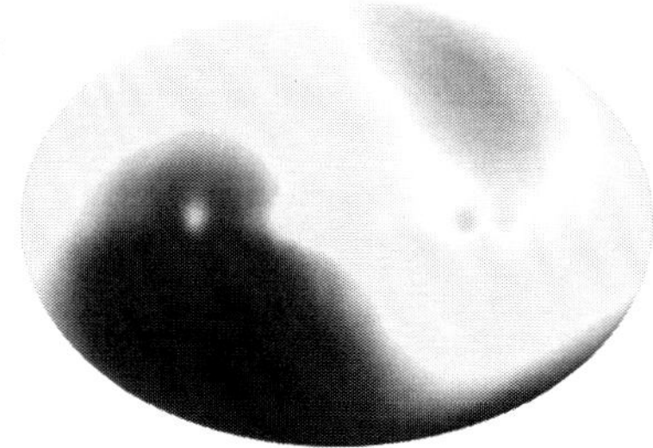

Figure 178. Red and Blue Shift

- *The Earth has a velocity of 378 km/sec relative to the cosmic microwave wave background radiation (PF-SRT). This is represented by redshift in one direction (Right) and a blueshift in the opposite direction (Left) as depicted above.* [10]

What this signifies is that we on Earth are not absolutely at rest with the PFSRT. It means we possess a velocity of 378 km/sec. relative to the PFSRT. This is extremely slow compared to the speed of light, nevertheless not zero. Additionally, it is also presumed that the majority of the galaxies, although not all, have a fairly low velocity with respect to the PFSRT. So they, as we, are almost at rest with the PFSRT.

Summary

To recap, in the actual universe, an observer (A, B, C) is either at rest or else at a velocity relative to the PFSRT. As such, each observer (object) is associated with a specific inertial mass and a given rate of time, both as a function of his/her velocity with respect to the PFSRT.

In addition, his/her perception of the motion distance to any given point in the universe is dependent upon his/her "time frame". Furthermore, for all observers, no matter what their velocity relative to the PFSRT, they still perceive the speed of light as c.

What is more, the observed wavelength of the light emitted from any object in the universe is a function of the observer's velocity (rate of time) relative to the PFSRT, the objects velocity (rate of time) relative to the PFSRT, the intrinsic wavelength of emitted light from the object, **and finally, the relative velocities of the observer and object with respect to each other**.

As for the later (in bold letters), this explains why light emitted from an object traveling towards the observer is blueshifted, whereas light from an object traveling away appears red shifted. This is defined as the Classic Longitudinal Doppler effect.

This is analogous to the sound emitted from a truck that approaches you, passes, and then recedes from you. The pitch of the sound drops as it passes you by. The higher-pitch sounds represent sound waves piling up as it approaches you (blue shift). And the lower pitch represents sound waves stretching out (red shift) as the truck passes and subsequently recedes from you. To most individuals with a minimal scientific background, it is obvious that there is a preferred frame for sound, which in this case, is the atmosphere.

Likewise, considering this new theory (PFSRT), the exact same function occurs but this time regarding light, with a **preferred frame of the ether**. What is interesting is this: In the past, this analogous relationship and connection was far easier for the non-physicist to assume, since he/she did not understand SRT. As for the physicist, the similarity was clear but obscured by the complexities and mathematics of SRT. Therefore, this obvious interconnection was then ignored.

8. SRT vs. PFSRT

1. SRT assumes that all inertial motion is relative to the observer.

PFSRT presumes all inertial motion is relative to the PFSRT.

2. SRT assumes, that relative to the observer, as the velocity of an object increases linearly, its inertial mass increases by an LT function. In addition, relative to the observer, the velocity of the object cannot exceed c.

PFSRT presumes that relative to the PFSRT as velocity of an object increases linearly, its inertial mass increases by an LT function. Furthermore, relative to the PFSRT, the velocity of the object cannot exceed c.

3. SRT assumes, that relative to the observer as the velocity of an object increases linearly, its "rate of time" decreases by a LT function.

PFSRT presumes that relative to the PFSRT as velocity of an object increases linearly its "rate of time"decreases by a LT function.

4. SRT assumes that relative to the observer, as an object approaches the speed of light, distance in the direction of motion, including physical length contraction of matter, decreases, (see Figure 179 below).

- *The illustration shows that relative to the observer, as an object approaches the speed of light, its physical length contracts.* [13]

PFSRT presumes that **only the perception of motion distance through space (ether) in the direction of motion** decreases as the observer's velocity increases relative to the PFSRT. It does not posit physical length contraction of matter in the direction of motion.

5. SRT assumes the speed of light is c relative to only the observer. In addition, it also presumes there is no preferred frame; thus all motion is relative. PFSRT presumes there is a preferred frame of the ether, wherein the speed of light

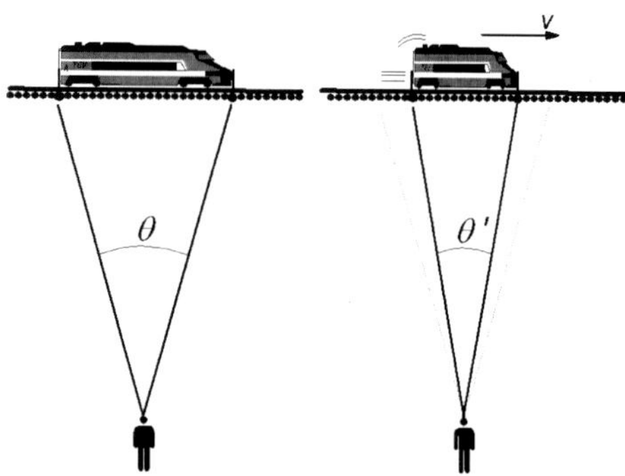

Figure 179. Length Contraction with Two Trains

travels at c. Even so, for all observers, no matter what their velocity relative to the PFSRT, they still perceive the speed of light as c.

6. SRT assumes the laws of physics are the same within all inertial reference frames. PFSRT also presumes the laws of physics are the same in all inertial reference frames.

9. Resolution of The Paradoxes and Inconsistencies Associated with SRT

SRT–the twin paradox problem.

Einstein's SRT assumes all inertial motion is relative. For example, imagine two astronauts (A and B) traveling in the far regions of outer space where nothing else exists, moreover, in opposite directions with respect to one another. Therefore, assuming SRT is correct, if astronaut A travels at .5c relative to stationary astronaut B, then this is no different compared to if astronaut A is stationary and B is traveling in the opposing direction, again at .5c.

Now given the postulates of SRT, furthermore, as these astronauts pass by each other, with respect to their different inertial frames, then A observes B as having increased inertial mass and a slowing in the "rate of time" and B vice versa. This is nonsensical, for by logic, both scenarios cannot be correct. In contrast with reference to PFSRT, there is no twin paradox conundrum, because there is a preferred frame–The ETHER.

Now, regarding the resolution of twin paradox problem, the author does not concur with the classical SRT explanation given by physicists, whereby acceleration and a gravitational field are evoked. In the author's opinion, since SRT involves only inertial motion, then the answer to the paradox cannot be a function gravity or acceleration, which is what physicists attempt to do, en erratum.

This new non-classical portrayal of twin paradox problem offered by the author better illustrates the conundrum, furthermore, devoid a solution relevant to the assumptions of SRT. But it can be explained with the presumption of an ether [PFSRT]; the preferred frame.

SRT–the simultaneity problem. [14]

"*In special relativity the relativity of simultaneity is explained with the following example. We have one frame of reference, a train moving from left to right with constant speed v relatively to the embankment, and second frame of reference, the embankment itself. On the embankment, there are points A and B and their midpoint M. On the train, there is the point M's. When M and M's meet each other, two lightning strike both A and B. The observer on the embankment sees that the two flashes of light meet at the midpoint M. But since the train is moving and the point M's with it, M's moves towards B and therefore, the observer on the train will see that the beam from B will arrive first at point M's and after that will arrive the beam from A. And so simultaneity is relative – for one observer the two events are simultaneous, but for the other, they are not.*"

So as presented above, referring to various diverse inertial frames, the perceived timing of events is different. On the other hand, if there is a preferred frame (not the observer), with an ether wind, then the above classic example can be explained by another methodology.

For instance, in the scenario where there is a relative ether wind with respect to the Earth Centered Frame (ECF)/Earth's gravitational field (EGF)/ether, then as a result, neither M or M' receive the flashes simultaneously. This is because M and the two lightning bolts possess the same velocity relative to the (ECF/EGF/ETHER) as a consequence of all three rotating synchronously along with the spinning Earth at its surface. This is assuming the train is traveling west-east and the flashes of lightning are in front of and behind the train, then it takes light longer to travel west-east compared to east-west.

On the other hand, M' possesses a different velocity with respect to the (ECF/EGF/ETHER) given the fact that while riding on the train M' is then traveling at a greater velocity with respect to the rotating surface of the Earth. As a result, M' velocity relative to the (ECF/EGF/ETHER) is greater than M. Therefore, the time interval of the asynchrony of the observed lightning bolts is greater for M' compared to M.

This alternative explanation of simultaneity as a function of the relative ether wind will be much clearer after reading chapters 2 and 3 of this article (GRT) and referred to again at that time.

As with all theories, given sufficient time, Einstein's relativity will eventually be overturned. And when it is, the whole world will then wonder why these inconsistencies were ignored; nevertheless the theory is still accepted, without question, as absolute gospel truth.

Notice, all the inconsistencies of Einstein's SRT vanish if its assumptions are modified with PFSRT. This modification includes a single preferred frame for the speed of light, motion of objects, rest inertial mass, the "rate of time,"and finally, the perception of motion distance, other than from the frame of the observer.

10. Lorentz Theory

Lorentz posited a theory with a stationary luminescent ether, somewhat similar to PFSRT with c relative to that ether and **physical** length contraction of objects (matter) in the direction of motion. In addition, this contraction is postulated to be a function of an object's velocity relative to a preferred frame [ether], and not with respect to the observer. (Figure 180 below). [15]

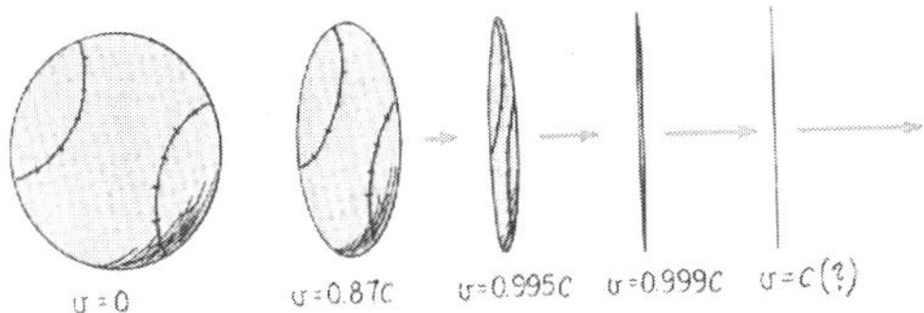

Figure 180. Length Contraction, Different Speeds

- *Relative to the preferred frame of the ether, as an object approaches the speed of light, its physical length contracts.*

However Lorentz's length contraction of actual physical objects has never been experimentally observed so remains unproven. In contrast, PFSRT presumes perceived distance through space in the direction of motion decreases as an effect of the observer's "rate of time" which in turn, is a function of the observer's velocity relative to a preferred frame (PFSRT). The key point is perceived motion distance through space, not physical length contraction of objects [measuring stick distance] in the direction of motion. PFSRT is more intuitive and logical, in essence, more consistent with common–sense reality. So given SRT, Lorentz Theory, and PFSRT, which theory is more compatible with reality and Occam's razor?

11. Conclusion

As stated in the preface, in essence, this new visual theory (PFSRT) combines Galilean transformation theory and Newton's theories (three-dimensional space) with Maxwell's EM theory (velocity of light of c relative to the observer) without altering any of them, but now from the rest frame ether of (PFSRT) not the observer.

In other words, Einstein's synthesis had to choose between Maxwell vs. Newton and Galileo. He either had to modify Maxwell's theory to make it compatible with the Newton and Galileo theories or vice versa. He chose the latter. Take note, this new theory (PFSRT) accomplishes almost the same outcome as SRT, but now from the frame of the ether rather than the observer, furthermore, visually, not mathematically.

Conceiving all this from a different point of view, then on one hand, regarding Einstein's SRT by definition c is relative to the only the observer. As such, the focus is on c, and all else [time and distance] revolves around this basic assumption, moreover, by using purely mathematical means.

On the other hand, vis–a–vis the new PFSRT, the crucial concept is the observer's velocity relative to the physical ether of PFSRT. In other words, there exists a preferred frame [PFSRT], but regarding that frame, both the *perception* of motion distance and the *perception* of the velocity of light are an effect the observer's time frame, which in and of itself, is a function of his/her velocity relative to the PFSRT. And as previously explained, if the observer's rate of time and his/her perceived motion distance are directly proportional to one another, then the velocity of light always remains at c for all inertial observers [d/t = c] irrespective of the observer's time frame.

In addition, assuming PFSRT is apropos, then, the observer's rate of time [velocity relative to the PFSRT] *proportionally* and equally effects the *perceived* laws of physics, again pertaining to all inertial frames. Thus, regarding PFSRT, as with SRT, the laws of physics are the same in all those frames.

Now, here is the critical difference: With SRT, c is relative to the observer, but with PFSRT, all is ultimately a function of the Ether.

So referring back to the excerpt from Appendix 1, as presented at the onset of this chapter, both Amber and you perceive the velocity of light as c. Recall, regarding that illustration, the definition of c, as well as the concept of distance, are both a function of time.

Therefore, as opposed to that SRT example where the assumption of c, from the observer's frame, determines time and distance [c = d/t], but only as a mathematical function; what is more, with no corporal attribute as for why, PFSRT alternatively posits this interconnection is a product of a true three-dimensional physical ether [PFSRT]; moreover, not just a mathematical equation.

CHAPTER 2 – GRT/PFGRT

Chapter 2 is not included in this paper

CHAPTER 3 – THE MICHELSON MORLEY EXPERIMENT (MMX) AND OTHER SPEED OF LIGHT EXPERIMENTS

Abstract

This is the third chapter of the article titled The Ether. The intent of the article is to revise the assumptions associated with Einstein's relativity theories, thereby postulating an alternate theory, somewhat analogous to Einstein's concepts, however, now compatible with the existence of the ether. As a result, relativity, and quantum mechanics, rather than being disconnected, are then a part of one overall unified theory.

This is the most important chapter of this article for it demonstrates that the local preferred frame for the speed of light on Earth is its own gravitational field/Earth Centered Inertial Frame/Inflow of Ether. Additionally, it gives explanation as to why the Michelson Morley Experiment (MMX), as well as other experiments, is silent as to whether or not the ether exists. Given this presupposition, the other four chapters in this article then have meaning, and moreover, merit.

12. Introduction

Chapter 3 is the quintessential subject matter of this entire paper, for everything else in this entire article depends upon what is presented in this chapter. That is, proof of the existence of the ether. Many former scientist (Maxwell and Tesla), as well as more contemporary physicists/individuals (Ives, Lindner, and Stillwell), believed or still believe in the ether. Even so, due to the fact that the vast majority of modern-day physicists presuppose there is no ether, their ideas have been ignored or alternatively dismissed.

For that reason, the primary objective of this chapter is to demonstrate that there is, in fact, an ether. So assuming it exists, all of physics including relativity and QM must then be reassessed, furthermore, rewritten, based upon THE ETHER. In addition, presuming its existence, the other chapters in this article have meaning, and moreover, merit.

In this chapter, all theories are based on the assumption that the Earth-Centered Non-rotating Inertial Frame/gravitational field/ inflow of space is the local preferred frame for the speed of light on Earth. Everything else depicted in this chapter derives from this basic assumption. Keep in mind that all three terms are synonymous. Additionally, it should be noted that the term "Inflow of Space"(ether) as defined in Chapter 2 is new and not generally accepted by mainstream physics.

Therefore, for ease of understanding, generally, although within this chapter not exclusively, I will use the phrase "Earth-Centered Non-Rotating Inertial Frame" (ECF) or else the Earth's Gravitational Field (EGF).

Numerous small linear speed-of-light experiments, when performed on the Earth's rotating surface, have demonstrated only isotropy. The most well-known is the MMX. Einstein eventually used its null result as the main foundation block for validating his relativity theories.

Given that, if it can be demonstrated that even in the presence of an ether wind, the MMX still produces the same null outcome; then it is silent as to whether or not it exists. As a result, relativity collapses.

Presented below are five observations and/or experiments that *together* demonstrate or, perhaps, even prove, that the ECF/EGF is the local preferred frame for the speed-of-light/"rate of time" on Earth. First, read and comprehend them. Then, in conjunction with what is assumed to be the overlooked physics of the MMX, they will be used to reveal the reason for why all second-order speed of light experiments of this type, when performed on the rotating surface of the Earth, exhibit isotropy. In other words, what Chapter 3 will establish is that, even though the ether wind exists, these kinds of small linear experiments are all inherently incapable of detecting it.

The five observations and/or experiments are listed below.

- 1. The Pendulum
- 2. Aberration
- 3. West-East, East-West satellite transmission
- 4. Hafele and Keating
- 5. GPS system

One

As previously described in Chapter 2, a pendulum placed in motion at either of the Earth's poles is perceived by the observer to rotate (precess), 360 degrees every 24 hours. Alternatively, a pendulum sited at the equator does not rotate at all. However, at the poles, it is not the pendulum that is rotating, rather it is the observer. What does this signify? It indicates the (EGF, ECF) does not rotate along with the Earth's axial spin. Essentially, this function is the product of the conservation of momentum within a non-rotating gravitational field. The non-rotating gravitational field also explains the Coriolis effect, for if the gravitational field rotated along with the Earth axial spin, then weather patterns, as observed, would not occur.

Two

See Figure 181 below. There is a phenomenon known as stellar aberration. So what is aberration? Here is an example. Assume that raindrops fall directly straight down to the Earth's surface. Therefore, relative to this frame, if you are located within a stationary car, then from your viewpoint, the rain appears to drop perpendicular to Earth's surface.

On the other hand, if the car possesses a transverse velocity, then from your perspective, the rain appears slanted towards the motion of the car. In addition, with respect to the ground, if you have no visual reference frame, and if you cannot feel acceleration, then as you move from stationary to a velocity, rather than you, the position/angle of the rain appears to change.

What this indicates is that there is a fixed frame for the rain (preferred frame) In this case, it is the atmosphere, whereby rain falls directly straight down to Earth, as depicted below on Figure 181.

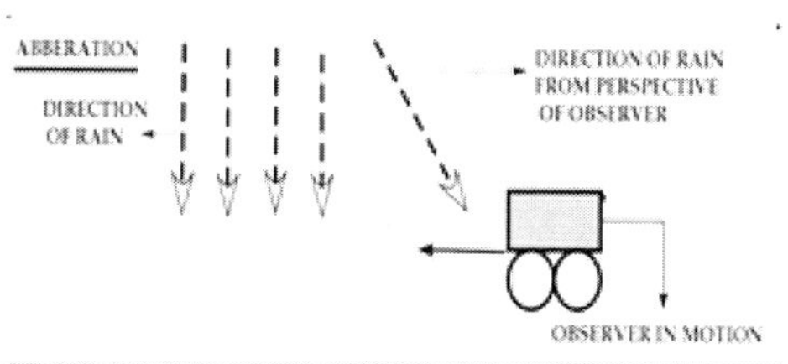

Figure 181. Aberration of Rain

- *Again, if rain falls straight down perpendicular to the Earth's surface, and if the observer within the car possesses a transverse velocity relative to the rain, then from the perspective of the observer, the rain appears slanted towards the motion of the car. This is aberration. It indicates there is a preferred frame for the rain, in this case, the atmosphere.*

Similarly, the identical phenomenon is observed with respect to starlight, called stellar aberration, as explained in the following quote.

"*If you watch the stars (using the necessary equipment) over the course of a year, you'll note that they move about in little ellipses. The paths of the stars over the poles (or more precisely, above the plane of the Earth's orbit) will be almost circular, while the paths of those near the equator will be flat. This effect is called stellar aberration. Unlike parallax, this affects all stars equally, no matter what their distance.*

"You'll note that stellar aberration affects all stars, so this effect is different from parallax. Since it equally affects stars that are at any distance from the Solar System, and since the effect varies with a star's distance from the Earth's orbital plane (an imaginary plane that intersects with the Earth's orbit), then we know that this effect is somehow due to the Earth's motion as it goes around the Sun each year.

"Stellar aberration is the effect well known by astronomers to cause stars to shift 20.5 arc seconds in their location in the sky. The amount of apparent positional change is governed by the time of year and location in the sky with regard to the Earth's orbit around the sun. The number also mathematically correlates perfectly with the Earth's speed around the sun compared to the speed of light.

"If you understand relativity, you should have immediately picked up that light between an emitter and an observer should have no relation with some third object. Yet we find stellar aberration is perfectly related to a third object; Our speed with respect to the sun. They have picked the sun as the center of a preferential reference frame and have no idea why they did it." Anti-relativity (no author).

For a more detailed explanation of aberration, the author refers you to this website. [16]

There exist at least two forms of stellar aberration as observed from Earth: annular (Sun) stellar aberration and diurnal (Earth) stellar aberration. Obviously, starlight travels within the Sun's gravitational field (SGF), then later within the Earth's gravitational field (EGF). Both are local preferred frames for the speed of light as corroborated by the following observations.

As the Earth orbits around the Sun, then its velocity and angle continually change relative to starlight located within the preferred frame of the (SGF). Consequently, as observed from Earth, throughout the time frame of a year, the position and angle of the starlight also continually changes. This is not stellar parallax, which is a totally different phenomenon. Below are Figures 182 and 183, which depict analogous forms of aberration. [17]

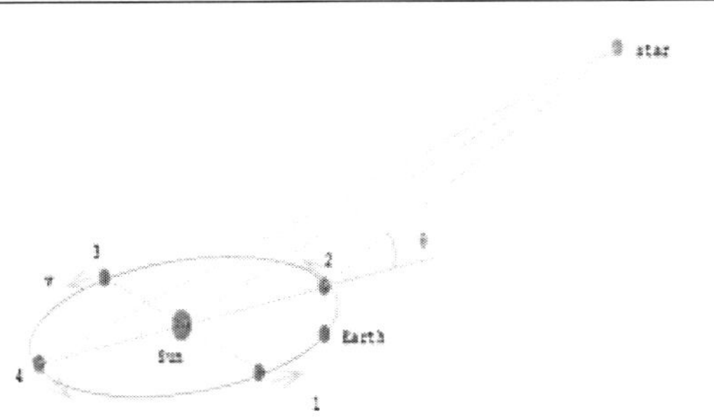

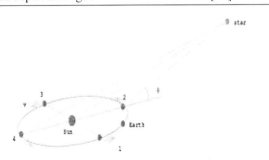

Figure 182. Stellar Aberration

- *The central larger dot represents the Sun with the Earth orbiting around it labeled 1,2,3,4.*
- *The smaller dot located to the far right portrays a star.*
- *As the Earth orbits the Sun, then as a function of annular stellar aberration, the apparent position of the star changes.*
- *Note this diagram does not depict solar parallax*

See Figure 183 below. In the same way as the Earth revolves on its own axis every 24 hours, then the observer, who is on Earth, changes his/her velocity/angle relative to the starlight located within the preferred frame of the EGF. Therefore, over the time span of 24 hours, the apparent position and angle of the starlight continually changes.

So what does this indicate? It signifies light is not relative to the observer. It means that there are fixed non-rotating frames where light travels within. What is more, they are preferred frames, identified by different names; one of which is called the gravitational field (inflow of space or ether).

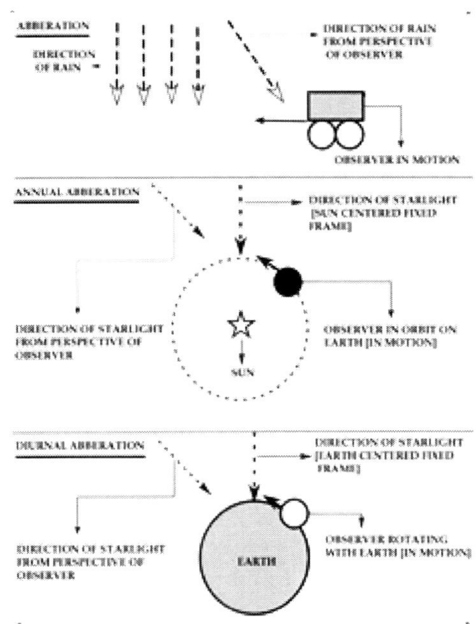

Figure 183. Rain, Annular, and Diurnal Aberration

- *Figure 183 demonstrates analogous forms of aberration.*
- *Top = rain aberration with atmosphere as the preferred frame.*
- *Middle = annular stellar aberration with the Sun's gravitational field as the preferred frame.*
- *Bottom = diurnal stellar aberration with the Earth's gravitational field as the preferred frame.*

Einstein's SRT can also account for stellar aberration, but SRT assumes the magnitude of stellar aberration is a function of the relative velocities of the observer vs. emitter. But notice this fact carefully, not all stars have the same velocity relative to the observer on Earth. So if

Einstein's SRT's assumptions are germane, then different stars should possess varying amounts of aberration.

However, this is not what is actually observed. What we perceive is this: Relative to the plane of the Earth's orbit around the Sun, no matter how far, and regardless of a star's velocity, with respect to the observer on Earth, all stellar aberrations are identical as already mentioned:

"The effect varies with a star's distance from the Earth's orbital plane [an imaginary plane that intersects with the Earth's orbit]. You'll note that stellar aberration affects all stars, so this effect is different from parallax. Since it equally affects stars that are at any distance from the Solar System, and since the effect varies with a star's distance from the Earth's orbital plane (an imaginary plane that intersects with the Earth's orbit), then we know that this effect is somehow due to the Earth's motion as it goes around the Sun each year." The paths of the stars over the poles (or more precisely, above the plane of the Earth's orbit) will be almost circular, while the paths of those near the equator will be flat. The number also mathematically correlates perfectly with the Earth's speed around the sun compared to the speed of light." Anti-relativity (no author). For this reason, SRT cannot be correct.

In contrast, PFGRT is consistent with actual observations, whereby annular stellar aberration is a function of the velocity/angle of the observer on Earth, relative to starlight located within the preferred frame of the SGF. So, with respect to this frame, all aberrations are the same. Again, this is called annular stellar aberration. In addition, there are two forms of stellar aberration; annular and diurnal. This duality cannot occur if the preferred frame for light of c is only from the perspective of the observer (SRT).

What is more, observer aberration also gives explanation for why, from the frame of the observer on Earth, the apparent instantaneous, but not real, acceleration effect on the Earth towards the Sun [see Chapter 2, speed of gravity] does not match the visual position of the Sun,. In essence, the apparent, instantaneous gravitational pull position of the Sun is about 20 arc seconds east of its visible position. This is a function of observer aberration of sunlight from the frame of the Earth as it orbits about the Sun. Notice, in this case, the preferred frame for light is the Sun-centered frame/Sun's gravitational field/Sun's inflow of the ETHER. This is analogous to the fixed frame for light relative to the Earth, its gravitational field/inflowing ether.

For further clarification and from another perspective, sunlight travels outwards from the Sun in the form of a symmetrical radiating sphere, and the observer on Earth, [which is in orbit around the Sun] is moving at a transverse velocity relative to that radially outward spherical frame, thus observer aberration.

In addition, the acceleration function of the inflow of space [ether] or as classically defined the gravitational field has only the appearance [not real] of an instantaneous so-called "pull effect" on the Earth [again see Chapter 2, speed of gravity]. This action is at a radial right angle relative to the Earth as it orbit around the Sun. And so as a result of these two different interacting factors, then from the perspective of the observer on Earth, the apparent instantaneous gravitation pull position [inflow of space] by the Sun exerted on Earth does not correspond to the Sun's visual position. Notice again in this instance the preferred frame for light is the Sun centered frame not the observer.

There is another factor to take into consideration, moreover, paramount in order to comprehend this aberration concept. Within the fixed frame of the SGF/EGF, light is captured or entrained by that frame, furthermore, in an inflowing non-rotating manner. So, inside that frame, if there is relative motion of the source and/or observer, then classic source vs. observer, aberration occurs as well as longitudinal and transverse Doppler effects.

In other words, a beam of a given length of light located within a fixed frame [gravitational field] can move longitudinally as well as transversely through that frame, even though still entrained by that inflowing frame. So light leaving a star traveling towards Earth is entrained [fixed] first by the star's gravitational field, then as it travels through the galaxy by its gravitational field, then by the SGF, and finally by the EGF. This occurs even though these separate gravitational fields [fixed frames] move at a velocity relative to one another.

In summary and for reinforcement, the gravitational field [inflow of space or ether] fixes the light within that specific frame but still allows for source and observer aberrations in that same frame. In addition, this same concept explains the transverse and longitudinal Doppler effects again within the same gravitational field frame. Take note, transverse and longitudinal Doppler effects would not occur devoid of same functional process that produces source/observer aberration.

Even though in erratum, observer aberration, specifically within a single gravitational field frame [Sun], was used by Bradley as a proof of the speed of light as c, what is more validating, only SRT (from the observer's reference frame). See quote below. However, in reality, it (c) is related to the reference frame of the Sun's gravitational field (PFGRT). In essence, Bradley calculated c correctly but mistakenly posited the wrong reference frame.

"In 1728 James Bradley made another estimate by observing stellar aberration, being the apparent displacement of stars due to the motion of the Earth around the Sun. He observed a star in Draco and found that its apparent position changed throughout the year. All stellar positions are affected equally in this way. (This distinguishes stellar aberration from parallax, which is greater for nearby stars than it is for distant stars.) To understand aberration, a useful analogy is to imagine the effect of your motion on the angle at which rain falls past you, as you run through it. If you stand still in the rain when there is no wind, it falls vertically on your head. If you run through the rain, it comes at you at an angle and hits you on the front. Bradley measured this angle for starlight, and knowing the speed of the Earth around the Sun, he found a value for the speed

of light of 301,000 km/s." [18]

It should also be noted that source aberration of binary stars has never been observed from Earth. There are several possibilities for this fact now posited.

First, perhaps this is because, again as observed from Earth, different fixed frames or gravitational fields [star, galaxy, Sun, and Earth] are all moving at different velocities relative to one another. This circumstance results in observer aberration of the binary stars together, functioning a single unit, but masks the two different individual source aberrations as those stars orbit one another.

In other words, from the Earth's observer frame of reference, differential source aberration of the binary system exists. However, it is markedly reduced from what would be expected, assuming light is emitted directly from the two stars to the observer on Earth without interacting with the different intervening non-rotating gravitational fields, all of which are traveling at differing velocities relative to one another.

Second, alternatively binary stars, which are orbiting one another, then generate a very complex single gravitational field [fixed frame] which may compensate, therefore negate, their different source aberrations.

Third, the emitted light of the source stars is in the form of a complex sphere [complex fixed frame], whereas from the observer reference frame on Earth, that light is in the shape of a pencil beam.

Fourth, source aberration of binary stars is based upon spectral analysis of light, whereas observer aberration is based upon starlight position. As a result, there may be unaccounted factors that do not make them equivalent.

These are possible explanations for why, from the reference frame of the observer on the orbiting Earth, observer aberration is measured *within* a single gravitational field such as associated with our Sun or else from starlight emitted from a single star. But on the other hand, regarding binary stars, again from the reference frame of Earth, differential source aberration is not apparent.

Three

Radio waves transmitted via satellite from Japan to the U.S. take a longer amount of time than vice versa. Similarly, radio waves that are sent, via satellite-to-satellite, around the Earth's equator, then back to their origin, take longer traveling west to east than east to west. So what does this all indicate? It signifies that the ECF/EGF is the local preferred frame for the speed of light. Thus, as a function of the Earth's axial rotational spin, relative to within the EGF/ECF, so it then takes light a longer interval of time to travel west to east as compared to east to west.

Four

See Figure 184 (Hafele and Keating)

"During October, 1971, four cesium atomic beam clocks were flown on regularly scheduled commercial jet flights around the world twice, once eastward and once westward, to test Einstein's theory of relativity with macroscopic clocks. From the actual flight paths of each trip, the theory predicted that the flying clocks, compared with reference clocks at the U.S. Naval Observatory, should have lost 40+/-23 nanoseconds during the eastward trip and should have gained 275+/-21 nanoseconds during the westward trip. Relative to the atomic time scale of the U.S. Naval Observatory, the flying clocks lost 59+/-10 nanoseconds during the eastward trip and gained 273+/-7 nanosecond during the westward trip, where the errors are the corresponding standard deviations." [19]

For the benefit of the non-scientist, this is the author's explanation of the Hafele and Keating experiment. Relative to the baseline clock sited on the rotating surface of the Earth, if one compares the amount of time it takes for the two atomic clocks to travel by airplane around the earth, from west to east as compared to east to west, the west-east clock takes longer. (Hafele and Keating). See Figure 184 below.

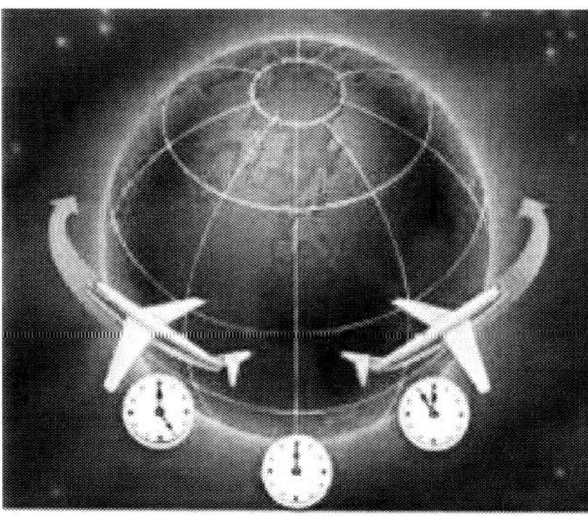

Figure 184. Hafele and Keating

- *With respect to traveling around the Earth, it then takes a longer amount of time for the clocks to travel west to east as compared to east to west (atomic clocks aboard aircraft).* [20]

What does this experiment signify? It indicates that relative to the EGF, the west-east clock possesses a higher velocity compared to the east-west clock. As a result, its "tic rate" is slower. This consequence can only occur if there is a preferred frame, EGF/ ECF.

The website [21] contains a video describing an experiment supporting the concept that the "rate of time" of an atomic clock is a function of its velocity relative to the Earth Centered Frame [EGF] just like the Hafele and Keating] experiment.

However, it is a more precise experiment. Nonetheless, the author of the website describes the experiment as a function frame dragging. Alternatively, it is this author's opinion that his conclusion is en erratum. The experiment actually demonstrates differential "time dilation" of an atomic clock as a function of velocity relative to the Earth Centered Frame/Gravitation Field/Inflow of Space-Ether.

As an analogy, an atomic clock positioned at the equator tics slower [1,000 mph relative to the EGF, ECF Ether] compared to an identical atomic clock located at a higher latitude [< 1,000 mph with respect to the ECF, EGF,

Ether]. This end result is a function of their different velocities relative to the non-rotating ether [EGF, ECF].

Five

The GPS basically proves PFGRT as correct. [See Figures 185 and 186 below, moreover the following citation.]

The following website [22] partially describes how the GPS functions.

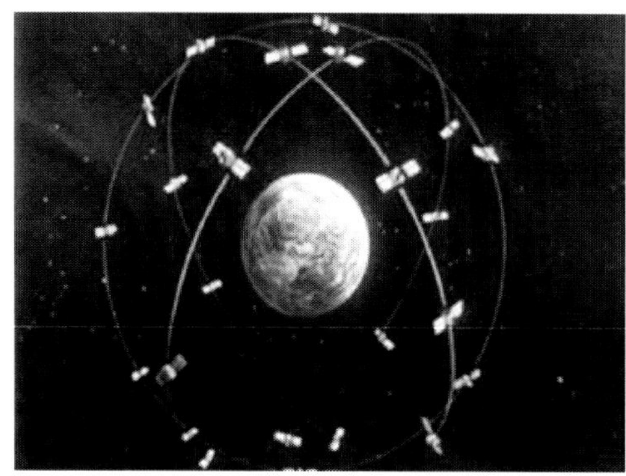

Figure 185. GPS System

- This is an illustration of the GPS system: *"Each GPS satellite transmits data that indicates its location and the current time. All GPS satellites synchronize operations so that these repeating signals are transmitted at the same instant. (They are synchronized with an Earth-bound baseline clock) The signals, moving at the speed of light, arrive at a GPS receiver at slightly different times, because some satellites are further away than others.* See Figure 186 below. [23]

This begs the question, by what methodology are the atomic clocks of the GPS synchronized in order for the system to function correctly? Physicists do use some of Einstein's relativity equations, nevertheless, only with reference to the (ECF), not the observer. Basically, they utilize two factors for synchronizing the orbital clocks with the Earth-based baseline clock: The first is the altitude of the orbit, and second, the velocity of the orbit. [24]

- *"The distance to the GPS satellites can be determined by estimating the amount of time it takes for their signals to reach the receiver. When the receiver estimates*

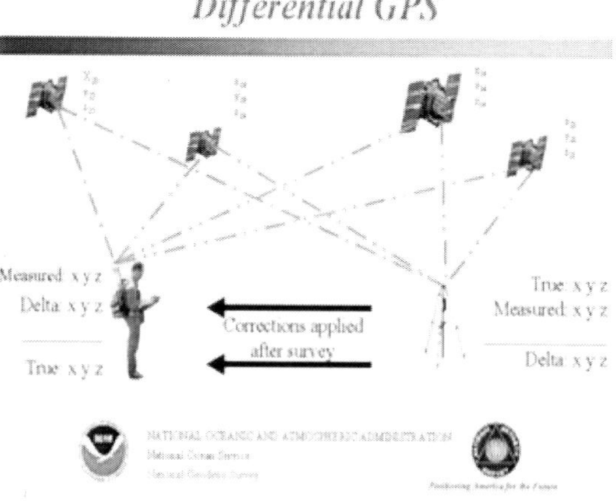

Figure 186. Another GPS System [24]

the distance to at least four GPS satellites, it can calculate its position in three dimensions".

- *"There are at least 24 operational GPS satellites at all times plus a number of spares. The satellites, operated by the U.S. DoD, orbit with a period of 12 hours (two orbits per day) at a height of about 11,500 miles traveling at 9,000mph (3.9km/s or 14,000kph). Ground stations are used to precisely track each satellite's orbit."* [25]

With respect to the first, the higher the orbit, the weaker the gravitational field, so the "tic rate" of the atomic clock increases. And for the second, the closer to Earth, the faster the orbital velocity, thus the slower is its "tic rate". Once again, the adjustments are made relative to the ECF but most importantly not from the perspective of the observer. With reference to the new lexicology of this article as defined in chapters 1 and 2, the synchronization process can be described this way. However, first in order to comprehend the following explanation, one must understand and accept the assumptions presented in those two chapters.

The inflowing ether (EGF/ECF) accelerates and self compresses as it streams in towards Earth. As a result, the closer a clock is to the Earth, the greater is the velocity/density of the inflow. Therefore, the clock's tic rate decreases. In addition, as the orbital velocity of the clock increases, the closer it is from Earth; then its transverse motion relative to the inflow also increases. And for that reason, its tic rate then again decreases.

But that is not all. The GPS system also uses the ECF as the preferred frame for the speed of light, not the observer. So, in order to determine the correct position on Earth, then relative to the ECF, both the orbital velocity of the satellite, as well as the rotational velocity of the desired location on Earth, must be factored in. Once again, this is not from the perspective of the observer.

What the GPS proves is this: The EGF/ECF is the **local** preferred frame for the speed of light on Earth, moreover, the frame that also determines the "rate of time". In contrast, presuming the GPS used the observer for the preferred frame, then in all likelihood, it would be too complicated to function properly. In that case, each satellite's clock would have a constantly changing velocity relative to all the other satellites, with their clocks, as well as to the Earth-based clock. Even so, theoretically, it could be made to work, nevertheless, only with the use of extremely complex mathematics. It is important to note that this would violate Occam's razor.

These five observations and/or experiments in conjunction basically prove that the ECF, EGF is the local preferred frame for both the speed of light, as well as the rate of time. In other words, the local preferred frame for the speed of light on Earth is its own gravitational field. This basic assumption will now be applied to the Michelson Morley Experiment (MMX).

13. The Michelson Morley Experiment (MMX)

The author has decided to make this specific section redundant, not for the sake of the physicist, for he/she will readily understand the concepts presented, but rather to underscore their significance. The author has composed it in this manner for the benefit of the apprentice. This is because, in the author's opinion, the concepts described here within are somewhat visually abstract, especially for the neophyte.

For that reason, the same concepts are presented multiple times and from different perspectives. Hopefully, for the novice, this repetitive methodology will aid in his/her ability to grasp the ideas presented.

As already described, large global experiments/observations all involve rotation within the EGF, but more importantly, they demonstrate anisotropy. On the other hand, small extremely high-quality linear experiments, performed on the Earth's rotating surface produced isotropy. Some of them were not pursuing the Earth's axial spin velocity. Nevertheless, they should have been sensitive enough to detect it. In fact, there have been so many that it is not realistic to assume that if there is a fault, it lies with poorly designed equipment or the experimenter.

Once again, with regards to the global experiments, there is irrefutable evidence that the local preferred frame for the speed of light is synonymous with the Earth's gravitational field. In addition, they directly measure the speed of light predominately in a vacuum. However, given that they all involve acceleration, rotation and curvature, they are then considered Sagnac experiments [GRT], thus not contradictory to SRT.

Viewed from another perspective, if a gravitational field is the **only** preferred frame for the speed of light, furthermore, as a product of mass [matter[, then all preferred frames for light must be connected with a sphere/gravitation field/acceleration of some sort. How could it be otherwise? And so given the above assumption, what other option is there?

In contrast, there is solid evidence derived from numerous small local linear experiments, when performed on the rotating surface of the Earth, that the speed of light is isotropic. But notice this fact very carefully. These second-order local experiments do not directly determine the speed of light, rather they measure "interval of time" as a direct function of "distance through the ether". The latter phrase is defined within this article as **geometry**.

Therefore, if one posits that there is a fundamental error related to this geometry, which has been overlooked, then this presumed fact explains the discrepancy between the global vs. local experiments. In addition, it is more likely that the fault lies with the local experiments, seeing as the global experiments are so overwhelmingly convincing, as well as practical. Furthermore, they directly measure the speed of light. What is more, there are some local experiments, [Brillet and Hall], which hint that the EGF is the local preferred frame for the speed of light on Earth.

MMX

Michelson and Morley were not searching for the Earth's axial spin velocity, rather the Earth's orbital velocity around the Sun [67,000 mph = .4 fringe shift]. In addition, the experiment was not sensitive enough [.04 fringe shift] to detect the Earth's axial spin velocity at the latitude of the experiment [<1000 mph =< .006 fringe shift] Nevertheless, many other super-sensitive high-quality second-order experiments have confirmed the MMX's null result.

This segment describes "overlooked physics," that when taken into account, produce a null outcome, for all second-order experiments of this type, even in the presence of the ether wind. Given the fact that the MMX is so well known, moreover considered by many as proof of relativity, it will be used as the model.

Before proceeding further, if one is not familiar with the MMX, then it will be highly helpful to peruse Appendix 4, which describes the MMX in much greater detail. Only then will one be able to fully appreciate the following assumptions and conclusions. In addition, for the beginner, viewing the YouTube websites listed below will simplify one's understanding behind the physics of the MMX. This is because, generally, it is much easier for the novice to clearly grasp its function by watching a visual presentation, rather than reading a written one.

- http://www.youtube.com/watch?v=7qJoRNseyLQ
- http://www.youtube.com/watch?v=uMaFB3jM2qs
- http://www.youtube.com/watch?v=Z8K3gcHQiqk
- http://www.youtube.com/watch?v=YPS02iShohE

On the other hand, if one already has sufficient expertise, then please skip to the paragraph beginning with the four asterisks located on Page 22.

Classical Interpretation of the MMX

Listed below are *modified* quotes describing the classical interpretation of the MMX written by Michael Fowler, Ph.D. Figure 188 is from the original MM paper by Michelson and Morley. With respect to this adapted interpretation, it is assumed that the EGF/ECF is the preferred frame for the speed of light as demonstrated by the global experiments. For that reason, there is a relative ether wind equal to the Earth's rotational spin velocity at the latitude of the experiment.

North

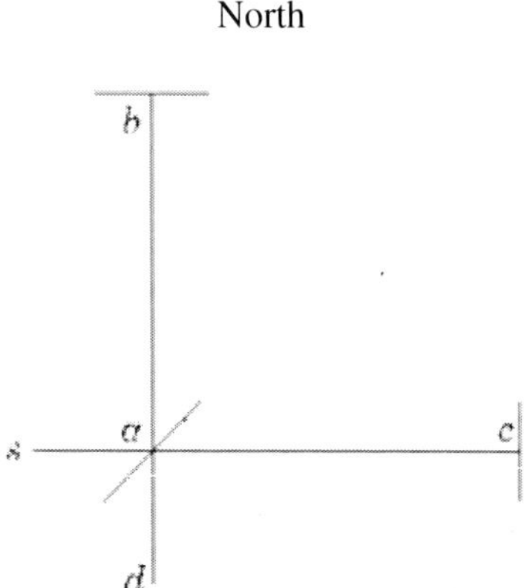

Figure 187. MMX SetUP

South

- *The source of light is at s.*
- *The 45-degree line is the half-silvered mirror.*
- *b and c are mirrors.*
- *d is the observer.*
- *The horizontal axis is west-east and east-west.*
- *The vertical axis is south-north and north-south.*

Below, find a more detailed explanation of Figure 188.

1. *The scheme of the experiment is as follows: a pulse of light is directed at an angle of 45 degrees at a half-silvered, half-transparent mirror, so that half the pulse goes on through the glass, half is reflected. They both go on to distant mirrors, which reflect them back to the half-silvered mirror. At this point, they are again half-reflected and half-transmitted, but a telescope is placed behind the half-silvered mirror as shown in the figure so that half of each half-pulse will arrive in this telescope. If there is an ether wind blowing, someone looking through the telescope should see the halves of the two half-pulses to arrive at slightly different times, since one would have gone more west-east and back, one more s-n and back. (The wave from west-east and back would travel a longer distance [time] than the wave from south-north and back.) To maximize the effect, the whole apparatus, including the distant mirrors, was placed on a large turntable so it could be swung around.*

2. *Michelson utilized a steady beam of light of a single color. This can be visualized as a sequence of ingoing waves, with a wavelength one fifty-thousandth of an inch or so. This sequence of waves is split into two, and reflected back to the central receiving mirror (telescope eye where the interference pattern occurs). One set of waves goes northward and then southward [a,b then b,a]. The other set of waves goes eastward and then westward [a,c then c,a]. Finally, they come together into the telescope and the eye (d). If the one that took longer is half a wavelength behind, then its troughs will be on top of the crests of the first wave; thus they will cancel, and nothing will be seen. If the delay is less than that, then there will still be some dimming. However, slight errors in the placement of the mirrors would have the same effect. This is one reason why the apparatus is built to be rotated. On turning it through 90 degrees, then the north-south waves through the ether wind and the east-west waves through the ether wind will exchange places. The other one should be behind. Thus, if there is an ether wind, if you watch through the telescope while you rotate the turntable, you should expect to see variations in the brightness of the incoming light.*

In addition, here is a second brief synopsis regarding the physics of the MMX found at the website: [26]

Also see Figure 188 below.

"In 1887 Albert Michelson and Edward Morley of the USA carried out a very careful experiment at the Case School of Applied Science in Cleveland. The aim of the experiment was to measure the motion of the earth relative to the aether and thereby demonstrate that the ether existed. Their method involved using the phenomenon of the interference of light to detect small changes in the speed of light due to the Earth's motion through the aether."

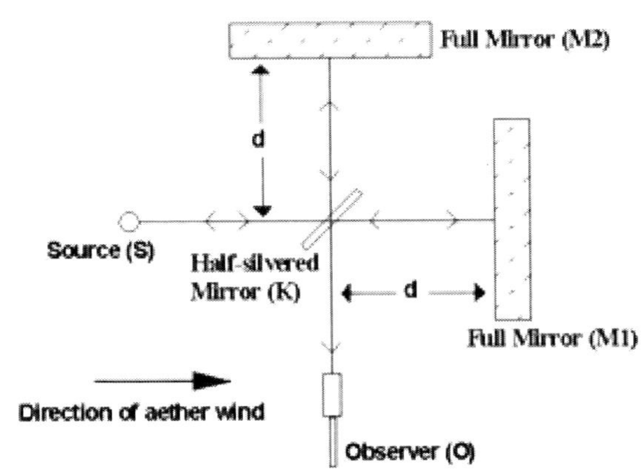

Figure 188. MMX Apparatus

"The whole apparatus is mounted on a solid stone block for stability and is floated in a bath of mercury so that it could be rotated smoothly about a central axis (5). The Earth, together with the apparatus, is assumed to be traveling through the aether with a uniform velocity u of about 30 km/s. This is equivalent to the earth at rest with the aether streaming past it at a velocity-u."

"In the experiment a beam of light from the source S is split into two beams by a half-silvered mirror K as shown. One half of the beam travels from K to M1 and is then reflected back to K, while the other half is reflected from K to M2 and then reflected from M2 back to K. At K part of the beam from M1 is reflected to the observer O and part of the beam from M2 is transmitted to O."

"Although the mirrors M1 and M2 are the same distance from K, it is virtually impossible to have the distances travelled by each beam exactly equal, since the wavelength of light is so small compared with the dimensions of the apparatus. Thus, the two beams would arrive at O slightly out of phase and would produce an interference pattern at O."

"There is also a difference in the time taken by each beam to traverse the apparatus and arrive at O, since one beam travels across the aether stream direction while the other travels parallel and then anti-parallel to the aether stream direction. This difference in time taken for each beam to arrive at O would also introduce a phase difference and would thus influence the interference pattern."

"If the apparatus were to be rotated through 90o, the phase difference due to the path difference of each beam would not change. However, as the direction of the light beams varied with the direction of flow of the aether, their relative velocities would alter and thus the difference in time required for each beam to reach O would alter. This would result in a change in the interference pattern as the apparatus was rotated."

"The Michelson-Morley apparatus was capable of detecting a phase change of as little as 1/100 of a fringe. The expected phase change was 4/10 of a fringe. However, no such change was observed."

"Thus, the result of the Michelson-Morley experiment was that no motion of the earth relative to the aether was detected. Since the experiment failed in its objective, the result is called a null result. The experiment has since been repeated many times and the same null result has always been obtained."

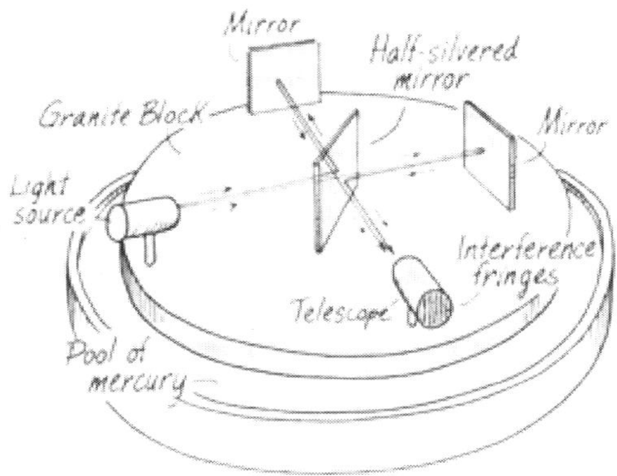

Figure 189. 3D-MMX Apparatus

- Figure 189 is a three-dimensional reconstruction of Figure 188.

Figure 190. Photograph of MMX Apparatus

****

Perhaps it will be considerably easier for the novice to comprehend the following classic explanation of the MMX, written by the author, since it is designed specifically for that segment of the population. Even so, for the physicist, this description will help clarify the error of the classic interpretation, since one must comprehend how the MMX actually functions, before one can understand the flaw of the overlooked physics.

First, assume the physical lengths of the arms of the MMX are absolutely equal. And second, presume that there is an ether wind. Therefore, the light, which travels within the "to-and-fro" wind arm, takes a longer transit time when compared to the crosswind arm. It is assumed the to-and-fro transit time is longer, given that light (c) travels a greater distance through the ether because of the ether wind.

Take note: "time" is a direct function of distance "travelled through the ether." In turn, distance is a function of geometry. From here on out, with regards to this chapter, geometry refers to the distance traveled "through the ether," not distance relative to the physical length of the arms of the MMX. Therefore, with reference to this concept, moreover, to avoid confusion, the word distance, as such, will be labeled in parentheses and with an asterisk; (distance*) = distance through the ether.

In essence, the MMX does not directly measure the speed of light, for relative to each arm, any potential gain or loss of the speed of light traveling in one direction is compensated by a loss or gain in the opposite direction. As a result, the speed of light is not directly measured, rather only time as a function of (distance*). If the preferred frame for the speed of light is the ECF (gravitational field) as proven by the GPS system, then the maximum measured anisotropy possible is located at the equator at 1000 mph.

The following Figures 191, 192, 193, 194 describe the classic explanation of the function of the MMX. They represent four different reference frames.

Figure 191 assumes there is no ether or else the MMX is at rest with the ether. With reference to this frame, it is as if the observer is standing adjacent to the MMX, moreover, with no discernment of the ether. Therefore, the illustration shows his/her perception of the pathways of the light beams with respect to the frame of the MMX.

Figure 192 posits a stationary ether. With reference to this frame, it is as if the observer is a part of the ether, moreover observing the pathways of the two light beams traveling through the ether.

Figure 193 postulates an ether wind. With regards to this frame, it is as if the observer is standing next to the MMX with no awareness of the ether wind. As such, the illustration shows his/her perception of the pathways of the light beams relative to the frame of the MMX.

Figure 194 posits an ether wind. With respect to this frame it is as if the observer is stationary with respect to the ether wind, furthermore, observing the pathways of the two light beams traveling through and with the ether wind.

So to begin with, refer to figures 191 and 192 below and the following dialogues. Again, assume the physical lengths of the arms of the MMX are absolutely equal and distance refers to distance through the ether, labeled (distance*).

Figures 191 and 192 presume there is *no ether* or else the MMX is at *rest with the ether*. In this setting, relative to the two arms, the (distances*) are equal. If so, then at the location of the detector (observer) the two light streams are in phase. Consequently, no interference pattern forms [**no dimming**], regardless as to whether or not the MMX is rotating.

Left Right

- *O= Observer (detector)*
- *S = Source of light.*
- *HSM = Half-silvered Mirror.*

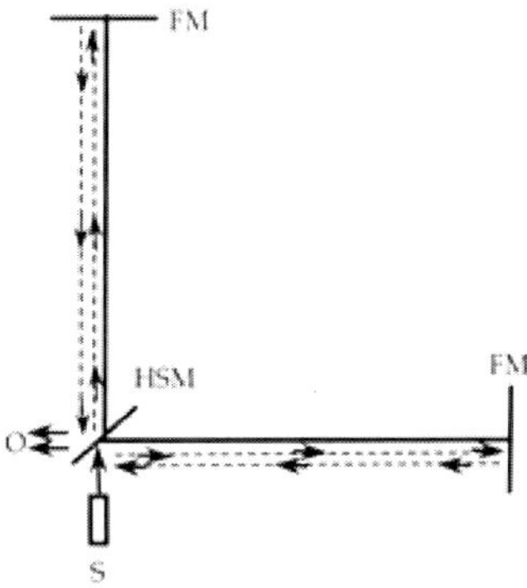

Figure 191. Two Paths of the Light

- *FM= Full mirror.*
- *Dotted lines with arrows = pathways of light beams.*
- *Figure 191 above depicts the MMX in the absence of an ether or else at rest with the ether, moreover from the reference frame of its own physical structure. The illustration shows the perceived pathways of the two light steams (denoted by the arrows) relative to an observer standing next to and observing the MMX.* [27]

Left Right

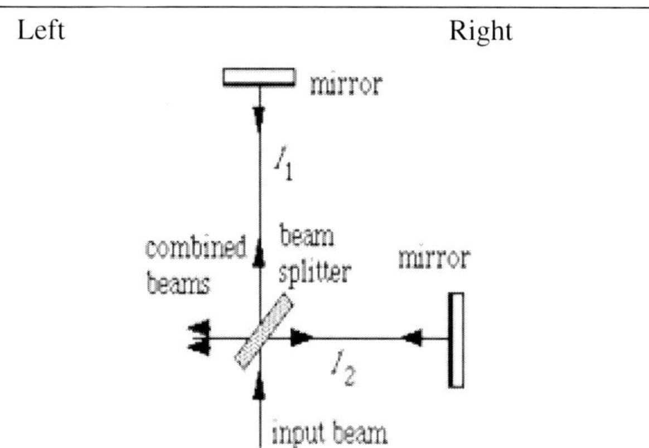

Figure 192. Two Paths of Light

- *Figure 192 above depicts the MMX at rest with the ether, moreover from the reference frame of the ether. The illustration shows the pathways of the two light streams, depicted by the arrows, as they traverse through the ether, In this scenario, the verticle arm (distance*) equals the horizontal arm (distance*). Therefore, no interference pattern forms, with or without rotation.*

See Figure 193 and 194 below and the following dissertations. Alternatively, if the *ether wind exists*, then the "interval of time" (distance*) that it takes for light to travel within the "to-and-from arm" is greater than the "cross wind" arm. This divergence produces an interference pattern at the location of the observer/detector (see Figure 195 left). Subsequently, during 360 degrees of rotation, then relative to the two arms, the (distances*) change.

Essentially, they exchange places every 90 degrees. As a result, over 360 degrees of rotation, there is a continuous alteration in the appearance of the interference pattern [**alternating brightness and dimming**]. This takes the form of a fringe shift with a sinusoidal wave pattern. See also Figure 195 (left to the right), as well as Figure 196.

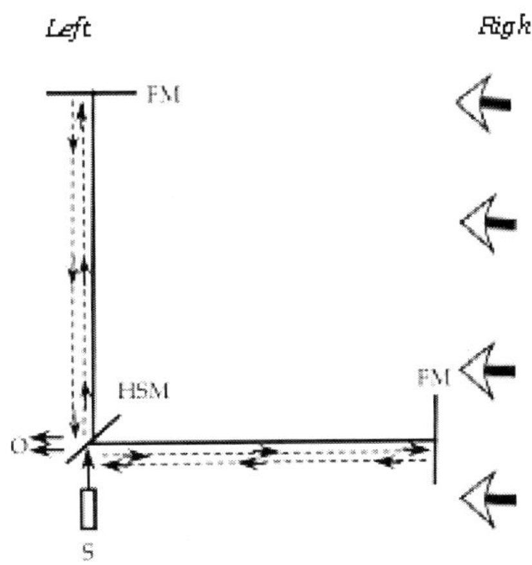

Figure 193. MMX with Aether Wind

- *Figure 193 above shows the MMX from the reference frame of its own physical structure, but now in the presence of an ether wind. Assume the MMX possesses a translational velocity relative to the ECF/EGF, from left to right.*
- *Therefore the* <u>*relative*</u> *ether wind is oriented in the opposite direction, from right to left (arrows on the right). Schematic demonstrates the perceived pathways of two light steams from the reference frame of an observer standing next to and observing the physical structure of MMX with no awareness of the ether wind.*

Left Right

- *Figure 194 depicts the pathways of the two light streams as they traverse through and with the relative ether wind, moreover, from the reference frame of an observer stationary with respect to that ether wind. In this instance, the to-and-from arm time (distance*) > than "the cross wind arm" time (distance*).*

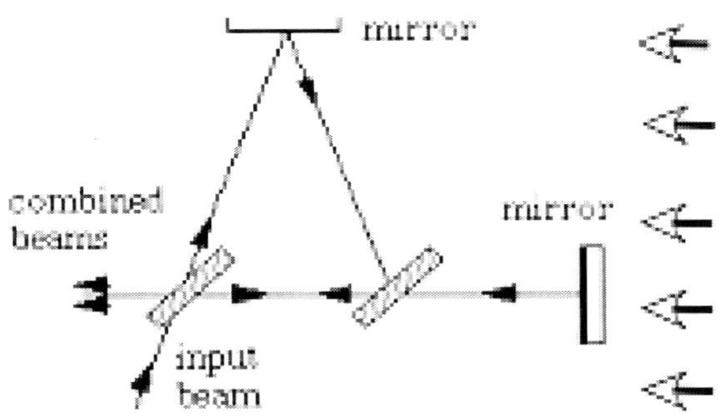

Figure 194. MMX with Aether Wind

- *Therefore, an interference pattern forms at the location detector/observer. In addition, as a function of rotation (360 degrees), there is then a fringe shift produced in the form of sinusoidal wave pattern. See Figures 195 and 196 below.*

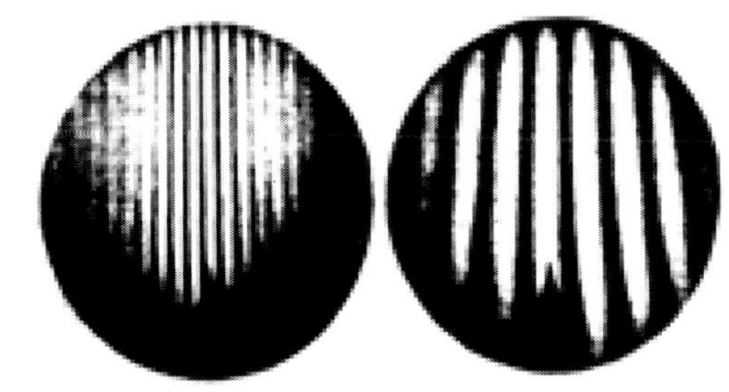

Figure 195. Interference Pattern

- *From left to right, the interference pattern changes which is called a fringe shift.* [28]

Figure 196. Graph

- *The graph is from the original MMX experiment paper. The change in the appearance of the interference pattern (fringe shift), during 360 degrees of rotation, takes on the form of a sinusoidal wave pattern as depicted above by the more pronounced dotted curved line.*

The major concept for comprehending the overlooked physics of the MMX is this. The interference pattern is not formed at the detector (observer). Rather, it is formed at the location of the half-silvered mirror. This is where the two returning/reflected, moreover, opposing wave-fronts first interface/intersect, and then interact at right angles to form the interference pattern. Subsequently, after this recombination at the half-silvered mirror, they are then fixed relative to one another. And once fixed, they travel parallel, moreover, in the identical direction, through the same ether to the detector (observer), even during rotation. See Figure 197 and the following discussion.

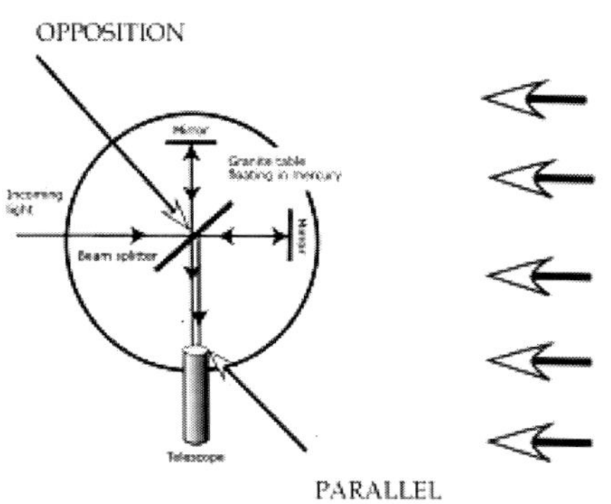

Figure 197. MMX with Ether Wind

- *Assume equal physical length of the arms.*
- *Presume an ether wind portrayed by the hollow arrows on the right.*
- *As opposed to the prior illustrations, the source and observer have exchanged places. This has no effect on the outcome.*[29]

Incorrect interpretation.

The observer located at the detector (telescope) falsely assumes, with respect to the two arms, that the two light waves are traveling parallel to one another their entire (distances*) (time). Take note, in actuality, they are not always physically in all segments travelling parallel their entire (distances*). However, mathematically expressed as a function of time with respect to the MMX equations, they are functionally parallel.

In addition. he/she also incorrectly presumes the interference pattern forms at the position of the detector (observer). Given these false postulates, then during rotation, the two light waves (distances*)(time) essentially exchange places every 90 degrees. This function is somewhat analogous to two vertical metal grates shifting back and forth for every 90 degrees, with the grates representing light wavelengths. Therefore, presuming an ether wind, this assumed effect, over 360 degrees of rotation, produces a fringe shift [presenting as alternating dimming and brightness] in the form of a sinusoidal wave pattern.

Correct interpretation.

However, in fact the interference pattern actually forms as a function of two returning light waves, which have already been reflected from the peripheral mirrors to the half-silvered mirror. Therefore, from the frame of the half-silvered mirror, they are then traveling in physical opposition to one another (right angle). The half-silvered mirror is the location where the interference first forms. So during rotation, from the frame of the half-silvered mirror, one arm progressively gains (x) wavelengths, while the other arm anti-symmetrically and progressively loses (x) wavelengths. Consequently, the configuration of the two opposing interacting wavefronts at their interface [half-silvered mirror] does not change, even though the (distances*) have changed. This process reverses itself every 90 degrees. Then, from the half-silvered mirror to the detector (observer), the two waves travel parallel, moreover, are fixed relative to one another, even during rotation. This is because at that interval of time, both waves are traveling physically parallel through the same ether. Therefore, overall, during rotation, there is no fringe shift even in the presence of an ether wind.

The most important facts to acknowledge are:

1. The interference pattern is observed at the detector, but not formed there. It is formed at the location of the half-silvered mirror.

2. The interference pattern is fashioned from two opposing waves, which have already been reflected from the peripheral full mirrors to the central half-silvered mirror. So from the reference frame of the half-silvered mirror, they are physically traveling in opposition towards one another (right angle).

3. For reinforcement, the interference pattern is not a function of two interacting parallel waves traveling in the same direction their entire (distances*), though the definition of parallel is only expressed mathematically as a function of time with respect to the equations of the MMX. Rather, as above, it is a function of two physical interacting waves traveling in physical opposition at the location of the half-silvered mirror.

At this juncture, before proceeding, it would be highly helpful if one viewed Figures 205 and 207. These illustrations demonstrate, that at 45 degrees, relative to the ether wind, the (distances*), within the two arms, are exactly the same. This is assuming equal physical lengths of the arms. Knowing and accepting this fact/assumption is a crucial step in order to understand the following explanation and descriptions.

See Figures 198 and 199, 200, 201 and assume all is oriented as shown. Here are the crucial concepts and descriptions regarding the overlooked physics of the MMX. This first description is of the classical, nevertheless erroneous interpretation.

Incorrect interpretation.

Once again, presume an ether wind and equal physical lengths of the arms as depicted. In this instance, relative to the two arms, the intervals of time (distances*) are unequal. Consequently, at the position of the detector or observer, where it is posited that the parallel light beams recombine, an interference pattern then forms. Take note again, in actuality, the two light beams are not physically travelling parallel their entire (distances*). Parallel in this instance is a mathematical function of time with respect to the equations of the MMX.

In addition, as a function of rotation resulting in a gain of an interval of time (distance*) in one arm vs. an anti-symmetrical loss of an interval of time (distance*) in the other arm, then over 360 degrees, a fringe shift is produced in the form of a sinusoidal wave. This fringe shift is depicted below in Figure 199.

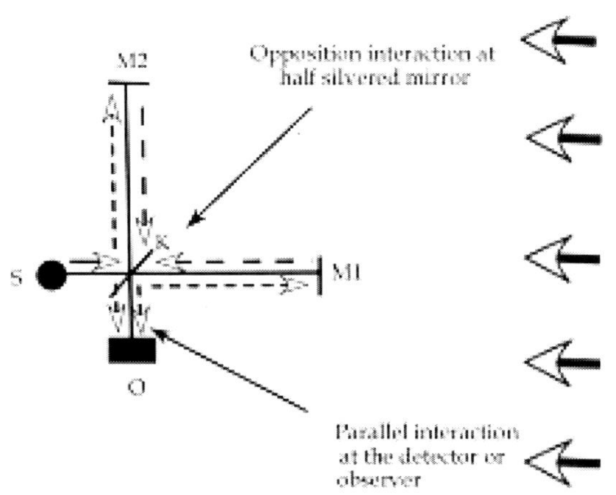

Figure 198. Parallel Interacting Waves with an Ether Wind

- *S = light source*
- *M1 M2 = peripheral full mirrors*
- *K = half-silvered mirror*
- *Arrows within MMX – direction of light waves*
- *Rows of hollow arrows to the right = ether wind*

For reinforcement, the incorrect interpretation is again presented referring to Figures 198 and 199.

Parallel interacting waves (Incorrect)

There is a fringe shift between A and B

- *The classical explanation assumes the interference pattern forms at the detector.*
- *Assume an ether wind with equal physical lengths of the arms.*
- *(Distance*) = distance of the light through the ether = interval of time.*
- *The straight vertical line represents the detector or observer.*
- *The two sets of waves represent the (distance*) (time) within each of the two arms. A = one set. B = the second set.*

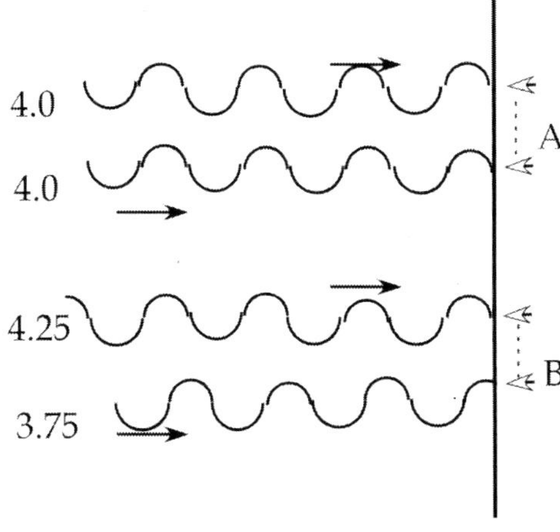

Figure 199.

- *A = The arms are oriented 45 degrees relative to the ether wind.*
- *B = The arms are oriented at either 0 or 90 degrees relative to the ether wind.*
- *At the location of the detector, the two waves travel mathematically (time) parallel to each other their entire (distances].*
- *Note, the illustration depicts parallel waves, but only as a representation of time with respect to the equations of the MMX .*

The following is again the classic, but erroneous, interpretation of the function of the MMX. Take note, the assumptions presented are false; therefore, the physics described below is incorrect. Refer to Figure 199.

Position A = 45 degrees relative to the ether wind.

At this position, with respect to the two arms, the "interval of times" (distances*) are equal. Therefore, at the location of the detector/observer, the two light waves are in phase. As a result, no interference pattern forms [no dimming].

Position B = 0 or 90 degrees with respect to the ether wind.

At these positions, after rotation from 45 degrees, relative to the two arms, the (distances*) are unequal. In this setting, the two waves are now out of phase, because during this rotation, one arm gains .25-wavelength (distance*)(time) (A top), while the other arm anti-symmetrically loses .25-wavelength (distance*)(time) (B bottom). So at the location of the detector (observer), an interference pattern forms. This process then reverses itself every 90 degrees. Therefore, as a function of 360 degrees of rotation, a fringe shift is produced in the form of a sinusoidal wave pattern [alternating dimming and brightness].

Correct interpretation.

Before proceeding, please see figures 200 and 201. Again, assume an ether wind with absolutely equal physical length of its arms. And all is oriented as shown.

In reality, the two streams of light waves, after being reflected from the peripheral full mirrors, are then physically traveling towards one another in opposition at a right angle. Their wave fronts initially intersect, moreover, interact, at the half-silvered mirror to form the interference pattern. Then, from the half-silvered mirror to the detector, they are fixed physically parallel relative to one another, even during rotation.

Assume there is rotation of the MXX. If the two light waves are traveling in opposition [Figure 201] and if one wave progressively gains (x) number of wavelengths (distance*), whereas the other wave anti-symmetrically progressively loses an equal (x) number of wavelengths (distance*), then at the true location of the interacting wave fronts (half-silvered mirror), there is no change in their interface. For the same reason, during rotation, there is no fringe shift [dimming], since this anti-symmetrical compensatory function prevents it.

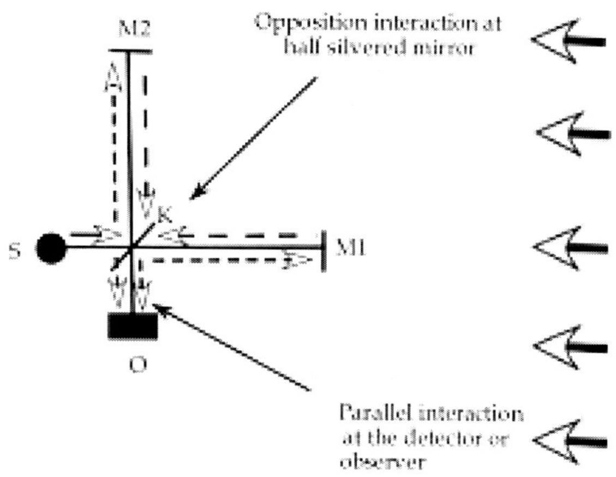

Figure 200. MMX with an Ether Wind

- *S = light source.*
- *M1 M2 = peripheral full mirrors.*
- *K = half-silvered mirror.*
- *Arrows within MMX = direction of light waves.*
- *Line of arrows to the right = ether wind.*

Once again for reinforcement, again the correct interpretation is presented now referring to Figure 201 below. The assumptions presented are true. Therefore, the physics described below is correct.

Opposition interacting waves (correct interpretation)

Left *Right*

A= 45 degrees B= 0 or 90 degrees

- *Assume an ether wind and equal physical length of the arms.*
- *(Distance*) = distance of the light through the ether.*
- *The straight vertical line now represents the half-silvered mirror.*

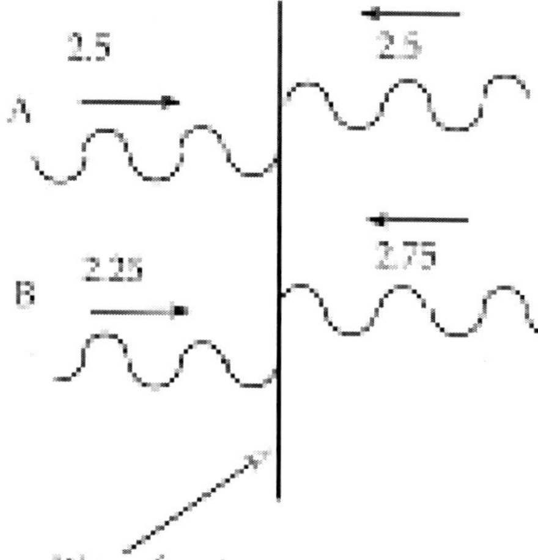

Figure 201.

- *The two sets of waves (left and right) represent the (distance*) (time) within each of the two arms.*
- *At the location of the half-silvered mirror the two returning waves are traveling in opposition relative to one another (actually at a right angle).*
- *A = The arms are oriented 45 degrees relative to the ether wind.*
- *B = The arms are orientated 0 or 90 degrees relative to the ether wind.*
- *The correct explanation assumes the interference pattern forms at the location of the half-silvered mirror as a function of two opposing waves.*
- *The opposing waves, as shown above, are a function of the two light waves traveling to their respective peripheral mirrors and then both reflected back to the half-silvered mirror where the interference pattern then forms. However, with respect to this illustration, only the reflective returning segment is shown.*

Position A = 45 degrees relative to the ether wind.

At this position, relative to the two arms, the (distances*) are equal. Consequently, at the location of the half-silvered mirror, the two light waves are in phase. As a result, no interference pattern forms.

Position B = 0 or 90 degrees with respect to the ether wind.

At these positions, after rotation from 45 degrees, then relative to the two arms, the (distances*) are unequal. In this scenario, during this rotation, one arm gains .25-wavelength (distance*), on the right side, while the other arm anti-symmetrically looses an equal .25-wavelength (distance*) on the left side.

As a result of this opposing anti-symmetry, at the location of the half-silvered mirror, where the two returning, moreover opposing light beams, first interact (right angle), the interface of the two waves does not change, even though the (distances*) have changed, Therefore, they remain in phase. This same function then reverses itself in 90-degree segments, throughout 360 degrees of rotation.

In addition, from the half-silvered mirror to the detector (observer) the two interacting waves then travel physically parallel in the same direction to the detector/observer. Furthermore, they remain fixed with respect to one another, with or without rotation. This is because at that time, they are both traveling parallel through the same ether (distance*). So given all of the above, then during rotation, no fringe shift is produced, even in the presence of an ether wind.

However, in the real world, the physical lengths of the arms are not absolutely equal relative to a single wavelength of light. So in reality, at 45 degrees, an interference pattern forms, but only as a function of the unequal physical length of the two arms. Then, during rotation the anti-symmetrical compensatory process just described prevents a fringe shift.

In summary

- *If the two streams of light waves are initially out of phase, related to **only** the ether wind, then during rotation, the anti-symmetrical compensatory function just described prevents a change in the interface. As a result, there is also the no change in the interference pattern. And so, during rotation, there is no fringe shift.*
- *If the two light waves are out of phase, in this case, **only** as a function of unequal physical length of the arms, then again, there is no fringe shift during rotation.*
- *Assuming there is no ether, once again as a function of rotation, there is no fringe.*

For all these reasons, the MMX is silent as to whether or not the ether exists. In summary, The MMX is incapable of detecting the ether wind. Voila! There you have it.

This concept is not easily visualized. For if it were, then it would not have been so easily overlooked. For that reason, a more detailed explanation is now provided as offered below in Figure 202 and the following dissertations.

Essentially, this re-explanation is not for the physicists, but for the benefit of the novice, the target population of this article. Carefully, follow the pathways of the two light beams with respect to Figure 202, which are described in the following paragraphs.

Opposition interacting waves (correct interpretation)

- *S = light source.*
- *K = half-silvered mirror.*

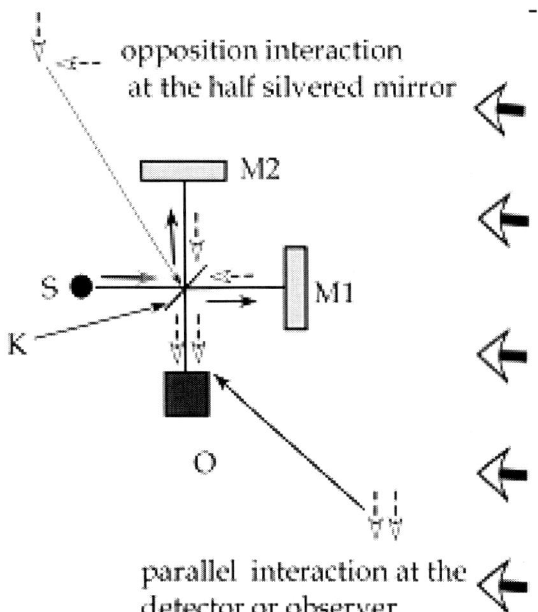

Figure 202. MMX with an Ether Wind

- *M1 and M2 – full mirror.*
- *O = Observer or detector.*
- *Blue arrowhead [adjacent to the circle] = direction of the single light wave before interaction the half-silvered mirror.*
- *Black arrowheads = direction of the two light waves towards the peripheral full mirrors.*
- *Smaller hollow arrowheads = direction of returning two lights waves after refection from the peripheral full mirrors.*
- *Larger hollow arrowheads to the right = ether wind.*

A single beam of light is emitted from the source (S), represented by the blue arrowhead [arrow adjacent to the black circle]. This light beam is then divided into two separate streams (black arrowheads) by the half-silvered mirror (K). They then travel to the peripheral full mirrors (M1, M2). Subsequently, the full mirrors then reflect the beams back to the half-silvered mirror. The smaller hollow arrowheads represent the two reflected returning light beams.

Here is the crucial point. When the returning reflected light beams first intersect, then interact (interface), at the half-silvered mirror, moreover, at a right angle, this is where the interference pattern is first formed. This interaction is a function of two light beams traveling in physical opposition-not mathematically parallel as a function of time. So from the reference frame of the half-silvered mirror and during rotation, as one light beam progressively gains wavelengths (distance*), while the other beam anti-symmetrically progressively loses an equal number of wavelengths (distance*), then the interface of the two waves remains unchanged.

This means the interference pattern also remains unaffected. In essence, during rotation, the (distances*) change, but the interference pattern does not.

Then, from the half-silvered mirror to the detector (observer) the two beams physically travel parallel in the same direction). Moreover, they are fixed relative to one another, since at this time they both are traveling through the same ether (distance*). Given all of the above, then as a function of the rotation (MMX), even in the face of the ether wind, there is no fringe shift.

The next two illustrations with their following captions more accurately depict the classical, although incorrect, interpretation of the MMX (Figure 203) versus the correct interpretation (Figure 204). Figure 204 is a more precise description compared to Figure 201; since the opposing wavefronts interact at a right angle relative to one another. In other words, it is easier to understand Figure 204 (90 degree opposition) after comprehending Figure 201 (180 degree opposition). This is rational for the re-explanation.

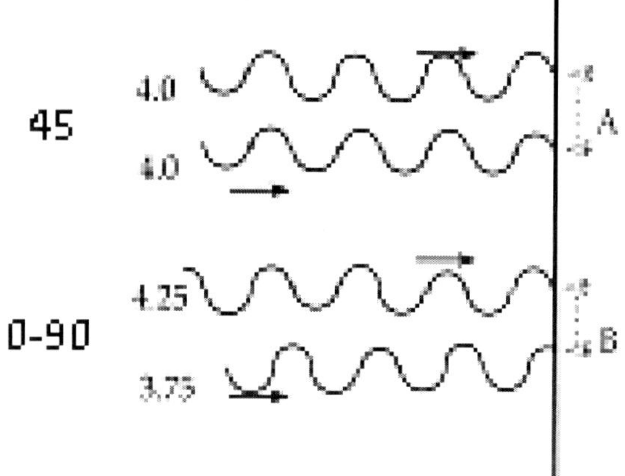

Figure 203. Parallel (time) interacting light waves (incorrect interpretation)

There is a fringe shift between A and B

- *Assume and ether wind with equal physical length of arms.*
- *(Distance*) = distance of light through the ether = interval of time.*
- *A Top: 45 degrees relative to the ether wind.*
- *B Bottom: 0-90 degrees relative to the ether wind.*
- *Note, illustration depicts parallel waves, but only as a representation of time with respect to the equations of the MMX*

Incorrect interpretation.

Figure 203 above is the incorrect interpretation of the function of the MMX. The assumptions presented are false. Therefore, the physics described below is then incorrect.

Classically, it is assumed, relative to the two arms, that the interference pattern is formed at the detector (observer) as a function of two interacting parallel waves, traveling in the same direction their entire (distances*), however, parallel only expressed mathematically as a function of time in the MMX equations.

Position A. (45 degrees). At this position, the two light waves are in-phase, since with respect to the two arms the "intervals of time" (distances*) are equal.

Position B. However, after rotation from 45 degrees, at 0 or 90 degrees (B), they are out of phase, since in this setting, relative to the two arms, the time intervals (distances*) are unequal. Therefore, an interference pattern forms. This is because during rotation, one wave gains an "interval of time" (distance*), while the other wave anti-symmetrically loses an equal interval of time (distance*).

This process then reverses itself every 90 degrees. Consequently, over 360 degrees of rotation, at the location of the detector, a fringe shift is produced in the form of a sinusoid. All of this is assuming, relative to the two arms, that the two light waves are traveling parallel (expressed as time in the MMX equations) in the same direction their entire (distances*), moreover, then recombine at the location of the detector (observer), both assumptions of which are incorrect.

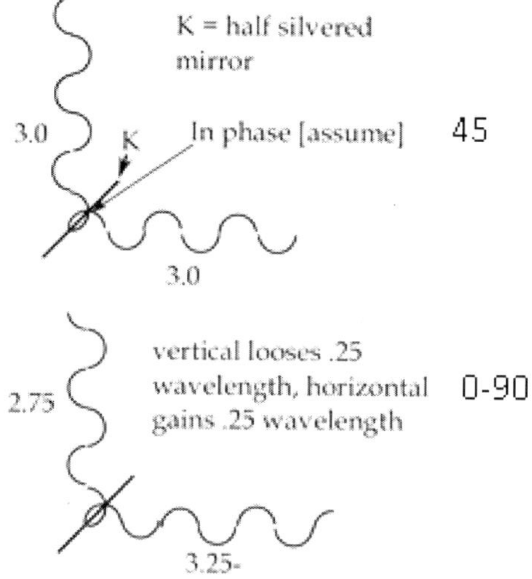

Figure 204. Opposing (time) interacting light waves (correct interpretation)

There is no fringe shift between A and B

- *Assume an ether wind with equal physical lengths of the arms.*
- *(Distance*) = distance of the light through the ether.*

- *Top = 45 degrees relative to the ether wind.*
- *Bottom = 0 or 90 degrees relative to the ether wind.*
- *The opposing waves, as shown above, are a function of the two light waves traveling to their respective peripheral mirrors and then both reflected back to the half silvered mirror where the interference pattern then forms. However ,with respect to this illustration only the reflective retuning segment is shown.*

Correct interpretation.

Figure 204 above is the correct interpretation of the function of the MMX. Take note, the assumptions presented are true; therefore, the physics described below is correct.

In reality, the interference pattern is formed where the two returning opposing wavefronts first intersect, which is at the location of the half-silvered mirror (K). These right-angled intersecting waves are traveling in physical opposition, not parallel (time in the MMX equations). So during rotation (top to bottom) one light wave gains .25-wavelength (distance*) while the other wave looses 0.25-wavelength (distance*). As a result, the configuration of the two interacting wavefronts at location K then remains unchanged. In essence, during rotation, the (distances*) change, but the interface of the two opposing waves does not. So, if the interface does not change, then neither does the interference pattern; therefore, there is no fringe shift.

Additionally, from K to the detector or observer, the two waves travel physically parallel in the same direction, moreover, are fixed relative to one another, because at that time, both waves travel through the same ether (distance*). Therefore, overall, relative to the detector (observer), during rotation, no fringe shift is again observed.

In the real world, the physical lengths of the arms of the MMX are not absolutely equal relative to a single wavelength of light. So in actuality, at 45 degrees an interference pattern forms, but only as a function of the unequal physical length of the arms. Then, during rotation, the anti-symmetrical compensatory process just described prevents a fringe shift.

Once again for the novice, Figures 205 and 206, 207, 208 below demonstrate, in the presence of an ether wind, that during the rotation of the MMX, due to the opposing anti-symmetrical compensatory function just described, where a gain of the number of wavelengths (distance*) in one arm is associated with an equal loss of a number of wavelengths (distance*) in the other arm, then no fringe shift is produced.

Notice, at 45 degrees, the (distances*) within both arms are the same, assuming equal physical lengths of the two arms. This explains position A in the previous illustrations. But remember in the real world, the physical lengths of the arms are unequal when compared to a single wavelength of light. As a result, in truth, at this position (45 degrees), the (distances*) are unequal, although only as a function of the different physical lengths of the arms. The underlying rationale for why the author chose to assume equal physical length of the arms is for simplicity of explanation.

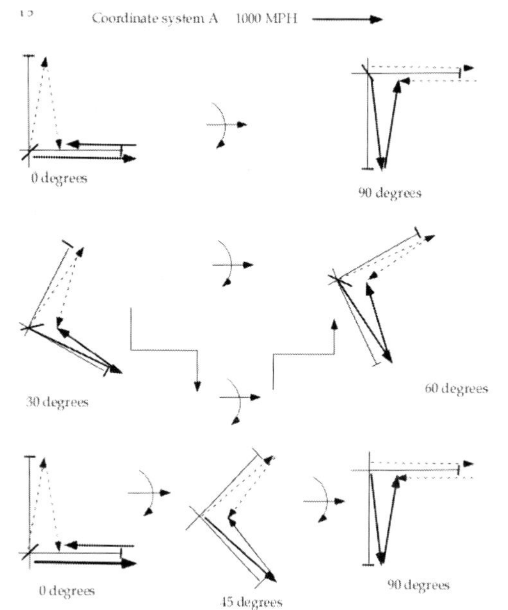

Figure 205. Opposing (time) interacting light waves (correct interpretation)

Assume an ether wind 1000mph from left to right.

Presume equal physical length of the arms. So at 45 degrees, the (distances) within both arms are then equal. Observe during rotation of 90 degrees.*

- *The dotted (distance*) exchanges places with the solid (distance*).*
- *Or the total number of wavelengths within the dotted arm exchanges places with the total number of wavelengths within the solid arm.*
- *Or the gain in the number of wavelengths within the dotted arm is anti-symmetrical with the loss in the number of wavelengths within the solid arm.*

- *The opposing anti-symmetry function of number of wavelengths then produces, during rotation, at the location of the half-silvered mirror, a stable interference pattern, regardless of whether or not there is an ether wind.*

One more time for the novice, this compensatory anti-symmetrical function is once again shown below in Figures 206, 207, 208, but now with even more clarity.

Notice: the (distances*) relative to both arms change; nevertheless, the interface still remains constant. As a result, there is no fringe shift during rotation.

Left *Right*

Hollow Arrows = ether wind

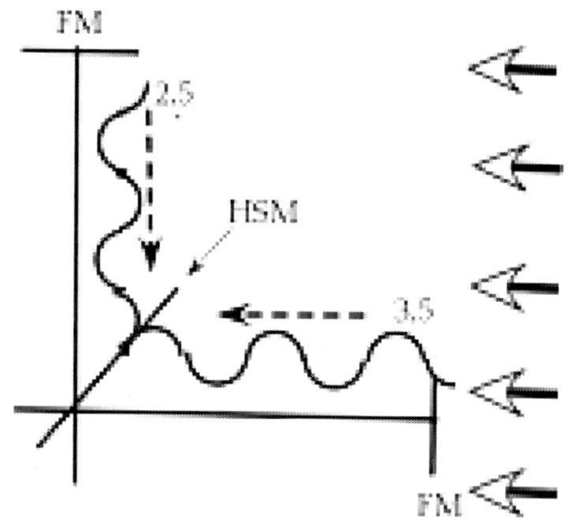

Figure 206. Opposing Interacting Waves

0 degrees relative to the ether wind

MMX is rotating clockwise.

- *The (distance*) with respect to the to-and-fro arm is greater than the cross wind arm.*

- *Notice, for the purposes of clarity of the illustration, at 0 degrees the two light beams at the interface (half-silvered mirror) are in phase. In reality, at 0 degrees, assuming an ether wind and presuming equal physical lengths of the arms, they could and would most likely be out of phase as a function of the extent of velocity of the ether wind.*
- *The opposing waves shown are a function of the two light waves traveling to their respective peripheral mirrors and then both reflected back to the half-silvered mirror where the interference pattern then forms. However, with respect to the above illustration, only the reflective returning segment is shown.*

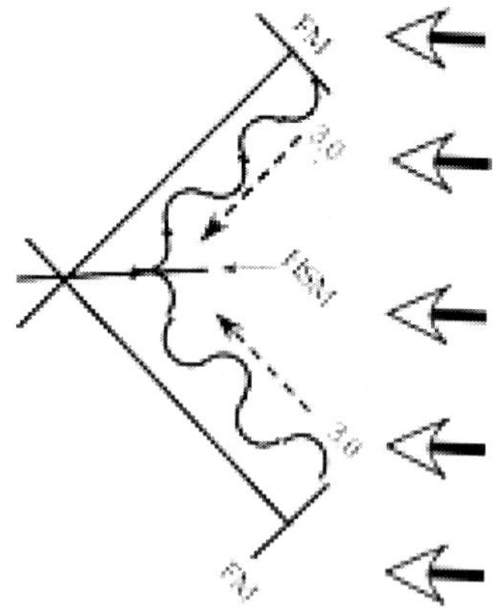

Figure 207. Opposing Interacting Waves

45 degrees relative to the ether wind

- *The (distances*) within each arm are now equal to each other. Nevertheless, the two light beams at the interface, (half-silvered mirror) are still in-phase. This is a function of a gain of a half a wavelength in one arm and a loss of a half a wave length in the other arm. There is no fringe shift.*

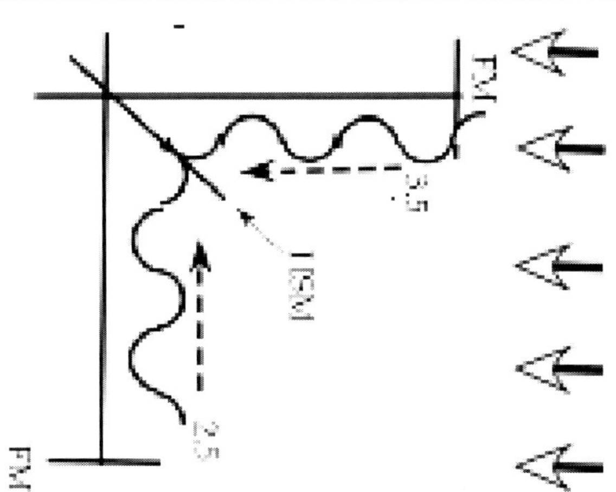

Figure 208. Opposing Interacting Waves

90 degrees relative to the ether wind

- *The (distance*) with respect to the to-and-fro arm is greater than the cross-wind arm. But now when compared to 0 degrees, the two arms have exchanged places. The two light beams at the interface (half-silvered mirror) are still in-phase. Again, this is a function of a gain of a half a wavelength in one arm and a loss of a half a wavelength in the other arm.*
- *Therefore even though, as a function of rotation, the (distances*) change, the interface does not. And, if the interface does not change, then neither does the interference pattern. For that reason, there is no fringe shift during rotation. In essence, even in the presence of an ether wind, the MMX is silent as to whether or not it exists.*

Summary

The classic interpretation of the MMX perceives the experiment from the reference frame of the detector (observer) as a function of the "amount of time" it takes for light to travel through the ether, relative to each arm. This interval of time is then mathematically correlated to the (distances*), involving two parallel light beams, traveling with reference to both arms in the same direction. Take note, in actuality, they are not travelling parallel their entire (distances*), but mathematically expressed as a function time with respect to the MMX equations, they are.

The incorrect interpretation is related to the following.

1. Relative to each arm "time" is a function of (distance*) (true). However, the (distances*) could be traveling mathematically (time) parallel (false) or in physical opposition (true).
2. The origin of the interference pattern is located at the detector/observer (false).
3. This is at the location where the two interacting waves travel physically parallel with respect to each other (true).
4. The origin of the interference pattern forms at the half-silvered mirror (true). This is the location where the two waves travel in physical opposition with respect to each other (true).
5. During rotation, the two parallel waves (mathematical — time), shift back and forth relative to one another, therefore, producing a fringe shift at the location of the detector (false).
6. During rotation, at the location of the half-silvered mirror, the interface of the opposing light waves remains fixed as a function of counteracting anti-symmetry (true).

In contrast, the correct interpretation perceives the MMX outcome from the reference frame of the half-silvered mirror. Therefore, relative to each arm, during rotation, as a function of two opposing, moreover, anti-symmetrical counteracting wave fronts, the (distances*) change; however, the interface remains constant. Consequently, as a function of rotation, no change of the interference pattern occurs. In other words, during rotation, there is no fringe shift even in the presence of an ether wind.

Epilogue

As usual regarding physics, it is not that simple. For instance, if the relative ether wind changes velocity between two different reference frames (defined as coordinate systems B and C in Appendix 4), then a fringe shift occurs as a function of moving from one frame into another one. Examples of two different frames or coordinate systems using the MMX relative to the ECF/EGF would be:

1. At the equator, sited on the rotating surface of the Earth, with one arm oriented south/north (S/N) and the other arm west/east (W/E), thus 1,000 mph with respect to the ECF/EGF—a relative ether wind of 1,000 mph.
2. On an airplane, traveling 600 mph, west to east, at the latitude of the equator with one arm oriented S/N and the other arm W/E, therefore: equal to 1,600 mph with respect to the ECF/EGF—a relative ether wind of 1,600 mph.

The two coordinate systems possess different velocities relative to the ECF/EGF, as such, different relative ether winds.

As postulated by this chapter, within each of the above two coordinate systems, the MMX is inherently incapable of detecting the ether wind for the reasons just presented. Therefore, during 360 degrees of rotation, with each separate frame, a specific non-changing non-sinusoidal interference pattern emerges. But between the above coordinate systems and in the fixed N/S, W/E orientation, the interference pattern then changes.

For example as above, if one carries out a MMX "sited" on the Earth's rotating surface, fixed in the S/N-W/E directions, and subsequently at the same latitude, in the same mode, on an eastward bound airplane traveling 600 mph, then between these two frames, a different, though constant, non-sinusoidal-shaped interference pattern emerges, with or without rotation.

Additionally, if one performs the experiment, S/N, W/E, first at the equator, at rest with the Earth's rotating surface, 1,000 mph relative to the ether (ECF), and second at the

South Pole, 0 mph relative to the (ECF), there will then again be a disparity in the shape of the interference patterns between these two frames.

This is because as the MMX increases its velocity relative to the ECF, moreover, as in Example 1 fixed and oriented S/N-W/E, there is a gain of (distances*) in both the to-and-fro arm (W/E) as well as the "cross-wind arm" (S/N). But it is proportionally greater in the to-and-fro arm. Consequently, there is a fringe shift as a function of an increasing velocity relative to the ECF but not as a function of rotation.

Take note, for ease of comprehension, the first hypothetical experiment described above is relative to only the fixed N/S-E/W orientations. However, in reality, this theoretical experiment could be performed in any direction (N/S, E/W-360 degrees) with the same results.

These imaginary tests, if carried out as actual experiments, and if confirmed, would be evidence of a relative ether wind. So, in fact, the MMX can detect the ether wind but not in context as originally performed. The author cannot emphasize this enough. This alternate experiment of the MMX, as described above, and if verified, would then invalidate relativity, furthermore, attest to the existence of the ether. Again for emphasis, as originally performed, the MMX demonstrated nothing. It is silent as to whether or not the there is an ether. But this alternative mode, if validated, then gives proof to the ETHER.

There is one further consideration the author wishes to make, and it is this: the misconception with regards to the classical interpretation of the MXX belies with the fact that the focus was on the mathematics of "time" as a function of (distance*). But time did not distinguish as to whether the two (distances*) are traveling parallel or in opposition.

And so, for that reason, the true visual function of the experiment was then overlooked. To somewhat paraphrase Maxwell, who believed in the ether, the main focus of physics should always relate to the true function, not the math.

In conclusion, given the new hypotheses, moreover, derived conclusions as just presented, the null result of the MMX as originally preformed does not invalidate Einstein's relativity, but is silent. On the other hand, it [relativity] collapses if this alternative MMX mode is verified. As a result, by default this leaves only the global observations and experiments, which represent true reality, whereby the speed of light is related to the gravitational field (inflow of the ether).

CHAPTER 3 (Second Part) - THE MICHELSON MORLEY EXPERIMENT (MMX) AND OTHER SPEED OF LIGHT EXPERIMENTS

Chapter 3 (Second Part) is not part of this conference paper.

CHAPTER 4 - QUANTUM MECHANICS (QM) AS A FUNCTION OF THE ETHER

Chapter 4 is not part of this conference paper.

CHAPTER 5 - EXPERIMENTAL AND OBSERVATIONAL PROOF OF THE ETHER

Chapter 5 is not part of this conference paper.

APPENDICES are not part of this conference paper.

The author expresses grateful appreciation to Donna Tucker and Robert de Hilster for editing this paper.

REFERENCES

1. Web Site: www.youtube.com
URL: https://www.youtube.com/watch?v=TgH9KXEQ0YU.
2. Web Site: www.youtube.com
URL: https://www.youtube.com/watch?v=9BFKqIoqSIYIt.
3. Web Site: www.youtube.com
URL: https://www.youtube.com/watch?v=TgH9KXEQ0YU.
4. Web Site: www.dummies.com
URL: http://www.dummies.com/how-to/content/einsteins-special-relativity.html
5. Web Site: Science Photo Library
6. Web Site: Wikipedia
URL: http://en.wikipedia.org/wiki/Inertia
7. Web Site: thegeneralfieldtheoryofphysics.com
URL: http://www.thegeneralfieldtheoryofphysics.com/wp-content/uploads/2011/12/Mass-Lorentz-Transformation-8-30-2008.jpg
8. Web Site: thegeneralfieldtheoryofphysics.com
URL: http://belate.wordpress.com/2011/02/17/aristotle-definition-of-time-in-physics/
9. Web Site: cosmology.berkeley.edu
url: http cosmology.berkeley.edu- 2FEducation-2FCosmologyEssays-2FThe- Cosmic-Microwave-Background.html
10. Web Site: cosmology.berkeley.edu
url: http://uvsmodel.com/pictures/CMBR
11. Web Site: thegeneralfieldtheoryofphysics.com
URL: http://www.ucolick.org/ bolte/AY4-00/ week9/time-dilation-graph.gif
12. Web Site: thegeneralfieldtheoryofphysics.com
URL: https://www.quora.com/If-fourth-dimension- is-true-how-could-one-draw-the-fourth-axis- perpendicular-to-the-other-3-axis-3d
13. Web Site: thegeneralfieldtheoryofphysics.com
URL: http://renshaw.teleinc.com/papers/simiee2/simiee2.stm
14. Web Site: thegeneralfieldtheoryofphysics.com
URL: https://www.physicsforums.com/threads/ problem-with-relativity-of-simultaneity -original-example.470129
15. Web Site: thegeneralfieldtheoryofphysics.com
URL: http://www.patana.ac.th/secondary/ science/anrophysics/relativity-option/commentary.html
16. Web Site: thegeneralfieldtheoryofphysics.com
URL: http://www.antirelativity.com/ stellaraberration.htm
17. Web Site: thegeneralfieldtheoryofphysics.com
URL: www.globalserve.net/ bumblebee/ geocentrism/aberration.htm
18. Web Site: math.ucr.edu
URL: http://math.ucr.edu/home/baez/physics/Relativity/SpeedOfLight/measure-c.html
19. Web Site: hyperphysics.phyastr.gsu.edu

URL: http://hyperphysics.phyastr.gsu.edu/hbase/relativ/airtim.html#c1

20. Web Site: worknotes.com
URL: http://worknotes.com/Physics/SpecialRelativity/TwinParadox/htmlpage9.aspx?print=true
21. Web Site: youtube.com
URL: https://www.youtube.com/watch?v=G-7ImOWnxQ8
22. Web Site: youtube.com
URL: https://www.youtube.com/watch?v=0n0T992ccik It is titled âĂIJHow Does GPS Work?âĂİ (2005).
23. Web Site: www.phy.ntnu.edu
URL: http://www.phy.ntnu.edu.tw/ntnujava/pics/gps-3.jpg
24. Web Site: worknotes.com/
URL: http://worknotes.com/Physics/SpecialRelativity/TwinParadox/htmlpage9.aspx?print=true
25. Web Site: www.pocketgpsworld.com
URL: http://www.pocketgpsworld.com/howgpsworks.php
26. Web Site: webs.mn.catholic.edu.au/physics/
URL: http://webs.mn.catholic.edu.au/physics/emery/hsc-space-continued.htm#M-M
27. Web Site: bit.ly/1YqtQfU
URL: http://bit.ly/1YqtQfU
28. Web Site: upload.wikimedia.org
URL: https://upload.wikimedia.org/wikipedia/en/c/cb/RealFringes.gif
29. Web Site: answersingenesis.org
URL: https://answersingenesis.org/astronomy/cosmology/twentieth-century-cosmology/
Web Site: upload.wikimedia.org/wikipedia/en/thumb/
URL: https://upload.wikimedia.org/wikipedia/en/thumb/d/d1/Michelson-Morley-887-Figure-6.png/300px-Michelson-Morley-1887-Figure-6.png

Author Index